JUNIATA COLLEGE

Uncommon Vision, Uncommon Loyalty

The History of an Independent College
in Pennsylvania
Founded by the Brethren
1876-2001

Earl C. Kaylor, Jr.

Published by Juniata College, Huntingdon, PA
2001

Juniata College Press

ISBN 0-9636610-1-9

Copyright © 2001, by Juniata College Press.
Juniata College
1700 Moore Street
Huntingdon, PA 16652

All rights reserved. Printed in the United States of America. Except as permitted under the United States Copyright Act of 1976, no part of this publication may be reproduced or distributed in any form or by any means, or stored in a data base or retrieval system, without the prior written permission of the Juniata College Press.

Cover and book design, typography & electronic pagination by Arrow Graphics, Inc.

For additional copies of this book contact:
Juniata College Bookstore
1700 Moore Street
Juniata College
Huntingdon, PA 16652
(814) 641-3381

In Memory of
Harold Bennett "H. B." Brumbaugh
(1911–2000)
"Mr. Juniata"
to Generations of Alumni

CONTENTS

Preface / *vii*

Acknowledgments / *ix*

1. Prologue: The Founders and the Struggle for Brethren Schools / *1*

2. Jacob Zuck—The Man and His Experiment / *15*

3. The College on the Hill / *28*

4. Others Take Up the Work: 1879–1888 / *45*

5. Rise of the Brumbaugh Dynasty: 1888–1893 / *63*

6. Juniata College Comes of Age: 1893–1910 / *77*

7. Student Life: Mid-1890s to Early 1900s / *102*

8. Toward a Greater Juniata: 1910–1924 / *115*

9. Bringing in the New Era: 1924–1930 / *139*

10. Surviving the Depression: 1930–1943 / *161*

11. Student Life During the Depression: 1930–1943 / *176*

12. A Quarter-Century of Dynamic Growth: 1943–1968 / *187*

13. Student Life: World War II to Late 1960s / *210*

14. Girded for the Second Century: 1968–1975 / *238*

15. Advancing into the Second Century: 1975–1986 / *262*

16. Priming for the Twenty-First Century: 1986–1998 / *302*

17. Juniata College at Millennium 2000 / *352*

Recapitulative Epilogue / *365*

Notes / *369*

Name Index / *383*

General Index / *395*

Preface

Several times Robert Neff, late in his presidency, approached me about revising and updating *Truth Sets Free*, my 1976 centennial history of Juniata, titled after the college's motto. I respectfully demurred each time. Retired from the faculty in 1991, I had just seen into print my biography of a great Juniatian, Governor Martin Brumbaugh, and did not yet feel back in a writing mood.

Then one midsummer's day in 1998, President Thomas Kepple, newly arrived on College Hill, called me into his office. He told me that he and Harold Brumbaugh, the alumni's elder statesman, had recently had a little tête-à-tête. Their conversation, he said, focused on the school's impending 125th anniversary year, 2001. The two of them thought, like Dr. Neff, that a reworked and expanded *Truth Sets Free*, long out of print, ought to be included among the big-year's publications. So President Kepple, in his gently persuasive way, put the matter to me, and I agreed. This volume is the outcome.

I reworked every chapter of *Truth Sets Free,* polishing diction, correcting mistakes, deleting—or adding—material, sharpening interpretive perspectives. The format of presentation, however, I left unchanged. Chapter 14, which deals with John Stauffer's presidency (1968–1975), underwent the most extensive revision. From that point on, the book is all new history. Because the new part covers more than a third of a century, and thus is more than a mere revision of *Truth Sets Free*, I have decided to give this history a new title. It is partially borrowed from President Kepple's inaugural address.

This latest recountal of Juniata's past, however, still falls into the same genre as *Truth Sets Free*. I intended both books to be a cross in style between those of the two earliest accounts of the college. David Emmert's *Reminiscences of Juniata College*, privately printed in 1901, is an anecdotal, people-centered, often droll, sort of memoir. By contrast, Charles C. Ellis's *Juniata: The History of Seventy-five Years, 1876–1946* takes a more institutional-oriented, matter-of-fact approach. Both books are topical in organization of material. Mine has been a narrative mode, in 1976 and now, progressing chronologically by presidential administrations. It is, of course, every bit as encyclopedic in scope as was *Truth Sets Free*.

As before, I do not, because of qualms as a historian, blink internal strains and issues. My book would not be a history if I had; it would be institutional propaganda. But I try to confront Juniata's past with honesty *and* compassion. In a recent article written for *The Chronicle of Higher Education* (Jan. 28, 2000), James W. Loewen laments how often colleges and universities distort history to avoid mention of conflict. A former professor of sociology at the University of Vermont and the author of two best-selling books about how Americans lie on historical markers and in textbooks, he titles the essay "The Shrouded History of College Campuses." He concludes by writing: "When institutions of higher learning tell their history fully and honestly, they also exemplify good historical practice for their students. In the process, they provide a much-needed lesson about the contentious, sometimes unpleasant, nature of truth." Juniata, of course, has long professed that fact of life, ever since adopting the motto *Veritas Liberat* in 1902.

In various ways I have tried to humanize Juniata as an institution by showing how people from *all* segments of its constituency have contributed to the evolution of a distinguished college. This includes the student-athletes, their coaches, and the whole sports program. At Juniata the term student-athlete is no mere cliché; varsity letter-winners often excel in their studies and graduate with academic honors. A great number have become loyal alumni, and many return to College Hill as trustees. Few college histories, if any, have ever treated athletics as an integral part of higher education. I think intercollegiate sports reveal an important aspect of a college's character.

I rather like the way I ended the preface in *Truth Sets Free,* although I have no recollection twenty-five years later where I came across the quotation. I wrote: "Someone has said that 'the potency of college memories lies in the fact that in those years we made the most memorable decisions of our lives.'" So I hope, as I did in 1976, that this 125th anniversary retelling of Juniata's distinctive past "evokes among Juniatians of all ages happy thoughts of days spent on College Hill."

ACKNOWLEDGMENTS

I have read that the University of Chicago Press forbids its authors from thanking any of its staff by name. If that ban applied to the staff of Beeghly Library at Juniata College, this page of acknowledgments would be drastically abridged. I owe a debt of gratitude to so many of them.

First of all, Library Director John Mumford readily set up a spacious workplace in the Archives for me. This meant encroachment upon Archivist Donald Durnbaugh's quiet sanctum, but he made me quite welcome. Donna Grove, library office assistant, sat at a desk just outside the Archives and helped me in countless ways to get what I was looking for. Always, too, there was Lynn Jones, library circulation supervisor, who as in my research for past books, willingly came to my aid no matter how busy she was. So did a duet of public service librarians, Robert Bleil and Andrew Dudash. These two young gentlemen could track down all kinds of minutiae for me, always promptly and in good humor despite my frequent intrusions upon their heavily scheduled days. Unfailingly they knew, smart as they are, what it was I was looking for, even when I did not. In a real sense, all of these professionals were partners in the preparation of this book.

Others of Beeghly locale gave me moral support, though they probably did not realize it. When I would sneak in the back door before the library opened every morning, Patricia Lightner, cataloging assistant, and Bethany Yocum, acquisitions clerk, gave my day a bright start with their cheery greetings. The summer of 1999, senior Julia

Krall, on work-study duty, would call out through the opened Archives' door, "Good morning, Earl," which was always an early-day tonic.

Elsewhere on campus, Evelyn Pembrooke in the alumni relations office gave my visits her immediate attention. Others kindly responsive when I needed them were Brett Basom in admissions; Darwin Kysor in career services; Carole Gracey and Philip Thompson in the business office; Violet Confer, Jane Croyle, Patricia Musselman, Lisa Wiedemer, Ronald Wyrick, and Marsha Frye Hartman in development; Margaret McChesney in academic records; Brenda Roll in external relations and marketing; Russell Shelley in the music department; Dawn Scialabba in Ellis Hall; Joanne Krugh in the provost's office; Renee Lucas in the J. Omar Good office; Christine Sowell in the Science Outreach Project office; and Jeremy Santos in the Juniata College Bookstore.

Nancy Siegel, curator of the Juniata College Museum of Art and blessed with a singular gift in visual history, was of immense aid in the selection of photographic illustrations. Rosann Brown, Juniata's publications coordinator/graphic designer, and college writer Valerie Gliem also had a hand in readying photographs for this book. It was always a delight to work with Administrative Assistant to the President Joanne Park. In Founders Hall Joan Parsons Engle, director of development research and operations, smilingly tolerated my unannounced presence or disruptive telephone calls countless times. The same was true with Cynthia Gilbert Clarke, institutional research specialist, who always put herself at my beck and call with no show of impatience.

Talk about patience! Sports Information Director Melvin Parker (everybody calls him "Bub") had to put up with my rifling through his file cabinets or record books days at a time. Engrossed though he might be at his word processor preparing a sports release, he answered my intrusive questions forthwith, unannoyed. My presence was a violation of his office privacy, yet he inevitably responded, "No problem." Two other alumni, Joseph Scialabba, former part-time SID, and James Hunt, retired editor of *The Daily News*, who filled in for a year in sports information, were very helpful. All the varsity coaches I sought out generously put themselves at my disposal: William Berrier, Lawrence Bock, Kathleen Collins, Jon Cutright, and John Mumford (in addition to heading the library, John is associate head men's soccer coach). Permilla Sloan and Belinda Zauzig in the athletic department office obligingly gave me help from time to time.

For the behind-the-scene story of how the William von Liebig benefaction came to pass, I am beholden to three longtime friends—Miriam and Eugene Brumbaugh and Beulah Baugher, who did their part to make it happen. And to David Hawsey, former Juniata vice-president and dean of enrollment, I tip my hat in thanks for researching figures on von Liebig's personal wealth and the net worth of his major foundation.

I deeply appreciate the ready support many administrators gave this history project: Presidents Robert Neff and Thomas Kepple, Vice-President John Hille, Provost James Lakso, Vice-President William Alexander, and retired Vice-President Harold Brumbaugh (now deceased). Alumnus William Alexander, for two decades mastermind of college finance and operations, often took time on the spur of the moment to answer my telephonic inquiries about the mysteries (to me) of fiscal and budgetary matters. To David Gildea, director of external relations and marketing, I am most grateful for all his support. And I cannot say enough about the help Pat Kepple gave me; as my copy editor, proofreader, and go-between with the publisher, she was truly a godsend.

On the domestic front, I am much obliged to Susan Kaylor Herrold, the family's computer guru, who was always just an e-mail or a phone call away, despite her busy roles of wife, mother, businesswoman, and civic leader. The greatest debt of gratitude I owe to my wife, Harriet. We have spent a good block of our retirement years collaborating on this history. She deciphered my handwritten manuscript, with its marginal additions running hither and yon, and put it in shape for the publisher via the word processor. I profited much from her criticisms (she called them "suggestions") of style and grammar. It could be said that this book, due to be published in 2001, is our anniversary gift to each other. On June 30, in the college's 125th year, the two of us will hold a special celebration of our own: fifty years as husband and wife.

Chapter 1

PROLOGUE: THE FOUNDERS AND THE STRUGGLE FOR BRETHREN SCHOOLS

James Quinter was in his sixty-third year when tapped to head the Brethren's Normal College. It was the summer of 1879. The Huntingdon school had just suffered a traumatic loss in the sudden death of its young principal and first teacher. The trustees, faced with a crisis, created the new office of president. Quinter was their clear choice to fill that post despite his advanced age. A churchman of singular stature, he had relocated his business to Huntingdon, the county seat, largely because of the college, and when it was incorporated he became one of its biggest stockholders.

But his fellow trustees turned to him for other reasons, too. Ever since the year 1856 his name had been vitally linked with educational reform in the Church of the Brethren. It was Quinter who initially forced the issue of higher education upon the church, sparking a revolution that culminated in the Huntingdon institution, the first permanent Brethren college. For two decades a tiny band of educationists looked to him for inspiration while carrying on a patient but hard-hitting propaganda crusade. They were stymied on every hand by antagonism, apathy, and failure, until their work took lasting hold on April 17, 1876.

Both Quinter and the cause of Brethren education had come a long way since 1856. When that year turned up on the calendar Quinter was a part-time pastor and backwoods schoolteacher in Southwestern Pennsylvania. He was a man of handsome features, with broad forehead, bushy eyebrows, and full-flowing beard. The forty-year-old preacher-teacher was living on a small, run-down farm provided as a parsonage by the George's Creek congregation in Fayette County. He was never one to quip or make small talk, and he seldom laughed. In later life, though, he always recalled his agrarian days with mirthful laughter, joking how the parishioners soon learned he was not "cut out" for a farmer.

Nobody, however, doubted his competence when behind the pulpit or in the classroom. He was one of Nicholson Township's most respected citizens, the examiner of those seeking teacher certification in the district. He was already known as a first-rate debater—sharp witted, eloquent, forceful, and devastatingly logical. Within the next half-decade he would emerge as the premier Brethren polemicist in that age of formal interdenominational debates.

But now Quinter, who had married at age thirty-four, was about to leave his flock of fourteen years and his pupils at Dogwood Hollow School, which he had organized in 1850 and which met in the local Mennonite meetinghouse. Sometime in midwinter he had announced plans to take up new duties as coeditor of the *Gospel Visitor,* the recently introduced Brethren periodical. After nearly five years this humble paper's pressroom was still a springhouse loft on a farm near Poland, Ohio.

When the *Visitor* had made its debut, Quinter began to contribute doctrinal articles under the nom de plume "Clement." (Brethren of that time frowned upon real-name bylines as a mark of vanity.) His flair for writing immediately caught the publisher's eye and soon brought him the offer of an editorial post. Journalism, as the future soon showed, gave Quinter an opportune way to reach a wider audience in a long-held personal cause of his: a Brethren "high school." Such an idea was tantamount to heresy in the thinking of most Dunkers, especially for one of their spokesmen.

Educational maverick though he was, Quinter never wavered in his advocacy. His own schooling had been necessarily meager, much to his everlasting regret. But he had nourished his hungry mind over the years with the impressive private library he was building up, husbanding every cent he could from a scanty income to buy books. He had been one of only a very few members of the denomination to take up public school teaching after the tax-supported systems became law—the late 1830s in his case. Now, twenty years afterward, there were still but a handful of teaching Dunkers.

BRETHREN LIFE AND THOUGHT

Brethren leaders of the Civil War era held no objection to a common school education (elementary grades) but dismissed the value of further learning. Traditionally, they were a simple people, welcoming the label "peculiar." Their religious heritage—the product of an Anabaptist-Pietist synthesis—derived from German ancestors who migrated to Penn's Province in the 1720s, the victims of persecution. (At first officially called German Baptist Brethren, the denomination changed its name to Church of the Brethren in 1908.)

Later generations of Brethren pioneered and followed the shifting frontier to settle together in little Dunker colonies, neighboring with their kind. ("Dunker" or "Dunkard" was a popular colloquialism for the Brethren, an English corruption of the German word "to baptize by immersion.") Dunkers, until the late 1800s, stayed on the farm or lived in rural villages, distrustful of the city. Some became storekeepers or learned a trade, but few entered the professions.

Their lifestyle, typical of kindred sects among the Pennsylvania German, cherished such values as nonconformity, nonresistance, refusal to go to court or take judicial oaths, frugality, and plain speech and dress. The sartorial badge of Brethrenism for men was the straight-collared coat, broad-brimmed hat, and full beard (sans mustache); for women it was the bonnet and prayer covering. In business transactions a Dunker's word was said to be as good as his bond.

From colonial times, therefore, the Brethren, unsophisticated and uneasy with distinctions of rank and title (everybody was either "brother" or "sister"), had manifested a deep-seated prejudice against an educated ministry. Originally it had been the need of a trained clergy that had spurred the wholesale founding of small denominational colleges during the first half of the nineteenth century. But not so with the sectarian Brethren; they refused to place any confidence in education or in a learned leadership. New Testament literalists, they naively argued that if learning was so important Jesus would have chosen some educated men for disciples and the Apostle Paul would have founded schools along with churches. Hence no intramural pressure whatsoever was generated for educating the Brethren cloth; when the church finally did enter the field of higher education it was for another reason.

Instead, the Brethren in those days operated under a system called the "free ministry"—whereby part-time preachers were elected from the ranks of the laity, receiving no salary. The highest ordained office was the eldership, attained by progressing through two lower probationary degrees. But for the bulk of elders and lower-degree ministers, nothing more than a rudimentary schooling answered all their educational needs until long after the Civil War.

Thus "worldly wisdom" came to be viewed with abhorrence by the elders controlling Annual Meeting. Three times between 1831 and 1853 the question of higher education was debated by the ruling elders. Each time they vetoed all schooling beyond the elementary level, condemning academies and colleges alike. For example, to the question in 1853, "Is it right for a brother to go to college, or teach the same?" the church fathers replied, "[W]e would deem college a very unsafe place for a simple follower of Christ, inasmuch as they are calculated to lead us astray from the faith and obedience of the Gospel."[1] The same warning had been given two years earlier about academies. Such, then, was the cultural milieu out of which James Quinter came and against which he would set himself a champion of liberal education over the next two decades.

BEGINNING OF THE BRETHREN SCHOOL MOVEMENT

In the shift from teacher-pastor to editor in 1856, Quinter discovered, quite by chance, a fellow heretic in Henry Kurtz, his quirky employer, who himself had been mulling over a school project. Kurtz, born and educated in Germany, was a defrocked Lutheran dominie turned Dunker. A hump-backed man addicted to the pipe, he had lost his pastoral license in the 1820s for flirting with communal societies. Soon afterward he joined the Brethren. Their clannish ways seemed to promise supportive human relationships like those professed by communitarianism. Overcoming stiff opposition in 1851 he brought out his monthly *Gospel Visitor,* the first authorized Brethren periodical (now called *Messenger*) and one of the oldest denominational magazines in America. At that time Kurtz was no doubt the best-educated member of the church.

Acting without delay the new editorial team informed the Brotherhood about their "contemplated school" in a rather novel fashion. Quinter, while on a debating tour back East, wrote Kurtz a letter setting forth ways of implementing their brainchild. Kurtz printed this correspondence in the March issue of the *Visitor* with parenthetical comment. The chief purpose of the school, the letter revealed, should be "to educate young brethren for school-teachers"; secondarily, it should serve as "an auxiliary for the advancement of Gospel truth."[2] Such an institution, it was pointed out, would ensure that Brethren children would not be "deprived of a vital element of education, namely the moral and religious," an educational element, the editors felt, lacking in the public schools.

But in launching the school, Quinter stressed, there was one important desideratum: the need for "well qualified teachers—teachers possessing both literary and moral qualifications." The assistant editor then proposed a plan for finding teachers of high quality. He wrote, "Send one or two young brethren to school to qualify them for teachers…I would prefer poor young men who look for success in life, to their own exertions, and the blessing of heaven." He concluded his letter by outlining alternative scholarship programs interested church members could adopt in helping those persons selected for this training.

The dissenting duo knew their school proposal would horrify the hierarchy of elders, but they sincerely believed that the church needed to come out of its cultural shell if it hoped to survive. As Quinter wrote in the heat of controversy, "Shall we as a denomination throw ourselves into a hostile position against the onward march of intellectual improvement?"[3]

There was ample evidence that more and more Brethren youth had educational aspirations and were kicking over the scholastic traces. Teaching had gained new status and stability under the state public school systems, and to many farm-weary Brethren boys it seemed to offer a ticket for escape. Some of them were finding their way to academies for their post-common school education. Until the 1890s the academy, not the high school, stood as America's dominant secondary institution. Academies were basically private schools, often with church ties, and dependent upon donations, endowments, and student fees for their support. In addition to serving as surrogate high schools, they performed the popular function of training teachers (state normal schools were just coming into vogue in the 1850s).

A recurrent theme in the Kurtz-Quinter argument was that many Brethren students, especially those who attended sectarian academies, ended up defecting from the church. This attrition alarmed the two reformers. (Brethren at mid-century probably numbered no more than thirty thousand, about a fourth of them Pennsylvanians.)[4] They were convinced that several good Brethren "high schools" would stop this drain of talented youth.

As expected, Quinter's letter drew immediate fire from *Visitor* readers. They argued that a church-backed school would do more harm than good. Nevertheless, the two publishers stood their ground, and in the September issue of their paper Quinter contended

> We think it not only right that the church should encourage such institutions in which our youth may acquire useful knowledge, but we think it is her duty—a duty she owes to her God, to herself, and to the rising generation, to encourage and build up such institutions.[5]

Despite the vocal negative reaction, they expectantly moved their press to nearby Columbiana, Ohio, in April of 1857, giving the following explanation to their reading audience:

> It was not only to increase our facilities to send out our Publication, that we desired a more favorable location, but the idea of establishing a school, a subject heretofore introduced, to meet the want of such of the Brethren who desire better opportunities than are now enjoyed among us for obtaining an intellectual and Christian education for their youth, to prepare them for the useful occupations of life, has not been abandoned by us. The propriety of an institution of the kind contemplated, becomes more apparent....[6]

But when a query on the "propriety" of a school came before Annual Meeting that May, it was put down with the verdict: "It is conforming to the world. The Apostle Paul says, 'Knowledge puffeth up but charity edifieth.'"[7]

In the June *Visitor* Quinter betrayed a hint of annoyance at the haste with which some business items on Annual Meeting's agenda had been decided. He implied that the school matter had received less attention than it deserved so that the delegates could bring the conference to a prompt end and leave for home. For the time being, however, he and Kurtz took refuge in the hope "that if it should meet the approbation of the Lord, the plan would in time be matured, and the various means for its expectations obtained."[8] Quinter, meanwhile, was distracted by his wife's failing health, and in October her death left him with a motherless daughter. Yet, the burden of personal problems did not remove him altogether from the school struggle; he still drafted trenchant editorials.

His adversaries built their case generally on two main fears. First, education would inevitably make the Brethren proud. No longer would they be willing "to stoop so low as to engage in the common kinds of labor, or mechanical arts, to make a living," wrote one diehard. Second, a school would lead directly to a paid and professional ministry. Dunker "free ministers," the same writer predicted, would be transformed into "gospel sellers," making merchandize of the Gospel,...[and] selling it to them that will pay them the most money." In response to the alarmists, Quinter restated the purpose of the school more broadly than he had originally. Contended the coeditor:

> The design is no more to qualify young men for the ministry, than it is to qualify them for farmers, or mechanics, or school teachers, or any of the avocations of life. The design is to offer to our youth the facilities for acquiring the various branches of useful knowledge which they may wish to acquire, in order that

they may be qualified for whatever calling in life their inclinations may profess....[9]

Patient journalism and effective behind-the-scenes lobbying finally paid off at the 1858 Annual Meeting. The editorial pair got the go-ahead nod for their pet project when the elders announced: "Concerning the school proposed in the 'Gospel Visitor,' we think we have no right to interfere with the individual enterprise so long as there is no departure from gospel principles."[10] What arguments carried the day were never recorded, only the terse sanctioning statement. It was a momentous decision for the church. A new era of Brethren educational history had dawned. Nevertheless, the antischool sentiment was far from dead at Dunkerdom's grass roots. The 1858 statement simply acquiesced in the establishment of secondary schools by church members. In no way did it imply that these schools should be regarded as official Brethren institutions although operated and capitalized by Brethren.

EARLY ABORTIVE SCHOOL VENTURES

Ironically, the honor of starting the first Brethren school did not go to Kurtz and Quinter. In April of 1861, just as cannon were booming at Fort Sumter, Solomon Sharp of Central Pennsylvania opened up a school in Mifflin County's beautiful Big Valley. A Mennonite convert to the Dunker fold, he borrowed money from his farmer-brothers and bought Kishacoquillas Seminary, a defunct Presbyterian plant located about ten miles from Lewistown (the brick building still stands, in good shape).

Sharp, quite possibly the first Dunker graduate of a state normal school, had earned a Bachelor of Elements degree from Millersville, Pennsylvania, in 1860, and with proper credentials in hand, he made known his ambition of becoming the headmaster of a normal school or academy. At the time of his decision to purchase the bankrupt Big Valley institution the twenty-five-year-old educator was the principal of McVeytown's grade school. While teaching there he had cursorily surveyed Brethren congregations in adjacent counties. He came across a goodly number of aspiring teachers who promised their patronage if he started a secondary school in the area. Thus encouraged, he took over the former Presbyterian facility and renamed it Kishacoquillas Seminary and Normal Institute.

Coeducational, Kishacoquillas aimed to prepare its students either to teach or to qualify for sophomore standing in college. It was the first Brethren-related school to offer a curriculum that included college-level work. The seminary also introduced Dunkers to a liberal education, its course offerings embracing the classics, higher mathematics, advanced sciences, music, oil painting, and foreign languages along with regular English subjects. Sharp operated his school until 1866, managing to survive the turbulent war years in black ink. But five years of sacrificial toil left him jaded and his wife's health broken, and so he sold it—but to someone outside the Brotherhood.

This pioneering Dunker pedagogue, who later achieved eminence as a geologist and put in stints as president of three Brethren colleges, left his mark on two of Juniata's future genitors. One of them was a farm boy named John Brumbaugh, a prize student of his at Kishacoquillas, whose experience there convinced the teenager of the need for Brethren schools. The other was twenty-year-old Jacob Zuck, whom Sharp took under his pedagogical wing at Millersville State Normal School, where he taught for a time after getting rid of the seminary. In 1868 Sharp moved to Tennessee to assume the principalship of the New Providence Institute at Maryville. When Zuck finished his studies two years later, he was very nearly lured into accepting a position as assistant principal at his former mentor's school.

Meanwhile, six months after Sharp had got his seminary underway, Quinter headed up a school of his own—but not in Columbiana as originally planned. Some friends of education in Southern Ohio bought a brick building in New Vienna and invited Kurtz and Quinter to start an academy there. Because the printing business was down at that time, the editors decided against risking a move to another location. But it was arranged for Quinter, lately remarried, to take charge of the school while still maintaining editorial ties with the *Visitor*. The New Vienna Academy, however, lasted only three years, closing in 1864, done in by wartime conditions and church resistance.

Despite the church's obscurantism Quinter did not despair, remaining confirmed in his Dunkerism. This was something of a curiosity, because as a progressive he often had to play the rebel, yet he never reflected the rebel's sense of alienation. His unwavering loyalty to the church was illustrated by an incident that took place shortly after the New Vienna Academy folded. An educated minister of another denomination heard the ex-academy head preach. At the close of the service he said to him, "You have too much talent to waste on those slow Dunkards." Replied Quinter, "You say they are slow; then I'll remain with them to help them."[11]

After the short-lived New Vienna venture, the proschool faction attempted nothing more until 1870 when a few of them in the Midwest tried to start a college at Bourbon, Indiana. Known as Salem College and taking Oberlin for a model, it billed itself as of "equal rank with the best colleges in Europe and America."[12] This latest undertaking had an auspicious beginning and finished its first year with 125 students. But internal discord developed, followed by legal entanglements, and the institution went under in 1874, at great financial loss to its investors.

THE BRUMBAUGHS ENTER THE SCHOOL STRUGGLE

Joining the educationists' cry soon after Salem College opened its doors was a pair of new voices: the Brumbaugh brothers, Henry and John. They hailed from Marklesburg, a village a few miles south of Huntingdon, in Woodcock Valley. In 1870 they had entered the publishing field with their paper, the *Pilgrim*. Two other Brethren periodicals were then in existence: the monthly *Visitor* (Quinter was now the editor and part-owner), and a weekly, the *Christian Family Companion,* established in 1864 by Henry Holsinger of nearby Tyrone. Holsinger's *Companion,* however, was stridently progressive and offended many Brethren who demanded another weekly with more temperate editorial policies. The Brumbaughs, tenderfoots in the printing trade, hoped to meet this need in a rival weekly publication. Henry Brumbaugh once characterized the *Pilgrim* in this way: "While it was aggressive and always on the side of liberal views, it did it in a way not to arouse antagonism or to engender strife among the church people...."[13] As reformers, the *Pilgrim* publishers, conciliatory yet plucky, were the psychological doubles of Quinter.

Henry Brumbaugh was his brother's senior by a dozen years and the ascendant member of their business partnership. Born on a farm along the Raystown Branch, he began teaching school at seventeen. During the late 1850s he attended Williamsburg Academy (private) in Blair County and Cassville Seminary (Methodist), on the other side of Terrace Mountain from his home, in Trough Creek Valley. The older Brumbaugh, slight of build, his bearded face accentuated by a large nose, deep-set eyes, and wavy hair, taught school for nine years. Until after the *Pilgrim* came out he lived on the homestead farm, helping to work it while making and peddling brooms as a sideline.

In 1855, when nineteen, he became a diarist and for the next sixty years kept a meticulous record of his private and public activities—even the dates, places, titles, and texts of all the sermons he ever preached (he was called to the ministry by the James Creek congregation in 1864).[14] A voracious reader, Henry Brumbaugh was a deviant Dunker from his youth—long before he pulled an un-Dunkerlike stunt in 1860 by eloping with his boyhood sweetheart (a Lutheran), counting down the days until the scheduled caper by coded entries in his diary. He read widely, not only in the Bible and theology, but also in literature, philosophy, psychology, and history. Music also gave him pleasure, and he learned to play the melodeon in defiance of the Dunker ban on musical instruments of all kinds.

John Brumbaugh, his broad face framed by a neatly trimmed beard, shared his brother's passion for a liberal education. He also attended Cassville Seminary, afterward coming under Sharp's tutelage at Kishacoquillas. After teaching school for a while the quiet, reserved twenty-year-old Penn Township native spent a few months as Holsinger's apprentice at Tyrone before entering into the *Pilgrim* partnership in January of 1870.

Within a year after the *Pilgrim's* maiden appearance, the Brumbaugh brothers emerged as ringleaders of a school movement in Pennsylvania, apparently drawing encouragement from the early successes of Salem College. In league with them was Henry Holsinger, the firebrand *Companion* editor whose radical stance would provoke a major schism within the church in another dozen years. The three of them conferred about the project for the first time on March 4, 1871, in Marklesburg.

This meeting inspired the initial Brumbaugh editorial on higher education and Brethren schools. They insisted that "a good liberal education would be an advantage to us all," lamenting that in the absence of a Brethren school "your unworthy Editors...were therefore necessitated to place ourselves under sectarian influences."[15] Such an experience, they observed, made them "no worse or better," but they would have preferred going to a school "taught by our brethren."

A second confabulation by the three men followed several months later, on October 19, this time with some district elders present. Several likely locations for a school were brought up: Berlin in Somerset County and four communities in Central Pennsylvania—McVeytown, Mount Union, Tyrone, and Martinsburg, all boasting rail service. Holsinger pressed for Berlin, near Meyersdale, where he had since relocated his paper, while the Brumbaughs favored Martinsburg, where they had plans to remove their business and introduce a secular newspaper. The *Pilgrim* editors pointed out that Martinsburg was set in a stronghold of Dunkerism and had available the building and grounds of the Juniata Collegiate Institute, then for sale.

The Pennsylvania school movement fell strangely quiescent after that midfall colloquy, probably because of little general support. Nothing more was heard editorially from the Brumbaughs on the subject for a whole twelvemonth—not until October 1872. John was then off studying at Millersville, and so it was Henry who broke the silence and tried to revive interest. In a forceful October 1 article he used Salem College as a model for the dormant Keystone State project. But it met with apathy among the readership.

By now, a close kinsman of the *Pilgrim* owners had entered the school fray, using buttonholing tactics rather than the power of the press. This was the Huntingdon physician, Dr. Andrew B. Brumbaugh, their cousin-german. An erstwhile teacher himself (nine years), the thirty-six-year-old surgeon was the first member of the Church of the Brethren to earn a medical degree (University of Pennsylvania, 1866). Before that, he had attended an academy near Newport, Perry County, and the normal school at Millersville. Born and bred on a Woodcock Valley farm, he was mechanically inclined, training himself to be ambidextrous—a skill that later stood him in good stead at the operating table. For a period of time he supported his family as a carpenter and cabinetmaker, all the while preparing himself for medical studies by poring over anatomy textbooks laid out before him on the workbench. Dr. Brumbaugh even learned tailoring in his youth and made his own wedding suit. He was a man of tremendous drive and wide interests, taking the words of Longfellow literally: "Life is real! Life is earnest!"—a line he liked to quote.[16] Dr. "A. B.," as everybody addressed him, was determined to have a Brethren school in the town where he practiced medicine. He saw the birth of the *Pilgrim* at Marklesburg as a logical step in that direction. Many times he was heard to say, "A paper and an advanced educational institution together at Huntingdon."[17] When discussing the subject, he had a habit of striking the palm of his left hand with his right fist for emphasis.

The good doctor bombarded influential Brethren with letters urging the need of an eastern school and Huntingdon as the place for it. He gladly made his downtown Washington Street home a way stop for church leaders passing through the area. Inevitably, houseguests were treated to a buggy tour of suitable school sites, especially vacant West End lots. All the while they had to listen to his spiel about the town's great virtues. Sometime in the early 1870s he took a five-year lease on two corner lots at 14th and Mifflin streets, which were to be used, his diary reveals, "for a mission school or church."[18]

His first choice of locations, though, was what is now the J. C. Blair Hospital knoll. One November day in 1872 he took Henry Holsinger up there, and that feisty descendant of Alexander Mack, father of the Church of the Brethren, fairly raved about the panoramic view it afforded. It was, indeed, a splendid site for a school! That night, in the comfort of the doctor's home, he wrote for his column, "Editor's Diary":

> Before we leave Huntingdon, we must not forget to mention the beautiful site for a College. About one mile west of town, is an elevation which appears to have been especially thrown up for some public institution. The scenery is grand beyond description. At a distance can be seen the mountains and hills, dressed in their coats of many colors, overlooking the tallest steeples that rise from the town at its base. If a Normal School should be wanted in that section of country, that Normal Hill is the finest location our knowledge.[19]

A couple months after Dr. A. B. and Holsinger took their carriage junket, John Brumbaugh, writing for the *Pilgrim* from Millersville, made a strong plea of his own for a school in the East. He observed that of the five hundred or so students at Millersville only seven or eight came from Brethren families. These young men did not "feel at home" at secular schools, he alleged, and went on to deplore the absence of Dunkeress classmates. He warned that there were too many "temptations" at nonsectarian institutions. The *Pilgrim's* junior partner minced no words in stating his position: "Since I have been here I am more than ever impressed with the necessity of having a school conducted by the brethren, and situated among the brethren."[20] But antieducationists kept bringing up the stock argument that "colleges lead pride into the church." One important elder in Franklin County about that time went around telling people—in the idiom of the Pennsylvania Dutch—"how higher education would spoil their sons, how they would come home from college dressed in fine broadcloth, wearing a high bee gum hat, swinging a little cane, and acting like dudes."[21]

A pointed *Pilgrim* editorial in April of 1873 dismissed such charges as baseless, begging the question. To those "aged brethren" frightened by innovations, the Brumbaughs countered with a warning of their own:

> Again, it is said to be something new, and therefore some object to schools. Schools among the Brethren may be something new....The subject and discussion of it, however, is nothing new, and indeed it is becoming old enough, if there is any virtue in age, to demand some attention. . . .
>
> Schools are nothing new. They have existed for centuries, and we as a Church, have, to a limited extent, availed ourselves of the advantages to be derived from them. This we may still continue to do, but unless we ourselves take hold of the work of education, the surrounding influence will certainly lead many, that may be bright and shining ornaments in the Church, away from it.

And to those who linked education to a professional ministry, the editorial offered assurances:

> There is an idea extant among part of the Brotherhood at least, that were we to establish schools the design would be to prepare our brethren for the ministry, and that our ministers would finally drift into the same channel with other Churches....We can assure you, brethren, that were this so, we would be among the number that would oppose schools.[22]

This editorial provided the first inkling of the kind of school the Brumbaughs envisioned. It advised against any "high sounding" name like "college" and simply recommended "Brethren's School." The implication was that it should be a grade between common school and college—an academy—and of course, coeducational, teaching the arts and sciences as well as the "humble principles of the Church."[23]

For some time now Dr. A. B. Brumbaugh had been importuning his *Pilgrim* relatives to relocate their business in Huntingdon instead of Martinsburg. Finally, early in 1873, they opted for the doctor's hometown. Their decision, reached while Henry was engaged in visiting possible school sites there, was aided by a dream he once described to David Emmert, Juniata's first art teacher. Emmert wrote in his delightful little book, *Reminiscences of Juniata College:* "So favorably impressed was the senior member of the firm by his study of the location that shortly afterwards he had a dream in which he saw a school full-fledged and a large body of students marching down one of the main streets."[24]

Huntingdon was then a bustling town of some three thousand souls and a station for two railroads. It seemed to them to give more promise for business growth than Martinsburg where their newspaper, the *Cove Echo*, had not fared too well. (The *Echo* was published from February to September 1872 under the supervision of an employee, who then bought them out.) And so, on April 1, Henry closed a deal with another Henry Brumbaugh, his first cousin, a prosperous Woodcock Valley farmer and brother of Dr. A. B., paying $250 for a West Huntingdon lot at 14th and Washington streets. He made plans to begin building on it at once.

Two days prior to Christmas, Henry Brumbaugh and his family moved into an unfinished three-story brick complex—half of it designed for living quarters, the other half for business. Eight wagons, supplied by relatives and friends, hauled the household goods and shop equipment the twelve miles to Huntingdon, while Susan, his wife, and three-year-old Harvey came by way of the Huntingdon and Broad Top Railroad. The unmarried John took a room on Penn Street above 14th.

Even though preoccupied with all the urgent problems that go with adjusting to new familial and business conditions, the Brumbaughs did not neglect the school question. Salem College's imminent demise at the turn of the new year, threatening to deprive the Brethren of their only school, fired them to push harder for one in Pennsylvania. Now ready to put their scheme to a test of popular support, they and their ally, Henry Holsinger, called a general meeting of interested members for March 16, 1874, at the Martinsburg Church.

A large gathering was on hand when that day arrived, the majority from the Central Pennsylvania region. Some prominent district elders, like the revered James Sell and Graybill Myers, spoke out persuasively in favor of a Pennsylvania school. But the opposition was represented, too, and a real difference of opinion surfaced. Henry Brumbaugh later told of one Dunker elder at the meeting who cornered him and Holsinger and said in all candor: "Well, brethren, I love *you* but I don't love your cause."[25] The consensus, however, was to push ahead on the project and capitalize the school on a joint-stock basis. Several potential school sites were nominated, but the list was finally narrowed down to three: Huntingdon, Martinsburg, and Berlin. Brumbaugh support went to Huntingdon, but despite the advantages of railroad services and basic public utilities (waterworks and gaslights), that community had no organized Brethren church. So it was ruled out. Martinsburg, in Morrisons Cove, was likewise dropped after it was decided to locate the school at the place which pledged the most money. The best the Morrisons Cove people could do on the spur of the moment was to raise only a few thousand dollars.

This left Berlin, sponsored by Holsinger and James Quinter, whose representatives came up with thirty thousand dollars in pledges. Further deliberation produced a name for the prospective school: the Brethren High School of Berlin. Other action set a subscription goal of one hundred thousand dollars, but no payments were to be collectible until the total amount was subscribed. Holsinger was appointed to direct the fund-raising drive. He was assisted by Solomon Sharp, who came up from Tennessee where he was then a professor at Maryville College. Central and Western Pennsylvania were thoroughly canvassed, as were parts of Ohio.

The *Pilgrim* men and Quinter (since the previous year the two other Brethren organs had been consolidated under him and headquartered at Meyersdale) put their papers solidly behind this latest school movement. Henry Brumbaugh made several trips to Somerset County over the succeeding months, consulting with Holsinger, Quinter, and other promoters on campaign strategy and progress.

Meanwhile, in April of that same spring, Lewis Kimmel—without fanfare or advance publicity—began his Plum Creek Normal School near the village of Elderton in Armstrong County. He and Oliver Miller, who had been Quinter's assistant at the New Vienna Academy, were the first two Brethren to earn liberal arts degrees (in 1859). Kimmel's three children were the only students to show up on the morning of Plum Creek's opening.

Plum Creek went ignored by the antieducationists, but "letters to the editor" poured into the *Pilgrim* office protesting the Berlin enterprise. These were scrupulously printed along with the far fewer favorable ones. The negative letters fretted about the "dangerous outgrowths of education," or reminded readers that the scriptures did not "authorize" high schools, or kept up the hue and cry about a professional ministry. All of which drove the Brumbaughs to editorialize a bit testily in early October:

> That a school among the brethren means a paid ministry and a hundred other evil prophesies has no real existence, save in the minds of those who have come to these conclusions....Hence we think it unsafe to think certain things and offer them as real, and as supports to our argument.[26]

JACOB ZUCK AND THE SCHOOL MOVEMENT

Though still $40,000 short of the projected $100,000 goal by year's end and in violation of the procedural plan adopted at Martinsburg, the Berlin Brethren decided to move ahead with a school as soon as possible. Holsinger got in touch with Jacob Zuck, a normal-school graduate pursuing further studies in Ohio, and tendered him the position of headmaster. Zuck had written a few proeducation articles for the church papers during the past year, quickly emerging as one of the leading apologists for the cause.

He traveled to Berlin early in January of 1875 to explore Holsinger's invitation. His visit almost ended in disaster, from the way he later told it. On the thirty-five-mile sleigh trip south from Johnstown, he and his host ran into a blinding snowstorm.

Apparently the sleigh bogged down in a deep drift, and, handicapped by his bad hip, Zuck nearly succumbed to the cold before reaching the safety of a nearby farmhouse.[27] But the Berlin scheme was destined to miscarry. First of all, Zuck's fragile health prevented him from taking over right away, and there was no one else available or willing. Years afterward, the schismatic Holsinger wistfully remarked that the Berlin movement "would, no doubt, have been successful had not Brother Zuck been attacked by one of his frequent indispositions just at the time when it was desired to open the school."[28] Then, on top of that, the depression of the 1870s struck with a paralyzing blow, and the ambitious fund-raising campaign began to peter out.

Thus, by the end of 1875, the educationists had little to show for all their industry and promotional activity over the past two decades. Lewis Kimmel's quiet work at Plum Creek, carried on in a remote rural locale and taken seriously by few, represented their only tangible gain to date. And so while the nation busily prepared for its upcoming centennial, Brethren schoolmen faced the future with no particular enthusiasm. But this picture would abruptly change in the months ahead—all because of a fortuitous incident.

On New Year's Day 1876 a young man with a noticeable limp got off the train at Huntingdon early that afternoon. A few minutes later John Brumbaugh and Eleanor, his wife of little over a year, heard a knock on the door of their apartment in the *Pilgrim* building, home for them since setting up housekeeping. The unexpected caller was Jacob Zuck, John's good friend whom he had gotten to know while at Millersville a few years back. Zuck, older than Brumbaugh by a year and a half, had returned to Millersville in the spring of 1873 for additional study in the sciences (he had graduated in 1870). But he also taught some classes and acted as a residence hall advisor. The two of them had taken to each other at once and afterward kept in close touch by letter or occasional visit.

Now, here was Zuck in the Brumbaugh home, on an impulse stopping off to pay his respects. John urged his visitor to stay overnight and entrain for home the next day, an offer gladly accepted. While the two comrades reminisced, their talk turned to the plight of education among the Brethren. The guest said, "I'm sorry, but there's surely a pressing need for a revival of educational work among our people." Then he sighed, "But the revival can only be brought about by hard work and sacrifice on the part of the friends of education."[29]

Both Brumbaugh and Zuck, it developed, thought Holsinger had been unrealistic in his grandiose expectation of raising one hundred thousand dollars from within the denomination so bitterly divided on the school issue. At this point in the conversation John Brumbaugh responded, "All's quiet now, and no effort's being made to start a school anywhere. Let's quietly start one right here. There are a few vacant rooms in the *Pilgrim* building that could be used for this purpose."

Zuck looked at his younger friend in surprise. He replied that "he had no money and that the income from the students he might get would not pay his boarding." To which demurer, his host retorted, "Do it on a small scale. You can board at least six months in my home without any charge. We'll not let you suffer."[30] Brumbaugh recalled, "I shall not forget how he looked me squarely in the eyes and asked, 'Do you mean it?'" The *Pilgrim* journalist affirmed his sincerity, and that ended their conversation on the subject. "For," said John in looking back after thirty-two years, "I felt the apparent absurdity of such a proposition and supposed he did also."

But two months later, in March, Zuck wrote his Huntingdon friend to say that the school proposition kept "ringing in his ears." He said, "I cannot see through the project financially, but am sure the Lord will supply our need. I feel sure we need a school, and if you brethren go on in sympathy and will stand by my work, I am willing to try it."[31]

Elated, John showed the letter to his brother and the doctor as soon as possible. They talked it over in the *Pilgrim* office. Analyzing the status of the school movement, all three concurred on writing off the Berlin endowment fund as doomed to failure. They also discussed Plum Creek and the apathetic response of Brethren to Kimmel's current appeal for scholarship aid. On the face of it all—what with an oppositionist church and a deepening nationwide recession—they had to admit that another school effort at the moment seemed a mad idea.

But Dr. A. B. had made up his own mind that they should go ahead, regardless of adverse odds. He proposed, his diary reveals, that *"we start a school here,* and ask for students only, and do such work that the school will commend itself."[32] The others "nobly" seconded the proposal, noted the doctor.

John was instructed to write Zuck and assure him of their cooperation. In his letter he reminded his former school chum how all three Brumbaughs had supported the Berlin cause even though they had worked to get Huntingdon selected as the school site. However, Zuck was advised, if he wished further confirmation on the attitude of the other two men, he should write them personally (which he did). The prospective teacher was also told that Henry would provide space in the *Pilgrim* building, John would guarantee free board, and Dr. A. B. would recruit students and furnish basic equipment.

Several letters were exchanged, in the course of which Zuck spelled out the nonsectarian policy that the school should follow while at the same time honoring Brethren customs. By then the month of March had passed, and only a few days remained until the announced date of the school's opening—April 17.

Chapter 2

JACOB ZUCK—THE MAN AND HIS EXPERIMENT

HIS EARLY LIFE

Jacob Martin Zuck, said Emmert in his *Reminiscences,* was the "dominant spirit" in the formative years of the college. Yet, to present-day Juniatians—familiar with his name but ignorant of his background, his dreams and aspirations, his severe physical disability—their alma mater's founding teacher remains much a man of mystery. Even Emmert, in concentrating on Juniata's genitive period, provides no biographical data and gives few clues to Zuck's character and personality. But from all the material that has come to light, he emerges, in the words of Henry Holsinger, as "an ambitious, energetic young man of push and grit."[1]

Born in a log farmhouse at Claylick, near Mercersburg, Franklin County, Pennsylvania, on October 29, 1846, Zuck was the second in a family of six sons and five daughters. When an infant (age two) he fell and injured his right hip, which lamed him for life. At first he walked with crutches but afterward was able to manage with a cane.

Sickly and crippled, he was spared the drudgery of farm work. This freed him to focus on an education. He attended the Lafayette District School, where an older brother taught, although his frail health kept him home much of the time. He probably never started to school until he was eight or nine. On his first schoolday he was tagged with the nickname "limpy." To one bully whose taunts cut deeply, the maimed boy shouted defiantly, "I can't lick you, and I wouldn't if I could, but I'll beat you in arithmetic before school is over," which, as it turned out, was not an idle boast.[2]

In 1863, at sixteen, he passed the examination that certified him to teach in Franklin County. As a teacher, he popularized interschool spelling bees. Meanwhile, the quietly devout Zuck joined the Welsh Run Church of the Brethren.

STUDENT DAYS AT MILLERSVILLE

Between 1867 and 1870 Zuck spent four summers and one winter at Millersville State Normal School. He paid his own way for the first three summer terms but borrowed money for the winter and summer terms of 1870, putting himself several hundred dollars in debt when he graduated that year. Originally he had no intention of obtaining a normal degree. As he wrote in a short journal titled *My Last Term at the Normal*, he had felt in 1867 that one session was all he needed to prepare for teaching, his "highest aim."[3] But one taste of formal education and he was hooked for good.

The twenty-four-year-old student, who roomed in Harmony Hall, did quite well his last year at Millersville, although trigonometry and Greek gave him trouble. In fact, he barely missed out as class valedictorian, so his diary claims. His one, all-absorbing extracurricular interest as a senior was the Normal Literary Society, the campus debating club. Fellow students elected him treasurer and critic but spurned him for president.

Usually abed by ten and up at five, he complained often of "headaches," and "feeling tired." "Seems I get too little sleep. Much study is a weariness to the flesh, saith the sacred writer," his diary reads for Wednesday, April 29. He had spells of depression and self-doubt, too. The previous day he had made the anxious entry: "Wonder if *I* can succeed as a teacher? Feel discouraged sometimes. Oh the future!" Two days later, on the 26th, he wrote, "I am pretty near tired of going to school. At times I feel almost disgusted, but at other times I am contented and love to be here."

Earlier, in January, he had seen himself in print for the first time, having written a piece for Holsinger's *Companion* called "Preach to Save and Sow to Reap." In April he submitted an article to Holsinger's juvenile paper, the *Pious Youth,* on the evil of smoking. It was followed in May by a second antitobacco essay. Thus was born Zuck the journalist, his pen to be put to increasing use with the passing of time.

A nonsmoker and teetotaler, the abstemious student was equally chaste in speech, once risking a bloody nose to censure a bunch of toughs for their profanity. It happened during a vacation break when he was on the train going home. Annoyed by the salty talk of some rowdies behind him in the coach, he scribbled the words "Why do you swear?" on a scrap of paper and threw it back to them. The accused, incensed at his temerity, shouted threatening remarks and challenged him to fisticuffs—an invitation, of course, he prudently declined.

Zuck, headed for life-long bachelorhood, was no woman-hater in spite of what he wrote in his senior-year journal: "During my school days at the Normal I succeeded quite well in keeping my mind on my books and off the girls." For once final exams were over in July and "after some deliberation and the advice of my chum," he decided to "go for" a girl named Lucie Stager, whom he knew and liked but never took out. He wrote her a billet-doux, then got cold feet and never sent it, missing, he later lamented, a "golden opportunity." And so, unable to "muster up enough courage to ask for a date," he would leave Millersville having "made but little progress" as a swain.

Sometime in the spring Zuck had written to Solomon Sharp, his one-time professor, inquiring about school openings in Tennessee. Late in June he received a letter offering him the post of Sharp's assistant at the new Providence Institute in Maryville. But he "desired something better," after learning the job paid only forty-five dollars a month. Influenced by a classmate, he accepted a grade school position in Schuylkill County for twenty dollars a month more.

Then, on July 21—a warm, sunshiny Thursday—twenty-seven graduates received their diplomas (Bachelor of Elements) in a day-long commencement program, each graduate giving an oration. Having earned "complimentary honors," Zuck spoke on the theme "The Spirit Supreme." His declamation, reported the Millersville *Daily Express,* was a "dignified, elevated production, carefully thought out, and delivered in a deliberate, impressive manner."

On the first Sunday after commencement, the new graduate attended services at his home church and visited with some of his "old friends." It was a distressing experience, at once sad and revelatory, dramatically illustrating for him the widening cultural gulf between educated Brethren and the rank and file membership. In his diary that night he was moved to say of his past companions:

> They are more like strangers to me than many of my Normal Acquaintances. Very little sympathy of feeling—or rather community of feeling—seems to exist between us. Mental culture is a strange term to many. Pity.

THE CAREER TEACHER

His teaching position that fall was in Donaldson, a mining town of about eight hundred then squarely situated in the heartland of Molly Maguire terrorism. In fact, James McParlan, the undercover Pinkerton detective who infiltrated the infamous Irish fraternal order and brought about its downfall a few years later, made Donaldson the first stop on his exploratory trip to the eastern coal regions to choose a base of operations. A polyglot "patch" made up of Dutch, Irish, English, and Welsh, it was nestled in a long, narrow valley that sliced diagonally through the Sharp Mountain range on a northwest-southeast axis.

Zuck arrived at Donaldson on Saturday, September 3, taking a spur of the Philadelphia and Reading Railroad to Tremont and then hiking a mile or so up the valley to his destination. His first impression of the dirty, rough and tumble coal town left him confused and shaken. The typical house was a duplex, "each side having two rooms down and one up" and "made crudely of hemlock boards, with weather stays over the cracks and no plastering, no ceiling, or wall paper."[4] His diary for that day reads:

> I find myself in the mountains and among the sooty miners. As the [men] came from the mines today they looked like Africans of the darkest hue. I hardly know what to think of the "Situation."

The newcomer took room and board at Lornison's Tavern at the going rate of five dollars a week. Before long the sensitive diarist admitted privately: "In one respect this is a very disagreeable place for me to live. My host is a rum-seller and I see spectacles about this bar-room sometimes that make the heart sick." There follows in his diary by a few days a description of a husband-and-wife drunken brawl in the tavern, the entry ending with the exclamation: "Whiskey! Whiskey! Whiskey!!!"

"Few persons of piety" were to be found in Donaldson, claimed Zuck, and consequently he made no close friendships. There was no church in town, and the only public worship service was a Sunday school, which met in his classroom. Occasionally he officiated in the absence of the superintendent. He spent most of his time alone in his upstairs room, except when at school. His diary speaks of a mountainside "retreat" that he frequented for private devotions, sometimes twice a day in his loneliness.

The school was only a few steps from his front door. He began with seventeen pupils, but the number increased when some of the "breaker boys," out on strike, came to classes later in the fall. His biggest discipline problem, though, was not created by any of these youth, no doubt reveling in freedom from their dawn-to-dusk, lung-clogging, face-blackening servitude, but by the sixteen-year-old daughter of his landlord, a perennial troublemaker. "If Alice Lornison were in Europe," he wrote in mid-October, "my school would be so pleasant."

Yet, insisted the determined schoolmaster in his diary, "I mean to have *my* way," concluding philosophically, "I rather like little things to turn up—give Experience—that's what I want." A good paddling, however, did the trick. "I think my use of the rod on last Thursday has had a wholesome influence on the school," noted Zuck, who rarely resorted to corporal punishment.

But another member of the fairer sex proved to be much more of a thorn in his side, this one a teaching colleague. The feud started with a halfway facetious article Zuck wrote for the Tremont *News*. Earlier, he had helped to organize a Union Teachers Institute, comprising the faculties at Donaldson and Tremont, and had been elected presiding officer. At the Institute's initial semimonthly meeting, he was irritated by certain "lady teachers" who whispered back and forth the whole evening. He singled them out for a mild rebuke in his write-up of the session for the local paper.

Said Zuck of his article afterward, "It created a frightful sensation among the teachers whose toes I have tramped." As a result, he fell into the bad graces of one of these women, who took umbrage at his audacity. "Of all the young ladies I have ever met," he confessed, "I can not think of one that was more disagreeable to me." He added, "She and I sometimes quarreled—or rather it was *sometimes* that we did not, when we should be so unlucky as to get together." Their relations, however, improved toward the last, and they parted at school's end with her farewell words "all is square between us."

To augment his income, Zuck ran a night school for ten weeks in the fall, picking up an extra sixty dollars. This allowed him to buy a new alpaca coat and hat in Tremont, his only major expenditure while in that coal-mining area. But classes were discontinued when they became too much of a drag for him. By Christmastime he was fed up with the anthracite coal regions and already applying at other places.

The next we hear of him is in the fall of 1871, now a grade-school principal in Mercersburg. But apparently a higher salary plus ambition enticed him back to Molly Maguire territory and a bigger position, even though the school year was almost a month underway. The *Mercersburg Journal* for September 28 reported that the local principal, having found a substitute, had resigned to become "superintendent" of the Tremont Schools in Schuylkill County. The position paid seventy-five dollars a month.

Tremont, its population double that of Donaldson, was a "truly live" community, boasted a hometowner in the *News* that October, with its "nicely graded sidewalks, elegant private residences, cozy cottages and everything about the place evincing a thrift and prosperity which makes one feel as if he could anchor there and feel at home." There were foundry and machine shops, buggy and wagon works in the coal town, and, to give it respectability, six churches: Methodist, Lutheran (English and German), Evangelical, Reformed, and Roman Catholic. Over four hundred pupils attended the six grades in the three-story brick school building under Zuck's charge.

While at Tremont the twenty-five-year-old administrator pulled a personality switch, turning out to be much less of a recluse than he had been at Donaldson the previous year. He introduced a front-page column in the *News*, a weekly, called "Educational Department." For this special feature, he solicited "brief, pointed and practical essays on literary and educational topics," hoping to convince "the general reader that the teachers, and their friends, are awake, and that they do not mean either to fall asleep or let others do so." Many articles were signed with his own initials, and sometimes he used the column to publish compositions by his best pupils.

Another of his outside activities was the recently formed Everett Literary Society, which met bimonthly on the third floor of his school. He was one of its regular debaters and on the committee that planned the program for its first anniversary the last week of February 1872. On that occasion he took the affirmative side of the resolution: "That we grow more happy as we become more learned"—not at all the opinion, he knew full well, held by the bulk of Dunker patriarchs.

In early July Tremont's principal left the eastern coalfields for good, after conducting a month-long summer select school in the borough. "Mr. Z.," the *News* gave notice on the Fourth, "will spend his vacation rusticating among the fragrant groves and verdant field of Franklin County—his native place." But Zuck did more than rusticate on the home farm. In August he slipped off to the big city (Philadelphia) to attend the four-day nineteenth annual meeting of the Pennsylvania State Teachers' Association. While there he joined a "grand excursion" to the New Jersey shore and took an evening ride past President Grant's cottage at Long Branch. Once back home he prepared full but separate accounts of the convention and seashore excursion for the *Franklin Repository* and the *Waynesboro Village Record*. He could not help putting in a plug for higher teaching salaries.

The fall of 1872 found Zuck back in Dunkerland, teaching grade school at Waynesboro, a town of about fourteen hundred not far from his birthplace. There was a brand new schoolhouse to greet him, the dedication ceremonies on October 4 covered by him for the *Village Record*. He shared an apartment that year with David Emmert, the eighteen-year-old son of a Dunker preacher, from Benevola, Maryland.

Emmert was then a patternmaker in a shop that manufactured farm implements. Later to be reunited at Huntingdon, the roommates discovered, said Emmert in his *Reminiscences,* "that we both traced our line of ancestry to the same great family tree."[5] But for Zuck there was another discovery of greater moment. In the Frick Manufacturing Co. employee he saw artistic genius of a rare order. For that reason the budding artist one day soon, at Zuck's bidding, would take his formative place in the annals of Juniata College.

In April 1873 when the school year ended, Zuck decided to go back to Millersville for the spring term. Those were the months when he struck up a second fateful friendship, this one with John Brumbaugh. In a Founders Day speech long after Zuck's death, Brumbaugh recollected the origin of their close relationship in this way:

> My attention was called to him, and I was led to seek his acquaintance, by a reference made to him at the close of the morning chapel service. The reference made to him by Prof. Brooks [the principal] indicated to me that he might be one of our own people, which he proved to be, and from that time on we were intimate friends. I spent most of my Sundays in his room....[6]

IN QUEST OF MORE DEGREES

While the two were keeping company the veteran schoolteachers suddenly came up with plans for the future that "greatly surprised" his Millersville friend as well as himself. He made this decision known in a letter to the editor, captioned "FAREWELL ADDRESS—To the pupils of the Grammar School," and published in the *Village Record.* Their ambitious teacher told his "dear Young Friends": "It is my design to devote a year or two more to hard study, so that I may be able to fill a higher position than any I have yet had." So on September 1 he entered the National Normal School at Lebanon, Noble County, Ohio, and enrolled in the scientific course.[7]

Soon after matriculating he sent off a powerful article to Holsinger's *Christian Family Companion,* published in mid-October and headed, "Educate or Perish." He took a different tack in his line of reasoning from other educationists, whose stand tended to be more defensive and less positive about the impact of learning on piety. Turning the oppositionists' argument around, Zuck asserted:

> Pure mental culture may not bring about religious convictions, yet it is favorable to the comprehension of religious truths and to an intelligent discharge of Christian duties. Hence, though the improvement of the intellect will not, of itself, fit us for heaven; yet the wilful [sic] neglect of that improvement may be one of the means of debarring us therefrom....Directly or indirectly we owe to education almost every one of the ten thousand blessings that we enjoy over and above what falls to the lot of what we are wont to call the "poor heathen in distant lands."[8]

He then turned his attention to the "need of having a good educational institution among us." His approach here was also novel. He built his case upon two points, the first one curiously suggestive of subtle proselytism. A school was imperative, argued the writer, "in order that we may hold and develop, not only the intellect that is now in the church and that seeks educational facilities; but also that which we can draw into the church by this agency, and by this alone." The second point, after a brief reference to "hundreds of our young people at other church schools," went on to speak of

> hundreds more not wishing to expose themselves to those influences, and having no where else to go, are allowing their God-given faculties to be dormant, thus curtailing their power, and placing themselves in the centre of a sphere of usefulness that *might* be a hundred times as large.

Several months after this article appeared in print, Zuck's health broke, obliging him to drop out of school the following May. John Brumbaugh, worried by the news, made a special trip to see his invalid friend at Claylick while he was recuperating. But home study and correspondence work enabled the infirmed Zuck to complete requirements for the Bachelor of Science degree by summer commencement time. He received his diploma on August 14, 1874, his graduating oration titled "Spanish Struggle for Liberty."

He was back at the National Normal in September to pursue the classics course. But because of a shake-up within the faculty, he transferred in November to a Professor Carver's Normal School at Medina, just west of Akron, Ohio. Once again, for health reasons, he was forced to leave school—sometime early in 1875—and return home. This was just after his near-tragic trip to Berlin through a Somerset County blizzard. Perhaps because of that ordeal his delicate health gave out for the second time in as many years, necessitating another prolonged convalescence at home.

In September, though, before departing Lebanon, he had written a long article for the Brumbaughs' *Pilgrim* on "A High School Among the Brethren." It was in answer to the denunciatory letters that had swamped the two Brethren papers once the Berlin High School fund-raising campaign began to build up steam. Deplored Zuck: "Some people are always fretting about the prickle; they never see the rose."[9] He ended his rebuttal by holding up the Quakers as worthy of emulation. Also a "peculiar" fraternity, he noted, "their character (simplicity and plainness included) is known and respected in all parts of the civilized world; their devotion to education and institutions of learning is equally well known."

He contributed another piece that September to Quinter's paper, called "The Idea of Utility."[10] A lover of poetry (his scrapbook, preserved in the college Archives, is pasted full of excerpted verse), he accused the stolid, pragmatic Brethren of a "low, materialistic idea of utility" in their rejection of esthetic values. He charged: "Whatever we cannot eat or wear or hoard, or in some way appropriate to ourselves, is of no use." "Are we not more than mere animals?" asked Zuck in his plea for an appreciation of the fine arts.

BACK TO THE CLASSROOM

His facile pen fell silent after his breakdown, and his career plans were left up in the air. But in late summer the rejuvenated Claylick native wrote John Brumbaugh about his appointment for the coming school year at Mt. Pleasant, Maryland, near

Boonsboro and Hagerstown. The letter betrayed a lack of self-confidence almost neurotic for a man of his age and administrative experience. It said:

> I am elected principal of a grammar school. I don't feel big enough for it, but I am going to make myself big enough, if my own personal effort will do it. The man who resigned is my superior. He is a college graduate, and I am told a Christian gentleman, so you see what it will be necessary for me to do in order to be a worthy successor. It is the first position tendered me since my graduation [from National Normal School] and, God being my helper, I mean to measure up to it.[11]

Indeed, the crippled principal, whose reputation "as a writer of ability" had preceded him to Mt. Pleasant, had no trouble measuring up. He added three subjects to the curriculum: geometry, physiology, and drawing. With respect to the last "branch," the *Boonesboro* [sic] *Odd Fellow* declared: "Prof Zuck has certainly been very successful in drawing, when we consider that none of his pupils ever drew before he came here, and I doubt if his scholars can now be beat in the country, especially in map drawing" (there is a booklet in the college Archives with samples of their work). He also encouraged the children in creative writing and arranged for the *Young Disciple,* a Brumbaugh Sunday school publication, to print an occasional essay of theirs. "As a disciplinarian," said the *Odd Fellow* of him, "he has rare abilities, leading instead of driving, thus gaining the love and respect of all his pupils."[12]

The Mt. Pleasant schoolmaster's performance won him a place on the program of the Teachers' Institute of Washington County, held in Hagerstown, December 20-24. His featured address was on the topic "How Much Geography Ought to Be Taught in County Schools, and How Shall It Be Taught?" The *Hagerstown Herald and Torch Light* described his presentation to eighty-five teachers as "marked by more than usual care; it evinced a thoughtful, exhaustive, and systematized classification of the subject and well digested plan of teaching it."

A week after the Institute came Zuck's New Year's Day surprise call on John Brumbaugh in Huntingdon, thus setting the stage for fast-moving developments over the succeeding three months. That impulsive visit, we saw in the previous chapter, led to talk of starting a school in the *Pilgrim* building as soon as possible. This was followed by a flurry of letters between Zuck and the Brumbaughs on the feasibility and nature of the proposed "experiment." Wrote Zuck in his scrapbook: "After a serious but very brief consideration of the matter I concluded to accept the invitation of the Brethren in Huntingdon, and to that end resigned my position as a teacher of the public school at Mt. Pleasant, Maryland, a few days before the regular time of closing." "On bidding farewell to his scholars, the *Odd Fellow* said of his leave-taking, "many of them shed tears."

The man the Brumbaughs had decided on to head up their trial school, though not yet thirty years old and frail of body, had excelled both as a teacher and a principal in the public-school system. He was obviously a Dunker of their ilk: ambitious, progressive-minded, capable, visionary, dedicated, devout. At the time, they could not have made a better choice from among their own people.

BEGINNING OF THE EXPERIMENT

So precipitately did the founders act that little advance publicity was given prior to the opening of what they chose to call the Huntingdon Normal Select School, the first in an array of subsequent names. The initial announcement was brief, carried by the *Pilgrim* on March 28, and simply read:

> Brother J. M. Zuck talks of starting a select or Normal School in our town, for the coming Summer. His object will be to give his pupils a good, thorough education, and also to prepare young men and ladies for teaching. Bro. Zuck is a man of fine abilities, being a graduate of the Penn'a State Normal, also of a leading Western school. Any of our brethren's children or any others, contemplating going to school during the coming Summer will do well to make calculations to come here as excellent facilities will be offered.

Fuller information appeared in the April 4 edition, emphasizing the existence of an active church (the Huntingdon Brethren had renovated a room in the *Pilgrim* building as a place for regular worship in June 1875) and indicating that students would room and board with members. "The design of the school," this latest announcement explained, "is not to teach religion but to educate; therefore in principle it will not be sectarian." It further stated:

> The departments of the school will be arranged so as to lead students from the elementary branches to a thorough knowledge of all the higher branches of an English education. Facilities will also be afforded for obtaining as thorough a knowledge of Latin, Greek and German languages as is usually obtained at Academies and Seminaries, and preparing them for teaching, for the active duties of life or for entering college.

Jacob Zuck arrived in Huntingdon four days before classes were scheduled to begin. He settled into a one-room apartment, rented for him by John Brumbaugh, directly across the street from the *Pilgrim* building. Only three students greeted him on Monday, April 17, instead of the expected fifteen or twenty. All were from the local area—two girls and one boy, Gaius Brumbaugh, Dr. A. B.'s fourteen-year-old son. The teacher refused to open a book the first morning until after he had led his little troupe to the first-floor chapel where the four of them knelt together in prayer.

The nation's economy was still reeling from the effects of the 1873 crash when Zuck, a slender, almost delicate man of average height with brown eyes, dark hair, and—at the time—beardless, began teaching that "experimental term."[13] Henry Brumbaugh lamented in the *Pilgrim* that while 1876, as the centennial year, should be a time of celebration, the country was mired "in a financial depression that it has been our lot seldom to experience." Huntingdon, its population now reaching upwards to five thousand, had not escaped the economic fallout. David Emmert's impression of the town upon his arrival in the fall of 1877 was one of patent depression everywhere:

> What a town! *Alba longa* (long white town): better *nigra longa* (long black town). For West Huntingdon stretched for a mile or more over a broad plateau and looked as if it had been in the full swell of a great boom sometime and had

been stranded by the subsidence of the tide. Here were vacant lots innumerable, with fences and without, signboards everywhere: "This lot for Sale. Apply to _____"; empty houses many, and boardwalks abominable. The streets were unpaved and muddy. The tall stack of silent factories told the story of industrial decline. Here and there were a few centers of activity. One of these was the *Pilgrim*, later the *Primitive Christian* office. The older part of the town was somewhat more improved, but in many places the pavements were laid with flat stones. There was no sewerage system and the streets were lighted, when at all, by coal-oil lamps.[14]

The legendary William Beery, an entering student in 1877, has left another first-hand description. In a letter dated April 11, 1944, and headed "Huntingdon as I Found It (Winter 1877–78)," he wrote in part about the West End:

> On all sides were old, black frame houses in which lived people who could afford nothing better, most of whom had been employees of the defunct car works. Some places there were old, dilapidated sidewalks, many boards missing. To mention one spot: on Mifflin Street, where Sammy Clemens and wife lived and kept store in the same little house, there was such a walk. They had a cow which roved around there to get the benefit of the grass that grew in spots. This cow seemed to take special pleasure in walking on the few boards and bare spots where the walk should have been, which resulted in making it perilous for a pedestrian lest he step into a hole in the walk, or something worse.[15]

Little wonder Zuck expressed misgivings the day before his school opened. To John Brumbaugh he confided, "I must confess I can't see the way to success in this enterprise, but I do believe it's right, and I believe God will show us the way as we go onward."[16] But on the morrow drooping spirits gave way to fierce determination, despite the poor opening-day enrollment. After the last class John Brumbaugh said to him, "Only three pupils! It looks small indeed, but I hear others are coming." Replied the teacher, "I'm not scared, and now since I've started, if I can have these rooms and am spared, I'll continue for one year. And if these pupils leave, I'll go out and compel others to come in." Then he went on to analogize with a twinkle in his eye:

> I feel tonight like my mother's old hen. Before I came up here, she told me of the trouble she had with her old hen. She was bound to hatch, whether she had eggs or not. But I'll do better than the old hen; I am not only bound to hatch, but I am going to have eggs, too. There are eggs that must be hatched![17]

For a hatchery, Henry Brumbaugh gave Zuck the use of a second-story flat, rent free, in the south half of the *Pilgrim* building. There were three rooms, one of which was converted into a parlor (14' x 18'), another into a classroom (14' x 12'), and the third into a small principal's office. From Zuck's scrapbook we also learn that Dr. A. B. furnished a table and two blackboards, John Brumbaugh a set of chairs, and the sober-miened teacher a bookcase he himself had made. A further scrapbook entry indicates that John Brumbaugh lived up to his promise to board his friend for whatever he could pay, which was nothing for much of the first year.

The Brumbaughs, persuaded that "our brother. . .is the right man in the right place," put their press at Zuck's disposal.[18] The May 23 issue of the *Pilgrim* introduced a column headed "Educational Department," edited by Zuck. He wrote in that edition: "Having had some experience several years ago in conducting a Department of this kind in a secular paper, I enter this new field with less reluctance than might otherwise be felt." The purpose of the column, he said, was to call the reader's attention "to our work in the educational field, and also what we may consider his duty in relation to the same," as well as present "selected articles as may be deemed wholesome" on "all matters relating to the cause in general."

In addition the *Pilgrim* on the 23rd carried a four-page circular inset on the "Huntingdon Normal School," published gratuitously by the Brumbaugh firm. An opening blurb about the school's location assured parents and prospective students that the "health and morals of the place are as good as can be found anywhere and much better than in most towns of the same size." Tuition was listed at seven dollars for a ten-week term and room and board in a private home at three dollars a week—rates "considerably lower than at most schools of the same grade," it was pointed out. The circular further advised that the curriculum would be modeled after that of "our best State Normal Schools." There was also a bit of long-range forecasting: "It will be our aim to extend the course of study until it shall include all the elements of a liberal education."

According to the little brochure the library, which was housed in a corner of the teacher's office, consisted of *Webster's New Unabridged Dictionary* and two encyclopedia sets: the sixteen-volume *Appleton* and the ten-volume *Chambers*. With a few more acquisitions, it was boasted, this reference library "will compare favorably with those found at some of our State Normal Schools."

In the parlor students could keep abreast of current events in "the fields of science, literature, art, politics or religion" through a collection of newspapers and magazines. Besides dailies, like the *New York Tribune*, the *Witness*, and the *Graphic*, there were "excellent weeklies, both secular and religious, pictorial and otherwise." The leading magazines included *Harper's, Lippincott, Scribner's,* and *Popular Science Monthly*.

As for "religious advantages," the circular mentioned "a comfortable church room in the *Pilgrim* building which will answer for a chapel" and that "Sunday school and Bible classes will be organized." Out-of-town students, especially Brethren, were expected to "frequent" all religious services. Affirmed the school's founders:

> Although no attempt will be made to teach or enforce sectarian dogmas or doctrines in the classroom, yet we have no sympathy with that pernicious system of education which confines itself to the training of the intellect and endeavors not to awaken and call forth the higher and holier impulses of the soul. Hence we shall employ every proper means to lead our pupils to realize in the deepest possible sense that the fear of the Lord is the beginning of wisdom.

By May, when the circular for 1876–77 went out, the enrollment picture began to look brighter. Ten more names had been added to the roster: six females and four males. Like the first-day three, they were all from Huntingdon County.

One evening that spring, probably in early May, Zuck was sitting at John Brumbaugh's dinner table, pensively eating. Suddenly he leaned back and said, "We must have a literary society. I want the students of this school to be able to get up and speak in public, and a literary society is essential to give drill along this line."[19]

That night he and Brumbaugh made out a program for the first meeting. It took place a day or so later in the chapel, but for some reason the distaff side was excluded. Curious, some of the ladies huddled outside the door and peeped through the keyhole, "not a little amused at the proceedings." Soon, however, someone came out, invited them in, and before the night passed membership was voted for all. The literary society soon became a powerful intellectual stimulus in the life of the infant school. Its programs, integrated with classroom work, featured declamations, lectures, and reading. Debate was not added to its routine until August, during the Teachers' Institute.

When the first term ended in late June screaming newspaper headlines told of Indian wars and the massacre of Custer's 7th Cavalry at the Little Bighorn River in Montana. But Zuck had problems of his own—money, not scalps. His ten-week income from thirteen students grossed a mere $53.95; his outlay amounted to $81.80. Nor did the Teachers' Institute that summer help to swell the school coffers. Only one student registered on the first day, and the six-week session closed with but a half-dozen in attendance.

THE EXPERIMENT GAINS SUPPORT

The school founders were hardly ecstatic when only fifteen matriculants reported for the fall opening on September 12. But at least a few were out-of-staters (from Virginia, Maryland, and even Colorado), and the roster now included Pennsylvanians from beyond the Juniata Valley, among them a brother of Zuck. Two made belated appearances in October.

By then the *Pilgrim* publishers had closed a deal that now brought a familiar personage among Brethren educationists into the inner council of the fledgling school. For most of two years James Quinter had hounded Henry and John to consolidate their printing business with his. Finally, in July of 1876, the Brumbaughs came to terms.

In October the two publishing houses were incorporated under the name of Quinter and Brumbaugh Brothers, with a capital stock of twenty thousand dollars.[20] Quinter, the senior partner, took over as editor-in-chief, and the *Pilgrim* building was made the firm's headquarters. The sheet of this merger was renamed *Primitive Christian*, its first number going out on October 25 to almost ten thousand subscribers. On Halloween Day Quinter moved his family from Meyersdale to Huntingdon. Later he was voted the first presiding elder of the local congregation.

In the first November issue of the *Primitive Christian*, Zuck's column lamented the lack of interest in education among Dunker belles. Bothered that his school was "too exclusively made of representatives of the male sex," the teacher wrote:

> We prefer to have both sexes, as we think the influence of each upon the other is beneficial. The idea of the co-education of the sexes is endorsed by most of

the Normal Schools of the country and is gaining ground in some of the leading colleges and universities. How long will it take our young sisters to catch a little of the educational spirit which characterizes the young women found in many of the schools of the country?[21]

Femininity might have been in short supply among Zuck's band of learners but not enthusiasm, especially for the literary society. Its weekly programs were attracting a nonacademic audience—from the *Primitive Christian* staff, the founders' families, and the town—wanting to take active part. This led to the formation of the Juniata Literary Society on January 13, 1877, with forty-nine charter members.[22] A constitution was adopted calling for annual dues of fifty cents. On February 3 Henry Brumbaugh introduced the *Juniata Literary Record*, the school's first paper, which circulated in manuscript form. A weekly, it was a ribbon-bound collection of prose and poetry submitted by members. Debate, however, was divorced from the exercises of the society for a time between 1877 and 1879. After then, to foster rivalry, Zuck arbitrarily divided the student body into three debate clubs: Bryants, Ebenezers, and Irvings.

Meanwhile, there were other promising signs that the "experiment" seemed to be working out. When the winter term began on November 21 the tiny classroom provided by Henry Brumbaugh was suddenly jammed to the walls with people. There were thirty-two registrants on hand, a one hundred percent gain over the preceding term. Students soon grew impatient with the overcrowded conditions and complained of being "too thick to thrive." Moreover, inquiries were coming in from Dunker bastions in the Midwest: Ohio, Illinois, Missouri, Iowa, and other states. Zuck now found himself in the painful position of having to discourage applicants for want of space.[23] He was forced to alleviate the situation by the time forty-five students enrolled on February 6, the first day of the spring term.

Fortunately, Zuck was able on short notice to rent the Burchinell place, a large, three-story house, one block away at 1224 Washington Street. It had been the home of Thomas Burchinell, the retired owner of a planing mill and sash factory. (The place was razed in 1971 by the Owens-Corning Fiberglas Corporation for a parking lot.) In 1877 this spacious building, only ten years old, contained two large rooms 14' x 30' and eight smaller ones, not counting the kitchen. One of the big downstairs rooms was used for classes, the other for a parlor. The upstairs space was utilized as a dormitory, and kitchen facilities enabled students to form boarding clubs, for which there had been a growing demand.

On Thursday, February 9, the school moved into the Burchinell House, the student body thereafter making the one-block trek each morning to the *Primitive Christian* building for chapel services. It was beginning to look as if the "experimental" stage had been safely weathered, and already the founders were making bolder plans.

Chapter 3

THE COLLEGE ON THE HILL

PLANS TO INCORPORATE AND BUILD

Even before relocating the school upstreet the four founders and their two new allies, Quinter and Joseph Beer, an editorial assistant, had conferred on several occasions about its future. The first meeting was in the office of the *Primitive Christian* on Monday evening, January 22, 1877. There was talk of building, and Zuck showed his own rough diagram of a structure he thought "would meet the wants of both the school and the church at this place."[1]

Zuck had awaited the evening of the 22nd with prayerful expectation, as John Brumbaugh discovered quite by chance. Only moments before they were scheduled to meet, Brumbaugh needed a magazine the teacher had taken to his room across the street. He walked over and knocked on Zuck's door, but there was no answer. Thinking his neighbor was out, he barged in and found him on his knees, absorbed in prayer. After a while Zuck rose and said, "This evening the question of the erection of a college building is coming up, and I thought I'd have a private talk with God about it."[2]

A follow-up meeting on Saturday of that week resulted in an open and free exchange about how much support could be expected from the church at large (which by then claimed a following of a little less than sixty thousand) and whether or not Huntingdon was really the best location for a Brethren school.[3] Quinter, at sixty the Nestor of the school fight, played the devil's advocate throughout the deliberation, leaving the others to plead for the county seat. Dr. A. B. argued for "having the school in close proximity to the leading Church paper" (there were two others). He further contended that Zuck's work "manifests no sign of decay but on the contrary exhibits every evidence of vigorous life and healthy and rapid growth." Henry Brumbaugh clinched the case for Huntingdon with the observation that "freedom from local opposition and interference is a point of much importance." Nobody could dispute that.

A committee of three (Quinter, Zuck, and the doctor) was appointed to draft resolutions organizing the Huntingdon Normal School as a joint-stock company and authorizing a fund-raising drive for a building project. The committee made its report to the Huntingdon Brethren on Thursday evening, February 2. Henry Brumbaugh then took it the next evening to a council meeting of the mother congregation at James Creek, which gave unanimous approval. (Not until 1878 did the local Brethren become an autonomous church group.)

The resolutions provided for a board of temporary trustees, the three committee members plus the Brumbaugh brothers and Beer. This board was given oversight of the financial campaign and charged with finding a school site. Ultimately there was also provision for a permanent nine-member board of trustees with staggered three-year terms. All had to be Brethren, and at least five of them had to live in the vicinity of the school. The trustees were to be elected by and from among the stockholders, one vote allotted for each one-hundred-dollar share. One thing the document made clear: although the school intended to honor Brethren tradition and doctrine, it would not be church owned or controlled. Organizing it on a joint-stock basis, people were told, would ensure its private status. In this connection Zuck was wont to characterize the school, a half-century or more before the term "church-related" came into popular usage, as "denominational but not sectarian."

EARLIEST FACULTY ADDITIONS, MERGER, AND CURRICULUM EXPANSION

While the trustees, in a display of wishful thinking, spoke of breaking ground by summer, Zuck faced the more immediate problem of coping with the doubled spring enrollment. To assist him he hired Phebe Weakley, a member of his graduating class at Millersville, to teach Elocution and Literature. He also made use of a student aide, Emma Miller, a Bedford County native with a Pennsylvania teaching certificate. (Her father, who had died when only twenty-five, had been a pioneer Dunker educator in the early 1850s.) Miss Weakley, a thin, hollow-eyed, plain-looking woman who wore her hair pulled severely back, was baptized a Brethren soon after her arrival. She replaced Henry Brumbaugh as the sponsor of the *Juniata Literary Record*.

By April 17, when forty-five students representing six states and eight Pennsylvania counties reported for classes, the trustees were deep in merger talks with Lewis Kimmel, pressuring him to combine their two schools at Huntingdon. As early as March 5 they had delegated Quinter to approach Kimmel on the matter; later, Dr. A. B. Brumbaugh also joined in the parleying. Wrote John Brumbaugh in the *Primitive Christian*: "They found him quite willing to confer with them on the subject, and also willing to make any sacrifice in order to remove anything that might be in the way of making a school among us a success."[4] Consolidation was effected the last week of April, and on the 26th a circular letter went out under Kimmel's name urging scholarship donors to transfer their support to the Huntingdon enterprise. Another public statement by Kimmel appeared in the June 12 edition of the *Primitive Christian*. Soon after that he donated fifty volumes from the Plum Creek Normal library, mainly reference works, and before long his name was to be found on the list of stockholders.

A month after the merger—on Thursday, June 28—closing exercises for the first full academic year took place in the Penn Street Opera House, conducted by the Juniata Literary Society. Advertised as "New, Entertaining and Instructive," it was an all-day affair, with morning, afternoon, and evening sessions. The *Local News* reported that in the evening Henry Brumbaugh spoke to a crowded house, giving "full and satisfactory reasons for the future success of the school." It further stated: "He believes the day is not far distant when the roll will contain the names of 600 or 1000 pupils."

The teachers' term opened on July 23 and attracted thirty-six registrants, thirty more than the previous summer. The publicity flier on this session reflected a touch of Madison Avenue hucksterism. It said magniloquently: "Those who are preparing to teach, or who wish to review preparatory to examination, will find it to their advantage to patronize the school that is destined to become the leading Educational Institution in this section of the State."

There came to help Zuck that term twenty-five-year-old Jacob Brumbaugh, Dr. A. B.'s youngest brother and an 1874 Millersville graduate. As yet unmarried, Brumbaugh had spent three years at Millersburg, Dauphin County, where he was lauded by the *Herald* for his "sacrificing work as principal of the High School." He had been induced by his older sibling to give up his monthly principal's salary of $120 to join forces with Zuck, taking the classes in science and teaching-methods. There was no promise of a regular income at first, and he roomed with Dr. A. B. until Founders Hall was built. Jacob Brumbaugh, who would become Zuck's right-hand man, was paid nothing until the following December. For five months' work he received the grand sum of fifty-five dollars a few days before Christmas.

Meantime, in midsummer, while railroad strikes bred mob violence in Pittsburgh and other eastern cities, bringing death and property damages in the millions of dollars, Zuck pushed for donations of books and equipment and sent out the circular for 1877–78. It announced a revised calendar of three unequal terms (fall, winter, spring) for the regular academic year and a six-week teachers' term. Tuition was hiked from seventy cents a week to seventy-five cents weekly. The minicatalog also set forth a list of "Rules and Regulations":

1. The use of Tobacco in any form is prohibited in the Building or upon the school premises.

2. All students, unless excused, must remain in their rooms during the evening study hours, and it will be the duty of the parties with whom students board to report promptly all violations of this rule.

3. Students from a distance are required to attend regularly the religious services held in the Chapel, unless there is a mutual agreement to the contrary.

4. All students are expected to join the Literary Society and to discharge faithfully all duties connected therewith.

5. Every case of absence or tardiness, unless promptly excused, will be regarded as a misdemeanor and will subject the delinquent to such discipline as the offense may seem to demand.

6. Students of the two sexes, other than relatives, must not meet privately except on business, and then only by permission of the Principal or some duly authorized Teacher. Lady students from abroad will not receive calls from gentlemen not connected with the school, unless the latter first obtain permission to make such calls.

The minicatalog explained: "The above rules and restrictions are deemed prudent and absolutely necessary in order that our school may attain that high standard of moral and intellectual excellence which we aspire to teach." Out-of-towners were told that the "omnibus" fare from the depot to the Burchinell place would cost ten cents, more if a trunk were thrown in. A two-page supplement was run off in August announcing the creation of three new subject areas: drawing, music, and languages (classical and foreign). David Emmert, the principal's former roommate at Waynesboro, showed up in September to teach drawing and oil painting. He had been approached by Zuck the preceding summer, the two talking while he, grease-covered, repaired a threshing machine. The death of his father, Emmert wrote in *Reminiscences of Juniata College*, prevented him from joining the "noble band of workers at Huntingdon" until the following year.

Almost at once, Emmert, whose facility in the graphic arts reportedly amazed James Whistler, set to work on what today is a collector's item: the 21" x 30" lithograph *View of Huntingdon*. Apparently, he was the one who did the ink drawings for Thomas Hunter, the Philadelphia lithographer. Available in July 1878, the picture gave a view of the town as seen from Shelving Rock, with vignettes of local buildings and dwellings arranged in the corners and along the margins. At three dollars a copy, plain or tinted (or one of each for five dollars), the proceeds from its sale went toward the library and "apparatus" fund.

To teach voice Zuck hired John Ewing, called by some the "father of Brethren music." An Ohioan, Ewing traveled among churches promoting congregational singing. The tuning fork was his sole instrument in that day of unaccompanied hymnody. He stayed on two years and had a profound influence on William Beery, who soon eclipsed his mentor as the church's best-known singer and composer.

For the classical and modern languages the principal turned to Hugo G. Olawsky, who had studied at the universities of Berlin and Breslau. He is the unidentified subject of the whimsical chapter "The German Professor" in Emmert's book. Olawsky, whom Zuck learned was temporarily staying with some farmers a few miles out in the country, was invited sight unseen to be interviewed for the language position. Emmert describes the school's first glimpse of the candidate in this way:

On a certain day he came. All horror—a tramp! Hair and beard unkempt, slouch and greasy hat, shabby and dirty clothes, pants tucked into his cowhide boots and a faded carpet-sack grip under his arm. The students stood aghast, and even Professor Zuck looked "sold."[5]

Nevertheless, when it came out that Olawsky was not only a German scholar but trained in the classics as well, he was taken on. Zuck, Emmert, and the students rounded up some clean clothes, prevailed upon him to bathe, trimmed his "shock and bristle," and took "real pride" in his spick-and-span appearance. But the German professor's tenure was very brief. Deprived of his beer stein he grew cranky after a couple of weeks. Soon his students rebelled, calling him "the old tyrant," and, said Emmert, even worse names. Finally, Zuck had to call him into his office for a man-to-man talk. Here is Emmert's description of the outcome:

> What was said in the brief interview none but the two professors ever knew. Then the door suddenly flew open, and out came the German professor like a thunderbolt. The students rushed aside; up the stairs he went, three steps at a bound; I followed to see what would happen. What a scene! The old man was in a rage. He threw off his shoes and banged them into a corner; he threw coat and vest and hat all over the room, and without taking time to unbutton his shirt, he seized it at the collar band, ripped it up the back, and sent it whirling like a flag of truce across the bed. I got out and hastened down the stairs to warn those below to clear the track for what was coming. In a few minutes he appeared clad in his old duds, and, with a jabber nobody could understand, and gesticulations which sent terror to the hearts of the timid ones, he rushed down the street and disappeared from view forever. Professor Zuck was convulsed with laughter, the boys were hilarious, the girls clapped their hands and hallooed, "Good-bye!"[6]

CHANGE OF NAME: BRETHREN'S NORMAL SCHOOL

Zuck and Emmert found themselves "roomies" once again the fall of 1877. Their apartment was on the third floor of the Burchinell House, a small dormer window letting in outside light. Its bare floor they covered with a "cheap carpet." At first the pair boarded out, but on Zuck's suggestion they joined one of the student clubs for their meals. The standard dish for supper, recalled Emmert, was "a sort of potato soup," invariably scorched. Even though the student body had grown to fifty-seven, Zuck had to scramble to make ends meet. As his roommate observed in his book: "It soon became evident that Professor Zuck was under great financial strain to equip the school, pay his teachers (small as were the salaries), add to the library and supply apparatus as necessity demanded."[7]

At the same time, the hard-pressed principal could write optimistically that the near future would likely bring some changes, not only in name but also in the school's academic thrust. In the *Primitive Christian* for September 4 he served notice with the following statement:

> We are especially anxious to have young brethren and sisters and Brethren's children come here. It was for this class that our school was started, and it is from this class that we would like to receive the principal part of our encouragement. We would like to make our school a Brethren's school in fact if not in name, and when that is accomplished we trust there will be no objection to our assuming the name that properly belongs to us. If there should be no valid

objections, we propose to call our school the "Brethren's Normal School," and if in due course of events the word "school" should give place to some other word, we trust the fitness of things at that time will justify the change.

By November the new name was fixed, and Zuck spoke of issuing "Certificates of Graduation" at the close of the current school year. He also advised *Primitive Christian* readers of plans to add a "Scientific Course," a more advanced program than the Normal English Course, and "to make some advancement in the Collegiate Department."[8]

THREATS FROM THE MIDWEST

But then came "an ambassador from the land of the setting sun," Emmert wrote, urging consolidation upon the trustees and the relocation of their school in a mid-western town eager to attract one. Emmert failed to identify the place in telling about this upsetting visit, but it was Ashland, Ohio, where the citizens had pledged ten thousand dollars toward the purchase of a twenty-eight-acre campus. This so-called ambassador, according to Emmert, was a man of great enthusiasm, eloquence, and persuasive power. The visitor told of an ambitious scheme to establish a college of the first rank, to equip, endow, and professor it, starting it as a booming success at once.[9] The Brethren's Normal School authorities were asked, "Why struggle through the long, trying period of experimental development?"

Ever since the Berlin High School fiasco Zuck and the Brumbaughs had been skeptical of "instant success" talk. Their operating motto was "little by little," Zuck once wrote, and this explains why they always referred to their initial efforts as an "experiment." As he said in his *Primitive Christian* column, playing upon words: "A mushroom may develop in a night, but Nature's *Normal plan* is 'First the blade, then the ear, after that the corn in the ear.'"[10] Nevertheless, when the said "ambassador" left with the threat: "Well, if you do not unite with us you will be swallowed up," Zuck fell into deep depression.[11]

In confidential talks with his roommate Zuck admitted anxiety about competition from another school and his "wavering faith" that enough funds could be raised in the East.[12] This fear was evident as early as the previous May, when the young educator, in reporting the Plum Creek-Huntingdon school merger, went on to plead:

> Let us unite and establish one school. Since we have made the move here at Huntingdon, we hear of other similar projects. Of course it is the privilege of any of our brethren who may feel to do so, to start a school, and is all right, but there can be nothing more detrimental to the cause. We have been laboring for years to establish a school among the Brethren, and hitherto have not been successful, and is it possible that we can start three or four at once! Our brethren should not think of this matter. If our school here were not in successful operation we would at once drop it, but as it is now pretty well established, and is apparently doing well, we feel that we should go forward. We wish all similar projects success, but if we have too many of them at once, it may be that none of them will succeed so well. Our motto would be, one at a time, and then build up others as they are needed.[13]

APPEAL TO THE TOWN FOR LAND

The Ashland visitor may have struck fear in Zuck's heart, but he also planted an idea in his fertile brain. On December 6 the *Local News* carried a long article from the principal's pen under the heading "An Address to the Citizens of Huntingdon in Behalf of the Huntingdon Normal." It was written with the trustees' imprimatur. Taking a cue from Ashland, Zuck wrote, "We now appeal to the citizens of the town to assist us by donating the ground needed for the building that we propose to erect next summer."

Shrewdly he informed the local merchants that the trustees foresaw not too far ahead a student body of some three to five hundred. Therefore, he estimated they would stand to benefit anywhere from $100,000 to $150,000 annually from school and student business. "Can our business men, our merchants, tailors, millers, butchers, bakers, etc., see no advantage in this?" he asked. In fact, argued Zuck, "Our students from a distance have already spent as much in your midst as it would cost you to buy the ground that we need for our proposed building."

He then mentioned that "other towns in this State, and at least one town in another State are bidding for the school," one community ready to put up twenty thousand dollars. In the last instance, of course, he was referring to Ashland, but the trustees were also discussing a deal with Jacob Oller of Waynesboro, an intimate friend of the three Brumbaughs. Oller was trying to sell them on the idea of buying the Clairmont Hotel, located a short distance east of Monterey, and converting it into a school building.[14] Berlin was another locality making overtures. Having called attention to attractive invitations such as these, Zuck went on to say:

> We reserve our answer to [these] propositions until we hear what Huntingdon is willing to do for us in the way of donating a proper school site. The best interests of the enterprise demand that this matter should be brought to a head without unnecessary delay, and hence we urge you to act promptly if you propose to act at all. We do not ask you for 10 or 15 thousand dollars, but merely for enough suitable ground upon which to erect the building, and also enough to permit the future growth and development of the enterprise.

Since spring the temporary trustees had been looking at several possible school sites in the Huntingdon area, one of which lay across the river. But by now, Zuck's article disclosed, they had narrowed it down to two sites, both of which were in West Huntingdon. The first location was identified as the twenty lots between Moore and Oneida streets on the west and east, 17th Street on the south, and extending north to the middle of the block between 18th and 19th streets (which took in two lots owned by Dr. A. B. Brumbaugh). "Site No. 2" consisted of the plot of ground bounded by the two alleys between Washington and Moore streets, and extending northward into the Taylor estate between 19th and 21st streets, including "the hill" (Round Top). The trustees, Zuck said, pulling no punches, would accept the first site "unconditionally," but there had to be proof of adequate water supply before they would agree to the second location.

The decision to ask the townspeople to donate land meant that the trustees had to play down the school's inherent Brethrenism. Thus, in his December 6 article, Zuck stressed that while the Normal was designed to meet denominational need, it was also committed to educating all applicants, "regardless of creed, sex, or social distinctions." Such rhetoric had a ring highly suggestive of today's affirmative action pledge. By way of further commentary he observed:

> We have already had students representing many different religious faiths, and we suspect that all have felt about as well suited as though the school were designed for them. We have thus far tried to respect the rights of all, and we shall continue to act upon the same Christian principle, believing it possible for a school to be denominational and yet not sectarian, in the bad sense of the word.

As for the teachers' term, said the principal, "We are not over anxious to have our school considered even denominational, but rather *professional* and *normal* in the highest and best sense of the term."

On Saturday evening, December 8, two days after Zuck's article appeared in the *Local News*, the temporary trustees took their case directly to the town fathers. They met with a number of civic leaders in the office of Col. William Dorris, a resident attorney for the Pennsylvania Railroad. According to the *Local News*, a committee of five was appointed that night to ascertain the price for "Location No. 2" and to organize a fund-raising campaign. Why the citizens' group made that site selection, given the reservations of the trustees, was not explained. Two days later the same newspaper reported that "some of the owners have already consented to donate their property," and Zuck informed *Primitive Christian* readers on December 18 that the ground was appraised at five thousand dollars and, most significantly, separated by a mile from the downtown area. Thus, he gave assurance it was a safe distance from "the places where students could come into contact with shows and other evil agencies."

THE SMALLPOX SCARE

All thoughts of school sites and subscription lists, however, were pushed aside before another fortnight. Early in December the borough was plagued by chicken pox, the severity of which, said Emmert in his book, "awakened a suspicion that it might be smallpox in mild form."[15] The first diagnosed case of this dreaded disease was found next door to the Burchinell House. Anxious Normal students tried not to notice the little girl "peering from the window with flushed and pitted face" as they passed by on the street. But with her recovery all fears faded, and on Saturday the 22nd, the students left for the holidays.

Then, during Christmas week, a smallpox scare swept the borough, peaking shortly after the turn of the year. A couple of physicians, one of them Dr. A. B., denied in the papers that the town had an actual epidemic on its hands. Still, rumors were rife. Students returning by train for the winter term on January 7 were shaken, miles from town, by the cry: "Smallpox at Huntingdon!" They heard wild stories of death and quarantine.[16] Upon their arrival they were met with the odor of disinfectant (carbolic acid) everywhere. The "Seven Orphans," as members of the Zuck-Emmert boarding club were dubbed, dutifully downed liberal doses of molasses and sulfur three times daily. Every day red quarantine signs went up on all sides of the school.

Less than a week after the vacation break, the "scabby foe" finally struck at Zuck's little band. The wife of a young minister from Virginia (he had entered in the fall of 1876) died of the scourge on January 12. Early the next morning, a damp and chilly Monday, the school met for a funeral service in the chapel. The grief-stricken husband was confined at home with his only child, a baby. That day classes did not meet in compliance with a ban on all public gathering enacted by town council on the 10th.

Students and teachers scattered, most to distant homes, a few girls to emergency quarters locally, and that plucky threesome, as we shall soon see, to their Trough Creek refuge. Before dispersing, the school made tentative plans to resume classes on February 18. Nevertheless, good-byes were spoken with heavy hearts. Wrote Emmert: "Before us lay the possible abandonment of the school enterprise."[17]

As the students were leaving, John Brumbaugh said to Zuck, "Well, if there's no hope at all, I suppose we must stop." But the doughty educator shot back defiantly, "Stop! No!" And then, in words soon to prove prophetic, he said, "We commenced this work as an experiment and nothing less than death will stop me, and if I should be stricken and die, I hope others will have the courage to take up the work and continue."[18]

On the following Friday, the 17th, Zuck and Emmert took their own "sorrowful leave." But not before they had tackled the problem of what to do about three of the "Seven Orphans." This trio, all Ohioans, were afraid that going home would mean never to return. On the evening classes were halted, Zuck, Emmert, and the Ohio "Orphans" were sitting together in the unlit parlor, their mood matching the darkness and gloom.

There was a quick rap on the door and in walked Jacob Brumbaugh. His "breezy spirit" was a timely tonic for the downcast quintet, and one of the boys got up and brought a lamp. Soon the group was bantering and laughing as the fate of the "Orphans" was weighed. The boys wanted to move in with some of the farm families close by and wait out the crisis. But, as Emmert later wrote, farmers were boycotting the town, "and it was not likely that even a dog from Huntingdon would be welcomed in their midst."[19] Then, recalled the art teacher:

> More in jest than in earnest some one said, "Boys, let's go to the mountains!" "There!" said Professor Brumbaugh, "that suggests something." Then he told us of a place far out in a deep mountain gorge—"The Forge"—where there were several old houses in fair condition, one of them lately occupied by the woodchoppers.[20]

Thus began the saga of the "Orphans' Retreat," so memorably told in Emmert's *Reminiscences*. The three boys lived out their six-week "exile" near the main picnic area of what is now Trough Creek State Park. According to William Beery's own account of that experience, the three "refugees" reached the "Forge Country" by train and wagon. Accompanied by Jacob Brumbaugh they took the Huntingdon and Broad Top Railroad as far as the Aitch Station. From there Robert Mason, Brumbaugh's brother-in-law, gave them a jolting lift the rest of the way in his spring wagon.[21] (The route they took from Aitch is now partly covered by the waters of the new Raystown lake.) Mason was the mailman who passed their ramshackle "hide-away" every day, delivering welcome letters from friends.

Both Emmert and Beery refer to frequent visitors, and so the "Orphans'" sojourn was not spent in utter solitude. One of their regular callers was a fifteen-year-old boy from Marklesburg, Martin Brumbaugh. "His greatest delight," said Beery, "was to take us on hikes up and down the valley and over the mountains to show us the sights." Much of the land was owned by his father, George. By their own admission, they had "a lot of fun."

Their enforced vacation brought hardships, too. Beery, who lived to be 103, wrote that each of them, in turn, came down with "an attack of something like the flue" [sic]. Severe weather that January further added to the drama of the occasion. As the future Normal School music professor remembered it:

> We had no way of measuring the temperature, but we knew it was biting cold some days and nights. During the day time we had no trouble keeping from freezing, with fire in the "furnace" [a cookstove] and vigorous exercise; some nights, with the weather somewhere below the zero mark and the fire gone out, it was different, but there being three of us in one bed we managed to survive without any serious consequences. Mr. Peightel, a sympathetic friend, spent a few of the coldest nights with us, which made "four in the same bed.[22]

BACK TO SCHOOL

Finally, word reached them that the school would reopen on February 25, a week later than planned. (The borough ordinance banning public meetings had been rescinded on the 6th.) That announcement, said Beery, "was the most welcome news that came our way in the time of our residence at the 'Forge.'" They hurried back, bringing in tow their mountain guide, Martin Brumbaugh of future national fame. The gangly teenager must have presented a comical sight with baggy pants stuffed down into high-top boots.

Other resident students were notified by Zuck through an open letter published in the *Primitive Christian* on February 19. He himself was still at Claylick, ailing and able to get around only on crutches and with great pain.[23] As a result he said his own return would be delayed (he did not come back until March 25). The other instructors, he indicated, would carry on in his absence. Zuck never disclosed, in the statistics he privately kept, how many returnees finished out the term. But apparently there were enough to reassure him that the school had survived the interruption. Furthermore, applications by early April seemed to augur a bumper crop of students for the spring term.

In anticipation of this surge in enrollment Zuck recruited a fifth faculty member: A. S. M. Anderson, a boyhood chum. Anderson was another Millersville degree-holder with further study at Mt. Union College in Ohio. He and the principal had grown up together on adjoining farms and attended the same country school as deskmates. Emmert wrote that the "very disability of Professor Zuck was an additional motive for the marked affection which Professor Anderson showed for him down to the day of his death."[24] The latter and Jacob Brumbaugh shared a third-floor room at Dr. A. B.'s. They had trouble sleeping in the same bed until they put a plank divider between them.

To accommodate the sixty-nine students that reported for the spring term, Zuck rented a second dwelling for a dormitory and boarding club. On April 4 the school tenanted the George Corbin house at 1204 Washington Street, a few doors south of the Burchinell House. Curiously, this other rental, which was used until the move to Founders, has gone unmentioned in all previous accounts of the college's embryonic stage (it was razed in 1960).[25]

HUNTINGDON COMES THROUGH

Concurrently with this onrush of students came the good news that townspeople were prepared to donate the asked-for plot of ground in West Huntingdon. For two months after the smallpox scare, business and professional men of the borough had done nothing about a building site. Their inaction finally provoked the temporary trustees into calling a mass meeting at the courthouse on Saturday evening, March 2, to bring the issue to a head. This call, which brought a response from fifty-some citizens, not only produced prompt action on donated land, but also gave birth to the Huntingdon Board of Trade (counterpart of today's Huntingdon County Business and Industry, Inc.). As the *Globe* put it, "the object of this organization was 'to advance the general business interests of the town, and promote the general prosperity of the citizens of the town and country.'" A twenty-man directorship was formed, to which Henry Brumbaugh was elected.

The directors were authorized to begin a subscription campaign at once for the purpose of securing "Site No. 2." Appointed chairman of the subscription committee was R. Allison Miller, who had sold his broom and brush factory, directly across the street from the *Primitive Christian* building, the year before. In a promotional spiel on March 4 the *Globe's* editor and proprietor, Alfred Tyhurst, laid it on the line to the borough businessmen. He urged:

> What is to be done in this direction must be done quickly, as the number of pupils has increased so rapidly that the present rented building is entirely too small, and, more than that, western towns have made very tempting offers to take not only the school but the *Primitive Christian* office away from us. If the school is permitted to go through lack of enterprise and liberality upon the part of our citizens, our town will lose at the least calculation $90,000 every year. Can we afford to lose the circulation of this sum of money in our midst?

That evening the board of directors met as a body for the first time in the grand jury room. Happily for the Normal School, the subscription committee reported that "Site No. 1" was now available at a price of thirty-four hundred dollars including legal fees. This tract, it was explained, covered sixteen lots, broken down as follows: five lots by the Huntingdon Building and Loan Association; seven lots by the Reverends M. R. Foster and M. L. Smith; two lots by Dr. A. B. Brumbaugh; and two lots by Dr. Homer W. Buchanan. The board, reversing its earlier recommendation, endorsed the committee's report. Said the *Globe*, "The best of feeling prevailed at the meeting, and it was the determination of all present to use every effort to raise the amount." The paper indicated that $2,040 had already been pledged to date.

The committee "worked like beavers," declared the *Globe*, for the rest of March before "their efforts were crowned with success." "They met with much discouragement," the paper acknowledged, "but Spartan like, they persevered." On Saturday, March 20, the solicitors made their final report to the Board of Trade, which then directed its treasurer to collect pledge payments and deliver the deeds to the school trustees. In due time, on Thursday, April 25, these deeds for the three-acre plot were turned over to Henry Brumbaugh, trustee president.

The founders could at last breathe a sigh of relief. For there was no question about their readiness to pull up stakes if the Board of Trade's campaign had fizzled out.

BUILDING ON THE HILL

Earlier, on March 11, once it was pretty evident that the local drive would succeed, the trustees had begun to draw up rough sketches of a main building. On that date *Primitive Christian* employee William Swigart became one of the six temporary trustees. An ex-teacher, he replaced Beer, who had left to join Henry Holsinger in a new publishing venture at Meyersdale. They agreed on a four-story T-shaped structure, the front facing south (not, as now, toward Moore Street), to which wings could be added when needed without marring the original plan. But Henry Brumbaugh and Zuck did not see eye to eye on size. Zuck submitted a diagram that would include a chapel. Dr. A. B. talked up the idea of a tower projection, for a buttress rather than for looks. The publisher had his way until estimates came in, none below eleven thousand dollars. After that the plans were scaled down closer to Zuck's dimensions (84' x 102') but with a tower entrance (12' x 18'). Zuck said of the building's design: "We aim at plainness, but do not wish to ignore correct taste or architectural skill and beauty."[26] Final plans were prepared by a Philadelphia architect who charged seventy-five dollars for his services.

On the first day of May the school plot—a potato patch the year before—was surveyed and the building staked off. A simple groundbreaking ceremony brightened Monday morning the 6th, the soil soggy and the day overcast. Wielding the shovel in turns were Dr. A. B., Henry and Jacob Brumbaugh, Zuck, Quinter, and the doctor's son, Gaius, representing the students. After the brief ceremony a crew of men immediately started to dig the foundation.

THE ACADEMIC YEAR 1877–78 ENDS WITH HIGH PROMISE

While the new site was humming with workmen, townspeople were getting more and more involved in the cultural life of the Normal. The Juniata Literary Society had grown too large for the chapel, and so, in April, it was decided to form two groups. One was exclusively for students with private programs: the Junior Literary Society. The other was made up of "town and gown," renamed Eclectic Literary Society, and held public exercises. Each group kept on file its own *Literary Record*. With one hundred members, the Eclectic Society adopted the motto "Onward and Upward."

This motto aptly epitomized the way things were going in general for the school as summer 1878 came and went. John Brumbaugh, who had assumed Beer's fund-raising chores, was on the road in Eastern Pennsylvania, enjoying good results in lining up stockholders (almost one hundred by August). And with more than fifty teachers in attendance, Zuck took satisfaction in his biggest summer session yet. Promotional literature now spoke of the "Brethren's Normal School and Collegiate Institute," identifying it as "A HOME, A SCHOOL, AND A CHURCH"—a phrase much-invoked over the next decade.

The school's first full-length catalog, a twenty-four-page brochure, appeared in August, flaunting the words "Collegiate Institute" on its title page. Under "Course of Instruction," it stated: "We aim to provide for a full Collegiate Course, but a shorter course has been arranged for those who desire to obtain a good practical education at a minimum of expenditure of time and money." The academic program for the four-year liberal arts course was laid out in detail. Every subsequent issue of the catalog carried it, despite the fact that nobody would show any interest for another two decades.

The Normal English Course was what the catalog really meant to put across. It set forth a two-year diploma curriculum designed to train teachers. But for "ladies and gentlemen of exemplary deportment," only a year's work might suffice. As for student supervision, the catalog scorned the "spy and police system" in vogue at many schools. At Huntingdon a "high sense of personal and individual responsibility" obtained. Those lacking this trait, it was suggested, "would do better to go to some College where the Professors have time to watch them." Instructors should be "personal friends" of students, the policy statement preached, and then ended with a word on the school's selective standards:

> In the educational problem, quantity and quality are both important factors, but we want it understood that we shall ever keep in view, *not so much the number as the spirit, character and influence of our students.*

While Zuck compiled the first catalog the temporary trustees, on August 2, petitioned the Court of Common Pleas for incorporation under the name Brethren's Normal College. The articles of incorporation differed from the resolution of the previous year only in specifying fifteen trustees instead of nine; otherwise, all provisions remained the same.

Late summer also saw Principal Zuck replace one faculty member and add another one. William Beery, one of the Ohio "Orphans," took over as music teacher for Ewing, who left for more training. Nicknamed the "sweet singer," he would teach part-time while working off his degree, awarded in 1882. Beery went on to give thirty years in all to the college, twenty-one as trustee. Among the Brethren he came to be revered as a composer of hymn tunes (more than one hundred).

In Daniel Flory, a third-year student at the University of Virginia, the school had its eighth instructor. Hired to teach the classics, German, and literature, Flory was let go the following summer because he was not enough of a "generalist." He proved his worth later, however. In 1880 he founded Spring Creek Normal School in Virginia, which evolved into Bridgewater College, now a sister institution of Juniata.

Every member of the faculty that fall of 1878—one woman and seven men—had somehow managed to escape matrimony.

THE CHARTER AND A FORMAL ADMINISTRATIVE SETUP

The school's third academic year opened on an expectant note. Zuck welcomed sixty students, and work on the new building pushed ahead rapidly. On Tuesday, November 18, the charter of incorporation cleared its last legal test, and the name Brethren's Normal College was made official. This happy event was almost celebrated under a cloud. Only the day before, John Richardson, a carpenter, fell from the cupola on the tower to the roof of the building, sustaining severe injuries. Fortunately he caught himself before falling to the ground and certain death.[27]

On December 24 Jacob Zuck took the 7:30 morning train for Ashland College on a goodwill trip. He found their building at about the same stage of construction as the one in Huntingdon. His guide was Solomon Sharp, his erstwhile don, who had been elected Ashland's first president. In writing for the *Primitive Christian* about this two-day jaunt Zuck admitted to his earlier prejudice against the Ohio venture, fearing that the Brethren might "ignore the work that has been done and yet remains to be done here among the hills of the good old Keystone State."[28] But now, the educator wrote, he desired "to form the acquaintance of some of our western educational brethren in the hope that something may be done to bring about greater unity of aim and effort." In return the *Gospel Preacher,* published by Ashland Brethren, paid Zuck this tribute: "The substantial interest now manifested by our brethren on the subject of the proper education of our youth is greatly owing to his unflinching energy and devotion to the educational cause."[29]

In February the temporary trustees gave attention to the administrative organization of the college now that the charter was official. At their meeting on the 28th John Brumbaugh offered the following motion, which passed unanimously:

The Principal

1. The Principal shall be President of the Faculty.

2. He shall have the general oversight of the School, and its working; direct its classification; administer the discipline, and attend to any special correspondence.

The Secretary

1. The Secretary shall act as assistant to the Principal by attending to the general correspondence of the School, the business transactions with the Students, furnishing their books, and performing such other duties as may be requested by the Principal as directed by the Trustees.

Dr. A. B. nominated Zuck for the position of "Principal and President," while Jacob Brumbaugh got William Swigart's nomination for "Secretary." Both were elected unchallenged.

THE MOVE TO THE HILL

Much of the trustees' time in the succeeding weeks went into ordering furniture and equipment for the building, which was fast nearing completion. Each room was to be furnished with a double bed, table, washstand, bucket, pitcher, basin, and two chairs. The trustees decided to purchase a piano and organ, to be used jointly by the church and college—a decision that bothered conservative Brethren for years to come. To make the best use of dormitory space the trustees ruled against private quarters for the principal and secretary; each had to share his room (and the double bed) with a student.

When the spring term began on Monday, April 7, seventy-five resident students (out of an enrollment of 102) had moved into the still unfinished building, pressing hard upon the carpenters, plasterers, and painters. "To help matters along," Emmert later recalled, "some of us who knew the use of tools quit the classroom some weeks before the moving day and turned carpenter to help complete the work on time."[30]

On a rainy Thursday afternoon, April 17, dedicatory services were held in the chapel. The local clergy participated and James Quinter preached the sermon. Jacob Zuck was in his glory. To some well-wishers at the ceremony's end, he allowed for the first time: "The day of success is dawning."[31] The "Building," its simple name before christened Founders Hall in the mid-1890s, stood out starkly in a bare field of shale and soil on dedication day. Emmert graphically describes the unattractive grounds at that time in *Reminiscences:*

> When the first pick was struck for the foundation of this structure, in the whole area of the campus to be, stood one lone stunted walnut tree. The soil was so thin that not a spear of sward-grass grew therein. Insignificant mosses, lichens, and such plants as endure severe drought, gave a tinge of tawny green to the hilltop. When school opened in the new quarters, we were practically in the middle of a plowed field. Fences were not yet built nor walks laid out, and not a tree had been set.[32]

In design and floor plan, the Building was as functional as an apiary and soon as much abuzz with activity. The basement contained the dining room, kitchen and pantry, the laundry, a storeroom, and three apartment rooms used by the steward and kitchen help. There was an underground cellar in the rear.

On the main floor were found the library, parlor, two classrooms, and the chapel, which could squeeze in about five hundred bodies. Zuck had his room and an office on the third floor over the library. The bookroom was across the hall. The women lived in a dozen rooms over the chapel, their wing screened off with a red muslin curtain. The top story housed the men. Besides the tower staircase, a narrow flight of steps wound down to the second floor just inside the Moore Street doorway. Stairs also ran down the back end, for exclusive use of women. Missing, though, were bathrooms and inside toilets. An outhouse behind the Building answered the latter purpose.[33] And sponge baths deodorized the body politic until tubs came along.

Outside, oil for kerosene lamps was kept in a barrel, strictly rationed. A Normalite could be ousted for disregarding the curfew hour in the use of lamp oil. In the early days a picket fence, running north from the chapel end, divided the "yard" into a "boys' campus" and a "girls' campus." The walk leading from the tower entrance was reserved for coed traffic exclusively. The fellows used the west entrance.

Two more bachelors joined the faculty when the college moved to the Hill. William Cotton, a brilliant orator skilled in shorthand and with striking Oriental features, came to teach Elocution and Rhetoric. The new mathematics instructor was Joseph Saylor, a Millersville graduate, like Cotton, who got to know Zuck there in 1873. Saylor, whom Cupid failed to waylay for another two decades, would spend thirty-two years teaching at the college, seven more than he put in as trustee. Cotton, a non-Brethren, left after two years and later became a federal judge on the West Coast. But he never lost touch with the little school set in the mountain fastness of Central Pennsylvania.

DEATH OF JACOB ZUCK

The euphoria everywhere evident on the Hill those thrilling April days in 1879 lingered on through the spring. Attention now began to turn to another historic event scheduled for July: commencement for the first graduating class. But early in May the college community was dealt a stunning blow by Jacob Zuck's untimely death. Ironically, it was the Building that led to his undoing, at least in the opinion of his colleagues. The dampness caused by still-drying plaster and the strain from extra stairs, they said, aggravated his deformed hip and apparently wore him down. Emmert and others worried about his "feeble state of health" and begged him to put a heater in his room (there was no central heating at first, only hall stoves). Emmert said, "He resolutely declined all extra attention on the ground that he would not have what the rest of us had not."[34]

Fatigued, he caught a severe cold that developed into pneumonia in his left lung. On Wednesday, May 7, the dying principal was carried in a chair to John Brumbaugh's house a few blocks away. Four days later, on Sunday the 11th, Jacob Zuck died at 3:30 P. M., dear friend Emmert holding his hand in a deathbed watch.[35] He was seven months past his thirty-second birthday. Quinter preached the funeral sermon the next day, but interment in Riverview Cemetery was delayed until Tuesday morning, after the arrival of Zuck's parents. Long-faced students acted as pallbearers.

On the day Zuck was buried George Phillips, a Virginian, dropped out of school. Reminiscing in 1911, he wrote, "When near the station, I looked back and said to myself. "What will become of the Normal?"[36] At first that was the question hanging heavy on everybody's mind. Could the still-struggling school survive the calamity of its founder's death? As David Emmert said, "To take up the thread of his thought and develop the enterprise which he had merely begun was no small task."[37]

Amidst the despair there were also expressions of hope. James Quinter had built his eulogy upon the text "The Lord will prepare a sacrifice." The grand old man reassured his dismayed audience: "Someone will take up this work where Professor Zuck laid it down. The seed sown in faith and watered with tears cannot fail of harvest."[38]

The evening of Zuck's burial the Huntingdon Brethren gathered on the banks of the Juniata River to observe the rite of baptism. Among a foursome of baptismal candidates was the seventeen-year-old Martin Brumbaugh. David Emmert's mother witnessed the scene, the words of Quinter fresh in her memory. As she watched she turned to Emmert and said, more prophetically than she knew, "That boy may some day fill Professor Zuck's place." She clung to her intuition till her dying day, shortly before the prophecy was fulfilled.[39]

Another onlooker at the baptismal scene was William J. Swigart, who shared the prescience of Mrs. Emmert. A habitual diarist like Henry Brumbaugh, he noted in his diary for that day of funeral and baptism: "A star has set—a new star has arisen."

For the newly baptized Martin, arguably Juniata College's most famous graduate, Zuck had been his teaching model, the man most responsible for steering him in a career in public education. The Normal's first headmaster, Brumbaugh once said, "Shook a lot of nonsense out of my head and put a few guidances [sic] into it."

Chapter 4

OTHERS TAKE UP THE WORK: 1879–1888

MEMORIALIZING ZUCK

Dr. A. B. Brumbaugh stood at the lectern-pulpit in the chapel, a prepared speech before him. The members of the Eclectic Literary Society waited for him to begin on that Thursday evening, June 12. It was to be their memorial service for Jacob Zuck. The doctor began by characterizing the late principal as an intellectual hermit, "whose brief life was wrapped up in books and study and teaching." Only such self-devotion on Zuck's part and his "determined will," the speaker said, made the Huntingdon school possible. "He pushed forward his work, thinking while others were idle, working while they were sleeping."[1]

No one who heard these words felt that the doctor had overstated his case. For not a single person in that audience could ever remember seeing the no-nonsense educator at play.[2] Dr. Brumbaugh ended his address on a prophetic note, indulging himself in some predictions about the future greatness of the college. He declared that it was destined to survive as a monument to its founding teacher. But more than that, he promised, "The time will come when the influence of this school movement will be felt from the Atlantic to the Pacific, and from the Lakes to the Gulf." That climactic sentence, however, never made the copy that afterward went to the newspapers; it was furtively deleted by David Emmert and other confederates. This made Dr. A. B. very unhappy. Emmert wrote of the incident in his *Reminiscences* and explained: "Some of us thought these utterances rather extravagant and felt that such a prophecy concerning so small an institution was almost ridiculous. . .[and] would be an injury to the cause at the time."[3] The ringleader, he kept "mum" and let the editorial staff of the *Primitive Christian* bear the blame for "butchering the manuscript." He confessed to suffering twinges of guilt every time the matter came up. Not until the doctor read *Reminiscences* in 1901 did he learn the truth about its author's part in the escapade.

One bright, moonlit night soon after the society's program, a few of the college boys mustered for prayer in the meadow below the Hill. There in a grove of elms, Gaius Brumbaugh, about to graduate, proposed that the students memorialize their deceased principal by some gift to the college. He suggested an oil portrait of Zuck. The prayer band thought it a good idea.

In a matter of days sixty-one Normalites contributed twenty-five dollars for that purpose. Probably on Emmert's advice they commissioned John Chaplin, a local mulatto artist who barbered for a living, to do the painting for nineteen dollars. Gilt framed, it hung for years in the Building parlor (now in Beeghly Library).

Such a thing was unheard of among the simple, frugal Brethren. The "taking of likenesses" was bad enough, and six times between 1839 (when daguerreotype was perfected) and 1879 the church condemned posing for pictures as vainglory. Photography was a still-touchy subject at Annual Meetings as late as 1903. And many judged it sheer prodigality to spend money on a painted portrait. It could well be that the Zuck canvas was the first one in the Brotherhood.

FIRST COMMENCEMENT

Gradually the trauma of Zuck's death began to ease, although his absence at the first commencement had a tempering effect on all activities. Bouquets were tabooed and there was no applause on orders from the trustees. Held on Thursday, July 10, it was a day-long, all-college affair that started at 8:30 in the morning. The chapel walls fairly resounded to a succession of essays, orations, recitations, declamations, and a variety of musical selections. James Quinter, who only moments earlier had accepted the new office of president, addressed the graduates in the evening and gave them their handwritten diplomas. His speech, transcribed by Prof. Cotton, who sat behind a screen near the rostrum, dwelt upon the utilitarian value of a liberal education. In making his perorative point, the hoary-headed president said:

> The best and most important thing in an education is not the amount of knowledge acquired, but the training which gives us control of our minds—the power of being able to apply the mind to studies, labor, and duties which the calling we select may require.[4]

Before the historic event wound up, Elder Isaac Price of Chester County, a long-time educationist and then the country's oldest postmaster—in both age and tenure—asked for the floor. (Quinter's first job after leaving school had been in Price's country store.) The local press reported that the seventy-seven-year-old patron gave a rousing impromptu speech, after which he donated a large Bible that long afterward rested in the chapel pulpit.

FIRST THREE GRADUATES

Bachelor of English degrees were conferred on three graduates, only one of whom (Gaius Brumbaugh) had shared with Jacob Zuck the excitement of that memorable April morning in 1876. He and the other two classmates, both women, went on to distinguished careers. Brumbaugh attended several medical schools, earning M. D. degrees from both Howard and Georgetown universities. Along with his private practice in Washington, D. C., he held a succession of medical posts in the federal government. Dr. Brumbaugh was a man of wide-ranging interests, but he was most notably a history buff. He was also an ardent genealogist and published a monumental study of the Brumbaugh families in 1913. A trustee for forty years, twelve as board chairman, he proved to be an alumnus par excellence.

The other two-thirds of the Class of 1879—Phoebe Norris of Gettysburg, Elder Price's granddaughter, and Linnie Bosserman, a Missourian—left their mark in the world, too. Phoebe Norris taught school for awhile and then entered the Postal Department in Washington, D. C. While there she studied medicine at Columbia College (now George Washington University) where she received her degree in 1891. A confirmed spinster and faithful alumna, she was elected vice-president of the Medical Association of the District of Columbia in 1907, one of the first women physicians to be so honored.

Linnie Bosserman (Grigsby), herself an off-and-on medical student, became a schoolteacher out West. Her fields were art and music, and she taught in Colorado and Missouri before going to an Indian school in Oklahoma. There, in the mid-1890s, she became the "happy bride" of the United States Commissioner of Courts.

FIRST PERMANENT BOARD OF TRUSTEES

By the time the Class of 1879 departed the campus on their separate ways, important changes had been made in the composition of the board of trustees and in the college's administrative setup. At their May 26 meeting the temporary trustees, in keeping with the charter, acted to elect a permanent board from among the stockholders. They drew up a slate of candidates and sent it out, announcing that the ballots would be counted on June 30. The majority of the charter board members were church elders. The three Brumbaughs and Quinter, of course, numbered among the trustees-elect. Henry Brumbaugh got the nod to be chairman, a position he would hold for forty years, until his death in 1919. His brother John put in forty-three years on the board, and Dr. A. B. twenty-nine. William J. Swigart, who over the years would also function as teacher, principal, and treasurer at the school, became the Methuselah among the original trustees in terms of service—a phenomenal six decades. Another noteworthy initial member was Jacob F. Oller, a wealthy businessman and church leader from Waynesboro, Pennsylvania. A generous benefactor of Juniata College, he left an eleemosynary heritage that members of his family carried on for generations to come.

JAMES QUINTER: FIRST PRESIDENT

Having organized, the trustees met again on commencement day, after the afternoon exercises, to name the administrative officers of the college. Jacob Brumbaugh, acting principal since Zuck's death, was elected to that position for another year. Then, in a surprise move, the trustees created a higher office—that of president. What prompted this step is not at all clear since the minutes for this meeting are typically synoptic. There is no evidence that the idea had ever come under prior review by the Huntingdon men. Probably the decision was dictated in large part by the fact that the other two Brethren colleges (Ashland and Mt. Morris) were headed by presidents.[5] And evidently the holdover trustees, who openly begrudged the rivalry of these western schools, saw in the presidency some kind of status symbol.

Such an interpretation gains more credence when it is noticed that the presidency was essentially a titular position for the next fourteen years—until 1893 when M. G. Brumbaugh assumed the office. The duty of the president during those years was to act officially for the college only on stated occasions, whereas at the two sister institutions he was the chief administrative officer.

Nevertheless, the new post demanded a man of mettle and intellectual stature, a man who could rally the shaken college community by symbolizing the spirit of the founders and the whole cause of Christian education. He had to be a man who could salve the wounds higher education had inflicted upon the Brethren.

Without hesitation the trustees turned to James Quinter, the sixty-three-year-old sage whose name was synonymous with the rise of Brethren schools. As David Emmert wrote of him: "His high standing in the church, his nobility of character and eminent qualities of mind and heart well fitted him for the position he was so unexpectedly called upon to fill. The influence of his life upon the students who came under his administration cannot be estimated."[6] But Quinter, nearing retirement age, resisted the presidential call. Henry Brumbaugh revealed in the *Primitive Christian* that his business partner acquiesced only with "great reluctance" and at the "urgent request of the Board."[7]

FACULTY

Under the new administrative plan the day-to-day operation of the college remained in the hands of the principal and his assistant, the secretary of the faculty. Except for a two-year hiatus, from 1881 to 1883, the principal's mantle rested on the shoulders of Jacob Brumbaugh from the time of Zuck's death to 1893, when the position was abolished. It was this intense, strong-willed administrator, only twenty-eight when he took over, who was the polar figure in the immediate post-Zuck decade. Short, with dark, piercing eyes, Brumbaugh bore the major responsibility in the Eighties for developing the curriculum, recruiting the faculty, and building up the enrollment. As Emmert said of him and his work:

> When it is remembered that these years covered the most critical period in the history of the educational work of the denomination, a period when the schools were on trial, when favorable sentiment was unorganized and criticism

was ranging with loose rein, the difficulties of the position can be imagined....Professor J. H. Brumbaugh's administration covered [Juniata's] youthful period and ended at the point when the young institution attained its majority, made its bow to the world, changed its name, enlarged its equipment and stood up to be counted as a college among the colleges.[8]

Jacob Brumbaugh, for reasons not given in the trustee minutes, opted to trade administrative chairs for a two-year spell. Between 1881 and 1882 he functioned as the first secretary of the faculty. William Swigart stepped in as principal for the interim. Joseph Saylor, the first regular college graduate on the faculty, succeeded Brumbaugh as secretary (he completed his studies at Ursinus in 1882). He held the office until it, too, was eliminated in 1893 along with the principalship.

Everyone taught for a pittance. In 1882, for example, Saylor was paid $450 a year plus room and board and assigned seven class periods a day. Public school teachers were doing much better than that. To help make ends meet while principal, Brumbaugh (a bridegroom in 1880) worked on the side as a special agent for the B & O Railroad, representing Western Pennsylvania. In the summers he peddled textbooks for the Butler Company.[9]

In the early 1880s it was jokingly said that the Brethren's Normal College amounted to a Millersville "annex" because of the number of its graduates on the faculty. Perhaps so, but because of low salaries—not till World War I years did senior professors earn as much as one thousand dollars—the turnover of instructors was frightfully high. Only Brumbaugh, Saylor, and Swigart gave stability to the faculty during the Quinter years. Phebe Weakley, a standby from the beginning almost, resigned in 1881 because of her rheumatic condition. William Beery was gone from 1885 to 1889, studying and conducting music institutes in the Midwest. And David Emmert took a nine-year leave (1883–92) to oversee and coordinate the work of two orphanages he founded at Huntingdon and Hagerstown, Maryland. The stockholders, however, recognized Emmert's value to the college and in 1884 elected him to the first of nine consecutive three-year terms as trustee. Emmert, always the gentle-spirited humanitarian, was a rare soul, never one to prostitute his artistic gifts for personal gain. John C. Blair, father of the paper tablet, found that out. Theirs was a staunch friendship, an intriguing union of small-town tycoon and good Samaritan.

Long since forgotten, the story of their relationship was first told publicly by Emmert in 1897, upon Blair's premature death at age forty-nine.[10] They first met in the fall of 1877, soon after Emmert's arrival in Huntingdon, when he stopped in Blair's bookstore on the Penn Street diamond. The two young men, only a year's difference in age, struck up a conversation. The storekeeper revealed his ambition to mass-produce some line of paper merchandise, at the time thinking it might be wallpaper. Obligingly the town's newcomer volunteered to make cuts of original designs for Blair's use. Thus began an acquaintance fed over the years by mutual admiration.

As they chatted that fall day in 1877 Emmert occupied himself in fashioning a pad, 5¾" x 8½", which he intended to use for taking notes while auditing Zuck's rhetoric class. For backing at the top he scrounged a piece of stiff cardboard. Then he took a stack of papers, trimmed to size, and clamped it together with four large carpet tacks, using an old-fashioned wire clinch borrowed from the bookstore owner.

It was this homemade pad that inspired the "Blair Tablet" and a whole new stationery industry. Emmert's friend had found his "line" and promptly forgot about wallpaper. At first ordinary carpet tacks like the ones the art teacher used fastened the "modest little tablet of common newspaper." Later, Blair employed copper tacks and after that glue, "a great improvement," Emmert wrote in the June 1897 issue of the *Juniata Echo*.

A year or so following, after the tablet had begun to catch on, especially in public schools, Emmert was Johnny-on-the-spot again. As he told it:

> One day as I entered the store [Blair] addressed me in a cheerful mood, "I want to improve these tablets; can you make a design for a cover with a Keystone as a trade mark?" We both seated ourselves on the counter and there on a piece of brown wrapping paper I sketched the design for the "Keystone Pencil Tablet." "That is just what I want, make me a cut at once," he said, without asking cost.

The resourceful ex-patternmaker got hold of a few dental instruments, visited a local blacksmith shop, and forged out most of the tools he needed to make the cut. By 1882 the Keystone trademark, still carried on one Mead Products item today, could be seen on stationery in many European countries and throughout most of the Western Hemisphere. In 1884 Mark Twain, from Hartford, Connecticut, dashed off a chit to the stationer turned tabletmaker saying: "Your packets are an unspeakable convenience. They make authorship a pastime!"[11] Supposedly Blair was so impressed with Emmert that he offered him half interest in the burgeoning business. But the gifted artist, at the time more excited about building orphanages than about making and marketing tablets, turned the invitation down.

It was a minor setback, then, to lose the services of Emmert and the others so closely identified with the school's origins. But this void was partly filled by a short, boyish-looking individual in his early thirties named William Swigart. As a lad, born in an old cottage along Jacks Mountain, he had led his blind father around Mifflin County selling pins and needles for a living. He attended Kishacoquillas Seminary and from 1868 to 1876 taught public school. A born preacher known for his precise articulation, he next worked in the *Primitive Christian* office before joining the faculty in March 1880. By then he was already on the trustee board.

Swigart, who at first handled a strange combination of subjects (Surveying and Elocution), would come to enjoy a strong and lasting friendship with Henry Brumbaugh. Ardent anglers, they whiled away many an hour in each other's company fishing the bass-filled waters of the old Raystown Branch. Between them, they represented a century of yeoman's service on the board of trustees. Swigart's sixty years, however, will likely stand forever as a Juniata College record. As Emmert approvingly said of this teacher-trustee midway in his career: "His life has been bound up in the life of the school, and of him, if of any one, it may be said, 'He is wedded to the work.'"[12]

Beginning with 1883 Dr. A. B. Brumbaugh, no less "wedded to his work," got catalog notice as a lecturer in hygiene. At first he made classroom visits only occasionally, but with 1885 one afternoon period every Thursday was set aside for him. A devotee of Dr. Dio Lewis, the famed temperance reformer, he dwelt much, in talking about hygienic living, on the "evils" of tobacco and strong drink.[13] And each year he favored the fellows with a special homily on the "bad effects" of masturbation. The doctor was also available to physiology classes, for which he sometimes performed vivisections on stray cats captured on campus.

The names of two women appeared with that of Dr. A. B.'s in the faculty listing for 1883. Huntingdon's Ida Pecht, a talented musician, was hired to teach piano and organ while completing her Normal course. (Two female instructors, each for one year, had handled instrumental music before her.) She stayed on for nine years, and when William Beery left, gave voice lessons as well. Another pair of female instructors took to the classroom within the next couple years. Harriet Wilson, of nearby Alexandria, took charge of the art department for one year. She belonged to a distinguished family of artists and was the sister of Dr. Jerry Wilson, a well-known portrait painter. Jacob Zuck had recruited their sister, Martha, on a part-time basis in the spring of 1877 before Emmert was able to come.

The catalog for 1884–85 names no art instructor, but the following year red-haired Cora Brumbaugh (Silverthorn), Dr. A. B.'s daughter, joined the faculty. She taught four years under her uncle-principal in this capacity, taking off the spring of 1886 to attend the Philadelphia Art School for Women.[14] In 1885 Elizabeth Howe (Brubaker), upon her graduation, became the third woman on the nine-member faculty for that year. A farm girl from near Lewistown, she was one of a family of twelve children. Her father, William, was a Dunker elder and served as trustee from 1883 to 1892. Three of her brothers and one sister would graduate from the college. She taught English grammar until 1894, and Emmert wrote, "During these years Miss Howe was a strong factor in the development of the intellectual and moral life of the school."[15] The staffing of the classics, however, proved most nettlesome. Six different men handled that department during Quinter's nine-year presidency.

Not only did low pay discourage non-Brethren members of the teaching staff from long-term commitments. Sometimes the quality of food served in the dining room created morale problems of its own for boarding faculty, to say nothing of students. There was so much grousing about the cuisine by the faculty in the spring of 1880 that the trustees called the guilty parties on the carpet. The minutes of that body reveal that the cavilers were "severely admonished concerning table etiquette and discussing victuals at the table."[16] Then in the fall, hardly before school had even begun, the boarders staged an open protest. This time it was the faculty that asked for a showdown. They presented the trustees with a list of culinary grievances, complaining of such things as "not enough meat," "steak and mush for breakfast but none for supper," "Knives too dull," "no sugar in the syrup."[17] The demonstration brought immediate results, and led to the hiring of an additional cook and raising the wages of each girl in the kitchen to $1.75 a week.

CURRICULUM

The catalogs for this period carried the curricula for three programs: the two-year Normal English (B. E.), the three-year Scientific (B. S.), and the four-year Classical. There were no takers, of course, for the Classical and only three completed the Scientific before it was phased out in 1896. The first to receive a B. S. degree beyond the B. E. was Martin G. Brumbaugh in 1885, a year after his election as superintendent of schools for Huntingdon County.

Well into the next century it was the custom to confer a Master of English degree on Normal graduates who had taught for two years, "maintained a good moral character," and paid a fee of five dollars. Virtually all students, therefore, pursued Normal English study. Its curriculum was fixed, since the trustees would have nothing to do with the elective reforms of Harvard's Charles Eliot and Michigan's James Angell at this time. Henry Brumbaugh flatly argued that most students were not mature enough to deal with such freedom.

A preparatory year for those needing it—and most did—was developed in 1883. Three years later the trustees imposed a comprehensive examination upon juniors. The seniors faced a visiting committee of four examiners, one of whom ordinarily was the county superintendent. From 1884 to 1890, of course, that county superintendent was the school's alumnus, Martin Brumbaugh. In 1884 the thesis, an early requirement, was dropped.

Normal English students of that time lock-stepped their way through the following curriculum:

PREPARATORY YEAR

FALL TERM—Elocution, Orthography, Penmanship, Political Geography and Map Drawing, Grammar, Arithmetic

WINTER TERM—Elocution, Vocal Music, Drawing, Grammar, Mental Arithmetic, Written Arithmetic

SPRING TERM—Drawing, Physical Geography, Lectures on Teaching, Grammar, Arithmetic, Algebra

JUNIOR YEAR

FALL TERM—Book-keeping, English Literature, History (U. S.), Grammar, Arithmetic, Algebra

WINTER TERM—Physiology, American Literature, History (U. S.), Grammar, Arithmetic, Algebra

SPRING TERM—Etymology, Botany, Rhetoric, Constitution (U. S.), Grammar, Geometry, Mental Arithmetic

SENIOR YEAR

FALL TERM—Mental Philosophy, Natural Philosophy, Latin, Rhetoric, Grammar, Geometry

WINTER TERM—Mental Philosophy, Natural Philosophy, Latin, Grammar, Astronomy, Science of Teaching

SPRING TERM—Mental Philosophy, Latin, Evidences of Christianity, Science of Teaching, Review of Studies

All textbooks had to be cleared through the trustees. American Literature classes, however, had no censorship problems with anthologies of Whittier and Longfellow, two "household poets" of that day. A Whittier-Longfellow symposium was held in the chapel in March 1885, an event of which Whittier was posted by some public-relations-minded Normalite (Longfellow was dead). In response, there came a little note of acknowledgment from the seventy-nine-year-old Quaker bard saying:

Danvers, Mass. 2d Mo. 15, 1885

I shall be glad if the students of the Normal College find something worthy of their interest in my writings. They have my best wishes.

John G. Whittier[18]

Except for the preparatory year, art and music, unlike literature, were offered as electives (this was the only concession on electives made by the trustees). Nevertheless, these areas of the curriculum attracted their share of votaries. The art department provided studio coaching (oils), but its staple offering was drawing and design, especially under Emmert's tutelage. Students of this "born artist," the catalog avouched, "cannot fail to make rapid progress in this highly essential...branch of education, giving culture to hand, eye, taste and judgment." Training in visual composition, it was pointed out elsewhere, had practical benefits, too. The experience would prove helpful "not only in the class-room but on the farm and in the workshop," since it involved exercises in mechanical drawing and industrial design.[19]

Elements of Vocal Music and Sight Reading was the music department's counterpart in popularity. In the winter term of 1883 the entire student body of fifty-two took this late afternoon class from William Beery. There were also private lessons in voice, piano, and organ. During the 1887–88 school year sixteen undergraduates (all but five were coeds) received piano and organ instruction, first made available in 1881.

This evidence of keyboard interest was another illustration of changing values among college-going Brethren youth. Church prejudice against playing musical instruments, both in homes and in churches, was still deep-rooted, and their use would remain a vibrant issue as late as the 1920s. In fact, the first catalog in 1878 echoed this provincialism: "We encourage our students to give their attention to Vocal music in preference to Instrumental."

The natural sciences in the 1880s never enjoyed qualified staffing. Subjects were meted out among available faculty. Joseph Saylor, a mathematician, made astronomy his bailiwick, and M. G. Brumbaugh taught all science classes during a one-year appointment (1882–83) while pursuing the Scientific course. Thereafter, a classics scholar might very well end up teaching botany. But nobody tackled chemistry; it was ignored.

Scientific equipment materialized very slowly in those non-laboratory days. In 1881 the college became the proud possessor of its first microscope, made possible by a fifty-dollar cash gift from a Western Pennsylvania patron. And another piece of scientific apparatus, a "heliotellus" (planetarium), cost the trustees forty dollars in 1884. The Boston dealer from whom it was bought hawked in business ads: "One of these can be seen at the Normal College, Huntingdon, Pa."[20] Beginning in the fall of 1887 physiology classes scrutinized the latest anatomical charts and had for their use several mannequins with movable and detachable parts.

Charges for a Normal education remained wonderfully stable between 1879 and 1888. Despite the nation's unprecedented industrial and economic boom in that period, tuition for a forty-two-week academic year increased but eight dollars, from $34.00 to $42.00. The cost of room and board reflected even less of an inflationary hike, rising from $115.50 to only $121.80.

Even though the summer teachers' term provided an additional source of income and its enrollment was holding up, the trustees abolished it in 1881. The reason given: "The time is too short to accomplish any effective work in giving culture to the teachers."[21] There was no effort to revive summer study until 1895.

LIBRARY AND SCIENCE MUSEUM

In the decade after Zuck's death, Dr. A. B. Brumbaugh took it on himself, among the trustees, to build up the library and develop a science museum. His son Gaius had a hand in these projects, too, while establishing his medical practice in Washington, D. C. Dr. A. B. made the catalog his chief organ for sounding the cry of need in these areas. "The importance of a Library of standard and miscellaneous works in an institution of learning, cannot be over-estimated," so went the catalog appeal year in, year out for books and money. The 1878 lithographic view of Huntingdon—as a premium—went with a donation of two dollars or more. And by way of recognition the names of all donors were printed periodically in the catalog. Even so, by 1888 the library still fell far short of a thousand volumes, much to the disappointment of the Brumbaugh medics, father and son.

In 1885 the Normal College Library became a repository of all federal publications, thanks to the pull on Capitol Hill of Dr. Gaius and Congressman Louis Atkinson. At the same time Huntingdon County historian J. Simpson Africa, then State Secretary of Internal Affairs, and Assemblyman J. P. Giles placed an up-to-date set of the Pennsylvania Geological Survey in the stacks.

The tiny one-room library was hardly a place of heavy traffic when the Building opened for business. For half a decade or more its holdings were kept under lock and key in glass-door cases.[22] Library hours were limited to Saturday morning, the only time books could be checked in or out. Each student could take out only one book every two weeks. Henry Brumbaugh's *Golden Dawn,* a short-lived Christian education journal, noted that just forty-five percent of the students were book-borrowers during the fall term of 1885.[23] Interestingly, the women outnumbered the men three to one in library use.

Later, before the end of the Eighties, library services materially expanded. A reference library was installed in the hall of the main floor, but after a few years it was replaced by separate collections (each of some 160 volumes) for the men and women on their own dormitory floors. The main library itself kept hours each afternoon, a convenience made possible by volunteer student help. For a quarter of a century after 1879 the care of the library remained in unprofessional hands. Gaius Brumbaugh, while a student, began to inventory the glass-cased holdings. His catalog recorded the call number and title of each book, its value and donor, and its case and shelf location.

The college relied upon student librarians until 1882, when Martin G. Brumbaugh became the first faculty member to take the title of librarian. He was, of course, a part-time assignee, Saturday-morning book checking his major duty. In 1883 Joseph Saylor, who over a span of two decades carried a heavy class load along with librarian chores, succeeded Brumbaugh. For many years this lovable, eccentric mathematics professor simply cataloged all works alphabetically in a ledger, both by author and by title. There was no card catalog or system of classification; not until the late 1890s did the methods of the American Library Association find acceptance.

During the 1880s the science museum received equal billing with the library in the college catalog. The nucleus of the science "cabinet" was Jacob Zuck's own collection of a few boxes, which he had displayed on shelves in his cramped office in the old *Pilgrim* building.[24] It contained assorted mineral specimens and some "natural curiosities." Among the very earliest benefactors of the museum was the Building's architect, S. D. Button. He contributed a "handsome collection of precious stones."

In 1884 the faculty and trustees raised forty dollars to buy an assortment of 126 mineral samples from all parts of the continent.[25] That same year the Smithsonian Institution added over one hundred marine specimens to the museum.[26] Deep-sea dredging by the Federal Fish Commission in the mid-Eighties enabled the Smithsonian to make supplemental donations. As with the library, all museum patrons received public recognition and a lithographic print of Huntingdon.

STUDENT LIFE

By modern standards the student mix during the 1880s was far from ideal. Naturally the student body was predominantly Brethren, although Catholics and other Protestants were certainly no strangers to the campus. In 1885 the college took public pride that enrollment figures included members of a half-dozen faiths.[27]

Because of the school's Brethren background and orientation students came almost exclusively from farm families, rural villages, or small towns. Through all the Quinter years only sixteen Normalites claimed residence in a city with a population of ten thousand or more. Thus neighboring Altoona, where railroad shops were just beginning to lure the Brethren, accounted for but five students. In an age when most people thought woman's place was in the home, men outnumbered their skirted classmates nearly two to one at the Normal. And, of course, no blacks at all were evident around the place. The trustees, in 1882, were bemused by that eventuality, however. Dr. A. B. entered the following reminder to himself in the board minutes for January 16:

> The case of our relation to the other Schools of the Church in relation to admitting colored persons in the School....[W]rite to Ashland and Mt. Morris asking them whether they would admit them into the building or as day students. Ask official reply.

What lay behind this inquiry, or what came of it, remains a mystery.

Enrollment statistics for this period indicate steady growth except for a slight two-year slump, 1882–84. The fall term always had the lowest enrollment, while the spring had the highest—a trend that would persist until after World War I when the college went off the trimester system. In the Eighties, however, the spring figures were usually two and a half times higher than for the fall. The reason for this variance was that most rural schools closed for the year by April, which allowed teachers to take advantage of the college's third term. Farm boys added to the winter attendance once the fall harvest was in, but then some of them would have to leave in March at term's end to help with spring plowing. Thus, for example, the registration figures for 1887–88 went: Fall, 47; Winter 71; Spring, 141.

Not until December 1886 did the trustees decide to keep fuller records—names, birthdays, home addresses—on all students. And only in 1883 did Joseph Saylor, as secretary of the faculty, begin to keep a registry of final passing grades.

Despite the maturity of many students and contrary to catalog claims of the "personal and individual responsibility" of students, the college adhered closely to the principle of *in loco parentis*. Criticism of the church or an unchaperoned date could bring swift disciplinary action. Levi Brumbaugh, though nineteen and a second-year student, was "sentenced" to Room 52 for a week and not allowed to leave the building because he had been caught strolling with Anna Diehl, his future wife.[28] The trustee minutes for August 19, 1880, reveal that one Johnstown coed was dismissed because of derogatory remarks about the church and keeping downtown company, both equally heinous in the eyes of the trustees.

Earlier in the year, during the winter months, an Altoona damsel had almost fallen into the latter sin but apparently was saved in the nick of time by trustee intervention. She received this letter, a copy of which went to her parents:

Feb. 6, 1880

Dear_____:

It has come to the knowledge of the Board of Trustees of B. N. C., the members of which are your brethren, that you have been invited to go out to-night in a sledding and sleighing party in promiscuous company, the character of which we know nothing, but associations which may lead you into company and places where it would be very improper for you to associate or be as a Christian. We claim the right, as it is our duty, to watch over you and advise you in reference to your conduct and association, and we request you, if any encouragement has been made, to recall the same and remain at your home or place where you will not be led astray, and we ask that in the future you accept no invitation to go away from the Building without consulting Brother Brumbaugh whose duty it is to watch over those under his supervision and who will take counsel of others if he does not know the character of your proposed associates.[29]

The use of tobacco also brought summary suspension. Warned the *Golden Dawn* in 1885: "Tobacco and cards go hand in hand."[30] Tippling, it scarcely need be said, was unthinkable.

In those days, of course, there were no organized sports or supervised games. Sometimes the fellows got their exercise by racing around the school block. Football was another favorite pastime of the boys. Among his papers M. G. Brumbaugh has left his personal recollection of pick-up football before that form of recreation emerged as a mad new college cult about the turn of the century. The game of the Eighties relied more on kicking, rugby style, than its modern-day version, M. G. recalled:

> We had no athletic games until 1880 when some of us purchased a round ball and kicked it about on 18th Street east of Moore. Some thought we were headed for perdition. We did not mind. The kicking went on merrily each evening. Lincoln Davis, Howard Keim, Will Livengood, Albert Trent, Samuel McCann and others led in this awful thing.

Later, some improvised gymnastic equipment—a trapeze, a set of iron rings, and a crossbar—was put up behind the Building.

The girls had no physical activity except jumping rope, and the trustees even frowned on it. Dr. A. B. Brumbaugh condemned the amusement as a "pernicious habit," which sometimes led to fatal brain or spinal disorders. He alleged: "As exercise it is not required among girls of the age indulging in it, and ought to be considered as cruelty to children and therefore prohibited."[31] Later he would change his mind.

Chestnut gathering, however, was legitimate outdoor fun for mixed groups in the fall—but not without faculty escorts. Once snow fell, sledding parties made good use of bordering streets and surrounding slopes.

The biggest social event of the year was the faculty reception, a very proper occasion, scheduled soon after classes started. Every September for almost ninety years—until the late 1960s—custom prescribed that students shake hands down a faculty line, the first "How do you do?" said to the president.

Single faculty members who lived in the Building monitored dormitory halls. Roommates slept in a double bed, the fortune of all until single beds became standard furniture in the 1920s. Dormitory life, especially for the men, apparently evoked its share of pranks and horseplay. Even Dunker roughhousing sometimes left destruction in its wake. Hence Dr. A. B. and John Brumbaugh deemed it necessary in March of 1880 to initiate weekly room inspections. At the same time, the trustees directed the principal to charge "liberally" for damage to rooms and furniture.

Formal student evaluation of faculty is a latter-day contrivance, but Normalites had their ways of keeping teachers on their toes, or of getting rid of them. After the legendary Prof. Olawsky, D. Melvin Long, a graduate of both Millersville and Shippensburg, became the second victim of student wrath.

Hired in the spring of 1882, he survived his first term unscathed, but in October of that fall the seniors rose up in rebellion. They petitioned the trustees for a hearing, protesting that the class did not consider Long "a proper teacher" to prepare them for the senior-year final examinations. A few days later, on Saturday the 7th, the trustees met with three class spokesmen. They accused Long, who was teaching English grammar, rhetoric, and the natural sciences, of being disorganized and unable to control his classes. Furthermore, they charged, he had difficulty communicating, made lengthy assignments, and had distracting mannerisms.

The standoff dragged on for nearly a week while the trustees conducted an investigation of their own. They gave the beleaguered professor a private audience the following Tuesday, at which time he denied all charges. His accusers, he said, had distorted the facts and, what is more, the three of them were blatantly cutting his classes. That evening, Long called the seniors together in an unsuccessful attempt at reconciliation. Failing, he tendered his resignation on the 13th, effective at once.

A few sparks flew when he delivered his letter in person to the trustees that morning. He argued in parting that he had been victimized because "he took classes that the other members of the faculty *could* not and *would* not take."[32] This brought a challenge from Dr. A. B., who asked, "They *could* not?" Long retorted, "Yes, they *could* not!"

Not until a meeting with the faculty later in the day did the trustees act on Long's resignation. Impressed by the "opposition in all his classes," they saw no other alternative but to accept it. The trustees, however, were at pains to make clear that Long's dismissal was not "on account of the Board's opposition to him." He left to head a private school of his own in Maryland and the Normal faculty absorbed his classes for the rest of the term. Even in that day, student clout was a power to be reckoned with.

A month or so before the Long imbroglio, David Emmert had supervised the erection of the Huntingdon Orphans' Home across 18th Street at the rear of the college grounds. The L-shaped brick and frame building stood in the campus area today occupied by Oller Hall and the Cloister. Emmert had begun his child rescue work in March 1881 in a small brown, unpainted house in West Huntingdon not far from the school. From the start Normal students proved to be "zealous missionaries" for the Home, Emmert said.[33] Some were present at the mid-week prayer service when the formal step to establish an orphanage was taken. The first winter, students donated three and a half tons of coal to the Home. The earliest of the Home's matrons came from among College Hill women of professed missionary leanings.

In May of 1884 Emmert, who then lived in Hagerstown, came to Huntingdon on one of his periodic visits to the orphanage. He spoke to the Normal students on the general subject of child welfare and urged them to organize an auxiliary to the local Home. The idea intrigued them, and they promptly brought into existence the Normal Helping Hands Society. The purpose of this auxiliary, its constitution stated, was "to co-operate with the Home at Huntingdon and other associated societies in the work of finding homes for children and to aid worthy poor children in securing an education."[34]

Students were just as ready to pitch in and help landscape the barren campus those maiden years. Each spring until 1882, Henry Brumbaugh's diary reveals, he made trips to the woods in the company of able-bodied collegians to search out sturdy saplings. Elms, oaks, and maples were dug up, hauled in wagons, and transplanted in the Normal yard, tended and watered by a "bucket brigade."[35]

IMPROVEMENTS IN THE PHYSICAL PLANT

The early 1880s brought a number of modern comforts and conveniences to College Hill. In the decade's first summer the hall stoves were taken out and central steam heating installed. College publications played this up for all it was worth: "There is no fire to keep up or ashes to carry away by the students." In March 1881, almost five years to the day after Alexander Graham Bell's historic summons to Thomas Watson, the trustees contracted for a telephone. The Huntingdon exchange of the Central Pennsylvania Telephone and Supply began operations the next month with thirty-five customers. Even though the number of domestic and commercial phones nearly trebled by 1883, the Building's three rings sounded so infrequently that the trustees almost dropped the service in 1887.[36]

The tower, at last, got a bell in the fall of 1884. For years to come the bell served a very practical purpose. It signaled all campus events: meals, chapel, church, and classes. A brick sidewalk was laid and a fence put up on two sides of the campus (along Moore and 17th streets) in the spring of 1886. When the borough waterworks began business that summer the dormitory halls and the kitchen were piped with hot and cold running water. Flush toilets were another convenience that came after 1888 when the Normal Building tapped into the borough sewer line. The ultimate convenience for that age—electricity—did not come to the Hill until after the turn of the century, even though the Huntingdon Electric Light Company held a charter since March 1887.

PUBLIC RELATIONS AND PUBLICATIONS

Four Brethren schools existed by the mid-Eighties, but within the Brotherhood the Huntingdon institution was by far the most suspect. Elder David Frantz of Illinois alighted on the campus for a passing visit after Annual Meeting in 1885. He explained: "I called to see that which is so much spoken against."[37] Another visitant the next year was Howard Miller, then a government employee and once Lewis Kimmel's assistant principal at Plum Creek. He wrote in the *Gospel Messenger* (formerly the *Primitive Christian*): "A wide rumor exists to the effect that the Huntingdon church and school are out of line with reference to the peculiarities of the Church." Then he added, in a well-intended but dubious defense of the college: "Such is not the fact, at least not to any considerable extent."[38]

In spite of church resistance, financial support did not suffer, and in March 1884 the trustees announced that the college was debt-free. Unfortunately this good news backfired, bringing a flurry of requests from stockholders for remittals on their investment. To head off this stampede Dr. A. B. Brumbaugh drafted and sent out a form letter. In convoluted syntax he said in part:

> We need, all, to recognize the fact…that the great work undertaken is really, merely begun; that a substantial nucleus, only, has been formed, around which we can concentrate our efforts, and where we can bestow of our means that we desire to consecrate to the Master's service, in the direction of the church's great need. No one should seek to withdraw the aid rendered, but each one should rather double, triple or even quadruple the amount already invested, and others, who have so far had no part nor lot in this matter, should come to the rescue, that additional buildings might be erected, and more thorough equipment secured.[39]

Apparently this letter did the trick and kept the stockholders from wholesale defection. For nothing more was said about it after that, and in another year the trustees even talked of attaching a wing to the Building, by then badly overcrowded.

If holding on to stockholders proved a headache in that generation, enlisting new ones could be just as discomfiting. Poetess Adaline Hohf, soon to marry William Beery, certainly felt that way. She coedited the *Golden Dawn,* a Henry Brumbaugh periodical, and in 1885 declared in one of its articles: "It required so much labor to produce the funds for the first building that no one feels like undertaking the work again, but the indications are that it must be done in the near future."[40] John Brumbaugh and William Swigart—but mostly Brumbaugh—were the men most on the road for the college at that time. Sometimes they met with outright defiance, but fortunately both of them had a saving sense of humor.

Brumbaugh once told of a trip he made to the southern part of Bedford County in this early period. There in one home he and a native ally had just about talked the husband into buying stock. But the man would sign nothing until he consulted with his wife, who was working in the cellar with her elderly mother. He excused himself, and moments later the men upstairs heard the man's mother-in-law say in a loud voice: "They are good-for-nothing, lazy scamps, and I'd tell them so, too!" The two solicitors were so intimidated by this outburst that they took to their heels, afraid to go back for some personal papers they had left on the kitchen table.[41]

More to the liking of the Huntingdon trustees than money raising was the publishing of their little eight-page paper titled *Advance*. Planned as a monthly, it came out in September 1883, edited by Dr. A. B. Brumbaugh. A chatty news sheet, it reported about the people, activities, and alumni of the Normal. It also ran articles of general educational interest contributed by faculty and trustees. The *Advance* was the first paper published by the college, but after five issues it appeared irregularly. In all, there were twelve numbers, the last one in August 1890.

Between 1885 and 1887 the college received extra publicity in the *Golden Dawn.* One of the purposes of this thirty-two-page religious and educational monthly was to promote Brethren colleges. In every edition there was space allotted for news from each of the four nascent schools of the Brotherhood. Only the Huntingdon Normal, however, took full advantage of this free publicity. To Henry Brumbaugh's regret, the *Dawn*, in many ways a superb periodical, turned out to be a journalistic dud and after two years was jettisoned.

ALUMNI AND THE ALUMNI ASSOCIATION

The ten graduating classes of the Quinter era produced sixty-five alumni, eighteen of them women. A statistical analysis of the postcollege employment of all alumni, based on class histories, shows they were a competent lot. As would be expected, nearly half of the graduates (thirty) went into teaching, two becoming county superintendents and three of them principals by 1888. Nine Normalites entered the business world and five went into medicine. Another five became ministers, while a few took up farming or studied law. A half dozen continued their education, a similar number became homemakers, and one was lost through death.

Few, if any, of these ante-Juniatians took a greater interest in their alma mater than Gaius Brumbaugh. Not surprisingly, therefore, it was he who proposed the idea of an alumni association in a letter to the *Advance*, printed in its March 1885 issue. He wrote:

> Washington, D. C., Dec. 1884
>
> Dear *Advance*:
>
> Permit me through your columns to urge the formation of an Alumni Association. Such an organization will rekindle the flame of devotion to the highest interests of the Normal; will foster a deeper personal interest among its membership; will form a nucleus for an organized body of active friends and supporters of our *alma mater*; and will afford annual seasons of great enjoyment. Then all will gather, or in thought turn from a distance, to greet each successive class, and to consider methods for furthering the equipment and development of the "B. N. C." I regret that such action was not taken at the last "reunion," of which in the August number you said, "It was indeed the most enjoyable occasion of the day...."
>
> Let each Alumnus at once address Prof. J. H. Brumbaugh, giving his or her desires in the matter. A number have expressed an earnest desire for such an organization, and I believe the sentiment is general. Let us band together and labor more earnestly to aid each other, and to foster the true success of the beloved Normal!
>
> (Signed) '79

Animated by this letter, six "Alumnists" and four faculty members met in the library on Saturday evening, June 6, and formed the Alumni Association of the Brethren's Normal College. The graduates were William Beery, Samuel Brumbaugh, George Falkenstein, John Keeny (all from the Class of 1882), M. G. Brumbaugh (1881), and Cora Brumbaugh (1883). Saylor, Brumbaugh, Swigart, and Francis Green represented the faculty. The group elected William Beery president and Cora Brumbaugh secretary for that year. In other business the newly formed body granted the faculty honorary membership and appointed a committee of five to draft a constitution: Beery, Saylor, Falkenstein, Green, and M. G. Brumbaugh.

As stated in the constitution they devised, the object of the association was "the mental, moral, and social culture of its members, and the promotion of the interests of its Alma Mater."[42] The document further provided: "All graduates of the institution may become members of the Association by paying an initiation fee of one (1xx) dollar and signing the Constitution." The bylaws called for a public program by the alumni on commencement eve, to be preceded by an afternoon business meeting. All organizations then had to have a motto. The alumni chose "On, and Forever Onward." At first—in 1886 and 1887—the association sponsored reception dinners in private homes. M. G. Brumbaugh entertained the class at his place (now the Baker Guest House) in 1886, and Dr. A. B. made his downtown home available the next year. After this, on-campus receptions became the custom.

QUINTER'S DEATH

James Quinter was closing out his ninth year as president when he died under dramatic circumstances at Annual Meeting on May 19, 1888. The seventy-two-year-old elder, who had rarely missed a yearly conference in the fifty years of his ministry, reached North Manchester, Indiana, about noon on Saturday the 19th. He had been ill for several days and almost called the trip off.

Soon after his arrival he went to a three o'clock preaching service in the tabernacle tent, looking pale and tired.[43] He was asked to close the meeting with prayer, and kneeling down began in a trembling voice: "We are glad to meet again. . ." Suddenly he stopped praying and those on their knees beside him noticed with alarm his deathlike pallor. They helped him up, and he stretched out on a table on the stage. Then he gasped a few times and passed away in the presence of three thousand shocked conference-goers.

Few men in the Brotherhood of that day enjoyed the prestige and affection accorded the college's first president. Dr. A. B. once said, "Elder Quinter is the purest man I ever saw."[44] And of his twelve years in Huntingdon, Henry Brumbaugh wrote:

> To both the Church and the school his being with us proved a great blessing, as he was in many ways, a father to both....Indeed, wherever and whenever he came in contact with either teachers or students he was a living model of uprightness and Christian propriety.[45]

Brethren higher education, though still on trial, had made great strides and owed much to this quiet but extraordinary man. It was too bad, on the rainy afternoon of Quinter's burial, that no one thought to quote the words he penned more than thirty years before. They had an epitaphic ring:

> We think it not only right that the church should encourage such institutions in which our youth may acquire useful knowledge, but we think it is her duty—a duty she owes to her God, to herself, and to the rising generation, to encourage and build up such institutions.

Chapter 5

RISE OF THE BRUMBAUGH DYNASTY: 1888–1893

HENRY BOYER BRUMBAUGH ELECTED SECOND PRESIDENT

On commencement day, June 28, 1888—a Thursday—the trustees met in the afternoon to organize for the coming academic year. Making his first appearance as a trustee was Martin Brumbaugh, the twenty-six-year-old school superintendent. The board elected him vice-chairman. They hoped to capitalize on his name and reputation in recruiting future students from the local area.

Two of the fifteen board members were now women: Annie Bechtel of nearby Hesston (1887–90), who never attended the Normal, and Wealthy Clarke Burkholder, then the school's matron (housemother for women). Mrs. Burkholder, a native of the Broad Top area, had little formal education. But in 1870, at the age of twenty-one, she went to live in Henry Brumbaugh's home where she learned to set type in the *Pilgrim* office. From 1876 to 1880 she edited the *Young Disciple,* a Henry Brumbaugh juvenile magazine. She was the first woman to purchase stock in the college and was briefly enrolled as a student in 1883.[1]

Indeed, the stockholders counted among themselves a high percentage of women. Well over one-fifth (thirty-nine) of the 176 shareholders between 1878 and 1888 were females. And as early as 1880 Belinda Stoner of Union Bridge, Maryland, had been chosen the first woman trustee. Between her term and Wealthy Burkholder's came two other women: Mary Grubb of Pottstown (1881–84) and Hannah Buck (1883–86), the wife of a New Enterprise farmer and merchant and a benefactress of the college after her husband's death in 1916.[2]

After reorganizing on the 28th the trustees then gave their attention to the most

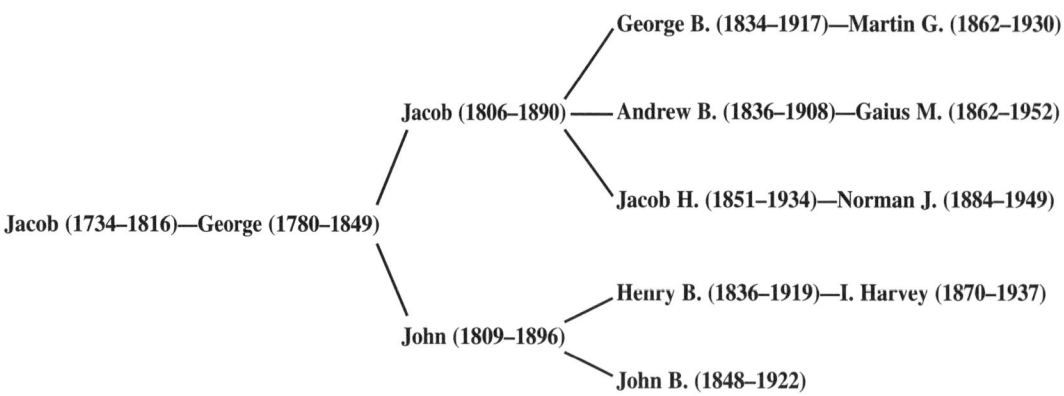

Early Juniata College Brumbaugh Lineage

important item on the agenda: whether or not to continue the position of president. A long debate ensued. William Swigart's motion to retain the post was seconded by John Brumbaugh but it failed by a vote of seven to five. Presumably the vocal element in favor of the presidency came from among the Huntingdon people and included some—maybe all—of the board officers. At any rate, the issue was not long put to rest by this vote.

Henry Brumbaugh's diary cryptically refers to a couple of short-notice parleys in his office over the next fortnight. Then on Thursday evening, July 16, a third consultation took place, this one minuted. All eight Huntingdon trustees were present and, after a lengthy discussion about the "difference of feeling in the Board," Dr. A. B. moved the election of the board chairman, Henry Brumbaugh, as president. Henry's other cousin, Jacob the principal, supported the motion, which carried unanimously, and the college had its second president—the result of a minor but uncontested coup on the part of local trustees. All of this was entered in Henry's diary in a most matter-of-fact way: "8:30—Had a trustee meeting. Elected J. H. B. principal and self president." At fifty-two, H. B. (all the founders and some early teachers went by their first two initials, a Brethren custom then) was a man of some means. But though known and respected throughout the Brotherhood, he lacked his predecessor's eloquence and charisma. He would have more time, however, to give to the presidency than Quinter had.

Five years earlier, in 1883, James Quinter and the Brumbaugh brothers had merged with a Midwest firm into the Brethren Publishing Company. With this consolidation it was decided to publish only one adult church paper—the *Gospel Messenger*—but operate with two branch offices, at Huntingdon and Mt. Morris, Illinois. Quinter was made editor-in-chief, a position he held until his death, and Henry Brumbaugh was named eastern editor. For some time the *Primitive Christian* building housed the *Messenger's* Huntingdon office. Then in 1885 it was moved downtown across from the Opera House on Washington Street. Finally, in the spring of 1890 the two branch offices were centralized at Mt. Morris. With the closing of the eastern office, Henry Brumbaugh, though still an editor, found his journalistic duties much less demanding in time and energy. Thus, much more than Quinter, he involved himself in the academic life and planning of the college.

FACULTY AND TEACHER-TRUSTEES

Under the second president the faculty was expanded and stabilized. To be sure, classical languages still presented problems. Two instructors were fired, one for "want of religious sentiment" and the other for dereliction of duty.[3] And the sciences continued to suffer from being farmed out among willing but unqualified faculty.

On the more pleasant side, David Emmert returned to the classroom, and four Brumbaugh kinsmen swelled the instructional ranks. Emmert, whose child welfare work had by then earned national recognition as the "Huntingdon Idea," came back in 1892 to teach biology and botany along with art. The Brumbaugh influx began in 1890 when Martin G. Brumbaugh, who had taken a fancy to stogies while school superintendent, became a permanent member of the faculty in English "on condition he stop smoking absolutely."[4] Two years later Harvey Brumbaugh, the president's son, began teaching Latin and Greek, finally giving the classic languages some rootage. A graduate of the Normal English (1886) and Scientific courses (1889), he had just received his A. B. degree at Haverford College. To the college and its friends, the classicist was always known as I. Harvey.

In 1893 Harvey was joined by his Uncle John, the president's brother, who taught in the newly created Bible department. John Brumbaugh gave up editorial work in 1883 after the *Gospel Messenger* merger, taking over as company treasurer and for a few years also running a haberdashery downtown. In 1888 he was called to the ministry by the Huntingdon congregation (later he was their pastor, 1903–10). He then spent the year 1889–90 in full-time study at Crozier Theological Seminary and the summer of 1893 with Dwight L. Moody, the celebrated evangelist, at his Chicago Bible Institute. Brumbaugh also took courses at Chautauqua, where such noted scholars as William Rainey Harper, president of the University of Chicago, held forth each summer in the company of popular lay leaders like William Jennings Bryan. Meanwhile, in 1889, the president himself, untrained in biblical studies except for Chautauqua courses, and self-taught in Greek, assumed professorial duties in the Bible department.

Those years ushered in the heyday of a unique core of men termed "Teacher-Trustees" by David Emmert. These individuals spent long days in teaching and weary hours at night wrestling with administrative and financial problems.[5] Nothing in the operation of the college escaped their corporate attention, not even the supply of toilet paper on hand. The men who served in this dual capacity were Jacob Brumbaugh, William Swigart, David Emmert, William Beery, Joseph Saylor, and Martin G. Brumbaugh. This list could also include others who taught part-time: the three Brumbaugh founders, Dr. A. B., Henry, and John.

CURRICULUM DEPARTURES: BIBLE AND BUSINESS

Henry and John's venture into the classroom came after the Bible department took shape in 1888, four years after Mt. Morris College had started one. The founding fathers had shied away from making the study of religion a part of the academic program because of Brethren fears of a professional ministry. But beginning in 1881 William Swigart, whose glasses always rode on the very tip of his nose, gave a required course called Evidence of Christianity. This course, the catalog said, set forth "proofs that the Bible possesses the authority of God, leading men to believe the doctrine which it teaches, and perform the duties which it enjoins."

Taught "without sectarian peculiarities," it was well received and seemingly aroused no open antagonism on the part of the church leaders in the district. Among the students it brought a demand for more Bible study. Quinter, mindful that Zuck envisioned a Bible program some day, pushed hard for it in his last years. Encouragement in that direction came from many friends of the college, like the one who wrote: "I have always been a strong advocate of your school, and have tried to secure for it patronage and money; but if you add a Bible department, I will work still harder."[6] Quinter died before realizing this goal, but the first catalog under his successor announced:

BIBLE DEPARTMENT

> When this Institution of education was started its founders had two leading designs in view. The first was that our children might have a place to go to be educated where they would be surrounded by the religious influence of our own church and people. And the second was, that our people might have a school where their children could receive, in connection with a literary culture, such religious instruction as is in harmony with our faith and practice.
>
> In accord with these designs, the Normal College, from the beginning, aimed to be strictly religious, both in influence and practice. But of late years we have been impressed with the necessity of making *religious teaching* a part of the *school work*. And to this end we now introduce the Bible Department.

The announcement went on to say that as yet there was no "established course" of study, but the catalog for 1889–90 spoke of two curricula in the field. The Eclectic English Course was intended for students "limited in time and means" and engaged in church work who could spend a term or two on campus. Nobody ever enrolled in the second program, the Diploma Course, since it required two full years of study and, perhaps to many, smacked of professionalism. Nevertheless, Bible study enjoyed instant popularity, opening the way for liberalizing the elective system. It attracted no less than thirty students the first year, nearly half of whom were women. By 1893 the number of registrants in the department had doubled. Not a few were enrolled in the Eclectic English Course. For decades no other department would outdraw Bible.

The second president also inaugurated an experimental program of adult religious education for the Brethren by means of annual Bible institutes. These institutes, the inspiration for which came to him while attending one at Chautauqua, were usually month-long and held in midwinter.[7] Promotional literature described the studies covered as meeting the needs of "ministers, Sunday-school workers, Bible teachers and all such as wish to pursue a regular course in Bible study and its kindred branches."[8] The first institute, or "special Bible term" as they were called, took place in the fall of 1890 on short notice and the attendance was small—six counting the two teachers. But by 1893 institutes were bringing to the campus nearly half a hundred from all parts of Pennsylvania and neighboring states. In later years the registration ranged as high as one hundred before the discontinuance of these sessions in 1925.

On the secular side, the most important curricular innovation of Henry Brumbaugh's administration was the creation of the Juniata Business College. The first step in the direction of business training occurred in 1882 when Joseph Saylor introduced bookkeeping as a required unit in the Normal program. Then, in 1886, the trustee minutes reveal that the board gave serious thought to some kind of coalition with the Altoona Business College, but they finally rejected the idea. No doubt lack of adequate space was the deciding factor, but in another five years the picture changed. A wing attached to the Building would make available plenty of extra room.

The next proposition for federating a business school with the college came in the spring of 1890. The instigator was George Snavely of Urbana, Ohio, a stocky, long-bearded man in late middle age. Jacob Zuck had lived in the Snavely home during his Lebanon Normal School days. His landlord, a Maryland native, was then a high-school teacher who later won two diplomas at business schools in the Buckeye State. He also had attended Bethany College and the University of Kentucky.

The trustees gave Snavely's proposal desultory attention until October when a committee reported back recommending a salary of seven hundred dollars for Snavely and giving him the use of two classrooms. Further bargaining granted Snavely the right to use the name Juniata Business College and to carry the title of "principal." But it was clearly understood his work fell "under the control of the Normal College." Also, "clubbing" by commercial students was prohibited; they were to take their meals in the dining room, the cost-conscious trustees insisted. Early in September Snavely's family moved into John Brumbaugh's old apartment in what used to be the *Pilgrim* building.

The Juniata Business College opened on September 14, 1891, and the trustees predicted that its debut would "mark an era" in the history of the Normal. During the first year Snavely prepared a fifteen-page brochure promising that "no effort will be spared to make the JUNIATA BUSINESS COLLEGE a useful, practical school." It spelled out the advantages of being associated with the Normal: the benefits of curriculum, library, literary societies, and religious influence. The United States was at the dawn of a new industrial era, the brochure proclaimed, and there was "growing demand for YOUNG MEN AND WOMEN of sterling good character" to enter the business world.

One page was devoted to the importance of a business education for women as well as men. It called attention to the fact that

> Lady accountants, cashiers, secretaries, clerks, amanuences, type writers, &c., are eagerly sought after, and such positions furnish lucrative employment. In addition to the value a practical education is to a young woman, it renders her

more independent and a better member of society; while it protects her against tricks and frauds in business transactions.

"Many a poor widow has had sad financial experience by not understanding business forms of law," readers were warned. "If to her other sorrows, she have added a consciousness that she has no knowledge of business, she is indeed at the mercy of others."

Snavely's promotional pamphlet further stated: "We *aim*, not only to make *good bookkeepers*, but to FIT THE STUDENT FOR ACTUAL BUSINESS LIFE, in the shortest time, at the least expense." Completion of the course, it said, would vary from three to six months, depending on the student's ability and background. The cost, including board, tuition, books, and stationery, was estimated at between $90 to $125. The course covered bookkeeping, business arithmetic, customs and forms, banking, business writing, business law, and correspondence. Shorthand (the Benn Pitman System) and typewriting were also offered. In the fall of 1891 the trustees bought a World typewriter—seventeen years after Remington placed the first machine on the market, early in 1874. Typing came of age in Pennsylvania in 1895 when a law was passed giving typewritten documents the same legal force as handwritten ones.

Prof. Snavely trained thirty-four aspiring businesspersons the first year, eight of whom earned diplomas. All were men, although five women took the secretarial courses (stenography and typing). Two females won diplomas in 1893, the first of their gender to do so. There were fifteen graduates in all that year, the second biggest class ever. Most early alumni of the Juniata Business College worked in the offices of small firms or were self-employed. A few, however, climbed close to the top of a large company—like Richard Blankley (1893) of Osceola Mills, Clearfield County. In 1900 he moved up to a main-office post with the Prudential Insurance Company of America, pioneer life insurers of blue-collar workers beginning with the 1870s (through small policies with weekly premiums collected by an agent).

In other academic advances under Henry Brumbaugh the catalog for 1889–90 reported that the trustees had authorized a diploma in music. It said: "Diplomas will be awarded by the Trustees of the College to students who have a good English education and have given satisfactory evidence of the requisite attainments in Harmony and Composition, and at least two other branches in this department." The "other branches" were Vocal Music, Vocal Culture, Piano, and Organ. There are no records to show how many diplomas were awarded in what the catalog called the "divine art" during that period.

ORIENTAL AND WAHNEETA LITERARY SOCIETIES

In April 1878, as noted, the college formed two literary societies. One was for Normalites only—the Junior Literary Society. The other, called the Eclectic Literary Society, was open to anyone—students, teachers, and townsfolk. By trustee resolution on September 11, 1879, the all-inclusive society reorganized under a constitution with bylaws and rules of order. Apparently the Junior Society dissolved at that time.

Over the next decade, as the student body expanded, the Eclectic Literary Society grew unwieldy in size. Consequently in January 1892 some of its members mustered the whole school, including trustees, on Friday evening the 15th to discuss re-forming into two rival societies. A committee of four was appointed to work with the faculty and trustees in the choice of appropriate names for the two groups.

The committee reported on January 30 and suggested "Zuck" and "Quinter" to everybody's satisfaction. But within a month this nomenclature was dropped since some students came to feel that competition tended to dishonor "two revered names." The two factions were then denominated Wahneeta Eclectic Society (Zuck) and Oriental Eclectic Society (Quinter). Both daughter guilds adopted elaborate constitutions that were printed and sold in hardback booklets. Each had a multipage section on rules of order. As the preamble of the Oriental Society stated, the object of these literary groups was, in addition to "mental improvement, the entertainment of our friends, and the cultivation of the amenities of social life," to provide "knowledge of parliamentary usages."

It is very hard for us today to appreciate the intellectual ferment and intense intramural rivalry generated by these literary societies. But students then had no intercollegiate athletics, no campus theater, no public events program. The two sodalities, therefore, filled a real cultural void and did much to quicken what at older schools was known as "college spirit." They provided an identity proudly professed; their officers were the BMOCs of that day, the equal of the Phi Beta Kappa key-wearer or the varsity letter-winner on other campuses.

Edgar Detwiler, who entered Juniata in 1902 and later became a prominent Brethren pastor, found the guilds still going strong when he matriculated.[9] As an entering tyro, he said, "You were soon approached by representatives of the two Literary Societies—the Oriental and the Wahneeta. It was not a difficult decision for me to make for scarcely without exception students from Bedford County belonged to the Oriental Literary Society." Young Edgar, like a good member, penned his share of compositions for the *Oriental Star*, rival manuscript paper of the *Wahneeta River*.

STUDENT LIFE

Overcrowded conditions during Henry Brumbaugh's first year in office forced student occupancy of the Building's basement and even the bell-tower attic. Despite these less than ideal dormitory accommodations, the *Advance* was pleased to note, the three terms passed without a single disciplinary case. It is a fact that the college never again enjoyed such a saintly spell. Campus mores nearly took a permissive turn of sorts under the second president. The trustee minutes for September 7, 1891, refer to William Swigart's motion that an area of the "Normal Yard" be open to students from supper to the ringing of the study bell each evening for "association." The motion never came to a vote, alas, although a few benches did get placed in the yard the following summer—for resting, not for flirting.

Nor were the trustees less disposed to relent on off-campus restrictions. College literature never failed to extol Huntingdon's environmental virtues—its healthful climate and its "pure, running, creek water, [which]has never been known to be the cause of any disease whatsoever." Still, it was privately admitted, the town had its dens of iniquity—among them the theater, from which the students had to be shielded. Hence, beginning with the 1887–88 catalog there annually appeared this notice:

> Parents and guardians are requested to grant no permissions to their children and wards to attend operatic and dramatic performances in the Opera House, as the Faculty reserves entire control of such matters.

Even the most biddable sons and daughters of that Victorian generation must have found campus regulations oppressive. Joseph Saylor, wearer of many hats, was the college postman and watchfully screened all incoming and outgoing mail. As one downtown lad, terribly lovelorn, wrote to Alphia Myers, "A letter addressed to me would certainly draw attention to you. While it is inconvenient to go to the P. O. yet it is much safer. The faculty are naturally suspicious of drop letters and are apt to inquire into their character."[10] Alphia had picked up this missive from its hiding place: an old fence post along the Warm Springs road.

With no apologies, the trustees fully intended to run a "College without temptation," the *Advance* said in December 1889. Where "professors are disposed to have a care for the social and religious welfare of the students," it insisted, "much can be done in the direction of guarding them against the snares and temptations that so often beset the unwary, in places where the mental training only, or with it the physical, receives the attention of the teachers." It is important, therefore, argued the *Advance*, that a "united effort" be made to discourage "the companionship of athletes and pleasure-seekers" if students are to be "guarded" from "dissipation" and "bad habits." In fact, the article concluded:

> Young men who have formed the habit of drinking intoxicating drinks, smoking, chewing, or snuffing tobacco, had better abandon [the scholastic life] before they begin, for their efforts in the direction of high intellectual training will be futile, and all their labors will result in disastrous failures. The best energies of the best minds, and brains, untrammeled by stimulants and narcotics is required to excel in study, and make high attainment; and the sacred precincts where the seat of knowledge is, will never be reached by those who persistently weaken their energies, and dwarf their ability by these things.

Thus the catalog for that period regularly recommended that tobacco-users "who contemplate attending school abandon [the habit] permanently before entering the school." Even snacking fell within the purview of trustee control, no doubt much to the distress of those plagued with ravenous teenage appetites. Nevertheless, the catalog advised:

> Boxes containing edibles are always injurious to the students receiving them; and, as an abundance of healthful, nutritious food is furnished all boarders at the Normal, we recommend to parents and friends that they do not send boxes containing edibles.

Dr. A. B. Brumbaugh, the most outspoken trustee on sumptuary vices and "clean living" at that time, also became quite a tub-thumper for a gymnasium and for adding physical education to the curriculum. Actually it was his son, in 1884 when in medical school, who first aired the need for a gymnasium. Gaius wrote to the *Advance:* "As a student at the Normal I experienced the need of systematic training." He stressed that "*physical* nature demands attention but little less than the *mental* and *moral*." His letter ended with the challenge:

> In behalf of the students, and in the interests of the Normal, I urge the recognition of this positive need upon its friends and patrons. A separate building could be erected and well supplied with the necessary apparatus at a moderate cost. A gymnasium will render possible a more perfect development of both sexes, and will materially add to the equipment and efficiency of the Normal.[11]

Such talk was a bit premature but the father made the son's cause his own. And when Ladies Hall, the annex to the Building, was constructed in 1890, he saw to it that one room was designated a gymnasium. A year later he said in an article for the *Juniata Echo* (it supplanted the *Advance* in 1890): "The necessity for a more thorough physical training of the young men and women of this age is becoming more and more pronounced, and the want of it recognized by the thoughtful."[12]

Dr. A. B. Brumbaugh deplored the situation in one large city where only one in seven of all applicants, he said, passed the physical examination. He advocated supervised exercise as early as grade school, lamenting the "slovenly physical habits" of most teachers. The trustee-physician went so far as to say: "A correct physical training of a child is far more important to it at the time it enters school, and for some years thereafter, than the mental training it receives during the same time." He concluded his editorializing by saying: "Every grade of the public schools and every place of learning should have its gymnasium and teacher in physical development."

What kinds of exercises took place in the Ladies Hall gymnasium were nowhere mentioned. But it probably included calisthenics and for the men drills with Indian clubs and dumbbells.[13] Though there was no formal or systematic instruction, the trustee minutes for March 3, 1892, do refer to a Miss Phoenix, who was "invited to come and give a talk and exhibition of Physical training." The opposite sexes, of course, under no circumstances made use of the gymnasium at the same time.

PROBLEMS OF WAYS AND MEANS

Steady growth after 1888, nurtured by a more diversified curriculum, brought enrollment figures to 195 by the spring of 1893. Reassuring as these statistics were, the trustees still rankled at a problem no less vexing in the year 2000: competition between high-cost private education and low-cost public education.

John Brumbaugh, as a trustee, vented his frustration through the *Juniata Echo* in 1891 when he wrote: "If…our people had a proper appreciation of our schools there would be no necessity for such competition."[14] He went on to observe: "The statement was made recently that in a certain State nearly one hundred of our Brethren's children are attending other schools, and why? Simply because some Normal School nearer home offers lower rates." Brumbaugh predicted that if "the School at Huntingdon were to put its expenses at $500 per year, or even half that amount, we don't suppose in a year's time it would have a dozen pupils." He cited the example of the Quakers and Baptists, who, he alleged, provided quality education at high costs and succeeded because those denominations were "interested in their own schools, and are jealous of church influence."

Thus, the president's brother repined: "Until our people can appreciate the importance of influence above the dollar, and as long as we must get our patronage by putting our rates below other schools, our work is going to be crippled." He said that even with high charges and the "closest economy, we can barely keep the institution moving," and closed with a tribute to the underpaid teaching staff, some of whom had received offers from other schools double their Normal salaries.

Balancing the books was thus an all but impossible feat for Treasurer William Swigart, when not preparing for classes. Operating expenses for 1889–90 came to $13,117.91, but income from all sources—room and board, tuition, books—totaled only $9,545.39. This represented a $3,000 increase in operating costs over the previous year and a $150 gain in income. Of course, putting up Ladies Hall did nothing to reduce the overhead. Instructional salaries for twelve faculty members, some of whom were part-time or teaching gratuitously, amounted to $3,453.65, a mere $7.27 boost over 1888–89. Student charges, however, remained unchanged from the Quinter administration: $1.00 a week for tuition and $2.90 for room and board.

LADIES HALL ANNEX AND CAMPUS ENLARGEMENT

With the Building peopled from bell-tower attic to basement recesses, the trustees took action on February 11, 1889, to begin construction of a four-story annex during the coming summer. By early May workmen were busy laying the stone foundation. Meanwhile, a new subscription campaign got going with Henry Brumbaugh's pace-setting pledge of five hundred dollars, followed by his brother John's two hundred dollars.

Across the river the Pennsylvania Industrial Reformatory was only weeks away from completion.

As yet, apart from twelve thousand dollars worth of insurance, little had been done about fire protection. There were still no permanent exterior fire escapes on either of the multistory structures. Back in 1881 William Swigart had been made a "committee of one" to "secure a pole or poles to make ladders for fire security." He did, and these ladders served both buildings until sometime in late 1893 or early 1894 when a set of landings and fixed stairs was attached to the chapel end.

Ladies Hall, as the wing was first dubbed, was ready for occupancy by fall of 1890 and erected at a cost of $12,889.56. The entire fourth floor was set aside for the Juniata Business College and the art and music studios. On the two levels below were dormitory rooms with the parlor and rest room located on the second level. Additional classrooms and the gymnasium took up most of the ground floor, which also contained two small apartments, occupied by the William Beery and John Brumbaugh families. The Brumbaughs lived in Ladies Hall until moving into a new house in November 1891 on the northwest corner of Mifflin and 17th streets (a vacant lot today).

In September of 1890 the trustees altered the entrance to the Building and fenced-in grounds by laying a diagonal walk from the tower to the corner of 17th and Moore (still in place today).[15] The original brick pavement, which ran straight from the tower landing to 17th Street, was taken up. David Emmert was commissioned to make a cut for the catalog showing these alterations and the new arch gateway. As yet no walk led from the west door to Moore Street.

The face of the "normal Yard" was further transformed in early 1892. This time, though, it was the doing of the Huntingdon Brethren, who shared in the use of the college chapel as its regular meeting place. Supervised by the president, their elder, the congregation put in a baptismal pool along the southeast corner of Ladies Hall. This eliminated the jaunt to the old baptismal site along the Juniata River near the present location of the ice plant. Many a Normalite was ritually immersed three times forward in the "Yard Pool" before Stone Church was built in 1910 with its inside baptistry.

For some time the trustees had been pondering the prudence of buying up land and buildings adjacent to the campus, both as an investment and for future expansion purposes. Though hard-pressed to meet mortgage payments on Ladies Hall, they decided to make the plunge at a March meeting in 1892. Over the next few years they obtained eight lots—all below the 17th Street campus extension, four on Moore and four on Oneida (the present location of Stone Church and the heating plant). In a highly irregular but pragmatic arrangement, considering the financial condition of the college, Jacob Brumbaugh procured the Oneida lots in his name, taking a college note for them.[16] The understanding was, of course, that he would sell them to the trustees at market value at any time in the future. It allowed him to make a profitable investment and yet kept the lots in trustee hands.

THE JUNIATA ECHO

The August 1890 edition of the *Advance* let fall expectantly that it was "about to enter upon an active stage of work, for education among our people, and our fraternity." But these words turned out to be its swan song because shortly after that the trustees changed the paper's name. On October 21 the board agreed that the *Advance* ought to be renamed and settled upon *Juniata Herald*. Then someone remembered that Mifflintown, some forty miles down river, had a newspaper so styled. And so they came up with the "poetic and beautiful" title, *Juniata Echo*—a salute to the "Blue Juniata" and the scenery of its basin, the first edition explained.

Started in November under the editorship of Dr. A. B. Brumbaugh, the *Echo* appeared quarterly until 1896, when it became a monthly. It was a more pretentious publication than the *Advance*, printed on larger sheets with three columns to a page. But the subscription rate—at twenty-five cents a year—was half that of its predecessor. The two papers at first differed little in content and format. To encourage good reading, the trustees offered the *Echo* free to all subscribers to any current popular magazines ordered through the college at a discount.

The *Echo's* editor preferred to think of it as essentially a literary journal rather than a campus newssheet, and this was reflected in time by the nature and scope of material printed. To gain professional insight and greater competence, Dr. A. B. joined the Pennsylvania Editorial Association, seldom missing its meetings and many times taking part in PEA-sponsored sightseeing excursions. He also represented the Normal in the Pennsylvania State Educational Association, a college publication body. By summer 1895 Editor Brumbaugh was boasting that the *Juniata Echo*, with more than three thousand subscribers, had the "largest circulation of its kind in the State."[17]

CHURCH ADVISORY BOARD

In 1890, toward the close of Henry Brumbaugh's second year as helmsman, the denomination instituted a procedure for keeping closer tabs on Brethren-run schools. It created an Advisory Board of three district elders for each school, charged with conducting annual visitations. The chief function of the board was to investigate the orthodoxy of textbooks and faculty and file a yearly report with Standing Committee, the ruling body of Annual Meeting.

The 1890 measure stipulated that all Brethren teachers "shall be in full sympathy with the principles and doctrines of the church, and shall conform to the order of the Brotherhood in their appearance."[18] It was further legislated that "at least once a year the doctrines of the church shall be specially held forth in a series of doctrinal sermons." This second requirement was no problem once the Bible Institute gained popularity and since the leadership of the local congregation was identical with that of the Normal.

The garb question, however, did present complications. Already the Huntingdon congregation had been visited by a delegation from Standing Committee in 1888 because of dress code violations. Some of the male members were sporting neckties and shaven chins, while a few women were seen in public wearing fashionable hats. Furthermore, senior class pictures provided clear evidence that most Dunker progeny were sartorially liberated. They were, however, far from being the cane-swinging "dudes" decked out in "bee gum hats" old-order parentage feared colleges would spawn.

Each year the college catalog listed the names of those on the Advisory Board. The first team review took place on Friday, December 18, 1890. Its subsequent report signaled the cordial relations that would always exist between the college and the committee. It read in part:

> Making due allowance for the peculiar circumstances under which an institution of this kind is placed, we have nothing to censure, but much to commend, believing it is doing a good work for the Church. We commend the school to the sympathy and support of the Brotherhood.[19]

For twelve years the chairman of the visitors was James A. Sell, a little-schooled but sagacious man and keen-minded almost to the day of his death at 102. He was widely known in the Brotherhood and throughout Central Pennsylvania as a preacher, author, poet, orchardist, and journalist. He was the first person in his denomination to publish a book of poems. His writings included the *Lost Children of the Alleghenies*, a true story still regarded as a classic by old-timers of the area. Elder Sell was also blessed with the instincts of an historian. He collected the data for the 1925 history of the Church of the Brethren in Pennsylvania's Middle District. He also assisted his son, Jesse, in preparing a general history of Blair County, published in 1910.

During this critical period when the college needed a sympathetic interpreter to the church, James Sell was its veritable tutelary saint. He had upheld the institution from the time of its *Pilgrim* building birth and became one of the most popular resource leaders at the Bible institutes. All four of his sons went to Juniata and many of his descendants can be found in the *Alumni Directory*.

ALUMNI AND THE SCHOLARSHIP FUND

By 1893 the Normal College had 102 alumni, of whom one hundred were living. Geographically they were scattered in two territories (District of Columbia and Oklahoma), fifteen states, and one foreign country (Mexico). Professionally, the profile of graduates had changed but little in five years. Over fifty percent were in public education, fourteen as administrators. Two were college presidents: Walter Yount at Bridgewater, Virginia, and, as of May 1893, Martin Brumbaugh at his alma mater. Only ten were in the ministry and thirty-seven had not yet been led to the altar.[20]

While many of these alumni had to work their way through the Normal with campus jobs, very few had received outright grants. It was not until the Henry Brumbaugh presidency that scholarship help was set up. The trustees, at William Swigart's urging, decided in April 1889 to approve ten scholarships for needy ministers or other "worthy young men" recommended by their church elders. They launched an endowment fund drive, selling stock in one-hundred-dollar shares. Each certificate had nine coupons attached that could be redeemed in tuition fees. Coming as it did hard on the heels of the Ladies Hall campaign, the fund, as conceived by the trustees, met with general indifference.

Ever since 1886, however, the Alumni Association had wanted to link itself to the college in a more meaningful way than merely by an annual meeting on campus. Soon after the trustee announcement in 1889 some of the resident alumni hatched the idea of a separate association-staked scholarship program. They appointed an ad hoc committee made up of M. G. Brumbaugh, Harvey Brumbaugh, and William Beery to draw up plans for an endowment fund and report at the annual meeting in June.

The scheme as finally adopted provided financial help for "worthy" students, women as well as men, in their senior year. This aid was actually a loan, to be paid back without interest on a time schedule mutually acceptable to the recipient and the fund trustees. Three trustees, one of whom must belong to the faculty, had charge of investing and disbursing all monies. A screening committee made up of the trustees, the president, and the principal selected those to receive grants.

At the June meeting of the association, with eleven classes represented and twenty-five alumni in attendance, pledges in the amount of $1,870 were raised. At six percent interest, this meant that about $112 was available for the first year, enough for two scholarships. By June 1893, fifty-one contributors had pledged $3,220 to the Alumni Association Endowment Fund. Twelve students over the past five years had benefited from the fund, seven during 1893.

HENRY BRUMBAUGH'S RESIGNATION

Henry Brumbaugh's diary for Friday, May 12, 1893—a clear, warm day—reads simply: "Resigned as President of Normal in favor of MGB." He was fifty-seven then and weighed a wiry 145 pounds. He lived in a new house he built at 411 17th Street (where the Humanities Center now stands) into which he had moved in September 1892. For another dozen years after his presidency, Henry continued on as dean of the Bible department. Finally in 1908 he left the classroom for good, two years into his seventies.

By then his nest had been well feathered. In 1897 the Brethren Publishing Company was dissolved and its assets transferred to the Brotherhood. At that time its stockholders, chief of whom was Henry, were earning an astonishing twelve percent in dividends.[21] Under liquidation terms, Brumbaugh received a cash settlement plus a handsome annuity based on a certain number of shares he had held in the company.

The college's second president was basically a loner, reserved and undemonstrative, and some people thought him cold and distant. Yet he was a man of equanimity. Though strongly principled, he nevertheless tried to avoid controversy. His partnerships with John and then with Quinter were remarkably harmonious.

As trustee whip for four decades, he won board esteem for his sound financial judgment. He was a founder of the Union Bank of Huntingdon (1894) and also of the Standing Stone National Bank (1902), in turn a director and officer of each. Over the years, entries in his diary note with pride, he always got the most votes at both banks as a director.

Henry enjoyed a long and varied career: preacher, schoolteacher, printer, editor, banker, college professor, trustee, and president. And not only did he help to found and shape the character of a college now a hundred and twenty-five years old, but he resolutely joined forces with those of broad vision struggling to reverse the policies of a denomination benighted by its sectarian part. The histories of two institutions, Juniata College and the Church of the Brethren, bear indelible traces of his formative influence and quiet courage.

Chapter 6

JUNIATA COLLEGE COMES OF AGE: 1893–1910

MARTIN GROVE BRUMBAUGH ELECTED PRESIDENT

"M. G."—as everybody called him—had just turned thirty-one when designated president-elect in May 1893.[1] For two months he demurred before making up his mind to accept the office. Already the college's most illustrious son, he had visions of greater glory outside the Brethren fold.

Then, too, there was the problem of his smoking. He was too fond of his pipe and cigars to shake the tobacco habit even for the sake of a college code. But he and the trustees worked out a *modus vivendi* (no smoking in public), whereupon he agreed to take the presidency, secure in his vice. The college made no announcement of his election until the November issue of the *Echo*. The paper described him as one "who brings energy, talent, and ability to take up the work."

One reason his predecessor, Cousin Henry, had stepped aside was because the trustees were eager to push the four-year classical course and to move the institution more decidedly in a liberal arts direction. They turned to the youthful Martin, with his splendid credentials, as the person best qualified among Brethren educators to carry out that goal. From the day he turned up in the company of the "Old Forge" refugees in the spring of 1878, his trustee-kinsmen knew they had a gem of the first water in the brilliant, winsome fifteen-year-old lad. An omnivorous reader, even of forbidden dime novels, he amazed people with his photographic memory.[2]

He began teaching public school at age sixteen in the Huntingdon area after a year's study at the Normal. He then returned to the Hill and graduated in 1881 with distinction, receiving the Bachelor of English degree. Following a few months of further study at Millersville, he came back to his alma mater as "Professor M. G." For the better part of two years (1882–84) he taught literature, grammar, rhetoric, and natural sciences. His first year back he also held the title of librarian.

Newly married in 1884 he won, by a single vote, election for Huntingdon County superintendent of schools as a twenty-two-year-old. No one in the Keystone State, before or since, became a superintendent so young. His recognition as an educator of promise soon became evident. He stood six feet tall and square shouldered, a striking figure with leonine head, dark craggy brows, and jutting, double-barreled jaw. He had sprouted a beard by this time to make himself look older. Because of his progressive ideas Brumbaugh soon became a favorite of Dr. Elisha Higbee, State Superintendent of Public Instruction.

It was Dr. Higbee who in 1886 recommended him for summer institute work in the state of Louisiana. The white population of that southern clime had rebelled against Reconstruction laws that imposed integrated schools upon taxpayers. Thus public education had gone neglected after the Civil War. Teachers were ill trained; the state had only two bona fide high schools in all of its sixty-four parishes. For a half dozen summers the young Pennsylvanian went south, visiting every part of Louisiana including the glamorous Crescent City itself, New Orleans. Not surprisingly, Brumbaugh was responsible for importing a dozen or more Brethren's Normal College graduates into the Louisiana school system during those years. Educators affectionately referred to them as the "Brumbaugh Infusion" or the "Pennsylvania Invasion." Some rose to high educational circles. One of them was John Keeny of Huntingdon, who in 1907 became president of what is today Louisiana Polytechnic University. As one prominent Bayou State educator said of Brumbaugh and his Hilltop cohorts: "Of all the schools of the North that have contributed to the growth and development of our public schoolwork in this state none has done so much [as the 'Infusion's' alma mater]."[3]

In 1880 Brumbaugh resigned the superintendency to return briefly to college teaching at his alma mater. The Huntingdon congregation made him a lay preacher shortly afterward. A spellbinder in the pulpit, the new licentiate never hankered for nor was ever elevated to the eldership. He preached his first sermon in the chapel on January 19, 1892, a raw, zero-degree Sunday.[4]

Between 1891 and 1894 he took full-time graduate studies, first at Harvard (where he hoped to study under William James but did not) and then at the University of Pennsylvania. When M. G. became president he stood at the verge of a Penn doctorate. He needed more time to complete his dissertation, a study of the post-Elizabethan poet and clergyman John Donne. (His was the first doctoral thesis on the dean of St. Paul's Cathedral written in America.) So, he delayed nearly a half-year—until January 1894—before actively taking over presidential duties. His Ph.D., granted the following spring, was the first one awarded to a member of the Church of the Brethren.

The new president could not have taken up his duties at a more inauspicious time. The country had been gripped since 1893 by the worst industrial depression in its history. The hard times would persist until the early months of 1897.

AN ABSENTEE PRESIDENT

Just when President M. G. was getting used to his new title the University of Pennsylvania stole him away—at least partially. He was selected to fill a part-time chair of pedagogy created by the Quaker City institution in 1895. It was he who had originally convinced Provost Charles Harrison and Penn's governing board of the need to furnish graduate and undergraduate work in education even if on a limited scale at first. This, on top of his superior academic record as an Ivy League Ph.D. (he made Phi Beta Kappa), placed him among the front-runners for the professorship when it was set up. He himself had touted Dr. Oscar Corson, Ohio's Commissioner of Common Schools, the man given first chance at the chair. But Corson declined and, turning the table, supported his own nominator. That was as far as it went; Provost Harrison had his man.

This was an awkward turn of events. It raised serious questions about Brumbaugh's commitment to his presidency. He divided his time between two places all the academic year 1895–96. Weekdays he spent in Huntingdon and weekends in Philadelphia for Friday night and Saturday classes.

It took the charismatic M. G. no time at all to cut a figure among his Penn colleagues. One of them much impressed with him was Edward Potts Cheyney, a leading historian of that day. Dr. Cheyney later became the university's official chronicler. Telling how the school of education got its start, he spoke of its first chairholder as "a man of great energy and competence" and a teacher of "much influence."[5] In short order, Dr. Cheyney wrote, "women and men alike came trooping to his classes."

Back at the college, however, the question of governance became a bit more ticklish when in June of 1896 the president let it be known he was moving to Philadelphia to live. On Monday the 22nd, according to Henry Brumbaugh's diary, he met with the trustees and "defined his future relations to the College." But nowhere in the records were these "relations" spelled out.

Needless to say, the trustees were in a predicament. To fill the administrative void they contrived the position of vice-president, giving it to Henry's son, Harvey. Dr. M. G. was on campus as much as possible over the next fourteen years—for important events, crucial trustee meetings, and to lecture. But not till 1924 did he again call Huntingdon his home.

As might be expected, the idea of their head man off living at one end of the state left everybody on campus wondering and uneasy. To bolster morale Dr. A. B. Brumbaugh stressed in an *Echo* editorial: "The success of the work and the prosperity of the school will not depend on the presence or absence of any one member of the devoted workers as long as there is a united purpose."[6] To some this sounded a bit like whistling in the dark, but time bore out the truth of Dr. A. B.'s words.

The college's third president perhaps found routine academic oversight and small-town life something of a bore in the afterglow of doctoral study in a metropolitan area. Quite likely the fire of his genius, soon to burn bright, would have flickered out had he not been able to escape from what to him must have seemed a stifling, parochial milieu.

Yet the totality of his devotion to the college and to the denomination that nurtured it was beyond question. In 1897 he dedicated his published *Juniata Bible Lectures on the Book of Ruth* to "the Church of the Brethren and Juniata College, the Church and School I love"—a sentiment he never tried to hide. In the end he probably did more for his alma mater as a truant chief executive than he ever could have by on-campus guidance. His name, influence, and contacts, to say nothing of his own generous out-of-pocket giving, enriched the college in countless ways.

ABSENTEE M. G. BECOMES PUBLIC-SCHOOL ICON

Upon landing the Penn professorship Dr. M. G. began to keep a hectic pace. None of his contemporaries made any bigger hit on the teachers'-institute circuit than he did. Though barely in his thirties, he often shared headlines with the famous. At one state teachers' convention in Ft. Wayne, Indiana, he sat on the platform with G. Stanley Hall, world-renowned psychologist and university president. As his reputation spread he was deluged with invitations to speak at high school commencements—some years thirty or more.[7] Religious, historical, and civic groups further crowded his schedule with speaking engagements.

Dr. M. G.'s way with words soon displayed itself in writing as well as oratory. In 1897 he and Dr. Joseph S. Walton, Chester County's superintendent of schools, prepared a supplementary reader, *Stories of Pennsylvania*, for the American Book Co. of New York City. This volume, one of a series on eastern states, put him in the company of such literary luminaries as Joel Chandler Harris (Georgia) and William Dean Howells (Ohio).[8] Within five months *Stories of Pennsylvania* had gone into its third edition. Then in 1899 came Brumbaugh's *Standard Readers*, a set of five graded textbooks. Their adoption, both by public systems and academies, was immediate and widespread. His *Fifth Reader* was especially popular and could be found in use long after World War I in many rural and urban schools.

By 1889 the indefatigable M. G. had become in his spare time an authority on the origins of his church. That year he authored *A History of the German Baptist Brethren in Europe and America*. It stamped him the denomination's pioneer historian and was a feat of prodigious scholarship. Some of the material for this monographic work had been gathered in the summer of 1896 while he was in Germany studying at the University of Jena. Most of his information, though, was searched out from a private collection of original manuscripts owned by Abraham H. Cassel of Harleysville, Pennsylvania. M. G. later saw to it that much of this valuable library went to the college.

Brumbaugh's history made the Brethren aware, as never before, of an important aspect of their past: the vigorous literary and intellectual activity of colonial ancestors. It revealed that the greatest cultural force among German-speaking colonists had been the Sauer press (a Dunker-family business), not Franklin's as historians thought. Moreover, it brought to light Dunker involvement in the founding of Germantown Academy and the fact that even much earlier, almost as soon as they had landed in Pennsylvania, the church fathers set up a school of their own, taught by a woman.

After his history came out Dr. Brumbaugh's academic and scholarly life was interrupted while he put in two years of government service. The summer of 1900 he was appointed the first United States Commissioner of Education to Puerto Rico. The Caribbean island had been ceded to the United States after the Spanish-American War and placed under military control. Then in May 1900 Congress passed the Foraker Act instituting civil government.

Secretary of War Elihu Root turned to Provost Harrison of Penn for help in locating some qualified person to organize a modern school system for the Puerto Ricans. Dr. Harrison immediately thought of his popular pedagogy professor and nominated him. But the Dunker professor expressed no interest, even though the provost promised him a two-year leave of absence. Secretary Root called him to Washington for a face-to-face talk. Brumbaugh still balked, so Root took him over to see President McKinley at the White House. McKinley played upon Brumbaugh's sense of patriotism, a basic theme in all the schoolman's *Readers*. He argued that, especially in the case of Puerto Rico, a teacher carrying a textbook could be as patriotic as a soldier carrying a gun. Forty-eight hours later Brumbaugh's wired acceptance was in the President's hands.

While on insular duty, Commissioner Brumbaugh, for obvious reasons, honored the college with only rare presidential homecomings. He did favor the *Echo*, however, with a succession of informative articles from Puerto Rico. They told of his work there, of the island's geography, its economy, its people and their history.

The commissioner lived in San Juan, the capital; his comfortable house adjoined the governor's mansion. By virtue of his position he held cabinet rank and was an ex-officio member of the territorial senate.[9] He found the isle, which had a population in 1900 of about one million, an educator's nightmare. Approximately eighty-five percent of the people were illiterate and not a single public-school building existed anywhere among the islanders. Classes were conducted in rented houses or rooms; most of these facilities were unsuited for the purpose.

Puerto Ricans saw dramatic gains in public education between 1900 and 1902. Brumbaugh's major task as commissioner was to reorganize and expand the elementary school system. Under his direction the enrollment in the grades increased by over one hundred percent. The number of school buildings multiplied from 616 to 876.[10] Thirty-seven of these were entirely new structures. In addition a high school was erected in San Juan and a Normal school in Rio Piedras (now the University of Puerto Rico). It was the commissioner's plan to use the Rio Piedras institution to train native men and women and rely less on foreign teachers (mostly from the United States). When he left the island, Puerto Rican teachers outnumbered their American counterparts by better than seven to one. There was no sizable "Brumbaugh Infusion," however, from the commissioner's alma mater to match that of Louisiana's. It was a deliberate policy so as not to show favoritism among the throng of American teachers. Only two alumni set sail for Puerto Rican classrooms.

His leave over, Dr. Brumbaugh resigned in 1902 despite the pleas of President Theodore Roosevelt, his political idol, whose biography he wrote in 1922. The San Juans, grateful for all he had done, named a street for him (Calle Brumbaugh). As for the populace generally, the press showered him with plaudits. The Puerto Rico *Herald* declared in 1901: "He has made himself popular throughout the island…and the people love and admire him."[11] That same year the San Juan *News* editorialized: "Some years hence the people of the island will be contributing a fund to erect a memorial to Martin G. Brumbaugh, the founder of our educational system, the mettle of our progressive isle."[12]

"El Señor Martino," as Puerto Ricans affectionately addressed him, went back to university teaching, and during the decade of his forties authored, coauthored, or edited a variety of works. All the while he traveled around the country lecturing at a punishing clip. He brought out several new readers and edited the Lippincott Educational Series and a history of Puerto Rico. A member of the Pennsylvania German Society, history-buff Brumbaugh wrote a biography of Christopher Dock, "the pious schoolmaster of the Skippack" who prepared the first textbook in America on educational theory. Probably his most influential book was *The Making of a Teacher*, published by Harper and Brothers in 1905. It became a best seller in educational circles and eventually went through eleven editions.

Then in 1906 scholarly pursuits once again took a back seat to administrative employment. In July of that year the Philadelphia Board of Public Education elected him superintendent of city schools. Brumbaugh's new position at once placed severe strains on his already tenuous college presidency, from which he now began to think of resigning. Being superintendent thrust him into the thick of a fight to modernize and upgrade the schools of Philadelphia, and Huntingdon concerns got less and less of his attention.

In 1906 the City of Brotherly Love ranked only behind New York and Chicago in population, but in per capita school outlay stood thirty-fourth among all municipalities.[13] Before he left office in 1914 Superintendent Brumbaugh had built up a school system that rated among the best in the United States. And in his judgment, after a trip abroad in 1913, it could even hold its own with Europe's *crème de la crème*.

Campaigning on the slogan, "A decent seat in a decent school for every child in Philadelphia," he was able to erect, in his first six years, twenty-eight new schools. The state's largest city became a model in vocational training, pioneered in special education, and led the way in promoting parent-teacher groups, in providing school lunches, in conducting night classes, and in developing playground facilities (a special crusade of the superintendent's). Other parts of his progressive program, such as practice teaching and a plan for junior high schools, made slower headway.

As Philadelphia's chief schoolman, Brumbaugh quickly gained a national reputation because of his liberal views and honest superintendence. His staff and the city's teachers adored him. One story has it that Woodrow Wilson, when he was governor of New Jersey and knew M. G., once pronounced the Philadelphian one of the three foremost public educators in America of that day.

M. G. TRIES TO RESIGN AS PRESIDENT

The Philadelphia job began to wear on his nerves and sometimes he reacted testily when there was pressure from back home for a presidential opinion or decision. Except in rare instances, the college authorities refused to act on crucial matters until after consulting him. They always did this by mail since he, to protect his privacy, never installed a phone in his Philadelphia residence.

In time an undercurrent of unrest began to tug at the faculty, and his no-show reputation as a trustee irritated some board members. Before long M. G. got wind of this morale problem on campus and decided to make a clean break with the college. Ever since 1899 he had been trying to shed the presidency but to no avail. So in a letter dated June 17, 1907, he resigned as both president and trustee. He said in explanation: "I hear from time to time that my relations to Juniata College, as its nominal president, and as a member of its Board of Trustees interfered with its normal development and its more effective usefulness."[14] That this might be so, he indicated, was a painful thought. As he saw it, the only solution was for him to sever all official connections with the college.

M. G.'s dual resignation shocked the trustees; no one wanted him to quit. They needed him too much. He had been their one and only link with Andrew Carnegie in getting a new library. On him hinged the hope for more help from that benevolent Scotsman. Moreover, the trustees had talked about using President Brumbaugh to cultivate John D. Rockefeller. Therefore, action on his letter was deferred, and Dr. A. B. wrote him urging that he reconsider. But his reply of July 10 was terse and adamant, insisting that he "meant" what he had said.[15]

Yet, in the end, he did back down, though there are no clues why. He stayed on as president three years more. But for him, apparently, it had been all over once, as superintendent of schools, he had moved into Philadelphia's City Hall. When asked to supply data for a biographical sketch in *Who's Who in America*, he listed the years of his presidency as 1894–1906.

HARVEY BRUMBAUGH: VICE-PRESIDENT/ACTING PRESIDENT

The anomaly of an absentee president for a decade and a half could have proved much more disruptive for the college had it not been for Harvey Brumbaugh, the president's second cousin who stoically and ably pinch-hit for him all those years. Although a de facto president, kindly, self-effacing Harvey knew his place in the batting order. Of the pair of them, it was all too clear who wielded the greater clout with trustees. Unintentionally, M. G. held charismatic sway over the campus and there was no escape from his haunting presence.

From 1876, when his father became identified with Zuck's work, Harvey had been a part of the institution. David Emmert recalled in *Reminiscences*:

> As we used to go in and out of the old Chapel in the publishing house at 1400 Washington street [sic], there frequently peeped at us around the corner a timid little boy whom we called "Harvey." He grew up serenely, a quiet and thoughtful youth, and when he came to mingle with the big boys on the hill the teacher of arithmetic had to stand him upon a chair that he might put his work in proper position on the blackboard.[16]

He was barely sixteen when he graduated with a Normal degree in 1886. Staying on, he became in 1889 the second person (after M. G.) to complete the Scientific course.

Then he was off to Haverford and a B. A. in 1892. That fall, a slender dark-haired youth of twenty-two, he was added to the Normal College faculty as a teacher of Greek and Latin. A year's leave of absence for study at Harvard bred a second B. A. diploma in 1895. It was the next summer, while at the University of Jena, that he was made vice-president when M. G. announced his plans to move to Philadelphia.

Three years later, in June 1899, spouseless Harvey was given the title of acting president.[17] This came at the end of another leave of absence during which he picked up a Harvard master's degree in classics. The year in Cambridge resulted in not only a promotion and a graduate degree but an *affair d'amour* that led him to the altar. His marriage, however, would have campus-shaking repercussions and involve him in a seriocomic episode, the scenario of which could hardly have been more paradigmatic of Victorian morality.

In looks, Harvey Brumbaugh was anything but a Lothario, what with his long, narrow face and large hawk nose on which usually perched a pair of round black-rimmed glasses. Before his first Harvard leave, the twenty-four-year-old professor was quoted in the *Echo* as lamenting: "Marriage for me is an unknown, indefinite vanishing factor."[18] His nuptial prospects bettered, however, in 1897 when he, the vice-president, began to court a Somerset County coed. Brethren both, they were soon engaged. But then came the fateful year's interlude at Harvard and his secret romance with Amelia Johnson, the daughter of a highly placed Cambridge family.

Their private wedding on Thursday, April 26, 1900, took the college community by complete surprise.[19] Prof. Brumbaugh had left Huntingdon a few days earlier supposedly to visit his father in a Philadelphia hospital. After a brief stopover there he sped his way to Boston town. In the meantime a batch of mail came to College Hill bringing the unexpected wedding announcement. Upon their arrival on campus two days after the ceremony, the bridal pair was given a lively welcome that included a roaring bonfire down on the ball field. That October they moved into a new house on the corner of Mifflin and 17th streets (occupied today by the history and religion departments).

Two years later Harvey Brumbaugh suffered a great indignity when his former ladylove dragged him into court on a breach-of-promise suit. The trial, which lasted four days, began on Monday, September 11, and engaged the services of no less than eight lawyers. Resorting to the law to settle personal disputes was a violation of Brethren teachings, as everyone knew. Huntingdon fairly buzzed with gossip over the scandal, and crowds shoved their way into the courtroom each day out of curiosity.

The acting president's ex-fiancée, who had been urged to take legal action by her angered brothers, was suing for twenty-five thousand dollars in requital. Defense attorneys argued that the engagement had been dissolved by mutual consent, which the plaintiff's counsel, of course, denied. Both sides submitted *billets-doux* as evidence. "These epistles," so observed the *Semi-Weekly News*, were "dignified in character, yet not lacking in fervor."[20]

They were also damaging to the Brumbaugh case. The trial ended at noon on Thursday the 14th, and the jury deliberated for four hours. By unanimous verdict it found against the defendant but reduced the amount of the claim to $9,250. The judgment gave the *Semi-Weekly News* an opportunity to indulge in a choice bit of moralizing, no matter that it was a gibe at the local college executive. The paper advised: "This decision may cause young men to thoroughly know their own minds before they make hasty propositions of marriage, or when such promises are made they may be slow to violate their word."[21]

Higher courts refused to overturn Brumbaugh's conviction, and for decades his suit was a textbook study at many law schools, Harvard's included. He was forced to declare bankruptcy. Never again did he hold property in his own name, his new home no exception. Thus he never paid out a cent to the jilted woman, but her brothers, one of them a Dunker preacher and former Normal student, would get back at her ex-suitor by and by. They would strike at him through a vengeful act against the college. Meanwhile, Mrs. Brumbaugh, a noble, refined woman, was emotionally scarred for life.

And so was Harvey, who was much too fine a man to be treated the way he was. But many Brethren were cruelly unforgiving. Though the Huntingdon congregation eventually advanced him to the eldership in 1907, he never won a place in the higher councils of the Brotherhood where he properly belonged. As for the college, the trial unfairly hurt his money-raising efforts among the Brethren ever after.

JUNIATA GETS ITS NAME AND BECOMES A LIBERAL ARTS COLLEGE

The name "Juniata College" (an M. G. idea) first appeared in public print in the *Echo* early in 1894. It had been adopted officially at the January board meeting of the trustees, who planned to legalize it later by amending the charter. This action came about in deference to a ruling of Annual Meeting against use of the term "Brethren" in naming a school. Place names, such as that of a town, were recommended.[22] (Of the existing six Brethren-founded colleges today, all are so denominated except Juniata.) The words "Brethren's Normal College" now passed into oblivion.

The eponym "Juniata" is of Indian origin. It is a corruption of "Onayutta," which means "Standing Stone" (a sacred obelisk of the Oneida tribe) that stood along the Juniata River in pre-colonial days. Moreover, legend holds that the river itself was named after a comely Native American lass. This shows, wrote Henry Brumbaugh in the *Gospel Messenger,* "that nature's children love and admire what God has made so beautiful."[23] And since much of this beauty can be seen from the bell tower, explained the top trustee, it was only natural to rename the college after a river. Thus Indian lore and local geography inspired the college's present name. In September 1896 the rechristening was made legal under a new charter.

The year 1896 was an important milestone in Juniata's history for another reason: that was when it became an accredited liberal arts institution. A state law, passed a year earlier, initiated a certifying board called the College and University Council. It also set minimum standards in terms of assets, facilities, and teaching personnel. There is some question whether Juniata technically qualified for accreditation under certain provisions of the act, but President M. G.'s magical influence with the twelve council members did the trick.

Though far from being any golden-dream college Jacob Zuck might have envisioned, Juniata now had a status of sorts. Its graduates automatically received a permanent state teaching certificate. And, jubilated the *Echo,* a Juniata B. A. meant admittance "without examination into the post-graduate departments of the great universities of this county and of Germany."[24] For a long time, however, earned doctorates were in short supply among the professorial ranks. (The college catalog in 1925 listed just three of them.)

CHARTER REFORM AND THE TRUSTEE BOARD

Ever since the late 1880s the trustees had fussed about some way of putting the college in the tax-exempt category. In June 1888 a committee was appointed at the annual stockholders' meeting to study the situation and recommend a plan of action. But nothing came of its work, and eleven years later the stockholders were still fretting about the taxation problem. As long as Juniata remained a joint-stock corporation—at least on paper—there was no legal ground for tax relief. Actually, the total value of college stock by the 1900s amounted to only fifteen thousand dollars.[25]

On February 1, 1904, the stockholders authorized the trustees to "make any legal changes in the charter necessary to further the interests of the College."[26] In another two years the trustees were ready to act and decided that, to dispel a general misconception on the part of stockholders and others, all evidences of private ownership must be abolished.[27] They came up with six points to stress in making their pitch to owners of stock certificates:

1. The money invested in stock was never intended to pay dividends but to be used to promote education.

2. In twenty-nine years no earnings were ever divided among the shareholders.

3. The college is able to go on because of endowment and current gifts.

4. The college is a "public charity" while technically the present charter makes it a business corporation.

5. Abolishing the joint-stock setup would solve the taxation problem.

6. This would also allay the misgivings which some philanthropists might have.

To recharter Juniata as a nonprofit institution meant the cession of every share (271¾ in all) before any court action could be taken. This proved to be a somewhat troublesome and dragged-out process. Once the trustees finally agreed to amend the charter, on January 28, 1907, M. G. wrote his cousin Harvey urging that John Brumbaugh

> get into the field at once and visit as rapidly as he can, securing either the complete surrender by endorsement on each stock certificate or secure proxies prop-

erly signed and witnessed in each case. As fast as it is discovered that the owner will not surrender in either of the two ways named you should let me know the name and number of the stock. Also in cases where the persons subscribed are dead and legal executors or administrators cannot be found to sign the surrender you should also then let me know the name and number of the stock. Each of those shall have to become a special action and the sooner we get them the better. Please hurry this matter as every minute is precious.[28]

The trustees spent months trying to track down all the certificates, not a few of which had been lost. Some had been sold without anyone's making a transfer on the stock records of the college. In the end most were ceded willingly and readily, but not all. A few persons, whose stock was inherited or bought from someone else, thought it had commercial value and resented being asked to yield it as a gift. And then there were the brothers of the girl Harvey Brumbaugh had jilted. Their chance to get revenge had come to hand at last. They held out for full redemption of their father's single share plus twenty-five years' interest (about $2,500).[29]

By year's end all stock had been surrendered, and on January 20, 1908, the trustees adopted a set of amendments to the charter. These revisions cleared the court on September 21. Under the amended charter, all stock was canceled and control of the college vested in a self-perpetuating board of trustees, still fifteen in number. M. G. had made sure that the revised charter was clean of even the most innocent sectarian allusions. This brought a mild protest from Harvey, who once wondered in a letter to M. G. whether it was "wise or necessary to remove all reference to the church."[30] But the president had George Henderson, the trustees' Philadelphia counsel and his close friend, on his side.

Because of them, two important changes were made in the charter. These made explicit the college's legal, if not actual, independence from the church. The first one expunged the provision that trustees had to be Brethren. The second one restated the purpose of the college. It amended the reference in the old charter preserving "the doctrines of the Bible as believed and practiced by the Brethren." It now read: "The purpose or design is to establish a college or institution of learning which will provide the young with such educational advantages as will fit them for the responsibilities and duties of life."

With reorganization came board-of-trustee bylaws for the first time, adopted December 11, 1908.[31] Honoring the charter, the bylaws eliminated a Brethren test for membership. But a "recognized religious character" remained the prime qualification. Familiarity with the college's history and its ideals was also essential. In addition to fostering the "intellectual life of the college on the highest possible plane of efficiency," it behooved the board to "direct and maintain the morale and religious life of the college in harmony with the principles...set forth in the Holy Bible." This was only window dressing, however, since nobody really intended to go out looking for non-Brethren trustees and for years never did. After the charter-reform years fewer trustees hailed from the local area, and faculty-trustees were much less in evidence. The precedent was also set at this time, as specified in the 1908 bylaws, for an annual written presidential report on the state of the college.

The board of trustees suffered a great loss not long after the bylaws went into effect. In January Dr. A. B. Brumbaugh, its enterprising secretary, passed away after an emergency appendectomy. At the time of his death patients owed the seventy-one-year-old surgeon, a large-hearted man, thousands of dollars. As someone said of him: "He is a good doctor, but a poor collector."[32] So overwhelming was the show of community mourning that his funeral had to be held in the Huntingdon Presbyterian Church, the only sanctuary big enough to accommodate the crowd. Dr. Gaius took his father's place on the board.

There had been a five-year hiatus after 1890 when women were absent from the board, but they were well-represented during the crucial years of charter reform. Mrs. Mary Geiger of Philadelphia came on the board in 1895 and served till her death in 1916 at age eighty-eight. She was a godsend in that day when the college needed generous donors. Her sister trustee for years was alumna Jennie Stouffer (Newcomer), a late-married schoolmarm and daughter of Elder Stouffer from Hagerstown. Elected in 1900, she gave the college thirty-eight continuous years, the longest tenure ever for a woman.

DIVERSIFIED CURRICULA: ACADEMY THROUGH COLLEGE

By century's turn there were three degree-granting programs: liberal arts, teacher education, and biblical studies. Three other courses of instruction (music, business, and the academy) conferred diplomas. For a short time, from 1896 to 1900, there was also a seminary course for women who had no interest in the professionally oriented Normal curriculum. Stressing languages, literature, and history, it was designed, the catalog said, "to give young women such liberal culture as will fit them for the varied duties of home and public life." The seminary program was discontinued when the Academy was started.

Liberal Arts

Anticipating accreditation, eight Normal graduates—all men but one—began the liberal arts course in 1894. A select group on campus, they were tagged with the moniker "posts" (postgraduates). Daniel C. Reber was the first "post" to receive the B. A. degree (in 1897), not long before he became the second president of Elizabethtown College. Charles C. Ellis, himself destined for the presidency of his alma mater, followed Reber the next year. The first woman to get a B. A. degree was Altoonan Mary E. Trout, in 1903. Meantime the B. S. degree was dropped in 1894 (although the Scientific course was continued for another two years) but revived in 1920.

Phasing out the Scientific course and doing away with the B. S. degree in no way meant a downgrading of the sciences, however. President M. G., an old hand with microscopes and other laboratory tools, made sure of that. Ever since becoming a trustee in 1894 he spoke out for strengthening that area of the curriculum. Thus from the start the course in liberal arts required some work in at least five of the natural sciences. Once the elective system was introduced in 1897, it was only another three years until advanced courses were being offered. Biology and mathematics led the way, with physics and chemistry next. Geology, though, remained a one-course field. In 1987 the science laboratories expanded and moved into part of Students Hall basement shortly after that building was erected. Next year the whole basement was pre-empted.

Among the sciences, astronomy, still the sideline of mathematics professor Saylor, persisted as the ultrapopular elective. In time there was talk of putting up an observatory on Round Top. John Brashear, the far-famed astronomer and precision lensmaker of Pittsburgh, aroused interest in such a structure while lecturing on campus in the summer of 1907.[33] But the stargazers never got their observatory although the college did acquire a brand-new five-inch Brashear telescope in 1909.

The elective system gave no less of a boost to the study of the social sciences than to natural science. By 1910 there were as many as eleven open slots for upperclass students. And so from one course each in psychology and economics the social science curriculum was expanded to include sociology and political science, for a total of seven courses in all.

There were also a few options in the humanities although art and music failed to qualify as credit-bearing electives. But it was the humanities, of course, upon which the arts curriculum was built. A breakdown of required courses in 1910 shows twenty from the humanities, three from the social sciences, and eight from the natural sciences. Language study began in the freshman year with Latin and either Greek or German. All students had to take two years of Latin and at least one year of German and French. There was one Bible requirement, two in history (both European), three in philosophy, and four in English and literature.

In the sixteen years between 1894 and 1910 the population of B. A. degree-seekers had grown from eight to forty-five, of whom nearly half were women. The all-inclusive fee for pre-World War I Juniatians ranged from $209.00 to $218.50, depending on which of three dormitories they were in.

In those early twentieth-century years Juniata was one of about five hundred degree-granting colleges in the United States. Of these, 350 had an enrollment of less than 160.[34] Ivy League colleges, among the nation's oldest, attracted about ten percent of the student pool (some 200,000) at that time.[35] Of the top ten in size as the 1900s dawned, Harvard headed the list with well over five thousand students, while tenth-ranked Johns Hopkins enrolled a few more than six hundred.[36] Only one out of every four hundred teenage Americans then sought a college education.[37]

The School of Education

The new century saw most state normal schools switch to a four-year curriculum, the better to prepare teachers for the multiplying numbers of high-school positions. Somewhat belatedly Juniata joined the parade, and in 1910 announced that the Teachers School had been reorganized under the name School of Education. Charles C. Ellis, with his recent Penn Ph.D., was made its dean.[38] In compliance with the state school code, aspiring high-school teachers and principals now had to take a fourth year of study. That meant the end of the old three-year Normal course in another year.

The Bachelor of English degree was withdrawn and replaced by a diploma. As before, however, the teacher-preparation curriculum still dwelt upon the needs of the rural school, reflecting student backgrounds and classroom ambitions.

As an alternative to teaching, the catalog promised, School of Education graduates could enter any college in this country. And when M. G. stepped aside the school had 159 on its rolls. It remained Juniata's very lifeblood during this time when liberal arts students came to the Hill in nothing more than a trickle.

The Bible School

That era's Juniata was a pacesetter among Brethren colleges in furthering theological education (as opposed to biblical), against which there was a church ban dating back to 1882.[39] The college's leadership came out openly for a trained clergy, expanded the curriculum in biblical studies, and added two degree programs. Juniata was the second of the sister colleges to engage a seminary-trained theologian and the only one ever to endow chairs in religion.

In 1897 the college introduced a three-year course that led to the degree Bachelor of Sacred Literature. At first there were no entrance requirements. By 1900, however, applicants were expected to have the equivalent of a high-school education. Involving the study of Greek and Hebrew, homiletics and hermeneutics, the Sacred Literature Course provided basic pastoral training, the first of its kind in the Brotherhood. There were twelve graduates, including three women, before the degree—but not the course—was discontinued in 1911. A diploma replaced the B. S. L. degree, after which interest dropped to practically nothing.

Meanwhile, in 1908 the catalog outlined a new four-year program offering the Bachelor of Divinity degree. It amounted to a bona fide seminary curriculum, much more professionally oriented than B. S. L. work, and admitted to study only those with at least two years of college. The B. D. program attracted no attention, however, for another decade. For one thing it was a bit ill timed. Granted, by then many Brethren were finding a professional ministry more to their liking. But the old bugbear of an educated, salaried pastorate still frightened a goodly number of conservative churchmen, most of them Pennsylvanians.

Then, too, there was the rivalry of Bethany Bible School (later renamed Bethany Theological Seminary and today the church's only graduate divinity school). Founded in Chicago in 1905 it had, because of its geographic location, a decided advantage in competing for Far-and Midwest Brethren. Later on, in the 1920s, when fundamentalism found a hotbed on the Hill, Juniata's B. D. program would take on life. Some came to see it as the church's answer to the modernism allegedly then taking sprout at Bethany.

However dormant its theological programs might have been, the Bible department was centric to the total curriculum, and as the years crept up on Henry and John Brumbaugh, M. G. and Harvey brought in new blood. Amos Haines, a graduate of Rutgers and the Yale Divinity School, came to Juniata in 1897. He was the church's second seminary graduate.[40] Haines was joined on the Bible staff in 1907 by Tobias

Myers, the fourth Brethren seminarian.[41] Holding degrees from Temple and Crozier Theological Seminary, Myers enjoyed two distinctions as a clergyman-educator. In 1891 he became the first regularly salaried full-time Brethren pastor—at First Church, Philadelphia. Twenty-three years a Bible professor, he became the first occupant of the college's oldest endowed chair.

This chair, in New Testament Literature and Exegesis, was made possible in 1907 by a gift of twenty-two thousand dollars from Mrs. Mary S. Geiger.[42] "Mother" Geiger, as people titled her, was a wealthy widow widely honored for her charitable, reform, and church activities. President M. G. had known and admired her ever since his doctoral days at Penn. It was he who cultivated her friendship for Juniata over the ensuing years.

The School of Music

Since first issuing diplomas in 1890, the music department made steady progress in upgrading its instruction. It was designated a "school" in 1906, along with Bible, education, and business, but this did not alter its status as mainly a service discipline. Like art, the extent of its academic offerings amounted to one basic course for the Academy and one for the School of Education. In 1904 the college hired its first conservatory-trained musician and five years after, when William Beery retired, the second. Both were women. With their appointments the school became increasingly involved with extracurricular music groups and performances. By 1910 the music staff was handling as many as eighty-eight students through private voice and instrument lessons.

The Business School

When the college was rechartered in 1896 the trustees did away with the name Juniata Business College. For a while it was called a "department" until made a "school" in 1906. A year or two earlier the future of business education on campus had hung in the balance. In November 1904 the trustees began to raise questions about the legitimacy of such a program, even in an adjunct relationship, within a liberal arts setting.[43] The following March they seriously considered wiping out the department at the end of the spring term.[44] But backing off, perhaps out of mercy for George Snavely, then dying of cancer, they decided to wait another year before making up their minds. Snavely died in September, at age sixty-three, the first to pass away while teaching since Zuck's death, more than a quarter-century before. Homer Sanger, a twenty-five-year-old Snavely protégé and college freshman, took over the department in January.

The next summer the trustees ruled against scrapping the business program. Sanger stayed on as its head until 1916. Business graduates took part in commencement exercises for the first time in 1907. Prior to then the principal had distributed diplomas in private. June of 1907 also gave rise to the Business Alumni Association. It disbanded in 1919 when all graduates of degree or diploma programs were made eligible for membership in the parent body.

The Business School flourished in the two decades after 1891, and by 1910 it could list 248 living alumni. Of this breed of Juniatians, over a third were office workers of some sort. Nearly as many were self-employed and a surprising number—about ten percent—had entered one of the professions. Sales, banking, and civil service attracted thirteen percent.

The Academy

Schooling beyond the grades was still a rarity for most *fin de siecle* Americans, and only as late as 1895 were second class cities in Pennsylvania ordered to have at least one high school. Moreover, current state compulsory attendance laws applied to few teenagers. Youngsters in rural areas were virtually denied a high-school education. This posed a real problem once Juniata was accredited. Most of its students came from the country, and at first some of them hoped to use the Normal English Course to get admitted to the college. But that meant dragging out their precollege training for five years in order to meet entrance standards. Many youth were discouraged by this prospect.

The faculty and trustees finally deemed it time to remedy this predicament. They introduced a three-year College Preparatory Course in the fall of 1899. In announcing this move the *Echo* said: "It is the purpose of Juniata College to prepare students, not only for the classical course…, but to train them that if they desire to go elsewhere they may have an equipment equal to that given by the best schools of the time."[45] Thirteen college-minded teenagers appeared on campus in September to enroll in this latest program.

The Preparatory Course was institutionalized as the "Academy" in 1901, when its curriculum was expanded to a full four years. The Academy had no separate buildings and no separate faculty. Nor was there any discrimination at first in the dormitory assignments. Beginning in 1907, however, all college men were housed in Students Hall. Academy pupils got few breaks in costs; except for tuition fees, which were fifty cents a week less, they were charged the same as collegians.

By 1907 the Academy had an enrollment of 109, second only to that of the School of Education by a few students and triple the number in the college. The trustees began to think hard about divorcing the Academy from the rest of the operations in every way—facilities, instructional staff, administration. On July 9, 1908, they met with the faculty to debate both the wisdom and the feasibility of such a step.[46]

A strong consensus emerged on this occasion for developing two different campuses. It was proposed to relocate the college on Round Top, leaving the old property for the use of the Academy. This proposal called for annexing the suggested site and the erection of two new buildings. The trustees were actively exploring such a plan when M. G.'s resignation in 1910 brought all talk of expansion to a halt.

Summer School

For many years after the teachers' institute was dropped in 1879, there was no interest on the part of the college to conduct a summer program on its own. But in 1896 M. G. pulled strings to bring to campus an outside organization, the Pennsylvania Summer School, which was based at Juniata each July for three straight years. Its two-week sessions exposed schoolteachers to a faculty of first-rate educators from all over the state. In essence, though, the school was only a glorified version of the old-time county institute and, as such, gave no academic credit.

In 1902 a pair of young professors, Perry Hoover and Charles Hodges, promoted the idea of a summer term that offered credit-bearing courses.[47] This was a novel idea in higher education then, although some places (like Chicago and Ursinus) had already taken the step. The trustees were hesitant at first, and both Hoover and Hodges had departed by 1909 when Juniata finally fell in line. The 1909 session enrolled thirty-eight students and course offerings came from the college, the Academy, and the School of Education. But summer work never drew very well and would be dropped in 1914 for a brief spell.

HOLDING A CORE FACULTY

The old teaching mainstays, Jacob Brumbaugh, William Swigart, and Joseph Saylor, were still around when M. G. called it quits as president. But gone were David Emmert (1905) and William Beery (1908). Meanwhile, a new crop of loyal Juniatians had moved into the classrooms. As noted, Amos Haines and Tobias Myers anchored the Bible department; both would teach for nineteen years. Charles Ellis returned in 1907, after an absence of six years (he previously taught 1894–1901), with a Penn doctorate. (An earlier one from Illinois Wesleyan in 1904 made him the fourth Brethren to earn that degree.) His was the only Ph.D. among the fixed faculty until Alphaeus Dupler and Charles Shively joined the ranks after World War I. Ellis, trained in education, would wear a variety of hats on the way to becoming president in 1930.

From Mt. Morris College came Oscar Myers in 1905, his B. A. and M. A. from the University of Michigan, to teach English and modern languages. This Lewistown native, a future church elder, spent thirty-seven years with the college. The last eighteen he put in as treasurer and business manager. In 1905 the *Echo* dubbed Myers, with his ready smile, the "Sunny Professor."[48] Students liked the "cheerio, man to man atmosphere" of his classes, the paper said.

Three other worthies were Allan Myers, Martha Shontz, and Frank Holsopple. Elder Myers, farm-born and –bred near McVeytown and an 1887 Normal graduate, brought stability to the sciences between 1893 and 1909. Afterward he replaced Dr. A. B. as trustee secretary, serving nineteen years on the board. Mrs. Shontz, who came in 1906, stepped into Emmert's shoes, and for the next fifteen years held a dual appointment as art instructor and matron. Alumnus Frank Holsopple (1891) taught English from 1901 to 1914 before leaving for other fields of endeavor.

Though doctorates were in short measure in that day, the faculty did their graduate work at some of the best universities in America and Europe. In 1904 the catalog began to list faculty credentials and where degrees were earned. From then on it carried names of schools such as Harvard, Yale, Penn, Chicago, Michigan, Rutgers, Vermont, Berlin, Leipzig, and Marburg.

NEW BUILDINGS

Despite the severe economic recession of the mid-Nineties and the lesser one of 1907, M. G.'s first presidency produced a major transformation of the campus. Its bounds were expanded sevenfold—to more than twenty-three acres. And by 1910 the campus complex consisted of seven buildings.

Students Hall

By 1894 the college had outgrown its classroom space. That October work began on a four-story brick building, 40' x 80', at the southeast corner of Moore and 18th streets. To drum up support M. G. penned a general letter for the *Echo* outlining a fund-raising strategem. He wrote:

> It is our belief that this building should be regarded as STUDENTS' HALL; and we desire to have all students of the College from its beginning, together with their friends, erect this Hall. To further this end we make to you this personal appeal to subscribe, for as many bricks, at one cent each, as you may feel able and willing to contribute....Surely we can contribute 300,000 bricks to this project.[49]

How well this plan paid off is not known, but it brought at least one enthusiastic response. From Chicago Elizabeth Howe, now a social worker, wrote the *Echo* editor that the children of her mission hoped to subscribe a good-size pile of bricks.[50]

Students Hall, designed by David Emmert and built under his eye, was completed by July of 1895. The basement housed the science laboratories and a gymnasium room. The library occupied the west side of the main floor; the east side was divided into two classrooms. There were four classrooms on the third story. The narrow two-floor projections at either end provided office space for instructors. The top level became a men's dormitory, fitted up for some twenty roomers.

In 1897 a stack room for the library, 16' x 26', was added to the rear of Students Hall. The two structures were joined by a fireproof transept, 8' x 16'. M. G. and H. B. Brumbaugh picked up the tab between them ($350 each) for this addition. When Carnegie Library was built the annex was converted into the biology laboratory. Then, following the erection of Science Hall in 1916, the two rooms were put to use for classes. Not till 1928, when the fourth-floor men were moved out, was all of Students Hall given over to instruction.

Oneida Hall

Oneida Hall, almost to a foot the same size as Students, was built in the spring of 1898. Fronting the campus, it abutted the south end of Ladies Hall, connected by an eighteen-foot transept that also served as the main stairway. (The south foundation wall encroached upon the outdoor baptistry, which was now moved to a spot directly east of the chapel.)

The college had long outgrown the old basement dining hall in the Building. Oneida was built chiefly to solve that problem. The new refectory, with high ceilings, large windows, and an open fireplace, was bright and airy. Occupying the entire main floor, its thirty-two tables could seat 269 boarders. On the evening of May 11, moving day, Henry Brumbaugh joined a jolly crowd for the first meal served there.[51] David Emmert remembered: "It was like coming from a dark cave into the open light of day."[52]

The kitchen and pantries were in the basement, from which food was sent up to the dining room on a large dumbwaiter. The upper two floors served as a women's dormitory, which relieved another overcrowded situation. A verandah off the third level overlooked the main campus. William Swigart was the one who came up with the name Oneida Hall. According to the *Echo*, "It received the appellation partly in honor of a neighborhood township and valley by that name, and partly because the street on which it stands is called Oneida street [sic]; but most of all, it was named in honor of a famous tribe of Indians that long ago hunted over these hills and valleys."[53]

Infirmary

In the early days the sick were cared for in their own rooms. Bunkmates carried in meals and dosed out the medicine. Then, for a few years, a college infirmary was located in a suite of rooms on the first floor of Ladies Hall. But there was too much noise, and late in 1899 a three-room cottage was remodeled back of Ladies Hall. It contained four single iron beds and a kitchen but lacked a bathroom. A trained nurse remained on call at all hours, answerable, of course, to Dr. A. B.

Gymnasium

Erected in 1901, the old gymnasium stood as a salute to student gumption and enthusiasm. For years there was grumbling at the lack of space for indoor team sports and vigorous gymnastic exercises. The low, cramped basement room in Students Hall hardly sufficed even for simple calisthenics. In December 1900 the students, with the blessing of sports-minded professors, formed a committee to plan and push for a gymnasium building. At first they thought in terms of a simple frame structure resting on locust posts. Then someone, dreaming bigger, suggested a dual-purpose facility: gymnasium and auditorium. This idea intrigued the trustees and by early next year they had caught "gym" fever, too. The *Echo* reported: "Mr. J. J. Oller of Waynesboro started the financial ball rolling by volunteering one-tenth of the entire cost of the structure."[54] The students "backed up their talk" by raising well over one thousand dollars in pledges and cash.[55] Nor did the alumni shirk in their generosity.

The brick building, with its steep, hip-shaped roof broken by gables, went up directly east of Students Hall (near the site of today's small outdoor bulletin board). Inside, a rostrum, created by the fifteen-foot extension on the east side, made the gymnasium a place for receptions, lectures, concerts, and commencement as well as athletic events. When used as an auditorium, it could comfortably seat on folding chairs an audience, by the *Echo's* estimate, of a few less than one thousand persons. Sweaty athletes, though, had to wait until 1908 before the basement got a shower stall and dressing room.

Carnegie Library

From the moment M. G. took office the library became the academic apple of his eye. In 1895 the erstwhile student librarian donated 315 volumes to the college. He saw to it that Mary Quinter, the late president's daughter, was made Joseph Saylor's assistant that year and urged her to introduce a card catalog and a system of classification. Her seven years in that position (she left for the mission field in 1903) gave the library a modern trend. In 1897 he helped foot the bill for the stacks-addition to Students Hall. At his entreaty that year, Mrs. E. C. Summers, widow of a local historian, turned over to the library on "loan exhibit" a fragment of the second Standing Stone.[56] (This historic relic, later donated to the college, is now on display in the museum.)

Two years later M. G. Brumbaugh acquired part of the famous Cassel collection for the college. Abraham Cassel was the remarkable Dunker antiquarian from Eastern Pennsylvania whom M. G. got to know while researching original sources for his study of Brethren origins. A stockholder, he had been a Juniata booster from the start; his daughter, Hannah, had put in a year of study back in 1877–78. Cassel's was one of the largest private libraries in the country. It contained over fifty thousand items, dwarfing many public and college libraries. Juniata got about a third of this collection—some eleven thousand books and four thousand pamphlets.[57] The bulk of it comprised existing manuscripts, letters, and diaries relating to the early Brethren. There was also a stock of rare foreign works, valuable colonial imprints, and almanacs galore. Thrown in as a bonus was the Cassel correspondence, three boxes full.

Getting his hands on this coveted miscellany cost M. G. a pretty penny. Cassel decided to sell off his library in 1898. At once the president began bombarding his septuagenarian friend with urgent letters.[58] He pleaded that the Brethren materials be kept intact and argued that Juniata was the place for them. The fireproof Students Hall transept, he contended, would ensure safekeeping.

Cassel agreed but there followed months of haggling before they finally settled on a selling price of $2,500. The college, with its Oneida Hall mortgage, was in no position to bear the expense. And so M. G. had no choice but to go it alone on a demand note, on which he made good in less than two years. The date of purchase was February 1, 1899. Later the Harleysville bibliophile refunded five hundred dollars of the purchase price to the college.

Building upon the Cassel collection, President Brumbaugh hoped to make Juniata the chief repository for Brethren publications, past and future. In 1900 he sent out circulars to one thousand ministers in the eastern part of the United States asking for old books, magazines, newspapers, almanacs, and anything else that might have been published by members of the denomination.[59] His project never panned out, but the Cassel library, preserved in the college Archives and the Treasure Room, remains to this day a veritable gold mine for church and social historians.

In 1904 the college came into possession of another collection: the Quinter library, donated by his heirs. It included about one thousand volumes, most of which dealt with theology. That year the college also hired its first trained librarian.[60] In the spring of 1904 Dr. M. G. offered to underwrite the cost for someone—a professional—to come in during the summer months and begin putting the library in order. He made this overture on condition the trustees continue the work. In June, Sarah Bogle, a Drexel graduate in library science, was appointed librarian. Along with her came classmate Mary Wilde, with the title of cataloger.

The team of Bogle and Wilde, with student help, put in long hours cataloging (by Dewey Decimal System) and setting up open stacks. In two years' time they had compiled Library of Congress cards for all books copyrighted since 1898. By 1907 Juniata had a "well cataloged and easily accessible Library," Acting President Harvey Brumbaugh could say in his annual report. At that time there were over twenty-eight thousand volumes on the shelves.

Those volumes, come 1907, had all been shelved in Carnegie Library, the proud showpiece of M. G.'s first presidency. It was the gift of the dwarfish steelmaster Andrew Carnegie, then the world's greatest philanthropist, retired since 1901. Believing that a man who dies rich dies "disgraced," the "Napoleon of the Smokestacks" dedicated the remaining years of his life to giving away his wealth for public libraries, pensions for professors, and other humanitarian purposes. In all he disposed of $350,000,000.

It might seem a pipe dream on the part of trustees at a small bucolic college, cash-starved and patently humble, to think the Scottish-born good Samaritan would be at all inclined to help with a new library. In their president, however, they had an intercessor of proven success in dealing with Carnegie. While Puerto Rico's commissioner of education, Brumbaugh had wooed the shrewd Scotsman into handing out $100,000 for a public library in San Juan. (It was one of only seven to be built with Carnegie money in the Western Hemisphere, outside the United States, before 1919.)

M. G. began his quest for a Juniata library in 1904. Unable to meet with the philanthropist in this country, he doggedly pursued Carnegie by mail on into 1905. At last the college trustees got the good news via an M. G. letter on March 22.[61] It said that Carnegie agreed to a grant of fifteen thousand dollars but on a matching-fund basis. (This was a policy he had originated in American philanthropy.) The college-raised money had to be used for maintenance of the proposed structure. The most amazing thing about the gift was that it did not come from the Carnegie Foundation but out of the steel baron's personal bank account.

The college acted posthaste. Within weeks, Edward Tilton of New York City had been commissioned the architect. The designer of most Carnegie-financed buildings, he had won world acclaim in the restoration of the Heraeum at Argos in Greece. Also, all summer and spring everybody on campus, it seemed, took it upon himself to go out and solicit matching-fund donors. The yield was worth it; by early winter $20,500 had been raised in cash and pledges.

A needs study, however, dictated a bigger library than originally planned. And so on September 26, M. G. wrote Carnegie at Skibo Castle, Scotland, his retirement estate, explaining the situation and asking him to increase his pledge. Carnegie wasted no time replying. On October 13 a cablegram came from his secretary that read:

> Mr. Carnegie...wants me to say that he will be glad to increase his allowance for [a] Library Building for Juniata College from Fifteen Thousand to Twenty-eight Thousand Dollars, as requested, in recognition of the progress you are making.[62]

The site of the library, the trustees agreed in June, should not be on the already crowded campus. They wanted a proper setting, one that would permit the building to face toward town. After much thought they chose the northwest corner of Moore and 17th streets. But there was one problem: Jacob Brumbaugh's brick home stood on that lot. The board vice president did not take too kindly to giving up his domicile, it was soon learned. He delayed for months, causing some bad feelings, before he came to terms. For a goodly profit he sold all his property across the street (three houses and six-and-a-half lots) to the college. This plus the purchase of David Emmert's property gave it ownership of the whole Moore Street block.

The cost of the library site added up to sixty-five hundred dollars. Once again, as in 1878, the college turned to townspeople for help. On November 2 David Emmert huddled with concerned citizens in the courthouse and outlined a trustee request. This time, though, there was no appeal for outright charity. The trustees proposed a seven-thousand-dollar, ten-year loan, interest free. The cash was to come from burghers and businesses through personal advances. But there was a slight catch. Should the trustees find themselves able to amortize this loan before it fell due, then the college was to get a five-percent rebate on each note.

The citizens group endorsed the plan and Emmert masterminded the canvass that followed. As an incentive President M. G. spread word that if the town responded he would give an equal sum toward campus expansion. In the spirit of 1878 the people of Huntingdon met the challenge, handing over the wherewithal in time enough.

Work on the library—architecturally a combination of Doric and Ionic—began in March 1906. Dedication ceremonies took place on Founders Day of the next year, a bevy of state dignitaries in attendance. The cost of construction came to slightly less than twenty-eight thousand dollars, leaving a small balance on the Carnegie grant.

It was M. G. who sparked the idea of memorial library windows in honor of Zuck and Quinter. Alumni and older students of the college made possible the Zuck window in the east wing; church leaders solicited the money for the Quinter window. These memorials were installed in late spring 1908.

CAMPUS EXPANSION

Beginning with 1899, when land along Oneida Street was bought for an athletic field, the main campus grew from four to nine acres in the next decade. For the bulk of this ground the college paid out better than twenty-two thousand dollars in all. But the parcel of it was a gift from President M. G. in 1907. True to his word, given when Huntingdon was solicited for Carnegie Library, he turned over to the college a tract of land valued at seven thousand dollars. This block-size plot north of Students Hall along Moore Street contained three buildings and extended east to the Orphans Home.

Then, through a series of real estate transfers early in 1909, the college, for a cost of $11,500, got possession of the Round Top terrain. It included the area between Washington and Moore streets and from 19th Street north to the foot of what is now Taylor Highlands. This brought college-owned acreage to more than twenty-four.

As noted, impetus for acquiring this area on the Round Top side of Moore Street came from the faculty-trustee conclave of July 1908, which had recommended separating the college and Academy. Then, too, there was a year-old commitment from the alumni to build a dormitory for forty or fifty college men.[63] Alumni Hall, its proposed name, and a combined administration-academic building would become the nucleus of an across-the-street campus. Before long, however, the trustees began backtracking on the idea. Obviously a two-branch operation would prove too costly. Morever, the growing popularity of public high schools raised real questions about the Academy's viability. Thus the matter was let die.

In the spring of 1909 alumnus George Wirt, then director of the State Forestry School at Mount Alto, volunteered his time to landscape the knoll and its slopes. He planted thousands of white pine seedlings on the west hill and hundreds of oak seedlings, both red and white, on the east hill. Along the Washington Street curb line he planted a row of elm saplings. Then he put in a double row of elms the whole way up to the crest of the knoll, forming a lane.[64] So it was that Round Top got its arboreal cover, much of which disappeared after World War II.

Long before Round Top belonged to the college, however, it had become a mecca for Juniata students every commencement week, the sacred site of a special vesper service. The custom of a sunset prayer service for graduating seniors began in 1894. A gratuitous suggestion by M. G.'s mother sent seniors from the foot of the knoll to its crown. The tradition of senior vespers continued after World War II. The hillock was named for Little Round Top, the rise back of Dwight L. Moody's home in Northfield, Massachusetts. Here the famous evangelist conducted vespers for college students attending his "life work" conferences. Campus delegates brought the name back and Juniata's "Round Top" was dedicated in June 1902.

Prior by a year or so to annexing Round Top the college got Pulpit Rocks, located along the old Alexandria Pike (near the present-day Smithfield Correctional Institution). These rocks, on an acre and a half of ground, were the gift of Huntingdonian J. Murray Africa in 1907.[65] In an earlier day the landmark was considered one of the East's natural wonders. Charles Dickens, who passed through Huntingdon in the 1840s, mentions the sandstone formations in *Notes on American Travels*.

CAMPUS FACE LIFTING

After nearly two decades, sometime in 1896 or 1897, the Building at last attained a name: Founders Hall. Originally Founders was not only nameless but also porchless. A fire law, requiring exterior doors to swing out, forced the trustees in 1905 to put a porch at the west entrance for protection against the weather.

In October 1899 a borough ordinance closed all alleys and streets—Oneida and 17th—that cut across the campus. The trustees then moved some buildings, including the soon-to-be infirmary cottage, on to the Oneida Street right of way. The 17th Street stretch was torn up, regraded, and that part of the grounds terraced. (A century later, in 2000, 17th Street would again bisect the campus.)

As the college domain enlarged, sidewalks became a necessity. The stretch between Students Hall and Founders was brick-paved in 1903 and linked with a walk to the gymnasium in 1905. The Students Hall-to-Moore Street "Diagonal," not yet a frosh taboo, remained a gravel path. In 1907 the campus area got sidewalks along both Moore and 17th streets. A pavement across muddy Moore Street was laid in 1907 between the main entrance at 17th Street and the library. Another crossing was put down the next summer farther up the block, directly out from the Founders-porch walk. Meanwhile, the old picket fence along Moore Street came down in 1906.

At the beginning of this century Juniatians still studied at night by light of kerosene lamps. Electrifying the campus was a prolonged, step-by-step process. Normal student George Wirt, the future pioneering Keystone State forester, noted in his diary for January 27, 1898: "Today they commenced putting wires in the buildings for electric lights."[66] The first wiring lighted the halls only, but the new gymnasium in 1901 had electricity from the start. In the spring of 1901 the Founders Hall office got a light bulb. The coeds then set up a clamor for an electric globe in the parlor. They got their way that summer. By early fall 1907 all dorms and classrooms had incandescent lighting, and oil lamps were shelved for good.

In 1910 the Huntingdon Brethren built Stone Church on the south edge of the campus. (Founder John Brumbaugh was the pastor.) The congregation took a ninety-nine-year lease on the site, a small annual rent assessed but never collected. (The lease was renewed for another ninety-nine years in 1998.) As before, when the Huntingdon Brethren worshipped in the chapel, Stone Church and the college had a close bond. Edward Tilton, architect for Carnegie Library, drew the plans for the new place of worship. He patterned it after a countryside Methodist chapel in England that had once caught the eye of Mrs. Harvey Brumbaugh.

TWENTY-FIFTH ANNIVERSARY AND EMMERT'S LITTLE BOOK

Latinist that he was, Harvey Brumbaugh should have known better. Nevertheless, the acting president allowed promotional literature to refer to 1901 as Juniata's Quadri-Centennial (the word means four-hundredth anniversary, not quarter-century). To make the most of the festal year, all celebrating took place during commencement week in June. Souvenirs abounded, among them the school's first wall calendar, a miniature, on which there was printed in bold letters, "Juniata: A College of High Standard."

Without question the choicest memento of the anniversary year was David Emmert's *Reminiscences of Juniata College: Quarter Century, 1876–1901*. While convalescing from a serious illness in 1900, he began to put on paper his personal memories of the college's early days. He started this little narrative with the idea of passing it on to his sons as a keepsake. Friends paying him sick calls were treated to chapters as they were finished. Soon everybody was urging him to put his "story-like history," the *Echo*'s apt description of it, into book form.

And so he did, underwriting the printing costs himself and filling the pages with over one hundred woodcuts and photographs. He wrote that if *Reminiscences*, a "record of incidents and experiences grave and comical, joyful and sad, shall lead anyone to understand better the motives and principles upon which Juniata, as it stands today, was founded, and the spirit in which it had gone forward," then the book had been worth his while.

Chapter 7

STUDENT LIFE: MID-1890S TO EARLY 1900S

STUDENT LIFE IN GENERAL

Latter-day Juniatians would hardly long for the daily regimen of the Gay Nineties, when their ancestors went from bed to class by seven o'clock (changed to 7:45 A. M. in 1904). *In loco parentis* was still very much the code of the day. Students looked upon Prof. Jacob Brumbaugh (they nicknamed him "Jakie," which he very much resented) as the campus snoop. He had an uncanny ability of catching miscreants red-handed on his prowls. And at mail call in the chapel Joseph Saylor, who expertly sailed letters into waiting hands, could sniff out envelopes addressed with fingers nicotine-stained. In 1902 the trustees reaffirmed, with his backing, the long-standing rule that tobacco users would be subject to dismissal or denied degrees.

But, of course, for most students then, as now, a special thrill derived from breaking campus canon. George Wirt's diary for 1897 tells of male students taking coeds up to their rooms, worry-free of tattlers. And in those days before the Liquor Control Board (LCB) card, callow Hilltoppers now and then slipped downtown for a draft or two at the Washington House.[1] Illicit drinking would persist as a problem despite the threat of tough penalties and the wrath of student prohibitionists.

Likewise vandalism, nowadays the woe of student deans, was not unknown in those less permissive times either. One of the worst cases of wanton destruction at Juniata occurred in 1908, making local front-page news.[2] For some reason the biology professor, Frederick Burt, got on the wrong side of a few students. One evening, during a Lyceum lecture, four of them broke into Burt's room. They destroyed many of his books and valued manuscripts, including his priceless collection of insects, the result of years of work. The books were smeared with ink and many of the pages pasted shut. The mischief-makers then tossed the books into a pile and dumped molasses and "slops" over them. Curtains were ripped from the windows and, along with the professor's clothes, soaked in the dirty water. With some sleuthing the scamps were identified and shown to the station.

Student social life at century's turn had strict limits. According to George Wirt's diary, chapel in 1898 was still a time to moralize on the impropriety of mixed couples walking up and down the street together. But things began to loosen up a bit in 1903 when men and women were allowed to fraternize for two hours every weekday (4:00 to 6:00 P. M.) and three on Sunday (3:00 to 6:00 P. M.). Another change toward "social amelioration" came with Saturday-evening partying, an innovation in January 1899. Held at first in the chapel and then in the new gymnasium, these get-togethers ranged from hunting peanuts to pulling taffy to intellectual games. But the favorite pastime, Edgar Detwiler remembered from his turn-of-the-century student days, was the Virginia Reel. Sometimes, reveals Wirt's diary, the fun on Saturday nights ended with devotions. Levity had to be tempered with piety.

For quick trips downtown after June 1907 Juniatians had the use of the "Toonerville Trolley." The electric streetcar line in West Huntingdon conveniently ended at Moore and 17th streets.

The new century bred the early tradition of Mountain Day. The first all-college outing was to the "Forge" in May 1896.[3] Everybody that day, reported the *Echo*, arose very early. Then they "ate a hasty breakfast, walked to the station, boarded a special train, crossed the Juniata River, rumbled southward over the Huntingdon and Broad Top, arrived at Marklesburg, climbed into big farm wagons, [and] jolted over four miles of indifferent country road." Finally they reached the creekside refuge of the smallpox exiles in 1877, their destination. By 1900 getting "away to the woods" had become a fall instead of a spring event. Henry Brumbaugh coined the phrase "Mountain Day," a Thursday, October 22, entry in his 1903 diary. So began in the mid-1890s a century-long alfresco tradition unique to Juniata among other American colleges.

On March 2, 1906, the trustees officially decreed what has become another Juniata tradition. Beginning that spring, April 17 was to be celebrated each year as Founders Day. Ever since, this event has marked a high point in the college calendar.

Up to 1898 Juniata had no common visible symbols upon which to build college spirit. Each class chose its own colors and motto, thus inspiring peer rather than institutional loyalty. The breakthrough came in 1898 when Dr. George Lyon composed the first *Alma Mater*. Then that June the college got its colors. "[This] marks," trumpeted the *Echo*, "another step forward" in Juniata's progress. "Blue and Gold…What does it mean?" the nameless writer asked rhetorically. He answered feelingly:

> [It means] that we recognized true devotion in the respect which students ofttimes pay to their college colors, that we now have an emblem which shall represent our own Juniata when we assemble in reunions and when we mingle with schoolmen from sister institutions…in short, it means animation, without which the scholar soon becomes a nonentity.

A quatrain followed this commentary, telling what the colors stand for:

> True as the blue
> And pure as the gold,
> Thus may our lives
> To their fullness unfold!

Another big day for insignia-minded Juniatians came in the fall of 1902. On October 25 Harvey Brumbaugh announced at a reception in the gymnasium that the faculty had officially adopted a motto, a seal, and a new college pin.[4] The seal and the motto were of the speaker's own devising. He explained that around the seal would appear the Latin words, "Sigillum Collegii Juniatienses." In the center would lie an open book. Above and below the book would be one word of the motto, "Veritas Liberat"—"The Truth Sets Free." This motto was based on the words of Jesus in the Gospel of John: "You shall know the truth, and the truth will set you free" (8:32). The "open book," the acting president said in his announcement, "has always been and ever shall be the only fountain and guardian of true knowledge, of truth."

As early as December 1899 the *Echo* makes passing reference to "the popular Juniata College pin" but gives no description of it. Apparently, then, one was in circulation before 1902, when it was redesigned. It now had a triangular shape with an old English J in bas-relief. In each of the two lower corners appeared one of the motto's initials.

All this ado about signets, colors, and mottos indicated a breaking down of Brethren bias against regalia. Perhaps the most obvious symbol of this liberation was the college flag, another 1902 novelty. The *Echo* took pleasure in how it waved "gayly," beneath Old Glory, on the flagpole outside Founders.

Other innovations soon followed. College seniors, disappointed in 1900 by a trustee order to show up at commencement as before in "citizen's clothes," for the first time paraded begowned across the gymnasium stage in 1904 to get their diplomas. Female graduates in non-baccalaureate departments wore white dresses for a special touch. Honorary doctorates were next—D. D.s (doctor of divinity) conferred on Tobias Myers and Amos Haines in 1905. The faculty, though, went slow on pomp for itself. Because of a strong difference of opinion (between old and young professors) they went without academic trappings at commencement until the late Twenties.

RELIGIOUS GROUPS

By the close of Juniata's first quarter-century, religious life, once the business of the local church, had come to rest largely in student hands. There were still college constraints, of course: compulsory Sunday worship (somewhere in town) and daily chapel. But the Brethren mid-week service had given way by 1890 to a student prayer group.

The first student religious organization was the Young Peoples' Missionary Society, started by the women of the church in May 1893.[5] The object of this group was "to educate young people to mission work, to encourage a living, active missionary spirit among them, by the reading and study of missionary literature and by contributing means in support of the work." Practically the whole school joined and under Harvey Brumbaugh, its first president, Elizabeth Howe's Chicago mission was made the group's main project. The next year brought a name change: Young Peoples' Missionary and Temperance Society. Teetotalism pre-empted the society's interest during the great prohibition fight, incited by the rise of the Anti-Saloon League in the 1890s, that culminated with the 18th Amendment in 1919. By 1917, with prohibition at hand, the society died out.

Meanwhile, students shifted their interest in missions from the home front to foreign fields. They organized the Volunteer Mission Band, allying with the intercollegiate Student Volunteer Movement.[6] The impact of the Volunteer Movement on idealistic American youth has no parallel in the nation's history, except perhaps the Peace Corps of the 1960s. It was a dramatic outgrowth of the late nineteenth-century foreign-missions thrust. As Uncle Sam's commercial and political influence spread abroad after the Civil War, the attention of Protestant churches was drawn to needy people beyond the seas. Soon they were out to evangelize the heathen peoples of the whole world.

Student enthusiasm for the "White Man's burden" was sparked in 1886 by Dwight L. Moody's conference center in Northfield, Massachusetts. There, one hundred collegians volunteered for foreign-mission service, and the delegates carried their enthusiasm back to local campuses. In 1888 this zeal was channeled into a permanent organization, the Student Volunteer Movement, which adopted as its slogan "The evangelization of the world in this generation." For the next three decades SVM would enlist the very ablest men and women on America's college campuses and send them to the far corners of the earth. Possibly the most outstanding product of the student missionary movement was Huntingdon's own Robert E. Speer, a Princeton graduate and Presbyterian layman.

Juniata's Volunteer Mission Band organized in March 1899.[7] The previous year three Juniatians—two students and Acting President Brumbaugh—had represented the college at an SVM convention in Cleveland. Then Robert Speer visited the campus and built up further interest. Dedicated to the Brethren mission field, all volunteers took the pledge: "It is my purpose, if God permit, to become a missionary. As to whether it will be in the home field or abroad, I await the further guidance of the Spirit."

Robert Speer once said that the great need for the world was "to be saved from want and disease, injustice, inequality, impurity, lust, hopelessness and fear."[8] The college solidly put its stamp of approval on this goal of all-out world salvation, a goal that Juniata, it was felt, had a duty to advance. The moral and educational call of the times, President M. G. told the stockholders in 1900, was to "meet the mission need."[9] Echoed William Swigart on the same occasion: "The mission work is a product of the schools. We need the men, the women properly educated."

Five "Volunteers" kept their pledges by 1904 and answered the missionary call, all to India. By March 1919 when the Band presented to the college a missionary-service flag—to hang in the chapel—twenty-six Juniatians had dedicated themselves to being foreign missionaries.

The early 1900s also gave rise to active student YMCA and YWCA chapters. But at first church and college officials offered resistance. The Brethren had long gone on record against local community Ys because they provided their membership with amusements. On campus the Y's forerunner was the Boys' Christian Band, started by Charles Ellis, then a student, in March 1897. Its members vowed to do "at *least one* good act for Christ each week."[10] A Girls' Christian Band organized in the spring of 1898.

In December 1901 a faculty-student committee petitioned the local church elders and the trustees for permission to begin a student Y chapter.[11] They argued that the "college movement" was "distinct" from community Ys since it operated under a different kind of constitution. The opposition responded in the October 1902 *Echo*: "Juniata did not yet consider it wise being identified with the YMCA." By 1904, however, the trustees and elders had changed their minds and sometime that fall a campus chapter sprang up. "Almost all boys and girls have joined," the *Echo* noted. Then in February 1907 Juniata women chartered themselves as the YWCA. It was the two Y groups that later introduced the custom of holding student-led worship services in the county jail. They also pioneered in Sunday-afternoon deputation services at outlying rural schoolhouses.

PHYSICAL EDUCATION AND THE RISE OF INTERCOLLEGIATE SPORTS

In 1897, when Students Hall still housed the gymnasium, the faculty instituted a regimen of daily workouts for their charges. Both men and women (but not together) made use of dumbbells, Indian clubs, and wands. After Oneida Hall became ready for use in 1898 the workouts moved to the old dining room in Founders basement. Dinner hour by then had been changed from five to six o'clock to allow more time for exercising. The new gymnasium in 1901, of course, made possible a vastly expanded program and the first paid "physical director."

In 1904 there was some form of organized physical training at 270 American colleges and universities. Seventy-two of them required it and another twenty-four gave credit. All the early physical directors crusaded for calisthenics credit. They failed at that, but in 1905 physical exercise did become a requirement (credit was not granted until 1923). Some enthusiasts imagined that they detected an "immediate" improvement in student health.

Outdoor sports got a big boost in the spring of 1899 when the college bought the Huntingdon Bookbindery on Oneida Street and made it into an athletic field. At that time, though, the field extended east only as far as Scott Street. A partial fence went up in the summer and the whole field was enclosed in 1905. Bleachers, seating a couple hundred, added spectator comfort in 1909.

For several years there had been both a Boys' and Girls' Athletic Association that looked after intramural events and an occasional town-gown baseball game. But in September 1900 the two groups integrated into the Juniata Athletic Association. The JAA set dues at fifty cents a year, and each sport—tennis, baseball, football, basketball, lacrosse—named a manager. An elected student had charge of keeping up the playing field and the tennis courts and purchasing equipment. Ewing Newcomer, inventor one day of the glass-lined thermos bottle, became the first student elected to this position.[12] JAA's big event of the year was "Field Day," an all-afternoon, all-sports affair. Even the faculty got a chance to show off their athletic prowess. It was JAA—urged on by the Rev. Haines—that set in motion the drive for a new gymnasium.

In 1902 supervision of the athletic program fell into the hands of a faculty committee. Through its members intercollegiate athletics came to Juniata. They hounded the trustees until permission was given in 1903 to compete in four sports: baseball, track, tennis, and basketball. (Football, banned as too dangerous even for intramural play in 1902, did not get its turn until after World War I.) But, it was stipulated, "all arrangements shall be made in accordance with the spirit of Juniata College" and "with schools who are responsible for the conduct of their students." Initially the physical director did all the coaching.

Juniata's first intercollegiate sports event was a home track-and-field meet with Susquehanna University on June 5, 1903. The Blue and Gold, taking but three first places, lost 60 to 41—all because, the *Echo* rationalized, Susquehanna was "bigger and better trained." Despite the final score, the person reporting was happy to say that no one, neither athlete nor fan, had spoiled the day by poor sportsmanship. Before long Juniata trackmen were winning more than their share of meets.

In 1909 the Juniata Athletic Association began to keep an official book on track-and-field records, including those set in previous years. Against Lock Haven in 1906 senior Norman Brumbaugh, son of Jacob and future esteemed Hilltop chemistry professor, ran the 100-yard dash in ten seconds flat. His record stood for sixty-six years.

Baseball holds the honor of being the oldest organized sport at Juniata, three games having been played in 1899 against local sandlotters. The June *Echo* issue that year carried a picture of the team posing on the steps of Students Hall, a big **J** on the shirt worn by each person. The Hilltop nine was also the first college team to play out of town, in May 1903. On that occasion the J-men opposed Rockview Academy at Shirleysburg. It was a two-hour trip by train and wagon, and the Juniatians, decked out in new uniforms, won 16 to 3. In 1904 there was a seven-game schedule involving three different opponents on a home-to-home basis. Next year, however, the team lost every game, with scores as bad as 18 to 2. The dismal season prompted the trustees to order a net batting cage to be used in the gymnasium when inclement weather disrupted outdoor practice.

Basketball, invented by Dr. James Naismith in 1891, was just a rising new team sport in the early 1900s. Juniatians began playing the roundball game competitively in 1904 against area high schools. Two first-stringers that initial season were Caribbeans: a Cuban and a Puerto Rican. The "Rooting Club" urged the team on at home contests. Their favorite yell was the "rocket cheer," with all the sound effects: s-s-s-s-ses and booms.

Juniata moved up to the college ranks in the 1906 season and was mauled. The *Echo* lamented in February:

> What is the trouble with basketball this year? There seems to be some missing links in the chain. If we are to have basketball, let us enter into it heartily, let us put up the best team that is possible....It is no disgrace to lose sometimes, but certainly some games should be won.

Perhaps one problem was the gymnasium's chilled interior. It went unheated until 1910, when it got a furnace of its own. (It was connected to the central heating plant in 1915.)

Basketball disrupted evening quietude and this gave the trustees some concern. At their January 27, 1908, board meeting they decided that the postgame meal for players should be "a lunch only, instead of a feast." The team was to eat as soon as possible after games so the dormitories could get "quieted down" all the earlier. In those early days "moral victories" were the usual fate of Juniata hoopsters. Not till World War I years did college quintets begin to enjoy an occasional winning season.

Tennis, a British petticoat import in 1874, was pretty much a pattycake affair seventy years ago compared to the vigor of play today. But it was the rage of the campus among both sexes, the ladies demurely returning service in toe-length skirts. In 1902 tennis courts had to be reserved a week in advance. Two years later students were up and swinging rackets at five in the morning if they hoped to squeeze in a few sets. And in 1908 the Tennis Association of Juniata College, with its 135 dues-paying members, imposed a one-hour limitation on court use per couple or foursome.

In 1896 the college put in its first court, of dirt, on the part of the campus where Stone Church now stands, then a corner lot. Two more courts were built the next year on the upper campus, behind where the gymnasium would go. And in 1903 another pair popped up at the foot of Round Top. Norman Brumbaugh's private court, just next door, got plenty of college use, too, as did the one near William Beery's place in the 1700 block of Moore Street. Never, though, did students dare a mixed match; tennis then was a sex-segregated sport on the Hill.

College-level tennis competition at Juniata began in 1907 but only casually—a couple matches with Lock Haven. The Hill's netmen that year included two professors, which understandably made Lock Haven unhappy. But the baseball team had filched their best players and this left the tennis squad short-handed. The sport got into full swing in 1910 with a five-match schedule, including three across-state schools: Swarthmore, Lafayette, and Lehigh. All three schools were played on their courts.

On March 25, 1908, the Juniata Athletic Association awarded the college's first varsity letters at a special chapel service. They were given in baseball, basketball, and track. Eight-inch block Js went to five college men; Academy athletes who made varsity teams received a smaller JC monogram.

Already on the American intercollegiate athletic scene unwholesome influences were at work. And the *Echo* in 1905, referring to a June article in *McClure's Magazine* on "The College Athlete," blistered the "win-at-any-cost" philosophy of college coaches and the recruiting pressure this created. In 1908 Yale helped set the pace in commercializing sports by putting up its thirty-thousand-seat football bowl. Said the *Echo* of Juniata, "Let us keep college athletics on a high level."

INTERCOLLEGIATE DEBATE AND PUBLIC SPEECH

Intersociety debate had long been an integral part of campus intellectual life. For a number of years the keen but polite rivalry of the Oriental and Wahneeta Literary Societies involved both college and Academy students. But the faculty came to feel that it would be better to have one society exclusively for collegians. And so the Juniata Lyceum formed in September 1899.[13]

Thanks to the Lyceum, intercollegiate debate got the green light in 1902. At once it took the campus by storm. At the invitation of Susquehanna University the two schools tangled in the Selinsgrove Opera House on April 25. The subject debated was: "Resolved, That the United States should hold permanent control of the Philippines." The Juniata debaters took the negative side and won handily.

Susquehanna lost out two more times to Juniata in that period. After one triumphant return from Selinsgrove, in 1904, Charles Vuille, the local auto dealer, and a gang of students met the debaters at the train station. He brought the victors up to campus in his "Tried and True" Cadillac (there were five motorcars in Huntingdon then), with horn honking all the way. Juniata colors were draped all over the automobile, which was trailed by the entourage of "rooters" singing college songs and giving college yells. A bonfire, the usual victory salute to Juniata disputants, soon blazed high on the athletic field.

In nine years Juniata won eleven consecutive debates before suffering its first loss, a close decision (2-1) in 1912, to the University of Pennsylvania.[14] Besides Susquehanna, other defeated colleges included Penn State, Bridgewater, Waynesburg, Swarthmore, and Westminster. The Lyceum arranged all intercollegiate debates at that time.

Ever since 1877, when Phebe Weakley came to teach Elocution, public speech had been an academic requirement. And orations, moreso than debate, had been the very lifeblood of all the literary societies. With the early 1900s oratorical contests became major events, attracting a large share of out-of-class time and interest. Cash prize awards fostered their popularity. For its members the campus Intercollegiate Prohibition Association began to hold annual oratorical contests soon after its founding in 1904. The winner got twenty-five dollars and represented Juniata at a state contest hosted by drys. Alumnus Eugene Carney, a North Dakota district judge, put up prize money for a contest each year between 1909 and 1924. Competition was open to all students on the Hill. Only collegians, however, qualified for the John M. Bailey prize, established by his wife and son in 1909 as a memorial to the distinguished jurist (the contest still attracts student declaimers today).

MUSIC AND PERFORMING GROUPS

Extracurricular music, vocal and instrumental, began to sound forth on the Hilltop with unprecedented vigor as the "Gay Nineties" passed into history. The two literary societies, Oriental and Wahneeta, each had choristers, and singing was a regular feature of their weekly programs. Ordinarily there were special numbers, from solos to choruses. And William Beery for several years had readied a choir at commencement time, recruiting Oriental and Wahneeta singers, many of whom took voice lessons from him.

But, apparently, the first major noncommencement performance by the choir took place at Christmastime 1897. A Beery-directed choral group gave the cantata *King of Kings* to a "delighted audience" in the packed chapel. From then on it became the practice for college choirs to present several musicals each year. The Beery songsters had grown to fifty voices by April 30, 1903, when they sang Mendelssohn's oratorio *Hymn of Praise*. In 1908 the choir assumed the name Juniata Choral Society.

With the arrival of Latinist Dr. George Lyon in 1896 college songs began to fill the campus air. This amiable scholar, with a University of Cincinnati M. D., set everybody to singing in his brief three-year stay. He composed many "local hits" himself, making good use of the college quartet whose existence he inspired in 1898.

In the spring of 1900 the quartet became the nucleus of a men's glee club. That summer the fellows published a booklet, *Campus Songs of Juniata*, dedicated to "Those who never sing, but die with all their music in them."[15] Most songs were Lyon compositions, some a mite maudlin by today's lyrical tastes. There was no music printed with the words, the songs set to familiar tunes. *Hail to Juniata!*, the original *Alma Mater*—written by Lyon probably in 1898—rated page one. There appeared old favorites like, *Bring Back My Bonnie, Old Black Joe, The Watch on the Rhine,* and *Rig-A-Jig*. Curiously the booklet, which sold for fifteen cents a copy, included the drinking song *There is a Tavern in the Town*. In 1904 the songbook was revised and enlarged, regarded by everybody as an indispensable article at any social occasion.

The Juniata Glee Club, twenty-four harmonizers strong by 1904, soon took to the road as ambassadors of the college. But this mission hit a sour note in 1908 when the trustees and the singers fell out over the "dress suit" question. Apparently reacting to outside criticism the trustees that spring forbade the group from wearing "dress suits [tuxedos] where this will be objectionable to our church people." A couple of club singers went to see some of the trustees. They protested, arguing that formal clothes added style to their concerts, but the trustees stood their ground. "Tuxes," so it was, had to wait till a later day.

Instrumental music also enjoyed some gains in that age. Piano students shared firsts with the choir on the evening of the *King of Kings* in 1897. Several keyboard solos had preceded the cantata; never before had student pianists performed publicly. The first piano recital as such took place in June 1898, featuring graduating seniors. Graduation recitals now became a tradition, enhanced in May 1905 by the purchase of a Steinway Grand piano (for $1,300). All-faculty concerts, however, were still a thing of the future.

In the fall of 1908 the music faculty put together a small orchestra. Later, all-college stringed groups began performing. The first time an orchestra (nine pieces) gave a public performance was in the fall of 1904. Next year a five-member group, calling itself the Juniata Concert Company, scheduled a couple out-of-town engagements. A full-fledged college orchestra, however, did not materialize until 1913. Beginning in 1902 musical groups like the Boston Concert Company regularly added professional entertainment to the public events' calendar.

EARLIEST FOREIGN STUDENTS

Juniata's first overseas student was Richard Arno Dassdorf, an army deserter from Saxony, Germany. Between 1897 and 1900 he earned a Bible School diploma. Dassdorf, then in his mid-twenties and disowned by his family, had lived with Abraham Cassel for a time after fleeing to America. A Lutheran, he joined the Church of the Brethren his first year on the Hill. He later told about his conversion in a published pamphlet titled *How I Found the Church of the Brethren at Juniata College*.[16] The "Flying Dutchman"—a nickname he good-naturedly accepted—paid his way at Juniata by doing odd jobs and teaching German.

From Puerto Rico came two students in 1900, sent at government expense by President M. G. Brumbaugh in his first year there as United States Commissioner of Education. In all, Juniata hosted ten islanders before they stopped coming in 1911. The most enrolled in any one year was eight—in 1902, when the Caribbeans organized a Puerto Rican Club. Two died while away from home, one of whom, James Laza, was buried in Huntingdon. Most took business courses or enrolled in the Academy; only one graduated with a B. A. degree. That was Juan Miranda in 1908, who then studied law at the University of Pennsylvania and became a successful Philadelphia attorney.

Two other nationalities were represented in the early 1900s. From Cuba came six students and from Guatemala, three.

A THRIVING ECHO AND OTHER PUBLICATIONS

In January 1896 the Juniata *Echo*, still a pacemaker among campus papers in the state, became a monthly (except August and September), and was enlarged to sixteen pages and repriced at five cents a copy. In October 1907 Dr. A. B. Brumbaugh, ailing and seventy-one, stepped down after seventeen years as its editor-in-chief. For the next half-dozen years or so the faculty manned the editorial post. After that editorial duties passed wholly into student hands.

There would be no pictorial yearbook until the *Alfarata's* debut in 1915, but an annual souvenir was not entirely unknown on the Hill. Three senior classes in the late Nineties put out little hardback books with inspirational titles: *Leaves of Industry* (1897); *Blossoms of Life* (1898); *Fruits of Virtue* (1899). Each one, however, largely featured class-day orations by Normal students, since B. A.-degree seekers were as yet few in number (four in those three years). The class books for 1898 and 1899 contained a group picture of all seniors (Normal and college) and a shot of the campus. The one for 1897 was illustrated with charming miniature woodcuts, probably the handiwork of David Emmert. No explanation was ever given why other classes failed to follow suit, but cost certainly had a lot to do with it.

In January 1904 the trustees inaugurated the *Juniata College Bulletin*, a quarterly publication. Explained the October 1905 issue: "The bulletin was begun as a definite and dignified means by which to present information about the college and its work to the public, and it is the purpose to make the different members expressive of the varied interests and activities of the institution." This new periodical gave the annual reports of the president and treasurer and carried faculty-authored articles on all sorts of academic topics. One of its quarterly issues was made the college catalog. Decades later the *Bulletin* would be taken over by the alumni office and made its official newsletter.

ALUMNI AND EARLY REUNIONS

An item under "Notes and Personals" in the *Echo* for July 1897 disclosed: "For several years the Ohio students of Juniata have been in the custom of holding a meeting to pledge anew their loyalty to their college and to strengthen the old ties of friendship with one another." This had reference to the first off-campus alumni reunion in 1894, held in the Buckeye State. Other alumni-studded areas soon followed with their own summer rendezvous. In 1899 Annie Brumbaugh, M. G.'s wife, planned to open their Philadelphia home for a day to Juniata friends. But she soon found that there was not enough room to accommodate the guest list and so she got the bright idea of entertaining them at the Belmont Mansion in Fairmount Park. The sixty-four who showed up on the afternoon of June 22 were treated to a meal of croquettes, deviled crabs, soft shelled crabs, lobster salad, potato salad, chicken salad, and other tasty fare. This epicurean repast was topped off with a fun-filled program, after which the Philadelphia Alumni Association organized, to be headed by M. G. The Philadelphians met again in 1900, but there was a lapse of two years while M. G. was in Puerto Rico.

The *Echo* recorded other summer reunions in 1899 and the creation of several alumni branches in Pennsylvania. There was one in Juniata County, and about eighty persons from Bedford and Huntingdon counties convened at Bedford Springs (called "the Carlsbad of America" by the *Echo*) on July 29. Later that summer a cluster of alumni gathered at Waynesboro. From this impromptu fellowship sprang the Pen Mar reunions, which by 1904 were attracting over three hundred alumni and friends from Southern Pennsylvania and Maryland. The park by that name near Waynesboro was their favorite gathering place as long as outdoor reunions lasted.

The early 1900s spawned several more alumni clans. One was formed in Somerset County in 1903, meeting at Meyersdale. Cambria County was added to the list in 1905. Lakemont Park, in Altoona, became the retreat of Blair County alumni in 1906. Meanwhile, Juniatians attending the Brethren yearly meeting took to socializing on one of the days as early as 1902. At all of the reunions, of course, someone from the college staff showed up to bring greetings. These gatherings were quite independent of the annual alumni meetings held at commencement time. David Emmert at the time was trying to promote area reunions through what he unimaginatively called the "Old Students Association." But the name never caught on and later, during World War I, some of the reunions discontinued.

John Wertz, a Johnstown schoolteacher, sired a remarkable alumni family of that period. He sent nine of his children, four daughters and five sons, to Juniata. To do so must have been a financial hardship for the schoolteacher. No doubt his offspring helped pay their own way with campus jobs or by an alumni scholarship. The Alumni Endowment Fund had made a little over one hundred loans since 1889, five a year. But the acting president's report for 1910 noted that thirty-eight were still outstanding, many long overdue. The Sisters' Missionary Circle of the Stone Church congregation set up the Women's Aid Fund for needy coeds around 1902, its assets amounting to more than two thousand dollars by 1910.

In 1902 a constitutional revision admitted Academy graduates into full Alumni Association membership. But Harvey Brumbaugh's proposal in 1908 for a permanent resident alumni secretary would go unheeded for another dozen years.

PRESIDENT M. G. FINALLY BOWS OUT

Arctic weather settled like a great frozen shroud over Huntingdon the early months of 1910. William Swigart said that he could not remember a winter like it. Ice was six inches thick on some streets. The cold hindered last-minute work on J. C. Blair Memorial Hospital, scheduled for a Memorial Day dedication. In April Harvey Brumbaugh took abed with a severe case of pneumonia. And before the summer was gone his father, as trustee kingpin, would get more bad news.

Under Harvey and his cousin M. G. the college had indeed come of age in the last seventeen years. Accredited in liberal arts, it had survived two hard depressions and grown to nearly 350 students (spring term). Its costs were but a fraction (less than a quarter) of those at Ivy League schools. Running the place had become far more complex, and in the fall of 1906 the acting president was given a private office, just inside Founders entrance. There, behind a big roll-top desk in one corner, he looked after college business. The roll-top desk has long since been gone, but Juniata's president today is still headquartered in the same office.

A strong Brethren constituency continued to give Juniata its identity. The local elders appeared annually on inspection visits until 1908. Then Annual Conference created a central Educational Board to care for the religious atmosphere of the existing ten Brethren colleges. Now the examining committee came out of this national board, and one area of campus life it scrutinized carefully was intercollegiate sports. Outsiders, it was feared, might infect the moral health of Juniata athletes.

Yet under the Brumbaugh cousins the college was no less mindful of other constituencies. The Juniata Valley, Harvey Brumbaugh pledged in 1905, would never be ignored as a prime recruiting area.[17] For many of its youth, he pointed out, the Huntingdon institution represented their only chance for a better education.

But as the new century wore on faculty morale dipped. President M. G. found more and more bad-humored letters in his mail, grumbling mostly about low salaries. In one letter to Harvey on the pay problem he wrote:

> But I wish you would lay before them the spirit of this letter, if not its words, saying that it seems to me that if they have the same devotion to the Church and to the work of the College for the Church as their predecessors have had, they will be ready to write the word "sacrifice" deep in their lives, for the sake of the cause that is eminently just. And if they protest against this advice on the ground that it comes from one who himself was not willing to make the sacrifice, let them remember that I made the sacrifice for ten years, and that ever since I have

been away I have sent back into the treasury of the College more money than I could possibly have earned had I remained in the Faculty.[18]

He ended by saying, not unkindly but sincerely: "There is the further fact that a man may be very successful in Juniata College who might not be equally successful somewhere else."

Meanwhile, M. G. had been given his pick of several college presidencies. This bit of information he left to posterity in a confidential memorandum among his private papers, dated February 28, 1910. The memorandum said nothing, however, about his refusal to be a candidate for chancellor of the University of Nebraska, despite strong pressure from influential friends. He spurned that invitation, so the *Echo* said, because he was "wedded to Pennsylvania."

Between 1907 and 1909, according to M. G.'s note, three schools approached him to be their president, all of which he turned down. One was Girard College in Philadelphia, whose overseers blinked the fact he was an active churchman and a preacher (Girard's charter banned clergymen from holding office). But, confessed M. G., "the 'pent-up' character of the place depressed me." In 1907 Penn State put in its bid with no better luck. His friend, the historian Edwin Sparks, got the job. Franklin and Marshall wanted him in 1909, but M. G. wrote: "I declined in loyalty to Juniata and in justice to my family. My present work, though more arduous, is more remunerative. I can give more to Juniata."

By 1910 years of overwork had begun to take its toll on Brumbaugh's health. He was worn down, and within that year he would have to take a leave from his Philadelphia post to rejuvenate. That spring, therefore, he decided to unburden himself of his alma mater's presidency, which, though nominal, did place some demands on his time and energy. Moreover, with all the talk about a new science building and an endowment push, he was afraid the pressure on him to get more involved would only mount. Quietly he let Harvey know of his intentions and that this time he would not back down no matter what.

In July the two of them in concert submitted letters of resignation. The trustees, knowing what M. G.'s name meant to college prestige, tried to head him off again by reshaping the administration. In August they voted him the title of chancellor, while naming Harvey president. But both men turned thumbs down on such an arrangement. Harvey was then asked–and agreed–to continue as acting president for the time being.

Chapter 8

TOWARD A GREATER JUNIATA: 1910–1924

ISAAC HARVEY BRUMBAUGH: DE JURE PRESIDENT

Harvey Brumbaugh had put up with a lot in his eleven years as acting president, running the college in M. G.'s shadow. But he was not a subservient person. In October he let the trustees know that they had better resolve the presidency forthwith or he was through. And so on March 6, 1911, forty-one-year-old Harvey was elected Juniata's fourth president. Curiously, not a hint of this election leaked out until William Swigart made it known at the first chapel service in September. In fact, M. G.'s resignation itself had been kept an absolute secret for a whole year. Hence Swigart's chapel announcement caught everybody off guard.

To the students he would always be "Professor Harvey," for he had been a popular teacher. On the basis of his time as acting president, the faculty viewed him as "naturally conservative" but a man of "genial affability," "approachable."[1] The news of his election drew "hearty applause" from the chapel audience.

CHARLES ELLIS MADE VICE-PRESIDENT

Back in 1890 the *Echo* said of a sixteen-year-old Normal graduate from Baltimore: "Mr. Ellis is not very large in stature, but he makes up for this in intellectual ability." Juniata's second B. A. winner in 1898, Ellis was cast much in the mold of M. G. Brumbaugh. An Illinois Wesleyan Ph.D. (1904) and another one from Penn (1907) had put him in select Brethren company. Like M. G. he took to the lecture platform, billed as the "Boy Orator." At first he made pedagogy his academic specialty, but with time developed a strong interest in religion as a disciplinary field.

Having taught at Juniata a few years before, Dr. Ellis came back in 1907, at age thirty-three, with no intention of staying. Soon other schools began to seek him out with attractive offers. Penn State, for one, pursued him in 1917 with a twenty-five-hundred-dollar contract, almost twice his salary at Juniata.[2] It was this across-the-mountain overture that prompted the trustees that June to make Dr. Ellis vice-president. With the promotion went a raise—all of one hundred dollars—but his income still fell short of fifteen hundred. For all practical purposes, however, Ellis's title was only honorific. His administrative duty mainly involved keeping an eye on Academy students.

Outsiders continued to look upon the vice-president as fair game over the next few years. Moody Bible Institute diligently sought him in 1919. The trustees wrote the Chicago school asking it politely, but pointedly, to stay away from Dr. Ellis since Juniata "could not afford" to let him go. Then in 1921 the trustees learned that more than one college was after him for their top position. The board promptly passed a resolution begging him to stay, which he did, having by then come to terms with his life at Juniata.

PLANS FOR A "GREATER JUNIATA"

As president, Harvey Brumbaugh liked to say he was running "A right little, tight little college."[3] By "right" he meant Christian, by "tight" he meant friendly, close. He gave fuller expression to this image of Juniata in a 1913 chapel talk:

> The small college with high ideals of training and character, but with moderate ambition in material equipment, led by scholarly and consecrated teachers, maintaining simple standards of living—the small college, with all the affection which the term implies because of the intimate association of its daily life, has yet a mission to the church and a message for the present-day world.[4]

In many respects a "moderate ambition" nicely characterized Harvey Brumbaugh's thirteen-year presidency. But it did produce the first major concerted endowment-fund campaign. Ever since 1903 there had been a long-range $200,000-endowment plan on the books—to strengthen certain departments, put up new buildings, buy additional land, and improve faculty salaries. The Mary Geiger endowed chair was part of this low-key effort, as was a gift of ten thousand dollars in 1912 from the Jacob Oller family of Waynesboro, honoring their deceased parents. But the trustees had gone about this plan in piecemeal fashion, first Carnegie Library and, beginning in 1910, the Allan Myers's canvass for a science building. It was one of Juniata's most liberal benefactors, the genial business executive, Joseph Oller, who prodded the trustees into an all-out endowment thrust.

At a board conclave in January 1916 Oller proposed an immediate drive for $100,000 and the formation of a special group, wider than the board, to carry it out. His suggestion won quick acceptance. A few days later President Brumbaugh "tore aside the veil that shrouds the future of Juniata" in a chapel talk, whipping up enthusiasm for the endowment goal. The *Echo* jumped on the bandwagon and in April put out a "Boost Juniata" number. It was this issue that coined the slogan for the campaign: "A Greater Juniata."

Echo student-editor John Baker (one day to become trustee chairman) asked representative Juniatians—a trustee (M. G.), a professor (Charles Ellis), two alumni, and a student—to submit articles forecasting "What kind of a greater Juniata" they saw in the distance. They were to look ahead forty years, to 1956, and dream. Most shared Dr. Ellis's vision, which was never totally realized:

> So if I might be permitted the magic wand for a day I would hasten to crown Round Top with an artistic and well-arranged group of college buildings sufficient to care for three hundred students and twenty-five professors and assistants. The value of this plant would be at least five hundred thousand dollars backed by an endowment of twice as much. Supplementing this of course would be the present plant caring for two hundred preparatory students.

The musings of one of the two alumni, though, focused on the "genius" of a liberal arts college, raising an issue that still keeps educators at odds. The Pittsburgh social science teacher wrote:

> [w]e realize that this age is demanding the "scientific," the "engineering," the "vocational," the "practical," in short the materialistic result from the educator; but it becomes the duty of some of us, it becomes the God-given burden of some choice small colleges in America to stand true to the wholesome traditions of the "humanities."

He was not denying the need for "technical" and "applied" education in the modern world, he said. But neither was he saying there is "nothing practical, useful, or applicable in the liberal or classical cultural courses." Juniata's "valuable" contribution to society, the public-school teacher contended, should continue to be that of sending out "a class of men and women who because of their rich training can hold key positions as teachers, preachers, missionaries, social workers, principals, superintendents, presidents, commercial masters, secretaries, reformers, and the like."

Out of the interest thus engendered came the group Oller had in mind: the Juniata College Extension Association for a Greater Juniata, formed on March 21, 1918. The organizational meeting was held in the Executive Mansion in Harrisburg, hosted by M. G., then the governor. The constitution and bylaws of the association were adopted and an executive committee of twelve members was elected from the college constituency at large. Governor Brumbaugh became president of the association, Joseph Oller its vice-president, and Harry Cassady, then the college pastor, the campaign director. His coworker was Galen Royer, who had just left the General Mission Board in Elgin, Illinois, to teach in the School of Theology at Juniata.

At Harvey Brumbaugh's prompting the association called the proposed fund the James Quinter Memorial Endowment, in honor of the college's first president. Its main campaign booklet was unapologetically leveled at a Brethren public. In fact, all the denomination's colleges were similarly engaged at the time in promotional work as part of a general Brotherhood program called "Church of the Brethren Forward

Movement." The booklet presented a list of twelve "FACTS," showing what the college had done for the church. The first eight gave a particularly impressive picture of Juniata's vital contributions to Brethren life and work:

FACT (a)

Of the missionaries who have been and are on the foreign field, Juniata has furnished 22.

FACT (b)

The presidents of six of our 10 colleges of the Church of the Brethren are Juniata Graduates.

FACT (c)

In the Middle, Western, and Southeastern Districts of Pennsylvania there are 36 fully supported pastors who are giving their entire time to the church; of these 28 are from Juniata.

FACT (d)

Of the 1,160 graduates from Juniata, 135 are ministers and missionaries of our church.

FACT (e)

Ninety-five young men have received the A. B. degree from the College. Of these, 44 are ministers in the church.

FACT (f)

Eighty-five per cent of our College graduates are members of the Church of the Brethren.

FACT (g)

Over 1,500 people have been received into the Church of the Brethren in the College Church.

FACT (h)

More than 50 young men have been elected to the ministry in the College Church.

Despite the war and then the flu epidemic, progress toward the goal of $100,000 was so encouraging that in April 1919 the trustees raised their sights by doubling the goal. By the end of 1920 the trustees had $100,000 in hand, and in April of the following year the second phase got underway.

The purpose of the 1921 campaign, it had now developed, was to meet the endowment requirements of the Middle States Association, whose accreditation the college was seeking. A representative of Middle States and one from the Carnegie Foundation visited the campus in February, and though finding things better than expected they had serious questions about the adequacy of the college's endowment (less than $400,000). The association's minimum for accreditation was set at five hundred thousand dollars.

The Greater Juniata Campaign took its start the week of May 31 to June 7. The local chairman was Chester Langdon, a graduate of Lehigh University and prosperous coal-mine operator. "Chet," soon everywhere to be known as "Mr. Rotarian," now began his long friendship with Juniata. More than 170 workers, many of them women, took part in the seven-day canvass. Once again the people of Huntingdon proved "true and generous," as the *Echo* put it, and by week's end over sixty-five thousand dollars had been subscribed.[5]

The appeal was then extended up and down the Juniata Valley with equally good success, although it took more time. A chart hanging in the chapel plotted the progress. By the end of the fiscal year 1923 President Harvey Brumbaugh could report going "over the top." This put all endowment funds at more than $507,000.

Some of the trustees had responded very generously. Joseph Oller, contributor to the gymnasium, to Stone Church, and to campus expansion, turned over a batch of securities valued at better than twenty-four thousand dollars. The governor himself came through with a bundle of bonds worth ten thousand dollars. From John Fogelsanger, a non-Juniata businessman from Philadelphia, the college got five thousand dollars for scholarship aid. One other substantial contribution came in during the campaign, unsolicited. This was a five-thousand-dollar unrestricted bequest in 1919 from the estate of Elmer Africa, president of J. C. Blair Co.

BOARD OF TRUSTEES: CHANGING PERSONNEL AND CHARTER REVISION

Some familiar faces disappeared from the trustee scene over the course of Harvey Brumbaugh's presidency. Henry Brumbaugh, the board's chairman for forty years, died on June 28, 1919, just past his eighty-third birthday. (M. G. Brumbaugh took his place as chairman.) The death of his seventy-four-year-old brother, John, on June 11, 1922, marked the passing of the last of the founders. David Emmert had already taken his earthly leave in 1911. And another old faculty-trustee, Joseph Saylor, became a retiree in 1913. Only William Swigart and Jacob Brumbaugh were left from the early days. (Brumbaugh stayed on as a trustee until 1934, Swigart until 1939, although both would soon retire from teaching.) Mary Geiger's death occurred in September 1919, ending her twenty-two-year tenure on the board. Elder Jacob Myers of Oaks, Pennsylvania, died in 1915, having served twenty-five years as trustee.

In October 1920 William Swigart, who had not taught in the last year, resigned as college treasurer, then a trustee post. The highest salary the veteran of forty-two years had ever received, as teacher-treasurer, was eight hundred dollars. His long letter of resignation included a recommendation for some sort of pension plan and other fringe benefits for the faculty.[6] He ended with the hope that Juniata might "steadily" continue to provide an "education free from the influence of extravagance and the contaminating evils so dominant in the world." After Swigart no one from the board filled the position of treasurer. From 1920 to 1924 the alumni director kept the financial records. Adie Ressler, who succeeded Swigart, and then Stoler Good held this dual appointment in those years.

In terms of years of service the only trustee old-timers left in 1924 were Jennie Newcomer and Joseph Oller, whose appointments dated back to the century's turn.

But some of the new blood showed remarkable staying power, too. Newton Long of Hagerstown, Maryland, served forty-eight years (1922–59). Waynesboro's John Fike, who moved to Somerset, Pennsylvania, became a thirty-four-year veteran (1923–57). John Fogelsanger would be a twenty-two-year member (1914–36), while Allan Myers's trusteeship (1911–30) ended at his death after nineteen years on the board.

Most of the others elected at that time put in at least ten years. Those who fell into this category were all Pennsylvanians: Perry Blough of Hooversville (1910–20); Henry Gibbel of Lititz (1911–27); Frank Foster of Philadelphia (1917–35); Lewis Knepper of Berlin (1919–33); Harvey Replogle of Oaks (1920–33); and William Gahagen of Windber (1922–36). Rounding out the list of inductees during the Harvey Brumbaugh era were Pennsylvanians Harry Sieber of Philadelphia (1919–27) and W. Emmert Swigart of Huntingdon (1922–26), and West Virginian Jay Ross of Huntington. Death cut short the tenure of two men elected just prior to Harvey's presidency: William Howe of Johnstown (1908–17) and Huntingdon's David Swayne (1889–98; 1908–11).

Not all of these board newcomers were happy about what had been done to the college charter in 1908. One source of displeasure resulted from the deletion of Brethrenism as a condition for becoming a trustee. Consequently the board's bylaws were amended in 1918 to reinstate this criterion.[7] Furthermore, the changes stipulated that in the event of dissolution the college would convey all its property to the Church of the Brethren. Through these revisions the reactionary element on the board sought to reaffirm Juniata's historic ties with the church. It was also responding to pressure from the denomination's General Education Board. At the time that board was investigating the charter to determine if it "safe-guarded fully the interests of the church."[8]

Some trustees got upset when the charter was not made to comply with the bylaws on the transferal of property. This issue led to prolonged debate. Chairman M. G. opposed inserting such a clause in the charter; William Swigart disagreed with him.[9] The M. G. faction won, but the controversy did lead, in 1923, to another reworking of that section of the charter on the college's purpose. Phrased by President Harvey, it stated:

> The founders of the Commonwealth provided for religious freedom and the extension of learning. The fathers in the Church of the Brethren were the first in this Commonwealth to print the word of God and thus lay the foundation for education imbued with Christian purpose. Believing that the principles of Christianity should be and can be taught, that the Christian motive should be the animating force in all teaching, the Trustees of Juniata College associate themselves to perpetuate good and sound learning distinguished by Christian principles that the youth of the Church and the State may be trained for such service as an enlightened mind and a quickened conscience may lead them to render to God and to man.

It has not been tampered with since. The charter was also altered to increase the number on the board to twenty-one.

THE PRE-WORLD WAR I FACULTY

By 1923 the last of the teacher-trustees—Emmert, Saylor, John Brumbaugh, and Swigart—had laid down the classroom chalk. But Juniata did not want for equally dedicated teachers. Still around were Charles Ellis and the two Myerses, Tobias and Oscar. And under Harvey, the president, this nucleus of regulars grew larger. They were joined by Clyde Stayer (1919–54) and Charles Shively (1920–43) in mathematics, librarian Lillian Evans (1918–52), musician Charles Rowland (1920–51), and Bunn van Ormer (1917–41) in philosophy. Others of lesser years of service who gave stability to the faculty were Alphaeus Dupler (biology), Perry Hoover (classics), Galen Royer (missions), Katharine Roberts (English), and Luella Fogelsanger (business).

Two supposedly entrenched professors of that period had to leave but not for reasons of incompetence. One of them was rum-foe Frank Holsopple (1891–93; 1901–14), married to James Quinter's daughter Grace. He made the mistake of backing the wrong gubernatorial candidate in 1914. He openly campaigned for M. G.'s Democratic opponent, Vance McCormick, who was endorsed by the Anti-Saloon League. The trustees considered this an unforgivable act of institutional disloyalty. So they quietly fired the English teacher. Holsopple then worked for the Anti-Saloon League for a couple years, after which he became president of Blue Ridge College in Maryland.[10]

The trustees summarily purged religion professor Amos Haines (1897–1916), even though the college had conferred on him one of its very first honorary degrees. Over the years his theology had taken a liberal turn. He began teaching about the latest scientific investigation of Old Testament books to discover their origins, histories, and original forms. This kind of scholarly criticism, college officials feared, undercut biblical inerrancy. Local trustees interrogated students of his in building their case for dismissal. In 1923 Haines wrote *No Creed: the Bible and Biblical Interpretation* to defend his stance as a scholar.

By 1924 the combined college-Academy faculty numbered twenty-eight. Six held earned doctorates, and there were eleven women teachers. One of the Ph.D.s belonged to Robert Mehl (1923–25), a chemist who later discovered the gamma ray.

Another belonged to Alphaeus Dupler, whose suicide in 1928 cut short a promising academic career. This biologist not only brought scholarship to his discipline for the first time at Juniata, but also gave vital administrative leadership. A church elder and only forty-four at his death, the tall, dark alumnus was asked to set up a registrar's office in 1911. Under him, in those academic deanless days, it became a position second only to the presidency in importance.

Then in 1921 the administration put him in charge of the summer program, dropped in 1914. The Department of Public Instruction had recently raised its standards for teacher certification, setting 1927 as the deadline for meeting the new requirements. And so the college hoped to benefit from the expected great rush of public-school teachers. In 1927 the Hill had the largest summer enrollment in its history—485.

Dedicated though most of the faculty were, they were far from indifferent about their standard of living. Tobias Myers, because of his endowed chair, became the first to break the one-thousand-dollars-a-year salary barrier in 1911, some while before most. A salary schedule, based on academic rank, went into effect in 1920—to which exceptions were made at once. Over the next few years two men in the chemistry department, both transients and with doctorates, received pay above the maximum level for their rank. Somehow the word got out and a quintet of stalwarts—Dupler, Shively, van Ormer, and the two Myerses—accused the trustees in writing of outright injustice, if not deception.[11] The board severely reprimanded the petitioners for questioning its integrity and refused to listen further.

The Harvey Brumbaugh presidency produced the first fringe benefit for the faculty. In 1916 the college adopted a sick-leave policy. It allowed full salary for the first eight weeks, half salary the second eight weeks, and nothing after that.[12] Although no pension plan yet existed, the trustees did have hopes of someday participating in a retirement program funded by the Carnegie Foundation.

The democratic character of the college had always discouraged any distinctions of rank and title. But the catalog in 1920 began to identify faculty by the three grades of professor, assistant professor, and instructor. The salary schedule introduced that year was correlated with these three ranks. But the old guard still successfully fought off the use of academic regalia on high occasions because they said it called too much attention to differences of station.

In those days the faculty chambered weekly (as it would to 1938). Its first set of extant minutes is dated September 23, 1915. The academic progress of problem students occupied most of the faculty attention, a reading of early minutes reveals. Disciplinary action, for a social infraction as well as low grades, was ordinarily a matter of corporate decision. A structure of standing committees, however, did exist to carry out faculty-set policies.

There were signs, meanwhile, that the technological age had reached the Hill. Staid Jacob Brumbaugh was the first to turn his back on horse-and-buggy travel. The spring of 1912 he put "Doc" out to pasture and could now be seen "going to and fro in his Buick."[13] Two years later Oscar Myers sported a horseless carriage (make unknown) of his own. And Benjamin Wampler, the music professor, hammered away on a garage, also bitten by the "auto bug."

JUNIATA MAKES THE GRADE:
MIDDLE STATES ACCREDITATION

Harvey Brumbaugh was elected secretary of the College Presidents Association of Pennsylvania in 1918. As a member of the executive committee, he knew all about new standards being set by emergent regional accreditation agencies. Though of late nineteenth-century origin, these agencies only began to exert their influence after World War I. Thus by the time the Middle States Association of Colleges and Secondary Schools (it was formed in 1885) initiated regional visits, the Greater Juniata Campaign was in high gear.

Juniata's visit, as noted, came in February 1921. The evaluators had some strong reservations, particularly about the endowment. They left without giving any guarantees. Middle States' first approved list came out the following November, but Juniata did not make it. The association also issued a supplementary register called the "gray list"—colleges that did not fully meet accepted standards but were making good progress toward accreditation. Juniata was on this one.

To keep the pressure on, college authorities warned that Juniata was "at the crossroads of her history." And President Harvey Brumbaugh impressed upon the trustees in February 1922 that "Juniata College cannot go independent of standards set by outside organizations if its graduates are to be accepted in professional fields."[14] The conditions for accreditation, advised Middle States, were fourfold: (1) physical separation of the Academy and college; (2) endowment of at least five hundred thousand dollars producing an income from twenty thousand dollars to twenty-five thousand dollars; (3) higher salaries; (4) more faculty with doctorates.

Steps had already been taken to meet the last three of these criteria. And at a trustee sitting in April the college set the year 1924 as the deadline for complying with the first one. Administratively even this move had been anticipated. In October 1920 Clyde Stayer assumed charge of the Academy as principal. The two faculties still overlapped, though each met separately for its own business, joining in a once-a-month congress.

In late May 1922 President Brumbaugh, armed with the April trustee action and an up-to-date "Greater Juniata" report, ran down the appropriate Middle States commission in New York.[15] Impressed with this latest evidence, the commission now took the college off the gray list. "Juniata Ranks As First Class College" shouted the overstated caption for the *Echo* article telling of the coveted promotion.

As a "first-class college," Juniata automatically qualified for recognition by the American Medical Association. The official word from the AMA came sometime in 1923. Alumnus Dr. Irvin Metzger (1894), president of the Pennsylvania Bureau of Education and Licensure, wrote a congratulatory public letter, printed in the *Echo*. He closed by saying: "The Juniata spirit, enforced by an adequate medical education, should make an ideal doctor. I should like to welcome more from my beloved Alma Mater."[16]

REORGANIZING THE CURRICULUM AND NEW PROGRAMS

A major regrouping and consolidation of academic divisions took place in 1918. The faculty reduced them to four: College of Arts and Sciences, School of Theology, School of Music, and the Academy.

College of Arts and Sciences

Still basic to the college was the B. A. degree, although this would gradually change after the B. S. degree reemerged in 1920. To keep up with the times the humanities added Spanish to the new department of foreign languages in 1916. Explained the *Echo*, this was done "in accordance with the trend of educational sentiment, which emphasizes subjects of commercial value as well as those of cultural training."

An overall curriculum built upon major/minor fields went into effect in 1922. Under this traditional scheme both B. A. and B. S. students had to declare one major (eighteen to thirty hours) and two minors (twelve hours each). In 1924 the catalog listed seventeen major fields: Bible, biology, chemistry, commerce and finance, education, English, French, German, Greek, history, home economics, Latin, mathematics, music, philosophy, physics, social science.

The college began operating in 1916 on the credit-hour system (120 hours total), but not until 1921 did it adopt a two-semester calendar (eighteen weeks to a semester). Upperclassmen of the early Twenties thought they had been unfairly penalized: the minimum passing grade for juniors and seniors was eighty (lowered to seventy-five in 1926). For all students, however, excessive cutting (more than one-tenth of the classes) meant debarment from the final examination in a course.

Meanwhile, the study of science got a boost with the establishment of the A. B. Brumbaugh Science Prize in 1916 for "proficiency" in physics, chemistry, or zoology. Then with the inception of a general science program in 1918, the B. S. degree reappeared. In 1920 one lone graduate got the B. S. diploma. But in another four years there were ten (all males), which represented about a quarter of the class.

One of the rising stars in the firmament of college curricula as the 1900s set in was "domestic science." The American Home Economics Association, organized in 1908, had given impetus to academic training in this field. Harvey Brumbaugh felt that such a program could serve Juniata's purposes, telling the trustees so in 1913. But until the projected science hall was more than talk, he advised against full-blown work—just a general summer course, like the one taught in 1912.

With Science Hall a reality, a home economics department got started in 1915. At first it offered a two-year diploma course, designed to prepare secondary teachers. Sloe-eyed Isabel Cook, Toronto University trained with further study at Wisconsin and Columbia, came to set the department up. Sixteen coeds enrolled the first year. With the fall of 1920 home economics blossomed into a four-year program leading to a B. S. degree. Its curriculum now broadened to train graduates for institutional jobs as well as to teach. By 1924 there were nineteen home economics majors.

Another of the period's departmental births was that of commerce and finance. With the divisional regrouping of 1918, the Business School had been absorbed by the Academy. Its offerings were drastically reduced; eliminated were all banking and accounting courses. In 1923 these reappeared as part of the college curriculum in economics. Herman Hettinger, a Wharton School graduate, played midwife to the department but left the next year. Harold Conner, also a Whartonian, then became the resident economist—until 1937—outlasting a whole cavalcade of departmental colleagues. Within the first two years twenty-four majors were lured into the field of commerce and finance, seeking the B. S. degree.

Like business, teacher training had also been demoted in 1918 to Academy-level rank. It still continued, though, as a four-year program. Then in 1923 education became a B. S. degree option and given full departmental status. Though there were only ten education majors in 1924, this statistic would soon take an upward leap. Practice teaching, first tried out in 1917 with the Academy, now became an annual ritual, administered in cooperation with the public schools.

School of Theology: Seedbed of Fundamentalism

During the years 1916 and 1917 the Bible School retrenched its B. D. program, but then, with the reorganization of 1918, brought it back. At the same time it took a more pretentious name: the School of Theology. Besides a B. A. Bible major and B. D. work, the school offered a three-year curriculum in Christian Worker's Training (for Brethren laypersons) that drew quite well. However, its three-year Bachelor of Religious Education program, instituted in 1920, came to naught. Dean Tobias Myers's School of Theology—whose staff some years numbered as many as nine—emerged in the postwar years as the most articulate forum of fundamentalism among the Brethren. Over the period 1918–31 the men of its faculty showed a zealous interest in teaching the basic doctrines of Christianity that went beyond distinctive Brethren tenets.[17]

The early 1920s marked the heyday of fundamentalistic thought and influence in American Protestantism. Harry Emerson Fosdick's heresy trial in 1922 brought the issue of orthodoxy to a head and branded him the despised symbol of undisguised modernism. (Fosdick was a liberal Baptist then pastor of the First Presbyterian Church in New York City. He subsequently went to Riverside Church, where John D. Rockefeller habitually worshipped.) Schisms rocked all but a few denominations. Antievolution laws swept the South, keeping Darwin out of the public schools. The climactic event of the modernist-fundamentalist battle was the sensational Scopes trial of 1925, when William Jennings Bryan and Clarence Darrow battled in court at Dayton, Tennessee. It became one of the most publicized legal cases in modern American history.

A distinction needs to be drawn, however, between fundamentalistic theology, which conservatives of all denominational genera could accept, and the brand of fundamentalism exemplified and preached by latter-day radio and television evangelists. Theirs is a self-righteous, intolerant, name-calling, hyper-emotional fundamentalism. The dignified men at Huntingdon were nothing like that, in character or in spirit. Nevertheless, they did take a dogmatic stance, feeling some uneasiness with the Church of the Brethren's historic noncreedal position and the silence of its leaders on the scientific and doctrinal issues of the day. The School of Theology was their answer to the alleged liberal learning of rival Bethany Bible School in Chicago. Of the Juniata theologians, Charles Ellis alone came to enjoy wide recognition in the larger, non-Brethren, fundamentalist camp. And it was he who nudged the college into taking a sympathetic stand. His biblicism had its roots in his two-year residency (1902–04) at Zion City, Illinois, forty-two miles north of Chicago. At that theocratic community, founded in 1901 by John Alexander Dowie from the down-under continent, Ellis was principal of both the preparatory school and the college. Dowie headed a sect called the Christian Catholic Apostolic Church and regulated Zion City by a series of strict "blue laws" that included the prohibition to eat pork or to use tobacco, liquor, drugs, or medicine. Dowie's writings (banned from the Juniata library by the trustees in 1900) argued that the earth is flat and held to an expectation of the immediate second coming of Jesus Christ. This latter doctrine, known as premillennialism, now began to shape Dr. Ellis's schematized view of the future.

He was not exactly welcomed with open arms when he left Dowie's utopia and returned to Juniata the fall of 1907. If some trustees had had their way Ellis need not have come back, but M. G. stood up for him and won a reprieve. The passing years vindicated the wisdom of giving the man a second chance. As time went on Dr. Ellis's interest in theology took an academic bent. For a year and two summers (1919–20) he studied at Princeton Seminary and Temple University. From the Philadelphia school he received in 1920 the B. D. degree in religious education. But this sojourn in theological study only confirmed him in his biblicism.

Beginning at this time he became a regular contributor to the *Sunday School Times* and the *Bible Champion*, two influential fundamentalist organs. His book, *The Religion of Religious Psychology*, was published in 1922 by the Sunday School Times Co., located in Philadelphia. It was later revised and reprinted (1928) by the Los Angeles Bible Institute, the West Coast sister of Moody Bible Institute—then the two educational strongholds of fundamentalism. Dr. Ellis taught at Moody in the summer of 1923, and even gave serious thought, as noted, to locating at the Chicago institution.

Private religion "is the plain biblical truth," insisted Ellis, the premillennialist and social gospel foe, one of whose heroes was the famed American evangelist, Dwight L. Moody. The social gospel theology, which Moody had deplored, equated the Kingdom of God with the progressive transformation of society. But for Moody—and Juniata's evangelical vice-president—all human history was a struggle between Satan and Christ. In their view of last things, social ills will never be cured until Christ comes to judge the world, destroy Satan, and set up his reign. Indeed, Dr. Ellis once felt constrained to say that actually the Bible contradicts the idea of God's fatherhood and man's universal brotherhood, the central belief of social gospel advocates.[18]

It was Dr. Ellis's firm conviction that Brethren colleges should become citadels of the "Fundamentals." In 1920 he wrote an article for the denomination's *Gospel Messenger* titled "A College Entrance Examination."[19] In it he raised the question: "Does the college with all its individual instructors hold and teach the following:"

1. The unique and infallible inspiration of the Bible.

2. The lost condition of all men by nature since the fall of Adam.

3. Redemption for men only through the death of Christ…, receiving in himself the penalty of man's sins and the necessary and holy wrath of God against sin.

4. The deity of Christ, different not in degree, but in kind from any so-called "divinity" that man has.

5. The virgin birth of Christ.

6. The resurrection of the body of Christ and of all men.

These points—plus the second coming, curiously omitted in the article—were the *sine qua non* of fundamentalism. Dr. Ellis concluded: "It is not always easy to answer for other individuals, but for the college and those who are its leaders it ought not to be difficult to answer."

For Juniata there was certainly no difficulty; the vice-president saw to that. From the time the School of Theology got its name, its watchword was "Loyalty to the Word." And in the section of the catalog that listed the religion course there appeared a ten-point doctrinal preamble that touched every orthodox base. Juniata College, readers were assured, "firmly believes in these fundamentals and emphasizes them in her teaching." This credal affirmation "gained favorable opinion" of the college, as testified by many alumni and friends.[20]

And the response to the statement outside the Brethren circles was no less favorable. From the editorial rooms of the *Sunday School Times* came a little note to Dr. Ellis in August 1924 saying: "We are constantly being asked to recommend a safe Christian college and it is a pleasure to speak a good word for Juniata whenever possible." Included was a brief testimonial from Miriam Dugan (Bryngelson) of Long Island:

> I must say that I find Juniata the most excellent little college in the world, and am most grateful to the Sunday School Times for recommending it a few years ago.[21]

In all, four Dugan sisters and a brother became Juniatians, three of the women as graduates. Scores of their fellow students would peddle bread as a summer job for the Dugan family's multimillion-dollar bakery business during the Twenties and early Thirties.

Over its seven-year life span the School of Theology graduated thirteen divinity students, the last one in January 1925. But its days were numbered. As early as 1923 sentiment began building in the Brotherhood to make Bethany Bible School the church's official seminary. M. G., Juniata's trustee chairman, led the fight against this maneuver in a losing cause. The general feeling at Annual Conference was that the Brethren should only have one seminary, and in 1925 Bethany was officially taken over by the church. The School of Theology then became the department of Bible and theology, and the non-liberal arts programs were all dropped. Its credal affirmation, however, remained in the catalog for another decade.

School of Music

For a time after the 1918 changes the School of Music still continued as an ancillary discipline. But in 1920 it gained departmental status as part of the liberal arts curriculum. Then with the introduction of the major/minor system in 1922, it qualified as an area of concentration. But department majors got the Bachelor of Music degree, not the B. A. Even before the Twenties music had not been a neglected study. Its staff had enough stature in 1918 to attract a two-hundred-dollar annual scholarship from the Presser Foundation of Philadelphia to train music teachers.

Between 1913 and 1917 the School of Music sponsored a "May Festival" each year. These festivals, the *Echo* said in 1915, are "an established event in nearly all Colleges and schools where music has a place." Prof. Herbert Harroun of Oberlin Conservatory was guest vocalist the first three years. As long as Peter Buys stayed around in those years (1912–19), the college had an orchestra of some merit. Trained at the Amsterdam Conservatory of Music and the Hague's Royal Conservatory, Dutch-born Buys, who had spent three years with John Philip Sousa, was Mount Union's bandmaster when discovered by Juniata. Buys would later win many honorary degrees and decorations and head the American Bandmasters Association. After his departure the orchestra had a checkered career until 1925, when it took a fresh lease on life.

Choral music fared better. In 1917 the Choral Society gave way to separate glee clubs for men and women. Then in 1920, with the coming of Virginian Charles Rowland, Juniata singers were put on the map. He introduced the annual concert tour his first year, one for each glee club (not till the 1930s would a mixed choir travel together). The bushy-haired director, ever the wit, took each group (the men in formal attire at last) to churches of constituent Brethren districts throughout the state. The Men's Glee Club went on the airwaves for the first time in March 1924 over radio station WFBG in Altoona.

The Academy and Its Demise

Along with education and business after 1918, the Academy also housed what was called the Expression Department (speech). Introduced in 1913, speech became a subdivision of the college's English department in 1924 when the Academy closed. Now that the Middle States' evaluation had doomed the Academy, the trustees came to see that their two-campus dream was unrealistic. To erect a whole new complex of buildings on Round Top and still hoist the endowment to where Middle States said it should be would require some monetary miracles. But the Academy was the only one the Brethren then had and the trustees as well as many alumni sincerely felt that somewhere within the Brotherhood there ought to be a good church-related preparatory school.

Beginning in 1920 the board made overtures to Blue Ridge College, then on its last legs, about working out a merger. The trustees had in mind making the Maryland school, whose enrollment was barely half a hundred, the Brethren academy. Juniata would trade its one hundred or so preparatory students for Blue Ridge collegians. A series of conferences took place—in Baltimore and Hagerstown—but in 1922 Blue Ridge decided to limp along on its own. That same spring Morrisons Cove Vocational High School, a private institution, got a visit from merger-minded college officials. These talks also fell through. And so on February 22, 1924, the trustees voted the Academy out of existence with the end of the current academic year. There were nineteen in the valedictory graduating class. Most of the other forty-three "preps" joined the growing ranks of high schoolers in their home areas.

ERECTION OF SCIENCE HALL

Once Carnegie Library and Stone Church had been erected, the trustees turned their attention to a science building. Allan Myers, a science professor and a board member, gave four travel-filled years to it, raising thirty-two thousand dollars. Two gifts in January of 1913 made his job easier: Joseph Oller's five thousand dollars and Mary Geiger's seventy-five hundred (Oller gave an additional five thousand dollars in 1915).

In the fall of 1913 a site was chosen: the upper end of the library block opposite Students Hall. Edward Tilton, by now a campus habitué, started working on designs the following spring. Excavation began in the summer, and on Founders Day 1916 (Juniata's fortieth anniversary) Science Hall was dedicated. One of the attending dignitaries, from a large university, was greatly impressed by what he saw. He said to Harvey Brumbaugh: "I am convinced that a dollar goes farther at Juniata than at any other college of which I know."[22] As originally laid out, the first floor belonged to physics, with the dynamo and electric room in the basement. Biology and geology shared the second floor. Topmost were the chemists, whose laboratory stenches clashed with the kitchen odors of the home economics girls.

SOCIAL REGULATIONS—FREUDIAN FEARS

By 1924 non-Brethren constituted more than two-thirds of the student body; the number would continue to decline. Over forty percent of those on the Hill came from the Keystone State. Forty-six Juniatians were on outright scholarships the academic year 1923–24, and scores more depended on loans and on-campus jobs.

At the national level, Calvin Coolidge moved into the White House, giving the Harding regime a badly needed moral fumigation. The Coolidge Twenties were delirious years, a paradoxical, bizarre decade. It was an era of technological revolution—the radio, the movies, the mass-marketed automobile. It was the age of Prohibition and KKK terrorism when the "business of America," as "Silent Cal" once said, was "business." It was also a time when American manners and morals went into convulsion. Victorianism was on its way out.

The "Roaring Twenties" swept with less fury over College Hill than over many other campuses. But the breakaway trend in fashions and values after the war was clearly evident. *Alfarata* photography documents rising hemlines, though not to "flapper" girl heights. Bobbed hair was common, lipstick less so. Every now and then the college pastor sermonized about "extravagant" coed dress. "Timely," was the faculty's stock response to these preachments.

For America's "flaming youth" the automobile was hailed as the symbol of freedom from restrictive nineteenth-century values. Guardians of public morals, however, decried Henry Ford's invention as "houses of prostitution on wheels." Obviously, the college powers-that-be felt the same way. The Students' Guide for 1921–22 stated: "Women students are not permitted to go automobiling in the evening and not during the day except by permission and with approved chaperon." And pity the poor fellow behind the wheel if a couple got caught joy riding.

"Lights out" was 11:00 P. M. One freshman wrote for the 1922 *Alfarata*: "We soon learned that there is nothing to do after sundown but to go to bed; nothing stays out after the retiring bell, except the trees on the campus." No doubt he knew better by the time he was a senior. After-hours trysting behind Ladies Hall became a common sport, no matter that the trustees tried to thwart it with better outside lighting.

The Victrola made its appearance when a room for men in Founders—as an asylum—became available in April 1916. The parlor got one later, for the women's listening pleasure. Dancing of any kind, however, with or without Victrola music, was a campus sin. Even the lively Charleston, so popular in America, had to be foregone.

Tabooed social outlets had hardly changed since the college's early days. Students perforce had to play cards surreptitiously. The basketball team in 1923 got careless and caused a poker-playing scandal. It cost the coach his job and three starters their positions. Cardsharps who played for stakes received no mercy; instant suspension befell them when snatched by the long arm of campus law.

As Freudian dogmas gained popularity in America, the college remained as determined as ever to patrol dating couples. Women and their escorts had to head for their rooms as soon as a campus event ended. Campus canon did allow senior coeds to go off-campus with dates once a week, juniors once in two weeks, and sophomores once in three weeks. Freshmen girls had a one-a-month quota always with a chaperone. All women were locked in at 9:45 P. M. On a Saturday afternoon, dating couples could go downtown. On Sunday, between 3:00 and 5:00 P. M., they could take walks within a defined territorial boundary: 10th Street to the hospital to the south side of Round Top.

The president was, in effect, the dean of students; he enforced all penalties. Until the time of student government (1922), resident faculty still supervised men's dormitories as live-in monitors. Mrs. Katharine Roberts, who came in 1922, was the first to be called dean of women (the original title of matron had been changed to preceptress in 1912). This beloved, white-haired teacher of English, held the position for eleven years.

Faculty-student relationships were kept stiffly formal. Students were almost always addressed as "Mr." or "Miss," rarely by their given names (and certainly not by nicknames, President Brumbaugh warned in 1919). The faculty never hesitated to correct a student on any occasion for a gaffe in speech or manners.

NEW YOUTH MOVEMENT: STUDENT SELF-GOVERNMENT

A Council of Cooperation (sometimes called Student Council) came into existence in February 1919 in an attempt to improve faculty-student communications. It grew out of student unrest over the daily schedule. Normally a student had six forty-five-minute classes or four classes and a laboratory. This load, it was argued, was overly heavy and academically counter-productive. Students wanted the faculty to adopt the system in effect at most colleges: three sixty-minute classes a day with two hours of outside preparation for each class.

The faculty stood firm, but a proposal from the juniors did result in the creation of the Council. It consisted of five students: two seniors and one from each of the other classes. The Council was so constituted as to guarantee at least one coed representative. For the first time the student body could speak with one voice and expect to be heard. In turn, the faculty established a three-man liaison committee. Good faith was presupposed on both sides. The *Echo* trumpeted: "This marks the beginning of a new era in the student life at Juniata. And why not? Co-operation is the advance-word of progress; and the spirit of democracy dominates in the new order of things following the war."[23]

In 1922 student leaders began to agitate for greater autonomy in regulating dormitory and campus life. Guided by Dean Roberts, they drafted a constitution that eventually gained faculty and trustee consent. The constitution called for two self-governing bodies, one for men and one for women. Both had eleven representatives: five seniors, three juniors, two sophomores, and one freshman. Each body drew up its own set of bylaws and social code.

What this meant was that the students were now empowered to regulate themselves and punish academic and social infractions by a system of demerits. They were not at liberty, however, to fix rules without faculty censorship. Nor could they enforce penalties imposed by the councils without prior approval. In point of fact, therefore, social restrictions remained as tight as ever.

Installation day was October 26, 1922, at the morning chapel service. What was heralded as the "New Youth" movement had at last brought democracy in full measure to Juniata, the *Echo* exulted, overstating the situation. One male Juniatian praised the college for this "expression of faith in the essential goodness of student nature." Ironically, however, the New Youth movement would help to hasten the resignation of the very person who backed it most—President Harvey Brumbaugh himself.

A RESTRICTED CAMPUS BUT NOT A DEAD ONE

Social life fell stagnant during the war years, 1917–18. A general exodus of men into military service or back to the farm depopulated the campus. The deadly end-of-the-war flu epidemic closed the school for three weeks the fall of 1918. (The epidemic raged worldwide and claimed a global mortality of thirty million lives. The disease killed 550,000 Americans, 54,000 of them Pennsylvanians.) Because of the manpower shortage intercollegiate athletics were all but suspended.

Up to America's entry into the war, however, social outlets on the Hill were far from nonexistent. Drama arrived at the campus for the first time in the spring of 1911. It came in the form of scenes from Greek plays put on by the Lyceum. But not with costumes, banned by a trustee decree. Shakespeare's *King Lear* and *Merchant of Venice* followed in 1913, now with props and period dress. Reluctantly the trustees let the junior class stage a full-length play in the spring of 1916. It was a current hit-comedy, *The Private Secretary*. Thereafter annual class plays, excepting the freshmen, took on the nature of intramural rivalry. This form of interclass competition ended after a drama club got started in 1926.

The year 1912 introduced Juniatians to a semester-end examination period and "blue books." It also marked the passing of the *Echo's* editorial care by a faculty member.[24] Ever since then a campus newssheet has been a student-body responsibility. Historically, however, most colleges like Juniata have treated their student-run newspapers more as house organs than full-fledged members of the press. Student journalists have been free to report and comment as long as they did not dishonor or disgrace the school. To be sure, after 1912 and until only recently the Hilltop press functioned under a heavy presidential thumb. More than one editor down through the years has been summoned to Founders Hall to face a very unhappy president.

Juniata got its yearbook in 1915—the *Alfarata*, named for the "Indian maid" of ancient lore. A senior project, it was dedicated to President Brumbaugh, "who has helped us to translate 'Veritas Liberat' in terms of life and character." M. G., then governor, got a special page as "Alumnus Pater Juniatiensis," which was loosely translated, "Our Intellectual Daddy." There was no *Alfarata* in 1916, nor for the three years 1918–20. After 1921 the yearbook became a junior class commission.

A May Pole materialized on the lawn in front of the gymnasium in 1916. Around it—in a climactic dance—forty girls in "flowing Greek gowns" interwove blue and gold streamers. But alas! the first queen and her attendants remained unidentified beauties. Next year's Queen of May, though, was the lovely Ruth Williams (Replogle), a senior from Royersford, Pennsylvania. (Consort Prince Charming did not become part of the festivities until later.)

The spring of 1916 was a time when many students made their first visit to the cinema. With trustee permission they saw David W. Griffith's classic film, *The Birth of a Nation*, an exciting but bigoted story of the Civil War and Reconstruction. Not till 1922, though, did the trustees purchase a movie projector for college entertainment.

Student activism was evident on the Hill long before the 1960s. After 1907, national prohibition became the social reform issue of the day. And Juniata could boast its share of zealots in the cause against "demon rum." They engaged in numerous local "no-license" campaigns, dedicated to the Anti-Saloon League goal: "America Dry in 1920." As for woman's suffrage, also well on its way to constitutional redress, it was long "the rule at Juniata," said the *Echo*. Hilltop suffragettes were no strangers at the downtown "Voters for Women" headquarters.

The General Information Contest, its cash prize funded by a nameless patron, was initiated in the spring of 1917. For decades the campus intelligentsia made it a prestigious challenge to win the prize. Thirty contestants competed the first time around.

After World War I the campus quickly revived. Juniata debaters continued their dominance in reasoned argument. In 1919 they began to receive credit for their out-of-class efforts. The overall debate record through 1924 came to twenty-three victories in twenty-nine contests. Women took to the forum in 1920, contending against Grove City College in a dual meet. The team argued the affirmative on the "closed shop" question, a major issue in industrial unionism. They lost on a split vote. In 1924 Juniata lady polemicists went undefeated in six encounters.

Club life flourished. In 1920 departmental clubs made their appearances as subgroups of the Lyceum: English; history and social science; music (in addition to the glee singers); science; modern languages. Still going strong were the on-campus debate club, the Lyceum, the Volunteer Band, the two Ys, and the Oriental Literary Society. The Wahneeta Literary Society, however, was not around (it folded in 1912). Gone also was the Intercollegiate Prohibition Society and its oratorical contest, now that the Eighteenth Amendment had supposedly made America "dry."

The Press Club took its rise in 1923, the inspiration of Prof. Herman Hettinger, on-the-side director of publicity. In the interest of a "Greater Juniata" its motto was: "Publicity Above All Things." A bevy of some seventy reporters, writers, and typists prepared and sent out regular news releases to over fifty papers in Pennsylvania, Ohio, and Maryland. Monthly, the hometown newspaper of every student received the latest write-up of college happenings.

Soon after the war dormitory-dwellers gained an added measure of privacy. Bunkmates literally split up in the fall of 1922, "roomies" no longer forced to sleep together. The men's halls got double-decked beds while the women were furnished with single "couch" beds.

"Carding" at Sunday evening Stone Church services remained mandatory. But New Youth students rebelled against compulsory attendance at Sabbath-morning Bible classes. This attitude was deplored at faculty meetings. The administration tried to crack down, inviting parental pressure—but to no avail. It was this minor rebellion that caused the faculty, in 1922, to lengthen the daily chapel period to a half-hour.

As extracurricular activities abounded as never before, "all around leaders" now came in for special recognition. Dr. Fred Hutchinson of Huntingdon established two annual prizes of twenty-five dollars in the summer of 1922. The winners were to be a senior man and a senior woman, chosen by popular vote, who contributed the most to the life of the College" in their four years on the Hill. The criteria were the same as those for the Rhodes Scholarship. These included force of character and leadership, literary ability, and participation in athletics. The first Hutchinson Award winners were announced at the 1923 commencement.

The campus intellectuals also made the limelight at graduation ceremonies in 1923. Before then the college had never given academic honors. But that year seniors with an average of ninety or higher graduated "cum honoribus." Out of a class of twenty-nine, four made the grade. However, beginning in 1925 "laude" was conferred in three Latin parts—cum, magna, summa—as tradition would have it.

Not only were the seniors of 1923 the first to graduate comrades "cum honoribus," but they introduced the "Torch Lighting" custom. At the conclusion of their Class Day exercises the Saturday before commencement they marched past President Brumbaugh, seated on a pedestal. In his hand he held a large lighted candle that kindled a smaller one carried by each senior. This was to symbolize the "light which they would carry from Juniata to their life work." The name "Candlelighting" soon substituted for "Torch Lighting." About this time the "Mantle Ceremony" was introduced, at the end of which the outgoing senior president placed the mantle of authority on the shoulders of the incoming one. The Candlelighting and Mantle ceremonies remained traditions to the end of the Calvert Ellis presidency.

ATHLETICS AND THE BIRTH OF FOOTBALL

Athletic facilities expanded to meet the demands of a growing intercollegiate program after 1911. The gymnasium gained added space with a rear addition in 1913. A grandstand, seating over one thousand, went up on the northwest corner of the athletic field the summer of 1914. Bought for seventy-five dollars, it came from the county fairgrounds. The baseball diamond, which originally faced west, was now reversed and given a professional look. It boasted a grass infield with skinned base paths. Around the fenced-in area ran the regraded cinder track. The rearranged athletic field sufficed until the coming of football, which created need for more space. With alumni help additional ground was acquired east of Scott Street in 1923. The borough then closed Scott between 16th and 17th streets.

It became the policy after 1911 to schedule only schools of college and university ranks, although exceptions were made at first. America's entry into World War I, of course, put a crimp in the athletic program. In the spring of 1917 the college reaffirmed the policy of using second-year Academy boys on varsity teams, a practice other colleges of the state were trying to discourage. For the duration, however, intercollegiate competition was drastically curtailed.

Postwar Juniata athletes gained a new sense of camaraderie through the varsity **J** Club. It organized on January 13, 1920, "to foster and create interest in College Athletics." Also, it jealously sought "to govern the promiscuous wearing of letters" by setting up rigid standards of eligibility.[25]

Athletics had become so much a part of campus life with the early Twenties that "Clean Sports" was named first in a list of college ideals the catalog began to feature in 1921. "Juniata," the catalog affirmed, "believes in the Roosevelt motto, 'Play the game, don't foul, hit the line hard.'" "In all contests," the statement went on, "Juniata will play hard to win" but not "to gain any honor unfairly."

Winning teams need good coaching, and in 1915 student "bench coaches" became a thing of the past. Ivan Bigler, an Academy alumnus, coached basketball and baseball that year. In 1916 the college brought in a professional for these two sports—Ward Putt, an ex-Hilltopper who played in the New York Eastern and South Atlantic baseball leagues. Ronald Kichline followed in 1922, turning out one of Juniata's finest baseball teams ever. It finished with a 13-6 record, amassing 196 runs to the opposition's 96. A trio of pitchers, including freshman-sensation Joseph Shaute, led the mound corps. The team, loaded with long-ball hitters, struck twenty home runs at College Field.

That July "Lefty" Shaute broke into the major leagues with the Cleveland Indians.[26] He threw his first pitch—as a seventh-inning reliever—against Babe Ruth in the second game of a double-header with the Yankees. Before the afternoon was over the rookie had fanned the "King of Swat" not once, but twice. The six-foot, 190-pound Shaute spent thirteen years in major-league baseball, with three different teams. He was a twenty-game winner in 1924 and ended his career with ninety-nine victories and an ERA of 4.15.

Shaute was not the first Juniatian to rise to the top in baseball, though he was the first to jump directly from campus. Two others, also pitchers, had earlier made the grade. William "Wild Bill" Ritter of McCoysville, Pennsylvania, a student in 1910, went up in 1912 for a four-year stay. Allen Sothoron of Bradford, Ohio, who pitched for the 1912 Juniata team while enrolled in the Academy, began an eleven-year major league career in 1914. Another pitcher, Perce "Pat" Malone of Altoona, played on Juniata's 1921 team, and seven years later was a moundsman for the Chicago Cubs. For thirteen years he was a major leaguer, part of that time with the Yankees and managed by Joe McCarthy. Not until the 1940s would another Juniatian give professional baseball a try out.

On the hardwood court, Juniata quintets, playing a schedule of as many as twenty games some seasons, were no pushovers. But there were more defeats than victories. Several hoopsters of that era later became trustees.

Women's basketball came into its own in the winter of 1922 (it had been tried earlier, in 1915). A six-game intercollegiate schedule was played the next year, which included Drexel, Temple, Indiana Normal, and Gettysburg. That 1916 sextet produced the first coed varsity letter-winners. And in 1924 women roundballers were assigned a training table of their very own.

Before the Twenties the track schedule never amounted to much despite good material. A relay team competed at the Penn Relay Race Carnival in 1916. They finished fourth in a field of eight. Clyde Stayer, one of the relayers and the record-holder in the 220-hurdles, became track coach when he returned to teach in 1919. Stayer-coached cindermen entered twice more in the Penn Relays and beginning in 1921 took part each spring in the Middle Pennsylvania Intercollegiate track-and-field meets. Out of the war years came a spikeshoe mark still supreme: Jefford Oller's 21.6-seconds time for the 220-yard dash in 1918.

As for Juniata netmen, they competed against college squads for the first time in 1917. But not until 1921 was tennis promoted to a varsity sport. The 1923 racket wielders, self-coached, were almost unbeatable, logging one of the best records in tennis history on the Hill. They won nine, lost two, and tied once. The team's captain was a slender nineteen-year-old senior named Calvert Ellis.

With the 1920s there came another varsity sport, one for the fall. Students had been pestering the trustees since before the war to give the green light to football. In 1919 they symbolized their feelings by making a campus fetish of a football bought with student funds. A determined lobby went to work as soon as school began the next September. For days the gridiron enthusiasts besieged the faculty and trustees before prevailing. Two top scholars did the most to turn the scales: John Montgomery and George Griffith, both to become distinguished physicians and Juniata trustees.

The student body raised over six hundred dollars for new equipment practically overnight. Roy "Pee Wee" Wolfgang, who would become a four-sport, twelve-letter man, then set out for New York City by train to make the necessary purchases, two empty trunks in tow. He went on the mission because he could ride free on his father's railroad pass. But who would be the coach? The question was answered in the person of Dr. Vernon Cecil, the chemistry professor, who had coached football for fifteen years at St. Johns College in Baltimore. A holiday was declared to level part of the baseball outfield, which was steeply banked, into a playing surface. Students pitched in with shovels, barrows, and wagons to make the dirt fly.

Then there was the matter of a schedule. Jesse Miller, student manager, went feverishly to work and in a few weeks lined up five games: Bellefonte Academy, Lebanon Valley (two), Albright, Shippensburg. The season opened on October 23. The blue-togged gridders won but once that first season: over Shippensburg, 28-0. The next Saturday Albright won 77-0. Juniata won six and lost twenty-two over the next four seasons. Lopsided scores were not unusual in football's nascent years. But there was no denying its mystique; from the very first kickoff it was for decades the reigning

Juniata sport. Coaches of the 1920s, though, never stayed around very long. Six of them came and went in that decade.

WORLD WAR I: OBJECTORS AND SERVICEMEN

The peace position has been the historic trademark of the Brethren. And from 1900 onward, as a militaristic spirit was increasingly displayed in the domestic life and foreign policy of the United States, the college took a strong stand in favor of pacifism and disarmament. M. G. Brumbaugh actively participated in the Annual Mohonk Conferences on International Arbitration. And in 1904 the *Echo* envisioned him one day on the Hague Tribunal where he could work "to make the principles of our Brotherhood a powerful factor in world peace."

William Swigart was no less a diligent pacifist. He represented the college in 1905 at a peace conference on the Goshen College campus where he read a major paper. In 1911 Annual Conference appointed a Peace Committee to educate the Brethren on the "sinfulness and folly of resorting to arms." The chairmanship of this committee went to Swigart. After Congress declared war on Good Friday, April 6, 1917, the denomination created the Central Service Committee to represent it in all matters pertaining to the draft. Its chairmanship also went to Swigart. The Central Service Committee worked closely with the other historic peace churches—Mennonite and Quaker—in gaining recognition for conscientious objectors. There was no provision in the draft law for pacifists, and it took months of mediation before they were allowed to perform noncombatant duties. M. G. Brumbaugh, then governor of Pennsylvania, interceded to help place many young Brethren men in alternative non-rifle-carrying military assignments. Meanwhile, Swigart and others on the Juniata staff visited army camps, counseling with resisters kept under detention. Some Juniatians were among the hundreds of those placed in guardhouses as war resisters. But the actual number is unknown.

Because of their peace heritage, college authorities refused to participate in a War Department program called the Students' Army Training Corps. This plan, announced in May 1918, made cooperating institutions a place for combined military and collegiate training. The purpose was not to interrupt the education of draft-age youth in technical and professional fields until necessary. But it meant the involvement of military personnel as instructors, and the presence of uniformed men—the symbol of war—was unthinkable to the trustees. Turning down the SATC program, they knew full well, would be costly in terms of male students.

The college did cooperate, however, with another national wartime measure introduced in late April 1917. The faculty rationalized it as a "moral equivalent of war." This was the effort to meet the food shortage, both at home and abroad, by mobilizing a temporary "Agricultural Army" in each state. Under this program undrafted young men could drop out of college with impunity by volunteering several months of farm work wherever assigned. They would receive full academic credit for the disrupted spring term. Any number of Hilltoppers answered this patriotic call. Because this worked havoc with the academic program, all final exams were canceled in June.

For most draft-age Juniatians, of course, patriotism meant military duty. A service flag with seventy-nine stars was place in the chapel by the YWCA on April 16, 1918. But other stars were affixed later; one of them represented Walter Eshelman. He was the first Juniatian to die in uniform, a flu victim, on October 2, 1918, at Camp Dix, New Jersey. The one Juniatian to fall in battle was Cloyd Davis, a marine from neighboring Petersburg. He was killed on the Blanc Mont Front in France on October 4, 1918. His sergeant found him lying at the base of a tree, a Bible clasped to his chest.

FURTHER CAMPUS GROWTH AND CHANGES

While work on Science Hall pushed ahead the summer of 1915, a new central heating plant, with a towering steel stack, went up next to Stone Church. The old boiler house behind the dormitories, its chimney toppled, was converted into the college laundry. Earlier, in 1912, M. G. Brumbaugh sold the college a corner lot (Moore and 19th streets) at the foot of Round Top. Then in 1921 the town council vacated all streets and alleys cutting across the Round Top tract. Next year the purchase of five lots below the Orphans Home further enlarged the campus ground. By then the college owned fifteen dwellings and a four-family apartment house east of the gymnasium. Included in its property holdings was Henry Brumbaugh's house, next to Carnegie Library, which the Oller relatives deeded over in 1921.

In the fall of 1922 the campus got a long-needed post office (in the basement of Students Hall) complete with 300 lock boxes. The narrow front stairway in Founders Hall was torn out in 1922. This alteration gave more space to the treasurer's office and added three dormitory rooms. But it took away the fun of rolling objects down the steps, to crash against the door of the president's office with a resounding thud. Ladies Hall, by petition of the women in 1922, was renamed Brumbaugh Hall in honor of the Brumbaugh group of founders. And with Coolidge prosperity came the paving of Moore Street between 17th and 18th in the summer of 1924.

NEW TWISTS TO ALUMNI RELATIONS

The immediate pre-World War I years saw the college take steps to better organize alumni relations and keep track of ex-Juniatians. In 1911 the alumni transferred their twenty-eight-thousand-dollar scholarship fund to the college endowment, still to be used for student aid of course. Then in 1912 someone broached the idea of quinquennial class reunions, or multiples thereof, at commencement time. The Class of 1898 set the example in 1913, on its fifteenth anniversary. Back in 1908 the corresponding secretary of the Alumni Association had been delegated special responsibility for building up the interest and support of former Juniatians.

Finally, in 1920 the Alumni Association took Harvey Brumbaugh's advice and appointed a field secretary, who, though part-time, would be paid. The position went to Allan Myers, science professor and trustee, and he began to put out the "Juniatagram," a mimeographed newsletter on college activities. He devoted some of his time to reviving local organizations that had fallen inactive during the war years.

Then in 1922 alumnus Stoler Good, a Waynesboro banker, became both college treasurer and alumni director. Within a year he activated several big-city alumni clubs: Chicago, Cleveland, Pittsburgh, Johnstown, Philadelphia, Reading, Washington, D. C. It was Good who planned the first Homecoming Day, November 3, 1923. The big event of the afternoon was the football game against Susquehanna, a battle royal. Unfortunately, the Blue and Gold came out on the short end of a 5-0 score. At half time the alumni paraded around the field, cheered on by the more than five hundred spectators.

The "old grads" came from all walks of life. But, because Brethren disliked litigation, law had never been a popular profession for Juniatians. This slowly began to change after the war, Juniata setting the example for its kin colleges. Of the eleven known law-schooled Brethren attorneys in 1923, seven were Juniata graduates.[27]

By then nine alumni had gone on to earn the Ph.D. degree. Two were women who took their doctorates at the University of Pennsylvania: Florence Fogelsanger (Murphy) in English (1917) and Frances Holsopple (Parsons) in psychology (1919). Both, top-ranking scholars, were denied a Phi Beta Kappa key because of their gender. Florence Murphy holds the distinction of being the first Brethren woman to get a Ph.D.

HARVEY BRUMBAUGH RESIGNS PRESIDENCY

From 1920 on some of the trustees became increasingly upset about campus discipline, which they felt was "far below what it should be." They saw Juniata as an "institution of the church" whose purpose should be to teach "true Christian piety."[28] The rise of student government particularly distressed them because of their fear that behavior might deteriorate completely. Troubled trustees began to put pressure on faculty members and the president, demanding that they show "more concern."

The president, because of three high-spirited daughters, tended to be quite lenient on the matter of campus mores. But the board-induced friction finally got the best of him and in February he asked for a year's leave, to be spent at Columbia University in study. The trustees honored his request unhesitatingly. But Charles Ellis balked when told he would be the interim man in charge while Harvey was gone.

For one thing, the vice-president did not take kindly to giving up his institute work. But more than that, he protested, it was an "unfortunate time" for President Brumbaugh to go away. There was the paramount problem—at least in Ellis's opinion—of student government and the need for someone to impose stricter controls. And just beyond the horizon, in 1926, loomed Juniata's semicentennial and all the dollar signs it conjured up.

Harvey was a tired administrator. Twenty-eight years he had run the school in one capacity or another. He needed to get away, and when Dr. Ellis threw up a roadblock he saw no way out except to resign. The trustees received his letter on June 2, 1924. His future relationship with the college was a matter to be determined later.

Chapter 9

BRINGING IN THE NEW ERA: 1924–1930

MARTIN GROVE BRUMBAUGH REDUX

On more than one occasion after 1922, complaints about the quality of student life besetting him from all sides, Harvey Brumbaugh had suggested bringing M. G. back to straighten things out. Perhaps the ex-governor, five years out of office, could awe the students into more respect for authority. And then when there seemed to be no solution for an administrative stand-in during his leave, the president pressed the idea on the trustees all the harder. At the same time he indicated a willingness to resign, thus opening the way.

Harvey Brumbaugh had given the board only a couple weeks' notice before it met on commencement day. Many trustees, however, thought that Harvey was right. M. G., their chairman, would be the perfect successor. And so they swamped him with mail, beseeching him to come to the "rescue of Juniata College," as Jennie Stouffer (Newcomer) put it.[1] She further exhorted, "You surely cannot close your mind to the fact that you are the man for the crisis." Philadelphian Frank Foster told M. G.: "You are the one man that can bring harmony out of discord, order out of the confusion that exists at the college."[2]

To this chorus of epistolary appeals Vice-President Ellis, to whom New Youth gains were something of a scandal, added a refrain of his own. He informed M. G. of a recent crackdown on the social code intended to leave student leaders "under no misapprehension as to the fact that all their authority is delegated to them from the trustees through the faculty."[3] He mentioned the need of a "capable watchman" and of "more campus light." It was important to him that the music rooms be moved out of

Brumbaugh Hall to keep men from "ever being on that side," and he "wished" that the women's dormitory was "absolutely separated." "The only opportunity I can see for permanence in the things we have started," Ellis stressed in closing, "is your acceptance of the presidency."

By law, M. G. could not succeed himself as governor, so he made his living as a lecturer. He spent the years 1919–24 criss-crossing the country in behalf of educational reforms.[4] He spoke out for required physical education in public schools and championed the cause of vocational training. He also traveled for the National Recreation Association of New York City, backing public playgrounds. And until its defeat he used the platform to campaign against universal military conscription, which had strong postwar support. The summer of the college crisis, however, he was scheduled to teach at Bates College in Maine, near his vacation home (Wayne).

His was a pro-forma election when the trustees convened on commencement morning. But there remained the matter of compensation. The college could not hope to meet his current income of seventy-five hundred dollars. The board proposed that he supplement his president's salary with lecture fees. But M. G. vetoed that expedient, with a knowing second from his wife. He finally agreed to five thousand dollars a year. For the first time the salary differential between the highest paid professors ($2,500) and the president amounted to more than a nominal figure.

In late June M. G. sold his Germantown home (for $40,000). His plan was to honor his summer commitment at Bates and his speaking engagements in the fall. He would then take office the first of December, making his Huntingdon residence a second-floor apartment in the new Mission Home. He importuned Charles Ellis to continue as vice-president, expecting to give more responsibilities to that office. And he made it understood that there would be a place for Harvey Brumbaugh after his year at Columbia was up.

M. G.: THE PEOPLE'S WARTIME GOVERNOR (1915–1919)

The board's decision to bring the sixty-two-year-old M. G. back to the Hill made Juniata the only small college in Pennsylvania ever to name a former governor its president. During the late war Brumbaugh had done honor to himself in Harrisburg. While some historians do not assess his administration as outstanding, none fail to laud him for his character and high sense of public calling.[5] How did it happen that a man of undisguised Brethren beliefs, whose ruling passion was public education, allowed himself to be put in the governor's mansion?

M. G., content to be the Quaker City's school superintendent, had never thought of getting involved in politics until William Vare, Republican boss of Philadelphia, put the notion in his head. Politically astute, Vare had the ability to read the "sign of the times"—the trend of the country after 1910 to place educators in public office.[6] Woodrow Wilson, Princeton's president, who went from governor of New Jersey to the White House, stood out as the classic example.

In 1914 Pennsylvanians had to elect a senator and the governor. Boies Penrose, head of the State Republican machine, declared his candidacy for reelection to the

United State Senate. But he was opposed to Vare and the Vare organization. The Philadelphia boss, however, foresaw that Penrose would have a fight on his hands to be reelected. This would be the first election of senators by the direct vote of the people. Furthermore, Progressivism was in its heyday, and Teddy Roosevelt had personally widened the breach between his followers and Penrose. Nevertheless, Penrose intended to dictate, as he had since 1904, the GOP slate for key state posts, most importantly the governorship.

A year or so before the election Vare decided to push an opposition gubernatorial candidate in the Republican primaries. If successful, this would be a telling blow in breaking Penrose's grip on the party. One day he asked his brother, Ed, what was the "most prominent school name" in Pennsylvania. "Brumbaugh," came the immediate reply. Vare said, "He's the man for us." His brother agreed.[7]

Six months before the fight started, Vare resorted to a clever ruse. He had M. G. speak before school and other civic groups, which later passed resolutions backing him. The cagey Quaker City politico rightly intuited that the state's thirty thousand teachers would constitute a solid Brumbaugh bloc and help attract thousands of independents that had left the Taft ticket two years before.[8] M. G.'s well-placed educator-friends played up the fact that he had been the leading member of the commission that drafted the School Code of 1911. This measure repealed every school law that had been passed since the beginning of free education in Pennsylvania. It substituted the new Code covering all phases of public schooling. Brumbaugh's strength developed in a rush; Vare had forced the Philadelphia schoolman upon Penrose.

Almost everyone on College Hill hailed with pleasure his entrance into politics. Some saw the White House at the end of the road for him. To them it was destiny-certain that he was the Republican Party's answer to Wilson. But others had misgivings, among them Charles Ellis. Ellis tried to talk him out of running for governor for fear he would get mixed-up in "gang" politics.[9] M. G. gave assurance, however, that there were no "entangling alliances." He spoke of himself as an "Independent Republican." To one Juniata alumna he wrote, "I have prayerfully gone into this contest." And in an open letter to the student body in April 1915 he said he had concluded it was his "Christian duty" to run.

He refused to do any preprimary campaigning. And he made it clear that he would reject the nomination unless it came as "the call of the common people, the people who work with their hands."[10] That call came in May when M. G. garnered four-fifths of the Republican vote (253,788), the largest ever recorded for a state candidate before woman suffrage. He received more than twice the votes polled by Vance McCormick, the victor of the Democratic primary.

On the campaign trail M. G. spelled out a thoroughly progressive platform, which included the ballot for women. He hit hard on the theme that as governor he would be "unfettered" and "unbossed in every way." Some three thousand voters in Philadelphia's Town Hall heard him one October night make his most caustic utterance against machine politics. He said, "I hate a boss as much as you hate a boss, and if ever a slimy thing throws itself in my path I will scotch it."[11]

For M. G. the wet-dry question was no less of a political problem than bossism. The ties between the GOP and the liquor traffic had long been close. Thus the Anti-Saloon

League, skeptical that Brumbaugh was his own man, threw its support to McCormick. But M. G. defied the state party, which counseled silence on the alcohol issue. He promised the drys: "I will do everything I honorably can to support local option." "No license" rather than blanket prohibition, he sincerely believed, was the "practical solution to a vital problem facing the people and legislature."[12]

A number of minor parties had also entered the field, and M. G. found himself caught up in a spirited campaign. But he won handily in November despite diverse opposition. His nearly 489,000 votes represented a solid majority. College Hill went wild the day after the election. The tower bell pealed the glad news. The faculty and students sent the governor-elect a congratulatory telegram. Classes dismissed. Parades marched all day. Speechifying filled in between parades. At night a huge bonfire, fueled by rubbish hauled in from all over town, lit up the sky from down on the athletic field. Brumbaugh's victory, however, was tempered with sadness. In July his wife of twenty years, the former Anna Konigmacher, had died unexpectedly.

In several respects his election was unique. No other Brethren has ever held the office of governor, and he was the second and last clergyman in the Commonwealth to do so. Moreover, no other career educator or college president or Ph.D. holder has ever become Pennsylvania's chief executive.

Though a progressive at heart, M. G. had to contend with the Penrose-controlled General Assembly and its conservative, stand-pat posture. In the end he vetoed 409 of its bills, a practice that earned him his so-so political reputation among historians. But Earl Kaylor's 1996 biography casts the Brumbaugh governorship in a more favorable mold.[13] The book argues that not a single one of the vetoed bills could be considered a substantive progressive measure. A great number fell into the pork-barrel category or were smugly passed but not funded. The intent was to embarrass the governor. By constitutional law Pennsylvania could not in those days incur indebtedness except by plebiscite. As the press put it, all the pork barreling deserved to be "meat-axed." The Kaylor biography challenges the accepted opinion of state historians that Brumbaugh the governor lacked a progressive agenda. It details at length his outspoken advocacy of a broad range of sociopolitical reforms that won him acclaim as the "champion of labor."

Ironically, Governor M. G., the peace-loving Dunker, found himself presiding over his native state in wartime. World War I overshadowed the second half of his four-year administration. Many Brethren criticized him when he mobilized the Pennsylvania National Guard, which went to France as the 28th Division and took part in some of the chief campaigns in the last months of the war. They felt he had breached the peace stand of the church. For him, signing the order had been an act of duty. In the end his sense of eternal right and justice triumphed over his Brethren ethic of pacifism. As he came to see it, the world's armed combat had been transformed into a holy crusade, because he believed God was on the side of the Allies.

In 1916 the Brumbaugh/Vare-Penrose standoff escalated into an internecine political feud. Vare somehow cajoled M. G. into running as the state's favorite son in the upcoming presidential race. Penrose bitterly fought this maneuver and tried to coerce him into quitting. He made public accusation about irregularities in financing M. G.'s gubernatorial campaign. His tactics failed, and the governor became one of eleven candidates nominated at the Republican convention in Chicago. He received twenty-nine votes on the first ballot, then withdrew and nominated Theodore Roosevelt, whom he would later idolize in a biography. Charles Hughes became the party's banner-bearer but he lost out to Wilson, who was reelected.

Pennsylvania's General Assembly at that time met biennially. So Penrose and his party minions openly set out to impeach M. G. in the 1917 legislative session. After his first wife died the governor bore the brunt of vicious gossip about his relationship with Flora Belle Parks. The Brumbaugh family had taken her into their home as a ward when M. G. was county superintendent of schools, more than twenty years before. A distant relative of his, she was a girl in her midteens when he became her guardian.

Attractive and socially refined, she made a perfect substitute First Lady for Pennsylvania's widowed governor. M. G.'s political enemies could see nothing innocent in his sharing the Executive Mansion with so comely a woman, almost young enough to be his daughter. Scandalmongers were silenced for the time being when they were married in February 1916, a month before he entered the presidential race.

Then in 1917 the Penrose faction publicized extracts from state records allegedly revealing extravagant personal expenses paid for out of public funds. The most sensational charge claimed that the people of Pennsylvania bore the cost of his 1916 bridal tour with Flora Belle Parks. Despite all the mud slinging, Penrose's vicious scheme never came to a test in the General Assembly. The maligned governor emerged from the trumped up scandal wholly vindicated but badly disillusioned with politics.

M. G.'S PROSPECTUS OF A "GREATER JUNIATA"

On the whole, the student body had felt a genuine affection for Harvey Brumbaugh. When he returned for M. G.'s inaugural he met with a rousing welcome at an evening celebration in the chapel. The seniors presented him with a watch-chain charm "as a token of the high esteem in which he is held by Juniatians everywhere." And three days later he was the guest of honor at their class dinner held in the Leister House (across the street from the railroad station).

Nevertheless, toward the end of his administration students had begun to complain about "screws being put on." And after his resignation an editorial in the campus paper predicted "more order and better organization" under the incoming president. Its scribe went on to voice the expectation that someone with M. G.'s background would "not long entertain some of the characteristic medieval narrow-mindedness which has long been present."[14] This was not meant to be so much an indictment of an ex-president as of the trustees and certain faculty members. Still it must have hurt the sensitive Harvey.

As a matter of fact, the new president, himself not fully sold on student government, saw his alma mater quite like his predecessor had: as a "tight little, right little college." His inaugural speech in January served notice on rambunctious New Youthers. In identifying "salient objectives" for the Juniata of his presidency, he said of the school:

It is a Christian College dedicated to the advancement of right living here and teaching that there is a hereafter of tremendous significance. It accepts the Bible and teaches that it is the key to the hope of immortal life. From this ideal, it should never depart. In this respect, the College is not only conservative but immoveable[sic]. The College wants not only to teach right but to do right. "Knowledge that is not refined into conduct is a curse, not a blessing."

He recognized the fact that the college students of the Twenties embodied a vastly changed set of moral and cultural values. Spiritual ideals, he lamented, lay "shattered" and "broken" in the wake of war, the American home and the schools in a state of moral decay. This gave rise, in his view of things, to a set of problems more complex than college administrators had ever before faced. But the values of Juniata had not changed, he asserted, and therefore the college "dedicates itself to a spiritual revival." During his presidency he hoped that it would be "counted among those agencies that stand in crisis for law, for country, and for righteousness." Here in this last statement he preveniently sounded the theme that he would later choose for the Jubilee Year: "Law and Law Observance."

M. G. made much of the point that Juniata "must remain small," a community in "close personal touch." He was, of course, taking over a campus sans Academy, its population sizably reduced. "Small" he translated into an enrollment of five hundred. By 1928 this mark, up a couple hundred over his inaugural year, had been reached and even slightly surpassed.

For reasons of his own, he did not see fit, in limning the "Juniata of tomorrow," to say anything specifically about the college's Brethren heritage, or its obligations as such. But never once during his second term did M. G. betray the slightest desire to lead Juniata out of the denominational fold. Indeed, in a 1929 letter to a Brotherhood dignitary he made emphatic his "trying here to build a school of the Church of the Brethren." He further stated: "We are certainly as loyal to its principles as I know how to make the school."[15]

Even so, he could get irritated at what to him looked like signs of undue church interference. In 1929, the doom of Blue Ridge College no longer in dispute (see Chapter 8), the church's General Education Board sought to keep Juniata and Elizabethtown from recruiting south of the Mason and Dixon line. Territorially, Maryland was reserved for two smaller schools in Virginia. But M. G. wanted Maryland declared "open territory." He argued that Juniata had already been forced to reach out into "other fields" for students because it had grown faster than the church. In strong words he let the people in Elgin, Illinois, know that he did not want the church "through any of its Boards or actions to cripple us in any way."

THE NOT SO GOLDEN JUBILEE

In 1925, at the close of its first half century, Juniata College owned a physical plant worth a half million dollars. Its endowment fund amounted to a few thousand more. Thanks to thrifty management, the school was solvent, not a cent of mortgage indebtedness owing on its grounds and buildings.

To accommodate the five hundred students optimally projected, there was need for added facilities and greater endowment income. M. G. and the trustees expected, of course, to exploit the college's semicentennial to the hilt. To build a men's dormitory and, most critically, to lift the total endowment to the million-dollar figure, meant a $750,000-Jubilee-Year campaign. In October 1925 the trustees engaged Ward, Wills, Dreshman, and Gates and Co., then the oldest professional fund-raising firm in the country, to direct the drive. The canvass proper began in mid-May and lasted two weeks.

Off campus, the campaign concentrated on three constituencies: the alumni, the church, and the community. The community, however, embraced more than the immediate river basin. It took in the whole two-hundred-mile stretch between Lancaster and Pittsburgh. Publicity brochures declared that Juniata College was "the only general college on the main line of the Pennsylvania Railroad."

On campus—among trustees, faculty, and students—there had been a precampaign solicitation. Nineteen trustees subscribed one hundred thousand dollars. The student-body canvass netted some thirty-three thousand dollars, an average of almost one hundred dollars a student. The senior class, which playfully labeled themselves "M. G.'s Sunbeams," had whipped up contagious enthusiasm among undergraduates. From the twenty-eight faculty members came subscriptions in excess of fifteen thousand dollars. Amazingly, not a single person in any of these groups refused to sign a pledge card. Overall, however, the Jubilee Campaign turned out to be nothing to celebrate. It fell far short of its goal by nearly $350,000.

M. G. had done his best to prevent failure. To set the stage for the May drive he had worked hard the previous month to make a grand occasion of Juniata's fiftieth anniversary. He built the events of Founders Day week around the theme of "Law and Law Observance." Robert von Moschzisker, Chief Justice of the Pennsylvania Supreme Court, was the featured speaker. In his own welcoming address the president spoke of constitutional law, of the responsibility of free citizens to state government. He hailed "education as the means and safeguard of American Democracy." From "Jubilee to Jubilee," he adjured, the college must always honor "in an enlightened way the values of our country."

Why this emphasis? Not because M. G. purposed to turn Jubilee Day into one of theatrical flag-waving. Patently he was out to contrive a fresh image of Juniata. He intended to show the larger world that his was not a backwoods institution, that neither the amorality of the Roaring Twenties nor the lawlessness seeded by Prohibition characterized the mood and manners of College Hill. Particularly, he hoped to make the college more visible to Pennsylvanians, to "firmly entrench" it, as he once said, in the "heart of the Commonwealth."

He brought to campus for the Golden Jubilee, not only jurists and legislators, but two Pennsylvania titans of business and industry. Howard Heinz of "57 Varieties," a close friend of his in ecumenical Sunday school work, got an honorary degree. So did M. G.'s life-long friend, Charles Schwab, then board chairman of Bethlehem Steel. Schwab showed up for his degree in a chauffeur-driven, topless Stutz Bearcat.

But the returns were practically nil. Heinz did make a modest gift, but Schwab proved closefisted, insulted by someone's lack of tact explaining Juniata's hopes for his philanthropic help. To M. G.'s great disappointment, it soon became apparent he lacked the Midas touch in cultivating men of wealth. He could get nabobs of Schwab-Heinz riches to campus (Bruce Barton, Josephus Daniels, Owen Roberts, William Woodin), but he could never open their checkbooks.

In the case of Woodin, the railroad-banking magnate and later Franklin Roosevelt's Secretary of the Treasury, the antics of silly students probably jinxed his 1929 Hilltop visit. Everyone knew why he was getting an honorary degree on Founders Day. Yet a gang of fellows stood outside M. G.'s office, stupidly chanting: "We want Woodin nickles."

No doubt Dr. Claude Flory, a retired Florida State University professor, has put his finger on why the president's well-to-do friends failed to give. As a Juniatian in the late Twenties, Flory fell into M. G.'s favor and was taken into the family circle. He once wrote, "I now realize that while the campus of those days looked all right to most of us country students it must have looked terribly unsophisticated—a hopeless educational investment—to men of national and international experience."[16]

At the time, optimism ran unchecked. The yearbook for 1927 was called the *New Era Alfarata*. The Jubiliee Year, it proclaimed, heralded the dawn of a glorious epoch for Juniata. M. G. wrote a page-long piece for this issue captioned "The Outlook in the New Era." One paragraph read:

> Accepting the challenge of the times and the demands of every prophecy concerning the years ahead we shall enter upon a New Era of service to God and society, resolved to keep close the first things of the Soul and adjust ourselves as fully as may be to the needs of the age. We shall not give up God, the church, the Christocentral life. But we shall adjust our offerings to cover the needs of right ordered living in the years to be.

ADMINISTRATIVE ADVANCES

M. G. was not a vindictive man by nature, as his gubernatorial feud with Penrose had plainly illustrated. Theodore Roosevelt called him a "woolly little lamb" because of his noncombative spirit. But soon after returning to College Hill M. G. found himself carping privately about a few of the geriatric but powerful members of the trustee board. He looked upon them as obstructionists, holding him back. In a weak moment one day he remarked to his golf partner while playing the Huntingdon links: "What we need is a few deaths on campus."

He once heard from someone who knew about his feelings toward these men. In a letter this person derided them and their alter egos on the faculty as the self-appointed "official Juniata Company." What more his friend had to say did nothing to assuage M. G.'s resentment. The writer confided:

> I know how they howl like hyenas when you go fishing or golfing. They try to know how many cigars you smoke and it makes THEM sick. They consider

themselves saints and everybody else a sinner. I wonder how you hold them to
an even semi-modern program in the administration of affairs.[17]

Fortunately these tensions remained latent. The majority of trustees, if less vocal, gave M. G. no problems. In 1927 the death of Henry Gibbel put Joseph Oller into the chairmanship. There came onto the board during M. G.'s second term another contingent destined for long tenure. Pennsylvanians all, they were Lewis Knepper, who in 1926 had joined the administration as field secretary (1927–39); Mrs. Florence Gibbel, wife of Henry (1927–56); Lloyd Hartman of Mifflintown (1928–51); Albert Horner of Pittsburgh (1927–1955); and Ross Murphy of Shippensburg (1926–60).

Soon upon his permanent return to the Hill, M. G. began to remodel college governance. In 1925 he introduced the trustees to the niceties of a budget. The next year he brought in a business manager. Prior to 1919 it had been the steward who looked after the physical plant and the food service. Another administrative innovation came in 1927 when Dr. Fayette McKenzie was made dean of men. Ever since 1925 M. G. had been talking about the need for a "moral and religious counselor," who, though an academician, would seek to promote himself as the *fidus Achates* of male students. The women, of course, had Dean Roberts. Dr. McKenzie, a sociologist, had returned to Juniata upon leaving the presidency of Fisk University, a black college in Nashville, Tennessee. All things taken into account, the wiry Scotsman, known for his wry smile and athletic interests, was a natural choice for the deanship.

As for an academic dean, however, M. G. could see no purpose. He and Vice-President Ellis, who now had more administrative say, teamed up to oversee the curriculum and the faculty. But not everybody could accept this, and personal tragedy befell the campus. Dr. Alphaeus Dupler had been dean of Bridgewater College before rejoining his alma mater in 1919. At Juniata, as registrar and director of summer sessions under Harvey Brumbaugh, he did the work of an academic dean, if lacking the title. Denied the deanship he aspired to and losing his summer sessions post to Harvey, back from Columbia, the father of four children took his life in a backyard shed in June 1928.

ACADEMICS

By the late 1920s high schools, of which there were then about fifteen thousand in the nation, had become an accepted part of the public education system. But little had been done about investigating how well high-school students were prepared for college. Nor had there been much study made of curriculum development at the postsecondary level. This task the Carnegie Foundation for the Advancement of Teaching took upon itself in the spring of 1928. It administered an achievement test to seniors at all Pennsylvania colleges and universities. Juniata's group, the result showed, ranked well up the list, slightly above average (Haverford came out on top).[18]

Hilltoppers were pleased by this performance. They interpreted it as an indication the quality of education at Juniata had not degenerated despite a tripled enrollment in the last decade. This was four times the average growth for colleges of Pennsylvania. Even so, President M. G. expressed the desire in 1929, now that the school had attained its goal in numbers, to concentrate on raising standards of admissions. Meanwhile, in January of 1927, Juniata had received other good news. The Association of American Colleges, patron saint of liberal arts institutions founded in 1915, had bestowed its blessings upon the Hilltop school.

From statistics on grade distribution it would appear that their professors did not overly coddle the New Youth. A change in policy in 1926 set up six grades, A through F, with E being conditional. Report cards still went out at six-week intervals. The statistical picture at the end of the first marking period the fall of 1929 looked like this: A (7.3%); B (30.3%); C (39%); D (16.3%); E (3%); F (1.8%); Inc. (23%). The higher minimum passing grade for juniors and seniors went by the board in 1929. In February 1930 the faculty adopted the quality point system, effective in the fall, to complement grades in computing graduation qualifications.

Dean Katherine Roberts and Harvey Brumbaugh urged instituting a dean's list. They cited Yale, Harvard, Radcliffe, and Haverford as places where the practice had found favor. At Juniata, with no academic dean, such a scroll became the "honor roll" in March 1928. Fourteen students—but only one freshman—had attained an overall first semester average of A- or better. "Professor Harvey" also got, in the fall of 1929, faculty sanction for "honors" courses (independent research projects). On the negative side of the academic picture, cheating scandalized College Hill. New Youth leaders shed copious editorial tears over this student frailty in the campus paper. To them the honor system, their fond hope, seemed an ever-remote possibility. There was essentially little tampering with the main lineaments of the curriculum. Areas of concentration, though, did undergo a bit of juggling. Philosophy was dropped (1927), and sociology replaced social science (1928). Speech was listed as a major for two years (1927–29). So that science students could take four laboratory courses, the number of hours in a major field went from thirty to thirty-two.

In 1928 a B. S. degree in music became available. Approved by the State Council of Education, it took its place beside the B.Mus., which never got Harrisburg's official stamp. The music department's growth plus the need for more dormitory space necessitated removing the music studio and practice rooms from Brumbaugh Hall. Two houses were eventually put to the department's use, one at 1821 Moore Street in 1924 and another up the block (1908) in 1929.

Home economics barely escaped being abolished in 1924, its doom seemingly sealed by presidential-trustee concurrence that spring. Harvey Brumbaugh had been disappointed at the discipline's retarded growth on campus and so called for cutting it out as soon as practicable, to which the board took no exception. But M. G., once in office, raised the yellow flag. He hired Dorothy Sayer (Pentz), a Penn State graduate, in the fall, and she quickly turned the situation around. Her toil won departmental deliverance. In September 1927 the former Henry B. Brumbaugh dwelling was converted into the home economics "Practice House." By then the program's staff had grown to three. The Practice House shift released space in Science Hall, which the chemistry department promptly moved into, adding physical and quantitative laboratories.

Founding Brumbaugh trio, pictured in the winter of their lives: Dr. A. B. (left) and his cousins, brothers John and Henry, the latter becoming Juniata's second president, 1888–93.

Founding principal Jacob Zuck strikes a Napoleonic pose—in his pre-Huntingdon years as a public-school principal/teacher. He was wooing one of the ladies behind him. Her death crushed him; he never married.

Faculty in 1879. Zuck, cane in hand, had grown a beard and adopted a straight coat, the marks of a properly groomed Dunker. Next to him is Phebe Weakley, his first fellow-teacher. Behind her stands Jacob Brumbaugh and, in the middle, Emmert.

The beloved David Emmert, shown here with his parents and one of his sons. An accomplished artist, he was a professor of many hats: drawing, painting, botany, and biology. He inspired the idea of a local orphanage and later became a national figure in child-welfare reform. In 1901 he wrote his delightful Reminiscences of Juniata College.

Jacob Brumbaugh, brother of founder Dr. A. B., poses here with his wife and their son, Norman Jodan. After Zuck's untimely death in 1879, the father served as principal until Juniata became a full-fledged college in the mid-1890s. The college would later owe, in part, its national reputation in the sciences to the demanding standards of the son, whom chemistry students dubbed—but not always affectionately— "Dr. N. J."

Founders Hall, erected in 1879 and, until 1897, called "The Building." This early-years photograph shows a white picket fence, visible on the left and right, which divided the "boys" campus from the "girls" campus. The Orphans Home can be seen in the background, its origin the result of a college prayer meeting led by David Emmert.

Class of 1879, picturing Gaius Brumbaugh, son of Dr. A. B. and future long-time trustee chairman. Seated are Linnie Bosserman (Grigsby), left, and Phoebe R. Norris.

Juniata's first gymnasium nears completion, 1901. It was located in the solid white rectangle shown in the 1901 diagram of the campus. Until 1940 the college used it as an auditorium for cultural events. Later, the locker room was converted into a student center ("Totem Inn") and a post office.

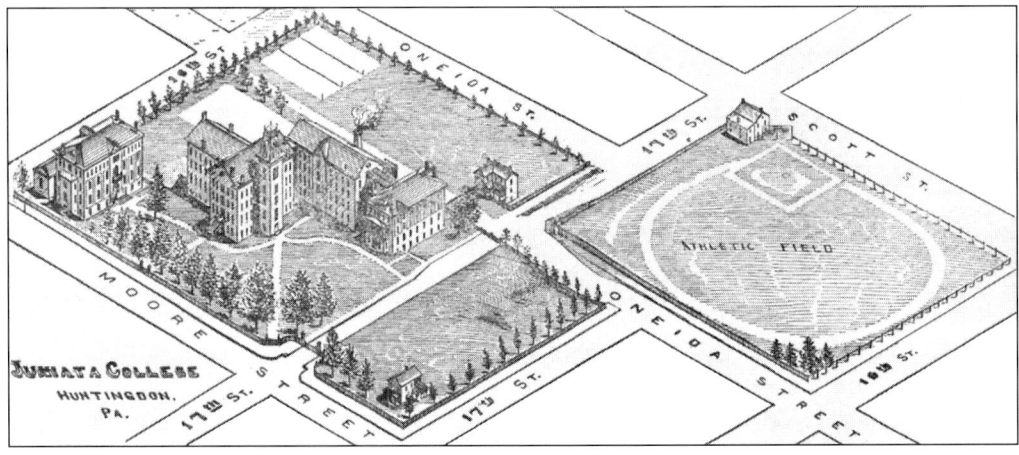

Catalog sketch of the campus, 1900. It shows three now-nonexistent buildings: Students Hall (on the left), the main academic building erected in 1895; Ladies Hall (later renamed Brumbaugh), annexed to Founders in 1890; and Oneida Hall, an 1898 extension. Both additions housed women (Founders, the men). First-floor Oneida became the college refectory. All three 1890s buildings, structurally unsafe, were razed in 1970.

All with beards take the front row! The faculty for 1907–08. The younger men have doffed the straight coat and shaved their chins.

James Quinter, first president, 1879–1880.

Alumnus M. G. Brumbaugh, third and fifth president, 1893–1910; 1924–30.

Alumnus Harvey Brumbaugh, son of founder and second president, Henry, fourth president, 1910–24.

Alumnus Charles Ellis (left), sixth president, 1930–43, passes college leadership to seventh president, alumnus son, Calvert, 1943–68. M. G. Brumbaugh, from a portrait of him while governor, 1915–1919, looks down upon the ceremonial handshake.

Alumnus John Stauffer, eighth— and first non-Brethren, non-cleric—president, 1968–1975.

Frederick Binder, ninth president, 1975–86.

Robert Neff—non-alumnus but Brethren minister— tenth president, 1986–98.

Thomas Kepple, Jr., eleventh president, 1998—present.

Harold ("H. B.") Brumbaugh, as he looked in his late seventies. He was a confidant to every president from Charles Ellis on, until his death in the millennial year. Over that six-decade span he emerged as a Juniata icon to alumni by the thousands.

The late William J. von Liebig, Juniata College's greatest benefactor to date. He made his fortune through the creation and production of textile devices used as grafts in cardiovascular surgery. The new Center for Science will honor his name.

A rendering of the 80,000-square-foot Center for Science.

A rendering of the Center for Entrepreneurial Leadership, to be located in the renovated current Brumbaugh Science Center.

A rendering of the Performing Arts Center, an addition to Oller Hall.

A rendering of Founders Hall after a planned renovation.

The millennial campus.

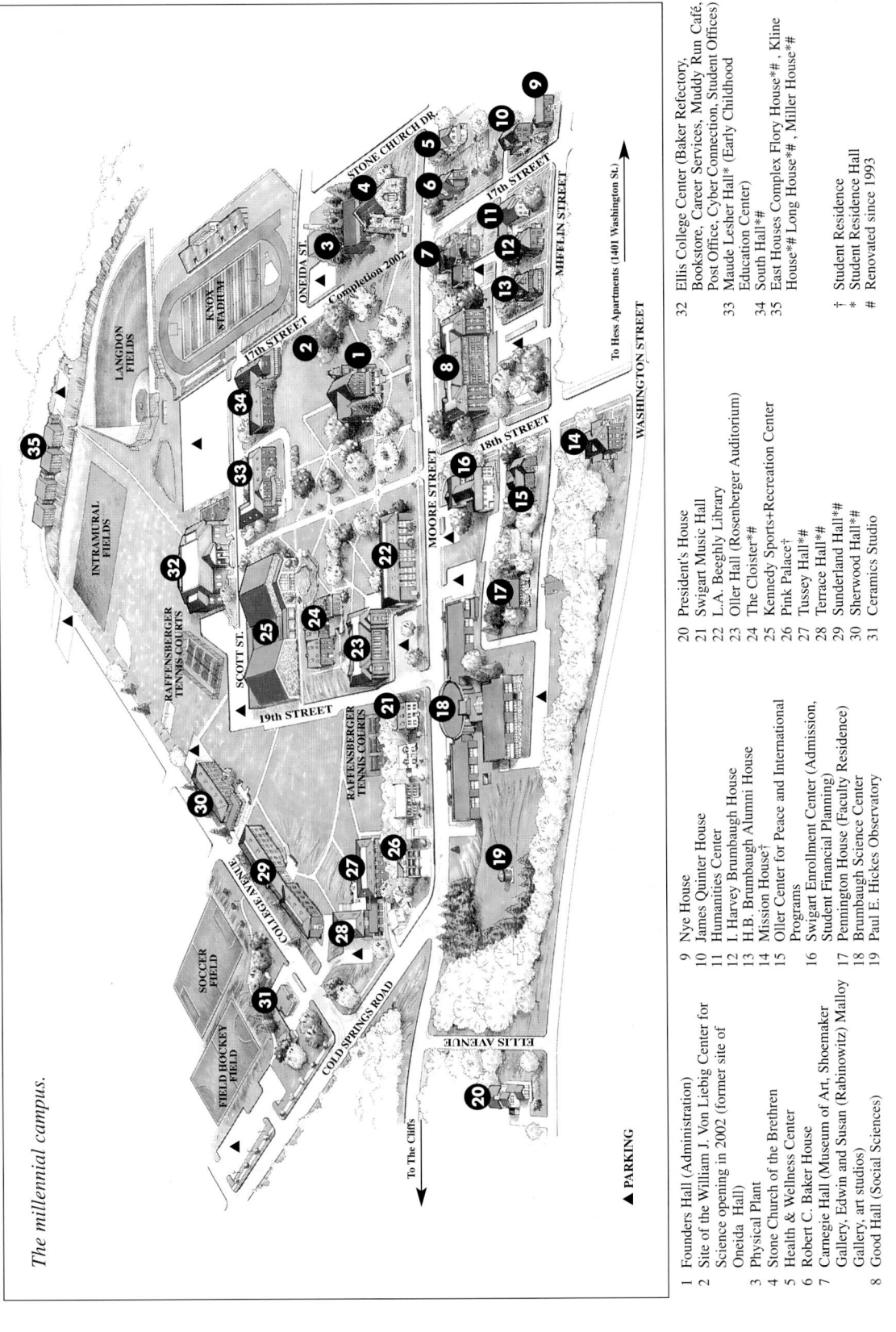

▲ PARKING

1 Founders Hall (Administration)
2 Site of the William J. Von Liebig Center for Science opening in 2002 (former site of Oneida Hall)
3 Physical Plant
4 Stone Church of the Brethren
5 Health & Wellness Center
6 Robert C. Baker House
7 Carnegie Hall (Museum of Art, Shoemaker Gallery, Edwin and Susan (Rabinowitz) Malloy Gallery, art studios)
8 Good Hall (Social Sciences)
9 Nye House
10 James Quinter House
11 Humanities Center
12 I. Harvey Brumbaugh House
13 H.B. Brumbaugh Alumni House
14 Mission House†
15 Oller Center for Peace and International Programs
16 Swigart Enrollment Center (Admission, Student Financial Planning)
17 Pennington House (Faculty Residence)
18 Brumbaugh Science Center
19 Paul E. Hickes Observatory
20 President's House
21 Swigart Music Hall
22 L.A. Beeghly Library
23 Oller Hall (Rosenberger Auditorium)
24 The Cloister*#
25 Kennedy Sports+Recreation Center
26 Pink Palace†
27 Tussey Hall*#
28 Terrace Hall*#
29 Sunderland Hall*#
30 Sherwood Hall*#
31 Ceramics Studio
32 Ellis College Center (Baker Refectory, Bookstore, Career Services, Muddy Run Café, Post Office, Cyber Connection, Student Offices)
33 Maude Lesher Hall* (Early Childhood Education Center)
34 South Hall*#
35 East Houses Complex Flory House*#, Kline House*# Long House*#, Miller House*#

† Student Residence
* Student Residence Hall
# Renovated since 1993

In May 1927 America had gone almost mad with joyful pride over the feat of a homespun, modest aviator named Charles Lindbergh, hero-conqueror of the Atlantic. The "Flying Colonel's" exploit was still the talk of Huntingdon when President M. G. went looking for someone to supervise Juniata seniors in their practice teaching. This search had been dictated by the Edmonds Act of 1921, which, as one provision for raising professional standards in the state, prescribed an apprenticeship for all aspiring high-school teachers. Before it closed in 1924 the Academy had afforded Juniatians convenient intern opportunities. But the placing of student teachers in the public system proved something of an administrative care. This was remedied in 1927 when Charles Smith, head of Mount Union schools, accepted the responsibility. Supervision finally reverted to the education department once and for all in 1933.

Pennsylvania's teacher-training program put the private college at a decided disadvantage. In 1926 the state transformed all the normal schools into teachers' colleges. As such, they received appropriations that covered the costs of engaging "critic" teachers as stipendiaries. Some independent colleges did not provide compensation, and it soon became evident that their students often got indifferent supervision as a result. For those institutions, like Juniata, which made recompense, students were penalized with an extra fee.

This whole matter became a great worry of the Association of College Presidents of Pennsylvania. For obvious reasons the Association turned to M. G., a member of its Legislative Committee, for a solution. He drafted a bill in the spring of 1929 that, if enacted, would have subsidized apprentice teaching for schools receiving no state aid. Backed by the Society of College Teachers of Education, it passed both houses of the General Assembly. But Governor John Fisher's veto signed the bill's death warrant, putting the issue permanently to rest. Not until 1958, when the all-inclusive fee went into effect, would Juniatians get exonerated from the student-teaching surcharge. (However, it was revived in 1976.)

The faculty initiated an on-campus night school during M. G.'s second presidency. Continuing education had been tried before, prior to the Great War. Evening classes were held in Altoona High School, but the experiment was short-lived.[19] Bible institutes, of course, dating to 1890, ended in 1915. Since 1919 the college had been conducting Bible institutes in local Brethren congregations in Pennsylvania. For a time (1923–25) a Religion Extension Service offered correspondence study with reasonably good results.

Then in February 1929 the Extension Department came about, thanks to an idea proposed by a college upperclassman.[20] Advance publicity called this local night-school initiative "Juniata's New Door of Opportunity." Classes met two nights a week on campus and tuition was fifteen dollars a semester, the same cost all Juniatians paid. Within another year the program had become extramural as well, with classes being held at outlying places within a fifty-mile radius. Business subjects came off as the most popular. Within a year's time adult education, both on and off campus, had fifty-seven names on its rolls (38 women, 19 men).

Sustenance for much of this New Era academic vigor flowed from a library in remarkable fettle. Since 1918 it had been the beat of alumna Lillian Evans, trained at

Drexel and Chicago. This gentle woman of quiet proficiency had practically doubled the number of holdings to forty-six thousand volumes within seven years. Among colleges and universities of the Commonwealth in the mid-Twenties, Juniata's library had risen to eleventh rank—"quite beyond," crowed President M. G., "what might be expected."[21]

NEW ERA FACULTY

By fall 1929, when the stock market went disastrously haywire, the faculty had grown to forty. Earned doctorates still numbered barely more than a half dozen. There were fourteen women, none of professorial rank. All but three were lowly instructors. Harvey Brumbaugh came back from his leave to teach Latin and education. His course, History and Trends of Education, became a perennial favorite with Juniata's future teachers.

New Era faculty recruits evidenced a liking for the Hill. Eleven of them put in stays of a decade or more. A half dozen taught between ten and sixteen years: Fayette McKenzie (sociology, 1925–41); Harold Conner (economics, 1924–37); May Keirns (Greek, 1929–41); Elmer Craik (history and government, 1924–36); Miriam Fackler (English, 1928–39); Harold Engle (biology, 1923–35). The other five had much longer careers, only one of them with a doctorate. Kansan Paul Yoder (1926–64) came from Maryland's Blue Ridge College. A physicist and Brethren preacher, he functioned as a one-man department for most of his career. From 1937 to 1944 he also directed summer school. Jack Oller (1928–65), son of trustee chairman Joseph, returned to his alma mater to teach French (and later Spanish). He became a European traveler and an ardent aficionado of varsity sports. From Canada came Margaret McCrimmon (1925–53), a Toronto native, to her first and only college teaching position. Another faculty habitué of Europe, the tiny linguist once said, "I always felt at home in the United States, but if I hadn't been so fond of Juniata I never would've stayed." Earl Dubbel (1926–54), a non-Brethren and barely five feet tall, brought solid Ivy League credentials (Harvard and Princeton). He became the Shakespearean of the English department. Norman Brumbaugh (1924–49), son of Jacob, failed his doctoral program at Harvard but redeemed himself at Penn in 1922. Dr. "N. J.," as students respectfully called him, never married. In the twenty-four years he was its head, the chemistry department rose to national prominence. Though a record-holder in track himself, he gave his sports-minded students no choice: it was either chemistry or athletics.

As yet, the faculty received no term contracts, only annual appointments. Norman Brumbaugh's reelection letter for 1930–31, stating a salary of $2,850, further read:

> It is understood that the faculty members are, in addition to the class work attendant upon election, to hold themselves ready at all times:
>
> First, to perform such services on Sunday in the Bible Classes as may be requested or assigned;
>
> Second, to assist the management in inculcating proper religious as well as educational standards in the College;

Third, not to be absent from class duties of the College without the knowledge and consent of the President;

Fourth, to attend all Faculty meetings unless excused for good reasons.[22]

Nor were sabbatical leaves then customary, though by 1929 President M. G. had pretty much wheedled the trustees into granting them. But his death and the deepening depression squelched any follow through. Nothing would be done about such a policy for another three decades or so.

LIFE AND DOINGS OF NEW ERA STUDENTS

"Huntingdon, Seat of Juniata College"—so two large signs, at either end of town, greeted tourists passing through on the William Penn Highway. Trustee Henry Gibbel had them put up in the fall of 1924. Countians still made up about one-fifth of the enrollment, most of them hailing from the county seat itself. Only a dozen or so out-of-staters set foot on campus each year. There was one overseas student, the first since before World War I, during the academic year 1925–26. He was Gisuke Kumada, a Japanese Christian. His wife died in March and he did not return the next fall.

In 1929 a year at Juniata cost, apart from laboratory fees, about $560. By then three local fraternal groups (Civic, Rotary, Elks) had swelled the number of loan funds available to deserving students. That of the Civicists was the largest of its kind in the Pennsylvania Federation of Clubs.

Commuting New Erans had it better than they could ever know considering the woeful lack of railway travel to and from College Hill in the millennium. Fourteen mainline PRR trains, eastbound, made daily stops at Huntingdon; this was two more than westbound ones. In addition the Huntingdon and Broad Top Railroad and the Petersburg branch of the "Pennsy" each provided passenger service twice a day.

Resident students, however, found their mobility somewhat checked. Night watchman John McCracken, "Mac" to decades of Juniatians, began his Cimmerian patrols in November 1924. The student government, taking alarm at "undesirable characters lurking around the dormitories," had asked for after-dark protection. The trustees complied, though as much concerned about enforcing campus regulations as ensuring campus safety. And so began the cat-and-mouse game—to last as long as a curfew obtained—between "Mac" and Juniata men. "Who is it?" he would call out of the darkness. At first he got in response all sorts of aliases, exploiting his naiveté. Early in the job he stopped William Shakespeare eight different times trying to sneak in late the same evening.[23] "Mac" was a much wiser night watchman after that. Because of him, few curfew breakers or other violators missed a next-morning presidential audience.

It soon became clear that M. G. was by nature no more of a nemesis to students than his cousin. He told the trustees in 1925: "I would much rather be an advisor to young men and women than the disciplinarian of defaulting students."[24] His letters to erring students were unfailingly tender, reflecting personal anguish over their misdeeds. They were liberally sprinkled with phrases like "pained me greatly"; "heartbroken"; "worried about it nearly all night." He wanted to be as open as possible with Juniatians. His initial months in office he held a series of give-and-take "chats" with sundry sectors of the student body. These presidential causeries sent campus morale skyrocketing.

Still, he had honest doubts about the effectiveness of student government. He said in 1927: "I am not sure yet whether it is the best method of disciplinary procedure." Sometimes, he feared, "this governing group fails to function wisely or even impartially."25 But he was far from ready to write it off, admitting: "Those governed by the Councils of the student body are for the most part amenable to their own government."

The councils were still bound by a Puritan-strict social code. Any open display of affection, no matter how innocent, rarely escaped an official reproof. M. G. wrote to one father in 1928: "Your daughter, throwing her arms around this boy in the public hall, was resented by every right thinking student." New Erans, however, won one concession: more room by several blocks for rambling off-campus. Now the ambulatory limits for dating couples stretched from the foot of Round Top over to the railroad, then down to Penn Street, and from there to Third, with Flag Pole Hill and the hospital the east-most bounds. Should they run into the president on their off-campus strolls, all students, the code specified, had to salute him by "tipping the hat."

To help orient Hilltop newcomers, the two Ys began to put out, in the fall of 1924, a pamphlet guide called the "Students Handbook." Two years later it was dubbed the "Scout" and, fabrikoid-covered, expanded to 152 pages. It was the bounden duty of freshmen to carry the "Scout" with them at all times, according to "frosh regs." Freshman intimidation was a New Era innovation. In the winter of 1925 the Men's Council formed a Tribunal of six seniors and five juniors. Their task was to cook up "customs" to impose upon first-year men. That February the "dink" (black with a green button on top) made its stigmatic appearance on the Hill.

How the Tribunal and upperclassmen lorded it over dink-pated frosh! Freshmen became the campus lackeys, at the beck and call of their superiors. They ushered, they worked on the athletic field, they raised and lowered the flag, they ran errands, they answered the telephone. They had to learn all college songs and yells, performing on the spot at the whim of any upperclassman. They had to attend all home athletic events and all mass meetings of the students, subject to roll call. No off-the-walk short cuts across campus for them. Freezing weather notwithstanding, they could not be seen in public with hands pocketed. They came last in all things—through doors, at the dining hall, at a table, in organizing as a class. The naïve fairly trembled at solemn-feigned Tribunal hearings. Punishment came in funny forms, though some felt humiliated by them. Men in skirts, glaring signs, and peanut-rolling episodes became familiar scenes of Tribunal justice at work.

Coed neophytes answered to the Women's Senior-Junior Court, a creature of 1926. Their badge of lowly status was a green band worn on the left arm. They, however, escaped the vassalage borne by men—except for reception room duty. But the keep-off-the-grass ban applied to them, as did memorizing songs and yells and compulsory attendance at certain functions. Unlike the men, first-year women got a helping hand, too. In 1926 the YWCA began to assign a "big sister" to each incoming freshman girl. The next year the administration pitched in to help with freshmen orientation days, the importance of which grew with the years.

Freshman customs, beginning with 1927, were removed each spring on Move-Up Day, the time for changing of the guard. Dropped in the early 1970s, this tradition issued from a March 1927 article in the campus paper. The article noted that "heretofore the transition from the old to the new has been uneventful" and called for much more "impressive" procedure. The paper's staff proposed a "brilliant occasion," about a month before commencement, "featuring installation ceremonies, public addresses, and athletic contest in the afternoon, an entertainment in the evening, and a general displaying of class banners, insignia, colors, and regalia." The plan got immediate support from students and faculty, cheered as "one more big step forward in Juniata's New Era program." The first Move-Up Day occurred on Thursday, May 12. One of its highlights was the groundbreaking ceremony for a new men's dormitory (the Cloister), in which each class had a hand with the shovel.

New Erans also pioneered the fall retreats, which in time developed into the student leadership conferences of the next half-century. In 1927 the two Ys, at the suggestion of the Stone Church pastor, Foster Statler, sponsored a student retreat a few days prior to the opening of college. It was held at Camp Myler, a Baptist-owned conference site near the breast of the Raystown Dam, where for a number of years the fall retreaters regularly gathered. Originally the emphasis of these "Camp Myler" conferences, as they were called, was religious. But in the 1930s they became two- or three-day diets when student leaders and faculty consultants, under Senate auspices, spent their time goal-setting for the year ahead.

With the New Era came a weekly campus paper: the *Juniatian*. The Press Club had begun to plump for a weekly in the fall of 1923 and circulated a questionnaire among alumni and students. The results gave proof of near-unanimous favor. But the administration expressed its fear that anything less than a monthly could not survive on a subscription basis. Student opinion finally prevailed.

The curtain number of the *Juniata Echo*, which had held sway for thirty-four years, came out in October 1924. The maiden issue of the *Juniatian* appeared on November 6. In its first year the *Juniatian*, which by May 1925 merited membership in the Intercollegiate Newspaper Association of the Mid-Atlantic States, claimed a circulation of about 550. Then, beginning in 1926, it was included as part of the incidental fees, which gave it financial stability. In another couple years the campus weekly would build up a readership of over 1,225.

A humor column, "The Tommyhawk," cropped up front page of the *Juniatian* on April 7, 1927. "Tommy Hawk" himself always remained anonymous until staff turnover on Move-Up Day. Nothing was too sacrosanct for his barbed banter. Only in 1926 did the fourth estate acquire its own much-needed inner sanctum on campus. It set up editorial offices in one of the basement rooms of Students Hall. There staffers of the *Juniatian* and *Alfarata* mingled with Press Club reporters.

Clubbing, meanwhile, as organized under the Lyceum, fell apart during the New Era generation. Of the five original interest groups, only two were still active the fall of 1926. And even the parent organization itself came to an end that September.

The *Juniatian* spoke out for recasting the decadent Lyceum system, which was purely literary in purpose, into one more conducive to relaxed sociality. It outlined a scheme that dissolved the old clubs and had the new ones take Greek letters or Indian names. There was the suggestion to keep each coterie small and intimate (twenty-five to thirty members).

The *Juniatian*'s ten-point reform plan won quick approbation as "another New Era project." Over the next three years it gave rise to the Alpha Club, Arts Club, Sigma Delta Club, Tapitawe Club, Le Cercle Francais, Chemical Colloquium, Home Economics Club, X Club (feminine fencing), Classical Club, Beta Tau Kappa, Ministerium, and Freshman Club. The two Ys and the Student Volunteer Group remained solidly entrenched, as did the dual glee clubs.

Another spawn of the "new Era project" was the Dramatic Club, redenominated the Masquers in 1927. It debuted early in the Jubilee Year with James Barrie's *Quality of Life*. Juniata thespians in 1927 began to compete in the Pennsylvania State Intercollegiate Dramatic Association contests, besides staging two or three plays on campus each year.

In December 1928 the Press Club renamed itself the Juniata College Press Association, to distinguish it from the social clubs. Its reportage now fell under the journalistic eye of the college's director of publicity. More than a hundred papers in four states and the District of Columbia received news releases. The JCPA was then the sole avenue to the *Juniatian* staff.

New Era debate, editorialized the campus weekly in 1927, was still "big time." The Jubilee Year enhanced its status as a major sport when it, like the *Juniatian*, was budgeted under incidental fees. In May 1927 Juniata got a chapter of Tau Kappa Alpha, the National Honorary Forensic Society, then with some sixty active locals. TKA thereafter assumed sponsorship of Juniata debate and oratory. The 1927–28 men's team argued its way to an impressive 12-3 record. The women sat it out that year, but they were back for the next debating season.

Oratory, debate's kin, enjoyed a kind of varsity status, too. Hilltop Ciceros, after persistent efforts, made the Eastern Pennsylvania Intercollegiate Oratorical Union in January 1927. Seven colleges, among them Penn, competed in the Union's annual tilt of words. There were also Blue and Gold entries in the National Contest on the Constitution each year. Likewise, Juniata orators participated annually in the World Peace Contest conducted by the Brethren colleges, the finals an Annual Conference event. At the intramural level, extempory speaking joined the John M. Bailey oratorical contest in 1926 as a second exhibition of declamation. Edgar Diehm established it as a prize-bearing memorial to his mother, Emma.

Instrumental music took new life and became notably popular among New Erans. About a fourth of them became involved in it for sheer pleasure, not credit. The orchestra, which had died out after Peter Buy's leave-taking back in 1919, revived in 1924 under Mrs. Mary Douthett-Deskey, the pupil of Leopold Godowsky. (Her husband, Donald Deskey, taught art at Juniata for two years, 1923–24, and later made quite a name for himself as an interior decorator. He designed John D. Rockefeller, Jr.'s home and New York City's Radio City Music Hall.)

Dr. Norman Brumbaugh became the orchestra's oboist and patron upon his return in 1925. (He invested over $1,540 of his own money in the orchestra by 1928.)

Instruments were privately owned or donated until N. J. importuned the president, in 1928, for college funding. M. G. came up with nine hundred dollars, justifying this outlay to the trustees by pointing out that the orchestra "directs the interests of all students to the right kind of music." Then came the punch line: "By the same token it discourages a liking for trashy jazz and dance music." In 1930 Conductor Karl Gilbert's (1927–37) orchestral group numbered in the forties and would stay at that number for some time to come.

"Trashy jazz," however, suffered no student neglect. A band in 1929, calling itself Kappa Phi Psi, specialized in the genre so popular everywhere during the Twenties. And "Klarinet" Tom Knepp, Juniata's answer to Rudy Valee, led another oft-scheduled troupe of jazz musicians.

Glee singers continued to make close harmony during the New Era. For many years the Men's Glee Club had featured a quartet, which in 1925 struck out on its own as the Varsity Four. The quartet gave independent programs and made special appearances. Not to be outdone, the Girl's Glee Club delivered its skirted version of four-voice parts the next year. Quartets, his and hers, remained fixtures on campus long after the 1920s.

Spiritual Emphasis Week was another New Era phenomenon. After three decades the special Bible session, which had once exerted a strong stimulus to campus religious life, gave its death rattle in December 1925. Its original purpose, an exercise in adult education, was now being served by the college in other off-campus ways. Moreover, its relevance had been lost on most students of that generation.

The Bible session's reincarnation as a more student-oriented spiritual experience—with messages on timely topics and opportunity for personal counseling—came about through a five-thousand-dollar gift by Mrs. May Oller Wertz of Waynesboro. It funded bringing in "recognized" clergymen and scholars able to relate to college youth. Dr. Andrew Mutch, M. G.'s Scottish friend and pastor of the Bryn Mawr Presbyterian Church, inaugurated the new approach, which, as Spiritual Emphasis Week, remained a regular campus event for the next forty years.

Men of the public press provided brainy New Erans with out-of-class sport befitting their intellect and abilities. Joseph Biddle, publisher of Huntingdon County's first daily newspaper, rescued the General Information Test in 1928 when the death of its previous patron threatened its cancellation. Biddle endowed the contest "to stimulate general reading and impress the importance of knowledge outside the curriculum." And President M. G.'s friend Edward Stackpole, owner of the *Harrisburg Telegraph*, set up an annual prize for the best student essay on the history and development of the Juniata Valley. Essayists locked pens for the prize until the early 1960s.

All the while, the "Gin and Jazz Age" confirmed college authorities in their desire to turn out a different brand of American. "Chivalrous Manhood, Womanly Deportment and Public Decorum"—these were Juniata's ideals of character and conduct, the catalog proclaimed in bold print. Certain prizes sought to uphold these qualities among Hilltop denizens. One of them, in memory of Justina Marstellar Langdon, was established in 1927, and went to "that girl in the College who best exemplified the spirit of helpfulness to others, gentleness of character and loyal devotion to the College." Another one, a 1928 memorial to Huntingdon's George Warfel, recognized two students, a coed and a fellow, who "give the best expressions of the grace of obedience as a fundamental virtue in religion, social life and business activities." (Langdon prize is current, but the Warfel prize ended with 1932.)

And, of course, for New Era conviviality there was always the College Inn a few doors downstreet—"Skip's" to all generations of Juniatians who crowded its compact interior. The first "Skipper" was Edward Gutshall, whose just-off-campus combination grocery store and snack shop had a mid-1920s opening. He had once been a conductor of the "Toonerville Trolley," hence his nickname and that of his café. Among the male habitués of Skip's Inn, Greta Garbo was by actual poll their favorite Hollywood pin-up actress.

The last four years of the New Era brought women the news (1926) they could join the American Association of University Women upon graduating. Those years also introduced a college ring (1928). Next year's seniors ordered what became the standard design for some while—blue cut stone with a Roman gold shank, an Indian head on one side and class numerals on the other.

NEW ERA ATHLETICS AND THE JUNIATA "INDIANS"

It was the Alumni Association that called for an Athletic Board of Control (ABC) representing the various Juniata constituencies interested in its sports program. This idea was adopted in the fall of 1928. The first seven-member board comprised the president, two faculty members, the football coach, an alumnus, and a student. These men passed on the intercollegiate schedule (student managers still did the scheduling for each sport) and framed athletic policies. (The ABC dissolved after World War II.)

The ABC made Lehigh University graduate Chester Langdon, the local leader of the Greater Juniata Campaign, an honorary member. Everybody on College Hill knew of his rabid interest in Juniata's sports program. The 1930 *Alfarata* was dedicated to him, "in truth, a loyal Juniatian." For many he symbolized the progressive ideal set for New Era athletics. His father, John, left the college ten thousand dollars for a new athletic field in late 1928. M. G. had gone on record the previous year for redeveloping the old playing site into a park and a residential area for college families. He envisioned Langdon Field being located on the north campus in the little hollow back of the new dormitory.

Son Chester put a Philadelphia architect to work at once. The plan was to fill in the hollow, which was started, and allow it to settle for several years. But then the Depression came along and the project was abandoned. The Langdon money, however, was kept on the books as a segregated fund. The original sum would grow sevenfold by the time Langdon Baseball Field materialized in 1963.

"Athletics for all" became the New Era slogan of the revitalized physical education department. The first full-time woman in the department was hired in 1927 (there had been part-time female directors since 1924). Another addition to the gymnasium in 1928, for coaching staff offices, brought the structure to its final size.

An extensive intramural program, both for men and women, now went into operation, built upon class rivalry. Through interclass sports—softball, basketball, hockey, soccer, track, volleyball—coeds had a chance to win their **J**. A Women's **J** Club had organized in the spring of 1926 when basketball and hiking were the only athletic outlets for the campus belles. Six hundred miles a year of hiking, a club sport beginning in 1925, earned a coed her Old English **J**.

Pre-New Era varsity teams had no mascot; they were simply the "Blue and Gold." Then in the spring of 1925 the *Juniatian* came up with the sobriquet "Indian." It was headlined in an article (April 9) about the opening game of the baseball season with Penn State. The Juniata nine were "Indians" the rest of the schedule. Who on the *Juniatian* staff thought up the nickname remains a mystery. It stuck in the fall in the paper's coverage of gridiron play, and "Indians" it was until the mid-1990s.

In football New Era Indians were not always the most fearsome. They were victoryless from October 11, 1924, to November 5, 1927 (though two ties). Who could blame the trustees for wailing that football "with all its disasters, losses, and problems…is…most perplexing for the college"?[26] Overall, the New Era gridders won 11 and lost 36 (1924–29), including no victories in 1925 and 1926. Their 5-3 season in 1929 stood out as the best won-lost log for the next eight years. And theirs was the only Indian eleven until 1948 to register four straight wins in a single season.

From the start football players had been honored each year by a YMCA-sponsored banquet for them. The Jubilee Year brought recognition to the sport in a very special way, President M. G. the instigator. He got Dr. and Mrs. Thaddeus Hyatt of Brooklyn, New York, "two very dear friends" of his, to furnish a trophy—a silver cup—to go each year to the student who excelled in three areas: "football, scholarship and character." Presidentially ordained, this award never lacked for prestige among the non-athletic ones. Stellar student-athletes of the gridiron would win the trophy each spring until World War II.

In retrospect, the New Era shines forth as a golden age in Hilltop field and track. Men of spiked shoes twenty-five times eclipsed standing college marks and bettered conference records in five events. Alden Holsinger (high hurdles, javelin, discus, shotput) was a four-time conference record-setter. His exploits in the 1928 Central Pennsylvania Intercollegiate Meet (CPIM) at Bucknell had all the glamour of a Frank Merriwell performance. Holsinger, thrice team captain, reset three CPIM records and one Juniata record, winning four first places and two thirds. (He also played football and captained the 1930 baseball team.)

The undefeated 1927 trackmen did their part to fill the trophy case Chester Langdon had recently donated. They were winners at the Penn Relays in April, not the last time Juniata spikemen would break the tape first in the City of Brotherly Love. In a downpour and ankle-deep mud, Juniata's "four horsemen"—Captain Harry Trout, Edward Apel, Ralph Leiter, Harry Bower—splashed to a sloggy victory. The college got a handsome bronze trophy, the fellows each a gold wristwatch. Two weeks later at Muhlenburg the team won the CPIM Class B trophy for the third consecutive year, which made the Blue and Gold its owners.

On a seasonal basis, New Era basketball broke even—three winners (1924–27) and three losers (1927–30). The 1924–25 team had the most wins, with a 9-6 mark. "Big, fast, smart and well-coached," was the *Pittsburgh Post*'s description of the Indians that year. The paper said further: "Few college teams have played in Pittsburgh this year that are better than Juniata."

Indian maidens, meanwhile, compiled a 12-19 six-year roundball won-lost record. The winning teams were in 1928 (4-2) and 1929 (3-2). For a couple years coed hardcourters were treated to a training table. The faculty, quite evidently, was no respecter of gender; more than one lady tosser ran afoul of academic probation.

New Era baseball won 49 and lost 42 but enjoyed only two winning seasons, 1926 and 1930. The worst won-lost record was in 1927 (4-9). The 1930 Indians went 13-2, making them, by the *Alfarata*'s rating system, "undisputed champions of the colleges of the Keystone State." Each player on the 1930 team wore a black band on the left sleeve of his uniform, mourning the preseason death of Dr. M. G.

Tennis, lamented the 1925 *Alfarata*, "is one sport on the decline at Juniata." Yet its overall six-year tally of fourteen wins and twenty-one losses was creditable enough. Curiously, the New Era netmen registered thirteen ties. For varsity and general Hilltop use, eight tennis courts served the campus by 1929.

NEW ERA CAMPUS LOOK

New Era dreams produced few direct physical changes on the Hill. Some alterations were minor but fraught with sentiment. A clock replaced the circular window on the front of Founders Hall: a gift from the Class of 1925. The Orphanage, an eyesore and standing less than a stone's throw from the Cloister Arch, came down the fall of 1929.

Other advances were of greater moment. Foresightedly, the trustees annexed more land adjacent to the campus. The purchase of three large tracts of ground netted seventeen acres, pushing Juniata real estate northward to Cold Springs Road and eastward to Warm Springs Avenue. These additions created an entire campus of slightly more than forty acres by 1926. It was necessary for the borough to close and cede to the college certain streets and alleys on these undeveloped properties.

Also, there was some college-related construction: a triad of building. But only one had a main-campus setting. Two were independently financed, and one of these had strings attached. First in order was the Mission Home, erected in 1925. Trustee Ardie Wilt, an Altoona businessman, popularized the idea of making Juniata a rent-free habitation for missionaries on furlough. He got the Brethren Sunday schools of Central Pennsylvania to raise twenty thousand dollars for that purpose. They built a two-story, brick-veneered, forty-eight-foot structure, which was then turned over to the college, owner of its corner site at Washington and 18th streets. When not occupied by missionaries, the four-room apartments, two on each floor, were rented out to married students or faculty families. One of the second-floor apartments became President M. G.'s home in 1924.

The Cloister came next, in 1928, the lone brick-and-mortar monument to the New Era's Golden Jubilee Campaign. At a cost of just over $140,000, it was designed to take care of 102 students. The architect was Edwin Brumbaugh, who enjoyed great success with his original interpretations of the German colonial style. He patterned the structure on the famous Ephrata Cloister in Lancaster, but with a brick exterior. M. G. said of his son's campus masterpiece: "There is nothing like it in college architecture in America. It will be distinctive of Juniata."[27] Until 1933, however, the Cloister, projected as part of a quadrangle in a new complex of buildings, had no name. It was simply "The Men's Dormitory" to everybody. The new men's residence released all of third floor Students Hall for academic use, the space remodeled into four large classrooms.

A President's House came last, but not for total college use until very recently. M. G., as a Mission Home occupant, found himself greatly handicapped in entertaining wealthy and politically high-placed friends he brought to campus, a fact he brought to trustee attention as early as December 1924. The board, sympathetic, commissioned Edwin Brumbaugh to prepare plans. But when estimates of construction costs proved excessive (over $30,000), nobody, including M. G., voted to go ahead.

The board, hesitant to incur a heavy mortgage, debated other housing options over the next several years. Finally M. G. took matters into his own hands. He put up twenty-eight thousand dollars and Joseph Oller twelve thousand, both gifts in the form of low-interest annuities. The college, which then assumed the mortgage for the house, donated three lots on the corner of Mifflin and 18th streets. Edwin Brumbaugh drew the plans, modeling them after the architecture of the Cloister. Finished the spring of 1930, the duplex (at a cost of $47,000) was planned with two separate entrances, one for each street. The Brumbaughs, as renters, would live upstairs, Prof. Jack Oller and his wife, downstairs. The house, however, was to revert to the college when the last of the original occupants was gone.

ALUMNI AND THE NEW ERA

At long last, in 1927, the alumni got a full-time secretary. In other developments a 1928 constitutional amendment made all nongraduate Juniatians eligible for association membership. And by 1930 two more cities were hosting alumni chapters: Harrisburg and New York. Several new countywide groups had New Era origins: Bedford, Blair, Cambria, and Huntingdon.

Out of the New Era came the Women's League of Juniata College, initially a quasi-alumnae organization. Mrs. Bunn van Ormer, who had been president of a similar college sorority, sparked its rise. The first League formed in trustee Bessie Rohrer's Waynesboro, Pennsylvania, home on April 14, 1928. Others would spring up at similarly strong alumni centers, all in Pennsylvania. These leagues, generous in college support, were products of the next decade. A Central Women's League was still twenty years away.

M. G.'S DEATH

Juniata's New Era president was going full stride as the 1930s came on. Outside honors still came his way despite his advanced age. He was state chairman of the Christmas Seal Campaign in 1928 and 1929. The latter year fellow presidents of Pennsylvania colleges elected him head of their association. When he died he had his heart set—even at age sixty-seven—on becoming State Superintendent of Public Instruction. He thought his friend Francis Brown, who had promised him the post, would be the next governor, but Brown lost to Gifford Pinchot in the Republican primaries.[28] The trustees had no idea what the president had in mind.

The first week of March 1930, M. G., after a thorough physical checkup, left for a vacation at Pinehurst, North Carolina, a mecca for golf enthusiasts where he was a familiar figure. He had suffered angina attacks for some time, but only a few of his friends knew this. On Friday afternoon the 14th he collapsed on the Country Club links at Pinehurst just after playing the eighth tee. He was taken to the clubhouse and then to the Carolina Hotel where he died at 1:30 P. M. M. G.'s body arrived at Huntingdon the next day. All college functions were suspended until after the funeral, Tuesday the 12th. The sudden loss of their beloved "Prexy" stunned the campus community. Samuel King, a future internist, had stayed on to teach chemistry before finishing his medical degree at the University of Chicago. He kept a diary in his early life, and it tells in poignant words his own deep sorrow, and that of the campus, the "solemn weekend" of Dr. M. G.'s death.[29] A more apt epitaph could not have been indited than the one penned in King's diary:

> I write all this about Martin Grove Brumbaugh because he is a true representation of the American ideal where a lad's initiative takes him from the humblest of circumstances through the help of Providence to real achievement and right living.

M. G. Brumbaugh died before he had a chance to move into the new residence he helped pay for. His interment took place at the original Brumbaugh homestead on a hilltop family cemetery near Marklesburg.

Chapter 10

SURVIVING THE DEPRESSION: 1930–1943

CHARLES CALVERT ELLIS: JUNIATA'S "ARNOLD OF RUGBY"

On Founders Day 1930 Deems Taylor, internationally famed composer whose father had once taught at Juniata (1880–81), was to have spoken and received an honorary degree. But M. G.'s sudden death so close to the event caused the trustees to cancel all arrangements. They met instead that day to name the next president.

Theirs was an obvious choice: Juniata's own vice-president. Dr. Ellis had been associated with the college almost uninterruptedly for forty-two years, ever since he first came as a student in 1888. Thirteen years vice-president, he was at the time probably peerless in Brethren higher education. As an educator, writer, and speaker his reputation ranged far beyond the Brotherhood. He was "long ripe for the presidency," declared Dr. Frank Graves, New York State Commissioner of Education, at inaugural ceremonies in October.

All Juniatians—and Brethren—knew him as "C. C." With his promotion the thirty-seven-year-long Brumbaugh dynasty came to an end. Over the thirty-eight ensuing years the Ellises—father and son—would make their family name respected in Juniata's annals of presidential succession. It was the father's lot, however, to steer the college through thirteen difficult years not only in *its* history, but in that of the nation.

At fifty-five, Dr. C. C., trim and distinguished-looking, was an unassuming man, though somewhat stern, who wore pinch-nose eyeglasses and high celluloid shirt collars. Husky-voiced, he had a throaty, infectious chuckle and, as a platform orator, was a master storyteller. The Chautauqua circuit and teachers' institutes, where he had been a sought-after name, would now occupy less of his time. Initially, though, his four-thousand-dollar president's salary meant a reduction in personal income, which before had been inflated by lecture fees.

Juniata's fifth president, like a true heir of classical Protestantism, believed in Luther's doctrine of vocation—that God "calls" Christians to particular tasks. Accordingly he put a theological interpretation upon the honor paid him by the trustees. In a letter to them upon his preferment he wrote: "I accept it as a call of duty to a service for our common Lord."[1] This notion of his presidency as one of divine trust came out again when he was formally inducted. He said, in the course of his brief remarks: "I accept this position as a God-given responsibility for which I shall expect to answer to Him in the coming Day, and with the hope that in His Providence I may find at the end of the way also a bit of reward for a duty at least faithfully undertaken."

On his desk, the new incumbent told inaugural-day well-wishers, he had placed the picture of Thomas Arnold, the mid-nineteenth-century headmaster of Rugby School in England. Dr. Ellis liked to identify the English educator, whom he had made the subject of one of his most popular Chautauqua lectures, as his "pedagogical patron saint." On Arnold's picture there was an inscription, which C. C. publicly vowed, would constitute his presidential motto. It read: "God grant that I labor with entire confidence in Him and none in myself without Him."

C. C.'S DESIGN FOR JUNIATA

In a real sense, then, Dr. Ellis conceived his presidency as inherently a divine commission. There was about his regime, as a result, always a certain note of urgency. He once said, "The consistent aim of this administration has been to justify to our friends and to all who learn of Juniata the term 'Christian College,' a designation for which we make no apology."[2] Upon becoming president he inserted a strong catalog statement that affirmed: "The college is distinctively Christian in spirit and teaching, emphasizing the beliefs and the ideals of character and conduct which are presented in the Bible." And to the trustees he gave the assurance early on that "the College is making a wider appeal to Christian people than [ever] before." The faculty continued to be selectively recruited from "Evangelical denominations," to use C. C.'s terminology, and from among candidates who were "active Christians" committed to the "fundamentals." Indeed, Juniata had the "right to expect…by virtue of her history as by the inevitable logic of events," the preacher-president declared one time, a teaching force of such character.[3]

As a "Christian College," Juniata justified its existence, Dr. C. C. was wont to say, only when engaged in shaping the character of students. Scholarship, though important, was not enough. Paraphrasing the Harvard naturalist Louis Agassiz, another of his teacher-models, he wrote while a novice president: "Laboratory and library, dormitory and dining hall, must not be strangers to the wholesale happiness of life that is unashamed to acknowledge God."[4] And when retired he said retrospectively of his hegemonic years: "May I make emphatic the fact that, whatever her shortcomings or the failures of individuals, Juniata has not been guilty of the impossible divorcement of Christian morality from the Christian religion."5

The all-vital factor in character building, ran the Ellis refrain, was the teacher. In a 1937 article for the journal *Christian Education*, President C. C. declaimed: "To conserve the permanent values we need more than scientific procedures and more than social goals; we need teachers whose faces are toward the light and whose feet are moving toward the goals of God."6 At Juniata he wanted professors to be an Agassiz, seeing God in the laboratory, or a Thomas Arnold, seeing Him in history. As one faculty member, a refugee from Hitlerian Germany, learned when called on the presidential carpet, even mild expletives like "damn" or "hell" were not then a public part of Hilltop vocabulary.

Free inquiry as an academic exercise and right was thus no more countenanced under Charles Ellis than it had been before. In Bible courses, for example, the methodology and theories of "higher criticism"—the scientific analysis of vocabulary, style, and historical allusions as a means of determining the authorship and composition of biblical books—were anathema. Any book or article questioning the uniqueness of Christ was banned from reading lists. A student in one of Dr. Ellis's own Bible courses who might raise a touchy, unorthodox point would get a piercing look from the man and this stock reproof: "Doesn't the love of Christ constrain you?" It was a shattering retort for most unsure Juniata skeptics.

Yet among the science faculty Dr. Ellis, a creationist by persuasion, made little attempt to muzzle the evolutionists. As a conservative-fundamentalist theologian he resisted, of course, the conclusions and implications of Darwinian biology because they seemed to strike at the very root of a biblically grounded faith. And as president he took a proprietary interest in what students were assigned to read on the subject of evolution. Thus when asked for an official statement from an irate alumnus or elder, he would always insist Juniata stood for creationism.

But C. C. was not ignorant of efforts on the part of evolutionists since long before the Thirties to harmonize their doctrine with the tenets of Christianity. Some of them were Bible scholars he respected, who saw no reason why creation as described in Genesis should be regarded as inconsistent with developmental theories. The *Sunday School Times*, in a necrological notice on his death in 1950, stated well his position on the historic tensions between science and religion. The paper said: "[He] sought never to compromise on the fundamentals of the faith, holding that although theories of science and religion may sometimes conflict, true science is in accord with the Bible, which is the unshakable and unchangeable Word of God."7

Though Dr. C. C. wanted the term "Christian College" to be Juniata's trademark, he never meant to disavow or play down the college's Brethren ties. In fact, no Hilltop president up to his time was more honored in the Brotherhood or gave greater service to the church than he. He was three times moderator of Annual Conference—1933, 1944, and 1950; only a handful of twentieth-century Brethren have been as often elected to that office. For several years he was a director of Bethany Biblical Seminary.

Most importantly, though, all through the Thirties decade he served as chairman of the denomination's General Education Board. During that time he did much to help unify the work of the then seven Brethren colleges. The Education Board under his chairmanship authorized an in-depth survey of these colleges by the executive secretary of the Association of American Colleges, Dr. Robert Kelly. The Kelly Report, published in 1933, "became a distinct stimulus to college improvement in the entire brotherhood," wrote Dr. Ellis in his 1947 Juniata history.[8] The college's raison d'etre, the Kelly Report quoted its president as saying, was "service to the Brethren Church" and "middle-class folk."

On the strictly academic side Dr. Ellis's proudest moment as president came in November 1940. At the chapel program on Wednesday the 27th, he said, "I am about to make the most important announcement I have ever made to any student body of Juniata College."[9] He then revealed that he had just received word of the school's recognition by the Association of American Universities, the highest accrediting agency in the United States. (The AAU discontinued its evaluation of undergraduate institutions in 1948.)

This had been his professed presidential goal since taking office. The decade-long dream, in unfolding, produced a fresh, imaginative curriculum, the strongest Hilltop faculty up till then, and sent more students off to graduate and professional schools than ever before. Juniata was the only Brethren college to be approved by the AAU. In 1940 less than one-third of Pennsylvania colleges had yet made its accepted list.

Then in 1942 the chemistry program brought the sanction of the American Chemical Society (ACS), adding another feather to Juniata's academic cap. Juniata was one of the first small colleges in the nation to make the society's list and as late as 1949 there were only sixteen of seventy Pennsylvania colleges and universities on it. By the time the elder Ellis made way for the younger the college had become well certificated. Besides having the approbation of the AAU and the ACS and being accredited by Middle States, the college was recognized by the Pennsylvania State Council of Education, the Pennsylvania Board of Law Examiners, the Board of Regents of the University of the State of New York, and the American Medical Association. Since the 1920s it also held membership in the American Association of Colleges. And in 1940 Juniata linked up with the American Council on Education, the principal coordinating organization for higher education in this country.

Juniata and the Church of the Brethren were not the only concerns of Dr. Ellis while president. He also wrestled with education problems facing the state of Pennsylvania. In 1931 the Superintendent of Public Instruction named him to a commission charged with the responsibility of developing a ten-year program for public education. This appointment lasted until 1935. From 1939 to 1943 he served on another Department of Public Instruction task force. His committee work over those years was largely devoted to the study of ways to improve the professional training and standing of Keystone State teachers. One noteworthy gain in this area as a result was a Teachers' Tenure Law in 1937 (amended in 1939) that assured a teacher, after a two-year probationary period, of a continuing position from which there could be removal only for cause.

For the year 1936–37 Dr. Ellis was elected head of the College Presidents Association of Pennsylvania, the organization of liberal arts colleges. This office thrust him right into the thick of the fight to guarantee a place for such colleges in the educational picture of the state. At that time there were fifty-seven accredited colleges and universities in Pennsylvania with approximately fifty-eight thousand students enrolled. Slightly less than ten thousand of these students were to be found at state teachers' colleges, of which there were fourteen. Lobbyists for this segment of higher education began to make ominous noises in the legislature, pushing to restrict teacher preparation in Pennsylvania to the fourteen tax-supported institutions.

Liberal arts colleges took alarm. Such an eventuality would deprive them of an educational enterprise intrinsically a part of their historical baggage. Their distinctive contribution in schooling teachers, it was argued, had always been one of a broad, cultural nature. By contrast the state teachers' colleges were perceived as being avowedly professional schools. Liberal arts colleges, the argument went, have given the prospective teacher an opportunity to wait, to weigh, to measure, to form a ripened judgment before deciding upon a profession.

Moreover, there was real fear, with a worsening depression, that eliminating their education programs would kill off or seriously cripple not a few struggling private colleges. To meet the competition and the threat posed by the erstwhile normal schools, heads of thirty-two privately supported institutions banded together in the Pennsylvania Association of Liberal Arts Colleges for the Advancement of Teaching. The association took the stand that preparation of secondary teachers should be left to their people, conceding the training of grade teachers to the state colleges. It further held that teacher programs in special fields, like music, home economics, commercial education, industrial arts, physical education, and art, should be given in institutions especially qualified for that work, as authorized by the State Council of Education.

The outcome of this particular public- vs. private-college spat was more or less a draw. Stiffer standards for teacher-training programs in all fields—elementary, secondary, and special—were established, and any institution meeting these standards had the right to prepare teachers. That has been the law of the Commonwealth ever since.

Juniata College, thanks to C. C. Ellis and Harvey Brumbaugh, played no bystander role in forging solutions at the state level on the teacher-training issue. Dr. Brumbaugh chaired the Association of Liberal Arts Colleges' important Committee on Code and Legislation. And Dr. Ellis, as the agent of more than one education interest in the hassle, was uniquely able to bring a broad, conciliatory perspective to the search for answers. All the while, an urgent presidential plea went out to the Juniata faculty at the start of each academic year. It called for one hundred percent membership in the Pennsylvania State Education Association, which boasted on the Hill an active chapter.

C.C.'S "BRAIN TRUST" AND FACULTY

The office of vice-president was abolished when C. C. moved up in 1930. The trustees, however, did offer the position to Harvey Brumbaugh. But he turned it down, questioning the usefulness of a double-headed command at a school of Juniata's size. The trustees came to see it his way, though they hoped to keep him axial to the operation of the college. And so, upon giving him an honorary degree (L.H.D.) they made him secretary of the board, to replace the retiring Allan Myers.

Dr. Ellis, for guidance in presidential decision-making, created an Administrative Council. At first there was, besides himself, Harvey Brumbaugh and Treasurer Oscar Myers. Campus insiders whimsically referred to them as the "Unholy Three." Later, upon Harvey Brumbaugh's death in 1937, Dr. Calvert Ellis, who succeeded to board secretary, joined the administrative troika. The college still had no academic dean, though Ellis the son virtually functioned as one by the end of his father's presidency.

Juniata came through the Depression fiscally battered, but intact, no paycheck having been so much as a day late, largely because of the purse-strings wizardry of brain truster Oscar Myers. He was an exceptional man. The former English professor, a bow tie his sartorial signature, never wanted to become treasurer back in 1924. He gave in to the trustees only out of a sense of duty. The 1930s brought him the ungrateful task of *not* spending money, and his tight control of finances helped save the college to serve another day. He developed an amazing capacity for stretching a dollar. He guaranteed college solvency by iron-handedly denying credit to fundless students. "Nickel Snatcher" some churlishly called the Brethren elder and State Sabbath School worker behind his back. Those in the know, however, were well aware of his countless Good Samaritan bursary acts. Many a time he salvaged a semester—or a degree—for someone by personally interceding for a bank loan or arranging for an on-campus job.

"Professor O. R.," as he was commonly addressed, died at age sixty-eight in 1942 while still in office. William Price, an alumnus (1884) and trustee nearing his eightieth birthday, filled his treasurer-council position. Earlier, as chairman of the board's finance committee from 1936 on, the Royersford, Pennsylvania, native had helped Oscar Myers institute a modern accounting system on the Hill. It was he who put the deeding of college real estate into order and developed for trustee use a more complete auditing method. In improving Hilltop accountancy he drew upon the expertise of Altoonan Charles Rice, then a teacher in the department of economics and business administration and a future trustee.

In 1936 Harold Brumbaugh, only three years out of Juniata, appeared on the administrative scene titled Assistant to the President. "H. B.," as he liked to be called, was a distant kin of the founding Brumbaughs. A confirmed bachelor, he built his whole life around Juniata, even in his many years of retirement. Before long he became alumni secretary (1939–62) and won his way into the hearts of Juniatians everywhere. Generations of graduates came to think of him, a born ambassador, as *Mister Juniata*. For many years he made the Cloister Arch his domicile. Tall and slim with wavy hair, he built up a tailor-crafted wardrobe that earned him the éclat of best-dressed man on campus.

In time, there developed a high degree of stability among noncouncil administrators, especially with the student deans. In 1930 Fayette McKenzie's deanship went to Warren Bowman, a Brethren elder with a Chicago Ph.D. in psychology. He left in 1935, later becoming president of Bridgewater College, to be followed by Clyde Stayer for the next twelve years. Deans of women in quick succession were Katharine Roberts, Liberty McClelland (1933–34), and Kathleen Gillard (1934–36). Then came

New Yorker Edith Spencer, a virtuoso in whistling, who stayed sixteen years. She would star as a whistler at many a social event. Spencer and Stayer began, in 1939, to keep an accumulative file on every student. Until that year the deans, besides their counseling and disciplinary duties, taught nine hours every semester.

As for the Depression-years professoriate, Dr. Ellis assessed his own administration as one "characterized by a strengthening of the faculty."[10] Aspirations for AAU sanction made this imperative. He hoped to appoint someone with a doctorate to head every department, which never quite worked out. Nevertheless, by 1937 there were seventeen doctorates scattered throughout a faculty of fifty (this figure dropped to nine out of thirty in 1943).

C. C.'s was the first faculty on the Hill to include women with Ph.D.s—four of them during his presidency. Under him three of these ladies, linguists all, unprecedentedly made the rank of full professor. They were May Keirns, a Chicago-trained classicist (in 1930); Emma Bach, a Johns Hopkins Germanist (in 1931); and Ida Kubitz, another Germanist from the University of Illinois (1936). The fourth doctoral holder was historian Bertha Leaman, with a Chicago degree. Professors Keirns and Kubitz taught at Juniata twelve and ten years, respectively. The other two chose to move on after short stays.

To the cadre of perdurable faculty members it inherited, the Ellis administration added, as time would prove, a sizable group of its own: eleven in all. Eight of them would stay on for tenures ranging between twenty-three and forty years. Four recruits strengthened the humanities: Harry Nye (Penn and Columbia, 1930–52) in history; Calvert Ellis (Yale Ph.D., 1930–68) in philosophy and religion; Canadian Harold Binkley (Harvard Ph.D., 1931–60) in English literature; and George Clemens (Penn Ph.D., 1936–42; 45-62) in modern foreign languages. The social sciences gained four members: Gertrude Butler (Columbia, 1935–69) in home economics; Edgar Kiracofe (Virginia Ph.D., 1935–60) in education; Kenneth Smoke (Ohio State Ph.D., 1938–46) in psychology; and Herbert Zassenhaus (Berne Ph.D., 1938–46), an economist who fled Germany with his Jewish wife. (It was Zassenhaus whom Ellis confronted on Founders Hall porch for using a mild expletive in public.) Three newcomers joined the science faculty: Homer Will (Pitt Ph.D., 1931–62) in biology; Donald Rockwell (Yale Ph.D., 1933–73) in chemistry; and Pressley Crummy (Pitt Ph.D., 1938–46) in biology.

During C. C.'s presidency, then, the college made major gains in professional strength. This was done by a balanced infusion of both Brethren and non-Brethren blood into the faculty. Already by 1936, however, church leaders were reporting that Juniata was unique among its sister schools because it had fewer Brethren on the faculty. For the academic year 1939–40 only fourteen out of a teaching staff of forty-six belonged to the denomination.

Dr. Ellis continued the practice of opening the first faculty meeting of the year with prayer. Beginning the fall of 1936, however, weekly meetings gave way to biweekly ones lasting no more than an hour generally. With October 1939 the faculty went on a monthly business schedule, the practice to this day. Standing committees were still appointed by the president rather than elected. The traditional trustee-faculty dinner, now a spring affair, originated as a fall mixer in 1932. That same year the college gave the faculty the option of being paid on a twelve-month instead of a ten-month basis.

The Ellis I era marked noteworthy advances in faculty fringe benefits. A retirement plan sponsored by the Teachers Insurance and Annuity Association (TIAA) went into effect the fall of 1938. TIAA had formed in 1918 to provide a fully funded, fully vested, portable pension system for college and university teachers. Group health insurance followed two years later. It was worked out through the General Education Board of the Church of the Brethren in cooperation with a major insurance company.

Typical of schools like Juniata, the faculty had a normal teaching load of fifteen hours a week. Only minimal encouragement was given for research and publishing. Still, surprisingly, fourteen professors in 1932 claimed authorship of a total of forty-one books and articles.[11]

The Depression made a conventional policy of sabbatical study impracticable. It was possible, however, for someone with seven years of service to take a leave of absence. During this leave the regular salary went on, but the professor had to provide, at his own expense, a substitute acceptable to the administration. Only two persons took advantage of this provision.

Faculty salaries at Juniata during the Depression were no better or worse than those at schools of comparable enrollment and endowment. Under the basic pay scale that obtained from the early Thirties on into the war years, professors got from $2,500 to $2,900; assistant professors from $1,000 to $2,500; and instructors from $1,300 to $1,800. This scale did not apply to the head coach and director of physical education, however. His salary was $3,500 for a nine-month's contract. Beginning in 1932 the faculty (and all college employees) suffered a series of paycheck cuts to ward off excessive deficits caused by declining enrollment. By 1936 these reductions totaled fifteen percent. Even as late as 1941 salaries were still off-scale by five percent at every rank. Still, the certainty of a paycheck made a smaller income bearable.

A NEW PHILOSOPHY OF EDUCATION

Midway through C. C.'s presidency Juniata was offering nine different programs, seven of which led to a B. S. degree. But the number of B. A. and B. S. recipients each year usually came out the same. The multiplicity of degree programs, most of which were designed for teacher training, was in large part due to state law. The majority of Juniatians were still going into education work—57.9 percent for the period 1921–31, according to one study of the vocational distribution of graduates.[12] In that same decade ten percent entered business, while 6.9 percent chose some kind of religious service, and 3.7 percent took up graduate study.

The 1930s, as noted, set on foot a liberalizing trend in the preparation of Pennsylvania teachers. This opened the way for wholesale curriculum reform at Juniata. A committee composed of Calvert Ellis, Harold Binkley, and Homer Will devised a curriculum, introduced in 1937, which stood for a quarter of a century. The committee was not unaware of the strong vocational outlook of most college students of that day—a fact of higher education in America that would only become more pronounced with time. It was their desire to develop a curriculum that would give Juniatians "enough contact with a liberal discipline to guarantee that [they] will be *men* as well as *craftsmen.*"[13] They reduced nine programs to one.

"What we now have," wrote Dr. Binkley about the committee's handiwork, "is the expression of what amounts to a philosophy of education with respect to this College."[14] He went on to explain: "The curriculum from which we changed was a curriculum accumulated to satisfy the demands of student upon the College; the one we have has been designed to meet the needs of a student in a liberal arts college." The inspiration for Juniata's new curriculum, which got attention in the *New York Times* for its novel features, was Dartmouth College, a pioneer in integrating liberal arts education.

Crucial to the operation of the curriculum was the alignment of departments, now grouped in three divisions:

> *The Arts and Languages*: Art, Classical Languages, English, French, German, Music, Spanish
>
> *The Social Studies*: Biblical Studies, Economics and Business Administration, Education, History and Political Science, Home Economics, Philosophy, Physical Education, Psychology, Sociology
>
> *The Natural Sciences*: Biology, Chemistry, Drawing, Mathematics, Physics

The freshman year was highly prescribed. All Juniata neophytes had to take three "integration" courses, one in each of the divisions: The Arts and Humanities; The Nature of Society; The Nature of Science. They rounded out the first-semester program with The Mind or a foreign language. In the second semester they followed up with introductory electives in each division chosen from a special list, plus Biblical History and continued language study. The curriculum further required that students take at least six semester hours beyond the work of the first-year program in a division other than the one in which they were majoring. The sixth and last course requirement was Ethics, for first-semester seniors.

The capstone of a Juniata education from now on was to be the comprehensive examination. (Actually, "comps" had been around since 1934, when Registrar Russell Stambaugh sold the idea to the faculty.) This final-semester ordeal, the catalog explained, was a "logical continuation of the principle, begun in the Divisional introductions of the first year, of integrating courses of study into a wider understanding of their mutual relations." Students sweated through six hours of "writtens" and an hour-long "oral." Three faculty members, one from outside the student's major division, made up the grand inquisition in each case. The examiners rated the combined test results with one of three possible markings: distinction, pass, failure. The last grade meant a delayed diploma, a minor tragedy that struck College Hill nearly every year. In most cases a retesting a few months later lifted the sheepskin penalty, but not always.

The 1937 curriculum boasted other innovative parts. It put a premium on "competencies" in certain academic areas, intending to prompt initiative. The two-year foreign language requirement, for example, could be met at any time through a special test. As for the "sacred cow of freshman composition," Dr. Binkley once waggishly wrote, it was "quietly and contentedly slaughtered" by the mid-Thirties curricular overhaul. A tutor plan or "conference program" replaced large-class instruction in which each student would meet a half-hour every two weeks with an English advisor. Not all of these advisors came from the English department: "the responsibility for using our language effectively is not to be limited to one special department," Dr. Binkley used to say. Papers were drawn from the integration course and other freshman offerings, allowing for more flexibility and relevance in the writing experience. Importantly, students could be exempted from writing conferences any time they attained a reasonable standard of proficiency. Division I graduates, of course, received the B. A. degree; those in Division III, the B. S.; Division II majors had a choice.

In 1942 the college went on a more or less three-term academic calendar—summer, fall, and winter—designed to allow students to accelerate and finish their work before being called into military service. It was now possible to graduate after three winters and two summers of study, or sooner.

THE ALTOONA EXTENSION CENTER

Almost from the start of its extension work under the directorship of Dr. Fayette McKenzie, Juniata College had been holding evening classes in the Altoona High School. The school board of that railroad city began to agitate for a junior college in 1930, and the University of Pittsburgh showed some interest in setting one up there. This alarmed Juniata's trustees, who protested that Pitt had no business interloping on another school's territory.[15] With little further delay, Hilltop officials began, on an experimental basis, a freshman-year college program on Blair County soil.

The Altoona Extension Center opened in September 1933, promotional literature billing the mother institution as "The College of the Juniata Valley." One tenth of the income went to the Altoona School Board for rental charges. Classes met late afternoon and in the evening. The first year sixty-eight Blair Countians entered the freshman program, other extension studies claiming another fifty students. On the night of Thursday, March 20, Altoona Juniatians met in the city's 8th Avenue Methodist Church for a special service. At that time they officially adopted an honor code and, with high ceremony, took the Athenian pledge, slightly modified, to signify their loyalty to the college and its ideals.[16] When the 1937 curriculum went into operation the freshman core courses and other basic first-year offerings took their proper place in the Center's academic program. Sixteen Hilltop faculty members, most of them department heads, made up the teaching force by then, at meager extra pay.

Between 1933 and 1939, 146 persons started their college work at the Center. About thirty of these Altoonans went on to graduate from Juniata. An additional 354 individuals enrolled in some kind of extension study during the same six-year period.

Meanwhile, Penn State signaled an interest in a branch college at Altoona. But Dr. C. C. successfully fought off any inroads by the Centre County land-grant school. However, sentiment for a junior college was strong in Altoona. Thus in late 1938 its Board of Education and Chamber of Commerce jointly petitioned Juniata to start one there. The city offered the college an unused school building rent-free while the Chamber of Commerce volunteered to raise the funds to equip it.

But after a careful study of the situation Juniata's trustees turned the offer down. Not only was there uncertainty about the future, but such a move, it was feared, might jeopardize Juniata's drive for accreditation by the American Association of Universities. With the college's leave Altoona city fathers then turned to Penn State, which began its operation of a downtown undergraduate center in the Webster Building the fall of 1939. Reported Dr. C. C. to the trustees after the decision to abandon the Altoona Center to Penn State: "While we cannot but anticipate a temporary disadvantage in our day to student enrollment, I am hopeful that ultimately we will reap some advantage in our upper classes."[17] Unfortunately his was a vain hope, the disaster of Pearl Harbor only months ahead.

OLLER HALL: DREAMS AND DISAPPOINTMENTS

Despite the Depression, the college was able to buy more land (athletic field addition), give some away, acquire new properties, renovate extensively, and, after a patient wait, put up a badly needed auditorium. Meanwhile, the Cloister got its name.

A flagstone walk in 1932 replaced the rotted boards laid out between the street and the "Men's Dorm," for which the trustees were still trying to think up a name. The next June they decided on "The Cloister," in recognition of M. G. Brumbaugh's interest in early Church of the Brethren history and the style of architecture. The trustees, in a patronymic gesture, then dubbed the Arch the Alexander Mack House (after the church's founder) and the Wing the Christopher Sauer House (after its most famous colonial leader). For some reason this nomenclature never caught on.

In 1932 the college got possession of the Tobias Myers place (for $8,250), across 17th Street from Carnegie Library, and in 1934 the Crownover corner dwelling (for $9,000) at 18th and Moore. A frame house behind Oneida Hall became the college infirmary in 1932, the asylum of the Hilltop sick for the next thirty-five years. An addition in 1937 provided two faculty apartments.

The Founders-Brumbaugh complex not only was remodeled by stages into the campus social center, but its transept gained a brick and steel fireproof stairway annex the fall of 1936. Ten o'clock most evenings would find the "fire tower," to use a student expression, a crowded mass of bodies, oblivious couples lining the walls in good-night embraces.

In 1939 the college converted the "love nest," which is what campus wags called the married-faculty apartment house behind the gymnasium, into a coed dormitory. Eighteen women, freshmen and juniors, moved into the building in September. The trustees named it the Geiger House in honor of Mrs. Mary Geiger of Philadelphia, Juniata's early benefactress.

Two years before, the trustees had deeded a small section of land to the borough for a playground. This patch, across Muddy Run below 16th Street, had been leased (one dollar a year) to the borough for recreational use when M. G. was president. He had promised that the college would eventually turn it over to the town, and the 1937 transaction honored that commitment. The West End public playground is still located there (next to today's Weis Market).

From a buildings-and-grounds standpoint, the one regnant dream of the C. C. Ellis years was the construction of a large music hall. Back in 1926 the college had first gone to the Presser Foundation of Philadelphia for help in such a project. Immensely impressed with the music program at Juniata, the officers finally made a proposal in January 1931 that seemed to assure the asked-for hall. The Foundation pledged fifty thousand dollars toward a one-hundred-thousand-dollar structure to be called, when erected, the Presser Music Building.

Wasting no time, the trustees accepted the offer and among themselves quickly raised more than twenty thousand dollars. By midsummer a few selected contacts had accounted for an additional twenty-one thousand dollars. Before the year was out Harrisburg architects had blueprinted a spired T-shaped edifice of American colonial architecture. With a seating capacity between 550 to 600, the auditorium was to stand on the present Oller Hall site.

Then came the setbacks, just when everything was falling into place. Excessive bids, which necessitated cost-cutting adjustments and many a revision in plan and specification, held up progress for another year. But the big blow fell two weeks before Christmas 1932. The Presser Foundation notified the college that the deal was off, at least until the Depression bottomed out. "Postponed, not canceled" was the way its heartbreaking communiqué read in reference to the fifty-thousand-dollar matching grant. As it turned out, the phrasing should have been reversed. For beginning in August 1937 the most precipitous economic decline in American history put the finishing stroke to the Foundation's good intentions. The stock market fell by forty-three percent. In all, the economy plunged about one-half as much in nine months as it had from 1923 to 1933.

Yet the college, with Rooseveltian optimism, went boldly ahead with other plans, right in the middle of this paralyzing mid-New Deal recession. The need for an auditorium and chapel was still there; so was studio space for the music department, which had to take over a third dwelling for that purpose, the Tobias Myers house. The fall of 1937 Pierce and Hedrick of New York City (Bayard Hedrick had a son at Juniata) directed a "national memorial campaign" to raise three hundred thousand dollars. Besides an auditorium and music hall the funds, to be collected over five years, were to go toward an endowed chair in education, named for M. G. Brumbaugh, and additional student scholarships. Huntingdon citizens contributed well over thirty-nine thousand dollars, exceeding the town's quota by four thousand. Altoonans grateful for the Altoona Extension Center, subscribed better than five thousand dollars. By January the nationwide drive had accounted for subscriptions totaling $145,000. But with war on the horizon that was as close as the college would get to its $300,000 goal.

"This is the first generation of students in ten years who will be able to see ground broken for a new college building on this campus," stated Dr. C. C. in a chapel announcement on a late October day in 1939. He then told of the recent trustee vote to construct a $130,000 colonial-brick auditorium, designed by the Altoona architect firm of Hunter and Caldwell. It was Dr. Ellis's idea to call the white-pillared structure

Oller Hall in honor of the Oller family, especially Jacob, an original trustee, and his son Joseph, the late board president. The architectural delight was dedicated at an impressive ceremony on Saturday, October 19, 1940. Governor Arthur James attended the event and spoke, introduced by alumnus William Livengood, Jr., Secretary of Internal Affairs. Despite the snowstorm and cold weather nearly twelve hundred persons braved the elements to be present for the service. The new facility now became the sanctuary of chapel services.

Oller Hall, an auditorium seating nine hundred, contains a large stage, a balcony, a projection booth, and two practice-organ rooms. The Hall's showpiece, however, is its Moller Organ, donated by alumna Rello Oller, sister of Prof. Jack Oller, in memory of their parents. *Diapason*, the national organists' magazine, rated the Moller Organ one of the best to be built in 1940.[18] Dr. Carl Weinrich, organist at Vassar and Wellesley colleges, designed it. Richard Whitelegg, then one of the outstanding tonal architects of the country, did the voicing. The Moller Organ has three manuals with thirty ranks of pipes (2,000 in all) and forty-three stops, including a set of chimes.

Within a year, artists such as Rose Bampton, leading soprano of the Metropolitan Opera, and the Tyrolean Trapp Family singers, directed by the young composer-clergyman Dr. Franz Wasner, had made Oller Hall appearances. Unfortunately it had not been ready for an April 1940 concert by Bela Bartok, the Hungarian composer-pianist on his second tour of the United States. The music department's Dorothy Domonkos, once a student of his, induced him to come to Juniata for the only college recital given on his tour. It took place in the gymnasium.

THE BOARD OF TRUSTEES OPENS UP

Joseph Oller's death in 1936 elevated Dr. Gaius Brumbaugh to chairman of the board. The Washington, D. C., physician had been the first male student (1876) and first male graduate (1879). He would wield the board scepter until 1952. The trustee meeting he presided over in the spring of 1939 proved to be quietly historic for the college.

One of the decisions that weekend opened the way for a broader representation of interests on the board. The board amended the charter to increase the number of trustees to thirty, but the most drastic changes came through bylaws revision in October. The major redaction allowed for one-fifth of the membership to be non-Brethren. This action greatly upset William Swigart, a month away from dying. He had always argued that "the College was founded by members of the Church of the Brethren and that in the early years money had been contributed on the condition that the College remain affiliated with the Church."[19] But his was the lone voice of protest. The board, however, made no change in the bylaws provision that, in case of dissolution, college property reverted to the Church of the Brethren for purposes of Christian education.

Two other significant reforms took place. One provided for the election of a college trustee by each of the supporting church districts of Pennsylvania: Western, Middle, and Southeastern (now the Atlantic Northeast). The other one allotted the

Alumni Association three elected board seats. Six trustees are still elected this way, each for three years, although as such they are not eligible for reelection. The first non-Brethren trustee co-opted by the board was Huntingdon's Chester Langdon, an Episcopalian. Chester, who had been a close friend of M. G.'s, would serve thirty years on the board. Before long other Protestants elected by the alumni joined him.

Other Depression trustee newcomers of the 1930s would give long, loyal years to the board: Samuel Hess of Huntingdon (1930–71), whose green-thumb touch did much to beautify the campus; Calvin Bowman (1936–55), a Johnstown educator; Mahlon Brougher (1932–50), a Greensburg pastor. The one man C. C. Ellis personally supplicated to be a trustee was alumnus John Baker (1936–87). Baker was then assistant dean of the Harvard Business School. The college had been running in a deficit for several years. On top of that, the endowment investments had badly suffered in the wake of the 1929 stock market crash. So Ellis felt the trustees needed Baker's financial acumen in making decisions about the college's battered portfolio. But the Harvard professor demurred, protesting: "You don't want me, C. C., I drink."[20] Ellis did want him, however, social drinker or not. Baker, who died in 1999 at age 103, finally relented and served on a trustee committee that made all the right decisions about the college's stocks and bonds. Baker's importance to the board would later be manifested in other crucial ways under Ellis the son.

"FRIENDS" AND ALUMNI

Their model the Waynesboro group, other Women's Fellowship Leagues sprang up during the Depression years. The Huntingdon ladies organized in December 1932. In subsequent years the women raised thousands of dollars for renovation projects and the furnishing of Oller Hall. The formation of similar leagues in Altoona and Johnstown followed in November 1936. A third, the Morrisons Cove League, took shape two months later. All the groups contributed liberally to the college.

Charity came from other sources, too, but for a different cause. The 1930s gave rise in many colleges and universities to groups calling themselves "Friends of the Library." Originally the purpose of these "friends" was to constitute a body of sleuths to uncover idle books in the private libraries of the community. Juniata's librarian, Lillian Evans, the woman behind the founding of the Huntingdon County Public Library in 1935, was the chief promoter of this latest Hilltop movement. The Friends of the Juniata College Library organized at a luncheon held May 15, 1937. The group, which soon began to issue its *Friends of the Library Bulletin,* adopted the custom of sponsoring commencement-time teas, often featured with a distinguished speaker. (Having a speaker is still in vogue but not the tea, and the time is now Alumni Weekend.)

A friendly interest in the college, however, was not much in evidence within general alumni ranks during the 1930s. In 1934 the college reported that only 470 former Juniatians out of 4,500 counted as dues-paying ($2.50) members. Indeed, statistics in 1935 showed that of the 2,475 actual graduates since 1879, the contributors numbered no more than 771. The last half of the decade evidenced a slight gain, but not much.

The college, though, did not want for ways of keeping in touch with former students. In 1931 it inaugurated Alumni Week in connection with summer school. This mid-July vacation of sorts, subsidized by the Alumni Association, was geared to offer graduates and others a "few days of intellectual refreshment, physical recreation, and good fellowship." There were eighty in attendance the second year, but interest began to wane after that. The last of these Alumni Weeks occurred in 1938. Five years before, meanwhile, the Saturday before baccalaureate Sunday had been designated Alumni Day. That annual meeting date would hold for the next half-century.

The college kept in touch with ex-Juniatians in two other ways—one of immediate import, the other more long-range. The Alumni Association celebrated its golden anniversary in 1935. For that jubilee event, its secretary and officers compiled what they titled, *The Alumni Record of Juniata College*. It represented a prodigious undertaking for that time. The edition tabulated the kinds of data printed in the college's latest *Alumni Directory* (1999). It even included detailed information about all of those known to be deceased. President C. C. wrote of the volume: "[I]t constitutes a noteworthy 'Who's Who at Juniata,' and, indeed, the only one so far."[21]

Another historic publication relating to alumni affairs also appeared in 1936, that May: *The Alumni Bulletin* (since 1999 known as the *Juniata magazine*). Heretofore the *Juniata Echo* and then the *Juniatian* had carried news of interest to, and about, alumni. The latter paper, beginning in 1928, had been devoting an entire page to such news. *The Bulletin*, issued quarterly from its inception, served as the college's chief periodical contact with alumni.

Radical changes in the organization and operation of the Alumni Association took place in 1939. That year Harold Brumbaugh took over as director. Constitutional revisions put the association under direct college control and into its budget. Annual dues were abolished and all Juniatians now automatically gained membership. Active membership, however, belonged only to those contributing to an annual major project. Choosing projects would be the responsibility of the Juniata Development Committee, which the board of trustees created in the fall of 1938. It was this committee, a representative group charged with looking after Juniata's fund-raising needs, that originated the One Hundred Club in 1939. A Will Judy idea, the club included all one-hundred-dollar donors each year. In 1943 the club reported thirty-eight contributors whose twenty thousand dollars or so amounted to more than a third of that year's total alumni giving.

Chapter 11

STUDENT LIFE DURING THE DEPRESSION: 1930–1943

PROFILE OF A DEPRESSION-PLAGUED STUDENT BODY

The early Depression year 1931–32 marked Juniata's largest enrollment in its history to that time: 534. M. G. Brumbaugh had left the college with a student body of 515. Trying as the 1930s were economically, the student population on the Hill, however, never took a precipitous dip. Overall decline in numbers did occur—from 534 to 402 by 1941–42—but the drop came in a fluctuating up-and-down curve. Actually, at the Depression's very depth Juniata was faring better than most small church-related colleges in the Keystone State, even those much older. For example, Juniata's enrollment in 1935 was 464, which compared very favorably with Albright's 343, Geneva's 458, Haverford's 326, Lebanon Valley's 396, Muhlenberg's 294, Susquehanna's 232, Thiel's 257, Ursinus's 455, and Waynesburg's 388. Sister-college Elizabethtown, twenty-four years younger, was struggling along with a full-time student body of 157.[1] Among the fifty-seven accredited colleges and universities of its home state, Juniata ranked twenty-second in enrollment in 1935. Indeed, five of the thirteen state teachers' colleges had fewer students than did Juniata that year.

Academic standards did not slip much at all in the fierce competition for students. By and large, over eighty percent of Depression-era Juniatians each year came from the upper two-thirds of their high-school classes (better than half from the top third). About ten percent of the freshmen brought either valedictorian or salutatorian laurels with them. Furthermore, Juniata's attrition rate was exceptionally low for a college of its type. The dropout count for each student generation of the 1930s never exceeded sixteen percent.

The first African-American to graduate from Juniata was Nancy Slaughter (Lee) in 1932. A local girl, quiet and soft-spoken, deeply spiritual, she went on to teach school. There would not be another black graduate until 1945.

When a threesome from the church's General Education Board paid a campus visit in 1936, two things impressed them about Juniata's student body. First, its social and economic status was manifestly highest of the Brethren colleges. Then, too, the predominance of non-Brethren students was all too obvious to them. All during C. C.'s presidency Juniata Brethren, though not outnumbered denominationally, never at any time constituted a third of the Hill's population. Behind them in descending numerical order came the Methodists and the Presbyterians, with the Lutherans somewhat fewer. All other denominations and faiths were only minimally represented.

Alumni brood, however, well populated the campus during the Thirties. In 1938, for example, there were sixty-four students (out of 476) one or both of whose parents had attended Juniata. The student body that year even included one fourth-generation and one third-generation Juniatian.

While President Franklin Roosevelt and Congress conjured up federal and state agencies of every alphabetical label to restore jobs and prosperity, a strange thing was happening on College Hill. Suddenly, by 1935, Juniata found itself somewhat out of character; it was no longer predominantly a residential school. About half the student body had become commuters, to cut down on costs. Day students who flocked in each morning on the "Pennsy" now had to take a bus from the station to College Hill, the "Toonerville Trolley" having been untracked in 1931. The commuting phenomenon would only be temporary, of course; after the war dormitory life regained its ascendancy. Fortunately the PRR, like most railroads, provided a "College Special" fare almost all of the Depression years. This reduced the cost of a ticket by as much as one-third.

To give prospective students a glimpse into college life and a look at Juniata, the college introduced Sub-Freshman Day in May 1939. Some three hundred high-school seniors witnessed May Day activities, under a clear blue sky on Saturday the 7th. The spring "prefrosh" visits became traditional and, in those ante-World War II days, the occasion for Dr. C. C. to name the winners of the competitive scholarship awards.

For years fourteen annual trustee scholarships had been granted on a basis of scholastic merit and financial need. But in 1933, in an all-out effort to attract quality students, the trustees created nine more, these based on a competitive examination. The testing for these scholarships was held only on campus at first, then later in certain high schools (mainly Camden, New Jersey, and Pittsburgh areas) as well. During the academic year 1934–35 one-third of the student body depended on some kind of financial aid or scholarship, an amount totaling well over fifteen thousand dollars. This was only eight thousand dollars less than that year's entire yield on its endowment, which had progressively eroded with the deepening economic crisis (by as much as $57,000 since 1929). Nevertheless, some forty specific scholarships were available in the mid-1930s. In addition, all high-school honor graduates got help as did all Church of the Brethren ministers and their children. Children of "evangelical" clergymen also qualified for limited aid.

By 1937 only about one-fourth of the students on the Hill were there on their own. "Everyone has some sort of work to do at Juniata," observed the campus paper, its editor impressed by all the self-help everywhere evident. Many Juniatians then had part-time campus jobs under the National Youth Administration program. (The NYA, an allied agency of the Works Progress Administration (WPA), would eventually aid 600,000 students in college and 1.5 million in high school.)

It was the practice of the NYA to assign students to projects that would not only benefit the college but also be educational to them personally. Thus someone interested in becoming a librarian might be assigned to the library's picture collection or to a clerical job. For 1937–38 there were thirty-three students working in the library, seventeen on NYA assignments. The aspiring biologist might end up making charts or preparing insect life-history exhibits for the biology department. And an NYA assistant in the English department likely made signs calling attention to colloquial and ungrammatical expressions. Others were assigned to projects that were academically unrelated. Some of them rebuilt tennis courts or refinished the gymnasium floor. The NYA allotment for 1939–40 amounted to $5,940, about a third of the total student aid. This form of governmental largess finally came to an end in 1942.

In 1940 a tuition remission policy went into effect for families of full-time college employees. The college rebated half the charges. For that year the cost of a Juniata education averaged about $689, up from the 1931 figure of $511.

On the whole, the vocational picture of Juniata graduates of the 1930s changed little from that of the previous decade. Slightly fewer went into educational work. There was a notable gain in medicine, however; forty-five Juniatians hung out M. D. shingles between 1931 and 1940. They got into some of the best medical schools in the East: Harvard, Johns Hopkins, Pennsylvania, Jefferson, Temple, Hahnemann, Pittsburgh, Maryland, and George Washington. Chemistry made a big jump, too, with thirty-nine careerists for the years 1938–42.

The classes of 1938 through 1942 produced 445 alumni. Of these, 132 went on to do graduate work upon or soon after leaving the Hill. In numbers the field of education was tops, attracting twenty-five. Medicine (22), the ministry (21), chemistry (19), and dietetics and home economics (16) followed in numerical order.

A college degree during the Depression, needless to say, was no sure passport to a good job. But Juniatians, like fellow collegians elsewhere, had a placement service to help them. One was set up in 1931, with Dr. Calvert Ellis the first director, at the cue of the Alumni Association. In 1934 its name became Bureau of Recommendations.

STUDENT INITIATIVE AND VITALITY

The 1930s brought a major change in the form of student government. Enforcing college regulations had soon lost its glamour for the heirs of the 1922 Student Councils. The responsibility for discipline was not only time-consuming but tended to heap odium upon those councilors conscientiously performing their duties. On petition of the students themselves, disciplinary functions, except for "frosh regs," were returned to the faculty in the fall of 1935. At the same time Calvert Ellis and the two deans, Stayer and Gillard, collaborated with Student Councils in creating the Juniata Senate. Student government would now take on a more positive image.

The new plan, which would stand the test of more than three decades of change on College Hill, aimed to centralize all of the many campus activities under one governing body. It stipulated a Senate composed of twelve student members and three faculty advisors (the two deans and an elected professor). The student members were divided into two groups—first, the officers: president, vice-president, secretary, and central treasurer; second, the chairpersons of social activities, women's house, men's house, freshmen, publications, activities, athletics, and religious activities. Officers and representatives had to be juniors and seniors nominated by the retiring Senate and elected by the student body.

Under senatorial auspices the social atmosphere quickened. Clubs of all kinds multiplied and flourished. Though coeds still lived under regulations limiting their frequency of dating, they enjoyed much greater freedom to keep informal company with men. Off-campus ambulatory perimeters now went by the board. To encourage on-campus socializing, the college remodeled the north end of Brumbaugh Hall in 1936, creating a large, open lobby flanked with alcoves and featuring an exquisitely mantled fireplace. This lounge area was comfortably furnished, and here sofa-cuddled couples would plight many a troth. The new parlor was stocked with table games, though banned from play on Sundays. In fact, a presidential fiat even forbade use of the social room itself during church hours.

Then in January 1943 the rear of the old chapel was converted into a recreation room, complete with Ping-Pong tables and ceiling-high closets for storing game equipment. Movable screens separated the two sections of the room, the eight rows of benches in the front part retained for special meetings and Bible classes.

The social code even made some small gains against long-tabooed vices. Tobacco-users got a qualified pardon; with 1935 men could smoke in the privacy of the Cloister, but only there on campus. A double standard, though, kept coeds under a no-cigarette ban. The administration now blinked card playing, for women as well as men, but the anti-drinking policy remained unchanged. Nor did the college give in to strong student pressure in favor of dancing. When the Senate forced a decision upon the trustees in 1942, the board felt obliged to stand firm "in view of the long-time traditions of the College and its historical connection with the tradition of the Church of the Brethren."[2] Every meal began with audible grace, student-prayed. The social code still bound men to wearing coats in the dining hall for the evening meal and on Sundays.

Dramatics, until the erection of Oller Hall, labored under the handicap of a cramped gymnasium stage and inadequate lighting and equipment. But student enthusiasm never lagged. Beginning in 1934 drama carried academic credit. As was the custom, the Masquers gave a full-length play each semester as well as occasional one-act skits. In 1938 student playwrights gave drama a satirical twist. That February All Class Night, a spoof on college life, made its debut as a tradition. After sixty years it is still a highlight of the campus social calendar each spring semester.

No extracurricular activity of the 1930s attracted a more avid following than music. The orchestra, still half-a-hundred strong, played in Oller Hall for the first time in

December 1941. A band of thirty pieces, after several false starts, finally took hold in the fall of 1935. The next year they played attired in Yale-blue sweaters, collegiate hats, and white trousers. Coeds became band members in 1937. The wind and percussion music-makers gave concerts as well as played at football games and pep rallies. In 1932 the A Cappella Choir, a consolidation of the Men's and Women's Glee clubs, began its long reign as the Hill's touring choral group. By 1940 orchestra, band, and choir members were all getting partial credit for their musicianship.

By then, too, Juniatians were singing a new *Alma Mater*. It began with a search for a different, original tune for *Hail to Juniata!*, the old *Alma Mater* arranged to be sung to *Maryland, My Maryland*. The new tune contest grew out of a Camp Myler proposal the fall of 1934. But the selection committee did not think much of the attempts at rescoring by contestants. So it recommended another song altogether: the familiar *To Juniata*, composed by Frank Ward back in 1926. Ward, who once taught history and political science on the Hill, wrote it for the Jubilee Edition song book. Prof. Charles Rowland had helped him set the lyrics to music. *To Juniata*, adopted by the Alumni Association in June 1934, still stirs memories of "days within her halls."

Debate remained popular among the men during the 1930s. Some years as many as eighteen forensic contests were scheduled. In the early Thirties Juniata teams were among the first to use the Oregon Plan in debating, before it became popular on the intercollegiate scene. The chief feature of the Oregon Plan was the cross-examination conducted by the second speakers of the respective sides. A first in the history of forensics at Juniata was what the Hill referred to as the "international debate." In November 1931 a pair of Juniatians squared off against two students from England on a debating tour of the United States. The Britishers—from University College, Nottingham, and St. John's College, Durham University—took the affirmative side of the query: "Resolved, That the world had more to fear from Fascism than Bolshevism." The Oregon Plan was followed, putting the Englishmen, who were unused to it, at a slight disadvantage, and the decision went in favor of the Juniata team. A second Juniata versus British debate took place the fall of 1935. The overseas visitors this time came from Cambridge University. Neither side won, since it was a split-team match-up. Women's debate, briefly revived in 1935 after a six-year lapse, fizzled out for good the next year.

Somewhat earlier—in 1933—the college began to liberalize its policy on required attendance at various religious services. Resident students were now given an option for Sunday worship; attendance could be either in the morning or evening, at Stone Church or downtown. In 1940 chapel went on a three-day schedule—Monday, Wednesday, Friday. At the same time Sunday school attendance was made voluntary. Nevertheless, excessive absences from church or chapel could bring suspension from college.

There was no let up on "frosh regs," however. Senate ordinances kept first-semester freshmen duly servile. The year 1937 brought them further hardships when the front steps of Founders porch and the diagonal walk from Student Hall to the street were closed to them. Freshmen coeds got bedinked at long last in 1940. Tribunal-harried men sometimes got a sympathetic word from their "Big Brothers," a freshman-orientation program that the YMCA borrowed from their campus counterpart in 1932.

It had been the Ys that originally sponsored the Camp Myler conferences each fall before college opened. With the 1930s these religious retreats began to take on a broader aspect. They became a time for student leaders and faculty consultants to grapple with campus problems, the Ys passing out of the picture. The tradition then developed for each Leadership Conference, planned by student government, to present the administration with a series of resolutions. Beginning in 1937 these weekend gatherings, which met before classes started, were for years held at Camp Kanesatake, the State Sunday School Association campgrounds near Spruce Creek.

Parents Day was an idea that came out of the 1936 Leadership Conference. Sponsored by the Senate, the first one took place on Saturday, October 17, that fall. The weekend attracted some 240 parents and friends to the Hill. Activities included a campus tour and a football game with Grove City in the afternoon (which the Blue and Gold won). Open-house visitation and a buffet dinner followed by a short musical skit in the chapel filled out the day's entertainment. The *Papoose*, a **J** Club publication, for years served as the official program for the annual visit by moms and dads.

Two other traditions, both Camp Myler inspired, had 1936 beginnings. In May of that year the junior class began hosting a reception for seniors, a practice observed every spring for nearly three decades. In October came the second tradition: the annual Firelighting Ceremony in the Brumbaugh social room in October. It intended to acquaint freshmen women with the Indian heritage that is Juniata's. To the slow, steady thump of a tom-tom Indian maidens advanced down the aisle to the fireplace. Then someone solemnly read the legend of Alfarata. The evacuation of Brumbaugh Hall after a new women's dormitory was built in the late 1960s put an end to this stately ritual.

Until the mid-Thirties the *Alfarata* circulated each year on a subscription basis. This kept the cost high, since many Juniatians chose not to buy one. But with 1935, by student vote, the price of an *Alfarata* copy (reduced to five dollars) was figured into the incidental fee. Now Juniata had a "college annual," declared the campus weekly, not just a "class book." That same year *Alfarata* editorship passed from junior to senior hands. The 1938 yearbook won a first-class rating from the National Scholastic Press Association (NSPA)—the only time ever. It was one of only thirteen annuals from colleges with an enrollment under five hundred to be so judged. The award-winning *Alfarata* illustrated the theme: "Juniata Through the Camera's Eye."

The year after the NSPA citation, Juniatians for the first time made the pages of *Who's Who in American Colleges and Universities*, an annual publication honoring graduating campus VIPs. The biographies of eight seniors were entered in the 1939–40 edition, five men and three coeds. In the mid-1950s, however, the faculty ceased making *Who's Who* nominations. The Student Government has ever since assumed that responsibility.

It was often the case that *Who's Who* entrants also got elected to the Honor Society. The Honor Society took wing the spring of 1942, its constitution largely the work of Dorothy Domonkos of the music department and historian Charles Read. A special faculty committee and President Ellis made the original selections. Often, the record shows, Honor Society members, as might be expected, won in the Joseph F. Biddle General Information Test. John Biddle and his sister, Josephine, had re-endowed the contest as a memorial upon the death of their father in 1936. Student interest in the test began to wane in the 1960s, though it was kept on the books until 1973.

The thirty-five contestants who sat for the Biddle prize the Saturday of March 28, 1936, had only days before watched flood waters rage through the lower end of town. The St. Patrick's Day catastrophe, with the river higher than during the great Johnstown Flood of 1889, saw houses, bridges, barns, and other property carried to destruction. It had rained in torrents for four days. All lines of communication with the outside world were broken, and for several days Huntingdon had no light, water, gas, or utility service. As Thelma Smith (Scott) wrote home, candles and lanterns on College Hill illuminated dormitory rooms and hallways, buildings had no heat for a day, drinking water had to be hauled in from Cold Springs, and commode tanks were filled with water pumped from Muddy Run.[3] Afterward WPA employees and Civilian Conservation Corps young men cleaned downtown Huntingdon and its environs, a chore that lasted most of a year.

THE SWARTZ DECADE IN ATHLETICS

With the early Thirties "Hoovervilles" began to dot the American landscape in a rash of urban sores and people by the hundreds of thousands went on relief, but varsity sports did not go begging on the Hill. Athletic scholarships had for some time represented a significant outlay. The trustees had been a little uneasy about a Carnegie Foundation study of athletic abuses in the late 1920s. Its report, which identified derelict colleges, happily made no mention of Juniata.[4] There were fifty athletes, almost one-tenth of the student body, on scholarships in 1931, each grant worth $150. The big three sports—football, basketball, and baseball—got the lion's share of help, track the least.

In December 1931 the Middle States Association (MSA) came out against all athletically based aid, charging colleges and universities with overemphasizing sports. An athletic scholarship interdict was set to begin September 1933, excluding those already committed. Juniata abided faithfully to the letter of MSA's law, though often there were suspicions that other colleges on its sports schedules had found loopholes. The college still attracted its share of good athletes, but the MSA ruling made it harder.

When Ronald Siersema left in 1930 to study medicine, Milford Swartz, then coaching at Dickinson Seminary in Williamsport, Pennsylvania, took over the athletic reins. Swartz, who wore a Knute Rockne-like pugnacious scowl, had been a three-sport sensation at Lebanon Valley College and later pitched three years in the International League. Coach Swartz was Juniata's man in sports a dozen years. In that time he made men's intramural sports an important part of campus life. He organized leagues in softball, touch football, volleyball, tennis, and track. The freshman-sophomore football game grew into a regular Homecoming Day spectacle. The full schedule of Hilltop competition climaxed each year with the traditional interclass meet.

Over the years other recreational facilities became available. Soon after he came, Swartz, a handball devotee, somehow managed to squeeze two courts into the gymnasium basement despite its low ceiling. Then by the fall of 1941 a golf driving range and four greens beautified the former wasteland on the northern edge of the campus as a means of reclaiming that swampland area. The war, however, put an end to further work.

Swartz was a hard-driving but well-liked coach. In football his scholarshipless gridders gave him an overall twelve-year record of thirty-five wins, forty-four losses, and five ties. His lone winning season was 1937, with a 5-3 log. Victories over arch foe Susquehanna still meant cancellation of Monday classes, a practice that began in 1929. A polio epidemic in Huntingdon forced the Indians to cut the first two games of their 1941 season. The Kiwanis Health Club at nearby Martin's Gap was the scene of Juniata's first (and only) football camp in 1946.

A plot of ground (400' x 150') purchased in 1931 extended the athletic field farther toward Muddy Run. As a result, in 1939 the football field was laid out so play would run east and west. That same fall, in time for Parents Day, the college erected a press box. It provided a public address system, wire service, and space on the roof for photographers.

The 1930s also brought changes in football rules, the most radical since the turn of the century. Reformers hoped to reduce the rising rate of gridiron injuries. Dropped was the "flying wedge" on the kickoff, the "flying tackle" and the "flying block." It became legal for the defensive team to use its hands. There was freer substitution. The ball was blown dead when any part of the ball-carrier's body hit the ground, except his hands and feet.

Swartz departed the summer of 1942 to direct a USO center in North Carolina, leaving the sport to Philip Snider. The genial Snider introduced the "T" formation, and three straight early-season wins produced a 3-2 first-year coaching record. Football was dropped the next fall; too many boys and the coach by that time had donned the Uncle Sam uniform.

Swartzmen on the basketball court recorded sixty-eight wins and ninety-nine losses. Their best year was 1932, with a 7-5 mark. The 1932–33 Hilltop team held Elizabethtown to but nine points in one game. As with the gridiron sport, the 1930s also introduced the nation to modern basketball. The fast break caught on; so did the one-hand shot. The man-to-man defense yielded to the zone defense, and in 1938–39 the center jump after goals would be abandoned forever. The 1940 Pennsylvania coaches and Associated Press sports writers named three Juniata cagers to the honorable mention list of that year's All-State Team. A Leadership Conference recommendation led to use of the Huntingdon High School floor the second half of the 1939–40 season, a school board courtesy renewed each year until Memorial Gymnasium went up in 1951. Jack Oller finished out the 1942–43 hardcourt season for Snider, who received a Navy commission in February. The Blue and Gold went 5-7 for the two coaches.

On the diamond Milford Swartz coached the Indians to eighty-eight wins, and suffered but fifty-one losses. Three times his Juniata teams were the Eastern Pennsylvania Intercollegiate Baseball League (EPIBL) champions—1932, 1933, and 1938. The EPIBL, the brainchild of students at Drexel Institute of Technology, organized in May

1931. Of the fourteen colleges invited to join the league, six decided to do so: Juniata, Drexel, Bucknell, Susquehanna, Ursinus, and Lebanon Valley. The 1932 baseball nine went eleven and two, the best diamond performance of the Thirties. After Swartz's departure, education professor Edgar Kiracofe became baseball coach in 1943 (he stayed on through World War II). Kiracofe's 1943 wartime nine recorded five wins and three losses.

Like baseball athletes, Juniata trackmen of the 1930s proved crowd pleasers, too. First-year Coach Snider's mile relay team in 1931, buffeted by a strong wind and pelting rain, captured a Penn Relay's first-place plaque. Plaques from the Philadelphia spring classic went to Juniata again in 1932, 1934, 1935, 1938, and 1939. The relay victory in 1938 gave the college temporary possession of the Rodman Wanamaker Cup (it went to the school that won three times). The 1938 team broke five Juniata field-and-track records. Two Indians of the C. C. Ellis era hold the record (since retired) for the 220 low hurdles; George Walton set it in 1935 at a time of :25.8, which Robert Mitchell tied in 1941. One of the Depression's premier trackmen was Daniel Geiser, a record-setting pole-vaulter in 1937 and 1938. An all-round athlete, he earned thirteen letters: four in baseball and three each in football, basketball, and track.

The war interrupted not only track and football but also tennis. During the 1930s the Indian netmen posted only two winning seasons. The sport was temporarily dropped in 1936, reinstituted, and then dropped again in 1943.

The Depression, not the war, dispatched the Hill's only coed intercollegiate sport: basketball. Overall between 1930 and 1935, Juniata sextettes ran up an impressive 16-6 victory margin. But the sport reverted to intramural status in 1935 when hard times forced other colleges to drop the sport.

Betty Fleck, assistant director of physical education, did much to diversify the women's intramural athletic program during the Thirties. She introduced field hockey in 1932, and the annual freshman-sophomore tilt became a big attraction the morning of Homecoming Day. A girls' athletic field, below Scott Street, got its first use in 1937, at once increasing the number of hockey enthusiasts.

In November 1938 Hilltop coeds organized the Women's Athletic Association (WAA) to take the place of their **J** Club. The WAA's motto, "A sport for every girl and a girl for every sport," had a familiar ring. It paraphrased the catchword of the Women's Division of the National Amateur Athletic Association, founded by Mrs. Herbert Hoover in the early 1920s: "A team for everyone and everyone on a team." Women athletes would now receive a WAA emblem instead of a **J**. Credit toward these emblems accrued not only from participation in intramurals such as hockey, basketball, softball, speedball, and volleyball, but also from individual sports such as Ping-Pong, badminton, tennis, skating, riding, hiking, shuffleboard, deck tennis, and others.

WORLD WAR II HITS THE HILL

During most of the 1930s American attention was centered on domestic problems. Yet foreign events occurring in the same period were to affect the United States even more profoundly than the New Deal. Aggressive military states threatened to dominate

Europe and Asia. Through 1939 and 1940 events in Europe moved swiftly—Germany overran Poland, occupied Denmark and Norway, then blitzkrieged through the Low Country and into France, leaving Great Britain isolated. Step by step the United States became involved on the Atlantic side, isolationism and neutrality giving way to British aid. And at the same time—in the Pacific—Roosevelt imposed stiff economic sanctions against Japan, then at war with China. *Juniatian* editorials took note of all this from time to time as "preparedness" talk grew louder.

In September 1940 Congress adopted the first peacetime conscription law in American history. The Burke-Wadsworth Act, however, deferred all draft age college men until the end of the current academic year. In all, fifty-five Juniatians, faculty and students, registered for the draft that fall. Otherwise, Juniata continued much as usual through the year, relishing to the hilt the many advantages of Oller Hall. The enrollment for the fall of 1941 showed only a slight decline.

Then Pearl Harbor—Sunday, December 7. America at war! The Juniata campus, like the nation, was momentarily stunned. On Wednesday the 10th, two days after Congress declared war, President C. C. spoke to the students in chapel on the subject "Our Attitude in the Present Crisis." Urging duty to one's country, he hardly sounded like a Brethren pacifist (which he was not—"conscience," he so often was to say, "works both ways on the question of military service"). Americans, his chapel talk stressed, have received many benefits from their government and "everyone ought to be ready to give back such help as he or she can render."

For yet a while the war touched College Hill in only minor ways. A committee on Civilian Morale, representing every segment of the campus, soon appeared, chaired by Dr. Ellis. In January some 250 professors and students began to study first aid under Red Cross instruction. War Time (President Roosevelt preferred this phrase to Daylight Saving Time) began Monday, February 9. Sugar rationing came in May and each dining room table was allotted a half-cup of sugar a day (each student one tablespoon full). All male students had to take part in a physical fitness program, at first three hours a week, later five.

But not for long could College Hill escape the sting of war's fury. The week before Thanksgiving 1942 came the sad new of Marine Lt. David Crosby's death. The handsome, wavy-haired Carlisle, Pennsylvania, English major had fallen on Guadalcanal, Solomon Islands. Then during the Christmas holidays word reached the Hill that Lt. Jack Shuck of Lewistown, Pennsylvania, had gone down with his Spitfire over Northwest Africa. Shuck, it was later learned, had bailed out and was alive. As a prisoner of war he eventually ended up corralled in the north compound of Stalag Luft III, the notorious German POW camp for allied airmen at Sagan, Silesia. There, one of six-hundred-odd conniving American and British officers, he became party to an incredible wartime story. For Stalag III was the prison camp that stunned the Germans with one of the most daring mass escapes of all times, since celebrated in book and movie as *The Great Escape*.

On Monday, February 15, 1943, the college gave twenty-eight Army Reservists a special sendoff that included a chapel service and individual New Testaments from the Student Volunteers. Four more men, three in the Army Air Corps Reserves and one in the Navy Reserve Corps, left the next week. And by mid-April, nineteen others had bade farewell to the Hill to enter various branches of the service. Three faculty members, one a woman, donned khaki uniforms in the early months of 1943. By fall Juniata's roll of men and women in civilian and military camps approximated 350 names. Of this number seven had been reported lost or missing in action, and at least fifty were in foreign service or in active duty on the high seas.[5]

As in the First World War the trustees allowed no military unit on College Hill. The War Department had approached the college as early as 1939 for permission to set up a flight school. But the trustees still felt bound by the Brethren peace position and said no to that tender and to other later ones. It cost the college dearly, of course, in terms of students and cash. Of the 249 students who enrolled for the fall of 1943, only sixty-five were men.

For the first time in untold years women invaded Founders Hall, third floor. The war year of 1943 brought Juniata's largest enrollment of resident women ever. This, said the *Alumni Bulletin*, was "attributable to the fact that Juniata is the only Pennsylvania co-educational college accredited by the Association of American Universities, with entire facilities and faculty personnel available for civilian higher education."[6]

September 1943 also marked the close of Dr. C. C.'s presidency. He had turned sixty-nine in July. Worries had piled up on his desk with every new month of the war and every added disruption of the civilian economy. Someone younger, he felt, should carry the college through the dark times ahead.

Chapter 12

A QUARTER-CENTURY OF DYNAMIC GROWTH: 1943–1968

FINDING DR. C. C.'S SUCCESSOR

When the trustee selection committee met in the spring of 1943 to choose Juniata's seventh president, the end of the war was not in sight and the future was very uncertain. The projection of student enrollment for the fall seemed bleak indeed—less than 250. Among the six-man committee there were some who feared the meeting would be a stormy one. The trustees were not of one mind on a lot of issues, especially on college regulations. The decision, everyone felt, hung on a "hinge of fate." The presidential transition must bring as little shock as possible to the college.

Moreover, opinions differed as to who the next president should be. Among the names considered, however, that of Calvert Nice Ellis, board secretary since 1938, clearly stood out. As Dr. John Baker, who was one of the committee members and then-dean of Harvard Business School, recalls that day in 1943, the leading nominee was "well known to all, was steeped in college tradition, [and] his educational background was ideal."[1]

Not all on the board—or on the faculty—at first jumped on the Calvert Ellis bandwagon. One colleague in particular, Dr. Norman Brumbaugh, voiced strong fears that the sciences would suffer neglect under the younger Ellis. And a certain trustee wondered whether he could raise money, or at age thirty-nine, had the "human touch" that marks the deft administrator. Said John Baker, "The trustees recognized that only the future could answer [such] questions."[2] And so on commencement weekend Calvert Ellis was unanimously elected president.

Getting him to accept was another story; he adamantly turned the offer down. Pressured, he asked for several days to think it over. Then on Monday, May 31, he closeted with the whole board to make a statement. He agreed to succeed his father provided he could continue on as manager of the D. Maurice Wertz Orchards in Franklin County. In 1940, upon his father-in-law's death, Dr. Ellis had taken over the management of the Wertz business, then the largest orchards (cherries, peaches, and apples) in the Commonwealth. (He would be a fruit grower until 1960 when the business was sold to Knouse Foods.) The trustees raised no objections to this extramural involvement and the matter of presidential succession was settled. The transition had been effected with smoothness and large good will.

CALVERT NICE ELLIS: A NATIONAL FORCE IN HIGHER EDUCATION

Born in Zion City, Illinois, Calvert Ellis never attended public school. His father had experienced a bad reaction (paralysis of his legs for a time) to his own vaccination and so denied the vaccine needle to the two Ellis boys. Their mother tutored them at home, and then they attended the Academy. A 1919 Academy graduate with some study at Princeton Preparatory School, Ellis received his B. A. degree from Juniata (1923) the year after his call to the ministry by the Huntingdon church (eventually he was ordained an elder). Pursuing graduate studies over the next nine years, he received a B.Th. from Princeton Theological Seminary (1927), an M. A. from Princeton University (1927), and a Ph.D. from Yale (1932). His dissertation on Karl Barth made him one of the first American scholars of that Swiss theologian. In 1932, turning down a position at Mt. Holyoke College, he heeded his father's invitation and joined the faculty of his alma mater to teach religion and philosophy. He made it plain, however, that he had no plans for staying, even though he built a magnificent home in Taylor Highlands in 1934.

Calvert, a warmer, more outgoing person than his father, of similar build but with sharper facial features, would go on to pilot Juniata for a quarter century. His has been the longest presidential tenure in the college's history. His years in office coincided with the dynamic postwar decades and the upsurge of higher education that attended them. Dr. John Baker put Calvert Ellis's long presidency in historical focus when he wrote:

> Dr. Ellis' administration covered many of the most crucial years in the history of American education. One world war and several smaller wars; too few students, too many students; Sputnik, with the upgrading of all education; changing social mores; restlessness among faculty and students; faculty shortages; inflation with its attendant financial problem; government aid and involvement and a host of other issues beset him and all other college presidents. Those were indeed exacting times and any president who succeeded in guiding his institution through this era successfully merited high praise.[3]

The name of C. C. Ellis was a familiar one to Pennsylvania educators, but as someone said of his son, "He helped mold the fabric of higher education in America."[4]

From 1944 to 1947 he was on the staff of the House Education Committee, which hammered out the guidelines for the first federal aid to private colleges and universities. He helped write the law popularly called the GI Bill (Veterans Education Act). The law allowed some six million "G. I. Joes and Janes" to use government funds for furthering their education. Over two million of them went to college. That influx into academe saved many small schools like Juniata, Calvert Ellis often said.

During the years 1944–47 he spent four- or five-day weeks every month in the nation's capital. He worked with sixteen other educators in an advisory capacity to the U. S. House of Representatives' Committee on Education and Labor. For twenty years in all Ellis testified periodically before Congress in behalf of higher education—a rare role for the president of a small college. Many congressmen and senators knew him quite well. Even Lyndon Johnson, after entering the White House in 1963, continued to call him "Cal." Jay du Von, then director of the College Housing Branch of the Federal Housing and Home Agency, told a group of Juniatians in 1963:

> Your president has a reputation for integrity coupled with vision which goes beyond the State of Pennsylvania and has made him one of the educational leaders of the nation. His wise counsel and advice are sought by the Federal Government on every important problem affecting higher education....[5]

While in office much of Dr. Ellis's off-campus time was given to the work of the Association of American Colleges (AAC). Established in 1915, the AAC represents some 870 liberal arts colleges, large and small, church-related and secular, public and private. From 1949 to 1955 he headed its Commission on the Arts, later chairing the Commission on Legislation (1961–64)—of which he was a member for eight years. In 1965 he was elected to the board of directors, and in 1968 became the association's national chairman. He was the fifth college president from Pennsylvania to be so honored.

He was no less active in the Middle States Association, over which he presided in 1965. He also served as director of its Commission on Institutions of Higher Education (1948–54). Seventeen times he led evaluation teams on their missions to colleges and universities of all sizes and sorts, including two great Protestant seminaries.

Nor was he without honor in his home Commonwealth. He headed the Pennsylvania Association of Colleges and Universities (1953–54) and the Foundation of Independent Colleges of Pennsylvania (1962–63). During 1965–66 Dr. Ellis was a member of the Advisory Committee on Higher Education to the State Board of Education. In 1966 Governor William Scranton appointed him to the Higher Education Advisory Committee to the Education Compact of the United States.

Like his father, Calvert Ellis gave liberally of his time to the church. Not an orator of his father's class, he was nevertheless an effective preacher much appreciated as a pulpiteer whether featured at Annual Conference or filling in for a rural pastor. He preached every Juniata baccalaureate sermon but one while president. He was moderator of Annual Conference for the year 1947–48, refusing other nominations for the position later on in the belief it should be passed around. For nine years he chaired the General Brotherhood Board (1948–54, 1966–67), the denomination's chief policy-making agency created in 1947. Dr. Ellis was a delegate to ecumenical church meetings in Amsterdam, Netherlands; Evanston, Illinois; and Lund, Sweden. And twice he toured various parts of the world to survey Brethren missions. Needless to say, Ellis the son wholeheartedly shared his father's pride in Juniata's Brethren heritage.

At the community level Dr. Ellis, a Rotarian, somehow found energy and time to carry other responsibilities. In 1936 he became a trustee of J. C. Blair Memorial Hospital, assuming board chairmanship from 1960 to 1962. The First Grange National Bank (now the Penn Central National Bank) elected him a director in 1946.

THE COMMITMENT TO A "SMALL COLLEGE"

The college that Ellis the son inherited in the fall of 1943 had an enrollment of 249 (178 women and 71 men). The total cost to a student for the 1943–44 academic year amounted to $674. The operating budget stood at $250,000.

The Calvert Ellis presidency would preserve the best of Juniata's past without limiting in any way the college's entry into the demanding revolutionary world of the 1950s and 1960s. Many small colleges in those decades, with the rising tide of students, burgeoned into universities with national constituencies, their church ties severed or neglected. But so far as Juniata's second Ellis was concerned, he would have been happy to preside over a college with no more than seven hundred students. He was heard to say this more than once. He believed the small college had been basic in our nation's life and history, a unique American tradition. In his inaugural address, "The Purpose of the Small College," he said:

> It is my conviction that the small, denominationally related college, rooted in local tradition has a significant role in America's future—a role the college has visioned but only partially grasped—to provide a basic education in the arts and sciences in an atmosphere friendly to the Christian faith.[6]

Only reluctantly, at trustee urging, did he watch the enrollment gradually climb to over eleven hundred by the time he retired. But it was a controlled growth. Seen in retrospect this was a wise policy, preventing the college from overexpanding during the student boom of the Sixties. Many colleges failed to act so deliberately and they met with financial chaos when the bottom dropped out in the early Seventies.

The success of a small college, said Dr. Calvert once in a commencement speech, is not whether it produces great persons, for that will rarely happen. "Juniata has never been a college for geniuses," he said, "although a few have survived!" He went on:

> Juniata will continue to admit students with intellectual capacity and then develop in them an appetite to know so they will accomplish more in graduate school and life than would have been expected when they entered college. I expect to live long enough to see educational institutions judged on the basis of what they do for students rather than on the College Board scores of their freshmen.[7]

Like his predecessors, Calvert Ellis constantly stressed that Juniata College was "Christian in purpose." The small liberal arts college, he believed, had a responsibility to develop sound habits and attitudes. He treasured the testimony of James Shook, a Reading, Pennsylvania, principal, who said, "I learned more in the university, but I got my set of soul at Juniata." In 1967, when student unrest was beginning to peak on the nation's campuses, he said in his report that year: "Juniata College believes that its constituency wishes certain standards to be taught...and that God places obligations upon us."

He usually spoke of Juniata as *church related*, seldom as *independent*. (It was he in 1939 who pushed the idea to give the three church districts representation on the board.) The steady decline of Brethren students bothered him. Yet he felt the times dictated against registering Juniata as a "denominational college" under a special state law enacted in the early 1960s.

With time Dr. Ellis built around him an efficient administrative staff; otherwise he could not have taken on so many outside obligations. But up to the very end his presidential style continued in the paternalistic vein of those who went before him. The Middle States team that visited the campus in 1962 referred in its report to "the family spirit which provides easy access that shortcuts organizational charts."[8]

Socially, though, this paternalism took special, intimate forms. From year one of the Ellis presidency, Calvert and Elizabeth entertained the faculty each spring. First it was at their elegant home, then, because of an overgrown faculty, at a variety of public places. In the 1950s the Ellises began taking faculty with new doctorates and their spouses on a junket to Erculiani's, fabled for its many-coursed meals, near Cresson. This was his unique way of prodding Hilltop people to see their doctoral studies through. In 1967 a record crop of Ph.D.s (five) plus wives sated themselves at presidential expense. (By 1968 forty-six percent of the full-time faculty had doctorates, not all, of course, Erculiani-induced.)

And it was Mrs. Ellis early in her husband's administration who brought faculty wives together for regular fellowship. "Juniata Dames," they called themselves. It was her concern that the women come to feel as though they belonged to the college, too. The Dames, as a sodality, lasted into the 1970s.

THE CALVERT ELLIS FACULTY

No Juniata president has transformed the campus to the extent Calvert Ellis did in the twenty-five years he held the office. Yet he took as much pride in the quality of the faculty he enlisted and kept as in the number of buildings he erected. As he told the trustees in his 1954 report to them:

> It is easy to become discouraged in the work of a college such as Juniata. There is not much that one can offer to his colleagues except hard work and modest financial remuneration. But it is thrilling to be associated with a group of committed persons devoted to the education of youth for service in tomorrow's world.

He did remark in his next year's report, however, about how hard it was to find professors willing to devote their careers to Juniata. (His presidential goal, though never publicly stated, was to build the faculty around a Brethren nucleus.) Even so, the passage of time provides evidence that he experienced notable success in bringing to

College Hill a faculty of enduring loyalty. In all, forty-five Ellis-appointed faculty members stayed on for two decades or more. Of this number, thirty taught for at least three decades and a half-dozen for at least four decades. To illustrate the stability of the Ellis faculty in another way, twenty-three taught under three presidents while a dozen have done so under their fourth. The names of these professors are as follows:

HUMANITIES

ENGLISH COMMUNICATIONS AND THEATRE ARTS: Clayton Briggs (Whittier M. A., 1962–90); Ralph Church (Columbia M. A., 1966–91); Esther Doyle (Northwestern Ph.D., 1945–75); Doris Goehring (Columbia M. A., 1965–90); William Hofelt (Rochester M. A., 1966–97); Richard Hunter (Princeton Ph.D., 1966–91).

FINE ARTS: Jack Troy (Kent State M. A., 1967-present).

FOREIGN LANGUAGES: Evelyn Church (Middleburg M. A., 1966–91); George Dolnikowski (Penn/Harvard M. A.s, 1954–88); Bernice Heller (Kansas M. A., 1955–97).

HISTORY: Elizabeth Cherry (Columbia M. A., 1962–98); Kenneth Crosby (George Washington Ph.D., 1947–80); Earl Kaylor (Penn State Ph.D., 1958–1991); Klaus Kipphan (Heidelberg Ph.D., 1965-present); Ernest Post (Michigan State Ph.D., 1959–1989); Philbrook Smith (Iowa Ph.D., 1954–97).

LIBRARY: Sarah Hettinger (Drexel B. L. S., 1944–64).

MUSIC: Donald Johnson (New York Univ. M. A., 1944–71); Mary Ruth Linton (Eastman M. A., 1942–51; 1963–89).

PHILOSOPHY: Robert Wagoner (Harvard Ph.D., 1965–99).

RELIGION: José Nieto (Princeton Ph.D., 1967-present).

SOCIAL SCIENCES

ECONOMICS AND BUSINESS ADMINISTRATION: Ronald Cherry (Princeton Ph.D., 1958–98); Herbert Miller (Harvard M. B. A., 1946–69); Thomas Nolan (Penn State M. A., 1953–97).

EDUCATION: Howard Crouch (Ohio State Ph.D., 1963–89); Miriam Schlegel Musselman (George Peabody Ed.D., 1950–75); Thomas Woodrow (Penn State Ed.D., 1967–97).

PSYCHOLOGY: Henry Masters (Kansas State Ph.D., 1968–99).

SOCIOLOGY, ANTHROPOLOGY, AND SOCIAL WORK: Paul Heberling (Penn State M. A., 1957–89); Duane Stroman (Boston Ph.D., 1963-present).

NATURAL SCIENCES

BIOLOGY: Robert Fisher (Cornell Ph.D., 1963–97); Kenneth Rockwell (Penn State Ph.D., 1960–99); Robert Zimmerer (Penn State Ph.D., 1961–93).

CHEMISTRY: Edwin Blaisdell (M. I. T. Ph.D., 1954–76); Eva Hartzler (Penn State Ph.D., 1950–76); Donald Mitchell (Vanderbilt Ph.D., 1967-present); William Russey (Harvard Ph.D., 1966-present); Paul Schettler (Yale Ph.D., 1967-present).

COMPUTER SCIENCE/CHEMISTRY: Dale Wampler (Wisconsin Ph.D., 1961–99).

GEOLOGY: James Gooch (Delaware Ph.D., 1968–99); Peter Trexler (Michigan Ph.D., 1962–89); Robert Washburn (Columbia Ph.D., 1966-present).

MATHEMATICS: John Bowser (Penn State Ph.D., 1961–97); Max Heller (Penn State M. A./Indiana Univ. (PA) M. A. T., 1958–97).

PHYSICS: Ray Pfrogner (Delaware Ph.D., 1964–98); Wilfred Norris (Harvard Ph.D., 1958–98).

Two other noteworthy Ellis-era faculty members came very close to twenty-year stays: Stone Church pastor-turned-sociologist Tobias Henry (Pitt Ph.D., 1946–65) and Dean Morley Mays (Virginia Ph.D., 1948–66). Both were alumni and birthright Brethren. Of the aforementioned forty-six professors, a dozen also had Juniata degrees: Bowser, R. Cherry, Dolnikowski, Hartzler, Hofelt, Kaylor, Linton, Miller, Norris, Pfrogner, Rockwell, and Woodrow. As for cradle Brethren, seven in addition to Henry and Mays could make that claim upon their appointments: Bowser, the two Cherrys, Kaylor, Linton, Norris, and Wagoner. By the year 2000 the faculty profile reflected a drastically reduced number of Brethren-born and alumni.

Much of the credit for recruiting the Ellis faculty should go to Juniata's first academic dean, Morley Mays. Trained in philosophy, Mays came back to the Hill in 1948 at the age of thirty-six. He soon won the respect of the faculty as a detail man and an expert on curricular matters. All during his deanship he served on evaluation committees for the Middle States Association, chairing a number of them. Twice he was a consultant for the Maryland State Department of Education and once for the New York State Department of Education. In 1963, when the college administration reorganized, he became one of three vice-presidents. Three times he was acting president of Juniata for brief periods. An ordained Brethren minister, he held a number of offices at the denomination's national level. He had hopes of succeeding to the presidency of his alma mater but got no encouragement from incumbent Ellis. Disappointed, he resigned in 1966 to become president of Elizabethtown College.

Donald Rockwell, then chairman of the natural sciences, was made acting dean while a search went on for Mays' successor. The fall of 1967 his appointment became permanent. The faculty loved Donald Rockwell, but he was not happy as dean. He much preferred the classroom, only a sense of duty and his deep affection for Calvert Ellis compelling him to make the sacrifice. He retired the spring of 1970, in failing health.

Meanwhile, over the years the problem of paying the faculty competitive salaries caused perennial concern. Salary raises came in increments of a few hundred dollars. A study of faculty income at eighteen Pennsylvania colleges with an enrollment between five hundred and one thousand in 1954 revealed that Juniata's average salary of forty-five hundred dollars was next to the lowest in the group.[9] Ellis pointed out to the trustees in his reports that year the injustice of paying beginning instructors within a thousand dollars of the salary of those who have given their lives to the college. By 1968, though, Juniata's scale ranked above the median for Pennsylvania colleges, except for full professors. The top figure for them on the Hill was then $13,500. The president's own paycheck totaled but a few thousand dollars more.

Expanded fringe benefits helped atone for modest annual increments. Social Security, which in 1951 was amended to include college employees among others, plus the TIAA/CREF pension plan, relieved some of the anxiety about the "sunset years."[10] Updated group life, hospitalization, and surgical insurance programs followed.[11] Then came major medical coverage.[12] The Ellis-Stauffer transition year added permanent disability insurance.[13]

Faculty housing—or rather the lack of it—had become a major problem by the late 1950s. The trustees seriously thought of putting up an apartment building to ease the situation. The spring of 1958 they voted to purchase up to six lots in the "Hollywood" section east of campus where a new $2.5-million high school was under construction.[14] These lots were to be sold at cost plus curb or street assessments to faculty members who wanted to build. The trustees again, in April 1967, authorized acquiring more lots—this time in Taylor Highlands—for the same purpose. Until the faculty got overly large the college gladly granted first mortgages to home buyers; later only second mortgages were taken on. The trustees also began to purchase more houses in the vicinity of the campus to be used as low rentals for faculty.

Up to 1964 faculty children got only one-half off tuition costs when attending the home college. In the early 1950s, however, Juniata had joined with several other institutions in a Faculty Children's Tuition Exchange Plan. The college pulled out of this consortium several years later because, as it turned out, the formula used for exchange did not balance out equitably for Juniata.

In 1964 the trustees introduced a plan staggeringly generous—unheard of at but a few schools. More than one above-par teacher has been saved for Juniata because of it. One part of the twofold plan is not unusual since other institutions have a similar tuition remission policy. It discounts for children of *any* full-time college employee all but two hundred dollars of tuition costs if they attend Juniata. But the unique feature of this plan (revoked in 1967 for future appointees but not for those already hired) was this: faculty and administrators' children could go to any college or university, where, in the event tuition was different from Juniata's, the grant was limited to the lower cost less one hundred dollars. The revocation of this latter benefit came about for good reason. In 1960 some unofficial census taker, probably the business manager, had reported a "baby boom" among the faculty and staff. The report tallied 135 future collegians of Hilltop parentage even then, the multiplying appointments and hirings of that decade still to come.

Calvert Ellis looked for other ways to build a loyal professorial cadre. In 1955 the college added the rank of associate professor. He saw to it that name professorships, most modestly endowed, did not long go unclaimed. The John Downey Benedict Professorship in English, named for a friend of the college killed in World War II, went to Harold Binkley in 1952 and to Esther Doyle in 1966. Donald Rockwell became the first Jacob H. and Rachel Brumbaugh Professor of Chemistry in 1958. It was established by the will of Dr. N. J. Brumbaugh, who left the major share of his estate to the college at his death in 1953. Miriam Schlegel Musselman, after a three-year lapse, inherited the Martin G. Brumbaugh Professorship in Education from Edgar Kiracofe in 1963. The Mary S. Geiger religion title, last held by the president himself, went to Earl Kaylor in 1966. Two others got name professorships that year. Evelyn Guss (Pitt Ph.D.) received the I. Harvey Brumbaugh chair in classics; it had never been claimed since established by the alumni as a memorial in 1938 (nor would it be assigned after Guss resigned in 1973). Wilfred Norris was named to the William I. and Zella B. Book chair in physics created in 1966. The donors were both alumni, the husband a former trustee and retired Penn physics professor.

By the time Calvert Ellis retired, the teaching craft was rewarded in two other ways. At his instigation the trustees approved a long-overdue sabbatical policy, a maximum of four a year. A sabbatical for a whole year meant half-pay, for six months, full pay. Then in the spring of 1968 the president announced the first cash teaching prize: the Beachley Distinguished Professor Award. Trustee Donovan Beachley, a Hagerstown, Maryland, furniture manufacturer, and his family endowed the annual honor. It would go to a senior faculty member exceptional in the classroom and active in college life and in community affairs. Historian Kenneth Crosby, with twenty-years' service, won the first award.

Institution loyalty on the part of *all* college employees got its share of attention during the Ellis administration. Administrators, faculty, and staff first celebrated Hilltop longevity at a Founders Day tea in 1949. Twenty-five Juniatians were honored for their ten years of service or more. The 10-Year Club, with induction rites spiced by brief humorous citations of anonymous authorship, has become a new Founders Day tradition. In the half-century since its inception there have been well over two hundred inductees.

The 25-Year Club, however, was an Alumni Association creation in 1961. Its first celebration took place at the alumni spring banquet that year and honored a dozen persons. One of them was Mrs. Anna Groninger Smith, the ever-pleasant, ever-efficient secretary to four presidents in her forty-four-year career (1921–1965). Induction into the 25-Year Club soon after became part of the Founders Tea get-togethers.

Out of the Ellis years has come another custom, this one saluting superannuated faculty members—and administrators with academic rank. The practice dates from 1960 when education professor Edgar Kiracofe retired. A colleague reads a valedictory eulogy in each case, to which the retiree gives a swan-song response of a reminiscent nature. A Juniata-monogrammed chair, presented by the college, represents a kind of unofficial passage into emeritus status for the recipient. This annual ritual, featured at a retirement dinner, takes place near the end of the academic year.

In the early Ellis years the president and the dean kept a firm hand on faculty governance. They named the personnel on standing committees. Not until 1954 did the faculty themselves nominate and elect their own representatives. Calvert Ellis, not the dean, presided at every faculty meeting. And until almost the very last Ellis year absences at those monthly meetings did not go unnoticed; the secretary kept an attendance record.

Needless to say, the faculty, no less than the students, need a registrar to keep academic order, assign classrooms, and maintain accurate transcripts. Occupants of this office during the Calvert Ellis quarter century were Pressley Crummy (1942–49), William Engel (1949–56, 1958–59), James Bray (1956–58), Hans Zbinden (1959–60), Ronald Cherry (1960–63), and John Hollinger (1963–69). Cherry, who took a leave from teaching economics to fill the post, began to translate some of the data collected in his office into useful statistical studies. His initiative paved the way for the first feeble efforts at institutional research and planning in 1966, the next year to be developed into a permanent position. In 1965 the administration remodeled the old chapel in Founders Hall and gave it over to registrar use. The office is still located there. Part of the renovation included a data-processing center and the installation of the college's first IBM machines.

During the Calvert Ellis years there was no tenure system. The trustees rejected the idea in 1961 in favor of three kinds of appointments: annual, term (three years), and indefinite. Indefinite appointments were automatically granted to full professors.

Faculty warhorses remember fondly the midmorning coffee break of the Fifties and Sixties held in the Faculty Club (now the Baker Guest House). Begun in 1950, this opportunity to fraternize lured in the teaching troops—and their bosses—each nonchapel morning between 10:00 and 10:30. The academic lull afforded a relaxed time to banter and gossip (or do business) for twenty years. Discontinuing chapel and imposing a different class schedule did in the klatch. But so far as bringing the faculty together across academic disciplines in a mood of camaraderie, nothing has taken its place.

By 1968 an increasingly cosmopolitan faculty had begun undermining what Calvert Ellis liked to call "Juniata's family spirit." Cliques had formed along age and interest lines, and more wives went to work. The once-a-month all-family socials, long a custom, had died out in the early Sixties. A sense of community, however, for many years has been fostered by the fall picnic. Through 1999 it was held at the Rockwells' estate, a few miles from the campus along Cold Springs Road. In the millennial year the picnic included the college staff and was held on campus.

PLAUDITS FAR AND WIDE FOR JUNIATA

When trustees conferred a surprise honorary doctorate on Dr. Ellis in 1963, his citation made the point: "During his lifetime and largely under his leadership, Juniata has reached its eminence in the world of liberal arts colleges." And so when incoming freshmen of that day answered the question Why Juniata? their responses invariably fell into the following order: (1) smallness; (2) scholastic reputation; (3) ideals of the college. Juniata, whose enrollment did not climb past one thousand until fall 1965, had by then got its share of far-flung recognition for the second category. The *Small College Annual,* first issued in 1948, included Juniata from the start as one of the "best" in the country. (Comparative guides to colleges and universities were then practically unknown.) In 1950 Juniata began appearing in *Good Housekeeping Magazine*'s yearly listing of notable small independent colleges, one of but thirteen in Pennsylvania. The College and Career Department of *Mademoiselle Magazine* rated Juniata in 1955 among 137 outstanding small liberal arts schools.

Earlier, in 1949, the Trytten Report, a five-volume study by President Truman's Scientific Research Board, had come out with kudos for Juniata. The report noted that many small colleges had, from 1936 to 1945, "contributed scientists out of all proportions to the number of their students."[15] It said that five colleges combined—Hope, Juniata, Monmouth, St. Olaf, and Oberlin—produced more candidates for doctor's degree in chemistry than did Johns Hopkins, Fordham, Columbia, Tulane, and Syracuse all together. In percentage, Juniata was rated eighth in the nation among smaller institutions.

Then in 1953 the Ford Foundation for the Advancement of Education gave the college high marks on another score. In a nationwide survey the foundation ranked Juniata among the top fifty colleges and universities with the best records for producing "young American scholars of promise."[16] Placing forty-third, Juniata was one of only four schools in its native Commonwealth to make the list, five steps above Penn.

The year 1957 yielded other statistical evidence of Juniata's academic strength. According to the National Research Council, 101 College Hill graduates earned doctorates (not counting the M. D. degree) between 1936 and 1956.[17] (The count went to 161 for the period 1920 to 1961.) A single banner year during Calvert Ellis's presidency was 1965–66 when a total of twenty-three Juniatians won doctor's chevrons.[18]

To attract good students the college had begun, just prior to the Second World War, to get into as many high schools as possible with a test prepared by the American Council on Education (ACE). It was the same one taken on campus by subfreshmen vying for Depression-years scholarships. After the war the college was getting into no less than 250 high schools, giving the ACE exam to as many as seventeen thousand college-minded students. Even the faculty went on the road to help administer these exams. The backbreaking chore of correcting them fell upon the college itself. Of 259 colleges and universities reporting in 1954, Juniata stood thirty-ninth in performance on the ACE test. In 1958 Juniata substituted the College Boards for candidates seeking admission.

Though good, the freshman Board SATs fell short of being superior. But the Ellis years reflected significant progress. The average verbal score of entering students rose from 476 in 1958 to 542 by 1967 and the average mathematics score from 515 to 571. This was well above the national performance. The new testing requirement, President Ellis had announced in his report for 1957, would not affect Juniata's commitment to its three major constituencies, "even if they do not have the highest academic potential."

At first in the postwar years, admissions was a part-time job, concerned more with selection than with marketing. Dr. Pressley Crummy was registrar and professor of biology while director of admission (1942–47). Melvin Rhodes combined admissions work with being dean of students (1947–52). Robert Newcombe became the first full-time director of admissions (1952–57), who now answered to the dean of the college instead of the president. Following him were Kenneth Wenger (1957–60) and Ronald Wertz (1960–63). Richard Kimmey in the next dozen years would bring Juniata's enrollment to its peak in that period.

THE CURRICULUM OF THE 1960s

Dr. Calvert's headship entertained two Middle States visits—in 1951 and 1962. These come at about ten-year intervals. On both occasions it was found that Juniata's virtues far outweighed its faults. The 1962 evaluation noted that the college's family concept "is important to students and faculty alike." It warned, however, that organizational shortcuts "inevitably invite friction." Juniata, its enrollment then just under eight hundred, "offers," said the re-accrediting report, "a program of studies that is good—not distinctive, but distinctive notes are there."[19]

Already in operation when the 1962 team showed up was an overhauled curriculum, initiated the previous fall. A faculty foursome, including Dean Mays, had spent three weeks at a Danforth-sponsored workshop at Colorado Springs the summer of 1959 restructuring the general curricular requirements. Faculty meetings the next academic year were given over to debate on the proposed changes.

The new pattern of education called for two basic courses, a yearlong one for freshmen and another for seniors. Freshmen took Great Epochs of World Culture, at first taught by Steven Barbash (Yale, M. F. A.), art instructor and the faculty's one Jew. Barbash, a flamboyant New Yorker, got his share of spoofing each year by freshmen in their All Class Night skit, as did the course itself and those who handled subsection discussion groups. Seniors had to take The Integration of Art, Knowledge, and Conduct, whose title later became The Nature of Man.

General education, long one of Juniata's commitments, stayed intact through the distribution strategy. Every student had to take four courses in each division outside his/her field of concentration, spread over two different departments. In 1965 the distribution requirement for Division III was changed, reducing it to three semesters of work in any two departments of which at least two semesters had to involve a natural science laboratory.

"Concentration" and "collateral" became the jargon for major and minor. Collateral courses, though, could cut across several disciplines. Dual concentration, in which a student attained a measure of depth in two different departments, became an option in 1964. It carried with it several alternatives with respect to the comprehensive examination.

Still retained was English conference. And requirements continued in foreign language, religion (upped to two courses—Biblical History plus a second—but reduced back to one in 1966), and physical education. Nor were written and oral comprehensives given up. Applied credit also stayed on the books—up to four hours for extracurricular participation in music. But journalistic activity, debate, and drama no longer qualified, as they once did, after the 1963 spring semester.

The Dean's List, which replaced the Honor Roll after Juniata got an academic dean, turned into two in 1964, a first (high honor) and a second (honor). The next fall midterm grades became obsolete, replaced by deficiency slips. A rather liberal pass-fail system (one p/f course per semester outside the field of concentration) went into effect in 1967. By then a variety of independent study opportunities were available to students. Few, though, took advantage of them.

The 1961 curriculum, of course, maintained the three-division structure. In 1963 division chairmanships, which heretofore had been largely honorific and of indefinite tenure, now went on a three-year cycle (as did department heads), the appointments made by the president. The intent was to vitalize the three posts, providing the dean of the college with closer faculty liaison in carrying out the academic life of the institution. An unintended result soon surfaced: divisional envy—especially toward the sciences, enriched by the post-Sputnik bonanza.

The humanities, with 20.9 percent of all majors in 1965, felt the most aggrieved. The administration responded by funding a double-faceted program worked out by the division: short stay artists-in-residence and a lectureship in comparative studies. Jack Gilbert, 1962 winner of the Yale Younger Poets Award (his would later become one of the nation's most eminent names in poetry), came as resident number one the spring of 1964. The first lecturer in comparative studies, beginning the fall of 1965, was Dr. Lawrence Abler, a young scholar from California who taught in the general areas of English and German.

Other gains came to the humanities during the decade of the Sixties. A modern language laboratory went into the I. Harvey Brumbaugh House in 1961. History, linked up with political science as a Division II department, split off and joined the humanities in 1964. (The religion department had already made the move.) At that time "Clio" was second only to biology in number of majors—108. The art department, which had been revived in 1953, got quarters befitting its dignity in 1964. (Until 1953 there had been no instruction in the graphic arts since 1921.) Before taking over renovated Carnegie Library the department made do in one of the Village's old barracks on Round Top. In 1966 the English department gave speech and theatre its autonomy. Russian, meanwhile, had been introduced back in 1961. The trustees, however, phased out music education in the fall of 1968, costs outweighing returns, the board explained. The emphasis now was to be on the cultural value of music for all students instead of teacher preparation.

At the same time Division II lost home economics. When World War II ended it had been the college's largest department. From 1947 to its demise the department occupied a white frame building, provided by the Federal Works Agency, which stood where what is now a vacant space behind Founders Hall. A little cottage close by served as the nursery. Finances dictated the fate of home economics.

Division II claimed the greatest number of majors the spring of 1968—35.9 percent of the college total. Education enrolled the most (122), thriving on what a 1966 *Juniatian* editorial called the "worst teacher shortage" in twenty years. Economics and business administration ran a close second (93). Sociology majors nearly doubled those of psychology (79 to 47) as President Lyndon Johnson's "Great Society" dreams made the job market in social welfare very promising. Political science, far down the column, got something of a boost when Juniatians were admitted to two off-campus programs in 1966: the United Nations Semester through Drew University and American University's Washington Semester.

In springtime 1968 about thirty-five percent of Juniata students were concentrating in some field of science. Biology majors by far numbered the most on campus (227). Chemists came in a distant second (61). Mathematics and physics were tied at seventeen. However, geology—introduced in 1962—had built up a following of twenty-nine. Its lowly departmental birth under Peter Trexler had taken place in the basement of Students Hall. By 1968, of course, Division III had settled into the Brumbaugh Science Center, a small-college wonder, then three years old. By that time the division had long been identified (since the early 1950s) with several cooperative programs in specialized fields at certain universities or hospitals. They included medical technology, engineering, and forestry. (The number of such programs would increase to thirteen come the millennium.)

What most quickened the envy of Divisions I and II in the early Sixties was the federal boon that befell the sciences after the Russians put Sputnik into orbit in 1957. Thousands of dollars, some for equipment but the lion's share for training undergraduates in research, flowed to College Hill. The National Science Foundation, the Atomic Energy Commission, and the National Institutes of Health made generous grants. From 1961 to 1966 the chemistry department conducted NSF-funded summer institutes for high-school chemistry teachers. Juniata's 1961 institute was one of only twenty-two conducted throughout the country under NSF auspices.[20]

A curricular innovation in 1962, though nondivisional in character, at first worked most to benefit the humanities. This was the Brethren Colleges Abroad (BCA) program. BCA originated as a cooperative junior-year program for foreign study at the instigation of the six colleges with a Church of the Brethren heritage. In its first decade BCA-host institutions were located only in Germany. In the year 2000 BCA operates in nine countries. Several Juniata professors have served as resident directors at the various overseas (Atlantic and Pacific) institutional sites.

The Will Judy Lectureship, established in 1958, provided the college with another nondivisional learning opportunity. The dog-magazine publisher intended his twenty-thousand-dollar gift to "supplement and enrich" Juniata's academic program by bringing to the Hill speakers of note from a wide spectrum of life: government, education, the arts, natural sciences, business, and other important fields of the public sector. For many years the choice of lecturers has been rotated among the three divisions.

A BOARD OF TRUSTEES THAT DARED

One of the most interesting aspects of his presidency, Calvert Ellis once observed, was helping businessmen to understand educators and vice versa. "Educators tend to be autocrats—there is no need to compromise," he said.[21] "Businessmen compromise constantly." Ellis had a way with men of affairs, and the rapport between him and the board of trustees remained exceptionally strong the whole of his twenty-five years as president.

He inherited more than a score of board members from his father's administration. But by the mid-1950s he was well on his way to shaping a board of his own design.

Some came to his attention when elected by the alumni or a church district. Others the board itself co-opted, twenty-three of them between 1944 and 1968. They would represent a wide range of business and professional interests. Two were women; fourteen were alumni. Their names appear below in alphabetical order under the decade of their initial election:

> 1940s—Percy Blough (1944–47; 1952–62); William Book (1946–49; 1951–62); George Detweiler (1947–50); Dale Detwiler (1949–1994); Denton Emmert (1959–62; 1963–75); William Flory (1946–69); Chalendar Lesher (1947–68).
>
> 1950s—Robert Baker (1956–76); Edith Hartman Cutrell (1957–95); Joseph Good (1952–94); Jewett Henry (1959–79); Robert Miller (1957–69); John Montgomery (1950–76); Paul Robinson (1959–76); Lester Rosenberger (1952–79); John Swigart (1950–89).
>
> 1960s—Charles Ellis (1966–91); Cecil Loomis (1967–81); Thomas Martin (1968–79); Thomas Miller (1967–79); Florence Fogelsanger Murphy (1963–68); Charles Rice (1967–77); John Stauffer (1967–79).

When Ellis became president, Dr. Gaius Brumbaugh, the last personal link to the college's inception, was chairman of the board. A trustee for forty years, the last twelve as chair, he resigned in 1948 at age eighty-six. Henry Gibbel, a Lititz, Pennsylvania, banker and insurance executive, took his place. (Gibbel's father had been Juniata's third board chairman.) A close Ellis friend and ardent fan of Indian football, Henry the son gave vigorous leadership for more than a decade. He died in 1959, still in his fifties. There followed a succession of figurehead chairmanships (one-year terms) until 1963. Then John Baker took the helm, chosen because the trustees felt he and the president "made such an effective team."[22] Ellis often said he never had a real "boss" until the day of Baker's election.

John Baker, a tall, suave, energetic native of nearby Everett, would chair the board for thirteen years. (In all he would serve as a trustee for fifty-one years.) His M. B. A. degree from Harvard in 1923, he remained there until 1945, first in a number of Business School positions and then as associate dean of the university. From 1945 until 1961 he served as the fourteenth president of Ohio University. Said *Time Magazine* in 1951: "A Yaleman founded the school, but a Harvardman put it on its feet."[23] The college in Ohio's Hocking Valley was in "shabby shape," John Baker discovered upon his arrival. "He searched like a talent scout," acclaimed *Time*, "for the best men he could find to fill the vacancies." The Baker administration provided Ohio University, founded in 1804, with its period of greatest growth, both physically and academically. Enrollment more than quintupled—to eight thousand—and thirty-two major buildings were added to the campus. In 1954, 1955, and 1956 Dwight Eisenhower appointed Baker as chief representative to UNESCO. He later conducted State Department studies of education needs in Cambodia and Colombia and in 1975 served as an advisor to the government of Iran. No one can properly assess what his experience and vision in higher education has meant to the board. Fortunately Calvert

Ellis had talked him out of abdicating as a trustee in December 1944 when he accepted the presidency of Ohio University.

Just before the Baker-Ellis team formed, the trustee bylaws underwent a significant revision. In 1959 the trustees amended them to read: "A majority of the elected members of the Board shall be members of the Church of the Brethren." This replaced the four-fifths prescript. The rationale: most trustees were alumni and well aware of the college's religious past. Also, most were Brethren, but some of them lived in places not churched by the denomination, so they had joined other Christian groups.

Something said by James Baxter, president of Williams College, had hit home with Calvert Ellis soon after he took office. Dr. Baxter wrote, while World War II raged at full fury: "The colleges and universities cannot go unreconstructed in a world undergoing a general reconstruction."[24] On the Hill these words inspired the Planning Commission, set up in 1944. It involved over one hundred persons—trustees, alumni, faculty—through associated committees, deliberating the aims and goals of Juniata once peace came. Out of the commission's study sprang the "Juniata Postwar Fund," approved by the trustees shortly before V-E Day. Its goal was one million dollars—for buildings and endowment. This was the first million-dollar drive in the college's history. It met its goal by 1953.

Yet Calvert Ellis could say that year: "The plight of the private college continues to be precarious."[25] And John Baker wrote from Athens, Ohio: "The small college of 500 students, which idealistically I admire, is no longer an economic unit."[26] There were deficits in the early Fifties as Juniata's enrollment, affected by the Korean War, dropped off sharply from a 1949 high of 710. Quoting the *New York Times*, Dr. Ellis told the trustees in October 1951 that more than half the colleges of America were operating on deficits caused by the draft and enlistments. Massive federal aid to higher education was still a decade away, but industry, at least, Juniata's president told the trustees in 1953, had showed signs of awakening to its responsibilities.

His comment referred to the work of the Foundation for Independent Colleges. This enterprise had originated in Indiana in 1952, and Ellis had helped bring its appeal to Pennsylvania. Juniata became one of thirty-six charter members, its president the foundation's first treasurer. The foundation still exists, heads of member institutions donating time each year to personal solicitation of commercial and industrial concerns. The money is equitably distributed among the free-standing colleges according to a formula.

In the fall of 1953, immediately upon the ahead-of-time success of the Juniata Postwar Fund, the trustees proceeded to move forward on the two-million-dollar "Build Juniata Program." The new ten-year initiative projected an enrollment of 750. In 1955 the trustees dared to increase the capital campaign to $2.5 million. The Ford Foundation added special cheer to the Hill's Christmas season that year by announcing a gift of $138,000. That was Juniata's largest single windfall up to that time. It went toward the support of faculty salaries.

For the first time in Juniata's history parents rallied as an organized unit behind a financial campaign. They formed DAJUMO (first two letters of Dad, Juniata, and Mother) in the spring of 1957. Said DAJUMO Chairman Benn Goodrich of Ridgway,

Pennsylvania, "There is need for the support, both spiritually and financially, from the parents."

In July 1957 President Ellis appointed alumnus Charles Bargerstock, an ex-Marine and Iwo Jima hero, to the new position of director of development. When he left in 1962 Harold Brumbaugh took up the work, forcing him to lay down his first love: alumni relations. The summer before Bargerstock's departure, Juniata received the largest bequest to that date from a Huntingdonian. Nonagenarian Allen Shaffner, a retired banker, bequeathed the college one hundred thousand dollars. His will designated the bequest as a scholarship loan fund in memory of his wife and sister.

That same year of 1961 the trustees dared to lift their sights again. In mid-campaign they raised the capital goal to $5,350,000. Board members themselves subscribed $248,830, and a "quiet campaign" netted $249,355 in Huntingdon. DAJUMO upped their gifts to nearly four thousand dollars in 1961. And the alumni responded by topping earlier levels of giving. The fiscal year 1963–64 produced a record in Hilltop charity—the first time gifts to the college exceeded one million dollars ($1,607,635).

In November 1964 Harold Brumbaugh gained a twenty-seven-year-old aide named Gerald Quigg. He was assigned to the Juniata Valley area. His personality and hard work earned him promotion to director of development in 1966 (when Brumbaugh became a vice-president). Quigg, therefore, guided the Build Juniata Program to its happy ending, completed sooner than expected and oversubscribed by twenty thousand dollars. All of this with only a minimum of professional fund-raising help—from American City Bureau—early in the going.

Over the previous half-dozen years the student population had risen thirty-three percent, to over one thousand. The faculty had more than doubled. The operating budget stood at $3.2 million—as against the $240,000 when Calvert Ellis became president in 1943.

Since September 1965, however, a Long Range Planning Committee, made up of trustees, faculty, and administration, had been looking into the future—beyond 1967. Among other things it projected, as the optimum enrollment, a college of 1,250 students. This called for more buildings, facilities, and a higher endowment. The cost of educating a Juniata student in the mid-1960s meant that eighty-five cents of every dollar was paid from tuition and fees.

Thus even before the 1967 Founders Day jubilation, the trustees had hatched another campaign. At the same time Dr. Ellis had gathered round him a President's Development Committee of thirty-three persons, all nontrustees. He charged the council with the task of representing Juniata to foundations, corporations, and potential individual donors during the course of the campaign. This latest capital drive, set at an unprecedented $10.1 million and to culminate in the college's centennial year, carried the name "Margin of Difference." Gerald Quigg coined the phrase. It meant, explained the president, that the hoped-for funds "will provide Juniata with that margin of difference in the quality of its education without which it could not successfully meet the challenges of the future."[27] Relying solely upon volunteers, the campaign got underway in April of 1968. The trustees, pledging over $370,000, again demonstrated their strong commitment to Juniata. When Ellis retired, the endowment had built up to $2,168,594, nearly a fourfold increase since 1943.

Who was responsible for reporting accurately the character and purposes of the development programs? For twenty years (1946–66) it had been William Engel. An experienced journalist, having worked on newspaper staffs in the Harrisburg and Pittsburgh areas, he came to the Hill as director of publicity. But other jobs were soon tacked on. Besides editing all college publications and writing countless news releases, he was registrar for eight years, kept faculty meeting minutes (1954–66), directed summer sessions (two years), announced Juniata football games on radio station WHUN for a decade, taught journalism, and advised the *Juniatian*. No wonder that paper said, when he signed "Thirty" to his press desk, it would take more than one person to fill his shoes. The *Alumni Bulletin* (Summer 1966) paid him fitting tribute when he resigned to become director of foundation appeals at Penn State. Someone wrote, ["He has been] the soul and conscience of Juniata's public relations."

Barnard Taylor, a professional designer and painter with a background in newspaper reportage, took Engel's place (1966–73). He assumed the title College Editor. The centennial logo, a tree sprouting from an open book, was his design. His graphic skills and instincts brought a fresh look to all college publications.

A CAMPUS BEAUTIFUL

A profusion of buildings stands as a monument to Calvert Ellis's presidency, though this was not what he necessarily wanted to be remembered for. Feverish construction was a phenomenon of the times on all campuses, he often said, dismissing his brick-and-mortar achievements. His presidential years, however, saw the main campus enlarge from forty to fifty-five acres, beautified by planned landscaping. The physical plant multiplied to twenty-four buildings, valued at more than ten million dollars.

The campus transformation began modestly enough. There was no major reconstruction until eight years after he became president. Some of the first buildings—government surplus—are gone. Sherwood Lodge, better known as the "Green Shanty," was a 1946 addition. An H-shaped barracks converted into a dormitory, it stood in the hollow behind the Cloister and housed eighty-six veterans. On Easter Sunday 1955 a fire destroyed the east wing (ignited by town children playing with matches). That summer a buyer dismantled the undamaged part. Sherwood Lodge, however, had encroached upon the unfinished golf course, which had suffered badly from wartime neglect. A campus links, it was soon evident, had no future.

The "Village"—for married ex-GIs—also went up in 1946, on the present site of Brumbaugh Science Center. It consisted of six buildings with dwelling units for twenty families. From the campus could be seen diapers on washlines, baby carriages on the grass, ice cards in the windows, and coal in outside bins. Later, after the veterans had left, faculty occasionally made use of the Village for housing. As noted, the art department also moved in. The once-peopled colony finally disappeared in 1964 to make way for science.

The immediate postwar years also saw M. G. Brumbaugh's old home, fire-gutted in January of 1945, reconstructed into the Faculty Club (1946); the college take over the I. Harvey Brumbaugh House (1947); and home economics barracked behind Brumbaugh Hall (1947). The I. Harvey Brumbaugh House became an extension of the library until the language lab was installed. (Later on it was also converted into offices for faculty linguists, and then, in 1972 turned over to public relations.)

High on the priority list of the postwar Planning Commission had been a student center with a refectory that could seat all resident students. That never developed, but an addition to the Oneida Hall dining room did (1950). Now over 470 could be served at one time. This ended, for a while at least, the two-platoon system of eating, a necessity since 1946.

Swigart Music Hall (1950), a private home last owned by Francis McSherry, president of the J. C. Blair Co., was a godsend.[28] The McSherry property was made possible through the gift of W. Emmert Swigart, son of William J. Swigart. The three-story structure, which still houses the music department, underwent extensive renovation in 1964 when the exterior (brown brick) was painted white and the front porch removed.

The big construction thrust lay ahead. The seventeen years after 1950 would see one building after another dot the campus—ten in all. It all began with the Memorial Physical Education Building (1951), erected in honor of the nearly seven hundred Juniatians who served in World War II. Designed by John B. Hamme of York, Pennsylvania, it was the forerunner of all later Pennsylvania gymnasiums and was the first of its kind to use an arched roof.[29] Folding bleachers, above which is laid a mezzanine indoor track, seat 1,080.

The old 1901 building now became the "Women's Gymnasium." Meanwhile, Elizabeth Ellis fretted. Not knowing the future, she feared that her husband's presidency would be remembered only for a gymnasium, while that of his father's for Oller Hall, a cultural center.

In October 1952, while Dwight Eisenhower and Adlai Stevenson squared off for the upcoming presidential election, Ellis carried good news to the trustees. He announced that outgoing President Truman had at last released forty million dollars for housing loans to colleges and universities under a law passed by Congress in 1950—a law Dr. Ellis had personally lobbied for.

Hamme-designed North Hall, on the eminence overlooking the northeast campus, became the second dormitory in the country to be partially financed by funds under the 1950 Act.[30] Erected in 1955 in two sections with a connecting lounge, it accommodates 128 students.* A structural problem (noise carried through the halls and rooms unabated) soon elicited pejorative nicknames for the dormitory: "Campus Albatross" or "Wart of Huntingdon County." (The problem has been remedied for the most part.) Architecturally, North Hall (renamed Sunderland Hall in 1997) set the pattern for all campus building to follow—contemporary colonial style of red brick in

---

* The maintenance building was a 1955 project, too—a two-floor concrete block structure next to the Heating Plant. Here are located the shops for carpentry, plumbing, and painting, and the Central Stores.

four blending shades. That autumn of 1955 the college changed architects to an Altoona firm, Hunter, Caldwell, and Campbell (later known by different names). All major buildings since have been their architectural creations.

East Hall (renamed Maude Lesher Hall in 1960), L-shaped and four floors high, reared up in 1957 where the Geiger House had stood.* Rooming 120 women, it has a dining room (for two hundred but now the Early Childhood Center), a lounge, and recreation area. The college infirmary, with medical facilities, was located here until 1998. Lesher Hall made media human-interest news when Capt. Will Judy, ever the imaginative alumnus, furnished a room "to be occupied only by titian-tressed ladies in honor of my wife, Ruth, herself an alumna."[31] Joan Greenwood (Metro), a senior elementary education major from New Jersey, was the first auburn-haired occupant of room 201 (not until 1964 did two redheads live together there). As recently as 1996 an Associated Press writer referred to "Juniata's gem" as "one of thousands of oddball endowments scattered around the country."

Sherwood Hall, a three-floor dormitory (for 120 students) east of North Hall, went up in 1961. Next year came L-shaped South Hall (for 150 students), at the corner of Scott and 17th streets, one wing overlooking College Field. This brought about the total evacuation of Founders and parts of Oneida. Faculty from Divisions I and II rushed in—except for art, music, and the languages. They commandeered third and fourth Founders for badly needed private offices, heretofore a denied luxury to most of them.

Now came a five-year respite in dormitory construction. But the Altoona architects were not kept idle; they had a library and a science complex on the drawing board. The Middle States reviews of 1951 and 1962 had each emphasized the deficiencies of Carnegie Library. President Ellis had been cultivating a potential donor for a new building ever since 1946. Over the years he and Harold Brumbaugh, on a tip by alumnus Edgar Diehm, had been making regular trips to Youngstown, Ohio. There they would call on wealthy industrialist, Leon A. Beeghly. Beeghly's grandparents had been prominent in the history of the Church of the Brethren in Ohio.

The Beeghly Foundation, however, was for years tied up in litigation with the government. In the end, the IRS lost and in 1963 Juniata got its library at a cost of over six hundred thousand dollars. Located along Moore Street but facing Memorial Gym it has space for over 200,000 volumes, numerous reader locations, and individual carrels for four hundred students. A decorative feature above the main entrance displays the seals of the college, the town of Huntingdon, and the founder of the Church of the Brethren in colorful ceramic tile. This was a gift of Stanley Davis of Lansdale, Pennsylvania. The second-floor William Emmert Swigart Treasure Room, with its rare books, incunabula, and first editions, holds great attraction for visiting scholars. Until the College Center was built, the bookstore took up most of the basement area.

---

* Three private residences were acquired during the 1950s for additional student housing, each named for a prominent person in Juniata's history. They were the N. J. Brumbaugh House (1953) at 1808 Moore St., the chemistry professor's actual home; the Emmert House, corner of 18th and Moore, for David Emmert; and the Saylor House, 18th and Mifflin, for Joseph Saylor. The "N. J. House" and the "Emmert House" also had faculty apartments. Dr. Kenneth Crosby bought the Saylor House in 1961 for his family home.

Mrs. Anne Catlin had come as director of libraries, a new position, in 1962 to take charge of preparing for the massive move to the new north-campus library location. In the spring of 1967 Juniata joined the Area Library Cooperative, then comprised of nine other Central Pennsylvania institutions (now seventeen). Mrs. Catlin called it "a model for interlibrary cooperation throughout the United States." Each college has developed an area of specialization.[32] For Juniata it is the Myers Science Library.

The old library, renamed Carnegie Hall (1964), was imaginatively redesigned as a fine arts center. The Col. Henry W. Shoemaker Galleries occupied the main floor for exhibitions. Upstairs, in the rotunda, went a historical museum, Harold Brumbaugh its founder. The rest of the building was given over to the art department for studio space and general classrooms. At first ceramics, including a kiln, had space there, too, until relocated elsewhere.

The site of a projected new science building was decided in 1958—west side of Moore Street where the Village stood. Blueprints showed a pretentious structure. The major breakthrough in funding came in 1962 when the Longwood Foundation of Wilmington, Delaware, announced a four-hundred-thousand-dollar challenge grant (then the single largest grant in Juniata's history, eclipsed the next year by Beeghly bounty). Brumbaugh Science Center (1965), constructed at a cost of $2.7 million, undoubtedly ranked as one of the finest of its kind among the nation's small colleges. Making use of natural topography, it is laid out in four elevations, three wings radiating from a large hub. The multiunit complex contains a chemistry wing (south), a biology wing (west), and a geology, mathematics, and physics wing (north). Since 1983 the north wing is also the location of the college computer center (which started out in the basement of Carnegie Library). The two-story circular unit at the hub has a four-hundred-seat Alumni Hall above which are two pie-shaped lecture halls.

By November of 1966 the college owed the government some one million dollars for federal loans.[33] On top of that applications had been made for another $1,150,000 in loans plus a federal grant of $250,000 for additional construction. One application was for the Tussey-Terrace complex (1966), a two-unit, L-shaped building connected by a one-floor social center, on the northwest section of campus. It provides room for 176 students. The complex also included an apartment for Harold Brumbaugh, who, as noted, for years had been ensconced in the Cloister Arch.

The other application pertained to what everybody at first called the Academic Classroom Building (1967). The college totally renovated the interior of the 1916 science building and enlarged it by adding wings at both ends. Air-conditioned like Beeghly Library and Brumbaugh Science Center, the structure contains more than thirty classrooms, several instructional laboratories, and over twenty faculty offices for the social science division. The humanities faculty now reigned supreme as office-dwellers in Founders' upper reaches. The language laboratories departed the I. Harvey Brumbaugh House for the basement of the new classroom facility. The Academic Building ended the Ellis phase of campus transformation.

After seventy-two years Students Hall, soon to be razed, now stood empty and silent. But not for long. Children from the Alexandria-Petersburg area, whose grade school had burned to the ground, invaded it the next year. Then it fell silent again, this time for good.

KEEPING AN EYE ON THE BOTTOM LINE

When the Ellises' presidential switch took place in 1943, alumnus William Price, nearing his eightieth birthday, became college treasurer. He died in 1949 and Mrs. Rhoda Metz Rhodes, assistant treasurer, ran the office until 1952. John Fike succeeded Mrs. Metz and handled Juniata's financial affairs as chief budget officer for the next nineteen years. Meanwhile, Hilda Nathan had been promoted to John Fike's deputy in 1952. She had joined the treasurer's office in 1946, a recent immigrant. She lost many relatives during the Holocaust, although able herself to flee Germany and spend the war years in England. (In 1969 she was elevated to chief accountant and retired in Juniata's centennial year.)

Also employed in 1946 was Paul Friend as business manager. A pre-war football standout for the Indians, he shouldered most of the responsibility for maintenance of buildings and grounds until 1963. The care of the campus then became the worry of Eugene Esterline (1963–73), with more construction ahead. Paul Friend gave twenty-one years to his alma mater in the business office.

CHURCH RELATIONS AND ALUMNI AFFAIRS

Annual Conference began helping out shrunken Brethren colleges, most of them worse off than Juniata, during World War II. For thirteen years after 1944 it made regular appropriations to each school—in Juniata's case about fifty thousand dollars altogether. The Brotherhood meant this funding more to symbolize church support than pay bills, especially after the wartime crunch.

Early in the postwar development program the college sought to bolster ties with the three church districts represented on the board of trustees. Alumnus Edgar Detwiler, a retired Brethren pastor, became director of church relations on a part-time basis (1948–57). Then in 1954, the Build Juniata Program well afoot, Clarence Rosenberger, called from a pastorate, joined Rev. Detwiler as a full-time partner.

Rosenberger, himself a Juniatian, who in 1945 had helped organize the first "Heifers for Relief" shipment and served as the "Zona Gale's" crew chief, spent fifteen years in the church relations office. He expanded the college's contact with the nearly 140 churches in the three districts. He introduced Brethren Campus Day, a Saturday of visitation by pastors and college-minded high schoolers, and began publishing a newssheet, the "Builder," in 1955. He arranged for Hilltop faculty, administrators, and student deputation teams to present "Juniata College Day" services in local congregations. It was his idea to make Juniata the repository of all Middle District historical records. (From 1960 to 1969 the Middle District Office had a Founders Hall location.)

For the quarter-century after 1943 contributions from the churches of the three districts increased from less than twenty-seven hundred dollars to slightly over twenty-eight thousand dollars. Ironically, however, the number of Brethren students declined from twenty-six percent of the enrollment to 12.8 percent for the same period.

In many of the district churches, of course, some alumni contributed to the college independently. Back in 1919 Charles Eliot of Harvard had said that a college had no right to expect financial assistance from others if its own alumni will not rally round its alma mater. Juniata graduates, between 1943 and 1968, gave their fair share of seed money. Twice—in 1963 and 1964—Juniata received achievement citations from the American Alumni Council. By 1968 alumni had contributed over two million dollars in the twenty-nine years since the annual giving program originated. That year there was a 36.6 percent participation, not the highest in the country but well above the national average of 17.9 percent. Averaged out, each Juniata contributor gave $81.72 more than his/her counterpart elsewhere ($118.64 to $36.92).[34] Will Judy, the nationally known dog fancier and publisher who had thought up the One Hundred Club, scored again in 1948 with the One Thousand Club. The Five Hundred Club had a 1966 debut. In 1967 it became the practice to call these three groups collectively "The Founders Club."

The spring of 1953 forty-seven seniors, their class treasury depleted and unable to do something to commemorate their days on College Hill, conceived a novel plan of systematic giving to the alumni fund. At the instigation of Ronald Cherry, soon to come back to teach, and Paul Good, of Youngstown, Ohio, the forty-seven became the "53 Investors Club." Each member promised to contribute $10 a year, to be invested over the next decade by a board of directors. At its tenth reunion, held at Motel 22, the Investors Club turned over its entire portfolio—worth $5,817.15—to the college as an endowment gift (for library books).

Two 1950s alumni succeeded Harold Brumbaugh as alumni secretary: William Martin (1963–66) and Glenn Zug (1966–72). They helped inaugurate a couple innovations during their time at the alumni desk. In 1964 Martin initiated the first telethon in canvassing potential donors to the Build Juniata Program. Then in midsummer 1966 Harold Brumbaugh acted as host guide for the first alumni tour—to Europe and England. By 2000 well over one hundred excursions had visited more than eighty countries. (Out of the tours grew the Passport Club, in 1974. The club's annual dinner meetings became a tradition during Alumni Reunion Weekend.)

By 1968 there were more than six thousand living alumni. The local associations numbered twenty-two, ranging from California to Florida to Boston. The alumni office kept track of Juniatians via two updated directories during the Calvert Ellis presidency, 1948 and 1958. These were the college's only Who's Who listings since the original one in 1935. Among them in 1948 appeared the name of William Beery, one of the Forge "Orphans" back in 1877. Every April 8 (his birthday) since 1940 he had sung over a nationwide network from station WLS in Chicago. In 1955 he was, at age 103, the oldest college alumnus in the United States (he died January 29, 1956).

Ten years before Beery's death the Juniata Women's League, combining the five local groups, consolidated into a central organization. Its charter meeting was held October 26, 1946. The League declared its mission to be "promoting the spiritual and financial welfare of Juniata College." The women underwrote a variety of projects to promote Juniata's cause over the years. Their annual spring "Continental Breakfast" lasted as a tradition to 1994.

Chapter 13

STUDENT LIFE: WORLD WAR II TO LATE 1960S

THE GI CAMPUS INVASION

The tides of battle had not yet turned the Allies' way when Calvert Ellis took charge on College Hill. In Europe, D-Day's cross-channel landing at Normandy, France, was still in the planning stages. In the Pacific the assaults on the Philippines—at Leyte and Luzon—would be a year away. The fall of 1944 found only sixty-five men on campus, which was not the lowest male population among colleges of similar size in the state.[1]

A spirit of "carry on" pervaded the student body of 295 that autumn. Enrollment would slip no further. At Christmastime the Senate and Lamba Gamma sent special greetings to all Juniata men and women in the service as "a gesture of friendship and loyalty." And Alumni Secretary Harold Brumbaugh kept in touch with them through the "Jay-Ce-O-Gram," a mimeographed newssheet.

Then came fierce fighting on German and Japanese fronts: the Battle of the Bulge, crossing the Rhine, Iwo Jima, Okinawa. The awful costs of war did not spare Juniata. The total number of students and alumni in the armed forces finally reached 675, of whom twenty-four would not return home.[2] A few from the Hill, perhaps less than half a dozen, served in Civilian Public Service camps as conscientious objectors.

At last came the fall of Nazi Germany in May 1945. In August the world learned of the devastation at Hiroshima and Nagasaki. The nuclear age had dawned. Five alumni had been connected with groups that did research on the development of the A-Bomb.[3] On August 14 the 110 summer students on College Hill heard the news of Imperial Japan's surrender.

Raymond Day, a Huntingdon preministerial student, had graduated two months before America celebrated V-J Day. He was the second—and only male—black student to get a Juniata degree up to that time. (Later, Rev. Day won national attention for his settlement-house work in Chicago, ending his professional life on the faculty at Wooster College, Ohio.) That fall of 1945, with Raymond Day gone, Juniata reverted to a campus devoid of a single black American.

The ex-GIs who returned to the Hill in September did not feel at home at first. They organized a Veterans Club to provide, reported the *Juniatian*, a "niche" for themselves, most of whom were "unfamiliar with present campus faces and organizations."[4] By spring veterans constituted twenty-four percent of the student body. That fall the enrollment soared to 573, doubling in one year. Of the 349 men on campus, 257 were discharged armed forces students of whom fifty-seven were married. Calvert Ellis was uneasy about what was happening. He wrote John Baker at Ohio University:

> I am…anxious that we accept only those veterans who will be able to do the work and be satisfactory graduates of Juniata. We find a number of men are applying for admission who actually are not fitted to carry forward college work satisfactorily. It is difficult to refuse admission and yet I feel that we must maintain our integrity as education institutions.[5]

Faced with a housing emergency, the trustees vetoed the use of trailers. They turned to off-campus rooms and, of course, army surplus buildings—the Village and Sherwood Lodge. The "Green Shanty," however, was not ready until October, and so for nearly a month eighty-six veterans bedded down in the old gymnasium. Their married counterparts in the Village organized the next year and elected a mayor, Richard March, a Scottsdale, Pennsylvania, biology student.

The number of veterans on the Hill peaked the academic year 1947–48, when over half the student body was there on the GI Bill. By 1949–50 only about one-fourth were former servicemen, the freshman class counting but twenty-one of them. The average age of students had declined, and campus leadership was passing to those coming directly to Juniata from high school. A total of 583 ex-World War II returnees had studied at Juniata by July 21, 1951, the cut-off date for the GI Bill. Scholastically the back-from-war Juniatians had proved more than equal to the academic task. A national survey in 1949 concluded college-going comrades were "curiously old before their time." The new breed of students replacing them struck Calvert Ellis—at least at first—as lacking their motivation.

CAMPUS LIFE DURING THE POSTWAR FORTIES

Veterans came back to a campus pretty much controlled by women. For the first time in its history the Senate drew up an all-female slate for president the spring of 1945. Myron Dunlavy in particular did not find the campus situation much to his liking after his discharge that year. He wrote a letter to the *Juniatian* titled "Are We Mice or Men?" It began:

> He [the veteran] is thankful to those courageous souls for their fine efforts in doing men's jobs during the emergency....
>
> However, the war is over and the women at Juniata, as well as women all over America, must relinquish many of their war-time jobs. It must be realized that women have an entirely different attitude than men toward many things and therefore are not as qualified as men in certain offices. Further, women should remember that men dislike domineering women.[6]

Who won the next election for Senate president? Glenora Edwards (Rossell), Myron's letter notwithstanding.

Uncle Sam's erstwhile warriors soon worked changes on the campus. They reveled in their newly gained freedom from the restraints of military life. They did not take kindly to civilian ones. After all, they were men now, not boys. With their return, for one thing, came college-sponsored dances. The first one (December 17, 1946) was discreetly arranged to be off-campus—at the Huntingdon Country Club. The *Juniatian* cryptically referred to it as a Veterans Club "party," a "semi-formal event," with "music furnished by a ten piece orchestra from Altoona." Some trustees were unhappy, but sixty-four-year-old Bessie Rohrer said the board had more important things to think about and to let the president run the campus. She silenced the issue forever. Next year, two dances were held on the Hill itself, one by J clubbers, the other by the veterans. The *Juniatian* did not now resort to euphemisms in publicizing them. Saturday night dances in the gymnasium became a regular part of the social calendar.

In other less unprecedented ways the peacetime campus came alive. In October 1945 the college bussed to Paradise Furnace for Mountain Day, last observed in 1941. Esther Doyle revived drama, a casualty of the war, in December of 1945. The reorganized Masquers, under her direction, staged Kaufman and Hart's *You Can't Take It With You*.

The A Cappella Choir, campused during the war years 1943–45, took to the road for its fourteenth concert tour the spring of 1946, Prof. Rowland still directing. The Rowland-conducted a cappellists had heretofore sung at chapel services in Oller Hall. But in the fall of 1946 Donald Johnson organized a Chapel Choir, made up of non-Rowland singers (in 1963 it was renamed Convocation Choir).

Mary Ruth Linton kept orchestral music alive from 1943 to 1945 through small instrumental ensembles. During 1945–46 Donald Johnson conducted a rejuvenated orchestra that gave three symphonic concerts. Then he turned the baton over to Herman Scholl, back after military service.

With October 1946 the familiar strains of *Washington Post* and the marked beat of the drum were heard on the athletic field for the first time since the war. Scholl's forty-five-piece Juniata Band, though led by five spirited majorettes, marched without uniforms (they had gone up in flames in the 1946 Faculty Club fire). On Parents Day next fall, however, moms and dads beheld the band newly accoutered in navy blue and gold.

Move-Up Day in 1946 took on another dimension. The Senate decided that the occasion should also "include a recognition service at which time awards for various contests, athletic achievements, etc., might be made." Then, as had been the custom, everybody adjourned from Oller Hall to the front campus. The sophomores lined both sides of the "Diagonal" while the freshmen marched through ending up on Founders' front steps where they gave forth with several cheers. Everybody sang the *Alma Mater* and all "frosh regs" were off after that.

A poll taken by the Senate in the fall indicated strong student disapproval of compulsory church attendance. The trustee committee that consulted with Senate officers refused to rescind the requirement. They expressed concern about preserving the "best traditions of the College" for the "spiritual welfare of students."[7] A year later, however, student resistance prevailed. The catalog now substituted the word *expected* for *required*.

Sadie Hawkins Day ("Ef a gal ketches you, then yo're hern") was a fall 1946 social innovation, climaxing with a square dance in the gymnasium. TWIRP Week, introduced two Octobers later, replaced Sadie Hawkins Day as the annual women-ask-men turnabout. TWIRP-ing went on every fall until the early 1970s.

Some dormitory rooms, when the 1946–47 school year got underway, were decorated with prints of famous paintings borrowed from the library. Art loan began in 1940 as a project of the Friends of the Library but was temporarily discontinued when Miss Lillian Evans was on leave during the war. The Juniata Women's League contributed eighteen new prints soon after its formation. The library still lends pictures—to anyone of the college community—from a collection expanded with the years. Room judging, initiated in 1945, became a Parents Day tradition that lasted into the 1970s. For a while the tradition included men's residences, but its inception and demise involved only women's rooms.

In March of 1947 Huntingdon got its first radio station (WHUN). President Ellis and the A Cappella Choir took part in the inaugural broadcast. The station's first program director was sophomore Cary Simpson, later to become head of his own radio network. Three College Hill alumni made up the initial staff of announcers. Until a campus station went on the air, WHUN provided valuable experience for Juniata students interested in radio. A half-hour each week was set aside for college-programmed shows.

Nineteen Forty-Seven also introduced Miss Homecoming I (Betty Kiracofe Weicht), a football-season tradition until 1990. That year Dr. Charles Ellis's book, *Juniata College: The History of Seventy Years, 1876–1946,* came off the press. The first husband-wife duo on the honor roll (John and Rosalyn Schell, both veterans) made campus news. And debate, dormant since 1942, started up again. The first postwar debaters compiled an impressive 9-1 record.

AMERICANZA, the first all-student revue to reach the boards at Juniata, was staged three nights in February 1948. A story of music from Indian days to mid-twentieth century, the production benefited the Juniata World Service Fund (JWSF), which hoped to bring a Chinese student to campus the coming school year. JWSF, the campus's own annual charity, first began in February 1944 and lasted through the Calvert Ellis era. It grew out of the Juniata Community Chest Drive, which went for the support of two Brethren missionaries. But with the outbreak of war, Juniata aid came to include the World Student Fund (for the relief of needy students in Europe and

China)—hence the birth of JWSF. Later JWSF divided its proceeds several ways, one of which was to bring a foreign student or two to the Hill. In 1948 students began the practice of making the fund's goal identical to the numbers of the current year.

On Capitol Hill in 1949 President Harry Truman's State of the Union address called for a program of domestic legislation he designated the "Fair Deal." Across the Pacific, the Communist Party seized power in China under Chairman Mao Tse-tung while the Marshal Plan saved many European countries from the same political fate. On College Hill the 4th Street bus stopped off at the campus every twenty minutes. Joseph Yoder, the Big Valley native who once visited high schools for Juniata, brought out his second novel about plain-folk youth, *Rosanna's Boys*, sequel to *Rosanna of the Amish* (1940).[8] The Associated Press and *Time* alerted the American people in May that senior Joseph Brady, who preached each Sunday at nearby Grier School for girls, had met with a dastardly deed. Someone had stolen 120 sermon outlines from his dormitory room. Soon after, quite mysteriously, the passel of notes reappeared on his desk. From Founders Tower melodic tones of carillon bells began to waft over a two-mile area heralding the Christmas season. Installed in Stone Church and played from the sanctuary organ, they still ring out every Sunday and on special occasions. W. Emmert Swigart donated them in memory of his parents, the William J. Swigarts of Juniata's nativity.

On the social scene, Skip's, popular as ever after twenty-four years, remained a favorite off-campus rendezvous, always overcrowded. Coeds went there to smoke, often in slacks, or shorts, which they could not wear to classes or laboratories. They still had to "sign out" when leaving campus; "lates" were prorated according to class (none for freshmen until Move-Up Day). Veterans drank and got away with it. The Senate still assigned tablemates in the dining room, except for weekends.

Also in the postwar Forties, Juniata alumnae, since June 1945, had full membership in the Association of American Women."[9] The 1948 Selective Service Act hung over the heads of men between the ages of nineteen and twenty-five. Baccalaureate had a Stone Church setting until 1950, and then it was Oller Hall. The average total cost for a residential student amounted to $835.

POSTWAR ATHLETICS

After a three-year hiatus, football returned to the sports calendar the fall of 1946, coached by Philip Snider. The Tower Bell did not toll a single victory that revival season (0-5-1). William Smaltz (1947–53), Penn State's prewar fullback great, led the Juniata gridders to a 12-8-1 record over the next three years. Several of his players won post-season Little All-America honors: David Croft (twice), Mike Dzvonar, Cecil Jackson, and George Smith. In 1947 Huntingdon's VFW Post 1754 relieved the Hill's YMCA of the annual football banquet. The veterans wanted to honor a team studded with former members of the military. The Post's fete took place each year for another quarter century. In 1949 the J Club erected an electric scoreboard on the east end of College Field; it remained there until Juniata's centennial year.

Basketball, winter middleman in the athletic program, held its own during the war years. Jack Oller teams won twenty-three and lost thirty from 1942 to 1945. Away trips were made in Oller's Mercury convertible, far from air-tight on a cold winter's night, and his more comfortable Lincoln Continental. The recently opened stretch of Pennsylvania's "Super Highway" shortened the travel time eastward. For the 1943–44 season Henry Eisenhart, a veteran and the team's leading scorer, broke the record for the most points in a single season. Philip Snider coached from 1945 to 1949, his first season's 13-6 record slipping to a four-year overall mark of 27 and 50. The 1947–48 squad set a Juniata record for the most defeats in a season—seventeen. Huntingdon dentist Arnold Greene, a fullback on Pitt's 1937 Rose Bowl team and former baseball professional, then took over the hardcourt helm. "Doc" coached basketball a dozen years (1949–61), longer than anyone else on the Hill except Milford Swartz, who had put in the same length of time. The Greene-coached 1949–50 Indians, employing the dentist's newly developed HAZ defense (an unprintable acronym for a variation of the zone defense), allowed the fewest points ever per game (62.7). But the team only won four games, losing thirteen.

America's National Pastime on the Hill suffered a one-year lapse (1945) during the war. But Coach Edgar Kiracofe's 1944 team won five and lost one, and his 1946 nine went eight and three. Near-sighted Henry Eisenhart, Juniata's basketball star, who got into the Army by memorizing the eye chart, played on the 1944 team, a recent discharge. Eisenhart could not see very well but he could throw hard, from portside. He was given a try-out with the Cincinnati Reds that May. Things did not work out for him, but they did for a fifteen-year-old kid who pitched in the same game as Hank—Joe Nuxhall. Bill Smaltz became baseball mentor in 1947, winning twenty-two and losing eighteen through the last three seasons of the Forties.

In 1946, after a four-year layoff, the Indians resumed intercollegiate competition in track. From then through 1949 Coach Snider's teams broke even in dual meets (6-6) and came in last in each of three triangular contests. But there was record-breaking talent among the lettermen in the persons of Joseph Beyer and William Murray.

Jack Oller introduced golf as an intercollegiate Juniata sport in 1947. The first lettermen were John Burych, Orville Dore, Jay McCardell, Blair Miller, and Harold Wagner. They split in a four-match schedule. But the second season, coached by Edgar Kiracofe (1948–53), Indian golfers finished with eight wins and an undefeated season. Their record in 1949 was almost as good (8-1-0).

Tennis, however, was the "black sheep" in Juniata's postwar athletic rebuilding program. Dropped in 1943, it returned for one season—1947, and then went ignored the next two springs.

Since Depression days athletically minded coeds were, for the most part, limited to intramural sports. But, beginning in the postwar years, the WAA did participate in occasional "playdays," both at home and away. This was the way it would be until the return of a women's sports program in the early 1970s.

The Hyatt Cup, long the highest honor accorded a Juniata athlete, was discontinued in 1946. The college replaced it with the Stanford Mickle Award—to recognize "that man of the graduating class who, like Stanford Mickle, loved athletics, participated and manifested a wholesome interest in sports, and contributed to the promotion of athletics at Juniata." Mickle, a high-school valedictorian whose parents set up the award, drowned his sophomore year trying to swim across the old Raystown Dam. His dream was to play major-league baseball.

THE NOT-SO "SILENT GENERATION"—THE 1950S

Thornton Wilder tagged mid-century college students the "Silent Generation." Others called them the "Beat Generation." Only "squares," went the stereotype, considered good causes and excellence worthy of their energies, time, and devotion. Excesses were expended in panty raids and hazing. The general mood on the nation's campuses was one of complacency, so declared critics. Said Calvert Ellis of college students in a 1955 speech at Philadelphia's Bellevue Stratford Hotel: they are "interested in preparing for a vocation"; they are "internationally minded"; young women are "interested both in marriage and a career"; they are "seeking a faith."[10] On College Hill social activism might have been absent, but Senate leadership all through the Fifties, calling for greater student responsibility, belied Wilder's label on many counts.

For Cold War-tense Americans the decade began under a cloud. In June the North Koreans suddenly struck across the 38th parallel. The United States, fighting under the blue and white United Nations flag, bore the load in what President Harry Truman called a "police action." But Lt. Ralph Harrity, first known Juniata alumnus engaged in the Korean conflict, wrote back: "It's a dirty, filthy war. The enemy takes no prisoners."[11]

For Juniatians everywhere June 1950 was mournful for other reasons. With Korea also came news of Dr. C. C. Ellis's death, a month short of his seventy-sixth birthday. Every yuletide season since his retirement he had entertained students with a reading of Dickens' *Christmas Carol*. Harold Binkley kept this custom alive till the mid-Sixties. At Christmastime, beginning in 1950 and for the next decade and a half, the Juniata Christian Association sponsored a party for underprivileged children of Huntingdon.

Spring semester 1950 the *Juniatian*, edited by senior Robert Smith, future Washington, D. C., newspaperman and biographer of Sen. Wayne Morse, won first-time critical acclaim from the Associated Collegiate Press (ACP). Honors came again, in that day when journalism carried academic credit, in 1955, 1957, 1958, and 1959. The "All American" rating in 1957, ACP's highest category, was based on excellence of news and sports coverage, features, headlines, style, photography, advertising, and editorial writing. Joan McClure (Hamm), a senior, edited the paper that year. The *Juniatian* of the 1950s produced a steady flow of insightful political commentary on world and domestic problems. It came from a bright ring of fellows made up of James Montgomery, Newton Taylor, Delbert McQuaide, Herbert Deucher, and Alan Quackenbos.

Mark Van Doren came to the campus to help the college celebrate its seventy-fifth anniversary. At that time some one hundred Juniatians on the Hill hailed from homes where grandparents, parents, or siblings were alumni. But the famous writer saw fewer

Juniatians than he would have the previous year. The Korean War was taking its toll on enrollment, which would not bottom out (at 586) until next year. For that reason President Ellis and the trustees seriously considered a ROTC unit of fifty men in science. Korean veterans began to return to College Hill in September 1951. The Veterans Club reorganized in 1954 and in another year had sixty-four members. The Korean Conflict GI Bill, however, was somewhat less generous than the World War II version. It favored low-tuition public schools.

The spring of 1951 inaugurated the prestigious Charles C. Ellis Memorial Scholarship. Established by friends of the former president and by alumni, it would be awarded to outstanding students irrespective of need. That spring also initiated the William Price Social Science Prize created by Mrs. Price in memory of her husband, the former trustee and college treasurer. The Price award goes to a graduating senior in the social sciences on the basis of a distinguished academic record.

Even as late as 1952, boyfriends could not accompany coeds when baby-sitting. The faculty decided to extend chapel period to fifty minutes four to six times a year to be used for special events. Music major Miriam Smith (Wetzel), enthroned as Juniata's first coed radio ham (call letters—WN3TBE), became upon graduation 1952's Miss Pennsylvania. At Atlantic City in the Miss America pageant that September she played Convention Hall's giant organ in the talent section. She was the first contestant ever to do that. Both student deans, Melvin Rhodes and Edith Spencer, left. Dr. James Penny replaced Rhodes and Mrs. Alice Dove moved into the dean of women's office. Dwight Eisenhower won over Adlai Stevenson in a landslide presidential election that November, and Korea, the "forgotten war," remained a Chinese puzzle.

Freshmen, beginning in 1953, were subjected to compulsory study halls three nights weekly the first semester (extended the whole year for those not attaining the magic 1.20 average). This Senate-approved academic help program went on a voluntary basis in 1956. On the 1953–54 Senate, for the first time in its eighteen-year history of Hilltop student government, were twins: Juanita and Lolita Carfora. At Christmastime 1953, students of all four classes began competitively to decorate designated areas of the campus, including Founders porch. The early 1970s put an end to this aspect of Christmas cheer.

The talk of the Hill in 1953, understandably, was the opening of Totem Inn in the basement of the old gymnasium. The dream of a Student Center began at Leadership Conference in 1952. Future Alumni Association President Russell Hill chaired the Student Center Planning Committee. With help from trustees and the administration, plans progressed rapidly. On March 2, after a lively kickoff assembly, "Operation Cooperation" got underway, supervised by John Dale, future trustee and benevolent Juniata patron. Over three hundred students appeared in work clothes with shovels, axes, picks, and hammers. Four busy weeks later the gutted basement was ready for skilled laborers to move in. They completed the remodeling over the summer.

Totem Inn, paid for in part by a Senate-imposed student fee, contained a snack bar, lounge and recreational area, bookstore, post office, a one-hundred-record jukebox, and television set. Robert Fisher, a local businessman, became the center's full-time manager (up to this time some member of the faculty had run the bookstore). In

November Juniata became a United States Postal Substation. Meanwhile, Russell Hill's plea, with coeds foremost in mind, that smoking be permitted in "Tote" got no support from President Ellis. His response: "Many parents of students, especially girls, disapprove of their children smoking, and one of the reasons that they are in attendance at this institution is that traditionally we have been concerned in this point of view."[12] Down the street, Skip's Inn would hang on for a while longer, mostly as a smoking den, but its days were numbered.

With spring 1954 came a campus radio station, built with student money. Physics major Eugene Hyssong of Altoona was the mastermind behind WJC. It started out in a 6' x 17' cluttered cubicle in the basement of Students Hall. But a regular broadcast schedule—8:00 P. M. to midnight daily except Saturday—did not begin for the twenty-watt-power station until September. (Overradiation caused WJC to be closed down temporarily in 1956, however, but the installation of a coaxial cable put the station on dormitory radios again.)

Spring 1954 also introduced a new policy for All Class Night, then sometimes held in the first semester. The types of skits were divided into four categories—history, music, drama, and comedy—to rotate every fourth year as theatrical themes. Commencement-day reports in June mentioned what everyone wrongly thought was the first Fulbright Scholarship to go to a Juniatian. The recipient was Wilfred Norris, a summa cum laude in physics and soon-to-be College Hill professor, who would study at the University of Tuebingen, Germany. (It so happened Fulbrights that year went to two other Juniatians, both from another era: Dr. Glenn Gray, a Colorado College professor, and Dr. Wendell McMillan, an agricultural economist. Congress enacted this postgraduate study abroad program in 1947.)

Coeds clad in Bermuda shorts and knee socks could be seen by fall 1955 at a few restricted places, which did not include the social rooms or front campus on Sunday. Also, on a trial basis, women had the privilege of visiting North Hall's lounge during designated hours over the weekend. January 1956 marked the last time a commencement would be held at the midyear convocation. For some reason, perhaps because of the 1954 Supreme Court decision on school desegregation and the more recent Montgomery, Alabama, bus boycott, the *Juniatian* got letters about the "conspicuous absence" of blacks in the dormitories.[13] "Comps" were under attack, a growing unrest with them becoming more evident. In the hottest Senate race in years James Stayer won on the third ballot in the March elections. And in an article titled "Grab for Grads," the *Alumni Bulletin* said that American industries during 1955–56 had sent more "talent scouts" than ever before on recruiting missions to college campuses.[14] Like most institutions, Juniata discovered that the demand exceeded the supply in many fields.

The year 1956 honored Juniata with its third Fulbright scholar: James Frysinger, a 1953 graduate. It was also a presidential election year and all the evidence that fall (mock student balloting and faculty poll) showed the campus three to one for "Ike," running for a second term. Two campaign whistle stops in Huntingdon brought Hilltoppers down to the railroad station in droves. Adlai Stevenson, the second-time Democratic hopeful, made an early October appearance. He was greeted by a delegation from the Hill and a banner: "Juniata College Chapter, Youth for Eisenhower-Nixon." Stevenson did not lack for a repartee: "I, for one, believe in the redemption of sins....And I believe the longer you are educated in college the more you'll vote Democratic."[15] Several weeks later it was Richard Nixon's turn. Sophomore Sandra Cohick of Whittier, California, the vice-presidential candidate's hometown, boarded the train to present him with flowers. This time hecklers carried signs touting the Stevenson-Kefauver ticket. The stir they caused, overplayed by the media, made newspapers all over the East and several radio broadcasts. The *New York Times*, which was supporting Eisenhower, devoted eleven column inches to a criticism of the incident.[16]

One of the Nixon baiters had been James Stayer, the Senate's dynamic president. The highlight of his twelvemonth tenure was the debut of a Campus Judiciary. Work toward this goal had started four years earlier as a step toward an honor system. The 1955–56 Senate, led by James Hunt, should be credited with working out the proposal for student self-discipline, which in the next-year October referendum won the approval of eighty-one percent of those voting. The jubilant Stayer had this to say about the "courageous" stand his fellow students took:

> Happily the Juniata student body has voted to make Juniata its community rather than its cage. If the ideals of this college are to become more concrete and its traditions nobler in our community, it is up to us to start thinking about honor and how real it can be in our personal lives.[17]

The purpose of the Judiciary, its constitution read, was "to implement the rules of college life in non-academic matters, to give the student body an explicit means toward self-discipline, and a greater opportunity for self-government, and to improve cooperation among our respective groups." The Senate president and the two student deans were automatically members. The Judiciary, however, elected the faculty representative. Hilltop history had run full cycle on the matter of disciplinary control since the 1920s, and the ultimate outcome would be the same.

The same fall of 1956, Juniata's Senate became a member of the National Student Association. And to stress how times had changed, George Fattman, editor of the *Juniatian*, wrote that senators of ten to fifteen years ago were preoccupied with coordinating club activities and carrying out simple projects. Recent Senates, he said, are "concerned with such projects as student self-discipline, the rising tide of young people seeking a college education, and the curriculum and how it is being presented."[18]

Even so, life on the Hill went on pretty much as usual in the post-referendum months. The freshmen, supervised by Delbert McQuaide, carried "Operation Recreation," a skating pond project on the eastern edge of the campus, to near completion. "Snowflake Lake" the freshmen named it, their privilege for being hard-working peons. And the first of many-to-follow "Ugliest Man" contests took place, the Senate president himself a candidate. A social calendar called the "Pow Wow" could be picked up each week in Totem Inn, giving the notice on what, where, and when things were taking place. Men forced to live off campus enjoyed free bus rides—gratis the college—to and from their downtown rooms. That was the last year of public transit service in Huntingdon, except for a cut-short experiment in another few years. In March students lined up in Memorial Gymnasium for free Salk polio vaccine shots.

Many Juniatians unhappy with the *Alma Mater* clamored for a special committee to come up with a better one. The new composition selected by the committee, with the Senate's imprimatur, did not make the grade with the faculty. The music department's blunt verdict: "No better than barbershop music." The 1956–57 academic year closed with a new student award: the Emma G. Wald Arts and Languages Prize. (In 1965 this became the John R. and Emma G. Wald Humanities Prize. Mr. Wald was a local manufacturer of reflective highway paint.) This prize is awarded on the basis of academic distinction in the major field of study. The year also ended with Juniata's fifth Fulbright scholar: biology-major James Martin.

By the academic year 1957–58 the college issued photo-bearing ID cards to students. But the most sensational story that fall was the Asian flu epidemic. It all began Sunday, October 6, when seven Juniatians took abed in the Lesher Hall infirmary. By Wednesday over forty students had the "bug," and before long beds overflowed into Lesher's dining hall and recreation area. Hi-fi sets and record collections made their appearance and supplied, the sick joked, "music to cough by." A temperature of 102 degrees was the admission ticket to medical care in the just-opened women's domicile. In all, 194 ended up in the makeshift infirmary, most staying three to five days. Many more were treated in their dormitory rooms. The college did not close, but the epidemic caused the cancellation of Mountain Day, two football games (although one was made up), and the postponing of Homecoming until Parents Day.

Sore throats, hacking coughs, headaches, and sneezes were momentarily forgotten on Monday night the 21st—a date also memorable. A "mob" of men rushed Lesher Hall intent on a panty raid, the Hilltop's first. They gained entrance, leaving some damage along their trail. More than a little displeased, President Ellis told the Senate: "I do not know of a single raid on a women's dormitory in a coeducational college which did not result in the suspension of those involved, and the administration cannot countenance the action of last Monday evening."[19] At an open hearing of the Judiciary, its first one, 150 students crowded into Founders chapel and heard the accused pair of "ring leaders" offer unshakable alibis. They were found not guilty. The October 21 *coup de main* would not be the last, but those of the future did not take on a storming-of-the-Bastille character. The fellows would simply stand outside shouting while obliging coeds dropped lingerie out the window. That panty-raid fall there were some three million collegians on the nation's campuses, up a startling forty-five percent over six years before.

On the Hill, where cafeteria-style breakfasts became the vogue upon Lesher Hall's opening, the Senate, now steered by McQuaide, promoted innovations of its own. Student proctors stood in for professors, upon request, at testing time—which included final exams. Periodic Sunday morning all-college worship services—to give resident students a "church on campus"—began in January. A Hilltop referendum added a thirteenth Senate post (chairman of educational activities). And President Ellis gave the green light for a formal midwinter dance, big band and all, to be an annual event beginning the next year.

As the Fifties decade waned to an end, College Hill rejoiced in the news that two graduating seniors had won, in successive years, a coveted Root-Tilden Scholarship.

The graduates were Delbert McQuaide (1958) and Charles Brown (1959); both had been Senate presidents and both would one day be Juniata trustees. Highly competitive and in 1958 valued at seventy-two hundred dollars, the scholarships were good for study at New York University's Law School. Only two a year were then awarded in each of the ten federal districts. In all, four Juniatians would become Root-Tilden scholars, three of them during the Calvert Ellis presidency.

The year 1958 marked the passing of two long-accepted Hilltop customs. When Miss Frances Mathias retired as college dietician, Crotty Brothers of Boston took over food service. Never again would a member of the home economics department plan and prepare the daily meals. Crotty Brothers began serving weekend suppers via a cafeteria line in Lesher Hall. This change further eroded the traditional coat-and-tie, sit-down evening dining. And before long table assignments would be a nuisance of the past. Then in October the president's Sunday morning class met for the last time. It had been a familiar Sabbath Bible hour, even once a required one, dating to the college's earliest years. But too many students were sleeping in on the Lord's Day and attendance had dwindled to a faithful few.

Juniatians in 1959, under an inclusive fee system introduced the previous year, were paying $1,525 for their education. A quarter of the student body received aid of some kind. But the National Defense Student Loan Fund, a Sputnik spin-off, was now available and hundreds of Juniatians would take advantage of its liberal terms in the years ahead.

ATHLETICS AND THE "GLORY YEARS" OF FOOTBALL

By the early 1950s Juniata belonged to several athletic conferences: the National Collegiate Athletic Association (NCAA), the Eastern Collegiate Athletic Association (ECAA), and the Middle Atlantic Conference (MAC). The MAC organized as a loose confederation in 1912 and then unified in 1952 as an actual league. Ever since, Juniata has been a member of the northern division (which has assumed a variety of names over the years) in all varsity sports. In 1976 the college dropped out of the ECAA.

The heyday of football on College Hill spanned most of the 1950s. Under three head coaches—Smaltz (1947–53), Robert Hicks (1954–55), and Kenneth Bunn (1956–62)—Juniata enjoyed gridiron success that even Notre Dame could envy. (Smaltz's seven seasons attained a record of 32-17-2; Hicks's two, 16-0-1; and Bunn's seven, 41-10-1.) In that span of sixteen seasons the Blue and Gold won eighty-nine games, losing twenty-seven and tying four. Those years accounted for the Tribe's only undefeated seasons—five of them: 1953, 1954, 1955, 1957, 1958. In Smaltz's final year the 1953 squad went undefeated (7-0), football's first. That season started the Indians on a twenty-three-game winning streak and its glory years. Hicks's 1955 gridders earned a Tangerine Bowl bid in Orlando, Florida, the college's first postseason appearance in any sport. On January 1 the Indians, outweighed twelve pounds per man, played the favored Missouri Valley Vikings to a tie before ten thousand fans. The glory years put Juniata on radio waves, play-by-play broadcasts carried first by WJC and then by WHUN.

A host of records, both team and individual, were set in the 1950s. College Hill got to watch a cavalcade of star players that decade. Fullback William Berrier three times made the Little All-America list (1957–59), and four of his individual marks are still on the Hill's record books. Other Little All-Americans of those years were Joseph Veto (1954), Barry Drexler (1955), Pat Tarquinio (1955), William Haushalter (1955), Charles Mullen (1956), John Staley (1956), Bernard McQuown (1957), Al Dungan (1959), and Robert Solomon (1959). Only Veto, nicknamed "Joe the Toe," was a first team All-American, the first of but two Juniatians to ever make the AP's number-one eleven. In addition, many of these players won All-Pennsylvania and Eastern College Athletic Association laurels. Charles Knox, a two-way tackle who co-captained the 1953-unbeaten team, did not make all-America honors. His glory would come later, however, as a coach in the National Football League.

The glory years produced the Goal Post Trophy in 1958, symbolizing football rivalry between Susquehanna University and Juniata. Six years earlier a gang from the Hill, in a frenzy of victory, tore down Susquehanna's goal post and hauled a seven-foot length back to campus. After some controversy the college authorities wisely converted the slab into a trophy, which still goes to the winning team each year for temporary custody.

Head football coaches on the Hill, until recently, also looked after baseball. During the 1950s Juniata's overall record on the diamond was seventy-six wins and fifty-four losses. The best seasons were 1952 (10-4), 1954 (10-4), 1957 (11-3), and 1958 (9-2). On Saturday, May 26, 1951, Earl Detrick pitched the only no-hitter thrown by a Juniata moundsman—against Lycoming. Until 1954 fans paid admission to watch the home team.

Basketball teams of the Fifties won ninety-eight and lost 101 for Coach Greene. The mid-1950s may not have been exactly glory years for the basketball teams, but they certainly were for Jacob Handzelek. As a guard he set eight records. Two still stand: career scoring average (23.8) and career points (1,950). Walter Vanderbush, a 6'6" center, played all four years with Handzelek and established records for most game rebounds and most career rebounds. His feat of thirty-three rebounds in a game has not been surpassed.

Track of the 1950s registered ten wins and thirty-one losses in dual meets. Snidermen did not take first place in any of ten triangular meets. Eugene Rothenberger, a four-year star, provided the one bright spot of that decade. His leap of 23' 1" in the long jump (1954) still stands in Juniata's record book, forty-six years later.

Back in 1936 Coach Snider had mapped out a cross-country course around the "little loop road," a distance of about 2.5 miles. Over the years the track team used it for fall workouts, timing themselves for the fun of it. Then in 1955 Juniata held three practice meets. By then the course consisted of 4.3 miles of hilly Huntingdon terrain. It began behind Memorial Gymnasium and finished in Sherwood Forest. The route covered Taylor Highlands, the woods along the ridge, Petersburg Pike, Cold Springs Road, and Warm Springs Avenue. From 1956 to 1959 Juniata harriers, paced by Donald Layman, Herbert Deucher, and Frank Hrach, hied themselves to a victory edge of twenty-one to one.

The Hill had reason to glorify golf in the 1950s, too, since Juniata linksmen swept to three MAC titles—in 1951, 1952, and 1954. Two titles and forty-five wins went with the coaching of Edgar Kiracofe (with only seven losses and one tie). Led by co-captains Raymond Korody and Robert Rhodes, the Juniata golfers in 1951 swept to a 10-1-0 record, the best ever. Alumnus William Germann, then general manager of WHUN and college trainer from 1947 to 1979, succeeded Kiracofe in 1954 and would coach golf the next quarter-century. Besides the MAC title that year, the squad won the fifteenth annual Western Maryland Invitational. The quality of play slipped somewhat after mid-decade, and the golfers of the Fifties ended with a 55-37 mark.

Tennis at mid-century ran through five coaches (four of them faculty members). The won-lost results, though, were not too bad: 31-49. The netmen of 1954 had one of the best seasons in the sport's history at Juniata, winning seven and losing one. The tennis courts behind Women's Gymnasium and at the foot of Round Top were clay and not in good shape. But in 1958 Horace Raffensperger of Elizabethtown, Pennsylvania, an officer of DAJUMO and father of two Hilltoppers, made possible the eventual construction of seven all-weather, hard-surface courts.[20]

Meanwhile, beginning the spring of 1950, athletics-minded alumni furnished loving cups to go each year to top-ranking athletes in each varsity sport. Still awarded, the six trophies are these: J. Harold Engle (football back); George L. Weber (football line); Jack E. Oller (basketball); J. Foster Gehrett (track); C. Blair Miller (golf); Charles F. Goodale, Jr. (baseball). Two other trophies came later in the 1950s: Calvert N. Ellis in 1954 (tennis) and C. Clifford Brown in 1958 (cross-country).

THE "NOW GENERATION"—THE 1960S

Students of the 1960s represented the first rush of baby boomers, those persons born in the United States during the great increased birthrate after the Second World War. They had no personal recollection of the Great Depression or the war years. They accepted the radio, television, jet travel, automobile, atomic energy, antibiotics, new medicine, and the wonders of science quite casually as though they had always existed. But American youth on most campuses during the Sixties decade reflected a deeper sense of social concern than the goldfish-swallowing, panty-raiding collegians of the Fifties. They became involved in many civil-rights protests—sit-ins, write-ins, drive-ins, lie-downs, marches—to protest racial discrimination in all of its insidious and patent manifestations. Social historians have labeled students of that period, however, the "now" or "me" generation, referring to their impatient attitude and indifference to social conventions of dress and manners. Young people of that stripe tended to resent and oppose external authority of any kind: political, military, and educational. Knotty social, domestic, and international problems turned them into intransigent absolutists.

The Sixties generation feared that colleges and universities, growing in leaps and bounds, were becoming soulless education factories. A preview of the disruptive struggles that were to break out in full fury in 1968 took place at the University of California four years earlier. Angry students staged sit-down strikes in university buildings, organized a "filthy speech" campaign, and generally disorganized the institution over a period of weeks. The crisis led to the eventual resignation of the university's president, Clark Kerr.

The war in Vietnam exacerbated the situation; many students considered the war immoral. Since college men were deferred from the draft, large numbers of young men without much interest in furthering their education enrolled merely to avoid military service. They tended to find the experience meaningless. By 1968 Lyndon Johnson and members of his administration were virtually barred from speaking on most campuses for fear of violent disruptions their presence might inspire. A nationwide left-wing group, Students for a Democratic Society, took the lead in organizing harassing tactics against government leaders in their speechmaking.

Some pundits of the social scene attributed student alienation to parental advice espoused in Dr. Benjamin Spock's popular books on child rearing, which, critics said, played down strict discipline. Parietal rules on college and university campuses were openly defied. At Juniata one spokesman noted in 1967: "The historical concept of *in loco parentis* is being challenged."[21] He went on to stress that on the Hill there is no

> lack [of] enthusiasm for the sexual revolution which is sweeping across the country. Juniata students are in the middle of it. The past patterns of behavior are considered "old fashioned" or "prudish." A new code for sexual conduct is being established. Students display their affections openly and talk more fully about sex....For some the free love movement has an appeal. We do not have an organized free love group on campus, but the undertone is there.[22]

In loco parentis, however, remained the college policy to the end of the Ellis administration. The women continued to "sign in" and "sign out." Lesher, South, and Brumbaugh-Oneida halls all had residence directors, to be "mother confessors" but also to be guardians. The men's dormitories did not each have a live-in director like North Hall; later a central director, who lived in one of the residences, watched over the fellows. Smoking outdoors on the central campus did not become a right of any member of the Hilltop community, no matter of what status, until fall 1967. The dress code went out at the same time regulations on the use of tobacco relaxed. But drinking alcoholic beverages anywhere on campus, at any college function, or on any college-sponsored trip still carried enforced penalties. One Senate president missed out on a June diploma when caught tippling just before commencement (he got his sheepskin in August).

The spring of 1960 warrants historical mention on several accounts. The *Juniatian* received an A-1 rating from the National Newspaper Service (NNS). This would be the paper's last homage paid by the NNS. Katherine Gillies (Dixon) had become editor-in-chief in February, the first sophomore to tackle the job. At the time the *Juniatian* had a circulation of over sixteen hundred. No one before or since had the good academic fortune of Richard Quinn, Senate president. He faced a choice among three dream scholarships: a Fulbright, a Danforth, and a Knapp (University of Wisconsin). The English major accepted the first one and the last one. Robert Rose, as a junior, won the first Richard M. Simpson Memorial Scholarship. (A Huntingdonian, Simpson had served in the U. S. House of Representatives from the state's 9th District for twenty-three years. His colleagues in Congress created the scholarship in his honor.) Rose, a history major, would become upon his graduation next year the fourth Root-Tilden scholar from Juniata. His future career in law would elevate him to the bench of the Nevada Supreme Court. In those first months of 1960, the women voted into existence a smoking room in South Hall. That semester also marked the birthday of Juniata's first literary magazine since the college's nascent years: the *Voice,* edited by Nancy Fitch. During the academic year 1964–65 Editor Dale Evans changed the name to *Kvasir*; he titled it after the poetic muse of Norse mythology. *Kvasir* is what students still write for today.

Fall 1960 the *Scout*, a companion of freshmen for thirty-six years, became the *Student Handbook* and in 1961, more poetically, *The Pathfinder.* The old run-down tennis courts behind Women's Gymnasium disappeared and the area leveled and seeded, an improvement the Senate had lately been calling for. State Police made Memorial Gymnasium home base for driving tests on certain days of the month. For over a decade students wended their way around cars of would-be licensees lining 18th Street. A camera was put to use in taking chapel attendance. Students sat in deep anticipation until they saw the lens sneakily emerge from near the top of the closed stage curtains. The audience reaction produced comic pictorial results, not to mention the bewilderment upon the part of the speakers who had no idea what was going on. (Other methods of taking a headcount soon replaced the camera.) Homecoming floats made their initial appearance in October when College Field was the scene of a football game with the Western Maryland Green Terrors. WJC, with its forty announcers, moved into the basement of Brumbaugh Hall.

Late October Vice-President Nixon, now pursuing the White House himself, enjoyed an uneventful whistle stop in Huntingdon. He had won handily over John Kennedy in a mock campus election, and Richard Caulk led a campus delegation carrying "Nixon-Lodge" banners to the station. The sophomore emceed prearrival ceremonies for a crowd that included two high-school bands and some Penn Staters. Mrs. Nixon accepted a bouquet of roses when the train pulled in, snow flurries filling the air.

But it was John F. Kennedy and his New Frontiersmen who rode into power in January 1961. Soon after taking office, Kennedy, by executive order, created the Peace Corps. Congress later made the Corps permanent by law. *Juniatian* editorials hailed the idea of volunteer Americans, especially young people, helping underdeveloped countries abroad.

The honor code was not a dead issue for the Senate, and under Richard Quinn one had been drawn up. It was the job of Ronald Vinson's senators to rally Hilltop support. The faculty voiced its strong approval. "Honor Week," a time of acquainting students with the code, ended on Tuesday, May 11, with a student referendum. The Senate set seventy-five percent as a minimum vote for acceptance. But the Quinn plan failed when only 57.1 percent favored it. At the same time the balloting on a second question indicated students would like to see some type of academic honor system instituted at Juniata College. And so the new Senate, John Rummel's, went to work on a revised system.

That June the college changed the day of commencement. From 1879 to 1921 graduation exercises had been a Thursday affair. From 1921 on they took place on Monday, the day after baccalaureate services. At that time both became the Sunday ceremonies of today.

A profile of entering freshmen for fall 1961 showed the sexes all but equals on combined SAT scores: women (1,067); men (1,056). The rigors of gymnasium initiation that Senate President James Hunt, back in 1955–56, had tried to outlaw, went out with the Class of 1965. No more mud, no more syrup. No more jeers, "Pray for rain, Frosh!" But other regulations remained in force, as did the "frosh-soph" Homecoming games to determine if dinks came off or stayed on another week. And "storming the Arch" continued to embroil freshmen in a fall donnybrook.

Calendar year 1962 started out with the student body rejecting a second revision of the honor code on January 9. The vote buried for good all senatorial hopes. By this time the Senate was in the bike rental business, and on a Saturday in late March twenty-seven Juniatians headed for Harrisburg in a bicycle marathon. It was to be a test of endurance. Sophomore Richard O'Connell, averaging fifteen miles an hour, reached the Capitol steps first, at 12:55 P. M., after a ride of six hours and twenty-five minutes. All was deserted. His first act was to hunt for a water fountain. Twenty-four out of the twenty-seven contestants, all males, made the ninety-eight-mile trip. O'Connell had done some winter training, and it paid off.

Two Masque plays, *Liliom* and *The Man Who Came to Dinner*, both directed by Prof. Bruce Spencer, caused a flurry of excitement over the question of censorship. Dr. Ellis thought *Liliom* "out of line," as did many of the college constituents. Not wanting to be a "censor" he nevertheless made it plain when the latter production took place: "We must be careful not to have profanity or drinking on the stage."[23]

Individual faculty members entertained in their homes nearly 450 students over the year, their hospitality partially reimbursed by the college under a policy dating back to 1955. (The policy was discontinued in the early 1990s.)

Innovations seemed to be the order of the year all of 1962–63. Homecoming Day featured a pregame parade through Huntingdon that included the Juniata and Huntingdon High School bands. Seniors Judy Carleton (Barnett) and Judy Fairweather (Young) started a kind of journalistic fad on the Hill—they were the first of three successive duos to coedit the *Juniatian*. In April students, clamoring for "big name" entertainment, brought to Oller Hall the Lettermen, popular recording artists. Ronald Smelser, in Germany for his junior year abroad, won the Senate presidency in an unprecedented write-in campaign. Thomas Paxton, a philosophy major, wondered why "there is no active student peace movement" on the Hill and urged the formation of one. A request from Class President Louis Browdy, Indian mascot of the football team, set the tradition of seniors wearing white (B. A.) and yellow (B. S.) tassels on their mortarboards at commencement.

The academic year 1963–64 had some new twists, too. For the first time in Juniata's history the faculty reception had no receiving line—a concession to the size of the student body. Chapel, or convocation as it was now being called, was scheduled once a week (Wednesday) and extended to forty-five minutes. The emphasis would be religious rather than a combination of worship service and cultural programs. Periodic public lectures and performances, by the same token, went under the rubric Focus Series. Juniata that fall was the first of the Brethren schools to employ a campus minister, the suggestion of a student Religious Convocation Study Committee. He was Robert Faus, a young Pennsylvania Dutchman with an endless repertory of jokes. The jolly reverend and his musically gifted wife, Nancy, soon won the hearts of all on the Hill. The house at 410 17th Street became the College Manse.[24]

Hardly had the Fauses moved in when, on September 19, "Book Switch" took place. Early morning of that day nine hundred students and faculty members began to move books, President Ellis leading the first group, from the old to the new library. Over sixty thousand volumes were moved by yellow, blue, and red teams under the direction of "traffic cops" headed by Dr. Ronald Cherry, wearing a big, black, broad-brimmed hat. The band provided peppy music and halfway through the morning there was a break for coffee and donuts. The operation took less than six hours, counting the midmorning break and an hour-long lunch period. At 2:45 P. M. Dean Morley Mays placed the last book, a biography of Zwingli, on the shelf. The tolling Tower Bell officially signaled the end of library moving day. Over forty students had won assorted prizes.

Then, on November 22, a concealed rifleman, Lee Oswald, killed President John Kennedy in downtown Dallas, Texas. The assassination shocked the Hill, as it did all America. Oller Hall had standing room only on the 25th, a national day of mourning, for a Juniata memorial service. The college community listened in sober silence as Dean Mays paid tribute to the first Catholic to occupy the White House. For many of them the tragic and senseless murder opened their eyes to the enormous capacity of evil in this country. The dean articulated their sentiments when he said, "May our rededication be not only a renewal of confidence in our American idealism, but also an act of contrition before God."[25]

Already the Senate of write-in President Ronald Smelser was hard at work trying to set up a system for evaluating courses. And Simpson-scholar Rodney Jones, son of missionary parents, had in September authored for the *Juniatian* an exceptionally perceptive two-part serial on Vietnam titled "Southeastern Sickness."

Senator John Fike, Jr.'s religious activities committee sponsored a three-day symposium on racial tensions in February. The committee made use of outside speakers and faculty. Then in March Elmer Maas (New York Univ. M. A., 1962–68), a philosophy professor and social activist, arranged for the Freedom Singers, a vocal group representing the Student Nonviolent Coordinating Committee (SNCC), to make two campus appearances. SNCC was a recent integration and civil rights organization that grew out of the 1960 sit-down movement in the South. This was not the last contact the Hill would have with this largely college-based movement.

One member of the Class of 1964 caused amused excitement when he drove off in a steamroller being used to pave College Avenue, which bounds the east campus. The Cloisterite learned how to control the machine by watching the operator through binoculars. One night he took his place at the levers and rumbled in toward town, thirty or more fellows draped all over the behemoth, which turned left on 18th Street, and with borough police in pursuit, came to rest against a tree beside Lesher Hall. A state trooper, not a local gendarme, made the arrest.

Another 1964 senior, Senate President Ronald Smelser, learned he had been designated a Woodrow Wilson Fellow, a coveted honor. Three other Juniatians would be designees over the next half-dozen years. Two of them got their fellowships during the Ellis II era: Janet Kauffman and Mary Harsanyi (Miller), both in 1967. Among other things, the Woodrow Wilson National Fellowship Foundation of Princeton, New Jersey, founded in 1945, has been committed to supporting students in doctoral programs. Smelser did his graduate work in European history, Kauffman in English, and Harsanyi in biochemistry.

Mountain Day had undergone a slight change by 1964, as the one at Colerain State Park on October 14 illustrated. The student-faculty softball game, a rivalry that came after World War II, had now been replaced by touch football. Moreover, the competition, involving some rough play, would hereafter pit seniors-only against the professors. The latter, after these encounters, limped into class on the morrow, bruises and abrasions all too evident. A new winter recreation made its appearance in December: skiing at Blue Knob, promoted by the Outing Club.

The Barry Goldwater-Lyndon Johnson presidential race remained a dead issue on campus. A few Hilltop Republicans did turn out when the Arizona senator's train made a whistle stop in Huntingdon. The candidate looked tired; his rhetoric fell far short of rabble-rousing.

Until the fall of 1964 a faculty committee chaired by the college treasurer administered the financial aid program. Historically, with the exception of a few honor scholarships, aid had been based on need. The number of scholarship funds had grown over the years to forty-one in 1964. There were also a number of loan funds, and many students received outright grants. And, of course, Hilltop jobs were available for earning part of school expenses. Approximately eighty Juniatians were then in the college's employ in some capacity. An Anti-Poverty Bill passed by Congress in the summer made possible further work-study grants, which would involve students in certain kinds of community activity. The aid program had now become too much of a burden for the faculty. So in September Robert Doyle, an assistant in admissions, became the college's first director of financial aid and placement.

Allotting financial aid had become onerous not only because of a growing student body, but also because of mounting governmental red tape. The post-Sputnik hysteria had demanded federal aid to education. Thus in 1958 Congress passed the National Defense Education Act (NDEA), which provided, among other things, long-term low-interest loans. The NDEA called for expenditures to higher education of about one billion dollars over the next seven years. Then in the mid-1960s Pennsylvania, like other states, established a Guaranteed Loan Program for college students from middle- and upper-income families.

By that time, Southern resistance to legal and legislative gains in race relations had aroused idealistic indignation on northern college and university campuses. And March 1965 witnessed the baptism of Juniatians into civil-rights protest action—and violence. A group of students and faculty, inspired by Harriet Richardson (Michel), a beautiful black woman, and Galway Kinnell, poet-in-residence, decided to join in demonstrations for voter registration in Alabama the week of the 15th. This was in response to a plea for help from SNCC. Plans called for a four-day, fifty-mile Selma-to-Montgomery pilgrimage. Supporters nominated by acclamation four leaders to organize the movement on campus: Miss Richardson, James Lehman, recently elected student body president, and Michael Marzio and Gary Rowe, both underclassmen.

Twenty-one persons, forewarned of the dangers that lay ahead, made the trip. Three Huntingdon pastors were in the group. A Hilltop company numbering more than one hundred marched from the college through downtown Huntingdon and bade farewell to those Alabama bound. There the Juniata people joined with hundreds of colleges throughout the nation at Montgomery, the state capital. Meanwhile in Selma, Martin Luther King and Ralph Bunche, two black Nobel Peace Prize winners, told the crowd that "no tide of racism can stop us." But the police tried. Mounted troopers and possemen assaulted demonstrators in Montgomery with cattle prods, clubs, and whips, tossing canisters of tear gas into their ranks. "Every white person in Montgomery would have killed us, with no questions on their part," railed Charles Lytle on his return.[26]

Several from the Juniata contingent suffered injuries. English professor Donald Hope received head wounds, was hospitalized, and released. The *New York Times* carried a front-page picture of Elmer Maas administering first aid to Hope after he was struck down. Galway Kinnell and the Rev. Gerald Will, one of the pastors (First Evangelical United Brethren Church), also took beatings. *Life* magazine that week in March printed a half-page photograph of Richardson (a future Juniata trustee), her brow furrowed from strain, tenderly wiping at Galway Kinnell's bloodied face. It was a photograph that angered many unsympathetic Juniata alumni and parents. (The *Life* picture later appeared in Michael S. Durham's book, *Powerful Day: The Civil Rights Photography of Charles Moore.*) On the way back the motor of one car was ruined after someone put sugar in the gas tank; its riders had to call home for money to buy another car. A highly emotional debriefing took place in Oller Hall on an evening soon after the Alabama demonstrators returned.

Another Hill group—sixty-four in all—traveled to Washington, D. C., on Sunday, March 14, to participate in civil rights demonstrations there. Juniata students carried signs proclaiming such slogans as "Freedom takes time—and time is running out," "United we stand, divided we fall," "All men are created equal." They also carried placards bearing the equality emblem. Some fifteen thousand protesters rallied at Lafayette Square. Nothing happened to mar the peaceful rally. Strains of *We Shall Overcome*, the "national anthem" of civil righters, filled the air the whole day.

Out of these experiences sprang SCORE, the Student Committee on Racial Equality, a campus organization that was open to faculty and administrators. Some of its projects included collecting clothing for the South and tutoring blacks in Huntingdon and Mount Union. It also worked with the Tri-County Anti-Poverty Program. Gary Rowe, a philosophy major, was the prime mover behind SCORE, his department professors, Frederick Brouwer (Yale Ph.D., 1964–67) and Elmer Maas, working closely with him.

The civil rights movement on campus, besides raising everybody's consciousness on race, said Michael Marzio, was "valuable for secondary reasons." It was "prolonging an aggressive turn" for change on the Hill. He had in mind the Senate-drafted "Suggestions to Faculty" concerning course structure and teaching methods. He also was referring to the unrest over Totem Inn. Students had returned the fall of 1963 to find the snack bar ousted and replaced by vending machines. Grumbling and Senate pressure never ceased over the next year and a half. By April the snack bar was back.

That was the month the Focus Series featured Arthur Schlesinger, Jr., noted historian and a former special assistant to a presidential pair: JFK and LBJ. He advocated "honorable negotiation" in Vietnam over the alternative of pulling out or escalating the war. At that time Dale Evans, editor of *Kvasir*, was fighting a skirmish of his own over censorship. The Student Relation Committee, made up of faculty and students, considered two proposed contributions to *Kvasir* in "bad taste" for a publication bearing the name of the college. The editor made certain concessions but he declared that the magazine, a creative outlet for College Hill, should not become a "tool of the administration's image-makers."[27]

The touring choir, always an image-maker for the college, got a special thrill on Sunday afternoon, May 16. That was the day the choral travelers sang at the New York World's Fair (the Tiparillo Pavilion). Their appearance climaxed a year of forty-two concerts. It was Director Donald Johnson's on-the-road swan song (his baton would go to Bruce Hirsch, Lincolnesque in looks and build). Some of Choirmaster Johnson's senior singers counted among the thirty-one percent of 152 graduates that planned to further their education. This was up eleven percent over the previous year.

The enrollment that fall exceeded one thousand. New on campus was Robert Holmes (1965–68), an administrative addition as coordinator of student activities. Holmes (later principal of the Huntingdon Area High School) was the man through whom students had to schedule student events: date, time, location, nature, and size. His job prepared the Hill for the kinds of responsibility that would befall the director of the College Center, a building then in the planning stages. Holmes began putting out a weekly *Calendar* each Monday.

The mid-Sixties seemed to reflect campus indifference toward student government. Said outgoing president James Lehman in 1966, "The biggest problem the Senate faced this year was proving to the Juniata College Community that the Senate is a responsible, committed body worth existing."[28] To his disappointment the election of new officers in February showed no hopeful change in apathy about student government. The lack of a voter quorum (60 percent, according to Senate bylaws) forced a re-vote. Then, too, three of the four executive offices had no opposition. Things went better, however, in the chair election. The Judiciary was in even worse shape. From 1957 to 1962 students almost always chose to be tried by their peers. But, in the years since, the Judiciary had lost the confidence of the student body. During 1965–66, for example, the deans reviewed sixty-eight out of seventy cases—an option to those accused of an offense. The *Juniatian* assessed the Judiciary's future as "dubious."

As the decade passed the halfway point, debate and the General Information Test made their permanent departure from the Hill. More interest at the time focused on what was happening at 1621 Mifflin Street. There, on February 11, Salut, Juniata's off-campus coffeehouse, opened to a more-than-capacity crowd. The place had once been a little grocery store, which the college bought and turned over to the students. With Senate funds a ten-member committee headed by the basketball team's towering co-captain Will Brandau, Juniata's folk-style Mitch Miller, began in September to renovate the frame structure. On opening night there were tables and chairs to accommodate fifty to seventy-five people, who paid a cover charge of twenty-five cents to get in. Murals, candles, and curtains were added extras promoting atmosphere. Waitresses took orders for tea, coffee, cider, and donuts. In the months ahead entertainment would include music, live and recorded, and poetry readings.

The musicians for the Grand Opening were the New Century Singers, Stephen Engle's popular campus group. The Hill first met them at an Oller Hall lawn folk sing for May Day weekend 1964. They cut three records, all original compositions, and traveled throughout the East and Midwest performing for colleges, high schools, conventions, service clubs, benefits, and other organizations. The New Century Singers won second place in an Inter-Collegiate Musical Competition at Lycoming College. Their final campus show was in May 1966. When the Oller Hall concert ended the student body presented Engle with a scroll recognizing his talents as a singer, composer, and director. Stephen's singers included, during their Hilltop existence, Susanne Judy (Wright), Robert McDowell, William Brubaker, Paul Morse, Patricia Dove, David Gould, Kirsten Miller (Gould), Donald Armstrong, and John Russell.

That same May students and faculty bussed to Shade Gap in southern Huntingdon County to help comb the woods for the "Mountain Man," who had kidnapped Peggy Ann Bradnick walking the lane to her home after school. It was a week-long search. The governor called out the National Guard, and the media kept the nation regularly informed on the hunt for the teenager. There was bloodshed, the kidnapper and an FBI agent left dead from gunshot wounds. But Peggy Ann was rescued, unharmed.

By mid-decade the college had come by several more endowed prizes, all of them extant. The Wilbur W. Oaks Prize (1964) honors a senior premedical student with a good academic record, pleasing personality, and with broad cultural interests. Mrs. Jane Swigart, wife of trustee John Swigart, established the award in honor of her cousin, a physician and surgeon. The Alice G. Blaisdell Prize in Geology or Mathematics (1966), established by Dr. Edwin Blaisdell in memory of his wife, honors a graduating senior with a strong academic record in each of the disciplines named in the title. The Charles M. Rice Accounting Prize (1967) recognizes a senior student outstanding in accounting. (Mr. Rice, a C. P. A. of Altoona, taught at Juniata 1932–43.)

A new administrator joined the Calvert Ellis team in the fall of 1966: Dr. Charles Schoenherr (Columbia, Ph.D.). He came from Wheaton College (Illinois) to fill the new position of dean of student affairs. Under his charge fell the dean of women, coordinator of student activities, campus minister, director of financial aid and placement, director of student health services, and the residence directors. Paul Heberling, dean of men since 1957, joined the sociology department, to become, in time, its anthropologist. (Deans, both men and women, had relatively short tenures during the Ellis presidency. After Clyde Stayer retired from the men's post in 1947, there followed

Melvin Rhodes (1947–52), Dr. James Penny (1952–57), and Heberling. Six women deaned under Ellis. Edith Spencer was succeeded by Alice Dove (1952–56), Barbara Bechtell (1956–60), Christine Yohe (1960–64), Clare Low (1964–67), and Frances Helms (1967–68).

Of special interest to the campus community upon Schoenherr's arrival, was the news that his mother-in-law, Mrs. Margaret Landon, had authored *Anna and the King of Siam*. The Landons had been Presbyterian missionaries to Thailand. Rogers and Hammerstein turned her story into a Broadway musical hit and Hollywood filmed it. Ironically, this big-screen hit was one of the last movies shown at the Grand Theater before it closed in the spring of 1962, leaving Huntingdon with just the Clifton for cinema buffs.

Coeds greeted the incoming Schoenherr with an organized protest over a spot check for improper weekend sign-outs. The *Juniatian* editorialized that the administration had no "legal, moral and ethical right" to determine students' personal moral codes. Pressure was building against what one letter to the editor called the "bulk of our Puritan and archaic conduct rules." The immediate result was the formation of SCOPE (Student Committee on Policy Evaluation) to deal generally with the question of *in loco parentis* and to recommend policy changes where necessary. David Gould and Paul Morse were the organizers of SCOPE.

At halftime on Parents Day skydiving Jeffrey Dunkle made a free-fall jump onto the middle of College Field. While the plane, which took off from Mount Union, circled two thousand feet overhead in a clear blue sky, Dunkle's father communicated by radio with the pilot. It was the sophomore's ninety-third jump, and he landed within six feet of his marked goal on the fifty-yard line. When he took off his jumping suit at midfield he was in full coat-and-tie dress, looking as if he had just come from a dance.

A couple weeks after this aerial show, in mid-November, came the annual JWSF drive. One of the charity's favorite money-raising gimmicks had been the tricycle race involving faculty contestants. No longer did JWSF determine its goal by the numerals of the year. And in 1966—in an effort to bring their humanitarian projects "close to home"—the Senate reduced its causes to two: the World Service Fund and the Disadvantaged Student Fund begun by SCORE.

In February students went to the polls in Totem Inn to vote on a completely new type of student government. Seventy-five percent of them said "yes" in ratifying the proposed constitution drafted during James Donaldson's Senate presidency. This constitution divided the governing body into four groups: executive, legislative, cabinet, and dormitory government. Only juniors and seniors served on the old Senate but now the sixteen-person legislature would consist of four students from each class. The legislature was to deal with campus problems. Another change related to the positions of treasurer and assistant treasurer. They were to be hired and salaried, not elected. The cabinet and dormitory government embraced the former chairs, and their responsibilities would now be purely administrative, not combined, as before, with legislation.

The Spring Carnival, held outdoors on an April Saturday night, had become something of a tradition by the late Sixties. The lawn between Totem Inn and Students Hall became the location of all sorts of booths. Carnival-goers had a choice from a variety of skill or try-your-luck games at five cents a turn. The Dunk-the-Prof booth was always one of the most popular. So was the Car Smash, scene of an old wreck decorated with names of the professoriate. Students could avenge themselves on particular ones with a twelve-pound sledgehammer. Afterward there was a dance and a drawing for door prizes donated by Huntingdon merchants.

William "Toby" Dills, Senate vice-president, was a senior now. Toby will be remembered as a *rara avis* for thinking up outlandish stunts. Jeffrey Dunkle's parachute jump was Toby's idea. Some say Lee Harvey Samseil, the fictitious character whose name cropped up carved on many a desktop, came from Toby's own brain. Dills was Lee's campaign manager for president of the United States. The *Juniatian* (May 17, 1967) even printed a diploma for Lee.

The name of Dills also came in the same breath with "marathon" once the lanky chemistry major from Wilmington, Delaware, arrived on the Hill. A Dills-directed football marathon (63 consecutive hours) received national attention in 1964 as did a Dills media-reported softball marathon (55 hours, five minutes) in 1965.

Toby concocted his most famous stunt, however, his last days on campus: "Mammoth Monopoly." That was how the Parker Brothers' blurb booklet, for a period of years, used to refer to Toby's version of the absorbing parlor game. It began on the sunny afternoon of Saturday, April 29, ingeniously using an entire block of campus sidewalks whitewashed to resemble the playing board. Each class used four oversized markers. There were also giant money, real estate, and property deeds. From atop the Students Hall fire escape, Toby roll-dropped dice made of large foam rubber. Below a sign read: "Beware of falling dice." Walkie-talkies and messengers on bicycles informed players of their moves. The news media had great fun with the story.

Students returned in the fall to be greeted by news of Calvert Ellis's letter of resignation. During the president's final months the college took a notably politic step vis-à-vis student-faculty teamwork. During the Leadership Conference at Blue Diamond Camp in September, the idea of student representation on all faculty standing committees—with voting privileges—came up. (This was already a fact of the Student Activities Council.) The student government drew up a petition, which Earl Kaylor, its advisor, and deans Schoenherr and Helms carried to the next faculty meeting. The Student Government (SG) proposal got due debate for several months. In February it passed, but with one modification: no student vote on the Faculty Council. SG agreed, since that council dealt with professional matters of no concern to the student body. (In time, this restriction was dropped.) In this quiet way Juniata gave a strong voice to its undergraduates in the areas of academic policy and the administration of their welfare. They were franchises that the majority of colleges and universities would much later vouchsafe—and then only after discord and with media coverage.

Ellis's terminal year, on the other hand, did not spare him from campus unrest over the Vietnam War. Prof. Maas, who helped form what was called the Vietnam Summer Committee, led a small band of Juniatians to a Washington, D. C., antiwar rally in October. (Maas would later take up company with the Berrigan brothers, the Catholic priests, who for many became the war's iconic protesters.) Then in November Sotirios Nicolopoulos surprised Capt. John Brennan, a Marine recruiter, by presenting him with a petition of 503 signatures in support of the war. Nicolopoulos, a Vietnam veteran, said the petition was evidence that the students who participated in the October Peace March on the Pentagon did not truly represent the prevailing sentiment on the campus. Yet a survey by mathematics major Linda Hartman (Bianchi) for an independent study in her minor, political science, indicated the Hill was of two minds about the situation in Southeast Asia. Her survey showed sixty-three percent of Juniata students disapproved of the government's handling of the Vietnam predicament.[29] But sixty-five percent opposed a withdrawal. Linda concluded that although a majority was unhappy about the present policy, they remained open to a negotiated settlement as long as it did not appear as a "victory" for the Viet Cong.

However, the antiwar faction on campus was at work in other ways than just marching around the Pentagon. They had become fans of dovish Sen. Eugene McCarthy of Minnesota, an idealistic and quiet-spoken ex-professor. His candidacy, taken seriously by few people, aroused countless numbers of college students. Hundreds of them descended upon New Hampshire for the state's early March presidential primary in what the media irreverently tagged the "Children's Crusade." The senator won, to the surprise of most politicos. Pro-McCarthy Juniatians and townspeople made a door-to-door canvas of Huntingdon alerting the local electorate that McCarthy was on the Pennsylvania primary ballot. Their watchword was "Make Pennsylvania Another New Hampshire." Among the Hilltop leaders were professors Maas and Sara Clemson, and students Christopher Moore, Marta Daniels, Michael Marzio, and Jeffrey Cawley. To "Be Clean for Gene" (another media label) the campaigners, both students and faculty alike, prudently gave up any sign of unkemptness. The Keystone State, to their dismay, did not turn out to be another New Hampshire.

It was becoming more evident by spring of Ellis's valedictory year that baby boomers had less interest in College Hill traditions than past generations. For the president the customs of Juniata were important because they signified a close-knit community that appreciated its heritage. It saddened him, therefore, that the Class of 1968 was the last one to observe the candlelighting and mantle ceremonies. Before many more years transpired, most traditions on the Hill would have vanished.

INDIANS OF THE 1960S

William Engel, the college's "Man Friday" in so many areas, showed the same kind of versatility in his own office of public information. Although not sports information director at Juniata, he prepared, beginning in the Sixties, an annual guide on all varsity athletic programs that became a model for small colleges. He also initiated the *J-Fan Letter*, a news coverage of each sports event that he sent to all alumni of the J Club. Juniata's first bona fide SID was Lillian Junas (1964–67), an assistant in the public information office. She was followed by David Leonard (1967–68).

The glory years of football had given that sport a major emphasis, and in 1960 James Harbaugh became Juniata's first full-time equipment manager. Over the rest of the decade he saw Kenneth Bunn and Fred Prender (1963–68) coach the gridiron sport much in the winning style of the Fifties (47-37-0). Prender, unsympathetic to the

Sixties' blasé attitude toward grooming, imposed a strict tonsorial code on his players: no flowing tresses. The Bunn-Prender teams also produced a crop of Little All-Americans: William Crowell (1963), fullback Mario Berlanda (1966), quarterback Donald Weiss (1967), and James Hartland (1968). Others of the 1960s posted record-making feats: quarterback Gary Sheppard; punter Grey Berrier; field-goal kicker Donald Corle; end Jeffrey Barnes; defensive backs Joel Delewski, Peter Straup, Randall Oeffner, and Barry Broadwater; extra-point kicker David Fleck.

All the while, Coach Snider's hill and dalers compiled an aggregate log of 61-31 before his coaching career ended in 1968. Between 1957 and 1963 the Snider harriers enjoyed five consecutive unbeaten seasons and ran up a thirty-eight-meet winning streak. From time to time, however, the cross-county course has been lengthened. Earl Samuel (1961–65) retired the record for the original 4.3-mile circuit (22:58:5), which began and ended in front of the press box on College Field. Another stellar long-distance runner of the Sixties was Richard Beard, Student Government president and thrice a Brown-trophy recipient, who in his junior year (1966) laid lasting claim to the 4.6-mile time (24:26:6). From 1967 to 1973 the course was 4.8 miles long, but the best time for it eluded a Juniatian.

Basketball had a harder time of it, three coaches posting seventy-two wins against 116 losses. Arnold Greene resigned after the 1960–61 season with a 103-131 won-lost total for a dozen years. High-school teacher Ralph Harden (1961–66), whose Hollidaysburg, Pennsylvania, teams had dominated the Mountain League for sixteen years, took over the Greenemen and relieved Philip Snider as athletic director. A first-rate administrator, he was bitterly disappointed with his five-year coaching mark of 27-61. His last season he termed a "personal nightmare" (2-15). Returning to high-school teaching, he never coached again. Fred Prender took his place in the AD's office but remained as head football coach. Keystoner Russell Trimmer, who led Middletown Area High School to 120 wins, twenty-one losses, and five championships in the Capital Area Conference over nine seasons, became Hilltop cage mentor. Trimmer, a truly great coach, had an exciting Jekyll-Hyde aspect to his personality. Off-court he was relaxed and easy going, a soft-spoken, likable man. But after the opening center-jump of a game he became a towel-throwing, chair-kicking, red-faced, referee-scolding Bobby Knight type of coach. But within two years he had Juniata back on the winning track. Visiting teams dreaded Memorial Gymnasium, the din of cheering fans deafening. The place got the epithet of "Snake Pit." The Trimmer quintets boasted a number of outstanding players such as rebounding stars Charles Robuck, first in average per game (15.5), and Leroy Mock, second (15.2).

Wrestling won varsity status in 1960, but unlike basketball just about broke even in wins and losses over eight seasons (36-38-0). Outsiders coached Juniata matmen until 1962 when William Berrier stepped in. Under him the Blue and Gold went 33-28. The second best season in grappling history on the Hill to that time was 1964–65 (7-3-0). Senior Duane Ruble, strongman of the unlimited weight class, won nine matches by falls. When a sophomore, Ruble won the first David L. Helsel Wrestling Award (and won it twice more). In 1968 Christian Sherk, the 145-pound grappler, himself among the Helsel elite twice, ran up an undefeated dual meet record of 9-0-1, the only Juniata wrestler to do so. He capped that with a second-place performance in the MAC championship meet, another College Hill first.

Golfers of the 1960s had good and bad seasons that evened out at 46-46-0. The first year of the decade was their best. They won nine and lost two and finished second in the NCAA Coast Regional Championships. John Vernocy, three times the C. Blair Miller-cup awardee, won ten of eleven in fairway duels.

The tennis team in 1960 won two and lost six. Then Dr. Ernest Post became coach the next year and promptly turned things around. Six of the next eight squads were winners, taking forty-five matches and dropping thirty-one. The 1967 season (8-1-0) was an all-time second best on the Hill. Stanley Conner and Larien Bieber each got the Ellis tennis trophy twice in those years. His last year, Bieber, a premedical student, also won the John E. Blood Memorial Award instituted in 1967. It goes to the senior athlete, who has earned four letters in any sport, with the highest academic average. John Blood, food director at Juniata, 1964–66, was a baseball fan while on the Hill, the unofficial "batting coach." He had written a book on Ted Williams.

Tracksters fell short of tennis's upsurge and from 1960 to 1968 won only twenty-six dual meets while losing forty-two and tying one. Still they had their shining days. In triangulars Snidermen took four firsts. Three of these came in 1963, Juniata's best overall track season ever, when the squad piled up ten wins to one loss. The season climaxed with a third place finish in the MACs, the highest showing until 1973. The Tribe of the 1960s, paced by the speed of Don Layman, Robert Berthold, Robert Gardner, Earl Samuel, William Williams, and John Stultz, shattered their share of records. But these all fell in the early 1970s. Philip "Mike" Snider retired in 1968. He had been a member of the athletic department—instructor, coach, director—since 1930 (except for a three-year hitch in the navy during the Second World War).

Of all the Hilltop sports during the 1960s only baseball turned up professional talent. Nineteen sixty was the year of the "bonus babies," stirring memories of the early Twenties when Joseph Shaute went with Cleveland. Donald Ross, the Tribe's third baseman and leading hitter, signed with the Baltimore Orioles for a bonus in excess of twenty-five thousand dollars after getting offers from twelve major league clubs. (Ross was traded to the Los Angeles Dodgers right after signing his contract.) William Berrier, who shared the Mickle Award with twin-brother James, an exceptional athlete in his own right, inked a professional contract with the Los Angeles Dodgers as an outfielder and received ten thousand dollars. The big surprise was Edwin Hoffman, a junior playing his first full season for the Indians. Hoffman, a left-hand hitting outfielder, signed with Cincinnati. In 1964 Grey Berrier, younger brother of identical twins William and James, signed with the Chicago Cubs. Only William Berrier stuck it out. He enjoyed a seven-year playing career that included Triple-A ball. He also spent twelve seasons managing minor league clubs in the off-months while associated with his alma mater in a variety of roles. Under coaches Bunn, Kaylor (1963), and Prender, diamond victories outnumbered defeats seventy-two to fifty-eight (one tie). In 1962 Anthony Faber captured the MAC batting crown. Gary Sheppard swung a bat to the MAC title in 1964.

For Chester Langdon and the athletic department, the spring of 1963 finally realized a twenty-five-year dream—separate baseball and football fields. Langdon Field (baseball), east of the old playing area, was ready first, in early May. But College Field (football and track) took longer, and the fall 1963 home gridiron games were played on Huntingdon's War Veterans Memorial Field. Gone now were familiar landmarks to Juniata athletes and fans for years: the old grandstand and the green, rickety fence that cordoned off the scene of play

Ellis-era athletics ended in a show of respect for a president who enjoyed sports and appreciated their place in the college's life. Robert "Bob" Richards, former Olympic pole-vaulting champion, a then-Brethren preacher, spoke to over 350 Juniata fans on Saturday night, May 25, at a banquet honoring Dr. Ellis upon his impending retirement.

Chapter 14

GIRDED FOR THE SECOND CENTURY: 1968–1975

CALVERT N. ELLIS RETIRES

Under Juniata's seventh president the enrollment had grown to twelve hundred. The college had a national reputation, and on the Hill Dr. Ellis enjoyed the respect of faculty and students alike. But the unrest that rocked campuses across the country had unnerved him, he privately confessed to friends. The resignation of President Kerr at the University of California in 1964—because of student-incited disruptions—particularly troubled him. Then the sit-in at Columbia University in April 1968, which caused at least 120 injuries, only confirmed his decision to step aside at age sixty-four. In August of that year, at an informal commencement exercise for summer graduates, he conferred the 3,304th and final bachelor's-degree diploma of his twenty-five-year presidency.

The last few months of his tenure coincided with a series of violent, deadly acts on the American scene. In April an assassin killed Dr. Martin Luther King, Jr. in Memphis, Tennessee, and in June Sen. Robert Kennedy met with the same fate in Los Angeles. At the time of Kennedy's death American armed combat in Vietnam, which he opposed, had become the longest war in United States history. Two weeks after Juniata's summer commencement, young antiwar protesters clashed with police and national guardsmen at the Democratic national convention in Chicago. Many of the agitators had participated in the Children's Crusade. In full view of television cameras hundreds of newsmen, bystanders, and participants were brutally beaten. The convention turned out to be the most violent in the nation's history.

JOHN N. STAUFFER: JUNIATA'S FIRST LAY PRESIDENT

Juniata, for most of its history, had been run by a Brumbaugh or an Ellis—all preachers. This men-of-the-cloth presidential regnancy ended in 1968. In his letter of resignation Calvert Ellis wrote: "Juniata needs vigorous leadership and new ideas for the years ahead which will be critical ones for the independent, church related, college."[1] John Baker responded for the board: "We respect his decision, but without him Juniata will hardly be the same." Chairman Baker knew that in the previous year three hundred college and university presidencies had gone begging.[2] But that was not what he had in mind when he acknowledged that Calvert Ellis would be a hard person to replace. He was talking about the man's rare qualities. Many of the faculty that Ellis recruited perceived him as a man of utter integrity, the prototype of a small-college president.

For the first time the search for a leader involved a faculty committee, an Ellis idea. It was all over in four months; in early March the Hilltop community got the word. As had been the case before, the trustees found among themselves a ready successor: fifty-two-year-old John Stauffer (Penn State Ed.D.). He was the first president not academically involved on College Hill beforehand. The towering alumnus brought to the office an impressive set of credentials. He had spent twenty-one years in administration at Ohio's Wittenberg University—as dean of students (1947–57), dean of the college (1957–63), and president (1963–68). A Lutheran layman, he had been the first Wittenberg president selected from within the faculty in sixty years.

To Dr. Baker, accepting Juniata's presidential call, the Palmyra, Pennsylvania, native wrote: "I have a deep sense of debt to Juniata as alma mater, a debt I have acknowledged but that I never expected to be able to attempt to repay."[3] And in an open letter to Wittenberg faculty and students, he said: "Those who do not understand the language of love for Alma Mater—who do not sense the respect and gratitude for Juniata that I have felt deeply since my student days—will not understand my decision."[4] Such were the sentiments of the man whom the Juniata alumni once elected their national spokesman (1959–60). Coming back to the Hill held added attraction, said Stauffer, because of Juniata's "academic reputation," the size and character" of its student body, its "commitment to liberal arts education." There was another persuasive factor:

> The structure and function of Juniata's board of trustees are, in my opinion, most desirable and defensible. While committed to the Christian tradition, the college and its board stand free from control by a church body. Juniata's tradition and present posture are favorable to the pluralism and the ecumenism appropriate to the needs of students.[5]

John Stauffer left behind a solid reputation in his adopted state. During his five years as Wittenberg's ninth president, the university, double the size of Juniata, made major advances on all fronts. Among Ohioans his name was known and respected everywhere in the field of higher education. At one time or another he had been a member or officer of every key educational agency in the Buckeye State. Active in church and civic affairs and a YMCA leader at the national level, Juniata's president-elect was also interested in the business community. He was on the board of directors of the Columbia Gas System, Incorporated, and also of the Cincinnati branch of the Federal Reserve Bank of Cleveland.

Trustee Baker shook his head in disbelief the day Stauffer's election was made public. He said to Earl Kaylor, chairman of the faculty search committee: "I never imagined it possible to talk John into leaving Wittenberg." With no pomp or circumstance Juniata's eighth president was installed the following October. He purposely dispensed with the more elaborate type of inauguration; the Installation Convocation involved just College Hill. "Simplicity" was his desire—to save "time and funds which can well be used elsewhere," he told the trustees. The former residence of Morley Mays, a modest white frame structure on 18th Street west of Moore, became the President's Home.

THE BEAT OF A DIFFERENT DRUMMER

The Stauffer years began, as noted, when "student power" had become a cause célèbre in academia. Against this background of ubiquitous alienation, John Stauffer pledged at his inauguration to create "a climate of mutual trust and respect" on campus. Quietly he began to work a major change in college governance. By Homecoming Day 1970 his goal of an "open" campus was a reality. That weekend students and faculty sat (as observers) for the first time on all trustee committees. Hilltop undergraduates, already yoked with the faculty, now participated at every level of the decision-making process.

There were other things he wanted to do at Juniata. He noticed how few blacks and members of other minority races were to be seen among the student body. He set out to correct this racial imbalance. But he had little success in what he viewed as our "society's most urgent domestic need"—educating disadvantaged youth.[6] Black Americans, though welcome and recruited, have found little at Juniata to interest them. Its rural setting has not been compatible with their urban rearing. (Nearby Penn State has the same problem.) Small-city and suburban nonwhites, however, have felt more at home on the Hill. What few of them that made their way to Juniata have been mostly males—and athletes.

Not only was John Stauffer anxious to guarantee an open and more heterogeneous campus, but also, as he once wrote, to assure that "henceforth Juniata College shall be in practice, as well as in fact, an independent institution."[7] Historically, as the president well knew, there have been three types of colleges and universities in the United States: independent, church-related, and church-owned. In Juniata's case, while the college had been related to the Church of the Brethren since its founding, it had no legal relationship to the denomination. In other words, Juniata had an independent board of trustees. Therefore, upon Stauffer's ascension as Juniata's chief the trustees began to rework the bylaws to make this explicitly clear. On May 10, 1969, the board unanimously adopted the revised document. Deleted was the proviso that a majority of the trustees had to be Brethren.

To further establish the college's independence, the trustees in 1975 took legal action to amend the charter. Unlike before, the Church of the Brethren no longer had legal claim to Juniata if it ever closed its doors. The charter now specified that the "institution's assets shall be assigned to non-profit educational purposes as determined by the Board and as further approved by the appropriate court."[8] The bylaws and charter revisions had nothing to do with distancing Juniata from its Brethren roots. Rather, the rationale behind the board action was to ensure that the college would never be denied federal funding because of any adverse future court ruling on the separation of church and state.

Stauffer's "new dream of what Juniata can become" included a recast curriculum, one relevant to the student of the Seventies. In the spring of 1969 he established a Task Force "to study the whole spectrum of the education program of the College." But that story will be told later.

NEW ADMINISTRATIVE BLOOD

"Youth" was an accent often heard in John Stauffer's speeches when he referred to his administrative team. Gradually, as openings occurred or new positions were created, he brought in his own people, most unfledged. This was to guarantee "vitality" and "continuity" of leadership, he explained.

When the search for an outside academic dean turned up no takers after Donald Rockwell resigned in 1970, the president decided the next one should come from within the Task Force. This faculty group, set up in the spring of 1969, had been charged "to study the whole spectrum of the educational program of the college." Ultimately the choice fell on Wilfred Norris, the Task Force chairman. Later, in 1972, the young physicist was made provost, a new office of larger authority. This was done to allow the president to concentrate his efforts on providing "general leadership." But it also released him to give more attention to the financial development of the college, which included increased political action in behalf of independent higher education both at state and federal levels. At any rate, back in 1970 Norris's immediate concern was to get the faculty to approve the Task Force package and implement it.

Youth could be seen everywhere in the Hill's hierarchy. In addition to Norris, there was Floyd Roller, who became business manager and controller in 1969. He replaced John Fike but did not get his title of vice-president. Foster Ulrich took Gerald Quigg's place as executive director of development in January 1970. (In 1968 Harold Brumbaugh had moved his vice-presidency from development to college relations.) In 1972 Thomas Robinson, an alumnus of only six years, succeeded Charles Schoenherr as dean of student affairs.* Then when Robinson left in 1975 Donald Hartman (Michigan Ph.D.), who taught philosophy, moved into that office. But he had the new title Dean of Student Services, which gave him supervision of the admissions office. The average age of these men in key administrative positions was—in 1972—just thirty-five.

---

* The title Dean of Women was expunged in 1968 when Delores Maxwell arrived as associate dean of students. After her there were Janet Cumming (1970–72), Karen Gabriel Stanley (1972–75), and Elizabeth O'Connell (1975–79).

MATTERS PROFESSORIAL

The faculty found John and Louise Stauffer to be more private than Calvert and Elizabeth Ellis had been. The Stauffers left the official partying of Juniata dons to the Norrises, Wilfred and Lona. Nevertheless, John Stauffer early won the utter trust of the faculty despite limited social contacts. It was he who—in 1970—marshaled the trustees into line on the matter of tenure. As a result, the board adopted the statement of the American Association of University Professors on academic freedom: "The free search for truth and its free exposition." (The AAUP had been founded in 1915 to advance the standards, ideals, and welfare of the academic profession.) The AAUP canon linked academic freedom to tenure—after a six-year trial period. Therefore, Stauffer acted promptly so that even faculty members without terminal degrees but who had been at Juniata a half-dozen years or longer received tenure in a blanket decree.

No sooner had Stauffer set foot on campus than he began talking about the need to do more to recognize superior teaching. An opportunity for this came in the form of a $250,000 challenge gift from the Charles A. Dana Foundation in 1970. The half-million-dollar endowment was to go toward establishing several supported professorships. Juniata, thanks to Gerald Quigg's alertness and persistence, became the fifteenth educational institution in the nation to benefit in this way from the philanthropy of Charles Dana, a Connecticut industrialist. Only three other Pennsylvania colleges had Dana professorships: Dickinson, Franklin and Marshall, and Lafayette. The original four Juniata Danas were Ronald Cherry, Esther Doyle, Eva Hartzler, and Earl Kaylor. At Juniata, as exemplified in these four appointments, the honor would be distributed among the three divisions in the future as retirements came along. Esther Doyle became the first of the Dana professors to retire, in 1975; historian Philbrook Smith succeeded her.

Meantime, the previous fall had given rise to what was then Juniata's only fully endowed chair, the J. Omar Good Visiting Distinguished Professor of Evangelical Christianity. Omar Good, a student on the Hill in the mid-1890s, was a Philadelphia printing executive who died in 1969 at the age of ninety-two. He willed one million dollars to Juniata, the then-largest gift made to the college. (The Academic Building, erected in 1967, promptly got a memorial name: Good Hall.) In addition, the nonagenarian's will left substantial residual funds, the use of which was to be determined by trustees of the estate, Mr. and Mrs. Lester Rosenberger of Narberth, Pennsylvania. A testamentary stipulation, however, directed that these funds be used for "the perpetuation of the Historical Triune Faith of Protestant Christianity."

Mr. Rosenberger, a soap manufacturer and a trustee since 1952, got the inspiration for a religion chair one morning while driving through the New England countryside. He envisioned "recognized authorities in the field of evangelical theology" as residents of College Hill teaching, writing, and available for off-campus lectures and preaching. There was to be a frequent turnover of scholars (no one staying longer than five years). Mr. Rosenberger worried about what was happening on America's campuses. Drugs and alcohol seemed to define college life. Bi-gender dormitories had become the vogue. State laws, making adults of eighteen-year-olds, had eroded the tradition of *in loco parentis*. On the Juniata campus compulsory chapel and required religion courses came to an end. Trustee Rosenberger feared that virtual student autonomy had bred a confusing array of conflicting beliefs and that collegians faced a serious crisis of values. The first Good-chair incumbent was C. Samuel Calian (Basel Ph.D.), then an internationally known theologian and author, and now, long-time president of Pittsburgh Theological Seminary.[9] The Good professor's salary ordinarily is on a level with that of the highest paid Dana holder.

So far as college endowments go, the J. Omar Good Fund is something of an anomaly. Its assets ($5,300,000 in 2000) must be kept segregated and separately audited, although the college is empowered to invest the Good portfolio. There is an independent, self-perpetuating set of trustees, three in number, which plays an involved role in the search and selection of candidates for the chair. They determine the annual budget and help foster religious life on campus in a variety of ways. There have been six Good trustees; three are deceased (the Rosenbergers and Calvert Ellis). The trustees at the millennium were Dr. W. Clemens Rosenberger, Dr. Nancy Rosenberger Faus, and Dr. Earl Kaylor.

At Wittenberg Stauffer had improved faculty salaries and benefits; he set out to do the same at Juniata. By the mid-Seventies, according to the AAUP report on small-college compensation, Juniata fell just short of the top-category for full and associate professors. At the other ranks, on a one-to-four scale, the college rated a "two."

Stauffer not only recruited young administrators, but he also inherited a young faculty. In 1975 their average age was forty-one. They numbered ninety-three (part- and full-time), about half with doctorates. Credentially, that represented a standstill since the Calvert Ellis presidency. Eight Stauffer-appointed professors have stayed the course to the millennium. They are, in alphabetical order by academic divisions, disciplines, and year of appointment:

HUMANITIES

ENGLISH: Mark Hochberg (Cornell Ph.D., 1970).

FINE ARTS: Alexander McBride (Cornell M. F. A., 1970).

PEACE AND CONFLICT STUDIES: M. Andrew Murray (Bethany Theol. Sem. D.Min., 1972).

SOCIAL SCIENCES

ECONOMICS AND BUSINESS ADMINISTRATION: James Lakso (Maryland Ph.D., 1970).

PSYCHOLOGY: David Drews (Delaware Ph.D., 1969); Dale Wright (Vermont Ph.D., 1969).

SOCIOLOGY, ANTHROPOLOGY, AND SOCIAL WORK: Robert Reilly (Marywood M. S. W., 1974).

At the president's bidding the faculty formulated bylaws for self-governance, still in force. These bylaws expelled certain administrators accustomed to voice and vote on academic matters. The faculty later reorganized their committee structure twice, coordinating it with curricular changes. The first time they created a monster, and committee work became all-consuming. Through the Personnel Committee they have a say in decisions about promotions, tenure, term contracts, and dismissals. But it has meant learning to live with constant evaluation from all quarters.

Despite heavy teaching loads and onerous committee work, several on the faculty of the 1970s authored or edited scholarly tomes: Esther Doyle, Earl Kaylor, José Nieto, Duane Stroman, Jack Troy, and William Vocke. The paintings of Alexander McBride and the pottery of Jack Troy did honor to the fine arts department at more than one juried show. In Brumbaugh Science Center chemists Donald Mitchell, William Russey, and Paul Schettler tackled one of the nation's biggest problems of that time: energy. In June 1973 President Richard Nixon created a White House-based energy office to expand research into new sources of power. Then in October the Arab oil-producing states declared an embargo on oil exports to the United States (lifted March 18, 1974). Federal funding enabled the chemistry department to conduct research on coal and hydrocarbon shale interaction.

A CURRICULUM IN FLUX

Academicians used to say in jest: "It is easier to move a cemetery than to change a curriculum." But that was before the time of student demands for "relevance" in their studies, before their opposition to "stultifying" required courses. These academic fidgets did some violence to that old saw about cemeteries and curriculums. Things began to loosen up with the onset of the Seventies. Curricular experimentation became the vogue almost everywhere in response to what many educators thought were legitimate criticisms. Juniata followed the parade. But it was John Stauffer who goaded the faculty into doing so, letting them march in whatever direction they thought best. At one of their first meetings after his arrival, he called for a "redesign of the academic program."[10] The following May he took steps to form a Task Force for that purpose. By then he had conceded to faculty-student pressure for a five-day class schedule, which Earl Kaylor had slipped into summer school during Calvert Ellis's presidency. (Ellis warned that class-free weekends would lead to an exodus of students, but Kaylor argued that Saturday classes were passé.) The shortened week was to take effect in the fall, ending a ninety-three-year tradition.

As for the Task Force, it labored for most of fifteen months puzzling out what might constitute an educational program that would "meet the needs of the 70s," in their words. From the faculty there were Elizabeth Cherry (chairperson after Wilfred Norris became dean), Sara Clemson, Donald Hartman, Esther Doyle, Robert Faus, Thomas Nolan, and William Russey. Student members were Karl Kindig, Michael Long, and Donna Roppelt.

The Task Force drew the whole campus into the study. Ad hoc committees abounded. Two "D-Days," (D-Day meant discussion day) with no classes, converted the Hill into a forum-of-the-whole. Debate seemed to go on endlessly—in homes, classrooms, offices, on the Hilltop lawns. At last a final report was ready, in September 1970. It reflected a basic, fundamental change in educational philosophy. For five months the

Mountain Day, a fall all-college outing, dates to 1896. Still a popular tradition, it is unique in the annals of higher education. Here, in 1907, college folk, fording Stone Creek, are on their way to gather chestnuts.

"Toonerville Trolley"—so students called it in reference to a comic-strip streetcar —began running in 1907. Here it is shown in 1919, parked at the corner of unpaved 17th and Moore streets—end of the line.

Pilgrim *building, birthplace of the college, at the corner of 14th and Washington streets. Classes began in 1876 in a little (12' x 14') second-floor room (left side) of this print shop. Henry Brumbaugh's family lived on the right half of the duplex. The building still stands, its exterior little changed.*

Burchinell House, the college's second site, 1877-79, at 1224 Washington Street. Rented, it was converted into classrooms and a dormitory. Zuck, pictured seated in the doorway, lived on the third floor (empty dormer window) with art teacher David Emmert. The house was razed in 1971.

Book-littered room of Lloyd Hartman (left) and Harry Sieber, in Founders Hall. Both students became trustees. Note the double bed (lower right corner), furnished in every dormitory room until 1922.

A tidy room in Brumbaugh Hall, circa 1903. A kerosene lamp stands on the table in front of the window. Incandescent lighting became a convenience in all dormitories and classrooms the fall of 1907.

Drama was a casualty of World War II, but English professor Esther Doyle revived it in 1945. Here is pictured a scene from the Masque production of Pygmalion (November 1947). At the millennium, flourishing interest in theatre has created need for more space, thus a planned addition to Oller Hall.

The first baseball team, pictured in 1899 on the steps of Students Hall. It is Juniata's oldest organized sport, in 1903 entering the ranks of intercollegiate competition. Harry Sieber, a catcher and future trustee (lower right-hand corner), said he started the sport at Juniata.

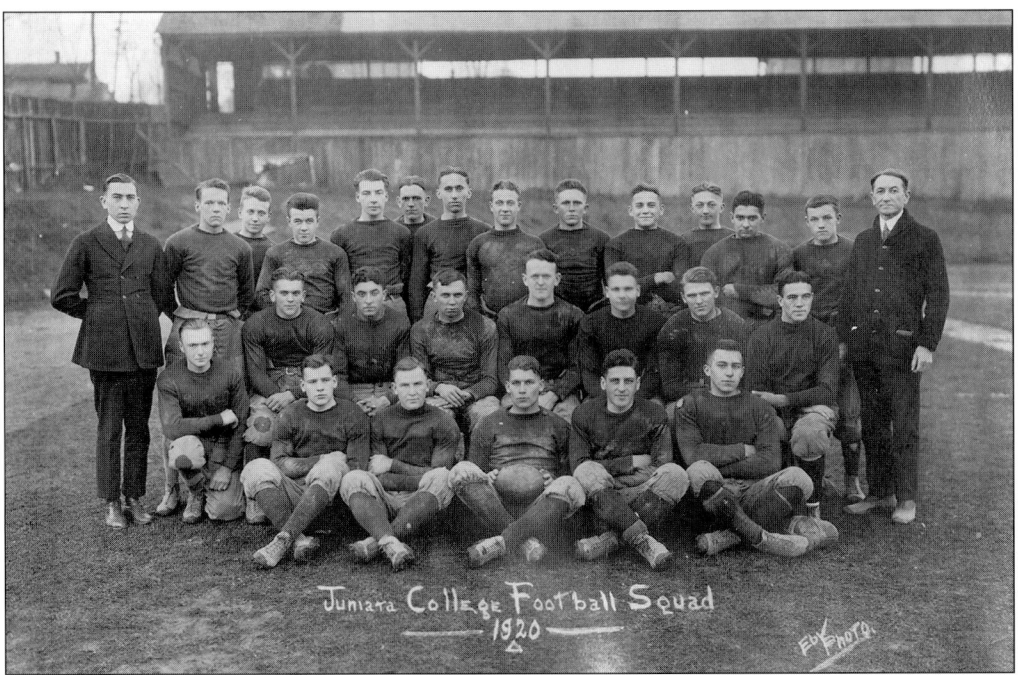

The 1920 football squad, Juniata's first, with the old grandstand in the background. Three players became trustees: George Griffith (seated, second from right); Jack Oller (row two, second from right); and John Montgomery (row two, fourth from right). Montgomery and Griffith attained prominent rank in the field of medicine. Oller and Harold Engle (on Oller's left) taught at Juniata—Oller all his professional life, Engle for ten years before becoming a dentist.

Two-time Penn Relay victors, 1938-39, shown here with their coach, Philip "Mike" Snider, one of Juniata's great athletes. Afterward, he served his alma mater thirty-eight years as coach of several sports and as athletic director.

Undefeated golf team (1948), which won 10 matches. The unhatted Orville Dore, standing to coach Edgar Kiracofe's left, received the Alumni Service Award in 2000.

Starting eleven at the NCAA's first Tangerine Bowl game, 1956. The outweighed Indians tied Missouri Valley (6-6) in the Orlando, Florida, classic. Five players made Little All-America: Barry Drexler (#47); William Haushalter (#57); Charles Mullen (#70); John Staley (#50); and Pasquale Tarquinio (#52). Robert Sill (#12) was elected president of the Juniata Alumni Association in 1982, and in 1990 received the Alumni Service Award.

Juniata's most famous gridiron athlete is pictured here: Charles Knox, a 1954 graduate. He later coached NFL teams in two West Coast cities: Los Angeles (twice) and Seattle. He is now an emeritus trustee after serving twenty-one years on his alma mater's board. Waiting patiently in line for an autograph—along with boys big and small—is the alumni office's Evelyn Pembrooke.

Coach Ernest Post's 1969 tennis squad holds Juniata's best record in that sport (10-1). One of the history professor's doubles players, a quarter-century later, made his mark in the world of science—physics Nobel laureate William Phillips (back row, fourth from left).

The 1973 Juniata football Indians, like the 1956 squad, also made NCAA Division III history. They played for the national championship in the first Alonzo Staff Bowl game (Phenix City, Alabama). Wittenberg University won handily (41-0), ABC covering the event live. The two co-captains, Louis Eckerl (#9) and Michael McNeal (#44), sit at the head of the team in this picture. Head coach Walter Nadzak anchors the left side while assistants Richard Reilly (yawning) and, behind him, Dean Rossi, anchor the right side.

In 1994 Juniata dropped the Indian mascot because of its racial implications. The faculty and Alumni Council strongly approved a name change; the vast majority of students and former athletes opposed it. Here some students are prepared to cast their votes on a new mascot from a list of five names (the alumni ballotted by mail). Juniata varsity teams are now called the Eagles.

Women's volleyball has long replaced football as the Hilltop's glory sport. Coach Larry Bock's teams have played in sixteen NCAA Division III national semifinals, finishing second four times in the finals. This is a photograph of the 1997 national second-place team. It had four first-team All-Americans on it: Colleen Carver (#3); Kristin Hershey (#1); Melissa Myers (#15); and Carrie Zeller (#9).

Head aquatics coach Kathleen Collins (standing, right) enjoyed a sensational 1999-2000 season. In all, nine records fell. Freshman Alissa Schneider (second row, second from right) posted the first MAC gold medal for a Juniata female swimmer.

The millennial year baseball team shown here won 23 games, the most for that sport. That number boosted coach William Berrier's total Juniata victories to 418. Berrier (far right), a sensational two-sport athlete (football/baseball) in the early 1960s, already has legendary status as a paragon of collegiate sportsmanship. He left professional baseball to return to his alma mater as assistant student dean, coach, and athletic director. On his right is alumnus George Zanic, a local attorney and former diamond standout, who will succeed the retiring Berrier. Two volunteer assistants (far left) are Huntingdon businessman Jack Lang (wearing sunglasses) and Dr. Craig Eisenhart, both former Juniata athletes.

Mud volleyball—a springtime event well on its way to traditionhood. The bemired outcome, as this photograph illustrates, is no respecter of persons or gender.

The Madrigal Dinner/Dance has been a popular tradition for over three decades. Here a student, one of many in a line, camps out the night before tickets go on sale to guarantee getting a couple for him and his date.

Storming the Arch—a fall tradition that goes back to post-World War II freshmen rebellion against hazing and other exacting regulations. These no longer applied if the assault on the Cloister Arch succeeded. Regulations have long been defunct, but the assault lives on. This 1998 photograph shows the charge underway, a look of fierce determination on the faces of the rushers.

May Day and Homecoming, decades-old traditions, once featured courtly pomp—with queens and princes and prettified attendants. In 1975 May Day dropped the theme of royalty and began honoring a "Woman of the Year." In 1990 Homecoming followed suit and became the occasion to salute a select group of students active in community-service projects. This 1992 photograph shows Pres. Neff posing with that fall's honorees. The women are (left to right) Victoria Masotta, Jennifer Serfass (Dean), and Rebecca Wentling. Behind them stand Andrew Loomis, Ayinde Alakoye, and Joel Meyer.

Gesticulating Robert Wagoner, a professor of philosophy, lectures students on Russian icons. Eleven of the forty-five sacred images in the exhibition he helped organize— at Eastertime 1988—are visible on the wall in Shoemaker Gallery. The display marked the birth of Christianity in old Russia a millennium ago. It later traveled to several prominent East Coast art museums.

The sign at the entrance to the college's outdoor Peace Chapel. The chapel was designed by Maya Lin, famous for her Vietnam War and Martin Luther King, Jr. memorials.

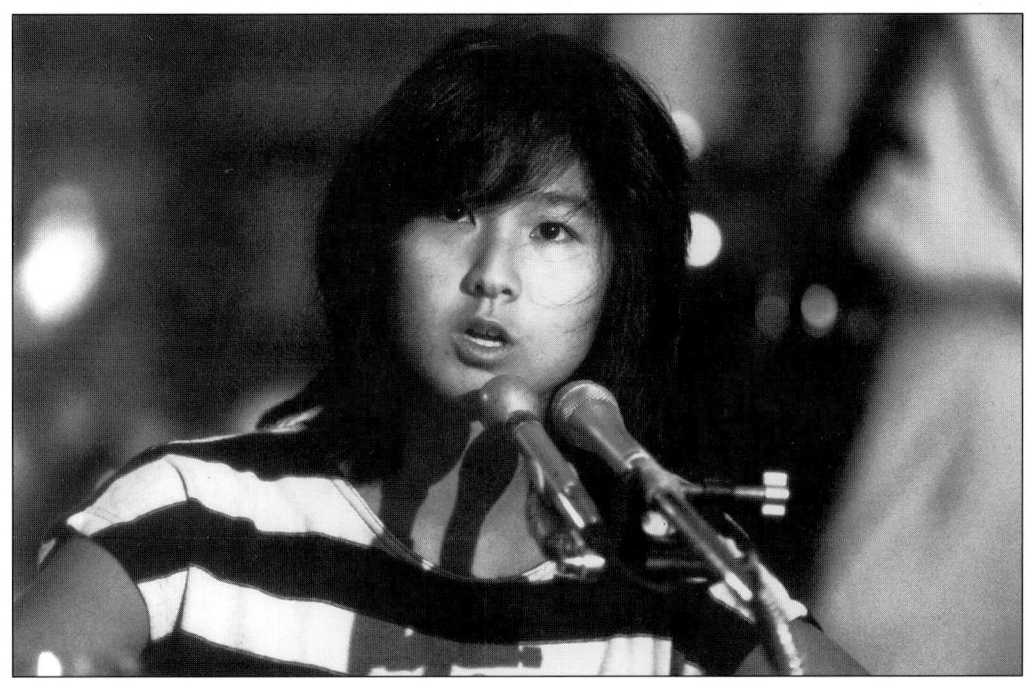

Maya Lin—at the podium, for one of her very rare public addresses, when the Peace Chapel was dedicated, October 1990.

The simple, hilltop Peace Chapel, created to blend in with the natural mise en scene, *is the site of this photograph. The occasion is a memorial service for John Baker, former trustee chairman and benefactor (with his wife) of Juniata's widely acclaimed peace studies program. The battered hat on the chapel table is a tender-touch reminder of the centenarian's fondness for this chapeau.*

In 1993 Juniata became the first college or university to contract with the United Nations to promote the peace issue. Here Andrew Murray, peace and conflict studies professor and director of the Baker Institute, is photographed (center, wearing glasses) addressing delegates to the first International Seminar on Arms Control and Disarmament. On his left is Johan Nordenfelt, then-director of the United Nations Centre for Disarmament Affairs. Nordenfelt, currently Swedish ambassador to India, was Juniata's commencement speaker in 2000, at that time receiving an honorary doctorate.

William Phillips, a 1970 graduate, won—along with two colleagues—the 1997 Nobel Prize in physics. Here placing an honorary doctor's hood on him is physics professor Wilfred Norris (left) and Provost James Lakso. The nobelist so esteemed Norris that he arranged for his undergraduate mentor to attend the prize ceremony in Stockholm, Sweden.

faculty joined issue over the document. Then they adopted it by a vote of 63-31-1, not exactly a mandate. The guinea-pig class was to be 1971's freshmen. Sophomores through seniors would continue under the old curriculum. Some thought this rushed things too much. The summer was given over to crash sessions for devising core offerings in the program. That initial year was hectic. The college operated on a two-track calendar, semesters and terms (the three-term calendar became standard the fall of 1972).

What had the Task Force wrought? In their words: to be human is to be "reflective," "interpretive," "decision-making." A very flexible program sought to develop these traits. Students, with close faculty guidance, could tailor their studies to individual needs and educational goals. There was to be an emphasis upon interdisciplinary study and team teaching. General education would no longer consist of a distribution pattern but of core offerings. The new approach, so hoped the Task Force, would make the transition from high school to college less traumatic. Thus much of the freshman year, the most innovative aspect of the curriculum, was to be ungraded. Modes of Thought and Methods of Inquiry replaced Great Epochs of World Culture as the academic rite of passage for fresh-on-the-scene Juniatians.

"Values—those criteria by which intellectual, aesthetic, and moral judgments are made": *that* became the shibboleth of teaching. "Value-centered education" became a new cliché on campus. Moreover, courses became "units."

With the new program came a shift in grading practices, for *all* students, not just for freshmen. Beginning with the era of student unrest, there unfolded a general trend to inflate grades in higher education. Many schools, like Juniata in 1971, dropped the D and did not enter failures on transcripts. The C was cheapened and no longer held respectable. Juniata never practiced easy grading to the extent many institutions did. Nevertheless, something had happened. A look at commencement programs reveals that, making allowance for an enrollment gain of three hundred, the number of honor graduates had increased over sevenfold in the twenty years prior to Juniata's centennial. There were four in 1956, nineteen in 1964, and twenty-nine in 1976, It is only fair to point out, however, that one Ivy League school in 1976 had more than two-thirds of its graduating class on the honors list.

The Task Force fully expected that the 1971 curriculum would enjoy a healthy life span of at least a decade. But, by the centennial year, the scalpel had been put to many parts thought ailing. What remained hardly resembled the one the Class of 1975 pioneered. The faculty mood had swung to the right, as it generally had at other colleges. Many professors felt that Juniata had designed a curriculum for the wrong student generation. The prevailing campus spirit in America, with the Vietnam War about to end and some progress made in civil rights, had turned more conformist and less confrontational.

Overhauling the academic program gave it more muscle. Probation came back. The freshman year became stiffer. There were now fewer ungraded units, and the D would reappear in 1977. Also, recent curricular changes indicated a return on the faculty's part to the old distribution philosophy of general education. Also, with the departing centennial class went the Program Review (PR), a weakened version of the old-fashioned comprehensive test. The PR, which just about any format fit, did not challenge students the way "comps" of old did, nor serve as an authentic educational experience. It could not be failed; examiners simply submitted a written evaluation to be filed with the student's transcript. The faculty came to feel no one was taking the PR seriously, that it was a waste of time, and voted it out of existence. (The old English conference plan also lost support and, in September 1977, would be replaced by a first-year-graded unit in basic writing.) All in all, the early 1970s were something of a registrar's nightmare. But Thomas Nolan, who had left the classroom in 1969 to take the job, managed to keep everything and everybody straightened out. Whatever the faults of the Task Force's curriculum, John Stauffer put it rightly: "Clearly the Juniata campus is a more exhilarating place than it was prior to the new program."

That was how a delegation from the National Endowment for the Humanities (NEH) felt on a visit to College Hill in April 1972. They spent two days on campus, impressed by what they saw. In time, Juniata received a NEH basic grant of $240,145. Supplemental amounts ultimately put the total at close to $340,000. Only eleven other colleges received NEH funds the same year. Juniata's grant, of course, was a vote of confidence in the curriculum, to be used to retool faculty, strengthen the library, and provide equipment and materials needed in special units.

Autumn 1972 fetched the regular ten-year review by Middle States. All went well, as expected. The eight-member team was intrigued by the attitude of Juniata students, who expressed "a belief in the future." This, they said, contrasted to the outlook on many campuses.[11] The evaluators' report suggested a rather novel administrative setup for a college of Juniata's size. It made sense, however, to Provost Norris, and so in 1973 he elevated the three divisional chairmen to assistant deans—to decentralize decision-making power and to improve internal communications. "Mini-deans," the faculty irreverently spoke of them at first. They formed the Deans Council. The three were Robert Wagoner (humanities), Duane Stroman (social sciences), and Dale Wampler (natural sciences). James Lakso replaced Stroman after one year, staying on as director of summer sessions. Stroman, out of deaning, revived continuing education, dormant since the 1950s. He geared the offerings to people in business services.

The times found the humanities in the doldrums, so far as majors were concerned. There was little consolation in the fact that this was a national trend. Rampant vocationalism had pervaded higher education, intensifying pressure for "career-oriented" courses and preprofessional training. Terrel H. Bell, United States Commissioner of Education, said in early 1976: "The college that devotes itself totally and unequivocally to liberal arts today is kidding itself. Today, we in education must recognize that it is our duty to provide students with salable skills."[12] President Gerald Ford himself called for a closer relationship between the life of the mind and the world of work.

Small private colleges, traditionally oriented toward the liberal arts, have always had to contend—especially during economic recessions—with the problem of job-minded students. But the debate over occupational preparation vs. liberal education had never been more heated. Stronger schools like Juniata, less worried about survival, hoped to be able to develop new relationships between the two approaches.

The humanities, however, were far from moribund. Ernest Post of the history department introduced Juniatians to the Urban Semester Program, sponsored by other colleges, whereby they spent a period of time in one of the nation's metropolitan centers. Clayton Briggs and alumnus Bruce Davis (today, executive director of theater arts for the Academy of Motion Picture Arts and Sciences) devised units on film. The purchase of a cluster of buildings behind North dormitory on College Avenue provided a "pot shop" and kiln for Jack Troy's ceramic students. The Fogelsanger-Murphy Lectureship in the Humanities, endowed at more than $85,000, brought in speakers, scholars, and artists for the division. Similar funds, the Calvert N. Ellis Humanities Series (1968) and the Edith B. Wertz Endowment for Support of Cultural Events (1973), went toward cultural programs of a broader, nonacademic nature open to the public. These gifts collectively evolved into the Juniata College Artist Series (JCAS) of today.

Division II's department of economics and business administration, as might be expected in light of the rising accent on vocationalism, ruled as king of the Hill by 1975. Its centennial eve's enrollment out-totaled once-regnant biology's by several score. Spring 1969, the department began its intern program, which put students out into the working world for eight weeks. In 1971 the Herbert A. and Marjorie F. Miller Endowment provided a benefaction of one hundred thousand dollars to support teaching in economics and business administration. Sociology held up well, its internships continuing to provide practical experience in a variety of social service agencies. The education department, historically a college pillar, continued to enjoy phenomenal success in placing its graduates. Its placement record bettered the average for all Pennsylvania colleges and universities by two-and-a-half times. In political science the G. Graybill Diehm Lectureship, honoring a man who gave thirty-five years as a Pennsylvania lawmaker and state Republican leader, began bringing distinguished speakers on political topics to the Juniata campus.

As for Division III, the college soon after the completion of Lake Raystown in 1972, got access to two parcels of land (totaling 800 acres) not far from where the "Forge Refugees" shivered through their winter's stay in 1877. (Lake Raystown is the largest impoundment wholly in Pennsylvania, with 110 miles of shoreline, about fifteen miles south of Huntingdon.) The land is leased from the Army Corps of Engineers. One parcel (365 acres) comprises the college's Raystown Environmental Studies Field Station. Robert Fisher, then the college's senior ecologist, took charge of the lakeside station. On it is a renovated log farmhouse built in 1825, which serves as field station headquarters and contains the Frank A. Pierce Laboratories. Pierce, of Ambler, Pennsylvania, a conservationist interested in the restoration of old buildings, donated twenty-five thousand dollars to the reconstruction of the early nineteenth-century homestead. A cove harbors a dock and a small fleet of boats. No other Pennsylvania college of comparable size can boast a lakeside field station.

There was another topic of concern on College Hill: world peace. The term "Cold War" still defined, as it would until the late 1980s, the arms-race posture of Soviet-U. S. relations. And despite a peace agreement in January 1973, the conflict in Vietnam had not quieted jingoistic support for military aid to block new Communist offensives in Indochina. Curiously the Brethren, as one of the historic peace churches, had never promoted the study of peacemaking in its college until 1948. In that year Manchester became the first college in the United States to offer undergraduate courses in irenology. At Juniata, Robert McFadden, religion instructor from 1955 to 1958 and a Manchester graduate, introduced the subject of peace as an academic offering. Brethren-historian Donald Durnbaugh (Penn Ph.D.), who taught on the Hill in the history department 1958–62, offered a course on The Church, State, and War.

Then in 1969 Mrs. Elizabeth E. Baker, wife of the trustee chairman, wrote President Stauffer pledging financial support for a peace studies program at Juniata. Both Dr. and Mrs. Baker had become strong advocates of universal disarmament. Mrs. Baker was not proposing that Juniata prepare "peace professionals." Rather she had in mind sensitizing young people from all academic disciplines to the realization that peace was everybody's business.[13] Her initial gift was a modest twenty-seven thousand dollars, a commitment that would in time grow to several million dollars.

European historian Klaus Kipphan took the initiative to implement a few department offerings under the rubric of peace in 1971 that dealt with the problems of war and its effects. Then in 1973 he chaired a joint student-faculty group under Provost Norris to develop an integrated, multi-disciplinary program. Two faculty members of invaluable assistance to Dr. Kipphan in the planning stage were chaplain Andrew Murray and sociology-religion professor Martin Clark (Harvard Ph.D., 1973–84). Peace and Conflict Studies (PACS) took its start as a structured academic discipline in the fall of 1974. Its stated purpose was to offer an interdisciplinary inquiry into the causes, nature, and consequences of conflict. By the centennial year peace-related courses enrolled two hundred students taught by ten professors from the perspective of their own academic expertise.

With all these curricular gains, the libraries, of which Robert Sabin, Juniata's science librarian, became director in 1972, were not ignored. National Endowment for the Humanities money went toward general education materials and a basic humanities collection. In the spring of 1969, the Friends of the Library, defunct for over a decade, made a timely revival. One of Juniata's greatest friends—in gifts of books and money—during the Stauffer years was the late Aaron Rabinowitz, a wealthy New York real estate executive. The Jewish tycoon, who died not long after getting to know the college, had been an admirer of Lillian Wald, the famous settlement house worker in Manhattan's poverty-stricken East Side. She had taken the philanthropist in tow in his boyhood. In 1974 the college dedicated a seminar room on the second floor of the Beeghly Library in memory of these two. To researchers' delight, it was head-librarian Sabin who created the Juniata Archives in 1973 with help from the Friends of the Library.

MARGIN OF DIFFERENCE PROGRESS
AND NEW PHYSICAL RESOURCES

The alumni and church districts continued to elect strong people to the board of trustees. However, the death or resignation of trustees on regular appointment created several vacancies. The board filled these with typically able and dedicated men, two of whom were non-Juniatians: corporate executive Thomas Martin (1968–86) and investment banker Edwin Kennedy (1969–94). Three others were alumni: Leroy Maxwell, Sr. (1961–64; 1970–81), automobile dealer Klare Sunderland (1970-present), and Prof. Jack Oller (1975–86). Calvert Ellis remained on the board after his presidency. Edward Kennedy of New York City, a director of numerous oil companies, succeeded Herbert Miller as the specialist on college investments.

All the while, the Margin of Difference Campaign moved successfully through Phases I and II, achieving its $5.3-million goal by 1973. The third and last phase took the name "Juniata Centennial Fund." The year John Stauffer resigned (1974–75), total support from all sources exceeded the two-million-dollar mark for the first time in the college's history. That same year voluntary support of the country's colleges and universities dropped about eighty million dollars.[14]

An important component of the record giving to Juniata was the Annual Support Fund (ASF), a Stauffer idea. The ASF was quite apart from the major campaign and was directed primarily at the alumni. No longer would the alumni undertake specific yearly projects as had been the custom. Said the president in 1969: "In the face of inflation the College is trying to fill a substantial gap between the cost of providing quality education and the dollars supplied by student fees and by income from the endowment."[15] At that time Juniata's endowment yielded a return of only $124,000 a year. William Swigart, Jr., local insurance executive and grandson of William J., chaired the initial ASF drive (1969–70)—for one hundred thousand dollars. All six drives during the Stauffer presidency exceeded their goals.

Some of the Margin of Difference funds, committed before Stauffer's arrival, had been earmarked for further Hilltop construction. A student center came first, completed the fall of 1969. The two-million-dollar structure, with its great columned portico, honors Charles and Calvert Ellis, Juniata's presidential family. Ellis College Center (also called Ellis Hall), the fifth campus building constructed by alumnus Paul Hickes of nearby Alexandria, is located at the foot of 18th pedestrian walkway.* The three-floored structure has since been the focal point of student life. It provides facilities for multiple services and houses a ballroom, lounge areas, bookstore, post office, dining room (the 690-seat Baker Refectory), and the Cyber Café (a wired snack area).

At Ellis Center can be found the organization that plans year-round cultural, recreational, and social functions: the Juniata Activities Board (JAB), composed of students and their advisor, Dawn Scialabba, director of campus activities. JAB is also responsible for all general policies relating to the use of Ellis Hall and its programs.

The last of the student residences the college would build, Hickes again the contractor, were the East Houses, in 1970. This dormitory complex, costing $1.6 million, is of modern architecture, thus quite different in style from the other post-Cloister residences. There are two buildings, each with four floors that provide a pair of apartment-like units on each story. (This was a practical consideration as much as an attempt at innovative dormitory living. The complex can easily be converted into rental apartments in the event enrollment ever drops permanently.) East Houses have

---

* The Hickes Construction Company also built Sherwood Hall, South Hall, L. A. Beeghly Library, and the Tussey-Terrace Complex.

been dedicated in memory of four trustees: William Flory, Joseph Kline, Newton Long, Sr., and Robert Miller. In 1975 more than ninety percent of the student body lived on campus.

The college's mid-century building spree ended in 1970, the year Hilltop residents saw heavy equipment move in and begin razing three early-years, central-campus buildings. Crane and swinging ball made rubble of Students, Brumbaugh, and Oneida halls that autumn. Only the Oneida Annex was spared demolition. Into it moved the business and accounting offices, while the print shop (formerly in a Founders basement nook) settled into the renovated ground floor. Then in 1975 the David Emmert House on the corner of Moore and 18th streets was demolished. Male students housed there used to sit on its porch-roof with their legs dangling through the balustrade along the edge of the roof, basking in the sun or bantering with passersby.

As the sixth decade ran out, the college acquired the Metz Poultry Farm in Oneida Township (1969). The farm, located on a ridge along Warm Springs Avenue not far from East Houses, had 170 acres of fields and wooded terrain. The trustees named the tract the John C. and Elizabeth Baker Natural Preserve. Later, the college enlarged the property to 315 acres, and in June 1975 the trustees renamed it the Baker-Henry Nature Preserve. Mr. and Mrs. Jewett Henry were major donors along with the Bakers in the land purchases.

Closer to campus, the college went about plucking up properties on adjacent blocks as they became available. One of them was the apartment building-turned-into-dormitory on the curve at Moore Street and Cold Springs Road. Students dubbed it the "Pink Palace" because of the exterior stucco's color. Twenty-seven buildings and 110 acres made up the Hilltop campus in 1975.

ALUMNI AND ALMA MATER LOYALTY

By year's end 1975 the college had 6,491 living alumni with known addresses. They could be found in every state and in twenty-seven foreign countries. Almost half of them contributed to their alma mater. In John Stauffer's first year thirty-five percent of the alumni gave; in his last year forty-nine percent were contributors, a record high. This display of support to Juniata merited, as it last had in 1963 and 1964, another brace of awards from the American Alumni Association. The one for 1970 carried a first-place citation (a trophy and $1,000) for besting the giving at 367 other small, private coeducational colleges in the United States. That year Stauffer instituted the Annual Support Fund, a new source of alumni giving. Its sole purpose was to supplement each year's operating budget.

An impressive record like this represented the efforts of scores of class agents. It also did credit to the office of alumni relations, which at that time looked after the twenty-three area clubs as well as guided the thirty-five-member national council. After Glenn Zug resigned as director of that office, Thomas Robinson (1971), Thomas Snyder (1971–72), David Kreider (1972–73), and Clayton Pheasant (1973–76) filled the post.

In 1971 the college began to honor alumni in two areas: achievement in career and service to Juniata. Ralph Leiter, a metallurgist with the Budd Co. of Philadelphia, his doctorate from Harvard and in 1957 president of the National Alumni Association, won the first achievement award. Cyrus and Isabelle Caulton co-won the first service award; their Bryn Mawr home was unlocked to all Juniatians and any college function, their time and energy freely at alma mater's beck and call. Cyrus, a retired RCA executive, had been national alumni president in 1960.

KEEPING BRETHREN TIES FROM UNRAVELING

By fall 1975 the Brethren constituted a mere 4.93 percent of the student body. Roman Catholics made up 18.81 percent of the enrollment, followed by United Methodists (11.45%), Presbyterians (10.43%), and Lutherans (7.64%). There were twelve Jewish students; foreign Juniatians on the Hill added up to a few less.

The sparse Brethren population on the Hill, in steady decline since World War II, had a simple explanation: economics. The comparative cost of a Juniata degree had forced countless youth of the church to go the route of state schools. Indeed, nationwide statistics for 1973 revealed that while the enrollment at more expensive private colleges and universities had stabilized or declined between 1952 and 1972, that of public institutions showed a 45.6% increase.[16] The absence of Brethren on campus had denied the college a personal liaison with local congregations. To address that communications gap, Stauffer created the Church Relations Council in 1969.

The Council's stated mission was to strengthen bonds with the denomination's three supporting districts. That same year Stauffer also announced the Alexander Mack Scholarship Fund, to be promoted under the slogan, "Help Send Brethren Students to Juniata College." (The church honors Mack, an eighteenth century German reformer, as its founder.) Within six years the fund had raised one hundred thousand dollars. The congregational giving of the three districts, however, would never, even to the present, total much over twenty-five thousand dollars a year. As in the past, the college continued to send student envoys to the local churches via the Deputation Club and the Concert Choir. Ties with the denomination remained intact in the person of the campus minister. When the popular Elizabethtown-alumnus Robert Faus left in 1971 he was succeeded by another winsome, talented Brethren—Bridgewater-graduate Andrew Murray. Guitar-strumming Murray already enjoyed a denomination-wide reputation as religious folk singer and songwriter.

JUNIATIANS OF THE STAUFFER YEARS

With the early 1970s the quarter-century-long academic boom appeared to be at an end. Federal support had been curtailed. Enrollments began leveling off, even falling at many institutions. At the same time the mood among collegians everywhere grew less contentious. There were many reasons for this change. The United States and North Vietnam signed a peace accord in 1973; the draft came to an end (January 1973); protest died down; the 26th Amendment (1971) gave eighteen-year-olds the vote; most states began lowering the legal age of majority in other ways.

Another amendment of the early seventh decade, this one to a federal statue, had in view protecting individual student's rights to privacy. The Family Educational Rights and Privacy Act of 1974, commonly known as the Buckley Amendment, was enacted to improve access for students to records about themselves and to restrict release of personal information without written consent. At Juniata the Buckley Amendment meant, for one thing, that grades were now sent home addressed to the student, not the parents. What happened then to this information became a matter of family resolution. The practice of many colleges and universities, however, has been to send grades to a student's campus address or have the student personally pick them up at the registrar's office.

Students everywhere reveled in the liberation from *in loco parentis* the latest batch of law, federal and state, guaranteed. These developments did not totally curb campus or political protests by collegians, Hilltoppers included, but by mid-century undergraduates had become pretty much a complacent lot. They expressed little interest in societal or ecological problems. Surveys showed that few of them would use their influence to change the political structure. This detachment from politics curiously prevailed at the very time the Watergate scandal unfolded and forced President Richard Nixon to resign in August 1974. Moreover, not only had the presidency come under attack for abuse of public trust but also Congress and various government agencies.

At the same time, the counterculture of the Sixties would leave a permanent impress on college life of the 1970s: sartorial indifference. Blue jeans and decorated tee shirts seemed to dominate the wardrobe of both sexes. Some students attended class barefooted. Coeds for the first time went braless in public and wore miniskirts. Shoulder-length hair on men became a common sight (except among athletes at Juniata).

On College Hill the 1970s bade farewell to many traditions, some institutionally ancient. Gone would be the weekly convocation, the faculty reception, the dink and "frosh regs," sit-down meals and table assignments, Move-Up Day, the recital of Leadership Conference resolutions to faculty and administration. There would be no more JWSF drive, no more Christmas party for children, no more midwinter formal, no more decorating the campus at Christmastime, no more TWIRP Week, no more room judging at Homecoming and Parents Day, no more finals in the Memorial Gymnasium. The May Day celebration remains but in a much-altered form. Gone are the queen and the prince, replaced by the Woman of Juniata College. In 1975 the first to be so honored were Cynthia Smith and David Amidon. On the other hand, one tradition was resurrected: the public reading of Charles Dickens' *Christmas Carol*. Perpetuated by Charles Ellis and later Harold Binkley, the practice had ended in the mid-1960s. Then, beginning in 1972, English professor Richard Hunter gave the famous Yuletide story a biennial rendition. His last reading was in 1990.

The campus locale changed in other, less drastic ways. An Oller Hall-lawn picnic now preceded Senior Convocation, referred to as "Academic Festival" or "Celebration for Seniors." The idea was to lure students into what had become an empty auditorium for convocation (with little success). The Convocation not only honored prizewinners but also became a time for seniors to make their own zany awards. The Masque disbanded, although Doris Goehring of the speech and theatre department struggled to keep drama alive. The Concert Choir, on the other hand, remained robust. Bruce Hirsch (Southern California, M. M., 1965–84) also drew upon student talent to make musicals a popular spectacle on campus. Ibrook Tower (Temple, M. M., 1974–95) regrouped the orchestra and the band. Clubs still had vitality, but those allied with a discipline kept most active. Religious organizations had dwindled to two: Juniata Inter-Varsity Christian Fellowship and Deputation Club. Once or twice a year the campus community, hardly in SRO numbers, assembled for an all-college worship service.

Will Brandau, Ellis College Center's first director, purveyed a host of social activities and public programs. A recent graduate, the basketball star (he would go on to own an amusement park in New York State) brought to campus many big-name entertainers: mimic David Frye, singers John Denver and Bonnie Rait, and groups like Seatrain, to name a few. He introduced Center-sponsored coffeehouse dances and weekly movies. The Brandau-conceived Raft Regatta—a race down the Juniata River in makeshift crafts—became a major Center-sponsored event. So did another Brandau-Center Board inspiration: the Madrigal Dinner for students. Today a seemingly fixed tradition, the Madrigal Dinner took root in 1970 in an attempt to capture the Yuletide spirit of the sixteenth century. From the J Club the Center inherited "Casino Night," a takeoff on Las Vegas. "Slave Day" also became popular—when freshmen, male and coed, were auctioned off to upperclassmen to perform various "domestic" duties in the dormitories. Salut, the coffeehouse on Mifflin Street, was re-dubbed "The Human Element" in 1968. Then, with the Seventies barely on the calendar, the college decided to tear down the dilapidated former grocery store that housed the coffeehouse. Thereafter the Center Board scheduled coffeehouse performances at various places on campus, including Ellis Hall. Eventually "Catharsis Lounge" in Sherwood Hall became a particularly favored locale.

The weekend exodus of students hurt social activities. To a certain extent, as Calvert Ellis predicted, the five-day class schedule had transformed Juniata into something of a "suitcase college." Students, of course, departed the campus by car. Huntingdon by the Seventies was practically devoid of public transportation. Two passenger trains stopped daily, one in each direction. The town had no buses, no taxis.

If keeping students on campus became a perennial problem, rounding up talent for student publications proved no less an enigma. Doing away with applied credit in journalism crippled communications. "The Last Juniatian," read the *Juniatian*'s headline on April 17, 1970, ironically the month and date of the college's origin. The situation had become desperate; no one wanted to write articles for the campus weekly. For a year thereafter a newssheet calling itself *Renaissance* appeared intermittently. One alumnus savaged it as "the most inarticulate, infantile, illiterate, and ineptly named journal to come off the campus in many a moon."[17] This was an overstated, if not an unfair, indictment under the circumstances. Then Scott Leedy came to the rescue the fall of 1971. He took it upon himself "to get the College newspaper back on its feet and functioning again." He succeeded, although the reincarnated *Juniatian* still had its problems at first. *Kvasir*, meanwhile, had its ups and downs and in the mid-Seventies reflected more interest in graphics than creative writing. The *Alfarata*, by contrast, never missed an issue.

Station WJC, like the *Alfarata,* survived in good shape. The mike and turntable always seemed to attract a full staff. In 1970 the "Voice of Juniata" began transmitting on cable TV, one of the first college radio stations to do so. Conrad Wickham, Larry Osborne, and Stephen Suplicki worked to make this possible. As yet, WJC broadcast only on the AM band. Since 1970 the station's staff had ensconced themselves in Founders basement, where the old print shop had been.

Summer school students in 1972 will not soon forget Hurricane Agnes. That tropical storm, while moving northward over the Atlantic, dropped 10.15 inches of rainfall over much of Central Pennsylvania in three days (June 22-24). High water marks in Huntingdon reached those of 1936, and at Mount Union overall damages totaled one million dollars. Juniatians, relieved of classes, helped out in rescue work throughout the emergency.

The year preceding Hurricane Agnes, Juniatians ratified a new Student Government constitution. Formerly, of course, all social events fell under the purview of the SG. But the College Center Board had, in the course of things, taken over much of the social program and its planning. Hence the need to revamp the constitution. SG presidents got along famously with John Stauffer. They appreciated the way he had opened up the campus. Twice they expressed their esteem for him with a gift related to his interest in Eskimo culture. One of those times was a surprise presentation at the last Juniata commencement he presided over. But openness encourages people to speak out, generates an atmosphere of dynamic tension as compromises are sought. The SG, therefore, could be confrontational. It pressed hard on the matter of food service and the quality of meals, causing the departure of two companies. The Hill's leaders lobbied successfully for nonacademic leaves of absences. And for a time things got tense over campus lifestyles and dormitory rules. SG agitation to abolish the senior-year comprehensives, or at least not make graduation contingent upon passing them, also paid off. In 1973 came unit evaluations, published in booklet form—a kind of Baedeker on what goes on in Juniata's classroom. Students elsewhere had been doing this for some time. But on the Hill unit evaluations lasted only one year.

The campus Judiciary, by then, had disappeared in its original form. It was given the new name of Judicial Board, and its members were not elected but appointed by the president of the SG and approved by the Senate. Juniatians, as in the past, would not inform on those who cheated or broke college rules. Virtually every hearing conducted by the Judicial Board still was a referral from the deans or resident assistants.

The Stauffer hierarchy, then, not only gave students a voice but also heeded them more often than not. Actually the most vocal element on the Hill when Stauffer became president was not the SG but a loosely organized group calling themselves the Student Action Group (SAG). They had already raised the battle cry of "relevance" in a confrontation with the trustees at the time of the board's dinner for retiring Calvert Ellis in May 1968.

The leading lights of the SAG made an interesting foursome: Marta Daniels, Kathleen Snyder (Johnson), Donna Roppelt, and Kenneth Smith. The best-known gadflies of their day, every one of them was very bright. They never held any elective office yet their influence was plenary. They worked behind the scenes, manipulating the faculty perhaps more than their peers in the cause of student power. So serious-minded were they that not one of them deigned to have a senior-year photograph in the *Alfarata*. They worked hard locally for Eugene McCarthy in the fall of 1968, his dovish stand on Vietnam to their liking. They were sincere idealists, advocates of personal freedom. It was for their kind, some said, that the 1971 curriculum was devised. In fact, they had a prolocutor on the Task Force for their point of view in the person of Donna Roppelt.

SAG, with Kenneth Smith the engineer, carried out Juniata's first real student protest directed at the college. On February 25, 1969, Beeghly Library was the scene of a "study-in." Some two hundred Juniatians refused to leave at closing time (10:00 P. M.). They demanded an extension of hours till midnight during class days. Deans Rockwell and Schoenherr showed up to represent the administration. The protesters made their point—and won. SAG, said Smith later, sprang up as a reproach to a "do nothing" student government. As he saw it, "A tremendous gap exists between the ideals of individuality taught in the classroom and the actual road of conformity students are forced to take in everyday actions."[18]

It was the Daniels-Snyder-Roppelt-Smith cartel that organized "Encounter '70," a colloquy during which the campus played host to approximately forty professional people. They "rapped" with students on a whole spectrum of subjects: air and water pollution, poverty, overpopulation, education, racial conflict, Vietnam, sex, the hippie scene, and more. "Encounter 70" went over big with Juniatians. The gadfly-four were also the moving spirits behind Division IV, a kind of "Free University," offering self-taught, noncredit work. But the new curriculum stole a lot of its thunder and it soon fell by the way.

Just as the "relevance" issue began to quiet down, unrest over Vietnam came to the fore. Students, faculty, and administrators cooperated in a demonstration called "Juniata Mobilization for Peace" on Thursday, May 15, 1969. Beginning at 10:00 A. M. Oller Hall lawn fairly echoed with the sounds of speech and song most of the day. Speakers ranged from Juniatians, including the president, to active members of national organizations. Musical entertainment filled in between speeches. One speaker-entertainer was John Sollenberger, who sang Arlo Guthrie's satire on the draft, *Alice's Restaurant*. The crowd, hundreds strong, gave him a standing ovation when he revealed his intention to turn in his draft card. To be sure, the "Hawks," who had a good turnout, did not let the day pass without getting in their word at the microphone.

That fall (October 15) Juniatians joined in observing "Vietnam Moratorium Day," a massive nationwide student antiwar demonstration. Starting with a Round Top morning rally, Hilltoppers rang doorbells all over Huntingdon, passing out peace literature and talking about the "madness" of the war. Afterward some two hundred of them attended a memorial service, conducted by Campus Minister Faus in Stone Church, for all who had died in the Southeast Asian conflict. It was outpourings like this all over the country that produced Vice-President Spiro Agnew's most notorious blast of adjectival invective. He tonguelashed the moratorium's leaders as being "an effete corps of impudent snobs who characterize themselves as intellectuals." A month later a second moratorium day attracted a crowd estimated at 250,000 (Juniatians among them) to Washington to march past the White House.

Then in late April 1970 Nixon ordered American troops into Cambodia. The North Vietnamese and Viet Cong had been using that neutral country for years as a springboard for troops, weapons, and supplies. The previous spring the President had promised in a televised address to withdraw United States forces over a period of time. To collegians the Cambodian invasion seemed to spell deeper involvement rather than withdrawal. It sparked dissent, immediate and red-hot, on the nation's campuses. The killing of demonstrators at Kent State University, in Ohio, by National Guardsmen on May 4 added to their indignation. A wave of faculty-student strikes closed down hundreds of colleges. Five days later huge crowds gathered in Washington, D. C., in an antiwar rally and to protest the deadly incident at Kent State.

The Cambodian and the Kent State news appalled many Juniatians. Wild talk spread over the Hill about proposed life-endangering demonstrations: picket the local armory, form a human blockade of Route 22, or set off explosives at some public place. Rumors circulated that outsiders were coming in to agitate. Stauffer and his staff debated what to do to forestall possible injury to Juniata students. They consulted with Jeremiah Eisenhour, Student Government president, and certain faculty members. Who could know or guess what might happen?

But Stauffer's mind was made up to suspend classes until the danger had passed. Early morning May 7 students found notices slipped under their doors telling them to leave campus before day's end. After breakfast the Hilltop community gathered in Alumni Hall for an explanation. Some of the faculty and students thought the president was overreacting. He readily agreed that might be the case, but he refused to risk student safety. A few parents and alumni mistook the May 7 decision to be a political statement against the war. Nothing was further from the truth. Students were called back on Friday, May 15, which allowed a week of classes before finals. The faculty gave their classes four options on grades and finals. Most of them took Option #4: credit with no grade or final.

While the Vietnam War kept the country's campuses stirred up, the early 1970s also brought revolutionary changes in student living patterns. Lowering the legal age of majority to eighteen in most states, as noted, rang the death knell for *in loco parentis*. Juniata changed with the times, too, the law on the side of the students. Also, no more would marriage automatically terminate a Juniatian's enrollment. Before, newlyweds had to petition for readmission. Thereafter a wedding band only required notifying the registrar's office of a change of status or name. Dean Schoenherr abolished curfews and adopted a flexible policy on visitation privileges. Juniatians could now choose among three dormitory plans—A, B, and C. Plan A was the most liberal, granting men and women the privilege of interdormitory visitation all hours, day or night. Plan B permitted some weekday visitation. Plan C allowed visitation only on weekends. Some residences would now house *both* men and women, already a dormitory choice at many other colleges. These housing patterns would not change much in the future.

Even though the counterculture values of the Sixties had impacted College Hill in benign ways—casual dress and open dormitories—they also had a malignant side:

drugs and drink. All college campuses encountered this problem. Juniata's student handbook, the *Pathfinder*, contained no policy statement on drugs until 1968, though they were in use before that. Apparently few Juniatians ever got into psychedelics like LSD. But "speed" (amphetamines), tranquilizers, and "pot" (marijuana) have been common chemical substances on the Hill. And Juniata did not lack for resident "pushers"—often from medical families, rumor had it. Sociologists of the time pointed out that this almost universal appetite of college-age youth for some kind of chemical crutch for the mind was but an extension of a "pill popping" society at large. Nevertheless, the *Pathfinder* warned that the possession and misuse of drugs could bring serious disciplinary action, including suspension.

Alcohol was the drug, however, that most confounded the Hill. A survey by sociology professor Duane Stroman revealed that many Juniatians of the Seventies came from families that drank alcoholic beverages. Yet the results of a questionnaire sent to parents in 1971 indicated that seventy percent of them opposed any change in the college's on-campus antidrinking policy. Student Government and the *Juniatian* took the opposite side. The administration was forced into an agonizing dilemma. A trustee committee wrestled with the problem but recommended no change in rules against drinking in the dormitories. For some of them it was a matter of strong moral conviction, and they could not countenance a liberal drinking policy. Other trustees thought it hypocritical to have a policy on alcohol but not enforce it.

That did not change the situation; Juniata was de facto a wet campus. Said one student, "You have to work to get caught."[19] Some student bingers, however, became abusers after a bout of drinking; they damaged college furniture and disturbed dormitory peace. These did get caught. Their defenders faulted the new curriculum—too much freedom, especially for freshmen. General dissidence over the curriculum and college policies led to Quality of Life Day on February 11, 1975. The administration and SG had jointly proposed this idea.

To promote the all-college event campus leaders formed Students-Teachers-Administrators Reaching Together (START). START organized mixed teams to visit each dormitory and college house, classes being canceled that Tuesday, for "rap" sessions. One purpose of the day, said SG president Carl Glaeser, was "to define a concept of wholeness of community, to seek a better relationship among segments of the college community." It also would try to get at the root of what Provost Norris had called the "at times cynical, at times hedonistic, and on occasion even barbaric" student attitude toward education and life. In the afternoon a panel reported at a packed Town Meeting in Oller Hall on the "gripes" uncovered by the teams. John Stauffer presided.

A second Town Meeting was held on the evening of March 26. It dealt with questions and issues raised at the first one. Meantime, between the two all-campus assemblies, the faculty had reinstated academic probation. When that was reported on the 26th Oller Hall erupted with applause by approving students. Professors sat nonplused at this unexpected response.

The Town Meetings were cathartic, and they did result in some changes. The director of Hallmark Management Services alerted the audience at one of the sessions about a dining hall problem. He reported that Juniatians were filching chinaware and table utensils at the rate of five thousand dollars a year. Theft did not cease, but it declined. As for alcohol, the college did not ease its official policy until the fall of 1975 with the coming of a new president.

The year before Carl Glaeser got involved with START, he and three other Juniatians—Gary Moore, Bruce Moyer, and Susan Rosshirt—took part in the third annual convention of the National Student Lobby (NSL) held in Washington, D. C. In late February 1974 they joined eight hundred other collegians from across the country as conventioneers. The NSL was founded to lobby for passage of legislation advantageous to students at both the federal and state levels. Two Juniatians, Rosshirt and Moyer, came away with top executive positions. Rosshirt, a junior, was elected a coordinator for six states and Washington, D. C., by virtue of which she became a member of the NSL national board of directors. Senior Bruce Moyer spent his last few months at Juniata as the first president of the Pennsylvania Student Lobby.

While administrators coped with a campus in social transition, donors added two more academic student prizes to the existing eight, and the college again graduated national scholarship winners. In 1969 the Women's League of Juniata donated the Rebecca C. Barrick Language Prize in honor of Miss Barrick, a former Huntingdon Latin teacher and long-time League member. It goes to a woman concentrating in language study (including English) with a distinguished record in her field the first three years. The William A. Schlichter Award (1970) is granted to a senior man of academic achievement, Christian character, and devotion to Juniata. The recipient must reflect the qualities of Schlichter, a sophomore who died in an automobile accident while driving back from a choir picnic in September 1969. Nineteen-seventy also brought word from the Woodrow Wilson Foundation that Juniata had graduated another designee, William Phillips, the future Nobel physicist. Then in 1972, after a hiatus of eleven years, political science major Karl Kindig became the fourth—and last—Root-Tilden Juniatian. His distinguished post-law school career would bring him back to College Hill as a trustee in another two decades.

Other worthy Juniatians, at the same time, benefited from sixty-eight endowed scholarships. In 1975 these yielded some sixty thousand dollars in student aid. Three years before, Congress had reenacted the NDEA as the National Student Loan Program. Later the federal government made available the Basic Educational Opportunity Grants Program. Beginning in the early 1970s the Pennsylvania Higher Education Assistance Agency (PHEAA) became another major source of student loans. By the college's centennial, access to federal and state funds had become a fixed option in meeting the costs of higher education.

INDIANS OF THE EARLY 1970s

The 1971 curriculum did away with required physical education but not the department. Aside from coaching duties, the department's staff now encouraged physical fitness through intramural sports. By fall 1975 sixty percent of the student body had become involved in a whole range of indoor and outdoor intramural games. Physical education lost its director when Fred Prender left in 1969 to be head football coach at Bucknell University. Earl Kaylor filled in as interim AD on a reduced teaching load to the end of the academic year. He recruited Walter Nadzak for the position and to be head football coach. Nadzak, who took over that summer, had been an All-Ohio Conference lineman and MVP at Denison University, then played professional football for a few years.

Prender's seasons amassed a gridiron tally of 30-19-0. His last year, Donald Weiss became a two-time All-American, who went on to play in the Canadian Football League. Nadzak, though an ex-marine, did not perpetuate his predecessor's barbering code. From 1970 to 1975 his teams won thirty-four, lost twenty, and tied two. He reached the high point of his coaching career at Juniata in 1973. That season he and his two assistants, Dean Rossi and Richard Reilly, coached the Indians (10-1) into the first NCAA Division III national championship game. Televised live by ABC, the title game, of all things, matched Juniata and Wittenberg University, the only two colleges in John Stauffer's *curriculum vitae*. The Amos Alonzo Stagg Bowl in Phenix, Alabama, hosted the teams. Pennsylvania Governor Milton Shapp wagered a bushel of apples against Ohio Governor John Gilligan's jug of maple syrup on the outcome. It was no contest; Wittenberg easily won (41-0). Despite the lopsided loss, Nadzak was named NCAA Division III Coach of the Year, the first from Juniata's athletic department to receive so high an honor. And the 10-2 mark remains the standard for victories in a season.

Nadzak-coached teams turned out a galaxy of MAC Northern Division All Stars during the Stauffer years. Three—Louis Eckerl (1973), tight end Peter Lentini (1974), and defensive tackle Stuart Jackson (1975)—earned MVP laurels. The same trio also made first team ECAC All-East, while Lentini was voted Little All-American. Robert Waggoner, a linebacker, holds the distinction of being one of only three Juniata gridders to earn All-Middle Atlantic Conference mention three years in a row at the same position (1970–72). He also made All-ECAC (1971 and 1972) and All-State in 1971. That period's defensive end, Raymond Grabiak, is the school's only two-time football first-team Academic All-American, in 1970 and 1971. Juniata's first African-American to receive this post-season honor, offensive tackle Maurice Taylor, joined Grabiak in 1971. In 1972 a Cyclone Fence enclosed College Field, which in 1975 got a new scoreboard with an easier-to-read clock.

Overall, the early Seventies were not as kind to basketball. Before Russell Trimmer left in 1970 (44-38 overall), however, he took the Blue and Gold to its first MAC playoff tourney, in 1968–69. He did it again the next year. Juniata finished fourth both times. Trimmer left in 1970, and his successor, John Swinderman, stayed through the 1973–74 season, leaving with a mark of 28-61. Seven of the players Trimmer and Swinderman coached rank among the college's top performers in scoring, rebounding, or assists: Charles Harvey, Oscar Hatchett, Mark Jula, Academic All-American John Smith (1970), Timothy Taylor, Leroy Wentz, and Donald Williams. Hatchett holds the all-time record in season assists (165). Carl Meditch, his system a throwback to Trimmer's, succeeded Swinderman, winning thirteen and losing twelve in 1974–75.

That won-lost mark was good enough for a berth in the MAC championship tournament (the team came in fourth).

Baseball struggled too, despite the coaching of William Berrier since 1969 (he would manage for the Dodgers every summer for another eight years). His teams for 1969–75 logged a 50–73 record. Centerfielder Thomas Streightiff made first team MAC in 1973 and upon graduation gave the minor leagues a brief try. (Thomas Dettore, who attended Juniata two years [1965–67] and played basketball but not baseball, pitched three years in the National League with Pittsburgh [1973] and Chicago [1974–75].) Men of the diamond appreciated an added convenience to Langdon Field in 1975: dugouts.

The mats of Memorial Gymnasium did not particularly favor Berrier's wrestlers, who went fifteen and sixty-five in the seven seasons since 1968–69. Their 8-3 tally that year, however, had been the best ever for Tribe grapplers. Heavyweight Peter Schuyler, 11-1 in 1970, entered the record books as Juniata's first MAC champion in any weight class. He had eighteen pins in three years, second only to Duane Ruble in 1960–64.

Golf and tennis each had one good season. Golf compiled a record of 39-34 in seven seasons, its best season being 1972 (9-0-1) when the team finished second in the MAC tourney. The whole team was named recipient of the C. Blair Miller trophy that year. Tribe netmen in that period of time logged a mark of 37-28. They went 10-1-0 in 1969, their best season ever. One of the racket wielders on the squad was the future Nobel physicist, William Phillips.

Track's overall record almost duplicated that of tennis's (38-29). But after Dean Rossi took over in 1973, assisted by Richard Reilly and chemistry professor Donald Mitchell, Juniata's field-and-track teams performed at a 19-7 pace. (There was a rapid turnover in coaches after Snider retired, until Rossi, who lettered at Penn State in the sport, came along.) Rossi's first squad won the MAC Championship, the only time ever. What is even more remarkable about Blue and Gold cindermen of the early 1970s is that they smashed fourteen school records in the seventeen track-and-field events of a meet.

All fourteen were registered just before the metric system went into effect, in the late 1970s. Four of them still stand. In 1972 the foursome of Joseph Coradetti, Carl Koval, Christopher Perry, and Michael Slough ran the Mile Relay in a time of 3:21:70. The next year Robert Zimmerman pole vaulted 14'8¾". Kim Witmer ran his record time of 49.0 for the 440 Yards in 1974. And in 1975 Calvin Shoenberger hurled the discus 147'2".

Cross-country runners, coached by the basketball mentor since Philip Snider days, fell short of breaking even in the won-lost columns (38-41). Dennis Weidler was the only Juniatian to run the 4.8-mile circuit faster than Richard Beard, in 1969; like Beard, he won the C. Clifford Brown trophy three times. In 1974 the cross-country course was lengthened to 5.6 miles, and that November, against Gettysburg, junior John McCullough set the best time for it (32.09).

After a four-decade interval, women's varsity sports made a comeback on College Hill. Congress passed Title IX in 1972, requiring schools that received federal money to provide equal opportunities—and funding—for female athletes. At Juniata reallocated budgeting revived three varsity sports for women: field hockey and basketball in 1973, and, in 1974, tennis. JoAnn Reilly coached field hockey the first year, followed by Alexa Fultz. Their combined two-year record was 4-8-1. Vernne Wetzel (Greiner) received the first Thomas B. Robinson Award in the ball-and-stick sport (1974).

Wetzel also got the first David and Gayle Kreider Award in basketball that year. This sport, by then played according to men's rules, had its revival under alumnus Patrick Frazier, a science teacher at the Huntingdon Area High School. He and his next-year's successor, Huntingdon Area Middle School guidance counselor Edmund Gargula, coached the maiden Indians to fourteen wins and seven losses in their first two seasons. Upcoming 5'9"-senior Mardi Frye (Dunklebarger) scored 157 points in the 1974–75 season, averaging 12.2 points a game.

Tennis got its Title IX start thanks to alumnus Ray Pfrogner, a Juniata physics professor and MVP netman in his own student days. His teams in 1974 and 1975 won five and lost four. The first Jack M. Haskell Tennis Award in 1975 went to Alice Herritt (Stenstrom), a sophomore.

Indian athletes, male or female, continued to get extensive coverage in spite of no SID after 1968. Charles Pollock (1974–81), a la William Engel, made sports news an integral part of his duties as director of public information. And in Mailand McIlroy, sports editor of the Huntingdon *Daily News* since 1952, Juniata had a loyal friend, who was as much a confidante to coaches as a reporter of what happened on field, court, or mat.

Chapter 15

ADVANCING INTO THE SECOND CENTURY: 1975–1986

JOHN STAUFFER RESIGNS

John Stauffer's letter of resignation on March 8, 1975, took the trustees by complete surprise; there had been no hint of its coming.[1] It impacted College Hill with the same shocking force. The president's letter revealed he suffered from a congenital heart condition and no longer had the stamina to meet the demands of his duties. Moreover, his cardiologist had advised him, after a recent physical evaluation, that "the work of a college president is no longer compatible with [your] health."[2] Privately, however, he confided to trusted friends that he had been diagnosed as being in the initial stage of "premature senility."[3] His resignation at age sixty came five years earlier than he had planned, so he asked to stay on in a less demanding position until he reached sixty-five. The trustees readily complied and assigned him general responsibilities in the development office. Stauffer himself thought it prudent, for the sake of his successor, not to continue as a trustee. In the end, he took early retirement in 1979, his dementia already taking its emotional and mental toll.

FREDERICK MOORE BINDER: FIRST NON-JUNIATA PRESIDENT

At age fifty-five, Juniata's ninth chief brought more presidential experience to the Hill than any of his predecessors upon taking office. He came a two-time president, having served at Hartwick College (1959–69), then a Lutheran institution in Oneonta,

New York; and at Whittier (1970–75), an independent college in California with a Quaker heritage. He spent the year 1969–1970 as Associate Commissioner for Higher Education of New York State. At Hartwick his leadership trebled the enrollment and the number of faculty. In ten years' time he oversaw construction of twelve new buildings. His five years at Whittier, Richard Nixon's alma mater, were no less distinguished. There, it was said, Binder (pronounced Bind-er) was not "the ivory-tower type of administrator."[4] He increased the college's endowment by more than twenty-five percent. At both Hartwick and Whittier he initiated major curricular and calendar changes. All the while, whether a New Yorker or Californian, he put his academic expertise at the service of numerous funds, foundations, and associations (national and regional) identified with higher education. Binder came to Juniata a cancer survivor.

A native of New Jersey, Binder, upon graduating from Ursinus College, went into the navy and served as a PT boat commander in the South Pacific (1942–1945). After the war he received his master's in American history and his Ph.D. in American economic history from the University of Pennsylvania. He taught for eight years in the history department at Temple University. Then from 1955 to 1959 he was academic dean and vice-president at Thiel College, a Lutheran school in Greenville, Pennsylvania. Prior to coming to the Hill he had published two books: *Coal Age Empire* and *The Serbian Assignment*, a spy novel.

The advisory committee to the trustees in the search for Stauffer's successor included fourteen members representing the faculty, students, and alumni. In the case of the faculty, according to the bylaws, the function of advising the board on the selection of a president (or other major administrative office) devolved on the Executive Committee. Over seventy candidates submitted applications. The board had already interviewed the leading nominee when Frederick Binder's belated, handwritten, one-page letter arrived. In it he said that when he was a young dean at Thiel College, Calvert Ellis had been his role model. The letter intrigued trustee Jewett Henry, the search panel's chairman.[5] All of a sudden the board had a new front-runner. A campus visit by the candidate ended the search.

Juniata never had an extrovert as president until it got a human dynamo in the person of Frederick Binder. Outspoken and outgoing, he was an earthy man. He had the stocky physique of an athlete (he lifted weights) and wanted to be called "Fred." He shook hands with a knuckle-crushing grip, spoke in a deep, booming voice, and would soon sport a Teddy Roosevelt-like mustache. For casual dress he often decked himself in western garb, from ten-gallon hat to cowboy boots. He and Martin Brumbaugh shared a common vice: cigars, except Binder brandished his in public. He became a vestryman at St. John's Episcopal Church soon after coming to Huntingdon, objecting strongly when the congregation got a woman rector. Like Calvert Ellis, Binder would chair or serve on numerous Middle States evaluation teams. He enjoyed classroom contact with students and from the start taught a course in American history every year, a practice he had followed at Hartwick and Whittier. For several years he regularly attended meetings of the history department. In 1979 he began broadcasting a fifteen-minute news program on Huntingdon's WHUN every Saturday called "Viewpoints." And, of course, he fulfilled community obligations by joining service clubs (Elks, Rotary) and representing the college on the hospital board.

Why Juniata for him, an Episcopalian? He found the college attractive, Binder said, because of "its outstanding reputation in the sciences and in all the pre-professional areas of liberal arts education and the strength of both its faculty and its board of trustees."[6] He also wanted to get back East: "It is good, finally, to be home again." As for his Huntingdon home, the president and his family (Grace and daughter Robin) moved into the former residence of ophthalmologist H. Ford Clark in Taylor Highlands. It had recently been donated to the college by Owens Corning Fiberglas Corporation and extensively renovated. The spacious house, a large den with a fireplace being added in 1982, proved ideal for entertaining Juniata people.

THE BINDER VISION FOR JUNIATA

Once in office Binder spoke of his strong belief in "the good, small, liberal arts college approach," namely, career preparation. Historically, he noted, this mission has been the main strength of schools like Juniata. Such institutions are invariably characterized by a "committed faculty dedicated to teaching and the individual students." He saw himself working to preserve Juniata's century-long legacy of career education. But, enviable as its record has been on this score, much remained to be done, Binder stressed. Thus as president, he wanted to take a new look at the curriculum, expand career counseling and placement, line up more business internships and community projects, and contract special arrangements with medical and graduate schools and hospitals. His immediate attention, however, would focus on admissions and retention. He said: "I believe them to be especially significant to the life and health of Juniata."[7] The future academic market place, he explained, did not look good because of an ever-shrinking applicant pool for several years ahead.

Quite aside from specific goals related to recruitment and attrition and service-oriented programs of study, Binder had a more general vision about his Juniata presidency. He articulated it in his first convocation address, titled "A Challenge for Juniata's Second Century." He dared the whole campus community—faculty, students, staff—to get involved in life-long learning, "here and now." He said a college or university has failed if it does not inspire "men and women to dedicate themselves to purposeful learning throughout their lifetime."[8] At Juniata he wanted to see a close intellectual relationship of student and professor in the classroom, in the laboratory, in all the rhythms and places of learning.

THE CENTENNIAL-INVESTITURE CONVOCATION

Fewer than one-fifth of all colleges and universities in the United States could lay claim to being one-hundred-years old in 1978. Plans for Juniata's centennial celebration began the previous year when President Stauffer commissioned Earl Kaylor to write a narrative history of the college. Kaylor envisioned his history as a hybridization of David Emmert's folksy, anecdotal *Reminiscences of Juniata College*, published privately in 1901 as a twenty-fifth anniversary chronicle, and Charles C. Ellis's commissioned conventional account, *Juniata College: The History of Seventy Years,*

1976–1946, written in preparation for the diamond anniversary in 1951. The centennial's *Truth Sets Free* came off the press in December 1977.

A novel memento of the golden anniversary began to take shape in the summer of 1975: the Juniata College Centennial Needlepoint project. Mrs. Calvert Ellis got the idea for it and enlisted twenty women to apply their stitching talent to it. Five feet long and four feet wide, the hanging portrays in Persian wool yarn some of the memorable buildings, scenes, and activities of the college's past one hundred years. Six central squares feature the centennial symbol, popularly known as "the book and the tree." Barnard C. Taylor, then the college editor, designed the emblem. The project made its public debut on Homecoming, October 11, in Ellis Center, where five hundred alumni and friends viewed its unveiling. For years the needlepoint hanging was displayed behind a large glass-fronted wall case in the main lobby of the Center. Today it is preserved in the college Museum.

The centennial undertaking that got the most pre-convocation publicity was James Lehman's multimedia show, *A Season of Good Favor*.[9] A 1966 Juniata graduate and free-lance writer-media consultant, Lehman utilized some 250 slides to illustrate a taped narration with background music that encapsulated Juniata's history in a perceptive, fast-moving production. *A Season of Good Favor* made the rounds of fifteen alumni clubs from Boston to Chicago between February and May.

As part of the continuing centennial celebration the college also published a journal, *Juniata Studies: Peace, Justice and Conflict*. Edited by English professor Ralph Church and history professor Klaus Kipphan, the publication was an outgrowth of the Peace and Conflict program. But it was also quite in keeping with Juniata's Brethren heritage of pacifism, a proper centennial emphasis. College Hill professors, all involved in the program, wrote articles expressly for the issue. Alexander McBride of the art department drew the cover design and did the graphics for it.

Other mementos of the celebration included the centennial pewter plate, an *Alumni Directory* (the college's third), and a Steven Barbash etching, "Mountain Day." Barbash, an artist-etcher who already had prints in the permanent collections of the Library of Congress, the Pushkin Museum in Moscow, and other galleries, had been chairman of the art department from 1960 to 1970. He struck two hundred impressions of "Mountain Day," which capture a forest scene near what had been his river-branch home before construction of the Raystown dam. The etching hallows Juniata's oldest tradition, one born of a tranquil past and a common love of nature.

No one involved in the early planning of centennial events, of course, expected them to include the investiture of a new president. But the trustees saw that it made symbolic sense, as well as practical sense, to combine Dr. Binder's inauguration with the centennial convocation, thus giving the May 1 occasion a second-century accent while taking pride in the history of the first century. Dr. James B. Rhoads, archivist of the United States, delivered the convocation address to a crowd of thirteen hundred in Memorial Gymnasium. Later in the program Dr. Binder, as the invested president, was presented with two new college symbols: the bronze Presidential Medallion and the Centennial Mace. The medallion, to be worn for all special ceremonies, features the college seal. (Each incumbent gets a replica for a keepsake.) The mace, a gift of the

National Alumni Association and designed by Barnard Taylor, had been lathed to shape by the E. B. Endres Lumber Company in Huntingdon. Heretofore the faculty marshal had borne a mere billy-club length of wood with a blue-and-gold ribbon attached. The yard-long, somewhat hefty Centennial Mace now projected solid authority. It had been hewn from a beam salvaged when the James Creek Church of the Brethren, congregational home of the Brumbaugh founders, was razed to make way for Lake Raystown. The head of the mace bears four medals: the college seal, Founders Tower, the Church of the Brethren's 250th anniversary seal, and Huntingdon's Standing Stone.

THE BINDER ADMINISTRATION: A TIGHT PRESIDENTIAL REIN

The centennial calendar year had hardly begun when Binder got the trustees' nod to restructure the administration, effective January 1, 1976. He deemed Juniata too small to operate under a dual-headed management system. So he restored the post of dean of academic affairs, thus changing Wilfred Norris's title. At the same time, the dean of students office became the office of student services, reporting directly to the president. This major change, Binder explained, allows "one office…[to] oversee all of a student's non-academic needs from pre-admission through placement" (including athletics).[10] Another principal change had the director of institutional research and planning, William Alexander, report to the president instead of to the chief academic officer. Alexander, an alumnus in the economics department and the director since 1972, further assumed charge of the whole data processing operation, formerly the bailiwick of the business manager-controller. As part of this restructuring plan, Binder also promoted Foster Ulrich, executive director of development, to a vice-presidency. In the spring of 1976 the president followed through on his promise to appoint someone full-time in career planning and placement. He brought William Martin back to be Juniata's chief vocational guidance counselor and contact-person with employment recruiters. Martin filled that position for nineteen years, until 1995.

The summer of 1976, however, Floyd Roller resigned, and that resulted in a division of duties in the financial affairs office that still obtains at the millennium. William Alexander took over Roller's position as business manager and alumnus William Rutter became the college's first controller. In Alexander's case, the move set the course of his career at Juniata in the quarter-century since, his responsibilities growing to vice-presidential status (1983). As for institutional research and planning, Cynthia Gilbert Clarke, a 1976 graduate, served as director until 1979, when Kevin McCullen took her place and in 1983 was titled by Binder as assistant to the president in that capacity.

It was Business Manager Alexander, soon after taking office, who created the position of director of personnel services and conferences in January 1977. The appointment went to Barbara Rowe, then director of the annual support fund. The maintenance employees had voted to join the local electrical union in the summer of 1972, a development that further complicated the legal environment arising from federal regulations and guidelines. Beyond that, Alexander saw the need for someone to be responsible for establishing and improving a full program of personnel service: hiring practices, evaluation procedures, staff development, union relations, affirmative action, personnel records, fringe benefits, and safety. At first Rowe also scheduled all college conferences, but after 1985 that responsibility was assigned elsewhere. She would look after personnel services until 1996, retiring in 1998 as part-time payroll supervisor.

Admissions, as noted, was an area the new president said needed close attention. William Asendorf put in a year as acting director under Binder, and was replaced by Thomas Snyder, who had formerly served in the admissions and alumni offices. Then in 1979 Gayle Wampler Kreider became the first female director of admissions (and the first to be titled dean of admissions) at Juniata. She held that position until the end of Binder's presidency. All three administrators were Juniata graduates.

The administration experienced a second major shake up at the top level in the spring of 1977. Binder never disguised his opposition to academic divisions. He told the trustees: "It is my personal conviction that in a small college divisions do exactly what they are defined to do, namely, divide."[11] He endorsed, he said, a "one college concept," in keeping with Juniata's self-image of a cohesive community. So he did away with the divisional structure and with it the need for mini-deans. Wilfred Norris thereupon resigned as dean of academic affairs to return to teaching.

Binder then appointed Donald Hartman to succeed Norris. Arnold Tilden (Temple Ed.D.), associate dean of students at Albright College, replaced Hartman in student services and would give that office stability for the next seventeen years. Binder promoted both Hartman and Tilden to vice-presidents in 1983. Hartman left in 1985, however, to be replaced by Joseph Stewart (Rochester Ph.D.). A physicist, Stewart had been dean of the arts and sciences at the University of Dubuque, Iowa. He came as a vice-president and stayed until mid-summer 1989, three years into the Robert Neff presidency. (Stewart once commented that, as a dean, he had survived five presidential successions.) Thomas Nolan ended his thirteen-year-turn in the registrar's office in 1981 to return to the classroom. James Westwater (Temple Ph.D.) came next, to be followed by Constance Collins (Syracuse Ph.D.) in 1984 and then Jill Shrum (SUNY B. S.) in 1986.

THE BINDER FACULTY

The faculty recruited by Frederick Binder, typical of Juniata, continued to provide a loyal core. Nineteen of them, all with doctorates or terminal degrees, have given from sixteen to twenty-four years of service at the millennium. Everyone reached the rank of professor. They are, by division and department:

HUMANITIES

FINE ARTS: Karen Rosell (Ohio Univ. Ph.D.), 1986-present

SOCIAL SCIENCES

ECONOMICS AND BUSINESS ADMINISTRATION: James Donaldson (Akron M. A./Syracuse M. B. A.), 1979-present; Edward Kaminsky (Kings M. B. A.), 1977–97.

EDUCATION: Fay Glosenger (Penn State Ph.D.), 1982-present; Kim Richardson (Temple Ph.D.), 1979-present.

POLITICAL SCIENCE: Craig Baxter (Penn Ph.D.), 1981–97.

PSYCHOLOGY: Ronald McLaughlin (Northwestern Ph.D.), 1985-present.

SOCIOLOGY, ANTHROPOLOGY, AND SOCIAL WORK: Susan Radis (Bryn Mawr M. S. S.), 1984-present.

NATURAL SCIENCES

BIOLOGY: Douglas Glazier (Cornell Ph.D.), 1980-present; Todd Gustafson (Wisconsin Ph.D.), 1976-present; Debra Kirchhof-Glazier (Cornell Ph.D.), 1981-present.

CHEMISTRY: Tom Fisher (Iowa State Ph.D.), 1976-present; Ei-Ichiro Ochiai (Tokyo Ph.D.), 1981-present; Ruth Reed (Virginia Poly. Inst. Ph.D.), 1976-present.

GEOLOGY: Lawrence Mutti (Harvard Ph.D.), 1976-present; Norman Siems (Cornell Ph.D.), 1980-present.

MATHEMATICS AND COMPUTER SCIENCE: Linda Sue Esch (Boston Ph.D.), 1976-present; Loren Rhodes (Penn State Ph.D.), 1980-present; Benjamin Sunderland (Penn State Ph.D.), 1982-present.

The Binder appointees dominated the list (seven of nine) of the younger faculty to win a new annual prize for junior professors (six years or less of service): The Lindback Foundation Award for Distinguished Teaching. They were business administration's Charles Wise (Pitt M. B. A.), 1978; L. Sue Esch, 1979; Ibrook Tower, 1980; Todd Gustafson, 1981; Laurence Mutti, 1982; Kim Richardson, 1983; Norman Siems, 1984; historian Thomas Baldino (Penn Ph.D.), 1985; Loren Rhodes, 1986.

As for the prestigious Beachley Distinguished Professor Award, there had been eighteen recipients since Kenneth Crosby, the first one in 1968. The seven during Stauffer's years were sociologist Paul Heberling, 1969; Dean Donald Rockwell, 1970; chemist Eva Hartzler, 1971; historian Earl Kaylor, 1972; English's Esther Doyle, 1973; historian Klaus Kipphan, 1974; chemist William Russey, 1975. The eleven Binder-era recipients were geologist Peter Trexler, 1976; economist Ronald Cherry, 1977; chemist Paul Schettler, 1978; biologist Kenneth Rockwell, 1979; English professor Mark Hochberg, 1980; chemist Dale Wampler, 1981; geologist James Gooch, 1982; economist James Lakso, 1983; sociologist Duane Stroman, 1984; biologist Robert Zimmerer, 1985; chemist Donald Mitchell, 1986.

Other worthy faculty members were honored with appointments to professorial chairs. Emerita Esther Doyle's Dana professorship went to Philbrook Smith in 1975 and retiree Eva Hartzler's to Robert Zimmerer in 1976. A fifth Dana chair was established for William Russey, to be effective the fall of 1977. As the other honorific chairs fell vacant, President Binder soon named replacements. In February of 1977 he awarded the Martin G. Brumbaugh Professorship in Education to Howard Crouch and chemistry's Jacob H. and Rachel J. Brumbaugh Professorship to Paul Schettler. Then in

1981 Ernest Post acquired Kenneth Crosby's W. Newton and Hazel A. Long Professorship of History and José Nieto became the Mary S. Geiger Professor of Religion and History. Earlier, in the fall of 1977, the trustees had changed the name of the I. Harvey Brumbaugh chair from classics to language (but no president has yet filled it).

At its September meeting in 1978 the faculty passed a motion to draft a constitution for the purpose of defining its responsibilities within the framework of a liberal arts college. Article I of this document sets forth two particular areas where the faculty has a major voice. One is to structure the college's educational program and to prescribe its graduation requirements, the faculty's historic role. The other is to ensure that each faculty member, whether tenured or untenured, retains the academic freedom as defined by the 1940 statement of the AAUP and adopted by the board of trustees on June 1, 1970.[12] The board voted its approval in May 1979.

A few faculty members belonged to the AAUP, but there never was much sentiment to create a chapter on the Hill. Many saw it as more a labor union than a professional organization. In the spring of 1979, however, the faculty aired the idea of starting some kind of on-campus group and in the fall, coincident with drafting a constitution, moved ahead on the idea. They called it the Juniata Faculty Professional Association. The JFPA saw itself as a forum to effect better communication among faculty members and between the administration and faculty. Its fifty-five members (about 70% of the faculty) represented a goodly number from all three divisions. There were three permanent interest groups: social events, creative activities, and benefits. The primary incentive behind JFPA was concern about salaries and benefits. The benefits groups set to work collecting comparative data. It reported that faculty salaries at Juniata averaged about nineteen percent lower than those at colleges with a comparable academic standing.[13] Only Ursinus had a lower average than Juniata.[14]

President Binder had only words of support for the faculty's compensation concerns. The salary schedule at that time was as follows:

Instructor:	$11,000—$15,000
Asst. Professor:	$13,000—$17,000
Assoc. Professor:	$13,000—$20,000
Professor:	$18,000—no ceiling

Binder pressed the trustees hard for substantial raises each year, and when he retired faculty pay had risen by one hundred percent. A senior Dana professor's salary, for example, went from $23,000 to $48,500 in eleven years. The college, at the president's urging, also assumed a greater share of TIAA/CREF pension costs and of premium costs for health and basic life insurance. Binder was also able, in 1983, to convince the trustees to rescind the limit of four sabbaticals a year. One fringe benefit he adamantly opposed and refused to countersign was the granting of second mortgages to any college employee.

Earlier, in the first fall of his presidency, Binder had formulated what he called the "Juniata Plan" for future contract and tenure decisions. John Stauffer had granted wholesale tenure to all associate professors that had been at Juniata more than six years. This had created an unduly tenure-heavy faculty, close to sixty percent. The Juniata Plan specified that the percentage of tenured faculty hereafter would be no less than forty percent and no more than sixty percent, with the administration attempting to maintain a tenured ratio in the range of fifty to fifty-five percent. The flexibility of this proposal allowed faculty members to stay beyond the magic six-year mark advocated by the AAUP but still be untenured. This is still the policy, so too the Plan's provision for one- and three-year renewal contracts, all contingent upon the recommendation of the faculty's Personnel Committee. The faculty endorsed the Juniata Plan by a sixty-one percent vote.[15]

A profile of the faculty in the fall of 1981 revealed a young to middle-aged professoriate. Of eighty-one permanent faculty by rank, twenty-two fell between the ages of fifty and fifty-nine and eighteen between the ages of thirty-five and thirty-nine. Only three were over age sixty. Forty-eight had doctorates (60%) and eight had other kinds of terminal degrees, for a total of sixty-four percent. This was up quite dramatically from when Binder became president. Then the percentage of faculty with terminal degrees stood at fifty-four. The number of full professors was twenty-four, nearly a third of the faculty. When Binder retired in 1986 the figure stood at thirty-three full professors, again accenting faculty longevity.

Because of the mounting number of long-serving faculty that would likely retire at Juniata, the Binder administration codified guidelines for granting emerita/emeritus status. In May 1977 the trustees approved the following criteria: the faculty member (1) shall normally have the rank of professor or associate professor; (2) shall have been employed a minimum of ten years, the work at Juniata being the last full time employment; (3) shall be retiring rather than resigning; and (4) must enjoy the esteem of the college community as expressed by the dean of academic affairs and president (and by the faculty Personnel Committee, if it wishes).[16]

The Binder years reflected evidence of a growing number of what the president called "teacher-scholars." He had reference to the tally of books and professional articles the faculty had seen into print, he himself a contributor of several book reviews. And, as before, the science departments continued to be a magnet for lucrative grants for research projects and sophisticated instrumentation. In February 1983 four Juniata PACS students in the company of Andrew Murray and two other classmates testified before the United Nations Commission for the University of Peace, one of the U. N.'s non-governmental organizations. They told the Commission members what they would look for in a graduate-level peace and conflict studies program. Students in the sociology department worked side-by-side with Paul Heberling doing archeological excavations at iron-making and Indian village sites.

The summer of 1986 a seventy-seven-year dream became a reality for the physics department. Ever since 1909, when the college purchased its five-inch refracting Brashear telescope, there had been the hope that "some friend will provide better facilities for use of the telescope in a permanent observatory."[17] Alumnus Paul Hickes, who did all the major post-World War II construction on campus, became that friend. The Paul E. Hickes Observatory, a brick structure with a rotating dome, built in 1987, stands on Round Top and houses three telescopes.

Out at Lake Raystown Field Station Robert Fisher, on a not-so-scholarly basis but an educative one nonetheless, introduced College Hill to the art of boiling down maple sap to produce syrup. A large stand of maple trees in the hollow below the farmhouse-station headquarters, still tapped and seeping every spring, had once been locally famous for the quality of its refined sap. Ever since the late 1970s, volunteers from the Hill—faculty, administrators, and students alike—each spring help in the boiling down process, the results of which many times show up in the form of containers of syrup or sugar cubes at the May trustee dinner.

Perhaps Juniata's most famous artist in residence of the Binder period was actress Nancy Kulp, star of stage, screen, and television. On television she played the role of Jane Hathaway on the long-running comedy series, "The Beverly Hillbillies." Said the president of her coming: "Ms. Kulp's presence at Juniata will provide our students with a unique learning opportunity. We continuously strive to enhance our academic programs, and having such a talented actress teach at Juniata will be a marvelous experience."[18] The Emmy Award nominee taught film and advanced acting and directed the college's spring theatrical production, William Saroyan's Pulitzer Prize-winning *Time of Your Life*.

The faculty had at its service three different head librarians during the Binder presidency: Robert Sabin, who left in 1978 after five years; David Eyman (Michigan Ph.D.), 1978–85; and Martin Wilson (1984–88). Eyman's tenure coincided with two major, unanticipated projects. In early 1982 the college discovered serious structural defects in Beeghly Library. It had not been designed to bear the excessive weight of over two hundred thousand holdings. This necessitated reinforcing the basement area and temporarily storing materials elsewhere on campus. The reconstruction was completed by the spring of 1983. The second project involved absorbing the Myers Science Library that same spring when the new computer center displaced it in the Brumbaugh Science Center.

Ten scholars in the field of evangelical Christianity held the J. Omar Good Distinguished Visiting Professorship from 1975 to 1986. Theologian Samuel Calian stayed on a second year (1976–77), to be followed by poet Chad Walsh (1977–78), biblical scholar Earle Ellis (1978–79), retired Presbyterian minister George Docherty (1979–80), philosopher Richard Mouw (1980–81), philosopher Merold Westphal (1981–82), historian Mark Noll (1982–83), historian Robert Clouse (1983–84), English professor Corbin Carnell (1984–85), and philosopher Bruce Reichenbach (1985–86).

A RESTRUCTURED CURRICULUM: DÉJÀ VU

Dr. Binder made it clear from the start that he was not happy with the curriculum that came with his presidency. A traditionalist, he had little patience with team-taught general education courses. They took professors out of their area of academic expertise, he believed, but also, in many cases, got faculty participation only begrudgingly. Tinkering with the curriculum began Binder's first year, three years later to get more serious.

The curriculum the faculty adopted in March 1979 had five primary goals. The first one perpetuated the Program of Emphasis terminology and structure: fifteen courses, five of them from the 300 level or above, hand-picked by the student and subject to approval by the curriculum committee of the faculty. The second goal aimed at developing writing and expression skills entailing four courses. All freshmen had to take a basic composition course the fall term. At least three additional courses had to be taken from a list published annually that further refined communication skills. A third component sought to develop analytical abilities and consisted of four courses. One, titled Logic and Language, was required of all freshmen in the second term. Students would then choose three other courses from a list primarily of courses from the natural and social sciences. The fourth objective intended to develop historical and cultural knowledge, again to be met through four courses. These would come primarily from the humanities. The last goal was designed to enhance students' examination of their own personal beliefs, pre-suppositions, and the decisions based upon them. This course was titled Senior Value Studies. The curricular overhaul did not get enthusiastic endorsement; Binder called it a compromise and the faculty voted only 27-13 to implement it. In the spring of 1984 the faculty acted to drop Logic and Language and agreed to modify Freshmen Composition, doing away with a single design.

The humanities division won two federal grants of its own in the Binder years that strengthened its curriculum and helped retool professors. Juniata had sponsored visiting writers since the early 1960s, but in 1981 it received its first-ever grant from the National Endowment for the Arts (NEA) to sponsor a writer-in-residence. Out of 123 NEA grants in 1981 only four went to Pennsylvania organizations. Then in 1986 Juniata's Peace and Conflict Studies Committee came into a grant of seventy-five thousand dollars from the United States Department of Education under the Hays-Fulbright program for a summer seminar in India on Ghandian approaches to conflict resolution. Fifteen professors participated, several from Juniata but also others from institutions in Pennsylvania and neighboring states.

In 1982 Peace and Conflict Studies at Juniata became a full, degree-granting program. Two years later the college proposed renaming the PACS program the Juniata Institute for Peace and Conflict Studies, giving it an institutional rather than a traditional departmental base. The success of PACS in a first decade's time sparked the idea for an institute with more ambitious goals. By the mid-Eighties the program had evolved into an interdisciplinary core of twenty courses in nine academic departments. Of the eighty-eight such programs in the United States at that time PACS had earned the reputation as one of the finest of its kind. To publicize the institute concept and add to its endowment, Dr. Murray staged a "swim for peace" at Lake Raystown. He swam twenty miles nonstop in fourteen hours and generated in excess of thirty thousand dollars in pledges.

Other curricular developments occurred during the Binder years. Among them was expansion of the Early Childhood Education program. In the fall of 1976 the college broadened the nursery school center into a laboratory and bona fide POE. The education department took over the whole lower level of Lesher Hall, and the college fenced in the outside area. Sally Ondrejcak (Penn State M. S.) and Jessiann Dortch (Wheelock M. S.) set up the laboratory and were the first to be in charge of it. Accreditation followed in early 1978. Social work became a POE option in 1976 and accredited in 1983. In the summer and fall of the latter year the college renovated the former science library in the rotunda of the Brumbaugh Science Center and installed an expanded computer system. The new facilities were ready for use when students returned from the fall break. Former chemistry professor Dale Wampler now became director of the computer center. Then in the 1984–85 academic year the college set up a modest budget for a writing center on a temporary basis. There was broad faculty support for a place where students could be sent for remedial work. The writing center soon became a fixture under the supervision of the English department. Also in the fall of 1984 the college created the position of Director of International Programs that carried assistant deanship status. It first went to Dr. William Vocke. The need for this office (half time at first) grew out of growing interest and participation in foreign exchange programs by Juniatians. Heretofore faculty volunteers had handled the various programs. By the mid-1980s Juniata accorded a multitude of foreign opportunities.

Two annual outreach programs of potential benefit to college recruitment got afoot in the Seventies and Eighties. Both of them involved public-school teachers and students from Central Pennsylvania. Division III initiated the Invitational Conference on Current Problems in Science in October 1973. All departments of the division participated. One purpose of the event was to show what science was like at a college with a strong reputation in the natural sciences. The faculty also gave lectures on a variety of topics and made themselves available for career counseling. In the mid-Eighties the "problems" approach mutated into a Science Fair, at which public-school students exhibited their projects.

The other still-thriving happening is History Day, a spring-1986 genesis at Juniata. The Pennsylvania Historical and Museum Commission invited Juniata to host the competitive occasion at the district level (Central Pennsylvania). History Day was conceived in 1974 by a professor at Case Western Reserve University in Ohio. Its intent is to encourage pupils, grades six through twelve, to learn more about history through the use of materials and methods of social studies, language, literature, and the arts. Students can compete on an announced theme, at their grade level in seven ways: papers, and, as either individuals or groups, in projects, performances, and media presentations. The competition takes place in the Kennedy Center and the presentation of awards, in Brumbaugh Science Center. By the mid-1990s the number of entrees had grown from the forty-six in 1986 to nearly 250.

Juniata's first experience in providing an academic encounter for an age group older by many decades than that of middle- and high-school pupils—the Elderhostel circle—occurred the summer of 1978. At that time a national program, the Elderhostel was launched in 1974 for men and women aged sixty and over. In 1978 sixteen Pennsylvania campuses participated, with an enrollment of seven hundred. (Nationwide, 126 campuses attracted over 10,000 retirees.) At Juniata the program entailed three one-week sessions taught by College Hill professors representing several disciplines. Of that first summer, Dr. Duane Stroman, then the Hill's Elderhostel director, said: "People raved about the quality of instruction."[19] Being applauded at the end of a class session unfailingly pumped up professorial egos. The number of senior citizens attending Juniata's sessions ballooned from thirty-nine to ninety-two in a year's time. College Hill Elderhostels were held until the Nineties, finally done in by declining enrollment because of lack of air-conditioned dormitories.

Another genre of institutional outreach—a cultural one—was the annual performing arts series at Lake Raystown's Seven Points Amphitheater (the pre-1998 structure) sponsored by Juniata and the Army Corps of Engineers. Begun in 1977 and directed each summer by Dr. Howard Crouch, the series looked to area residents and groups for talent: vocalists, bands, individual instrumentalists, or dancers. In 1989, when Crouch retired, Juniata withdrew as a co-sponsor of the lakeside entertainment.

The fall of 1983 marked the time for another visit by a team from the Middle States Association of Colleges and Schools. Juniata's reaccreditation process got underway in 1980 with the customary self-study, which was completed in March 1982 and submitted to Middle States. The nine-member evaluation team visited the campus October 10-13. President Binder received word the following February that Juniata had received full accreditation for another ten-year period. The team praised Juniata as "academically strong and fiscally sound."[20] Its report said: "There is strong indication that Juniata College is addressing immediate student needs and interests and is continuing to prepare students for the useful occupations of life."

Over the years Juniata's mission to prepare students "for the useful occupations of life has translated into a substantial number of alumni earning Ph.D.s," reported the April 1983 issue of the *Alumni Bulletin*. The *Bulletin* cited a recent study on the baccalaureate sources of the Ph.D.s at 867 four-year private undergraduate institutions between 1920–80. Juniata placed 82nd in the nation in the actual number of alumni who hold Ph.D.s (436 out of 7,232 alumni). The raw data placed Juniata in the top ten percent of the schools studied compared with twenty similar Pennsylvania institutions, such as Albright, Bucknell, Gettysburg, and Franklin and Marshall. Among these kindred colleges Juniata ranked first in the percentage of alumni who held Ph.D.s.

More kudos came Juniata's way in 1985 and 1986.[21] *Peterson's Competitive Colleges* listed Juniata both years as among 316 colleges and universities that annually have more qualified applicants than they can accept. In 1986 the book, *Best Buys in College Education*, selected some two hundred four-year institutions out of two thousand "that offer high quality education at reasonable cost." In Juniata's profile the book noted the high acceptance rate into graduate school of its alumni. A third publication, *U. S. News & World Report*, listed Juniata as one of the ninety best liberal arts colleges in the country. That put Juniata in the select company of such institutions as Amherst, Williams, Oberlin, Haverford, and Swarthmore. Only two Pennsylvania colleges were included in all three publications.

SECOND-CENTURY TRUSTEES
MAKE FUND-RAISING HISTORY

In Juniata's centennial spring John Baker, recently turned an octogenarian, stepped aside as trustee chairman. He had helped guide the college through its greatest period of growth during his thirteen years heading the board. Without doubt his most enduring legacy is the Baker Institute for Peace and Conflict Studies at Juniata College. Dr.

Baker and his wife Elizabeth had been at the forefront of the peace and conflict studies movement in the United States for many years. It was their vision and financial generosity that launched the PACS program on College Hill in the fall of 1974. Though giving up his chairmanship, Baker remained an active trustee until 1987.

The board elected C. Jewett Henry, a Huntingdon attorney, 1929 alumnus, and trustee since 1959, as Baker's successor. But Henry's tenure was cut short by his death in 1979 following an extended illness. Charles C. Ellis, senior vice-president of RCA and a 1940 graduate, became the next chairman. (He was a first cousin of Calvert Ellis.) Though a corporation executive all of his career, Ellis had a genuine interest in higher education. When he received the college's national achievement award in 1989, his citation read, in part: "If we could create an archetypal graduate who possessed all of the positive attributes to be derived from a liberal arts education, that graduate would be Charles C. Ellis."[22] Ellis chaired the board until his death in 1990.

Eighteen new members were co-opted by the board of trustees during the Binder period. This exceptional number in just eleven years' time was because of a charter change in May 1982 stipulating a board membership of not less than thirty-one and not more than forty (an increase of 10). Expanding the board made it possible to look for younger individuals and achieve greater geographic diversity. Eight of the eighteen co-opted still served in 2000: Donovan Beachley, Jr. (1982-present); Charles Brown (1976-present); Harold Brumbaugh (1970–95); Clay Burkholder (1980–93); John Cramer (1982-present); Philip Cronemiller (1985–96); Earl Croner (1975–98); Henry Gibbel (1973–76; 78-present); Warren Groff (1976-present); Charles Knox (1978–99); W. Newton Long, Jr. (1976–96); Edwin Malloy (1978–98); Jack Oller (1974–86); Wayne Patterson (1986–98); Garry Pote (1981–99); W. Clemens Rosenberger (1979-present); Vincent Sarni (1979–95); Betty Simpson (1984–2000); and Robert Wagoner (1982-present). All were alumni except Vincent Sarni (whose son was a 1978 graduate) and Edwin Malloy, the first Jewish trustee. Out of this group would come the board's millennial leader, John Cramer. Two other trustees elected by alumni in the early 1980s, George Cruser and Marie Zeller, would later become co-opted members.

When the eight-year, $10.1-million Margin of Difference Campaign reached its goal in December 1976, Vice-President for Development Foster Ulrich began preparing the trustees for the next capital-gains effort. Ulrich, who was promoted to the rank of colonel in the Marine Corps Reserves while at Juniata, projected a multifaceted campaign for the next decade. The trustees took no action until the fall of 1979 when they approved a thirteen-million-dollar, ten-year development program. Dubbed "The Century II Campaign: An Investment in Excellence," CIIC was the largest fund drive in the college's 104-year history. CIIC had six objectives: campus development and renovation of existing buildings; endowment growth; scholarship assistance; program enrichment; and on-going support of the academic program. At that time Juniata had its largest enrollment ever—some 1250 full-time students.

Foster Ulrich left the summer of 1982, and Clayton Pheasant, then at Elizabethtown College, returned as vice-president for advancement ("development" became "advancement" in 1983). Pheasant had previously served the college in alumni affairs from 1976 to 1981 as director of development and church relations. Then in 1985 alumnus Charles Kensinger was appointed director of development to work with Dr. Pheasant. By 1984 CIIC had already amassed ten million dollars in commitments. To maintain momentum the trustees opted to boost the campaign goal to twenty million dollars by the end of the 1980s.

TRUSTEES ADOPT A MODERN MISSION STATEMENT

The founders of the Brethren's Normal College stated in the original charter of 1878 that they "associate themselves to perpetuate good and sound learning distinguished by Christian principles that the youth of the Church and State may be trained for such service as an enlightened mind and a quickened conscience may lead them to render to God and to Man." In 1896, when the school's name was changed to Juniata College, the trustees made the amended charter to read:

> The purpose or design is to establish a school or Institution of Learning that will provide the young of both sexes, with such educational advantages as will fit them for the duties and responsibilities of life, at such place, and under such influence as will not prejudice their minds against any of the doctrines of the Bible as believed and practiced by the Brethren.

By court order this third article of the charter was amended in 1908 to say: "The purpose or design is to establish a College or Institution of Learning which will provide the young with such educational advantages as will fit them for the responsibilities and duties of life." Fifteen years later, as noted in Chapter 8, a reactionary element on the trustee board, urged on by President Harvey Brumbaugh, replaced this brief statement with a much longer one that reaffirmed Juniata's Brethren heritage. The revision also reincorporated that part of the original article that mentioned a college committed to "Christian principles."

This rewrite of 1923 has never been altered. But the Binder administration sought to sidestep another charter amendment through a mission statement to be published in the college catalog. The committee of administrators (including the president) and faculty that drafted it reported to the trustees in the spring of 1978 that a mission statement was the first and essential step in long-range planning. The trustees redacted the committee's rather lengthy formulation and reduced it to three sentences:

> Juniata College is an independent, co-educational college of liberal arts and sciences founded in 1876 by members of the Church of the Brethren to prepare individuals for the useful occupations of life. The College continues to prepare students for meaningful careers. It seeks also to instill in them those qualities of character and intellect which will encourage them to strive for excellence in their personal and professional affairs and thus to enable them to achieve satisfying and beneficial lives.

This statement of institutional purpose first appeared in the college catalog for the academic year 1981–82. Its shelf life would only be another seven years.

CIIC AND THE KENNEDY SPORTS + RECREATION CENTER

The Century II Campaign focused first on a $4.5 million, sixty-thousand-square-foot annex to Memorial Gymnasium, itself to be extensively refurbished. The student body had more than doubled since 1951 when the existing athletic facility was built. Frederick Binder knew when he became president that Juniata desperately needed a new sports-recreation center if the college expected to increase its enrollment and emphasized that need to the trustees early on.[23] The architectural firm of Hayes, Large, Suckling, and Fruth designed the building and the Paul Hickes Construction Co. erected it—the names of both businesses synonymous with Juniata's post-World War II physical expansion. The college conducted a formal groundbreaking ceremony on July 27, 1981, and two years later dedicated the structure on Juniata's 107th Founders Day.

The board named the new "colossus," as the president called it, in honor of Edwin Kennedy and his deceased wife, Ruth. Kennedy had been a motivating force when plans for the annex were in the initial stages and served as honorary chairman of the first phase of the Century II Campaign. The Kennedy Center includes a six-lane swimming pool, a two-station gymnasium, a wrestling-judo gymnastics room, and a large multipurpose room. Renovations to Memorial Gymnasium provide equal locker facilities for men and women, a weight-training room, a dance studio, coaches' offices, and a first-aid training room. Many of these sections of Memorial Gymnasium and the annex were named in honor of the trustee-donors who played major roles in making the new complex a reality.

DANA HUMANITIES CENTER

The project to create the Dana Humanities Cluster began in early 1976 when the college received a one-hundred-thousand-dollar challenge grant from the Charles A. Dana Foundation. Later the Kresge Foundation, the L. B. Smith Foundation, and the Pew Foundation made major challenge grants. By December of that year, thanks to Foster Ulrich and his development staff, Juniata had not only met but also over-subscribed the challenge by twenty thousand dollars. The plan called for developing a mall-like collection of humanities buildings along 17th Street between Mifflin and Moore streets. It involved the renovation of Carnegie Hall and four McKinley-vintage houses—the Faculty Club, the Manse, the I. Harvey Brumbaugh House, and the exterior of the Nye property. The plan also included demolishing the old Home Management House and building a new Humanities Center on that site.

Renovation and remodeling projects on the existing five buildings were finished the fall of 1978. The history and religion faculty moved into their new offices in the I. Harvey Brumbaugh House and the philosophy and the speech and theatre people into theirs in the Manse, renamed the L. B. Smith House. (Later the Peace and Conflict Studies faculty also took offices there.) Carnegie Hall continued to serve the fine arts. The Faculty Club was renamed the Robert C. Baker House for the late trustee and brother of John Baker. Meanwhile, Allensville Planing Mill began construction of the Humanities Center in 1978 and completed its work the next spring. The dedication ceremonies on Founders Day in 1980 stressed Juniata's continuing commitment to the humanities and to liberal arts education. The new colonial-style edifice houses special seminar rooms, a lounge, classrooms, and faculty offices. In the summer of 1979 it had become the domain of the English and foreign language departments. Their trans-Moore Street migration left Founders Hall permanently abandoned by the faculty. The cost of putting together the Dana Humanities Cluster came to about $700,000.

THE JUNIATA COLLEGE CONFERENCE CENTER AT WILLIAMSBURG

On March 15, 1985, Dr. Binder announced that the Westvaco Corporation had donated about seventy acres of well-maintained land in Williamsburg, some twenty-five miles southwest of Huntingdon. Westvaco operates a paper mill in Tyrone and an envelope plant in Williamsburg. The property includes the corporation's former clubhouse, two other residential structures, and a freshwater spring. (The spring produces about eight million gallons of water per day.) This gift, which gave a great boost to the Century II Campaign, had been under discussion for several years by the college and the corporation. Westvaco and prior companies had owned the buildings and grounds for about a hundred years. Known as the "Big Spring" property by local people, its main structure is of mansion size, colonial in design, and once was the residence for Westvaco's Williamsburg paper mill manager.[24] When mill operations ceased (circa 1970) the grand home became a corporate conference center or "clubhouse," as employees nicknamed it. Donald Clem, manager of the mill in Tyrone, said of Westvaco's decision: "In making this major commitment, we are expressing our confidence in Juniata's future and the many new possibilities that the center will open for the college and community."[25] In June 2000, however, the Williamsburg property was sold for 1.4 million dollars in a public auction.

THE PENNINGTON HOUSE

When John Stauffer resigned, the president's house was located at 415 18th Street, which had once been the home of Dean Morley Mays and then William Swigart, Jr. In 1975, as noted, the Binder family moved into the current President's Home in Taylor Highlands. The 18th Street dwelling was assigned to the J. Omar Good visiting professor. Five years later the college came into possession of the John and Blanch Pennington house at 1829 Mifflin Street. The large gray-stone structure had been built in 1936 and later acquired by the Penningtons, who admired Dr. C. C. Ellis and liked the idea of living across the street from him. Mr. Pennington, a retired navy commander, for many years was superintendent of what was then called the Huntingdon Correctional Institution. He died in 1960. His wife lived until 1977, bequeathing the property to Juniata in memory of Dr. Ellis. Bronze tablets, outside and inside the main entrance, witness to that tribute. In 1978 the college began renting the "Pennington House," as everybody refers to it, to the J. Omar Good Fund to be occupied by its visiting professor.

FOUNDERS HALL AND OLLER HALL GET REVAMPED

In December 1978 the admissions office moved from the ground level of Founders Hall to the vacated house at 415 18th Street, which had undergone some minimal renovations. This shift allowed public relations and development offices exclusive use of that part of Founders. The move by the admissions office spared its own staff a half year of dislocation. For the architectural firm of Shafer and Slowick of Pittsburgh (they designed the Dana Cluster and Center) reported in the spring of 1979 that historic Founders Hall was structurally unsound. The trustees could not bring themselves to consign the hundred-year-old building, the first on campus, to the wrecking ball. To do the restoration work they hired the Hughes-Crawford Company, Inc., from Altoona.

The Altoona company concentrated on six major areas where it was necessary to buttress the wooden timbers used in the original construction. The roof trusses needed to be reinforced with steel. New roofing went on and the exterior masonry repointed and thoroughly coated with silicon sealant to prevent further water penetration. Some areas of the interior were refurbished. The third and fourth floors, now free of faculty offices, were sealed off to minimize stress on the upper-level timber joists. In the meantime all administrative offices temporarily relocated in other campus buildings. The president himself worked out of the Robert C. Baker House. By New Year's 1980 the restructuring was done, at a cost of $385,000. Fittingly, the final sizable gift toward the restoration of the 101-year-old building in the fall of 1980 came from centenarian Beulah Mierley, then Juniata's oldest alumna.

Oller Hall, as the center for campus cultural events, is one of the college's most "public" buildings. Built in 1940 it had begun to show its age; even the *Juniatian* complained about its run-down condition. Unlike shoring up Founders in one grand effort, the college carried out a wall-to-wall, floor-to-ceiling, new-roof rehabilitation in stages, commencing in 1978. The ten-year face-lift, including the complete restoration of the Moller organ in 1981–82, cost the college nearly $325,000.

MORE OFF-CAMPUS HOUSING AND OTHER PROPERTIES

With the escalation in enrollment the college resorted to utilizing two off-campus buildings as dormitories. The trustees converted the Mission House into a dormitory in 1979. Then in 1980 they purchased and renovated a large apartment house, once a broom factory directly across from the original Pilgrim building at 1401 Washington Street, for the same purpose. The catalog refers to it as the Hess Apartments.

In the spring of 1984 the college obtained two other properties. One was a gift from alumnus Dr. Robert Patrick and his wife consisting of a lodge and six-and-a-half acres in nearby Diamond Valley. It has become a popular retreat for Juniatians of all stripes and a much-used facility for the economics and business administration department. The second property had an interesting history. When all the private dwellings on Scott Street had been razed to make way for Maude Lesher Hall and South Hall, one lone house stood undisturbed across the street. The little green cinder-block building had been built as a workshop in 1945 but eventually became the home of Mr. and Mrs.

Marshall Sier. When Mr. Sier died in 1978 the college attempted to buy the place from his wife, Zada. But she adamantly refused, and not until her death in the spring of 1984 did the executor of her estate sell it to the college. The little A-roofed cottage, of course, was soon after leveled.

Juniatians justifiably take great pride in the beautifully landscaped campus that has evolved since the 1950s. But College Hill did not escape the Dutch Elm blight that struck the eastern coast forty years ago. In three years, 1973–76, Juniata lost 101 of the diseased trees, eighty-three of which died in one year. By the college's centennial all the stately elms (170) on the main campus had to be removed. The Calvert and Elizabeth Ellis Tree Program made possible one hundred plantings for the centennial year (one tree for each of the college's one hundred years). On April 5, 1976, Mt. Etna Nurseries of Williamsburg, with student help, began setting in a variety of trees: Pin Oak, Sweet Gum, Canadian Hemlock, Red Oak, Flowering Crabapple, White Pine Redbud, White Flowering Dogwood, and Japanese Red Flowering Quince. Edwin Kennedy underwrote other plantings of 110 trees and shrubs: Hick's Yew, Canadian Hemlock, English Boxwood, and rhododendron.[26]

Since the early 1960s seven men have had the responsibility for looking after a main campus that in the millennium includes thirty buildings and 110 acres. Four of these men had supervision over all sectors of the physical plant—buildings and grounds—until 1981: Don Schaaf (1962–63), Eugene Esterline (1963–73), Kenneth Rabenstein (1973–77), and James Quinlan (1977–84). John Linetty, who had been assistant dean of student services in charge of housing and security since 1977, replaced Quinlan. Before Quinlan left, John Hardy had assumed oversight of landscaping and lawn care as part of his duties. Mark Langenbacher, a Penn State graduate in horticulture, succeeded Hardy in 1988.

ALUMNI ASSOCIATION: AT HOME AND ABROAD

In July 1976 Clayton Pheasant became director of development and church relations, turning over his old position of director of alumni affairs to David Kreider, his former assistant. The Pheasant-Kreider team reported at the time of the transition that a record number of alumni had contributed to the Annual Support Fund for the fiscal year 1975–76—3,114, or forty-eight percent of ex-Juniatians. The year 1976 initiated the first twenty new scholarships to be funded by the Annual Support Fund. This perennial evidence of institutional fealty caught the attention of Edward B. Fiske, editor of 1985's *Best Buys in College Education*. He wrote: "At a time when the national average for donations by graduates hovers between 22 and 25 percent, Juniata's average in the last decade is more than 40 percent and has been as high as 50 percent. That's a measure of the intense loyalty the students feel for Juniata."[27]

In the fall of 1971 the Founders Club subdivided into a third category: one-thousand-dollar donors. In 1979 the three clubs ($1,000, $500, $100) transmuted into circles: Presidents ($1,000 or more), Patrons ($500-$999), Associates ($250-$499), and Builders ($100-$249). By 1986 the Founders Club claimed over sixteen hundred in these four categories. In May of that year came the elite Quinter Society, its roster limited to those whose annual giving had reached five thousand dollars or more a year. Quinterians become permanent members when their lifetime giving equals or exceeds one hundred thousand dollars. There were fifty-six charter members of the Quinter Society in 1986.

The idea of reunion classes raising funds for campus reconditioning came about in 1976 from the Class of 1926. A variety of projects materialized, including contributing to the centennial tree-planting program. The Class of 1934, at its fiftieth reunion, made possible the crescent-shaped brick wall, which bears the name of the college in large anodized letters, at the corner of Moore and 18th streets.

Allegiant alumni involved themselves in the life of the college in non-financial ways. In April 1977 about forty ex-Juniatians participated in the Hilltop's first "Career Fair," set up by William Martin from the planning and placement office. The fair, held biennially, gives students a chance to ask candid questions about their areas of vocational interests. The success of the first one prompted an amendment to the Alumni Council Constitution in the spring of 1979 that added a standing committee on career planning and placement. Alumni were already conducting seminars recently introduced by the economics and business administration department for their majors. Though the seminars were dropped by the 1990s, alumni still are invited to give lectures to the department's classes.

Former Juniatians also volunteer to help out with the Alumni Admissions Program, which began in 1979. They attend college nights at high schools not covered by Juniata, make phone calls to potential freshmen, and host prospective students in their homes. In 1982 there were as many as 150 alumni volunteers. At the millennium the program remains a valuable arm for the admissions office, which has on file a list of about a hundred names of willing recruiters.

Institutional loyalty is further evidenced in the number of alumni children that keep popping up on College Hill. In the academic year 1976–77 the Juniata lineage of three students traced back four generations. Sixty-seven had mothers or fathers with Juniata degrees (fifteen claimed both parents). Four had brothers or sisters currently enrolled. There were three siblings on the Hill in the school year 1983–84: the Palmer sisters, Cynthia, Dorothea, and Deborah of Bel Air, Maryland. The most remarkable case of a Juniata family in recent history is that of Mrs. Hayden Woodworth of Boothwyn, Pennsylvania. Her story and that of John Wertz's at the turn of the century (see Chapter 6) are unique in the annals of higher education. She sent all seven of her children to Juniata between 1964 and 1981, six of them graduating: Gail and Gwen (1964), Eric (1970), Stephen (1972), Philip (1974), Elizabeth (attended 1978–79), and Amy (1981).

Sometimes Juniata loyalty takes offbeat but charming twists. Will Judy, as noted, established a scholarship for a red-haired coed, which got the college avid attention from the print and broadcast media. The same thing happened in 1977, when Mrs. Mary F. Beckley bequeathed a scholarship for left-handed students. She met her husband at Juniata while playing tennis in 1919, their freshman year. The two were paired because they were southpaws. NBC's *Today* show on December 8 made the nation familiar with both the Beckley and Judy gifts. As President Binder said, Mrs.

Beckley's singular bequest reflected her "strong attachment to the college." "Very often, he went on, "it's these personal feelings which keep Juniata growing."[28]

The *Alumni Bulletin* got some attention of its own two years later. Competing with other four-year institutions with less than three thousand students, the *Bulletin*'s series of 1978–79 earned a national honorable mention in the 1979 contest of college publications conducted by the National School Public Relations Association (NSPRA). The NSPRA cited the *Bulletin* in the "Alumni News" category, the first national acclaim extended the periodical.[29] In January 1983 the publication began coming out regularly in a glossy, colorful cover.

That June David Kreider, after thirteen years of service to the college, the last seven as director of alumni affairs, resigned. Dorothy Lehman Hershberger, a well-known Juniatian since her graduation in 1950, succeeded him. She had been an alumni representative to the board from 1978–81, a member of the Alumni Council, a member of the Church College Relations Council, chair of the 1977–78 Annual Support Fund, and assistant general chair of the Century II Campaign. In 1981 "Dottie," as everybody knew her, received the prestigious Alumni Service Award. At the time of her appointment she had been assistant director of alumni affairs and director of church relations since June 1982. By this time Mrs. Hershberger worked out of the Harold B. Brumbaugh Alumni House on Mifflin Street, the former Samuel and Ada Gehrett home next door to the I. Harvey Brumbaugh House. The college had bought and remodeled the Gehrett place and moved the alumni operations there in the fall of 1979.

GENERATION X MAKES ITS APPEARANCE ON CAMPUS

Generation X is what Douglas Coupland labels the group born between 1961 and 1971 in his novel of that title (1991). The members of this generation, reaching their earning power in post-Reagan America, are the first to grow up totally environed by technology—computers, remote controls, VCRs. Technology became the biggest factor in their work and play. As depicted in Coupland's novel, the Xers resent the hippies-turned-yuppies of the Eighties, their materialism, their moral bankruptcy. The life style and mood of the Generation X characters portrayed in the book seem to brand them as slackers, spokespersons for a new genre of Bohemianism.

The fact is, Gen-Xers have grown up and are now running companies. They are not the slackers Coupland made them out to be. If, as the novelist argues, older baby boomers did hand them a platter empty of possibilities, then the post-baby boomers proved they could be aggressively innovative, successful risk-takers. For example, the first four classes of Juniata Gen-Xers, from 1983 to 1986, seem to have done quite well in the workaday world and early on in their alumnihood became generous supporters of their alma mater. In the fiscal year 1991–92 the number of donors in those four classes averaged thirty percent. Six years later the *Report of the President* listed over thirty-seven percent of the class members as donors. For 1997–98 the Class of 1985 gave at a rate of 40.3%. The total giving for that four-year period by the initial Gen-Xers jumped from $18,377 to $31,416. Seen in the context of the times, this is an admirable example of beneficence on the part of young adults raising families.

One placement director, referring to the job market at the time Juniata's first Gen-X class completed its senior year, said: "You don't want to be a college graduate in 1983."[30] Another placement chief said that 1983 "has been the worst employment market in my 25 years in the profession." Job offers were down an average of thirty-four percent from the 1982 level, or a whopping forty-one percent from 1981. And in May 1985 the *Juniatian* ran an article that predicted half of that spring's college graduates in the United States would not have jobs when they left school. Admittedly these data do suggest a relatively empty platter, that the only kinds of work opportunities available were what Coupland termed "McJobs"—"low pay, low prestige, low benefits, low future." Be that as it may, the initial wavelet of the X generation at Juniata, as at most colleges and universities, did not graduate into being the aimless, find-solace-in-the-California-desert, embittered twentysomethings Coupland writes about, though born and reared in the same time frame.

The earliest Gen-Xers came to College Hill the year after a national survey (Astin Report) of first-time freshmen indicated that 83.3 percent of de novo Juniatians cited the college's academic reputation as the most important reason for coming here. Only 54.8 percent of students from all four-year colleges gave that as a prime reason. Not surprisingly, given Juniata's reputation in preparing graduates in the fields of health services, 19.2 percent of the male freshmen gave premedicine, predentistry, or preveterinarian as their probable course of study, while seven percent of coeds did. The national response was 4.3 percent and 1.8 percent, respectively. Of all freshmen at Juniata, men and women, 21.6 percent planned a medical degree of one kind or another. Nationally only 6.5 percent had this as a goal.[31] Among upperclassmen that academic year of 1978–79, 16.5 percent had POEs in prehealth fields.

The enrollment then had reached 1153 (650 men, 480 women). Tuition, room, and board totaled $4,905, but by President Binder's last year the general fee had doubled to $9,894, compared to the $8,029 average all-inclusive cost at other four-year colleges in the United States.[32] In 1978 seventy-three percent of the student body were Pennsylvanians, New Jerseyites constituting fourteen percent of the other out-of-staters. Thirteen came from foreign countries and ten were African-Americans. In 1975 the *Juniatian* mentions that a Minority Student Union had formed a few years before but was not active. The *Pathfinder* for 1974–75 lists for the first time a Black Students Organization under "clubs," and the only photograph ever of a group of black Juniatians (twelve) appears in the 1975 issue of the *Alfarata*. The organization is last mentioned as a club in the 1975–76 *Pathfinder*. (Juniata would never enroll more than a dozen blacks in any one year from the mid-Seventies to the millennium.)

As for clubs and organizations in general during the Binder years, students could find a wide and varied spectrum of social and extracurricular activities. For the year 1974–75 there were the following:

Music—Juniata Choral Union, Concert Choir, Pep Band, Concert Band, Chamber Orchestra, Wind and String Ensembles.

Professional Clubs—Barrister Club, Mathematics Club, Pennsylvania Student Education Association, Scalpel and Probe (Biology), Society of Physics Students.

Interest Clubs—Camera, Outing, Chess, Juniata Speleological Society, International Cultural Relations, Black Students Association.

Religious Organizations—Juniata Inter-Varsity Christian Fellowship, Deputation Club.

Honorary Groups—Honor Society, Tri-Beta (Lambda Epsilon of National Biological Society), Tau Epsilon Sigma (honor service club for students who have demonstrated academic ability, extracurricular participation, and leadership), Delta Epsilon chapter of Alpha Phi Gamma (journalism), Varsity J Club (athletic letter-winners), and Sigma Pi Sigma (national physics honor society).

By 1986 several new clubs had been added to this list: American Chemical Society, Amateur Radio Society, Andy Lawson Geological Society, Campus Women's Organization, Circle K, Conservation Club, Indoor Soccer Club, J. C. Cycling Team, French Club, Jewish Student Association, Juniata Executive Club, Order of the Arrow Outing Service (Laughing Bush), Psychology Club, Ski Team, Saturday Night Alternative Program (S. N. A. P.), Student Business Organization, and Young Republicans. For a time in the 1970s and early 1980s club sports had a strong following —Judo, Lacrosse, Trap and Skeet, and Ice Hockey—all of which scheduled intercollegiate competition.

Gen-Xers came to a campus where students, like Juniatians before them, got involved in community projects in various ways. The Social Service Club, for example, organized in 1977 by students with POEs in social work. They befriended children at the Crawford apartments, a low-cost housing complex, and helped out residents of the DeForrest building, a recent high-rise for the aged. In time, the club expanded its activities to include other forms of volunteer social work. Another group, Circle K, dedicated its social outreach to those with mental and physical problems and the elderly in the community. Organized in 1970, Circle K performed essentially the same functions as Key Club, a high-school service organization, only on the college level. Both clubs were student arms of Kiwanis International. Circle K's biggest project in these years was the Multiple Sclerosis Marathon each year, a fund-raiser that included such activities as volleyball, cards or board games, rocking in rocking chairs or dancing for twenty-four hours. In 1983 Circle K's marathon raised $3,125.44, eighty-two Juniatians going sleepless for two days.

Students had other, non-club ways to identify with human need, at home and abroad. In the spring of 1983 eight Juniatians belonged to the Huntingdon Hook and Ladder Company. One of the octet was a coed, Robin Crust (Boyer). Hilltop students had been Huntingdon fire-company volunteers since the early 1970s. A student project of these years that has become a tradition is the Meal for CROP. CROP is an acronym for Christian Rural Outreach Program, originally founded by the Brethren. Through twenty-three regional offices, the relief program works to make people in the United States aware of the extent and nature of world hunger. The campus meal, introduced in May 1975 on the suggestion of Campus Minister Andrew Murray, asks students to give up their dinner tickets, which are then sold to people in the Huntingdon area, usually through the churches. Ninety-five percent or more of the students willingly forfeit a Baker Refectory meal for this occasion.

Social awareness sparked student involvement in two international causes of that first post-Vietnam decade: banning nuclear weapons and protesting apartheid. On Saturday, April 26, 1980, over sixty Juniata students, accompanied by Andrew Murray, joined twenty-five thousand participants in the March for a Non-Nuclear World in Washington, D. C. Protesting the use of nuclear weapons and energy, Juniatians marched under their banner, "Better Active Now, Than Radioactive Tomorrow." The Hilltop delegation went to the nation's capital sponsored by the Peace and Conflict Studies Committee, Conservation Club, and Center Board. On Wednesday, April 24, 1984, Gen. William C. Montgomery of Vietnam War fame and Harvey Wasserman, journalist and anti-nuclear activist, debated the nuclear-freeze issue in Alumni Hall. From time to time other experts such as Paul Warneke and Dimitri Simes lectured to College Hill audiences on the nuclear-arms subject or on other aspects of the Cold War. Other speakers on international problems included then Sen. Mark Hatfield of Oregon and Sen. Joseph Biden of Delaware.

On October 13, 1984, Juniata students, professors and their children, together with Huntingdon residents marched five kilometers in an effort to raise funds for the Pennsylvania Campaign for a Nuclear Weapons Freeze. Many Americans had become alarmed that President Ronald Reagan had made little progress in reaching any nuclear arms agreement with the Soviets since Strategic Arms Reductions Talks (START) began in 1981–82. Juniata students took to marching again in April 1986. Thirty-five of them got up at 5:30 in the morning on a day of drenching rain, ate a breakfast of bagels and donuts, and set out for Washington, D. C. The march, organized by United Campuses to Prevent Nuclear War (UCAM for short), proceeded from the Calvary Baptist Church in Chinatown to Pennsylvania Avenue and ended up at the Capitol with a rally. Between five and six hundred collegians participated, Juniata's delegation apparently the largest turnout of any college in the nation. Hilltoppers carried a banner reading "Star Wars is a leaky shield." Symbolizing what the marchers thought to be the inability of the Strategic Defense Initiative (SDI), or "Star Wars" program, to protect the American population, many in the crowd toted leaky umbrellas.

On the other issue—racism—the political problem of South African apartheid first got serious attention on College Hill in mid-February 1986. At that time Timothy Hoch, a senior, led an informal group of concerned students in drafting and circulating a petition regarding the possible existence of college financial investments in South Africa. At the same time, the Student Government got involved. SG designated Lynn Basham (Fleisher), Michael Wojcik, and Amy Coursen to prepare a letter to the board of trustees setting forth SG's official position on the subject of divestment in South Africa. The letter, unanimously approved by the Senate, read, in part: "A great deal of unanswered questions have been posed to the Student Government, and as a representative body of these students, we feel it is our obligation to make the Board of Trustees aware of this concern."[33] By then, a group of concerned students had organized an Apartheid Awareness Week, March 16-20, supported by the peace and conflict studies department. The week of events included lectures, movies, videos, and readings of speeches by South African President Botha and jailed African National Congress leader Nelson Mandela. Anti-apartheid campus citizens that spring bade farewell to the Binder presidency still in the dark about college investments in South Africa. They would resume their quest in the fall.

Juniatians resorted to petitioning out of concern not only about a far-away racial problem in South Africa but also about a matter right on campus: administrative-student-body relations. In May 1987 the students circulated a petition signed by 630 members of the Hilltop community (60% of the student body and 4 professors). The complaints fell into four categories: (1) rules and regulations adopted by the administration without student input; (2) the president does not support the general education program despite faculty and alumni backing for it; (3) lack of communication among segments of the college community; and (4) a decrease in academic freedom.[34]

Gerald Keenan, editor of the *Juniatian*, presented the petition to the executive committee of the trustee board on May 12. Chairman Jewett Henry appointed a special committee of three trustees to review the problems covered by the petition. The committee met with twenty-two students, twenty-one faculty members, five staff persons, and Dr. Binder. It absolved the president of infringing upon academic freedom, got his consent to improve lines of communication—through weekly lunches with the Student Government president and an open-door policy an hour or two a week—and concluded that "President Binder deserves the support of the Board of Trustees."[35]

The *Juniatian* has always been the organ of campus dissent, as it was in the spring of 1978. And, as always, the paper has had to beg for writers. A front-page article in the February 6, 1976, issue declared that, for lack of copy, the *Juniatian* "has currently reached its lowest point in quite some time." The column lamented that two weeks previously the paper did not go to press because of so few articles. In December 1978 Editor Jamie Pirrello made the same pleas for writers, noting that for the first time Prof. Ralph Church was currently teaching a course on Journalistic Writing. Coincidental or not, the quality of writing for the *Juniatian* showed improvement, it gave attention to current international and national news, and its layout of photographs, cartoons, sidebars, and advertisements certainly put no editorial staff to shame. Beginning on October 20, 1983, psychologist Jay Buchanan (Penn State Ed.D), appointed Juniata's first counselor for students in 1978, wrote a guest column that soon became a regular feature. His commentary, captioned "Counselor's Corner" the fall of 1985, addressed timely issues affecting Juniata students. Buchanan left Juniata in 1995.

The *Alfarata* had some hard times of its own, but they were financial woes. It faced a deficit of $2,600 in the fall of 1978, a dilemma President Binder solved out of his own executive account. The yearbook's business staff met the same problem the following year. Because of poor planning and lack of appeal, 130 copies of the 1979 *Alfarata* went unsold, for a loss of one thousand dollars. In 1981 seniors for the first time had to pay for their own yearbook—ten dollars a copy. Then the 1984–85 *Alfarata* publication, because of the editor's negligence, did not go to print until nearly a year later.

Juniata's radio station fared quite well during the eleven years of the Binder presidency. In March of 1978 WJC gave way to WKVR-FM (91.7), the new system's quality and strength boosted by a transmitter and an antenna atop Brumbaugh Science Center. WKVR-FM had reliable power within a ten-mile radius of the college. That November station manager George Meyer announced that, come next summer, the station would relocate from the basement of Founders Hall to two rooms on the ground floor of Ellis Hall. The new area, one room of which had been known as Plato's Cave, would accommodate a production room, conference room, lobby, record library, and office space. The transmitter and antenna were to be moved from the Science Center to Ellis Hall. In October 1981 WKVR nicknamed itself "The Voice-V92," which later became "The Voice-V103" by late December. For the academic year 1982–83, according to the Voice's skipper, Brian Check, headed for a career with Philadelphia's WOGL Radio/CBS Inc., seventy-two percent of the student body opted for V103 as their most listened-to radio station.

Juniatians opted also to keep alive all the traditional special events inherited from the Stauffer administration. Mountain Day, however, underwent a change in 1980. No date was announced beforehand, bringing back the way it was originally done. The reason for the change was twofold: to discourage students and professors from using the day off to catch up on neglected work and to ensure nice weather. Students soon resorted to strategies to discover the date of the holiday, among them phoning bus lines to see when buses were reserved or checking with park rangers (the secrecy applied to the date, not the place). For a time a few years later, the college announced in advance several possible dates for Mountain Day in response to complaints by professors that the surprise ploy, among other things, caused them problems in scheduling tests. Since the early Nineties, however, the tight-lipped policy has again been the rule. The events of the day over the years came to include two touch-football games—faculty vs. seniors and Cloister vs. Sherwood—and the tug-of-war between classes.

One very popular tradition had an unwelcome demise and another had a mucky origin. In early May 1986 the Pennsylvania Fish Commission and Waterways Patrol issued the college an ultimatum: sign a document that would "indemnify and save harmless" the state and make Juniata the liable sponsor of the Raft Regatta. A Commonwealth law prohibited operating a water craft under the influence of alcohol, a law the college was not aware of. Not signing would make tipsy students—and the administration—open to arrest. By this time, however, another outdoor spring craze was ready to take the Raft Regatta's place: the mud volleyball tournament. A Juniata Executive Club idea, the springtime ritual got its start in May 1980. Each year since, the college prepares a quaggy court just below Sunderland Hall, where players—to the sound of rousing music—stomp, jump, and carry on in ankle-deep mud. The custodial staff resigns itself each year to the mire and mess carried into the dormitories even though mud volleyballers can hose down before heading for their rooms.

All Class Night (ACN), said by some students to be Juniata's greatest tradition, almost became a dead tradition like the Regatta. In March 1978 the Center Board put the night of student spoofs on probation. The "unruly" behavior of the audience and casts the previous year was a fiasco "in the opinion" of many onlookers. The 1978 skits easily passed the test, but the play performances for the following year barely did. But the "childish" conduct (a *Juniatian* epithet) of a lot of students before and after the plays again carried celebration too far—food fights in Baker Refectory, damage in one dormitory, and drunken and disorderly behavior in the audience. As a result, the Student Affairs Council (SAC) recommended by a 6-2 vote to cancel All Class Night in the future. SAC, however, reversed itself a week later (5-2), thus salvaging the tradition, dependent, however, upon a new alcohol policy for the college. Also, a review committee, composed of the four faculty class advisors and Dr. Linda Sue Esch, was given the responsibility of screening the class scripts for theatrical quality. In addition the SAC set guidelines about tolerable behavior, charging members of the Weight Lifting Club with authority to act as monitors (but not as bouncers) in controlling the audience. The reforms worked, and, as the *Juniatian* said of 1980s ACN: "The overall atmosphere of the evening is changed from 'rowdy' to 'classy.'"[36]

As noted, taming ACN's tendency toward rowdiness meant re-evaluation of the current alcohol policy, which had undergone a series of revisions since Binder came as president. During the summer months before his arrival, Donald Hartman, then dean of students, drafted a more liberal stance on drinking, yet to be approved by the trustees but which appeared in the *Pathfinder* for 1975–76. In effect it permitted the use of alcoholic beverages only in dormitories. Of this concession, the president told the *Juniatian* in its first issue of the year that he found the proposed policy "quite acceptable." "It is very similar to ones I've seen at other colleges," he said. Trustee minutes do not indicate any official action.

When Arnold Tilden replaced Hartman as dean of student services, the alcohol policy underwent scrutiny. Dr. Tilden gave more emphasis to keeping parties "self-contained" in rooms as well as on prohibiting the sale of alcohol. The new guidelines specifically stated that "Hallways and bathrooms are not to be used…to accommodate the overflow from social gatherings in individual rooms." This was to prevent parties from infringing upon the "rights of the minority." The spotlight again focused on Juniata's alcohol policy in March 1978 when the Student Affairs Council sought to reinstate hall parties. The proposal, with the explicit support of less than half the student body, was rejected by the administration on the advice of legal counsel. Todd Kulp, Student Government president, said he would like to see administrators "stress the majority instead of the minority," and admitted he was "extremely annoyed and disturbed." *Juniatian* articles, however, accused the administration of being inconsistent in enforcing the no-public-areas-use of alcoholic beverages.

In May 1979, at SAC's initiative, a new policy allowed the use of dormitory lounges for parties where the keg size exceeded one quarter per room, although kegs were outlawed on residential floors Sunday through Thursday. In the fall of 1980 an additional guideline stipulated that non-alcoholic beverages must also be present at every party in a ratio of 15:1—that is, for every half keg of beer, one gallon of non-alcoholic drinks had to be served.

In January 1984 a 6-1 ruling by the Pennsylvania Supreme Court had serious legal implications for colleges and universities in the state. The decision made liable companies and private individuals who served alcohol to drinkers under the age of twenty-one. If injured while intoxicated the minor could sue for damages. This court ruling led to a major change in Juniata's alcohol policy. On Wednesday, October 31, Dean Tilden spoke to an open forum in a Baker Refectory filled to capacity. He announced that, beginning with the winter term, possession or consumption of intoxicating beverages would be prohibited in public buildings and lawns and fields on campus. Moreover the new policy banned kegs from all dormitory parties. Such occasions had to be "self-contained" (to a room), and no intoxicants could be available if anybody under twenty-one were present. It had been a tug of war for a whole decade between the students and administration about the use of alcohol at social gatherings. The college policy had been progressively liberalized, but it was the courts that had the last word.

Studies show that approximately ten percent of the population in the United States have alcohol-related problems.[37] It can thus be assumed that ten percent of college-age youth are similarly afflicted. For that reason the student affairs office formed the Committee on Alcohol Study and Education (CASE) in the fall of 1977. Eventually the program adopted the motto: "If you choose to drink, then drink responsibly." Its first project was a workshop for resident assistants to help them deal with alcoholic Juniatians. Next autumn CASE conducted a seminar open to the entire campus on myths about the benefits of alcohol and the biological and sociological effects of drinking. In September 1979 CASE incorporated an alcohol-education session into the Freshman Conference Program. In 1980 and 1984 CASE sponsored an Alcoholic Awareness Fair in the spring on Detwiler Plaza. Booths, information tables, and a non-alcoholic bar were set up to help educate students. The State Police gave presentations and the Tri-County Drug and Alcohol Agency erected a booth of its own. The 1984 fair was funded by Boost Alcohol Conscience Concerning the Health of University Students (BACCHUS). BACCHUS had been impressed by CASE's efforts in 1983 during the "3D's Week" (Don't Drive Drunk).

A high court decision indirectly affected the solution to one dormitory-life poser, but the college had to resolve another residence-hall dilemma on its own. Student enrollment stood at 1,074 in the fall of 1975 dropping to 1,016 by spring. But the figures increased steadily after that, with slightly less than 1,300 by the academic year 1980–81. With 1,183 resident students the fall of 1982, the highest number ever, dormitories were operating at roughly seven percent over capacity. The college was housing 157 more students on campus than it did in 1975, a fifteen percent increase. Many freshmen that fall found themselves assigned to one of ninety-six triple rooms.[38] Despite a tuition rebate for this inconvenience, many freshmen felt "cheated," the *Juniatian* reported.[39]

To ease the housing crunch, the college looked to dormitory space off campus. In 1979 the administration readied the Mission House at 18th and Washington streets for student occupancy. That fall the college purchased what came to be known as the Hess Apartments at 1401 Washington Street (across from the Pilgrim building, where Jacob Zuck first held classes). The following spring it was renovated into ten flats to accommodate thirty-six students—but only upperclassmen. Each suite had a kitchen, bath (some two), living room, and bedroom. This did not eliminate, however, the need of three-to-a-room on campus. The expectation of enrolling over 1300 students—and a greater proportion of women—for the fall of 1980 forced the administration to plan to house women in the Cloister Arch.

Cloisterites rebelled, Richard Mayher articulating their grievance that coeds in the Arch would destroy the "all male Cloister tradition." A petition circulated by women and signed by ninety-one of them, declared: "LET THE MEN HAVE THEIR ARCH!" On a drizzly May 1 afternoon thirty to forty men, one with a megaphone, held a protest rally at the Cloister organized by Mayher. The sodden protesters chanted "Free the Arch!" and after a while marched to the porch of Founders, this time chanting, "We want Fred." To the surprise and cheer of the crowd, the president and then Housing Director John Linetty walked out and greeted them. But the powers-that-be held their ground. As many as twenty-seven women would be domiciled in the Arch come fall, if need be, they said. (At the millennium coeds are still in the Arch, and some students, by choice, still share triple rooms.)

Frustrated, Mayher and two rebels placed most of the blame for the Cloister decision on the Student Government, which was given a voice in the ruling. This was hardly the kind of reaction newly elected SG president Todd Kulp had in mind three years earlier when he said his major goal was to "bring back an interest in Student Government." He also opined that campus apathy in the past traced to having "no real issues to fight for." SG quickly latched on to two causes: vocal advocacy of a liberal alcohol policy and support for the student petition that went to the trustees concerning the need to rebuild lines of communication on campus.

When Douglas Klepfer's turn as SG president came in 1980, he said he intended to make the Senate a "more visible" part of College Hill. His idealism, however, was shaken by what the *Juniatian* termed "Senate Hookey." Unexcused absences on the part of senators at regularly scheduled meetings had become something of a scandal. William Blose, during his term (1978–79), responded to senatorial absenteeism with a Senate bylaw that authorized the College Governance Committee to monitor attendance. Despite a clause in the Senate constitution providing for impeachment of a member who failed to fulfill the duties of office, this never happened. So SG presidents, of the early Eighties at least, had to put up with a governing body some members of which were habitual truants. *Juniatian* editorials did identify delinquent senators, but its pages made clear that Student Government as a whole was both a "visible" and faithful campus lobby for its electorate.

Meanwhile, two new faces joined the student services staff, one more "visible" than the other but both very much a part of campus life. When Will Brandau left as director of Ellis Center in 1972 alumnus Bruce Bader first and then Sally Pennington filled the position. In March 1976 the administration decided to eliminate the position and upgrade the qualifications for it. The new job description included counseling and advising and major responsibilities for nonacademic programming. Wayne Justham (New Hampshire Ed.M.) began work on May 1 with the title of Assistant Dean of Student Services and Director of Programming. He stayed on for ten years.

The other staff member was Jane Brown, the new college nurse. The first mention of a resident nurse in the college catalog appears in the 1932–33 issue. When student enrollment started to climb in the 1960s the administration added a "senior" nurse. "Resident" R. N.s were either Juniata students themselves or the wives of students and thus of limited stay on campus. The senior nurse was older and sometimes stayed longer, such as Helen Woods (1962–72). Jane Brown, previously employed in obstetrics and the operating room at J. C. Blair Memorial Hospital, came of Helen Woods' mold and would give Juniata the last seventeen years of her nursing career. She made it her mission to build trust in the College Health Center. It was Nurse Brown who first organized in 1978 what became the biannual Health Fair (later, Wellness Day) with the help of the Scalpel and Probe Club, held on the mezzanine of the Kennedy Sports + Recreation Center.

Three other women in student services, although by virtue of their office more visible on campus than Nurse Brown, were those whose predecessors were once titled dean of women. When Elizabeth O'Connell left as associate dean of student services in 1979, Susan Trombley (1979–82) replaced her with the same title. But Julia Keehner (1982–86) came as assistant (later associate) dean of services for residential life.

Dean O'Connell, the spring of her departure, plumped the idea of a women's program on campus. It was not until January of 1980 that Prof. Janet Lewis, Patricia Cook, and Elizabeth Miller held the first organizational meeting. They called themselves the Women's Programming Organization. Thirty to forty coeds and a faculty member or two began meeting once every two weeks and made plans to be chartered by Student Government. The group took that step in the fall but under the name Campus Women's Organization (CWO). The CWO offered a chance for women, professors and coeds, to get together to plan activities and discuss topics of special interest to their gender. In the mid-1980s CWO rechartered itself as the Women's Action Committee.

By that time Dean Arnold Tilden's staff had introduced a wholly new type of transcript, one that listed a student's co-curricular activities. Commenced on an experimental basis in the spring of 1983, the Co-Curricular Transcript (CCT), still a current option, serves to provide corporations and graduate or professional schools with a description of the skills a student derives from social, athletic, dormitory, or leadership experiences outside the classroom. The transcripts are then placed on record in the Career Planning and Placement Office along with the standard academic transcript. For the academic year 1983–84 eighty-one students worked up a CCT, less than seven percent of those enrolled at Juniata. That level of minimal participation has remained constant in the two decades since, a historical fact disappointing to the placement office.

The academic transcripts of Binder-years Juniatians, however, were no cause for disenchantment. Retention was a worry but not a great problem. In 1983 sixty-seven percent of the class graduated, which was still well above the national average. A study indicated that the college-wide grade-point average for 1982–83 was 2.69 (C+). Of the 266 seniors at 1984's commencement ceremony, eight received their diplomas magna cum laude, while eleven graduated cum laude. The combined mean score on the SATs had risen steadily to a respectable 1,058 for 1983–84, compared to the national average of 921 and the state average of less than 900.[40] Thirty-four percent of the Class of 1983 planned to attend graduate/professional schools.

To attract and keep students of superior academic ability the Binder administration initiated the merit scholarship program in 1976. Heretofore student aid had been based primarily on financial need; by the centennial year there were eighty-seven need-based scholarships listed in the catalog. After that, the college would make a number of grants on the basis of merit and other criteria stipulated by benefactors, some to freshmen, some to upperclassmen. The first two such merit grants were the Brumbaugh-Ellis Presidential Scholarships (10) and the Annual Support Fund Scholarships (20). The criteria for both awards included class rank and achievement on entrance tests. By 1986 the number of merit scholarship funds had grown to twenty-two. Historically a student receiving financial aid in the form of a grant or scholarship was not permitted to bring a motor vehicle to campus or to the Huntingdon area. But that restriction ended at the beginning of the 1978–79 school year.

One prestigious non-Juniata scholarship won by three studious Hilltoppers was the Andrew Mutch Scholarship given by the St. Andrew's Society of Philadelphia. The scholarship honors a Scotsman who was a friend of Martin Brumbaugh's and the pastor of the Bryn Mawr Presbyterian Church. M. G. often had Dr. Mutch on campus, and it was he who inspired the Hill's Spiritual Emphasis Week, once a long-time Juniata tradition. Favoritism, however, played no part in the choice of Juniata's three Mutch Scholars. The competition is keen, candidates applying from all Pennsylvania colleges and universities. (Juniata first began competing in 1978.) The scholarship, covering practically all expenses, entitles the undergraduate to a year at a Scottish university. College Hill's trio of Mutch honorees were Mark Hysong (Aberdeen, 1978–79), Heather Zimmerman, née MacCrindle (St. Andrews, 1981–82), and Alan Thomas (St. Andrews, 1984–85).

During Binder's presidency the list of academic awards and prizes had lengthened to twenty-four, eight of them donated during his term. The Rufus Reber Prize was established in 1975 by Mrs. Ada R. Gingrich as a memorial to her brother, an alumnus and military physicist. The Raymond R. Day Social Science Prize (1976) honors Juniata's first male African-American graduate and is awarded to a student whose Program of Emphasis is in the area of sociology or urban studies. Through an endowment funded by Dr. and Mrs. John Baker in 1972, the first Baker Peace Studies Prize was awarded in 1977. It recognizes the academic achievement of a student who is "significantly" involved in peace and conflict studies. The first Russia Book Award was made in 1977 but did not become a funded prize until 1980 and wasn't listed in the catalog until the 1983–84 issue. The Victor Kamlin, Inc. firm of Washington, D. C., established it to recognize excellence in Russian studies. Since 1980 the American Association of University Women Award, provided by the Huntingdon chapter, goes to a deserving woman graduate from the local area who plans to further her education. To encourage cultural and artistic development among students, Vila Gardner Metzger in 1981 endowed three art prizes in her name to be awarded each year to those students who, in the opinion of the art department, have produced the most outstanding art works. Another prize established in 1981 is the Samuel J. Steinberger, Jr. Memorial

Award—by Thomas H. Knepp in memory of his friend and Juniata roommate. It is presented to a student who is either the tympani player in the college orchestra or a freshman of demonstrated exceptional ability in mathematics. The last accrued prize of the Binder era, the Rockwell Chemistry Award, was endowed in 1984. It honors the memory of Donald M. Rockwell, for more than fifty years a member of the Juniata faculty, including his years as academic dean. Colleagues, alumni, family, and friends contributed to this endowment. Its prize recognizes that senior chemistry student who has excelled in the study of the subject and has advanced the interests of the department and the wider life of the campus community.

From the day he assumed his College Hill presidency, Frederick Binder repeatedly adverted to an imminent crisis in college recruitment. He warned that the last classes of graduating baby boomers would leave an acute replacement void, a sharp decline in college enrollments, and sagging national SAT scores. This forecast is why at the very outset he stressed the necessity of an aggressive recruitment program, keeping a close watch on the attrition rate, and expanding scholarship opportunities. Thanks to these concerted actions Juniata at first "bucked the trend," as Binder told the trustees, when falling enrollment figures became a nationwide fact. On College Hill, as noted, matriculation numbers peaked at an all-time record high of 1,318 the academic year 1982–83.[41] But then the fact hit the Hill, and the numbers began a steady decline over the last three of the Binder years to a little over 1,100. The enrollment slippage did not let up for another decade, bottoming out at 1,050 by the late Nineties.

RECOGNIZING THE IMPORTANCE OF ACADEMICS IN COLLEGE ATHLETICS

For colleges like Juniata that offer no athletic scholarships the term student-athlete has long defined their varsity programs. The movement to balance sports and academics began in 1952 when General Telephones and Electric (GTE) created its Academic All-America Teams Program. The purpose is to reward individuals who excel in two very competitive areas: the classroom and the playing field. The program works through the College Sports Information Directors of America (CoSIDA), an association of some eighteen hundred professionals in the United States and Canada. The Academic All-America selection initially recognized student-athletes on university-division football teams.

Since 1952, however, the program has expanded to other university sports. Then in the early 1970s it added a college division for men's varsity teams. Later came women's athletics: basketball in 1979, followed by volleyball, softball, and the "at-large teams" (the so-called minor sports, like wrestling and track) in the early 1980s. Fall/winter at-large teams were added in 1995. To be eligible, student-athletes must be nominated by their sports information director, hold at least a 3.20 GPA average on a 4.00 scale, be starters or key reserves in their varsity sports, and have attained sophomore athletic and academic standing. Juniata began making nominations in 1970, and immediately had three Academic All-Americans, as noted in Chapter 14, in football's Raymond Grabiak and Maurice Taylor and basketball's John Smith.

ATHLETIC GLORY REDUX:
THANKS TO WOMEN'S VOLLEYBALL

Football at Juniata enjoyed its "Glory Years" from 1953–59 when five teams went undefeated on the way to a 50-2-2- record. But women's volleyball has given College Hill two "Golden Decades" of winning seasons *sans pareil* since 1977, when the sport had a varsity genesis. Its only head coach from that year to the millennium has been Lawrence Bock, a Penn State graduate. In 1977 Bock was a loan officer at the Union National Bank in downtown Huntingdon who joined the administrative staff in 1982 as director of financial aid. In time his would become one of the most recognized names in collegiate volleyball.

"Larry's Ladies," as the *Juniatian* dubbed the coed volleyballers, piled up a 328–62 record in its first nine seasons. In MAC Tournament play 1977–1980 Larry's Ladies finished second once and third three times. From 1981 on, however, the Bock women have captured the MAC title every single year—nineteen of them. In National Collegiate Athletic Association (NCAA) competition, Bock's teams finished second, third, or fourth once and fifth twice during the Binder presidency. In those years Bock himself was named national coach of the year in 1984 by the American Volleyball Coaches Association (AVCA), the first of four times he would be so-honored.

Larry's Ladies soon began winning individual national honors of their own. Juniata's initial AVCA first-team All-American was Colleen Ireland (1981). After her came Susan Barker-(Hildebrandt) and Claudia Tweardy (Serfass) the next year and Beth Hoppel (Barnett) in 1985. As a senior, Hoppel was named to the NCAA championship all-tournament team. Ekanong Opanayikul made AVCA second-team All-America in 1984. As for the Hill itself, Peggy Evans holds the record for career aces (381), compiled over the four years 1981–84. Claudia Tweardy set the record for single-season aces (145) in 1982. The first Arthur P. Evans Memorial Award for the most valuable player, established by Mrs. Evans and daughter Peggy, went to Priscilla Grove (Gibboney) in the spring of 1977, while volleyball was still a club sport. Much of the credit for the advent of coed varsity volleyball belongs to Grove, who, along with Coach JoAnn Reilly and teammate Marjorie Morgan, did much to whip up campus interest in the athletic event.

The other women's fall/winter varsity sport, basketball, played two more seasons under Edmund Gargula (16-17) before the as-yet-unwed Nancy Harden took over as head coach. She had lettered three times in both tennis and basketball at West Chester State University. Her father, Ralph Harden, had been athletic director and men's basketball coach at Juniata in the early 1960s. Under Harden the daughter the lady Indians went 101-80 from 1977 through the 1985–86 season. Her nine-year tenure as coach (1977–86) would be the sport's longest by several years and the most successful. Harden, married to William Latimore in 1978, led her 1979–80 squad to a 24-4 best-record-ever and a trip to the American Independent Association of Women's national quarterfinals. Her final team went 16-6, reaching the NCAA regionals and earning her Women's Basketball Coaches Association district coach of the year for the second straight season. She served as assistant athletic director from 1982–86 while coaching three sports.

Two Latimore-coached players rank as topmost career performers. An All-MAC star in 1980–81, Julie George (McCormick) remains number one in rebounding (1,130) for an average of 13.6 rebounds a game. She played four years, 1977–81, ending up an eight-letter winner in basketball and volleyball and with two athletic awards, the Bargerstock and Kreider. The Charles Bargerstock Award was established in 1977 in memory of the first man to win the Mickle Award and Juniata's one-time director of development. It recognizes leadership in women's sports and contributes to the college's overall athletic program and to the college as a whole. George earned CoSIDA All-Academic honors her junior year and first team Division III All-America Women's Sports Foundation (AWSF). Ranking second to her in these categories is Susan Grubb, who owns two summital spots of her own. Another four-year performer (1984–88), Grubb leads in career steals (292) and blocked shots (182). Nancy Zinkham, a 1980 graduate who also earned four letters in basketball (and three in volleyball), achieved CoSIDA academic honors, AWSF honorable mention, and All-MAC her senior year. She still ranks near the top of the school's career charts for assists, steals, blocked shots, rebounds, and points, respectively.

In football, Dr. Binder's college sport, Juniata played to a 56-47 record during his presidency. Walter Nadzak left to be head coach at the University of Connecticut in 1976. His assistant, Dean Rossi, coached three seasons, winning fifteen and losing thirteen. Rossi resigned in January 1980 to assume fund-raising responsibilities for the college's new Sports + Recreation Center. Later that spring he became a professional football scout. In his eight years on Juniata's athletic staff neither of the two sports he coached—track and football—involved a losing team. In March 1980 Rob Ash, offensive coordinator at Cornell College (Iowa), was named Rossi's replacement. Ash, a *summa cum laude*, Phi Beta Kappa graduate of Cornell, started four years there at quarterback, being named first-team Academic All-America in 1973. Ash's second year at the gridiron helm earned him the "Coach of the Year" accolade. Overall, his Binder-era gridders gave him a 29-28 mark.

Two football standouts of the mid-1970s-early 1980s made Associated Press Little All-American honorable mention—Peter Lentini (1974) and David Murphy (1984). Lentini starred as a tight end and Murphy as a flanker. Murphy, a four-year letter-winner in both football and baseball, remains one of only three players in the school's history to earn All-MAC first-team honors three times. Teammate Jeffrey Miles, like Murphy, was a four-year letterman in football and baseball. Twice he was named a MAC All-Star as a gridder, and he still holds the school record for his ninety-nine-yard kickoff return for a touchdown against Western Maryland in 1981. As for career school records, four players of the Eighties hold five of them: quarterback Michael Culver—passing completions (406), passing yards (5,799), and total offense (6,834 yards); defensive back Mark Dorner—interceptions (26 for 443 yards); Timothy Reed—punting average (38.5 yards); and David Murphy—receiving yards (2,710). Nine of the 1995 Indian gridders received all-conference honors: Richard Howey, Gino Perri, Robert Yanckello, Steven Berger, Michael Schaffner, Thomas Kalinyak, Michael Culver, Robert Crossey, and Michael Cottle. Another top performer, Steven Lach, was a three-year starter at free safety who has been an assistant defensive coach at his alma mater for the past two decades.

To the delight of the Phi Beta Kappa coach, three of his chargers in 1985 earned GTE Academic All-America honors. They were running back Ian Malee (3.35 GPA), a prelaw student; defensive end and premedical-major Louis Komer (3.37 GPA); and linebacker Robert Crossey (3.50 GPA), another premedical major who led the team in tackles (114) and in 1986, like Raymond Grabiak in the early 1970s, became a two-time repeater.

Beginning in the mid-1970s, college baseball resorted to aluminum bats, a budgetary consideration (aluminum bats do not break). Batters would use them exclusively for the next quarter-century. Some have argued that the use of the lighter-weight, more flexible club inflated batting averages and increased home-run production. Indian diamondmen of the Binder decade seemed to find aluminum bats a boon, winning 139 and losing 111. In nine of those eleven seasons the Indians won eleven or more games, twice recording twenty victories. Coach Berrier's best seasonal winning percentage ever came in 1983 when his club posted a 20-7 finish for a .741 mark. The 1980 diamondmen captured Juniata's first MAC sectional baseball crown but lost to Upsala in the MAC playoffs. The next spring, going 20-10, the Indians broke the record for wins in a season (the old, 16, having been set the previous year) and won two titles: the MAC Northwest Section and the ECAC Southern Regional. (Juniata withdrew from the ECAC in 1976, but then re-entered in 1981 for just one year.) Then the 20-7 squad of 1983 won the MAC Northern Division diadem. Twice Berrier's nine defeated the Nittany Lions of Penn State—13-10 in 1983 and 10-9 in 1985. Twice also his teams got NCAA bids, in 1978 and 1980, but were eliminated early. In 1985 Berrier notched his three hundredth diamond victory at Juniata.

Over a score of Berrier's players made first- or second-team MAC All-Stars. Two gained the honor twice: pitcher Richard Howey in 1985 and 1986 and third baseman Stephen Poska in 1984 and 1985. Centerfielder Jeffrey Miles, however, made MAC All-Stars three times from 1980 to 1982. In 1981 he was named to the American Association of College Baseball Coaches All-America third team. His .509 batting average that year led the nation in Division III.

In men's basketball Carl Meditch coached two more years, resigning in 1977 after a three-year career at Juniata with a 33-37 log. Huntingdon Area High School roundball coach, Patrick Frazier, who had launched women's basketball on College Hill in 1973, succeeded to the vacated position. Frazier, an All-MAC as a senior at Juniata, lettered four times and started every year. Not since 1949, when Philip Snider stepped down, had an alumnus guided Juniata basketball. The college's twenty-second cage mentor, he continued teaching biology at the high school. His four years as head coach produced a 29-59 mark. To replace Frazier the administration promoted Daniel Helm, an assistant coach and head trainer, to the hardcourt job. A two-time cage MVP at Indiana's Franklin College, Helm later played and coached for two seasons in the Belgian professional league. In all, Helm led the Indian cagers for nine seasons; for the five Binder years his teams went 38-80.

Two Meditch-Frazier cagers won All-MAC honors. Tay Waltenbaugh, a 6'7" center who transferred from American University in 1975 and played two years, made All-MAC first team his 1976–77 season. Roger Galo, a guard, gained year-end MAC recognition three times—1976, 1977, and 1979. The latter year he was named to the first team as well as making the ECAC All-East first-team list. Gallo ended up second only to Jacob Handzelek in career scoring (1,692 for an average of 19.2 points a game). He and Academic All-American Robert Musser, his fellow guard, came to be known as the "Twistin' Twins." In tandem, they were the highest-scoring back court combination in Juniata's basketball history. In 1979 they teamed up for a school-record seventy-five points against Delaware Valley one January night, only to score seventy-three against Kings College four games later. Musser's classwork as well as his spectacular play made him Juniata's second basketball Academic All-American (1978–79).

A highlight of the 1983–84 season for the hardcourt squad was spending their Christmas holiday in Belgium. The twenty-three-member party spent twelve days in Europe, the first athletic group to travel overseas. Belgian friends of Coach Helm helped arrange the tour. The Tribe played six games, one on Christmas Day, against club teams. They also enjoyed a full sightseeing itinerary—Paris, Brussels, the North Sea coast, and Belgian medieval castles.

As for Binder-era grapplers, they rolled up a record of 57-77-6. In 1985 the NCAA presented William Berrier with a plaque as a tribute to his twenty-five years as a wrestling coach at Juniata. In the 1979–80 season Berrier wrestlers grappled to 11-4-1, the sport's best record ever and the best since the 8-3 mark ten years earlier. Juniata had some stellar matmen in the years between 1975 and 1986, like three-hundred-pound Scott Simmons (11-4-1 in 1975–76), Chris Young (18-6 in 1982–83), Keith Sherbine (13-2 in 1982–83), and premedicine Richard Noll, whose feats on the mat (16-4 in 1983–84) and in class (3.50 GPA) earned him the title Academic All-American. But nobody excelled the wrestling career of future dentist Joseph Paskill. In the 1977–78 season he went 15-2-1 at 142 pounds and advanced to a triumph at the MAC Championships. Only Peter Schuyler had ever won fifteen. Next year Paskill (22-4) eclipsed Schuyler's season and career victories set in 1969–70. He finished the 1979–80 season undefeated, a Juniata first, for a four-year career mark of 70-15-3. His All-American honors in 1979 also gained him another Juniata wrestling first. And his NCAA Postgraduate Scholarship, the first to a Juniatian in any sport, was one of only six granted in the Division III "Other Sports" category. Paskill had compiled a 3.875 GPA out of a possible 4.0. The senior mat standout won his third Helsel MVP and easily captured the Blood Award for athletic and academic excellence. Needless to say, he graduated *magna cum laude.*

Tennis aficionados as well as the two varsity teams had cause to applaud in the spring of 1976, when the college installed "club-caliber" lighting at the Raffensperger tennis courts. Club-category outdoor lights are superior to recreational lights but not of tournament quality. Coin-operated meters control the use of the system.

The men netters saw their mentor of two decades, historian Ernest Post, step down after the 1980 season. He had produced a dozen winning teams over those twenty years. His final overall record was 102–92. Football coach Rob Ash took over the spring sport and further guided Juniata's netmen to a 46-70 Binder-presidency mark. Two racket wielders of that time each won the Ellis Tennis Award twice: Gavin Ford in 1975 and 1976 and Donald Rice in 1980 and 1981. Only two others before them had been MVP in consecutive years.

Women netters, in the meantime, suffered nine losing seasons out of eleven, recording twenty-eight victories and fifty-three losses. Nancy Harden Latimore took over coaching duties from Elizabeth Herritt in 1978. Herritt's record for her three years ended up 4-8. Her sister Alice Herritt (Stenstrom), a prize physics student, won the first three Haskell MVPs. As a senior (1977), she and junior Carolyn Seltzer (Diercksen) made history when, as a doubles team, they walked off with the college's first title in MAC women's competition.

The men's track-and-field athletes under four different coaches—Rossi till 1979, Thomas Roguish (1980–82), David Turnball (1983), and Alan Hartman (1984–86)—enjoyed some sensational seasons. Overall the thinclads won thirty-two meets and lost thirty-two, but in 1981 went 8-1 (the best since 1965's 10-1), 5-0 in 1979, and 6-1 in 1981. Dean Rossi's own seven-year coaching record gave the college an unprecedented forty wins out of fifty meets. In October 1982 the oval track on College Field went from cinders to an asphalt surface and was laid out in meter distances. Dedicated to the memory of Jefford Oller, a trustee from 1966 until his death in 1974, the refurbished track was made possible by his wife, Anne. The 1918 alumnus set a time for the 220 Yards never broken (21.6). With the conversion from yards to meters for track events, his record has been retired.

The decade from 1976 to 1986 saw some latter-day "Ollers" set some new field-and-track marks. Robert McNelly, as a freshman in 1976, became the first Juniatian to earn a berth in any sport in the NCAA Division III National Championships. In that 8-1 season McNelly tied Joseph Coradetti's time for the 440 Intermediate Hurdles at 54.3, set four years earlier. At the nationals, where the distance became 400 meters, he barely missed a spot in the finals. McNelly did not run in 1977. But in 1978 he won the 400 Meter Intermediate Hurdles at the MACs, setting a new time of :53.9. Again he went to the NCAA nationals, but did not reach the finals. Earlier he had copped another Juniata record at the Pitt Invitational with a time of :53.5. A repeat MAC champion in 1979, with a Juniata record time of :52.67, he again qualified for the NCAA National Meet. Once more, however, he faltered before the finals. But at Juniata he was voted MVP in track in all three of his seasons.

Six other thinclads gave stellar performances in those years. Gino Perri, a sophomore in 1984, placed fourth in the javelin throw at the NCAA Tournament, which earned him All-American status. (Athletes have to finish at least in sixth place to get All-American honors.) In his fourth-place finish, the highest for a Juniatian at the nationals, Perri threw the spear 220'5", an unbroken Hilltop record at the millennium. In 1986 he captured two MAC championships—in the discus and shot put events. He set a MAC record in the discus that year with a hurl of 155'4" and took his third straight put title. At the NCAA nationals he failed to make All-American in either event. Four track-and-field Indians of that day, like Perri, set records later broken. John McCullough did it in two events, the Two Miles (1975) and the Three Miles (1976); John Voler in the shot put (1981); Thomas Hoffman in the 1500 Meters (1981); and Thomas Cable in the high jump (1984). Eric Biddle, a football star and a MAC champion in 1982 in the triple jump, still holds that event's College Hill record—48'6".

Another men's spring sport—golf—went 44-56-1 in eleven seasons. In 1978 William Germann put in his last year as golf coach, ending a quarter-century on the links for Juniata with a career log of 120-131-1. His teams won the MAC title in 1954 and finished second twice, 1960 and 1972. Alumnus Wesley Lingenfelter filled in the next year, to be succeeded by co-coaches Dean Arnold Tilden and Dr. Duane Stroman. Their 1985 team posted the best won-lost mark (7-2) since 1954. The two of them, professor and student dean, compiled a .500 won-lost count in seven years—29-29-1. In the spring of 1980 Steven Stroup, a perennial MVP in the game, became Juniata's only golf medalist at the MAC Championships. Under adverse weather conditions Stroup played eighteen holes in just seventy-seven strokes, which netted him a first-place tie. The next year the MAC medalist and his teammates spent the winter-term break in Pawley's Island, South Carolina, for "Spring Training." The team itself, with lots of help from the coaches, organized the trip, the first ever for Juniata golfers.

Men's cross-country chalked up a winning margin of 54-47 from 1975 to 1985. The harriers were 8-2 in 1979, the best since going 6-1 in 1962. As Carl Meditch would be the first to admit, he was but a nominal head coach of cross-country; basketball practice in the fall interfered with other sports interests. The de facto coach was chemistry professor Donald Mitchell, his assistant. The Meditch-Mitchell three-year combination gave the Indians twenty-nine victories and fourteen losses. When Meditch departed in August 1977, Dr. Mitchell became the declared head coach. He mentored five teams—student coach William Shuler subbed in 1981 (2-4)—with an overall tally of 25-19. Joel Brown, a teacher at Southern Huntingdon High School, handled the squad the remainder of the Binder years.

Among the standout harriers of the late Seventies-early Eighties were John McCullough, William Shuler, and Thomas Hoffman. McCullough got the Clifford Brown Award three successive times—1975, 1976, and 1977. In the early 1980s William Shuler dominated the cross-country scene. As a sophomore in 1979 he broke the home-team record for the Indian's difficult, hill-infested 5.65-mile course in a time of 31.18. As a senior he bettered his own mark by a hundredth of a second. Also a track star—he set the record for the 800 Meters in two minutes flat—the speedster became only the seventh Juniatian to win three MVPs and the Mickle Award. Track luminary Thomas Hoffman, himself a cross-country MVP, broke Shuler's home-course record on Homecoming Day 1982 with a time of 29.16.

Soccer, promoted from a club to a varsity sport in 1978, struggled for eight years. Coached by German-language professor Klaus Jaeger, the booters suffered from a perennial drought of goals, winning fifteen and losing ninety. Future pharmacist Jacob Sherk won the first Francis Zimmerman Soccer Award in 1981.

Women's field hockey did somewhat better over ten years under three coaches (35-59-19). Roslyn Hall came as aquatics specialist and field hockey coach in 1982 when Nancy Latimore moved up to assistant athletic director. Her four teams registered a mark of 8-26-10 but in 1983 had its best season to that time (5-2-4). In 1979 Nanci Young, a sophomore, stopped eighty-one percent of opponents' shots at her goal. Next year the stingy goalie and three of her teammates were named to the Coaches' All-Star MAC team: sophomore halfback Barbara Pearson, freshman Elizabeth Abel, and sophomore halfback Clair Warmerdam. All were first-team selections except Warmerdam (honorable mention). Juniata had more all-stars than any other conference squad.

In the early 1980s Athletic Director Berrier got permission to upgrade three women's programs from club to varsity level, bringing the number of athletic teams to sixteen. Women's cross-country moved up first, in 1980, coached by William Latimore, a Huntingdon high-school teacher and husband of Nancy Harden. In many ways, credit for popularizing the coed sport belongs to Evangelia "Teddy" Lyras. The 5'5" brunette became the first woman to run a cross-country meet at Juniata. She did this during the men's half-time meet at the Homecoming football game in 1975. She ran at all the Indian home meets, since the NCAA allowed a team to take just nine runners to away events. She made it her stated mission to get a "girl's" track club organized at Juniata. So it was that out of her demonstrated passion for running—and ability at it—the "Lyras dream" of Juniata women competing at the intercollegiate level did come true. Indeed they competed impressively well, running up a victory margin of forty-four to nineteen under three coaches by 1985. Irene Chamberlain, a J. C. Blair Hospital nurse and well-known local long-distance runner, succeeded Latimore in 1984, and men's cross-country coach, Joel Brown, stepped in the following year. The maiden Indians were undefeated in 1981 (6-0) and then went on to record a 10-2 season in 1982 and a 12-5 season in 1984. Carolyn Andre (Beck) won the initial women's cross-country award in 1981, the first freshman to win an MVP honor. She would win it three times more and, in 1984, the prestigious Bargerstock Award. Two freshmen sensations, Kathleen Duffy, and Carol Tendall (Carmon), paced the team to its 10-2 mark in 1982. That year Tendall set the record time for the 5000 Meters (18:32). The next year Duffy, who had set two course records, at home and at Allentown, got the MVP nod, the only year Andre did not. Also on the MAC co-championship team was another superb runner—senior Nancy Roach (Gurdak). A Bargerstock Award winner in 1983, Roach ran on a pair of record-setting MAC championship relay teams that year. She garnered eight varsity letters—in basketball (4), cross-country (3), and track (1)—as a College Hill athlete.

In 1981 softball came next in the parade of women's varsity sports, also coached by William Latimore. His lady softballers gave him a six-year won-lost mark of 40-38-1. Third-baseman Gwendolyn Heidecker, a sophomore, became the sport's first MVP. Their winningest year was 1986, going 13-6. That season's pitching ace Kathleen Bednarczyk (Walch) tossed a no-hitter, five shutouts, and ended the season 13-3 with a sterling .074 ERA. Also the 1986's Janet Robison (Bumbarger), a senior, earned All-America second-team honors for her .433 batting average, having led the team in hits (26), runs scored (27), and home runs (5). The Indian shortstop that spring won three sports honors: the Bargerstock Award, the Kreider Basketball Award, and, for the second time, the softball MVP award (which that year got a name, thanks to alumna Judith Rodgers Pheasant, wife of Clayton Pheasant).

Women's track entered varsity competition in the spring of 1983 as the sixteenth Indian team. Roslyn Hall coached the sport until 1984, when Alan Hartman, a Mount Union high-school teacher, took it over. Their combined mentorship produced a 14-18 log over four years. Peggy Evans, a nine-varsity-letter-winner in volleyball, basketball, and track, quickly emerged as the infant sport's sensation. Women's track in its first year saw her cop MVP honors in the MAC Championships. In 1984 she earned the title All-American with a fourth-place finish in the triple-jump competition at the NCAA Tournament, leaping a distance of 33'8½". The next year she made Hilltop history again by capturing first place in her specialty at the NCAA finals. This time the national champion cleared 37'1½", setting a new Division III mark. In all, the 1984 Homecoming Queen set ten school records in women's track and field. At the millennium her times of 12:69 in the 100 Meters and 26.06 in the 200 Meters, both clocked in 1984, stand unbroken. Her teammate, Carol Tendall, ran the 5K in a time of 18:49.83 in 1983, which also has gone unbeaten to the year 2000.

Cheerleaders have long been part of the athletic scene on College Hill, primarily at football and basketball games. Over the years their ranks, with few exceptions, were supplied by coeds. In 1982 these vivacious ladies at last got due recognition. The first Jill Muir (Klinger) Award, donated by her husband and friends in memory of Mrs. Klinger—a 1960 alumna and a four-year-cheerleader—went to Ellen Zaleskie (Daulerio).

Despite the growing number of varsities and the absence of a full-time sports information director since 1968, publicity about the athletic program at Juniata did not go neglected. This was particularly the case when Charles Pollock was director of public relations, from 1974 to 1986; he doubled as a SID, a function he enjoyed. For the years 1978–79 four of his sports guides—for football, men's basketball, cross-country, and field hockey—were selected as the NCAA Division III's "Best in the Nation" by CoSIDA. A fifth Juniata entry—for volleyball—received honorable mention. Juniata had the most first-place entries among competing schools. Only one other school—Division I's Notre Dame—had more than one "Best-in-Nation" designation (five).

After Pollock left, James Hunt, an alumnus and the editor of the Huntingdon *Daily News*, pinch-hit in the SID role for the school year 1982–83. Freshman Joseph Scialabba lent Hunt a hand that stand-in year. Then in 1983 President Binder promoted David Gildea, college editor since 1981, to the newly created position of associate director of public relations and publications. In that post Gildea assumed responsibility for the college's sports information operation. He left for graduate work the next year. Tracy DeBlaze (Huston), a 1985 graduate in communications and volleyball's MVP in 1984, took over as SID among her other college-publications duties the summer she graduated.

A few years earlier, in the spring of 1977, Athletic Director Berrier organized the Juniata Indian Club, a support group comprised of letter-winners, alumni, and friends of the college. It became the practice for members to dine together each noon before a home football game. Commencing the fall of 1977 the Indian Club published "Smoke Signals," a mimeographed newssheet, issued periodically, that covered the various seasonal sports. In 1992, because of campus concerns about ethnic and social stereotypes, "Smoke Signals" became the "**J-Club Newsletter**."

Chapter 16

PRIMING FOR THE TWENTY-FIRST CENTURY: 1986–1998

FREDERICK BINDER RETIRES

In May 1984 Binder informed the trustees of his plans to retire two years hence—on June 30, 1986. By then he would have reached his sixty-fifth birthday, marking twenty-six years as a college president (eleven at Juniata) and forty years total in higher education. As a person Binder had many winning qualities, but as president he had the reputation of being a gruff taskmaster, quick with the put down and the trenchant missive. Yet he was just as ready to laud the administrative staff, always by name, in his annual reports to the trustees.

Thanks to the Binder-style presidency, the college found itself in fine fiscal fettle by the mid-1980s. Over the past decade or so the operating budget grew from $5.8 million to nearly $13.9 million, balanced every year. The nagging interfund debt of nearly $1.3 million that Binder inherited had been all but liquidated when he retired. The book value of the plant increased from fifteen million dollars to $16.6 million. Fifteen million dollars had been raised over the six years since 1982. For 1985–86 gifts to the college totaled more than $1.8 million, third highest in its history. The Annual Support Fund for that year gleaned $278,000 from alumni, the most to that date. The endowment figure more than doubled—from $6.1 million to nearly fifteen million dollars. Faculty salaries had become more competitive, fifty thousand dollars the top figure. Student enrollment had reached record numbers, although for 1986–87 matriculations had slipped to just over eleven hundred. Financial aid escalated to $1.3 million, more rapidly than the rise of tuition.

To find Binder's replacement the trustess appointed a Presidential Selection Committee in May 1985, chaired by Henry Gibbel. The committee consisted of seven board members and an advisory body of faculty, students, and alumni, its convener to be biology professor Kenneth Rockwell. For the first time in a presidential search the college also engaged a professional consultant, John Synodinus from Eastern Pennsylvania. Said Chairman Gibbel: "Higher education is faced with challenges of unprecedented magnitude in such areas as enrollment management and maintaining academic standards from now through the 1990s. The next fifteen years are going to be very critical times for private colleges...."[1]

By fall more than one hundred applicants had sought the job. In mid-October the search committee chose six candidates to interview; three were then brought to campus for a public visit. Two were incumbent college presidents from the Midwest, the third a church official. The trustees, in a not-so-common gesture, gave the whole faculty a collective but nonbinding voice in the presidential pick. Some professors were openly leery of a churchman with no academic administrative experience as Juniata's chief—*and* Brethren at that. As a result the faculty gave the two sitting presidents the preferential vote. One of them, however, withdrew his name and the other turned down a formal offer from the trustees. That left Robert Neff, whom the board elected president on December 30. He assumed his duties July 1, 1986, having turned fifty the previous month.

ROBERT WILBUR NEFF: JUNIATA'S TENTH PRESIDENT

Although not an alumnus, Neff found himself domestically surrounded by alumni all his life. Both parents received degrees from Juniata, as did his wife Dorothy, née Rosewarne, and their son C. Scott and daughter Heather. His father taught Bible studies and philosophy on College Hill from 1946 to 1949. (During those years young Robert became the baseball team's batboy.) Neff himself, aspiring to become an agricultural missionary, graduated from The Pennsylvania State University in 1958 with a B. S. in agriculture. He won a Danforth Scholarship to Yale where he went on to get his B. D. (1961), M. A. (1964), and Ph.D. (1969) degrees.

Ordained a Brethren minister in 1960, the then-divinity student ministered at two Congregational churches in Connecticut from 1958 to 1961. While working on his doctoral dissertation he taught a year at Bridgewater College in Virginia (1964–65), then completed it at Bethany Theological Seminary in Illinois (since moved to Richmond, Indiana). There he spent a dozen years (1965–77) as a professor of Old Testament. After that he served the Church of the Brethren as general secretary for nine years. As the denomination's top executive officer, he was responsible for a budget of fourteen million dollars and a staff of more than four hundred. During his tenure he emerged as an ecumenical leader; he held key committee positions on the National Council of the Churches of Christ in the U. S. A. and on the World Council of Churches. At the same time, he was a director of Bethany Theological Seminary and served on the denomination's Committee on Higher Education. He had authored several articles for church and scholarly publications.

Neff was asked by a writer for the *Alumni Bulletin* soon after he took office why he applied to be president of Juniata. He responded that he had been encouraged to do so by a number of alumni and friends of the college. He went on: "[I] felt that my skills and personality matched the needs of the College at this particular time."[2] Neff saw himself as a "people person," "committed to a consultative style of management."[3] He had always "dreamed" of teaching at a small liberal arts school, he said, and "I felt that this position would enable me to return to an environment for which I had been trained to serve."[4]

To the question What are your goals for the college? Neff said:

> To maintain the excellent academic quality and character of Juniata College; to insure that humanities occupy the appropriate place in the curriculum in a small liberal arts college; and to enhance the international character of the college curriculum and thus assist students in becoming global citizens.[5]

He had also addressed the question of presidential designs at his debut press conference in January, his appointment recent public news. He said he planned to push the "issue of values and life's goals." Diversity, later a watchword for the Neff presidency, was not mentioned explicitly though implied by the term "values."[6] As for the college's curriculum, he expressed overall satisfaction; he saw only a need for "enhancement" of programs. At his first convocation, in August, the new president pledged himself to strengthening the "sense of community" on campus. He also intended to work hard at improving "town and gown" relations, which had suffered in recent years. He emphasized that another part of his mission included making Juniata better known outside Pennsylvania, especially in the Mid-Atlantic States—his sales pitch: "A beautiful gem hidden among…beautiful hills."

Neff's inauguration took place on Saturday, April 4, 1987, capping a weeklong schedule of events. A freak, unseasonal weather front, however, had roared into Pennsylvania come Friday night. By Saturday morning predicted snow had piled up inches deep in Pittsburgh, Philadelphia, and other places north and south in the state. But in Huntingdon Mother Nature delivered a torrential rain, not snow, that caused a major power outage. State Sen. Robert Jubelirer spoke at 10:30 A. M. in a dimly lit Alumni Hall with a mute public address system.

Then came word that Dr. Ernest Boyer, the keynote speaker and head of the Carnegie Foundation for the Advancement of Teaching, had missed his flight between Pittsburgh and the Blair County Airport. But, the college learned, Boyer was on his way to Huntingdon through snow over a foot deep in places—by taxicab! Just minutes before the processional was scheduled to begin (2:00 P. M.), Boyer entered the Kennedy Sports + Recreation Center Memorial Gymnasium. When introduced, the famed educator received an ovation, no less a tribute to his valiant effort to be present as to his eminence in higher education.

The theme of the inaugural ceremony was Education with Vision and Values. Boyer, who for the previous five years had been listed by *U. S. News & World Report* as one of the top ten educators in the nation, spoke on "Discovering Connections." In keeping with the inaugural theme, he said: "I believe that all worthy goals we pursue in education are best expressed in the simple word "connections."[7] He went on to emphasize that the quality of collegiate education "must be measured by the spirit of community...both in the classroom and beyond the campus too."[8] His parting words were, "The connectiveness of things is what the educator contemplates to the limit of his capacity."

Boyer's speech resonated with Juniata's tenth president. Neff's first *Report of the President* to the alumni said that Boyer gave "eloquent voice to the challenge that stands before Juniata College today."[9] He saw his initial year as an attempt to exemplify interrelatedness on campus—connections between professor and student, between classroom and living, connections to the world, to the ecumenical religious community, to the alumni and friends. This vision would drive the Neff presidency. "Community" would become Neff's favorite descriptive word of College Hill.

THE NEFF ADMINISTRATION: SLACKENED PRESIDENTIAL REINS

Frederick Binder's administrative style had been to arrogate control to himself, Neff's to delegate it. Twice Neff reshaped the Hilltop leadership to that end. In time he brought back a provost with amplified duties. He also bestowed on a new vice-president for college advancement much broader internal authority over activities other than fund-raising.

The day of the long-term chief academic officer on College Hill ended in 1966 with Morley Mays and his eighteen years of deaning. Donald Hartman's eight-year term as faculty chief during Binder's presidency has stood as the longest in that position in more than three decades. Five deans served under Neff, two of them on an interim basis. Joseph Stewart left his vice-presidency in the middle of the 1988–89 school year, to be succeeded on an interim basis as dean by Dale Wampler for the spring term. Stewart's vice-presidential heiress was Karen Sandler (Penn Ph.D.), 1989–94. Sandler, a former professor of French, had been associate provost at Gettysburg College. She became the only female officer of Juniata College to date.

Alumnus Robert Hatala (Yale Ph.D.) replaced her with a broadened title: provost and vice-president for student affairs (1994–97). A chemist, Hatala had a long career as an academic administrator in Florida, Maine, Tennessee, and, most recently, New Jersey. A new management structure went into effect with his arrival. That same spring of 1994 Arnold Tilden had resigned, and so, besides academic affairs, Provost Hatala assumed charge of Tilden's bailiwick: student services and the strategic planning process. The new structure aimed at effecting greater integration between academic programs and student services. At Hatala's departure, James Lakso, a Juniata economics professor, was made interim provost. His appointment became permanent in 1998, with no change in the provost's expanded role.

Before the Hatala-Lakso sequence, student services had been under the care of Dr. Arnold Tilden for seventeen years (1977–94). When President Neff became concerned about the need for strategic blueprinting, he assigned Tilden the new title of Vice-President for Educational Planning and Services in the spring of 1987. Then, with Tilden gone in 1994, Neff revived the post of dean of students—to be the provost's man Friday in that area of operation. It went to Kris Clarkson (M. S.) in 1995, the current dean. The previous year, James Donaldson, a business administration professor, assumed Tilden's duties for institutional planning and research.

For sixty-nine years, ever since 1922, there had been a woman of some deanship status as a coequal voice in overall student governance. That ended in 1997. The succession of women after Elizabeth O'Connell left included Susan Trombley (M. S.), 1979–81, Julia Keehner (M. S.), 1981–86—both ranked as associate dean as was historian Elizabeth Cherry, an interim appointee from January to June 1987—and Nancy Van Kuren (Ed.D.), 1987–91. Dr. Van Kuren was the only female since Frances Helms (in 1968) to be fully titled a dean in the student affairs office. Since 1997 there have been no women deans of any rank, only directors (three). Currently the sole assistant dean is Daniel Cook-Huffman (M. A.).

Two years before Hatala's arrival, Neff had initiated an earlier reorganization plan. Clayton Pheasant resigned from college advancement in 1991. Neff named Donald Moyer, an expert in community and regional economic promotion, to replace Pheasant. In 1992 the president regrouped four offices under Moyer's ward: admissions, advancement, alumni relations, and college communications. (In 1995 the word "marketing" was added to Moyer's vice-president's advancement title.) Neff explained that this initiative would allow the college to pursue a "cohesive and aggressive marketing strategy." All advancement staff and functions were now grouped in the same suite of offices, located in the basement of Founders Hall. For the first time a computer network system linked the whole fund-raising/publicity corps. The alumni office, however, returned to the Harold Brumbaugh Alumni House on Mifflin Street after nearly a decade in Founders' bowels. Admissions stayed put at the corner of 18th and Moore streets.

There, after Gayle Kreider (later Pollock) resigned in 1986, three directors held forth until the office's sphere of supervision increased in 1995. All three of them were alumni: Richard Phalunas (M. A.), 1986–87; Charles Kensinger (M.Ed.), 1987–91, who shifted over from development; and Carlton Surbeck (M.Ed.), 1991–95. David Hawsey (M. B. A.), the first non-Juniatian in twenty years, came in April of 1995 as dean of enrollment (the latest name for admissions). At that time the new dean was given charge of all areas of student enrollment—matriculation, financial aid, and athletic and national recruitment. Hawsey's M. B. A. degree in marketing and management information systems and his established record in the field of admissions gave him unique qualifications to oversee Juniata's enrollment strategies. In 1997 the college promoted the towering dean (6'6" tall) to associate vice-president for advancement and marketing.

Moyer resigned in 1997, and Foster Ulrich returned to his old haunts on an interim appointment for the next two-and-a-half years. All this while, Kevin McCullen, whose forte became rounding up grants from foundations and industry, had moved from institutional research to director of advancement in 1985. His knack at that craft earned him a promotion to an associate vice-presidency 1991. He resigned in 1998, his place taken by Joan Parsons Engle, titled Director of Development Research and Operations. Meanwhile, institutional research analysis had gone neglected for a dozen years after McCullen moved into fund-raising. Then Cynthia Clarke returned to her old position as a research analyst in 1997, reporting directly to the president. Dr. Ronald Wyrick had come on the advancement staff in 1992 as director of planned giving. His predecessor had been Kay Stephenson Cramer. In 1999 Wyrick was designated an associate vice-president for college advancement and marketing.

Public relations remained lodged in the Harold Brumbaugh Alumni House. When Charles Pollock laid down his duties there in 1983, Robert Howden had taken them up, staying until 1987. Robert Nordin replaced him for one year, his position labeled Director of College Communications. Then David Gildea, formerly college editor and Howden's associate (1981–85), returned with a master's degree in 1988, collecting Nordin's title. In 1996 Gildea's office was renamed External Relations and Marketing.

The office of business affairs, at the millennium still presided over by Vice-President William Alexander after twenty-five years, did not itself escape management changes. In 1995, to help ease the college's financial plight, Oneida Hall joined the concerted effort of staff reductions in all administrative areas. It cut the number of its chief personnel from fifteen to the present nine. The fall of 1993 it had leased out management of the campus bookstore to Follett College Stores, Inc., of Oakbrook, Illinois. It is the largest bookstore chain in operation, with over four hundred stores nationwide in the mid-Nineties. The last of Juniata's own bookstore managers was Scott Himes, 1977–94. His predecessor had been Robert Fisher, whose career dated from the early 1960s. Since 1995 Follett's agent for this pivotal Hilltop operation has been Jeremy Santos. One other management shift took place that year: student financial planning moved from the aegis of business affairs to that of college advancement.

Except for that one year, Oneida Hall enjoyed a fair degree of stability in its hierarchy during the Neff administration. Alexander, of course, has remained a steadying presence. William Rutter, Juniata's first controller, served ten years to 1986, resigning because of poor health. John Jones briefly succeeded him (1986–88). Michael Christy then put in a few months in 1988 to be replaced by Philip Thompson, the current controller. Personnel services got a name-change—to Human Resources—when Gail Ulrich took Barbara Rowe's place as director in 1997. And in 1999 John Linetty resigned as director of the physical plant.

During the Neff presidency two annual awards were created to honor non-faculty employees. The first one, the Anna Groninger Smith Supporting Staff Award, was set up in 1990 and named for the woman who gave forty-three secretarial years to four different presidents before retiring in 1964. Its initial honoree was Jodee Ruby, secretary to the academic dean. The second guerdon, the Lucy M. Calhoun Award for Distinguished Administrative Performance (endowed as a memorial by her son, Ted J. Long, a friend of Juniata), went to Barbara Rowe in 1993. (Like mother, like daughter—Mrs. Rowe is the mother of Mrs. Ruby.)

NEFF REBUILDS A SUPERANNUATED FACULTY

Just as it fell to Calvert Ellis's lot to build a faculty of his own in the Fifties and Sixties, so did that contingency characterize the Robert Neff presidency—but for a different reason. Juniata of the mid-century, like every other college and university of that era, faced a meteoric surge in enrollment. In the past decade and a half, however, the college endured a steady stream of retiring professors, most of them veterans from the Ellis years.

The *Juniata College Catalog* for 1998–99 shows a faculty of seventy-five full-time classroom instructors for that academic year. Of that number, thirty-nine came under Neff, more than half. Most were in their early or mid-thirties. For the academic year 1996–97, fourteen new faculty members were hired, a striking one-year influx of new blood. Never have faculty credentials been so impressive. Seventy-one of the seventy-five hold terminal degrees (96%), sixty-one being doctorates. There are twenty-two women on the full-time force (29%), seven of whom are full professors. Neff credits Dean Sandler for the new faculty's strength. Still, the overall faculty roster—including administrators with academic rank, librarians, and those on leave or sabbatical—is absent an African-American but does list three men of Asian lineage.

The steady dwindling of the old guard over the past decade opened up more tenure slots. By 1999 ninety-one percent of the faculty was tenured or on tenure-track. (In the spring of 1990 thirteen individuals were granted tenure in one fell swoop.) Vanishing veterans and the arrival of a baby-boomer faculty helped bring the top-heavy rankings into better balance. Beginning the fall of 2000, for the faculty as a whole, the distribution figures fall this way: professor (36); associate (21); assistant (21); instructor (3).

Still, there are twenty-four classroom troupers with a quarter-century or more of service as the millennial year draws nigh. Eleven of them will have registered between thirty and thirty-nine years by the time 1999 is history. One husband-and-wife faculty pair has given nineteen to a single biology position, a unique way to control costs. They are Douglas Glazier and Debra Kirchhof-Glazier, both now full professors. Their shared classroom duties have intrigued many an academic dean at other colleges looking for ways to keep a strong faculty on a tight budget. Actually the first spousal set to split an appointment at Juniata was Tom Fisher and Ruth Reed, in 1976, also full professors today. Chemists both, they, like the Glaziers, were Binder employees. Fisher and Reed, however, got separate contracts after four years when their common teaching position was expanded to support two persons.

In retrospect, the Neff presidency has vindicated itself vis-à-vis the fears of some faculty members back in 1985. There were those who suspected the incoming churchman might have a bias toward recruiting Brethren professors. This suspicion was unfounded since Neff had a long record of espousing ecumenism. The fact is, he appointed only two birthright Brethren, both noncommunicants. In the year 2000 just four professors have come out of the founders' religious heritage. (For that matter, Neff never hired a single chief administrator of Brethren roots. Indeed, of the whole administrative staff at the millennium, only Ronald Wyrick and the new chaplain, David Witkovsky, are of that stock.) Many on the faculty, however, have joined the Stone Church congregation on the campus and have become leaders or otherwise active members. Nor did the faculty become ingrown with Hilltop alumni since 1986; the 1998–99 *College Catalog* carries the names of four Juniatians, only one of them hired by Neff.

PROFESSORIAL HONORS, CHAIRS, DOINGS, BENEFITS

The Beachley Distinguished Professor Award, dependent in part on years of service, did not of course go to any Neff appointee. The names of those so-honored since 1986 include Russian's George Dolnikowsky (1987); philosopher Robert Wagoner (1988); psychologist David Drews (1989); mathematician L. Sue Esch (1990); sociologist F. Robert Reilly (1991); German's Klaus Jaeger (1992); chemist Ruth Reed (1993); physicist Norman Siems (1994); geologist Laurence Mutti (1995); English's William Hofelt (1996); art's Karen Rosell (1997); and historian Elizabeth Cherry (1998).

In 1988 the Beachley family established a second award: Distinguished Academic Service. The eleven to win this honor, none of them Neff people, have been music department's Mary Ruth Linton (1989); Elizabeth Cherry (1990); chemist Donald Mitchell and peace studies' M. Andrew Murray, both 1991; education professor Thomas Woodrow (1992); physicist Wilfred Norris (1993); biologist Robert Fisher (1994); chemist Paul Schettler (1995); education professor Kim Richardson (1997); education professor Fay Glosenger (1997); and economics and business administration professor James Donaldson (1998). Three individuals have come by both Beachley citations: Cherry, Mitchell, and Schettler.

The Lindback Distinguished Teaching Award, after a run of seven years, became the Junior Faculty Award in 1994. Naturally the earliest honorees during Neff's term came from the Binder faculty: biologist Debra Kirchhof-Glazier (1987); education's Fay Glosenger (1988); psychologist Ronald McLaughlin and art's Karen Rosell, both 1989. But, in only four years time, those tabbed by Neff took over totally: political scientist Gary Aichelle (Virginia Ph.D.) 1990; education's Connie Maclay (Penn State Ph.D.) 1991; chemist I. David Reingold (Oregon Ph.D.) and communication's Donna Weimer (Penn State Ph.D.), both 1993; geologist Keith Mann (Iowa Ph.D.), historian David Sowell (Florida Ph.D.), and anthropologist Peter Peregrine (Purdue Ph.D.), all three 1994; political scientist J. Jackson Barlow (Claremont Ph.D.) and historian David Hsiung (Michigan Ph.D.), both 1995; peace studies' Celia Cook-Huffman (Syracuse Ph.D.) 1996; music's Russell Shelley (Penn State Ph.D.) 1997; and education's Grace Fala (Penn State Ph.D.) 1998. Karen Rosell of the art department became the first person to win both the Beachley and the Junior Faculty teaching prizes.

For two years there was also the Sears-Roebuck Foundation Teaching Excellence and Campus Leadership Award. It went to the theatre arts's Ryan Chadwick (Ohio Univ. Ph.D.) in 1990 and in 1991 to philosopher Janet Lewis.

Retirements during the Neff years left four vacancies in the Dana professorships. Historian Earl Kaylor's chair went to department colleague Klaus Kipphan in 1991, biologist Robert Zimmerer's to L. Sue Esch in 1993, economist Ronald Cherry's to English's Mark Hochberg in 1998, and historian Philbrook Smith's to psychologist David Drews in 1999. Esch, Drews, Hochberg, Kipphan, and chemist William Russey represent 120 years of dedicated teaching and scholarly activity on the Juniata College campus.

As the tally of retirees mounted, two name professorships fell vacant. Also, in 1998 a new chair was established in chemistry. In 1997 Ernest Post's W. Newton and Hazel

Long Professorship in History, unfilled since 1984, went to David Hsiung. Thomas Woodrow retired in 1998, and his Martin G. Brumbaugh chair in education devolved upon Fay Glosenger. In 1998 Dr. Ei-Ichiro Ochiai became the first occupant of chemistry's H. George Foster Chair. Mrs. Eleanor Foster, a 1936 graduate, endowed the professorship ($925,000) in memory of her husband.

The J. Omar Good Distinguished Visiting Professorship of Evangelical Christianity continued to attract eminent conservative Protestant scholars. They included Dead Sea Scrolls expert John Trever (1986–87); biblicist W. Ward Gasque (1987–88); church historian Donald Durnbaugh (1988–89); philosopher Robert Roberts (1989–90); feminist theologian Lauree Hersh Meyers (1990–91); political theorist Paul Marshall (1991–92); clinical psychologist H. Newton Maloney (1992–93); English professor Corbin Carnell (1993–94) for a second turn; social ethicist David Gill (1994–95); poetess Jill Pelaez Baumgaertner (1995–96); Civil War theologian/novelist Kent Gramm (1996–98); biologist Margaret Gray Towne (Jan. 1999-May 2001). In 1997 the J. Omar Good Fund sponsored a book of essays on religion and higher education titled *Should God Get Tenure,* published by the William B. Eerdmans Company. Sixteen of the twenty-one visiting professors at that time contributed to the collection, edited by David Gill. The volume also contains a biographical look at benefactor J. Omar Good, whose endowment after a quarter century has grown to five million dollars.

Not since the John Stauffer presidency had a faculty member without a terminal degree been appointed a full professor (Thomas Nolan in 1973 while registrar). And only three associate professors in the subsequent quarter-century were promoted to the top rank upon receiving emeritus status: Romance language's Jack Oller (1965) and Russian's George Dolnikowski (1988), and history's Elizabeth Cherry (1998). In the spring of 1987, however, the trustees established a new policy for active faculty members lacking terminal degrees. It endorsed promoting practiced teachers to full professor who "demonstrated outstanding work in their fields."[10] Two individuals—anthropologist Paul Heberling (1988) and English's Ralph Church (1990)—have been promoted under this policy over the last dozen years, both shortly before retiring.

The Neff years boasted a teaching faculty as actively engaged in research and publishing as during the Binder presidency. Scholarly articles went out nonstop from College Hill. The Hill's professoriate also continued to bring forth books: political scientist Craig Baxter; historians David Hsiung and David Sowell; philosopher Robert Wagoner; psychologist Dale Wright; chemist Ei-Ichiro Ochiai; potter Jack Troy. Alexander McBride sold three of his canvasses to the Pepsi Company. The paintings became part of a famed collection exhibited at the soft-drink industry's headquarters in Purchase, New York. There they share the spotlight with the works of such luminaries as Pablo Picasso and Willem de Kooning. In the spring of 1990 Dr. Craig Baxter (author of eight books and thirty articles) was instrumental in creating an exchange program between the United States and Bangladesh. The agreement created the American Institute of Bangladesh Studies (AIBS) to be headquartered at Juniata College. (Other schools involved in AIBS are Penn, Columbia, and Chicago.)

Dr. Baxter also wrote a proposal in 1990, under the auspices of PACS, that won the approval of the Fulbright-Hays Groups Projects Abroad Program. It supported a group study/travel seminar in the Soviet Union for five weeks. Fifteen faculty members—six senior professors from Juniata, the rest from other colleges and high schools—participated in the seminar. The group got to see contemporary life in the U.S.S.R. just months before its communist government collapsed.

Two years prior, during the Easter season, Juniata had opened an exhibit of Russian icons in Shoemaker Gallery at Carnegie Museum. Robert Wagoner and George Dolnikowski from the humanities division collaborated in organizing the exhibition. This display of sacred images marked the millennial year of Christianity's birth in old Russia. In the Soviet Union the official millennium celebration began June 12 in Moscow. Juniata's "Icons of the Golden Age" consisted of forty-five specimens from the fourteenth to the fifteenth centuries. For the whole next year this homage to the Eastern Orthodox faith traveled to the Washington Cathedral in the nation's capital, to New York's Interchurch Center, to Pennsylvania's Lafayette College, to College of the Holy Cross in Worcester, Massachusetts, and finally to Pittsburgh's Frick Art Museum.

In the 1990s five Neff-hired faculty members received Fulbright grants, that number a tribute to the quality of classroom instruction Juniata was attracting. Music's Donna Coleman (Eastman D. M. A.) spent the summer of 1992 as a senior Fulbright scholar in Australia. The summer of 1997 Spanish's Henry Thurston-Griswold (Texas Ph.D.) and peace studies' Celia Cook-Huffman used their joint grant to take fifteen secondary and post-secondary educators on a group travel seminar to Costa Rica. Then in the spring of 1998 two faculty members in the political science department got separate Fulbright grants. Jackson Barlow spent a year in the Czech Republic at Masaryk University and at Technical University, both in the city of Brno. The scholarship to Emil Nagengast (Pitt Ph.D.) enabled him to participate in a German studies seminar in Bonn for part of a summer.

In another area of the campus, Juniata science professors have been doing research with students—and co-authoring papers with them—ever since the early 1960s. It started first with chemistry, under Donald Rockwell. Then as funded research projects multiplied over the subsequent years, virtually every member of a science department began churning out scientific papers. Many have been prolific at applying for grants, too. For example, chemist David Reingold, between 1988 and 1996, received funding of more than $325,000 for his research in the synthesis of non-natural products.

In terms of grant proposals, the gold medal belongs to chemistry's Donald Mitchell. He is the mastermind—and only director—of Science in Motion, initiated in 1985. Over the succeeding years, this novel science outreach program has induced the National Science Foundation to allot it as much as $2,280,000 and the state of Pennsylvania another $1,500,000. The goals of Science in Motion, according to Dr. Mitchell, are to upgrade the knowledge and skills of science teachers, to provide them with increased access to modern instrumentation, and to give them greater hands-on experience.[11] In 1988 Science in Motion took to the road, literally. Two cube vans, one for chemistry and one for biology, travel to as many as fifty schools every year. Each vehicle, equipped with the latest scientific equipment, is driven by certified teachers in the respective fields.

The mobile science on wheels started out to serve the rural school districts of Central Pennsylvania. In 1983 the project expanded to include the Monongahela River Valley region of Pittsburgh (ended in 1999). Soon the vans were reaching two thousand students in thirty-five school districts. In November 1992 Dr. Mitchell received the "A+ for Breaking the Mold" citation from U. S. Secretary of Education Lamar Alexander. The award recognized innovative schools, programs, or individuals for "breaking the mold" to change and improve education. The next year Mitchell was named one of the nation's four exceptional teachers of science, chemistry, and engineering at the four-year college level. (The other three were from the universities of Michigan, Northwestern, and Purdue.) This prestigious Catalyst Award, established in 1957, is sponsored by the Chemical Manufacturers Association.

Juniata College received national visibility as a result of this creative venture. In November 1993 Peter Jennings featured "Science in Motion" in an "American Agenda" segment on ABC's World News Tonight. (It got five minutes' coverage.) The ABC news crew, headed by Education Correspondent Bill Blakemore, spent four days shooting the story in Central Pennsylvania. All that time Blakemore kept saying, "Why didn't somebody think of this before and why isn't it being done across the country?"[12]

In some places it is. Alabama has modeled a science-on-wheels program after the one at Juniata, which helped set it up. Delaware has adopted the idea, and other institutions—like Pennsylvania's own Gettysburg, California's Occidental, Indiana's Purdue, and Illinois' Chicago State—have also taken to the road in an effort to visit high schools cumbered by outdated laboratories.

Small wonder that Juniata became the host site of the annual State Science Olympiad beginning the spring of 1992. This contest is sponsored by the Pennsylvania Science Teachers Association. Students compete in thirty-two science events at the high school and middle school/junior high levels. The top team from each category represents Pennsylvania in the National Science Olympiad.

In 1988, the year that "Science in Motion" motored up, Academic Dean Joseph Stewart told the trustees that Juniata's aging faculty will be reaching retirement age at a time when a new supply of faculty members will be at a low point. Hence, "entry-level faculty members will require higher salaries," he said.[13] After a nominal salary increase of two percent at the end of Neff's first year, faculty compensation began to lag. So the trustees authorized a new salary range for the 1988–89 academic year.[14]

Rank	Number	Low	High	Median
Professor	37	$28,000	$55,000	$37,400
Assoc. Professor	23	25,000	40,000	31,500
Asst. Professor	15	22,000	32,000	26,000
Instructor	–	19,000	26,000	–

The *Juniatian* for September 9, 1993, carried a front-page article titled "Study Shows JC Salaries Low." It was a reprint from the July 11 issue of the Altoona *Mirror*. The *Mirror* story noted that faculty salaries at Juniata, with an enrollment of 1,134, averaged $39,800. The reprint went on to say, based on information published by the American Association of University Professors (AAUP): "Juniata lags behind other liberal arts colleges of its size in most pay categories." (For instance, Neff's salary of $96,467 for 1992–93 was markedly lower than that of presidents at comparable colleges—about twenty-four percent less.)

The budget crunch for 1995–96 caused a wage freeze as well as a reduction in administrative staff. At its April 28, 1995, board meeting the trustees promoted nine faculty members but with no increase in salary. Subsequent salary adjustments brought Juniata's faculty compensation within ninety-five percent of the means of nine peer colleges by 1998. There was also an attempt at internal equity, paying similar salaries to persons of equal rank. In 1999 the AAUP reported the following compensation data for Juniata's faculty:

Rank	Avg. Salary	Avg. Compensation	% Increase
Professor	$57,600	$72,500	6.7
Assoc. Professor	43,000	55,300	6.7
Asst. Professor	37,500	47,700	6.9
Instructor	32,300	–	–

Comparatively, Juniata's percentage of salary increases over the previous years was highest among its competitors at every rank. In some cases it was as much as four percent more.

As the above data show, average fringe benefits cost the college from a low of $10,200 per assistant professor to a high of $14,900 per full professor. Costly, too, are post-retirement benefits. In 1996 the value of tax-free post-retirement benefits totaled $2,047,915. That May the trustees acted to cut the college's outgo in this area by nearly $870,000 a year. Employees would have to share premium costs. The action, of course, upset the faculty—and the supporting staff—especially on the heels of a wage freeze and a modest raise.

President Neff appointed an ad hoc committee from diverse segments of the campus to come up with a compromise plan. The trustees then rescinded its May 1996 changes and adopted another option, which did not, however, fully meet the ad hoc committee's expectations.[15] A grandfather clause exempted faculty and staff members with twenty years or more of service from bearing the full cost of post-retirement medical and insurance premiums. For those that had been at Juniata less than two decades, the cost to be borne by them was prorated according to a formula based on the date of their hiring. All faculty members and staff employed after January 1, 1999, would not be eligible for college-paid post-retirement benefits. But they could participate in Juniata's group plan, currently Blue Cross/Blue Shield. In compliance with the federal Age Discrimination Act of 1986, the college has no mandatory retirement age for its employees.

In May 1997 the trustees adopted a policy dubbed "Annual Performance Review of Faculty." Implemented that fall with faculty approval, the policy's primary purpose is to promote accountability and performance. It also has implications for salary considerations. The process entails numerous steps and much paperwork and eventually ends up on the provost's desk for his signature. An unanticipated positive result of the review policy, Provost Lakso told the trustees after the first-year test, was that it was useful in the overall department-planning process.

Since fall 1990 there has been a Juniata College Emeriti Association. It was the brainchild of education's Howard Crouch and Russian's George Dolnikowski and includes retired administrators as well as faculty. The group meets regularly and operates under a constitution and set of bylaws. The emeriti have established a fund for planting trees in memory of deceased members. (A memorial book, profiling departed ones, is kept in Beeghly Library.) At the millennium there are thirty-four retirees and/or their spouses who live in the Huntingdon area.

MILLENNIAL KUDOS TO JUNIATA'S ACADEMIC QUALITY

The national acclaim Juniata has enjoyed in the last quarter of the twentieth century calls to mind the prophetic words of Dr. A. B. Brumbaugh one hundred and twenty years ago. He said, at the memorial service for Jacob Zuck, Juniata's founding teacher: "The time will come when the influence of this school movement will be felt from the Atlantic to the Pacific, and from the Lakes to the Gulf."[16] Some on the Hill bowdlerized the passage from newspaper copy because it struck them as outrageous to make such a claim for a school a mere three years old.

But a century-and-a-quarter's time has proved the good doctor more historically farsighted than his Hilltop colleagues. Juniata College now points with pride to its regular inclusion in surveys and guides that have given it a place of national prominence in higher education: *Peterson's Competitive Colleges* (fifteen years in a row); *Barron's 300: Best Buys in College Education; U. S. News & World Report; Rugg's Recommendations on the Colleges; College Research Association of Biologists' Directory.* In its "Year 2000 Annual Guide," *U. S. News & World Report* (August 30, 1999) ranked Juniata among the country's 122 superior liberal arts schools. A recent issue of Loren Pope's *Colleges That Change Lives* listed Juniata among forty highlighted colleges. Wrote Pope, former education editor of the *New York Times*: "[Juniata] has a powerful sense of mission. It has a powerhouse faculty trained at the top universities." A dozen years earlier, in 1987, the Carnegie Foundation for the Advancement of Teaching had classified Juniata as a Liberal Arts I institution. That put the college among one hundred and forty highly selective institutions of its type in the nation, eighteen of them in Pennsylvania.

Further testimony to Juniata's character lies in the record of alumni that have gone on for graduate and professional education.[17] Data recently provided by the National Research Council placed Juniata in the top ninety of 914 private, non-doctoral degree-granting institutions in the percentage of graduates that earn doctorates. The same study put Juniata in the topmost two-and-a-half percent of 518 American colleges in the number of chemistry graduates that have obtained their Ph.D.s. For biology graduates, Juniata ranks in the top eight percent and, for earth science graduates, the upper seven-and-a-half percent. As previous chapters have noted, alumni have frequently received coveted graduate fellowships. More recently, in 1995 and in 1997, a graduate won a Fulbright Fellowship, and in 1997, 1998, and 1999, a Juniata student received a Goldwater Scholarship. For the 1999–2000 academic year, two students studied abroad on National Security Education Program Undergraduate Scholarships. Eleven Juniata undergraduates have been St. Andrew's Society of Philadelphia scholars since the award's inception two decades ago, spending a year of study in Scotland.

Perhaps Juniata's national reputation is strongest in several preprofessional fields. Over the past several years nearly ninety percent of the Hill's applicants have been accepted to medical, dental, optometry, podiatry, and veterinary schools. Since 1993 over ninety percent of Juniatians that applied got into law school. Placement statistics are also impressive, especially in the areas of education, community service, and business and industry. Of all students registered with the college's placement services, according to a recent survey, ninety-three percent were employed, in graduate school, or otherwise engaged in activities as planned within six months of graduation.

THE NEW CENTURY'S CURRICULUM

President Neff's first year coincided with a return to the semester system. Since he found the curriculum he inherited quite satisfactory, he saw no immediate need to press for curricular revisions. In 1987, however, the faculty did add a required course in computer literacy and one in international studies. Midway through his tenure the college underwent the recurrent decennial Middle States reaccreditation process. Juniata gave eighteen months to preparing the customary self-study, the actual visit taking place in November 1992. As in the past, the visiting team found many strengths and few problems.

The Pennsylvania Department of Education made a concurrent accreditation visit that month of November. Teacher certification programs in the Commonwealth must be reviewed every five years. The visiting team's report had high praise for the education department's people and performance. It noted: "To merely say that the college is fulfilling the goal of preparing professional education personnel would be a gross understatement."[18] Juniata received thirty commendations in the report, a remarkable laudation.

By that time the education department had originated "New Visions" (in the summer of 1988), still ongoing at the millennium. It is a week-long summer camp for gifted and talented students in grades four through seven. New Visions campers are housed on campus and participate in two academic experiences and one recreational activity. Later, to accommodate those who outgrew the program, the department introduced "Voyages" for youth in grades eight, nine, and ten. These students take only one academic class besides engaging in an athletic exercise. Department chair Fay Glosenger has been long-time director of these two popular programs.

The overall curriculum audited in 1992 by two visiting teams changed little until the mid-Nineties. Students continued to tailor much of their academic programs via the Program of Emphasis (POE). There were still core-curricular requirements that guaranteed distribution of courses—in freshman composition, in the natural and social sciences, in certain general education offerings, and in the humanities. In place too was Senior Values Studies (SVS), which encouraged students to reflect upon their personal moral and ethical standards.

During the 1994–95 academic year, at the instigation of Robert Hatala, the new provost, the faculty began to reevaluate the entire curriculum. A major overhaul resulted and was implemented the fall of 1996 for the millennium class. Among the casualties were SVS, General Education (GE) as such, and the traditional freshman English I and II courses (units are now called courses again). Freshmen now take a three-module College Writing Seminar that introduces them to computer technology and library resources as well as to advanced composition. As a follow-up, students must take more writing-based and speech-based courses and also meet a basic competency in statistics and mathematical skills.

Distribution has not been abandoned. Students must complete six credit hours of coursework in each of five areas: fine arts, international studies, social sciences, humanities, and natural sciences. Nor has the POE been scuttled; it remains virtually the same as before. On the other hand, with the elimination of SVS has come a Cultural Analysis Core. It is team-taught and interdisciplinary. The 1998–99 *College Catalog* describes this two-part capstone core as being "designed to develop the necessary skills to identify, understand, and analyze culture." It purports to prepare students to think critically about the different aspects of culture, both Western and non-Western, as manifested through literature, art, science, and sociology.

Major curriculum revision and the problems of operating on two academic programs—three years in this case—always complicate the work of the registrar. William Duey (Shippensburg M. A./Geo. Washington M. B. A.) can attest to that. A retired army colonel, Duey succeeded Jill Shrum Pfrogner in 1993. He had come to Juniata in 1988 to teach business administration.

As Neff-era registrars, Pfrogner and Duey saw several academic programs either broadened or introduced. Since the early Seventies, international studies developed from marginal interest to, under Neff, one of the most important thrusts of the college. In 1987, as noted, international studies became a component of the distribution requirement in the curriculum. The year before, a chapter of Sigma Iota Rho, the International Relations Honor Society, had organized on campus. Then in 1989 Juniata affirmed a strong commitment "to provide an education within a global context…and enhancing the international dimension of the college."[19] Two years later the faculty added an International POE to the curriculum. In 1992 Neff announced that Juniata had made explicit its pledge to promote international education in its revised mission statement. The sentence reads:

> As a member of the international community, Juniata extends the student's academic experience into the world and encourages the free and open exchange of thought among peoples from different cultures and nations.

Ante-Neff presidents had involved Juniata in Brethren Colleges Abroad (begun in 1962) and the one-for-one exchange programs (primarily for science students). No Juniata president prior to Neff, however, advocated so imperatively the international perspective in education as he did. Pivotal to Neff's campaign to internationalize the campus was the leadership of Provost Robert Hatala. As vice-president for academic affairs at Ramapo College in Mahway, New Jersey, Hatala had been a major force in making Ramapo worthy of its slogan: "The college for a global education."

By 1995 there were nineteen different overseas programs available to Juniatians in as many as eleven countries. At that time over five hundred Hilltop juniors had spent a semester or summer overseas. In 1996 the college began offering an International Studies Certificate to recognize students with a significant exposure to a non-American society through study in another country. At the eve of the millennium Juniata annually sends an average of seventy to eighty students abroad to study.

The international program works both ways; students from abroad come to College Hill. Since 1994 Juniata has ranked second among a group of highly rated liberal arts colleges in Pennsylvania in the percentage of students from other countries. For the 1998–99 academic year students from twenty-three countries studied at Juniata. Many international students come to the Hill in need of further English study. In 1994 the college appointed William Helz (School for International Training M. A.) to be the first director of English as a Second Language (ESL). Helz resigned in 1997 and was followed by Elizabeth Smolcic (Georgetown M. A.). In 1998 ESL became the Intensive English Program (IEP). The change of name came about, explained Smolcic, because IEP "also includes utilizing English skills for courses in computer skills, ceramic arts, and cultural analysis."[20] Furthermore, foreign students learn about American life firsthand by excursions to urban and rural areas and various cultural events.

Just as Dr. William Vocke, first head of the International Programs Office (IPO), came out of Good Hall's classrooms, so did his next two successors. Dr. Kim Richardson of the education department served six years in that position (1990–96); historian Dr. David Sowell put in three years. Both directors returned to their former faculty stations. The aggressive leadership of the first three IPO directors built up the international programs to the point where the college needed to hire a full-time dean to supervise it. That person is JoAnn deArmas Wallace (Wright State M. S.), who brought to the Hilltop a decade of administrative experience in study-abroad operations. Since 1995 Jarmilla Polte (New York City College B. A.), former supervisor of the three language laboratories (removed in 1997), has been the principal student advisor in the IPO.

Another college-defining program the Neff presidency inherited and gave a big boost was the study of peacemaking (PACS). In the spring of 1989 the president renamed the program The Baker Institute for Peace and Conflict Studies. It honors John and Elizabeth Baker, the original benefactors of peace studies at Juniata. Two years later the MacArthur Foundation of Chicago awarded the institute a grant of one hundred thousand dollars. Since 1971 PACS' endowment has increased from a modest twenty-seven thousand dollars to over $3.6 million.[21]

The faculty has never wavered in its support of PACS, which today involves twelve departments and one-third of the faculty. Thanks to Dr. Andrew Murray's leadership from the start, Juniata's peace program "is the most campus-embracing in the country." So wrote Dr. Ted Herman of Colgate University, founder and director emeritus of peace studies there, who also extolled the Hill's PACS as "the best undergraduate peace program in the country."²² There are now over two hundred colleges and universities in the United States that offer academic credit in irenology, a select one hundred of them offering a major in the field. PACS' motto is "Si vis pacem...para pacem" (If you want peace, prepare for peace). This motto has found expression at Juniata in more than one way. In 1987 the Baker Institute helped found and continues to support the National Peace Studies Association, an organization of more than two hundred academic and non-academic institutions. Juniata's Andrew Murray has held the highest offices in the organization and is recognized as one of America's leading authorities in the field of peacemaking.

Juniata during the Neff years also became the first educational institution to have a contractual agreement with the United Nations to promote the peace issue. From 1993 to 1997, in union with the United Nations and the International Association of University Presidents, Juniata sponsored an annual International Seminar on Arms Control and Disarmament (ISACD). The two-week sessions were held at the college's Conference Center in nearby Williamsburg. They were targeted primarily at university scholars from developing nations but were also open, in special cases, to government officials. The faculty for the ISACD seminars came from among global leaders of various backgrounds on the subject of arms control and disarmament.

On Saturday, October 14, 1990, the Baker Institute celebrated a special occasion: the dedication of the Elizabeth Evans Baker Peace Chapel. Located in the Baker-Henry Nature Preserve adjacent to the campus, the chapel's site had long impressed Mrs. Baker as Edenic, the perfect place for some kind of simple peace shrine that blended with the alfresco scene. The Bakers engaged Maya Lin, designer of the Vietnam Memorial in the nation's capital and the Civil Rights Memorial in Montgomery, Alabama, to be the architect for an out-of-doors chapel. Maya Lin's parents taught at Ohio University, her father becoming academic dean during the presidency of John Baker. Her two most famous memorials have marked her as a minimalist artist, a concept she brought to the design of Juniata's Peace Chapel. It is a series of salt and pepper granite stones, rising from the earth on a grassy knoll, to form a large circle for group meditation. The stone circle encloses a slight depression. Several hundred yards away, on a higher knoll, is a small copse from which there is a magnificent view of the ambient hills. This spot is for private meditation. The circle of stones is visible from the copse but not vice versa. This set of sites anchors a fourteen-acre area.

Three other special academic programs were initiated, not inherited, by the Neff administration. The earliest, Program for Area Residents (PAR), began in 1987 and offered half-tuition to citizens of Huntingdon County out of high school five or more years. Then in 1989 Neff expanded the discount plan to include residents of seven other Central Pennsylvania counties. For the academic year 1998–99 thirty-five of these older, non-traditional students took classes at Juniata.

In November 1995 the president announced creation of the Juniata College Institute of Civic Affairs. Self-supporting, the institute is directed by Samuel Hayes, Jr., former Republican majority leader of the Pennsylvania House of Representatives and now State Secretary of Agriculture. Hayes, a state legislator for twenty years, serves without pay. As time allows, he teaches courses in the departments of education and political science. He is also available to help students find business and government internships.

The third academic development had to do with a new department: environmental science and studies, added in the fall of 1998. This was the culmination of an interdisciplinary program in environment studies introduced four years earlier. At that time Neff said the program would be "a genuine synthesis of the social sciences, humanities, and natural sciences."[23] It would not be strictly applied science, the president emphasized, but would demand that students approach environmental issues from all academic perspectives. The core faculty of this unique department consists of Paula Martin (Massachusetts Ph.D.) and Charles Yohn (Penn State M. S.), director of the Raystown Field Station. The *College Catalog, 1999–2000* listed sixteen professors from eight departments as supporting faculty.

In the realm of higher education, perhaps no innovation has had more of a revolutionary impact than technology. At Juniata the process of integrating modern-day educational technology across the whole campus began in 1994. Two years before, Middle States evaluators had pointed out that Juniata lagged somewhat behind in techno-cultural advance. Consequently, Neff appointed the Information Technology Task Force (ITTF) in June 1994 to formulate plans for better utilizing technology on College Hill. The ITTF came up with a blueprint hyped as "Technology for the Year 2000 and Beyond." The technological transformation on campus over the past half-dozen years, according to Neff, has "put Juniata in an enviable position among peers in higher education."[24] It now pervades every sector of the Hill—from classrooms to dormitories, from Beeghly Library to Muddy Run Café. In March 1996 David Fusco joined the Juniata staff as network manager (replaced in 1999 by Arthur Manion).

Implementing an all-campus, fiber-based network provides a variety of teaching-learning strategies. The distance learning center in Good Hall, named the Gump classroom in 1996, enables students to take courses at more than twenty colleges and universities.[25] By the same token, Juniata professors can telecast their courses to other institutions. Eight classrooms have been wired to the campus network to permit faculty to utilize computers for instruction. Henry Thurston-Griswold, for example, uses computers to teach Spanish. And Belle Tuten (Emory Ph.D.) uses them to teach history. All professors, of course, have college-placed computers in their offices.

For students there are five laboratories that provide a total of one hundred and twenty fully networked computers. In the fall of 1997 Dean of Students Kris Clarkson put out a clever brochure that encouraged parents to buy students "a computer rather than a car." That October 378 Juniatians owned their own PCs.

Beeghly Library upgraded its services with computer-based card catalog and research sources that include several state-of-the-art engines. Commencing in February 1994 the library now relies on the bar code system for checking out books. Such technological advances became a duty head-librarian John Mumford (Shippensburg M. A./Drexel M. S.) took over from his predecessor, Peter Kupersmith (Texas M. L. S.). Mumford moved up from public services librarian in 1995, after Kupersmith's seven-year tenure as Beeghly's top man.

Indeed, Juniata College was recently ranked 138th of all colleges and universities in the Yahoo! Internet Life Survey of "America's Most Wired Colleges." The survey identifies the nation's top Internet-connected higher-education schools.

STRATEGIC PLANNING, MISSION STATEMENT, DIVERSITY

At the trustee meeting in April 1987 President Neff expressed concern at the lack of long-range planning by the college. He announced that he had appointed three committees to help shape Juniata's future. He appointed Arnold Tilden to oversee that process with a new title: vice-president for educational planning and student services. All sectors of the campus had representation on every committee. One committee, on internal assessments, dealt with guidelines suggested by the Middle States Association. This self-study always comes at the five-year mark after a college receives its ten-year accreditation by Middle States and was due in October 1987. Another committee examined outside factors that affect the college, the source, so authorities say, for three-fourths of all changes in higher education.[26] The third committee rewrote the mission statement, rejecting the terse 1980 version. As noted, one of its four paragraphs delineates a latter-day Juniata with an institutional purpose more in line with its stated commitment to global education.

In the spring of 1989 this second paragraph of the 1987 mission statement became the rationale for a task force on diversity. The president appointed Charles Kensinger, then director of admissions, as its chair. Like so many predominantly white colleges and universities, Juniata had never been very successful in attracting and retaining minority students. There had never been a black professor on the Hill and only ever two staff members. This dearth of a minority presence on campus, declared task force chairman Kensinger, betrayed the language of paragraph two in the mission statement. He cited specifically the value Juniata places on "the free exchange of diverse ideas" and "the free and open exchange of thought among peoples from distinct cultures and nations." Moreover, he said, diversity on College Hill would better prepare all students for America's heterogeneous society once they leave Juniata.

The final report of the task force contained thirty-four recommendations for achieving a diverse campus community. The document did not view diversity as primarily a matter of race or ethnic origin. For the task force, the word also applied to age and religious beliefs. At its May 1990 meeting the trustees gave their stamp of approval to the policy that commits Juniata to a multicultural campus.

The Hilltop took major steps to abide by the new diversity policy. Several groups were established: an African-American Student Association, the Forum (for PAR students), a Multi-Cultural Committee for the Center Board, and African-American Alumni Association. In January 1992 Juniata held its first-ever convocation on the birthday of Martin Luther King, Jr., now a tradition. In February the campus recognized Black History Month—now another tradition—with a provocative play, *Our Black Men Are Dying and No One Seems to Care*. The next month the faculty adopted a resolution recommending to the trustees that the Indian mascot be changed. The faculty also added a course to the curriculum titled World Literature, which focuses on non-Caucasian writers of other cultures. On Homecoming, in October, the college permanently broke the forty-two-year tradition of crowning a queen. Instead, to avoid a sexist perspective, the queen and her court were replaced by nineteen students that received community-service awards. Already in 1990, two African-Americans were on the board of trustees.

Eventually, in the fall of 1993, diversity gave rise to Alternative Ways of Loving (AWOL). AWOL's moving spirit was Grace Fala (Penn State Ph.D.), assistant professor of speech communication. This chartered club, says Fala, "aims to increase understanding and support for the gay, lesbian, and bisexual community."[27] The club has attracted a sizable following not only among students but also among the faculty and staff.

Unfortunately, at the millennium, a decade after the task force report, the campus is no more racially diversified than it was in 1990. Blacks are absent from the administration, the faculty, and the staff. Moreover, the racial origins of the student body have remained constant, as the following table shows:

	1989	1999
Black (non-Hispanic)	12	10
Asian	11	12
Hispanic	9	7
Native American	3	0

Today's multicultural lineaments of College Hill, however, are more in keeping with Juniata's institutional *Weltanschauung*. Three current members, as noted, are of Asian heritage, while the Hill's international student census has all but doubled in ten years—from thirty-seven to seventy-one. In 1989 exchange students hailed from eleven foreign countries; in 1998 from twenty-four.

RECASTING THE BOARD OF TRUSTEES

Robert Neff not only had the rare chance to rebuild an aging faculty, he also faced the contingency of replenishing a venerable board of trustees. His presidency perdured the retirement of eleven long-serving members and the deaths of nine incumbents, two of them the presiding officer. The trustees that took emeritus status were Donovan Beachley, Sr. (1945–85), John Baker (1936–87), John Swigart, Sr. (1950–87), Calvert Ellis (1943–89), Harold Brumbaugh (1979–94), Edith Cuttrell (1957–94), Dale Detwiler (1949–94), Joseph Good (1952–94), Newton Long, Jr. (1976–96), Vincent Sarni (1979–97), and Wayne Patterson (1986–98). The nine who died in service included Charles Ellis (1966–90), Raymond Day (1988–91), Phyllis Henry (1990–92), Clay Burkholder (1980–93), Edwin Kennedy (1969–94), Earl Croner (1952–96), Delbert McQuaide (1994–96), Philip Cronemiller (1985–96), and Andrew Vance (1990–97).

The two chairmen who died at the board's helm were Charles Ellis and Delbert McQuaide. Ellis, dead at age seventy-one, led the board for thirteen of his twenty-four years as a trustee. His colleagues elected Klare Sunderland, one of Central Pennsylvania's leading businessmen and a board member since 1970, to Ellis's vacated post. Juniata experienced some of its most dynamic growth during Sunderland's six-year tenure as chairman. Twenty-four new trustees came into office in that brief span of time, retirements and deaths having taken a heavy toll. (Part of the rapid turnover is explained by the fact that the six trustees allotted the alumni (3) and the church (3) serve for three years and are ineligible for reelection.) Health problems prompted Sunderland to step aside (but not off the board) in the spring of 1996. The incoming chairman, Delbert McQuaide, a student leader on campus in the mid-Fifties, practiced law in nearby State College and served as general counsel for the Pennsylvania State University and Milton S. Hershey Medical Center. He brought a new organizational structure to the board, codified in a revised set of bylaws the spring of his election. His bout with cancer prematurely ended his one-year chairmanship in February 1997. He died at age sixty.

The trustees then turned to Harrisburg attorney John Cramer, board secretary since 1984. Cramer, a *magna cum laude* Juniata graduate, earned his law degree at Harvard. His election conformed to the college's 125-year tradition: all board presidents have been men and have been Juniatians and/or members of the Church of the Brethren.

Despite the influx of so many new trustees during the Neff presidency, twenty-one board members in the spring of 1999 had served ten or more years. The election of eleven of them hearkened back to the Binder years: Charles Brown, Charles Knox, Edwin Malloy, Garry Pote, Donovan Beachley, Jr., John Cramer, Henry Gibbel, W. Clemens Rosenberger, Warren Groff, Klare Sunderland, and Robert Wagoner. The rest came as co-opted members during Neff's time: Anne Baker (1987), Barry Halbritter (1987), the late Betty Finnegan Simpson (1984–87; 1988), F. Samuel Brumbaugh (1987–90; 1990), George Cruser (1982–86; 1991), Frances Hesselbein (1988), William Hershberger (1989), Harriet Richardson Michel (1989), Thomas Pheasant (1988–91; 1991), and Marie Zeller (1985–88; 1989).

Only once since the 1982-bylaws change has the board reached the full complement of forty members—1993–94. In the ante-millennial year of 1999, the count was thirty-seven. Seven were women—five being at-large members, the other two an alumnus and a church representative. Two African-Americans became board-nominated trustees: Harriet Michel and Dr. Maurice Taylor.

In May of 1997 the trustees established two new awards in recognition of outstanding dedication to Juniata College. The first one, the John C. Baker Award for Exemplary Service, came about upon the recommendation of the Alumni Council. It honors either individuals or organizations and is not necessarily an annual event. It is "reserved for appropriate candidates as they arise." Nominations may be initiated by the Alumni Council, the award generally being presented during commencement ceremonies. There have been a pair of Baker Service awardees: Delbert McQuaide (1997, posthumously) and Harold Brumbaugh (1999).

The second award, the Presidential Medallion for Meritorious Service, is granted at the discretion of the president in consultation with the trustee chair and the head of the board's committee on advancement and marketing. It is an annual award—also either to individuals or organizations—and may be presented in any setting but preferably at commencement time. The two recipients of the medallion so far have been trustee Robert Wagoner (1997) and retiring provost Robert Hatala (1998).

That October of 1997 the board revitalized the old Development Council and renamed it the Trustees Council. As before, practically all of the members—sixty-seven out of seventy-three—are alumni. Chaired by Dorothy and Rex Hershberger, this auxiliary group's mission is to identify and help cultivate large-donor individuals for the opening years of the twenty-first century.

SURVIVING A MID-NINETIES BUDGET CRISIS

Having overcome the financial stringencies of the mid-1970s, the college enjoyed seventeen consecutive years of balanced budgets—until 1992. Several reasons accounted for the sudden budgetary problems. One was the rapid growth in financial aid; eighty-two percent of Juniatians need college assistance. Other factors included the large number of Hilltoppers studying abroad, interest on new college loans, increases in medical insurance premiums, sustained major dormitory renovation, and lower enrollment for eleven years. Then, in August 1992, a fourteen-percent cut in state support for higher education removed over ninety thousand dollars from the revenue side of the budget. Student enrollment that autumn totaled 1,030.

Historically at Juniata, a strained budget developed when personnel costs (e. g., salaries, benefits, etc.) exceeded fifty-eight percent of the total outlay. In the spring of 1993 personnel costs had reached sixty-two percent, but the trustees capped that spending at sixty percent. President Neff now turned to the old Strategic Planning Committee for recommendations to bring the "budget back in line." The committee's charge: keep all college-wide compensation below $9.9 million. (The operating budget for the 1992–93 fiscal year had been twenty-four million dollars.) The deadline was April 15. In the area of academics the recommended solutions included immediate reductions in the music department, elimination of the theatre POE, and, by July 1994, termination of five other faculty positions. Also, some services were "out-sourced"—the bookstore, as noted, and health care (to J. C. Blair Hospital). The college cut the support staff by six persons—and two more by July 1994—and reduced the number of part-time employees.

These emergency measures did not suffice to end the budgetary woes. The executive committee of the trustees, meeting on February 25, 1995, projected a budget deficit of $1.8 million for the coming fiscal year. It challenged the administration to further reduce costs and present the trustee board with a balanced budget by the 1996–97 school year. In early April the president called a mandatory meeting of all non-union employees. Warning that Juniata, as a private college, "is struggling for survival," Neff went on to talk about decisions to cut back on counseling services and to reorganize the career planning and placement office and the development office. For the faculty, as noted earlier, there would be no pay raises for one year, even for those promoted. The administration and its staff would likewise be subjected to a wage freeze. These fiscal-reorganization decisions reduced the budget deficit to $850,000. Several budget problems persisted for the next two years before the administration could project a $20,836,000-balanced, but tight, budget for the fiscal year 1997–98. By then the student enrollment had increased to 1,177.

Looking for alternative sources of revenue in the course of its financial stress, the administration resorted to a rather novel compact for a liberal arts college of Juniata's national stature. In 1997 Neff invited DuBois Business College (DBC) to establish a branch campus on College Hill. The president saw this venture as an economic boost for Huntingdon County as well (he was, by virtue of his college office, a member of Huntingdon County Business and Industry, Inc.). The privately owned business school, its main campus located in DuBois, eighty miles northwest of Huntingdon, was founded in 1885. DBC offers associate degrees in a variety of business programs. Operating out of a college-owned house across from the Stone Church, the school shared afternoon and evening classroom space in Good Hall. The joint venture, however, only lasted until January 1998. Because of a dramatic surge in enrollment, DBC purchased the old borough building at 10th and Moore streets and relocated there, its current branch quarters in Huntingdon.

By the time of the DuBois Business College-Juniata entente, however, the administration had been following an endowment-spending policy adopted by the trustees in October 1987. It is similar to a system used by many well-managed colleges. In Juniata's case, the policy originally provided that spending from the Endowed Pooled Investment Fund in any given year be equal to five percent of the moving average of the last five years' market value. The intent of the policy is to create a more predictable endowment income for use in the budget. The five percent figure in 1987 was seen as intentionally conservative, permitting reinvestment of income and striking a balance between present and future needs. For the fiscal year 1997–98 the trustees increased the expendable average from five to 5½ percent and, for each of the two years since, to six percent.

THE TRANFORMATIONS CAMPAIGN AND TRUSTEE BENEFACTION

The Century II Campaign (CIIC) reached its goal of twenty million dollars by November 30, 1987, more than thirty months ahead of schedule. During the Eighties Juniata would raise twenty-one million dollars, doubling its fund-raising performance of the Seventies. President Neff advised the trustees in the fall of 1990 that Juniata would need to triple the efforts of the 1980s in the coming decade. On May 1, 1993, a budget crisis bedeviling them, the trustees accepted the challenge and voted to undertake a thirty-million-dollar comprehensive capital campaign: endowment ($9 million), facilities and campus modernization ($8 million), education programs ($9 million), Juniata Fund ($4 million).

The college's most ambitious fund-raising leap ever, it took the name "Transformations: The Campaign for Juniata." The label betokened a metamorphosed Hilltop that would carry it into the twenty-first century with "state-of-the-art" instructional and residential facilities. Its kickoff took place in the coming October, its conclusion projected for June 1996. Short of their goal at that date, the trustees extended the campaign until September. That month Vice-President Donald Moyer triumphantly reported that campaign gifts and pledges had exceeded expectations; $36,581,389 had been raised. Forty-six trustees (and their spouses) over those three-and-a-half years contributed approximately six million dollars, or twenty-two percent of the total. Three husband-and-wife trustee couples each gave a million dollars or more: the John Dales, the William von Liebigs (two million), and the Klare Sunderlands. A trio of trustees and their wives committed a half million dollars or more: the Dale Detwilers, the William Swigarts, Jr., and the Robert Wagoners.

TRANSFORMING THE CAMPUS

In January 1990 the executive committee of the board of trustees recommended to President Neff the advisability of engaging a campus planner. That person's charge: to put together a ten-year master plan of renovations, siting of new buildings, and landscaping with a view to the needs of the twenty-first century.[28] The college signed a contract with Cho, Wilks, and Benn of Baltimore in December. President Neff appointed an advisory committee, drawn from every constituency group on the Hill, to work with David Benn, the campus planner. By May 1991 the consultant's prospectus was ready, presented to the board, and approved. Eight years later, under President Thomas Kepple, the transformation of College Hill, as blueprinted by the master plan, was finally completed.

Renovation of residence halls, however, began immediately. Except for the Cloister, built in 1928, the six other main-campus dormitories dated to the Fifties and Sixties. All of them badly needed to be restored. But modernizing the seven dormitories meant a great expense—many millions of dollars more than it had cost to build them. North Hall, for example, was built for three hundred thousand dollars in 1955, then refurbished for $1.7 million in 1992. The college spent two million dollars to restore the Cloister to its original architectural charm, inside and outside. Five years were given to residential renovation, 1991–1996. Several other buildings got lesser reconditioning attention.

William Swigart and his wife Patricia—each to be elected to a three-year trustee term in the late 1990s—moved the transformation program along with two timely gifts. Their half-million-dollar pledge made possible a new wing and extensive renovations to the admission house at 18th and Moore streets. The Martinson Group, an architectural firm from Easton, Pennsylvania, patterned the remodeled house after a similar building at Susquehanna University. The college broke ground for it in April 1995, dedicating the new facility as the William E. Swigart, Jr. Enrollment Center on May 3, 1996.

The Swigart's second gift expanded the main campus and transformed the local geography. In 1995 they deeded to the college the Winton Hill property, a four-acre plot adjacent to the pottery shed along Cold Springs Road. This unanticipated transfer of land opened welcomed options for the master plan: additional parking spaces to replace those lost once 18th Street was closed and sorely needed sports areas. The Martinson Group drafted the landscaping plan; the outcome put in motion a swarm of heavy earth-moving machinery. The old farmhouse had to be razed, the swale in front of it filled, and the high knoll on which it stood graded into two split-level playing fields. The project, completed the fall of 1999, gave passersby on Cold Springs Road a panoramic view of J. C. Blair Hospital nestled into the western flank of Lion's Back.

The Winton Hill project was only one of several major transformation measures begun under Neff's presidency but completed under that of Kepple's—most notably the revamping of Carnegie Hall and the Brumbaugh-Oller House adjacent to Swigart Enrollment Center and carrying out the main-campus quadrangle/ring-road concept.

ALUMNI: THEIR NUMBERS GROW; THEY GIVE; THEY GAIN A NOBELIST

Victor Rini graduated from Juniata in 1970. He returned in 1995 for his class's twenty-fifth reunion and afterwards was moved to write a letter explaining "why Juniata College has remained such a large and positive influence on my life." He wrote of the "communal unity" Juniata graduates feel, traced to an "empathetic spirit" that pervades the Hill and cannot be described in the college catalog. Then he declared, "Whatever the reason for it, this spirit which fosters such strong ties among alumni of all ages is rare in modern society. But at Juniata it is found in abundance."[29] That is precisely what education-journalist Loren Pope had reference to in his 1996 book, *Colleges That Change Lives*. He noted how so very "eager" Juniata alumni are "to help and to contribute financially."[30]

At the brink of the new millennium, alumni numbers have surpassed the 11,500 count. For the seven years 1992 to 1999 their record of giving totaled $24,067,739. This represents sixty percent of all gifts for that span of time. Much of the credit for this performance properly belongs to those who headed the alumni affairs office during Neff's presidency. Dorothy Lehman Hershberger, appointed by Dr. Binder, served as the alumni's chief until 1993 (although she remained on call in an advisory role for a couple years more). Non-Juniatian Kenneth Dudzik, director of development, took over her work until he left, in 1995. Lynanne Schaeffer, his replacement in 1996, got a new title: Director of Alumni Development. She is a 1983 Juniata graduate and stood at the alumni helm at the century's turn. Meanwhile, three alumni directories were updated in the post-Binder years—1988, 1993, and 1999—making eight in all since the first one in 1935. Overseas-alumni produced a directory of their own in 1995. It was completed in time for the Tenth European Alumni Reunion, held in Brussels, Belgium.

In 1993 the annual-support program was rechristened The Juniata Fund. Beginning in the mid-Eighties, the program, originally for alumni only, was expanded to include other sources of philanthropy, much to the benefit of budget making. From 1995 on The Juniata Fund has received more than a million dollars a year ($1,271,256 for 1999). From a low of thirty-one percent participation rate for 1987–88, the level of contributing graduates increased to forty-four percent ten years later. Twice alumni giving to the annual-support cause reached forty-five percent—1990–91 and 1993–94—far above the national average. This type of added-on funding first got a full-time promoter with the appointment of Nan Hunt in 1988, releasing the director of development from personal involvement. Her successors were Elizabeth Dahmus (1990–93), Nancy Hess (interim, 1993–94), George Mayley (interim, 1994–95), and Joseph Scialabba (1995–99).

Class fund agents (CFA) number among a large group of volunteers that have remained close to the college. Historically, their role has been to challenge classmates, year after year, to "pay back" Juniata for the quality of undergraduate education they received on the Hill. Their dedication has helped keep their alma mater perennially among the nation's school with the best alumni-giving records. Some CFAs have performed a long time: for example, William Swigart, Jr. for a half-century, Henry Gibbel for over four decades, and Jack Buckley, Janet Claycomb Dodge, and Patricia Janusz Shreiner, each for over three decades.

Not to be ignored have been the presidents of the Alumni Association. In the one hundred fourteen years between 1885 and 1999, ninety-seven men and women have headed that national post (some for more than one term). But not until 1971 did a woman hold the presidency. There have been nine others in the years since, Dr. Jodie Monger (Gray) the 1998–99 incumbent.

As noted in other chapters, alumni have always volunteered their time and expertise in other ways. In the fall of 1988 the recruitment office created the Juniata Admissions Volunteers (JAV). This program, among other things, maximizes alumni participation by using Juniata graduates in a widening geographical search for prospective students. Some JAV members are late-1940s' graduates, like Jack Buckle and Orville Dore; others of the current one hundred twenty-four volunteers come from every decade after that. In another area of volunteerism, Darwin Kysor (Ph.D.), who became director of career services in 1997, has a list of over four hundred and fifty alumni to draw upon in helping to counsel and place Juniata seniors as they look to future employment. Also, as of 1995, former Juniatians participate in five-year cycle departmental reviews. They engage in similar periodic evaluations of certain administrative offices.

Kirstin Adams Brandt, a 1992 graduate now living in Denver, Pennsylvania, is not yet an alumna volunteer, but she holds another distinction: she is a sixth-generation Juniatian. Her family's Juniata roots go back almost to its beginnings, to great-great-great grandfather William Schrock, 1882–83. One of her Hilltop alumni ancestors was the Rev. Lewis Knepper, who became field secretary for the college (1926–29), alumni secretary (1929–30), and a trustee (1919–34).

Harold Brumbaugh—who came to be known as "Mr. Juniata" because of his ageless work with alumni—captured playful international media attention in 1993. For sixty-one years, as a student and then an administrator, he had lived in a residence hall on campus. He moved back into Cloister Hall in 1936 three years after graduating, staying there for thirty-two years. He relocated to an apartment in Terrace Hall in 1968. Then in September 1993, at age eighty-two, the long-time dormitory dweller went to Westminster Woods, a Presbyterian retirement community on a wooded knoll off Cold Springs Road, one of its first residents. *U. S. A. Today*, in both its national and overseas editions, featured Brumbaugh's story. *The Chronicle of Higher Education*, television and radio stations, and newspapers all over the country also deemed it a newsworthy human-interest story.

Another alumnus, a much younger man, also made international news: Juniata's first nobelist, William Phillips. The 1970 graduate shared the physics medal jointly in 1997 with two other scientists for their work in developing methods to cool and trap atoms with laser lights. His doctorate from MIT, Phillips is employed at the National Institute of Standards and Technology in Gaithersburg, Maryland. A devout churchman with a dynamic personality and ready sense of humor, the nobelist is quick to praise the professors he studied under at his alma mater, those in the humanities no less than those in the sciences. He does, however, single out Dr. Wilfred Norris as having been a major influence on him in the study of physics. To show his intellectual indebtedness, Phillips obtained a ticket for his former Hilltop mentor to attend the prize ceremonies in Stockholm, Sweden. The Nobel Laureate, recipient of the Alumni Achievement Award in 1998, was the speaker at Juniata's 120th commencement the next year.

JUNIATIANS AND THE WANING TWENTIETH CENTURY

The last decade or so of this century has not conferred any label on college-age young people. Some social observers have suggested the Y-Generation, but this nomenclature has not taken hold. Researchers at UCLA's Higher Education Research Institute, however, have turned up disturbing data that does place a stigma on the twentieth century's latest student generation. They found college freshmen in the fall of 1995 shockingly impassive about social issues and political reform.[31] Only 28.5 percent considered keeping up with political affairs important, an all-time low, compared to a high of 57.8 percent in 1966. Few freshmen cared about "influencing social values" (38.2 percent) or "cleaning up the environment" (22.5 percent). Only 33.4 percent thought it critical to promote "racial understanding." And even less—twenty-three percent—planned ever to participate in a "community action program." This is a sobering profile, but it hardly characterized the mentality of Juniatians as the 1900s faded into history.

Robert Neff greeted a student body of 1106 his first fall; the enrollment numbered 1204 his last year in office. During his twelve-year tenure the cost for room, board, fees, and tuition increased from $11,800 to $22,460. That was not out of line with what was happening at peer colleges in Pennsylvania. Financial aid made a similar dramatic increase, so that by 1997 one hundred percent of all freshmen showing need received help. The average financial-aid package of all students determined to have need amounted to $15,088 by the late Nineties.[32] Overall, about eighty percent of Juniatians get some kind of funding assistance at the present time. And Juniatians have an exemplary history of repaying their federal loans, it should be said. They have a mere .04 percent default rate while fellow collegians nationwide, according to a 1999 report, cheat the government at a rate of 8.8 percent.[33]

Historically, most students on the Hill were first-generation collegians. That is no longer so true; still, in the year 2000, about twenty percent of Juniatians fall into the first-in-family category. In the fall of 1997 fifty-six percent of Juniata students were women. Interestingly, in recent years, women make up about sixty percent of the freshman chemistry class. Wrote Loren Pope of this fact, "Juniata has an outstanding record of inspiring women to become scientists and doctors."[34] As in the past, many Juniatians come from rural areas. Although the student body in 1998–99 hailed from thirty states and twenty-three foreign countries, seventy-six percent claimed the Keystone State as home ground. The average combined SAT scores of unconditionally enrolled freshmen rose from 1059 in 1989 to 1154 in 1998. (The national average in 1996 was 1016.) Juniata continues to recruit standout high-school graduates each year. Twelve valedictorians and six salutatorians enrolled in 1998, members of a freshman class with an average 3.67 GPA on a four-point scale.

At Juniata, students tend to stay and get their diplomas. In the ten-year period 1987–96 the year-to-year retention rate for freshmen averaged 83.9 percent. For sophomores and juniors the percentage was 90.6 and 90.4, respectively. Of some 250 colleges at that time, many in direct competition with Juniata, not one had a retention rate as high as eighty-four percent. Juniata graduated 70.1 percent of all first-time freshmen that matriculated between 1987 and 1992. Nationwide, the graduation rate for all colleges was thirty-five percent, for private colleges sixty percent.[35]

Though diploma-minded, most Juniatians, as this history has shown in chapter after chapter, do not share the blasé attitude of latter-day collegians vis-à-vis social needs and civic duties. In fact, the latest curriculum purposely underwrites the virtue of a social conscience. A Service Learning course offers up to four hours credit for volunteer community involvement. Students also participate in service activities through three primary clubs: Circle K, Habitat for Humanity, and JC Outreach. Many of the other student clubs and organizations (there are seventy-four in 1999), however, also have demonstrated a sense of social awareness.

Of the big three, Circle K's annual activities are already a matter of record. JC Outreach, organized in 1990, provides volunteer services to the Red Cross, Special Olympics, and the American Cancer Society. Habitat for Humanity is one of Juniata's largest clubs, with over one hundred members in 1998–99. It began as a community service project initiated by a group of seniors in 1988, then was chartered two years later. The club's goal is "to eliminate poverty housing in Huntingdon County through service and education."[36]

Its members hold the annual fund-raising Shack-A-Thon in which they sleep—during a January night—in cardboard boxes to dramatize the cause of homelessness. Over spring break Juniata's Habitat for Humanity has, since 1996, participated in the "Collegiate Challenge." This is an event that involves more than 6,500 students, who travel to as many as one hundred and forty host sites to build homes each spring. Thirteen Juniatians spent the 1999 spring break in Columbus, Georgia, doing construction work.

Since 1987, Juniata has made its athletic facilities available to the Area J Special Olympics for various sports events. Circle K organized the first track-and-field contests for the mentally retarded athletes, at that time held in May. Then, on a weekend in February 1988, the college hosted the Pennsylvania State Special Olympics Volleyball Competition. William Huston (M.Ed.), director of programming and conferences, was responsible for bringing the tournament to College Hill. This event was unique because it was the only state-level tournament completely supervised by students. Juniata was host again in 1989.

Now, however, Juniata reserves a mid-October weekend for Special Olympians just from Central Pennsylvania. The occasion includes both indoor and outdoor games as well as a closing awards ceremony. For several years JC Outreach made the autumn classic one of its prime projects. Today the responsibility for it lies in the hands of Jenell Patton, coordinator of community service. More than a hundred students volunteer their time to this athletic weekend every year. Volunteerism of this kind, the *Juniatian* once observed, demonstrates that Juniata students care about "the growth and development of others."

Other service-minded groups of a recent origin, to add a few more examples, include the Conservation Club, Emergency Services Club, Environment Science Society, Health Occupations Students Association, Student Health Advisory Committee, and Voice! Activists for Human Rights. The Conservation Club, since 1994, participates in PennDOT's "Adopt a Highway Program." Its clean-up route is a couple-mile or so stretch of nearby Petersburg Pike. Beginning in 1990, as noted, Homecoming has been set aside as the day to honor not a queen, as the tradition had it, but a group of students chosen to receive Community Service Awards. These Juniatians are seen as exemplifying the highest ideals of helping others.

Needless to say, the campus ministry has never hesitated to witness for the "love your neighbor as yourself" motif, whether that neighbor is here or abroad. That message was heard as often from Chaplain Torin Alexander, an African-American, as from Andrew Murray, whom he succeeded in 1994. Murray that year had made the shift from the chaplaincy to full-time professor in the peace and conflict studies program. Alexander, educated to be a physicist with a master's degree in that field from the University of California, received a divinity degree from Union Theological Seminary. He soon became a regular visitor to the two local state correctional institutions for the Quaker-founded Pennsylvania Prison Society.

In 1987 the Good trustees began funding the J. Omar Good Protestant Campus Minister as the chaplain's adjunct. Community service became a major interest for those individuals who have filled this position. Recent college graduates, they have come to College Hill from an organization known as the Coalition for Christian Outreach. The Coalition, among other programs, prepares its members to serve on college campuses in a variety of roles for short periods. The Good campus ministers have been Chris Noyes (1987–89), David Satterlee (1989–92), Roger Johnson (1992–95), and Jenell Patton (1995-present).

Roger Johnson came expressly to devote his stay to organizing various types of community-service projects. Today, Jenell Patton, besides her Good ministry, functions as the college's community service coordinator under the provost. The campus ministry office, through the Service Learning course, sponsors a domestic trip and an international trip in alternate years. Work-project travels have taken students to New Mexico, Haiti, and inner-city Pittsburgh. The 1999–2000 schedule has Juniatians going to Honduras.

The campus ministry's annual CROP meal helps keep a community service-minded College Hill also aware of world needs and issues. So does the current curriculum's accent on multiculturalism and study abroad. Robert Neff arrived on campus to find anti-apartheid sentiment still at a boil from the previous spring. The fall editions of the *Juniatian* in 1986 ran a series of thoughtful articles on South Africa's racist stigma. They were written by reporters like Alayne Unterberger, Jeffrey Buttimer, Amy Coursen, and John Deppen. On October 10, 1986, a group of concerned students held a candlelight vigil on the lawn in front of Oller Hall. That Friday occasion marked National Student Anti-Apartheid Protest Day.

On September 10 of the following year the Human Concerns Committee, chaired by John Deppen, sponsored "South Africa: Voices from Juniata." The program commemorated the death of Steven Biko, who was beaten to death ten years before on that date. Again, as in the spring of 1987, the students petitioned to see the college's list of investments. This time the board agreed to open the portfolio only to discover that Juniata *did* have investments in South Africa. The next month, at the regular fall board meeting, the trustees voted "to invest in companies in South Africa only if they are signatory to the Sullivan Principles."[37] (This code—a voluntary pledge by U. S. firms—banned any investments other than those in black-owned firms or companies applying the fair-labor standards.) The board's integrity impressed students and quieted the anti-apartheid voices.

To be sure, however, Nelson Mandela's freedom in February 1990, after twenty-seven years in prison, got prominent front-page reportage in the *Juniatian*. Ella Stofile, a native South African student on campus, wept in joy at the news. The release of the black South African activist also prompted an editorial by Coeditor Michele Johnson. What could Nelson Mandela's liberation possibly mean to Juniata students? she asked. Her answer: By simply being aware of "injustices in our world...we are that much closer to a solution."[38]

Other world developments also roused responses on campus. American photojournalist Catherine Bauknight presented a slide show on the massacre in Tian'anmen Square, Beijing, China. The June 3 blood bath (250,000 killed, according to Red Cross reports) quashed a demonstration for democracy by Chinese students.

Operation Desert Storm, the code name for the Persian Gulf War to free Kuwait from Iraq's occupying army, captivated the interest of Juniatians in the early months of 1991. American history courses, especially, devoted class time to the "high-tech" blitzkrieg conducted by the armed forces of the United States and twenty-seven other nations. Most students supported this country's dominant role in the campaign. "Support Desert Storm" banners went up and the American flag appeared at dormitory windows; there seemed to be a resurgence of patriotism on campus.

But not all on campus that cold, wet night of January 16, when the Middle East War broke out, applauded the involvement of U. S. troops in the military action. A group of one hundred fifty students, faculty, staff, and Huntingdon residents marched around College Hill and downtown in silent protest. Sixteen Juniatians traveled to Washington, D. C., on January 26 to join 75,000 other pro-peace demonstrators.

Many more Juniatians opposed the School of Americas, a military training base for soldiers from South America. In April 1997 Father Roy Bourgeois, founder of the School of Americas Watch, spoke to an enthusiastic audience on campus. His visit was co-sponsored by the Spanish department and the Baker Institute. Father Bourgeois declared that "the school was responsible for training some of the worst human rights violators in Latin America, and the world."[39] For years critics called it the "School of Assassins."

Father Bourgeois, a Maryknoll priest and Vietnam veteran, had worked for five years in the slums of La Paz, Bolivia. His stirring speech set Jeremy Souder, a Student Government freshman, to drafting a petition to send to Sen. Arlen Specter (R-PA). It urged Specter to support closing the Fort Benning, Georgia, training site. Souder collected 365 signatures of students, faculty, and staff; he presented the petition to the senator in person when the lawmaker visited Huntingdon on April 3. The army still operates the controversial SOA, but its curriculum has changed to reflect the democratization of Latin America. Nevertheless, protesters could still be found on College Hill in 1999. Late November, three professors and twenty-six students joined twelve thousand demonstrators at Fort Benning in peaceful lamentation for the dead.

As noted in the previous chapter, the Hilltop's concern for world relief gave rise to the CROP meal each April. A quarter-century old in the year 2000, it has become a bona fide tradition on the serious side. As for other kinds of traditions, a random poll of students in November 1991 ranked Springfest as the most favored one. Mountain Day and Madrigal Dinner tied for second. Storming of the Arch came in third. This September ritual dates to the late Forties, when World War II veterans, who lived in the Cloister, began asserting a kind of campus territorial imperative. Those were the days of "Frosh Week," a time given to initiating freshmen into college. Soon after the war Cloister-dormed GIs decreed the Arch off-limits for the dink-pated during that week. One postwar year, a group of freshmen rushed the passageway and fought its way through. That ended all hazing activities for the year. Hazing has long since been outlawed on campus, and for a time the assault on the Arch lapsed. Then in the mid-1960s, for some reason, the practice came back.

Sometimes the storming got very physical and caused injuries. In 1995 the administration forced the men to take certain precautions, or else the tradition would end. The Rugby team has for some years guarded the Arch, and it was ruggers Michael Streicher and Steven Van Mater who negotiated the safety measures. Participants must now also pay a one-dollar fee that goes to a campus or town charity. In 1996 the stormers included not just fresh*men* but also fresh*people*; for the first time women (five) joined in the male-dominated tradition.

Two new annual events, begun in 1988, became popular during the Neff years. One of them, Lobsterfest, has endured uninterrupted and seems destined to traditionhood. It is a Labor Day-weekend celebration to usher in the new school year, held on the Sunderland/Sherwood lawn. Everyone on College Hill is welcome to feast on seafood, listen to live music, and enjoy all the company. But the other event, a mid-winter formal dance, died in its adolescence. It began as the Presidential Ball, but in 1996 the president's office turned over the responsibility for planning the event to the student affairs office. At that time, also, the venue shifted from Baker Refectory to the ballroom of the Huntingdon Elks Lodge. The last dance there was in 1998. (The Kepple administration currently has no plans to revive an annual dance-and-formal-dress occasion.)

A few other quasi-traditions have sprung up—like the Rugby team's decade-old Pig Roast at Lake Raystown's picnic grounds—that do not get entered into the college's official calendar. Happily, the Neff era saw the revival of an old seasonal custom that had gone ignored since the 1970s: campus decorations at Christmastime.

The *Juniatian* frequently printed pieces on the history of popular traditions during the Neff presidency. But a shortage of reporters continued to dog the paper perennially, which was no new story. Some years, recruiting sports writers was the biggest headache for the editors-in-chief. Interestingly, all the chief editors were women except two. (The trend has been for a coed to head the paper.) One of the exceptions was Christian Brosz. When he put his name on the masthead in 1991, he declared, "I want to turn this place upside down." In his valedictory article he wrote that his editorials had "created strong emotions." His combative editorship also produced a first-rate college weekly. But he, too, admitted: "We still don't have enough writers to cover all the events that go on around here." By the mid-Nineties editors began to rely more and more on articles by the College Press Services and syndicated cartoons to fill out the pages. Early in 1995 the *Juniatian* went on a bi-weekly publication schedule, which it still followed in the millennial year.

Beginning in September 1991 and on through April 15, 1995, the *Juniatian* ran a weekly feature titled "Killing Time." A frequent contributor was Mumia Abu-Jamal, an inmate at the Huntingdon State Correctional Institution. He had been sentenced to death in 1982 for killing a Philadelphia police officer. The conviction and death-row appeals of the onetime Black Panther and popular radio reporter became a cause célèbre the world over. Even Pope John Paul II pleaded for a retrial. In October 1999 the United States Supreme Court turned down Mumia's appeal; the Pennsylvania governor set an execution date for the upcoming December, later court-stymied.

Why the *Juniatian* chose to invite Mumia to write a regular column is not clear. A sidebar in the September 19 issue implies sympathy for the inmate's appeal, noting that his trial was "rife with irregularities." What is intriguing about the Mumia case is that it involves Philip Bloch, a Huntingdon Vietnam veteran and 1993 graduate of Juniata. While a student, Bloch befriended the incarcerated Philadelphian through his work with the Pennsylvania Prison Society. A few times Bloch contributed articles to "Killing Time" in place of Mumia. After graduation, he became a vocal defender of his prisoner friend.

Then Bloch himself made sensational news in the summer of 1999, giving Juniata publicity in the process. In a *Vanity Fair* magazine interview and on national television he revealed that Mumia had once said "yes" to him when asked if he regretted killing the police officer. Why did Bloch go public? Because, he said, of his "disgust" with the tactics of the convict's defenders, who vilified the policeman as "some rogue cop." This heaped calumny on the man's wife and made *her* the "underdog," he felt.

The *Alfarata*, like the *Juniatian*, is a repository of changing history on the Hill. A change for the *Alfarata* itself came in the form of "high tech" early in the Neff years: Taylor's Vision Electronic Publishing System. The Vision Series software now enabled the staff to produce all aspects of the yearbook on computer—write articles, design pages, compile indexes, and record income and expenses. Computerized yearbook technology made it easier for the editorial staff to expand the textual content of the *Alfarata*. More than one class had reason to be pleased with their editions, each a fine specimen of photojournalism and its pages interspersed with lively commentary.

The *Alfarata* had long had a permanent office, but *Kvasir*, Juniata's literary magazine, did not. Its staff finally moved into one the academic year 1997–98. At that time *Kvasir* compiled a tribute issue, which reprinted some of the best works submitted by students since 1964, the periodical's birth year. In 1991 the staff introduced *Kdavir*, an alternative magazine featuring "political and social satire, dark humor, bizarre thoughts, and twisted philosophies." As it turned out, the publication's name phonetically predicted its prompt demise.

By contrast, WKVR, Juniata's largest club, has hardly been moribund. After nearly two years of waiting and hoping, the station received good news from the Federal Communications Commission (FCC) in October 1987: the campus would be back on the airwaves soon. In April 1986 the FCC had notified WKVR it would have to vacate its current 103.5 frequency because Huntingdon's WRLR 106 FM wanted to move its transmitter. College Hill now tunes to 92.3 FM, a frequency that makes WKVR a Class A station, fixed forever on the dial. In the fall of 1997 a thirty-thousand-dollar, two-hundred-foot tower behind Ellis Hall replaced the eighty-foot one on the roof of Ellis. This giant steel structure propelled the aging station into the twenty-first century. It increased the broadcast area of Power 92 to a distance of sixteen miles from campus. The station continued to transmit from the basement of Ellis Hall.

Very much alive, too, was Student Government, although its leaders sometimes despaired over its lack of vigor. SG twice reworked its constitution (1989 and 1996), not counting an amendment or two, in attempts at reform. Two major problems bedeviled the organization: "sleeping members" and financial conundrums. The 1996 constitution got at the problem of senatorial nonfeasance by ceding more power to the executive officers while reducing that of the Senate. No constitution change could solve the other problem. As the *Juniatian* pointed out in May 1998, the plethora of clubs created a budgetary nightmare for SG. More than seventy chartered and unchartered clubs—one for every seventeen students—made adequate funding a selective process.

Apathy remained a perennial problem; in 1993 only one candidate ran for president, two for vice-president, and none for treasurer. Nevertheless, SG was led by a dedicated and competent cadre over the Neff years. They kept the campus well informed of perceived problems—from parking space to bigger recycling bins, from lack of playing fields to better campus safety and security, from physical plant needs (like handicap ramps) to causes of student stress, from food service to the college mascot.

Residence halls, represented by twelve senators, often cropped up on the SG agenda. The umbrella dormitory renovation project, beginning in 1991, brought the topic of triple rooms to the fore again. Sixty freshmen tripled up that fall. In September 1996, because of reasons more than construction, over one hundred twenty freshmen had two roommates.

SG could do little about overcrowding, but it did take the initiative on another dormitory sore point: residence hall pay phones. In early 1992 SG footed the bill for installing two phones each in Tussey-Terrace, South, and Lesher. Now students could make free local phone calls, the college picking up the monthly tab.

Three years later, however, the college began installing the Rohm phone system in every dormitory room on the main campus. All the old pay phones were pulled out (one for every forty students), each room now to be billed separately. A restive SG was partly behind the departure of Hallmark Management, provider of campus food for twenty years, in the fall of 1992. In its place the college engaged the Marriott Corporation (now Sodexho Marriott), the current food service.

Student Government had nothing to do with the new smoking policy that went into effect on March 9, 1992. The administration took that initiative, prompted by increasing publicity about the harmful effect of second-hand tobacco smoke. President Neff appointed a Smoking Policy Task Force in September 1991 that conducted a campuswide survey. Eighty-eight percent of the respondents indicated they were non-smokers, but only thirty-two percent favored a smoke-free campus, while forty-nine percent supported designated areas for smokers. The new policy prohibited smoking in classrooms, laboratories, hallways, restrooms in public areas, and twelve buildings. No restrictions applied to self-contained faculty offices or certain administrative and staff offices. Other designated smoking areas included the south alcove of Baker Refectory and a section in Totem Inn.

Much more controversial, as might be expected, were attempts to further curb the alcohol policy. Binge drinking had reached dangerous proportions on college campuses by the 1990s, resulting in fatalities. A study released by Harvard's School of Public Health that decade identified forty-three percent of college students as binge drinkers—a total of three million. The study also indicated that a third of all collegians enter college with binge-drinking problems.[40] To binge means to drink five or more beers (four for women) at least once in a two-week period. Students do this "not to get silly but to pass out," said Penn State President Graham Spanier.[41] Spanier sparked a binge awareness campaign in the fall of 1999, leaguing up with one hundred thirteen college presidents. The campaign featured a full-page advertisement in as many as fifteen national newspapers.

At Juniata, so the 1997 *Alfarata* reported, eighty-two percent of the student population consumed alcoholic beverages. Twelve percent drank only liquor, fourteen percent only beer, seventy-four percent drank both. Men imbibed more often than women. On the average, the *Alfarata* mentioned, Juniatians spent as much as twenty-five percent of their income on alcoholic beverages. Nationwide, to put these data into context, students spent $5.5 billion on alcohol each year, more than they spent on all other non-alcoholic beverages—and books—combined.

The Committee on Alcohol Study and Education (CASE) continued to keep College Hill informed about alcohol abuse. Each year it sponsored events such as pre-Madrigal non-alcoholic cocktail parties and "Punchbowl," a campus game show about the detrimental effects of drinking sprees. Every fall CASE also observed National Collegiate Alcohol Awareness Week, instituted in 1983. Juniata's policy to allow chartered clubs to furnish alcohol at lounge parties, as noted in the previous chapter, was changed in the fall of 1985. A court decision that year imposed social-host liability in cases where drunken drivers led to accidents. (The decision applied to minors, but neighboring states were considering cases where people were over twenty-one.) Therefore, Juniata clubs were forbidden to serve intoxicants, thus safeguarding the college from being considered a social host. The 1985 policy, however, did not restrict individuals from bringing their own beverages to the lounge parties.

In July 1988 the Pennsylvania legislature passed a bill that expanded the definition of furnishing alcohol. This new definition went beyond serving inebriants to minors; it also made liable anyone allowing underage persons to drink on their premises or property. Juniata College felt it needed to rewrite some parts of its alcohol policy in order to be in compliance with the state law. The administration made the following major changes: (1) only those students twenty-one or older may drink or possess alcohol on campus; (2) anyone having a party becomes the social host; (3) no kegs will be allowed in student rooms or dormitory lounges; (4) students must carry proper identification and show it when asked by college personnel. Along with the rewritten drinking policy came stiff sanctions for violators. No college, large or small, has worked harder than Juniata to educate its campus about responsible alcohol use or to provide alternative activities.

Juniata continued to do well also in recognizing student academic achievement. The Neff administration added thirteen more awards and prizes to a list that numbered thirty-six in 1999. The first one was the Accounting Plaque, awarded in 1988 to a student excelling in that discipline. The next one was the Class of 1989 Endowed Award, a senior-class gift that honors an outstanding junior involved in co-curricular activities with a GPA of 3.0. The Merck Index Award, of 1990, goes to an outstanding chemistry student planning to attend graduate school. An award was set up by the American Institute of Chemists, in 1990, to go to a senior in chemistry, biochemistry or chemical engineering. Three were new in 1992: The Art History Award; Friends of the Library Award; and the Donna Richie Van Antwerp Biology Award (a memorial to its namesake, an alumna of 1972). The three added in 1994 included the Juniata College Creative Writing Awards (in poetry and short fiction), the Native American Culture Award (to a junior who fosters interest in Indian issues), and the Tutoring Award (one to a writing center tutor and one to a peer tutor). The year 1996 introduced the Carroll C. Arnold Award in Communication that honors a renowned professor in that field. To honor the memory of a former member of Juniata's economics and business department, Dr. John Baker established the Herbert A. Miller Award in 1998 to be accorded a graduating senior interested in finance and business. (A pair of awards materialized during President Thomas Kepple's first spring convocation, both of them for budding chemists: The American Chemical Society Award in Analytical Chemistry and the American Chemical Society Award in Organic Chemistry.)

Academic recognition came to Juniatians in other, off-campus ways. Diversity, though not very successful in terms of numbers, did attract some minority students of solid scholastic ability. Mary Fortson, a Mount Union native, was one of only forty college students in the nation (only two were Pennsylvanians) to receive a prestigious Minority Leaders Fellowship for the summer of 1989. She spent ten weeks in Washington, D. C., in an intensive educational experience. Active in a long list of campus, church, and community activities and a member of the Juniata College Honor Society, Ms. Fortson made the registry of *Who's Who in American Colleges and Universities,* the *National Dean's List*, and *Outstanding College Students of America.* She became a high-school English teacher in Hagerstown, Maryland.

A pair of other minority students achieved academic recognition in the Neff years. Lynn Merritt-(Nixon), from Baltimore, was named to the first Health Care Financing Administration's Outstanding Scholar Intern Program, in 1992. Only twelve college students met the rigorous standards, which included a 3.5 GPA for all undergraduate courses. Miss Merritt, who majored in urban planning, was involved in a number of campus activities. With a master's degree from the University of Michigan, she took up work in the profession in which she interned. Silver Spring, Maryland's Ayinde Alakoye received Juniata's second Minority Leaders Fellowship, for the summer of 1993. A member of the men's varsity volleyball team and student representative to the board of trustees, Mr. Alakoye also served as chair of the Multi-Cultural Planning Committee and president of the African-American Student Association.

Two more examples of exceptional academic achievement came in the persons of Susy Atkins and Jennifer Sill. Ms. Atkins of nearby Alexandria was one of ten recipients of the 1993 Pennsylvania Association for Adult Continuing Education Award (PAACE). The PAACE Award recognizes outstanding adult students in higher education. Ms. Atkins, a single mother, enrolled at Juniata early in the Program for Area Residents (PAR), graduating with a degree in communication. A stellar student, she worked various part-time jobs, was involved in several community activities, yet participated fully in campus life. She was instrumental in forming The Forum for adult students at Juniata. She now works in Harrisburg.

Pittsburgh's Jennifer Sill, a 1995 *magna cum laude* graduate in international studies/anthropology, was named a Fulbright Scholar that spring. The Juniata Honor Society member had spent the 1993–94 academic year studying at Philips Universitat at Marburg, Germany. With her Fulbright travel grant and teaching assistantship, she taught English in a German high school and did research on Germany's relationship to Eastern Europe after the fall of the Iron Curtain. She is now study abroad advisor at the University of Pittsburgh.

A variety of cultural events—drama, dance, vocal/orchestral music, lecture—continued to enrich Juniata's academic program. World-famous people spoke on timely topics. For example, in 1986 Betty Williams, Nobel Peace Laureate, talked about nonviolence and her work in Northern Ireland. Yevgeny Yevtushenko, the Soviet Union's most celebrated contemporary poet and political maverick, twice visited the campus, in 1987 and 1991. The latter year he spoke at commencement and received an honorary degree, the first ever conferred upon a foreigner by Juniata. Maya Lin, renowned for her funerary architecture and designer of the Baker Peace Chapel, gave the convocation address in October 1990. It was one of the shy artist's very rare public appearances.

Campus-generated cultural experiences abounded. Theatre arts, although the mid-Nineties budget plight threatened temporary cutbacks in its staffing, got energetic leadership from Doris Goehring (who retired in 1990); Ryan Chadwick,1988–94; James Casey (Western Illinois M. A.), 1991; Margaret Kelso (Carnegie-Mellon M. F. A.), 1994–97; and Andrew Belser (Virginia Tech. M. F. A.), 1997-present. A *Juniatian* review of a drama production in November 1993 averred: "No doubt Juniata College has a theater troop that any grad school (and some German Community theaters) would envy." At the cusp of the millennium, Andrew Belser said he wanted "to develop the role of the theatre to what it once was."

All Class Night—drama at a different level—had meantime reformed itself of the riotous conduct and salacious skits that almost ended its existence in the early 1980s. The passing of the century, therefore, found the popular comic theatrical acts a healthy tradition.

The music department faced a budget crisis of its own in the 1990s. But, like theatre, strong leadership gave it new life. A variety of musical opportunities—bands, ensembles, choirs—allowed students creative outlets at the new century's dawn. The Wind Symphony, directed by 1996-newcomer Diane Bargiel (Michigan State M. M.), played three concerts a year. The thirty-member group hosted the first High-School Honors Band in the academic year 1995–96. This invitation welcomed the best instrumental players from the New England Area to perform with the Wind Symphony.

Choral music has traditionally been the ambassadorial medium for Juniata. Joseph Figg (North Texas State Ph.D.) was choir director from 1984 to 1991. Under conductor Russell Shelley, Figg's successor, the music department created five choral groups: Concert Choir, Alumni Choir, Choral Union, Chorale, and Chamber Choir. The Juniata Chorale is comprised of singers from the other four choirs. The Alumni Choir is a group of thirty-some voices from among graduates, their spouses, and friends of the college. The Concert Choir, the traditional touring chorus, performed at some venerable venues under Dr. Shelley: Washington National Cathedral (twice), Chicago Temple, and, in New York, at St. John's and St. Patrick's cathedrals. One of only five college choirs invited to give a full program at St. Patrick's that year, the Juniata College Concert Choir performed for its largest audience ever. Both the touring singers and the Choral Union, which includes vocalists from the Huntingdon area, perform twice a year, once each semester.

Since the early Nineties Juniata choruses have been taking European tours— the Alumni Choir in 1993 (Germany, Austria, and Italy); the Concert Choir in 1994 (Germany, Austria, and Czech Republic); the Alumni Choir in 1995 (England, Scotland, and Wales); and the Juniata Chorale in 1997 (Eastern Europe). Conductor Shelley hopes to establish a biannual overseas touring schedule for the Concert Choir. To that end, Mr. Alfred Hockley, in 1998, created the H. Alfred Hockley Concert Choir

International Tour endowment in memory of his father. Alfred Hockley, the father, a 1929 graduate, had been a member of the Juniata Glee Club. The Hockley Fund helps make the international performing experience affordable to choir members, who must bear some of the travel expenses.

The cultural life of the campus was immensely enriched on April 7, 1998. On that date President Neff officially accepted the Worth B. Stottlemyer Collection of Art. It was donated by 1951 alumnus Dr. Quayton R. Stottlemyer, a retired Du Pont research chemist, who inherited the private art collection from his father. The largess consists of about four hundred paintings, prints, drawings, and portrait miniatures. They represent the works of renowned American and European artists spanning the seventeenth through the twentieth centuries, many of which have never been seen in public.

Robert Neff experienced many happy moments as president, like the one in April 1998. But he also had to deal with two tragic losses, one at the beginning of his presidency and one toward the end. Both involved the accidental deaths of two popular students. Senior Carolyn Stambaugh was killed on the Baltimore Beltway the first week of the 1986–87 academic year. She was run over on the median strip by a motorist while she sat outside her car waiting for someone to come and repair a flat tire. She was a four-year starter on the women's volleyball team and Student Government treasurer. Juniata held a memorial service for her on Sunday, August 31, in Memorial Gymnasium. The Student Government along with her family, friends, and volleyball teammates, endowed an athletic award in her name; it goes to a woman athlete and student leader with strong academic credentials. In April 1988 two birch trees were planted in her memory in front of East Houses, where she had lived for three years.

On Friday, January 17, 1997, the Juniata College community gathered in Oller Hall at a memorial service for Scott Orr, a junior mathematics/chemistry major. He had died one week before Christmas of accidental asphyxiation. At the memorial service Mrs. Nancy Orr said of her son: "I am so grateful he came here; he loved your school."[42] A black gum tree grows outside Cloister Hall in his memory, planted by his dormitory friends. Scott Orr's death was the first one on the Hilltop campus in Juniata's history. Only a handful of students have died while enrolled, most as a result of vehicular accidents off-campus.

After over a year of silence, carillon bells again rang out from Founders Tower on Easter Sunday 1998. A generous gift from the Swigart Foundation and some funding by the Stone Church congregation set the chimes to ringing anew. The Westminster Old English Bells system is directly connected to the organ in Stone Church.

FAREWELL TO THE INDIAN MASCOT

Athletic teams, as noted in Chapter 7, have been known as the Juniata Indians since 1925. The student newspaper used the name in a sports story and it caught on, an unofficial dubbing. The first person to publicly question the appropriateness of the Indian mascot was President John Stauffer, in 1972. In a letter to the *Juniatian* that April, he expressed concern about the racist implications of the college's nickname.[43] The recent civil rights movement had made Americans more aware of prejudicial stereotypes. At that time a student or professor would attire himself in fake buckskin and a headdress at football games and do a war dance to animate the fans or celebrate a touchdown. Drums provided tom-tom rhythmical beats.

While Stauffer did not believe this kind of mimicry necessarily depicted Native Americans in a "negative way," he thought it time to seek a new name. Other colleges and universities, such as Stanford and Syracuse, were currently dropping their Indian nicknames. Stauffer announced his appointment of a special committee for the purpose of choosing a new mascot. Student Government, however, never pressed the matter of name-change, nor did any person on the Hill become vocal in support. So the renaming issue faded away. Nevertheless, the profile of an Indian head did not appear on football helmets or team uniforms after 1972.

Then in the fall of 1988 the student Human Concerns Committee put the issue back on the campus agenda. Sophomore Christopher Forney, the committee's spokesman, wrote a short piece for the *Juniatian* titled "Does Juniata Need a New Mascot?" He said he was offended and "shamed" to see Juniatians wearing T-shirts at an intramural championship game depicting a hatchet-wielding Indian doing a war dance.[44] But the letter sparked no outrage, although the Diversity Task Force raised the mascot issue in 1989 as part of its deliberations and kept the matter alive.

President Neff was of a strong mind that the mascot was inconsistent with the educational mission of the college to espouse diversity and multiculturalism. A poll by Student Government in November 1991, however, showed that eighty-two percent of the campus population favored keeping the Indian mascot. (At that time seventy campuses in the United States still went by the Indian sobriquet.) Student leaders feared the administration was taking unilateral action in adopting a new mascot. Neff appeared before Student Government that November, giving assurance his office would make no decision without student input. He made plain, nonetheless, that he was personally committed to a mascot change. "No matter how much of an effort is put forth," the *Juniatian* quoted him as saying, "there is still a negative portrayal."[45]

Student Government created a committee that fall to look at possible solutions that would "appease" opponents of the nickname and end the conflict. But before the committee could report back, the faculty, by over a two-thirds vote the second week of March, advocated a change in the mascot. Two months later, the Alumni Council did the same thing, unanimously. The student Mascot Committee finished its four-month investigation in the period between the faculty and Alumni Council votes. Its report to the Senate won total acceptance. Among other things, the report recommended that Juniata retain the Indian mascot and, on a two-year trial basis: (1) offer a general education course on Native Americans; (2) set up a scholarship in the field of Native American Studies (which the college already had) and an annual award recognizing a student who furthers better understanding of Indian life and culture; and (3) publicize the fact that Juniata will not portray the mascot in a disgraceful way. The students based their argument on the premise that the college's name derived from an Indian word; therefore, they reasoned, keep the present mascot but depict it in a form that reflects institutional pride.

Firm in its stand that the Indian symbol must go, the administration made no move to compromise. In effect, the college had no mascot. It is surprising how many students, some of them nonathletes, felt bereaved without an identifiable institutional nickname. Brenda Stark in her editorial for the January 28, 1993, edition of the *Juniatian* bewailed "the way in which our mascot was taken from us." Students should be the ones to take the initiative, she argued, not the administration. She lamented: "I was proud to be called a Juniata Indian, but now we are no longer the Indians, except perhaps in our hearts." Kathleen Vedock, an art history/premedicine major and a star swimmer, agreed. She said, "Before they took away the Indian mascot, a new one should have been decided on."[46]

At its May 1, 1993, meeting the trustees directed the president to appoint a composite committee to consider what the new mascot should be, and "to determine ways that Native American culture can be preserved on campus." President Neff did so in October. The committee established certain criteria relative to the genius of the surrogate mascot. The Indian replacement should not symbolize any one racial, ethnic, cultural, or religious group, nor be based on gender. Otherwise, it could reflect strength, courage, bravery, heritage, geography, or fauna of the region. Students and alumni were invited to submit nominations.

By early 1994 the Mascot Committee had narrowed a long list of suggested names to five: Eagles, J-Hawks, Muskies, Rattlers, and Wolves. Every one of the five choices had some relation to the American Indian roots of Central Pennsylvania. Students voted in Ellis Hall on February 16 and 17; the alumni had until March 8 to return their ballots by mail. The tally showed that 3,700 votes had been cast, the nickname of Eagles getting the majority (no actual count was ever given).

The final decision rested with the board of trustees, meeting on Saturday, April 30. Before going into executive session, the trustees invited two alumni to express their objections to adopting a new mascot: Albert Blough, a 1958 graduate and onetime Senate vice-president, and Robert Sill, Class of 1959 and stellar fullback on the Tangerine Bowl team. The trustees then took a written ballot, twenty-nine voting to ratify the Eagle as Juniata's mascot. A motion that the adoption be made unanimous failed; three voted no and one abstained.

The selection of a mascot for the college may seem like a rather trivial matter. But few issues, if any, on College Hill had ever stirred such deep emotions—anger, sadness, disappointment, even alienation. Many believed the college had succumbed to the "fad of 'political correctness' for its own sake," as Prof. Paul Heberling, Juniata's anthropologist and authority on the history and prehistory of the Juniata Valley, put it. Charles Goodale, first baseman on Juniata's 1938 baseball championship team, a self-confessed "proud Juniata Brave," and the donor of the annual baseball award, denounced the "biased" ballot that excluded the name Indian.

President Neff addressed the alumni's mixed reaction when, in announcing the board's decision, he implored: "It's time to begin the healing process and recognize that the Board has acted in the best interest of the institution in the mission to educate students. We invite all those associated with Juniata College to cherish the past and join us in celebrating the future."[47] A scholarship and annual award, as noted, remain in place. Most pre-1994 Hilltop athletes have since made their peace with the new mascot, but, like *Juniatian* Editor-in-Chief Brenda Stark, they remain Indians in their hearts.

TRANSFORMATION OF ATHLETIC FACILITIES

Robert Neff proved to be every bit Frederick Binder's peer in the presidential support of Juniata sports. He not only transshaped the campus, but he also gave hearty endorsement to upgrading and expanding athletic facilities. Centre County Judge Charles Brown, Jr. persuaded fellow trustees to give attention to these matters at their May 3, 1986, meeting. At its spring meeting the following year, the board approved projects to construct new stands at College Field and resurface the Jefford Oller running track with all-weather composition material. The board also made plans for improvements in Memorial Gymnasium and the Raffensperger tennis courts. It appointed colleague Charles Knox, then-head coach of the Seattle Seahawks professional football team, honorary chairman of the one-million-dollar fund-raising campaign. In 1988, on a Hurricane Hugo Homecoming weekend, the college dedicated the 3,500-seat Knox Stadium and the re-laid Oller track in a drenching rain.

The last major athletic project, totally unforeseen, involved re-landscaping the ten-acre Winton Hill property along Cold Springs Road into two new varsity playing fields. The gift of ground in 1995 from William and Patricia Swigart provided one site for men's and women's soccer, the other for women's field hockey. Also quite unexpectedly, the athletic-improvement program had acquired Nautilus weight-training equipment in the spring of 1988. Thanks to a lead from trustee F. Samuel Brumbaugh, Juniata purchased a defunct Nautilus club's apparatus for one-third the original cost. Trustee Brumbaugh, though one of the trustees to vote against the Eagle mascot, never wavered as a fan of Juniata athletics. In 1997 he and his wife Martha contributed three hundred thousand dollars to an enlarged fitness center named in their honor. The state-of-the-art 5,470 square-foot workout area features fifty-five pieces of modern strength, cardiac, and freeweight/bodyweight equipment. Said Athletic Director Lawrence Bock, "From an athletic standpoint, we are viewing the facility as a tool to fully develop our athletes...From a student, faculty, and staff point of view, it is a knockout facility and a great place to spend time, get fit, stay healthy, and be strong."[48] The Samuel and Martha Brumbaugh Fitness Center put Juniata on a short list of the finest Division III facilities in the nation.

JUNIATA COLLEGE SPORTS HALL OF FAME

The idea of a College Hill hall of fame for athletes dates back nearly half-a-century, to William Engel, director of publicity and sports information. It did not come to fruition, however, until the mid-1990s, when Vice-President Donald Moyer began to urge a recognition program of this kind. He once said, "There are many colleges and universities that have some form of an athletic hall of fame." And because Juniata had "such a strong athletic history and tradition," he thought it natural that College Hill should have one, too.⁴⁹ Part-time SID Joseph Scialabba (1988–96) took the initiative to bring about William Engel's dream in 1995.

According to bylaws, enacted June 27, 1995, the purpose of the Sports Hall of Fame is "to honor men and women who have made outstanding contributions to the athletic program." Ten members make up the selection committee: director of athletics, sports information director, and representatives from the coaching staff, faculty, J-Club, and alumni. The bylaws specify three categories for eligible candidates: (1) Juniata athletes (graduates and non-graduates, living or deceased), who have earned two or more varsity letters, their eligibility to start ten years following their class year; (2) athletic support personnel (coaches, trainers, managers, etc.), who are eligible after ending service to the college or, if the service came in a student role, ten years following the nominee's class; and (3) friends, special contributors, or others who have been associated with Juniata athletics for ten or more years. The third category, to date, includes the late Mailand McIlroy, former sports editor of Huntingdon County's *The Daily News;* William Engel; the late trustee Joseph Good and his wife Jane; and two deceased popular oft-honored alumni, Cyrus and Isabelle Caulton.

There have been five classes of inductees since 1995. In all, the five classes honor sixty-five persons, most of whom have been mentioned in the narrative account of athletics in this history. Fourteen of them are women. Plaques representing each individual, giving pertinent data, are displayed in the Hall of Fame room located in the Alumni Lounge of the Kennedy Sports + Recreation Center.

ATHLETICS: VOLLEYBALL'S TWO DECADES ON THE SPORTS THRONE

The eighty-six-year-old Middle Atlantic Conference, the nation's oldest small-college conference, was reconstituted for the 1993–94 academic year. The presidents from sixteen colleges and universities agreed to a plan that provided for two eight-member leagues, Commonwealth and Freedom. A championship playoff between the two league winners would now determine the overall MAC titleholders in most sports. William Berrier, Juniata's then-athletic director and MAC president, helped devise this proposal for conference champions. Neither MAC restructuring nor a new college mascot detoured volleyball from dominating the Hill's varsity scene during the Neff era. That was true no matter what the team's gender might be once the men began varsity play in 1990.

Between 1986 and 1997 the women won 495 times and lost 73 times. Coach Lawrence Bock, since 1977, had coached his "Ladies" to a 785-131 mark. Six times the America Volleyball Coaches Association (AVCA) voted him Region Coach of the Year in the 1980s and 1990s. The AVCA, twice more after 1984, named him National Coach of the Year (1989 and 1993). *The Volleyball Monthly/ASICS* selected him as its national coach in 1988, 1991, and 1993. Then in 1994, Bock joined fourteen others as the inaugural body inducted into the Pennsylvania Volleyball Coaches Association Hall of Fame. (His entire 1981 and 1993 squads are also inductees.)

The Blue and Gold won eighteen straight MAC championships in his career by the end of the Neff presidency. And every year since 1981 "Larry's Ladies" had competed in the NCAA Division III Tournament. As semi-finalists, they were runner-up in 1993, 1996, and 1997, four times in all since 1981.

A varsity sport with the phenomenal won-lost record of women's volleyball obviously had a host of stellar players. Since 1980 sixty-one Indians/Eagles had been voted MAC all-stars, forty-five of them beginning with the 1996 season. Twenty times a Juniatian made first team AVCA All-America since 1986, seven others the second team. The long list of first-team stars included third-time Beth Hoppel (Barnett), 1986 and 1987; Catherine Miller (Gilkey), 1987; Melina Selby (Sterner), 1989; Rhonda Bygall, 1989; Christy Orndorff (Osmun), 1991, 1992, and 1993; Larissa Weimer (Crum), 1991; Heather Blough (Pavlic), 1992, 1993, and 1994; Nicole Firestone, 1993; Jacquelyn Rebert (Wolfgang), 1995; Robin Diehl, 1996; Kristin Hershey, 1997 and 1998; Melissa Myers, 1997; Colleen Carver, 1998; and Carrie Zeller, 1998. Kimberly Hannig was named a MAC All-Academic for the 1991–1992 season. Nine of these All-Americans also made the Asics/Tiger list: Hoppel, Rebert (twice), Selby, Weimer, Blough (three times), Firestone, Orndorff, Diehl, Myers, and Hershey. Three from the above two All-America rolls hold Juniata volleyball career records: Firestone (2,021 kills and 4,554 attacks), Bygall (620 blocks), and Blough (6,331 assists).

Men's volleyball entered the varsity fold in 1991, starting with a cast of club players. Larry Bock coached the squad for five years and logged a 78-79 record. Strong recruiting classes quickly turned his squads into champions. Playing as an independent in the Eastern Intercollegiate Volleyball Association (EIVA), Juniata captured the Association's championship three straight years, 1992–94. (Men's volleyball is not a varsity sport in the MAC.) When Bock replaced William Berrier as athletic director in 1995, Dennis Hohenshelt took over the head coaching position for the 1996 season. His team won eighteen and lost seven, which is the program's highest single-season winning percentage (.720). Ryan Patton's turn came next, the present coach. Patton, an alumnus who starred in the middle for Juniata from 1992 through 1994, responded by leading the Eagles to a 33-26 overall record for the 1997 and 1998 seasons. His 1997 squad played to a third-place finish at both the EIVA title games and the inaugural Molten Division III National Championship.

Several Juniatians made EIVA Division III All-Star teams since 1992: Maurice Thomas (1992); Mark Knaub (1992 and 1995); Jeffrey Fischer (1993); John Baranowski (1994); Eric Gerko (1994); Christopher Fazio (1994, 1995, 1996, and 1997); Timothy Shawaryn (1995, 1996, 1997, and 1998); Roderick Kirby (1998); Andrew Kurl (1998); and Kevin Moore (1998). The men volleyballers often schedule Division I and II schools, and Fazio was tabbed first-team All-East at the Division I level in 1996 and 1997, while Shawaryn copped first-team honors in 1998. Fazio first received national notice in 1995 and 1996 when *Volleyball Magazine* named him a Small College All-American. The same publication crowned him Division III Player of the Year in 1998.

Football, the sport from which volleyball stole College Hill perennial thunder, put together a 50-72 twelve-year tally during the Neff presidency. Four coaches had a turn at the gridiron helm. Robert Ash left in 1988, winning twenty-one and losing eight over his last three years. His nine-season record was 51-36-3. Dr. Bradley Small, his doctorate in physical education from Springfield College in Massachusetts, moved up from defensive coordinator to replace Ash. As football's sixteenth mentor, he coached three seasons (12-17-1). Coaches seventeen and eighteen were alumni: former defensive coordinator Christopher Coller from 1992 to 1994 (6-23-1) and Thomas Gibboney (after his nine-year 60-32-6 tenure coaching the Huntingdon Bearcats) from 1995 to 1997 (10-19-1).

Despite football's mediocre record, Juniata produced thirty-five MAC first-team all-stars. Defensive back Mark Dorner won the Conference's MVP award in 1987, the year he also earned even a more prestigious honor: AP first-team Little All-America. Dorner also garnered Kodak's All-America College Division first-team listing, as had Steven Yerger, an offensive lineman, in 1986. Three players won Division III all-star accolades from Hansen's *Football Gazette*: split end Michael Cottle in 1988, defensive back Brian Giachetti in 1991, and defensive lineman Chad Zaring in 1996. Zaring, twice, in 1995 and 1996, took MAC plaudits as Defensive Lineman of the Year. Two Juniata records were set during Neff's time, both against Widener but nine years apart. In 1988 Keith Watson kicked a fifty-yard field goal and in 1997 Matthew Eisenberg returned a punt eighty-six yards. As student-athletes, offensive lineman Joseph Hobolinko and linebacker Christopher Rosenberry were named to the MAC All-Academic team, for the 1991–92 season.

The baseball team since the mid-Eighties has taken a spring trip south (one year to California). Now other MAC nines head toward warmer climate for pre-season practice games, taking away any early competitive edge. Still Coach William Berrier's squads collected 157 victories against 191 losses and one tie. Berrier himself twice merited MAC coach-of-the-year title (1990 and 1991). His 1991 unit won a record twenty-two games (22-8) and shared the MAC Championship with Moravian College, a play-off unable to be scheduled. Twelve Juniata diamond standouts made the MAC all-star team one or more times for the dozen years of Neff's presidency. Michael Reed, a MAC first-teamer, also made Conference All-Academic honors in 1989 and 1990 as well as being on the GTE/CoSIDA academic list for 1989.

Basketball could boast no coaches-of-the-year, but several hardcourt stars earned first-team MAC honors. Dan Helm resigned in 1990, his teams winning ninety-one (including two forfeits) and losing 131 over nine seasons. Two years before resigning, Helm took his charges on a second European trip—to many of the same places where they had played in 1983. James Zauzig, Helm's assistant and head football coach at Tyrone High School (1977–85), became basketball's twenty-fourth pilot. His teams went forty-four and 102 over the next six years.

Rick Ferry succeeded Zauzig in 1996, winning ten and dropping thirty-eight through the 1998 season. Ferry came to Juniata from Susquehanna University after serving seven years as an assistant coach with the Crusaders program. Graduating from Susquehanna in 1985, the 6'5" four-letterman in basketball holds an M. B. A. degree from Ohio University. Ferry took his 1998–99 Eagles on an overseas playing trip of his own—to England and Scotland.

Juniata's major winter sport put forth a clutch of its own stellar performers, on the floor and in the classroom under Helm-Zauzig-Ferry coaching. Four Juniatians were chosen to MAC's first team: guard Wayne Paul (1987); forward Jay Nicholson (1992); guard Casey Craig (1996); and forward Timothy Lonesky (1998). As for Hilltop career records, four roundball stars have left their marks: guard Shawn Habakus (1986–88) in assists (449) and steals (149); forward Craig Instone (1991–94) and forward Robert Sharkey (1992–96) in blocked shots (78); and guard Casey Craig (1993–97) in three-point field goals (177). As students, forward Joseph DeBlase netted All-Academic kudos from both the Middle Atlantic Conference and CoSIDA in 1989, as did forward David Welker in 1992.

Women's basketball experienced a succession of seven different head coaches from 1986 to 1999: Kathleen Quinn (M. S.), 1986–89 (17-29), Kelly Sparr, 1989–90 (10-13)—while Quinn was on maternity leave; Quinn/Stanley Risser, 1991–92 (Quinn was 3-3 and Risser was 12-4); Risser, 1992–95 (31-33); Amelia Fort (M. A.), 1995–96 (4-18); Fort/Joseph Scialabba, 1995–96 (Fort was 0-20 and Scialabba was 0-3); Jennifer Reimer (M.Ed.) 1997–98 (5-16); and Amy Buxbaum (J. D.), 1998-present (5-16). The won-lost tally in those years added up to 100-158. The 1991–92 team won seventeen and lost eight, the second best season since the 24-4 feat of the 1979–80 women's Blue and Gold.

College Hill fans watched some of Juniata's greatest female hardcourt athletes of that period. One of them, Susan Grubb, is already in the Hall of Fame and a couple others are well on their way to it. Grubb (1984–88) is one of only two women (joining Nancy Zinkham) in the Juniata top ten for career scoring, rebounding, steals, blocked shots, and assists. She is the all-time leader in career steals (292) and blocks (182). Twice, in 1986–87 and 1987–88, she made All-MAC and was Northwest Section MAC Player of the Year in 1987–88.

Annette Hoffman (1989–93) is certainly Hall of Fame-bound. She holds a mass of single-game, season, and career marks. On the career level, her 2,269 points (24.1 average per game) ranks first by nearly a thousand. She stands second in blocked shots, third in rebounding and three-point field goals, and fourth in steals. Moreover, Hoffman also registered ninety-two ten-point games, sixty-six twenty-point games, twenty-five thirty-point games, and three forty-point games. Her 744 successful field goals and 723 free throws rank tops. She was a MAC all-star four times, twice named its Player of the Year (1991 and 1992). For the 1991–92 season she earned Kodak's All-American laurels. Her teammate, Stephanie Haines, also won All-MAC mention in 1992.

Two other women basketball stars of those years left impressive career records. Forward Kerry Stefanko (1992–96) remains on top in career three-point field goals (140), sixty more than her closest rival. Point guard Dana Patete (1988–92) is number one in career assists (560), two hundred sixty more than runner-up Nancy Zinkham. She made the MAC All-Academic team for the 1991–92 season.

One of the women's turf sports—field hockey—reached some record heights despite a few rough seasons. Huntingdon high-school teacher Kathleen Quinn (1986–91) coached that sport to a 42-32-8 mark, while Assistant Athletic Director Jill

LaPoint (M. S.), 1992–97, led the women to a 49-51-2 tally. Caroline Gillich (1998-present), an All-American at Lock Haven University, posted a 9-9-0 mark her first year. Quinn's 1988 squad set a school record of twelve wins, tied by LaPoint's 1996 team. A bevy of field-hockey standouts of this period became MAC all-stars: Amy Oiler (1987); Jill Schadler (1988, 1989); Carolyn Sheedy (Seckinger)—1989, 1990, 1991; Joanne Thomas (1989); Amy Blough (1990); and Renee Rine (1992). Rine's career thirty-nine goals tied that of Kathleen McGowan (set in 1986–89). McGowan, besides being tied with Rine for career goals, also holds the record for most season goals (36). Nina Mathers (1993–96) set the standard for career assists (34). Mathers was selected a Division III All-American three years in a row between 1994 and 1996 from the South Atlantic Region. Jessica Emrich received the same honor for the 1996 season. President Thomas Kepple's inaugural year would see Juniata produce four field hockey MAC All-Academics: Allyson Kenyon, Melissa Ketrick, Candace Sanders, and Hope Woolcock. In addition, Kenyon, Sanders, and Woolcock were tabbed with Division III National Academic Squad honors from the College Field Hockey Coaches Association. In the category of on-field play, forward middlefielder Danielle Young was an All-Conference and All-Region pick in 1998.

The other women's turf sport—soccer—entered varsity ranks in 1994, bringing Juniata's athletic program to twenty teams that year, nine of them for women. There have been three coaches: Kimberly Severs (1994), Amy Fort (1995–96), and Donald Herlan (1997-present). The three seasons of Severs/Fort resulted in a trio of wins, thirty-one losses, and three ties. The Herlan mark through three seasons stood at 9-38.

As for male booters, this sport registered just one winning season since its varsity start in 1978. Men's initial soccer coach, Dr. Klaus Jaeger, posted a 24-120-7 record over eleven years. The team was co-coached in 1989 by Christopher Noyes, the J. Omar Good Protestant Campus Minister, and John Mumford, then a staff librarian, later head librarian. That squad won one and lost twelve. Since then Mumford has been head coach. His nine years at the soccer helm gave this sport a 50-115-10 mark through 1999. The 1992 team's record of ten and nine gave men's soccer its best season ever and its first .500 or better campaign. Future dentist Stephen Grater, in 1988, won MAC honorable mention. He was also named the Hill's MVP in swimming that year and garnered the John Blood Award as the senior student-athlete with the highest GPA.

Lady softballers, meanwhile, were mentored by a succession of five coaches over the thirteen seasons, 1987–99: Huntingdon businessman Richard Scialabba (1987–92), alumnus Michael Culver (1993–94), Huntingdon elementary-school teacher and former Juniata star female athlete Annette Hoffman (1995), Catherine Parker (1996–97), Richard Scialabba again (1998), and group therapist Betty Streightiff (1999). Women of the diamond won eighty-four and lost 182 under these coaches. Scialabba's dual stints notched fifty-one victories and seventy-eight losses. Three softball athletes earned special honors: Jennifer Wade went on MAC's academic honor roll in 1988 and, in 1992, Melissa North not only was a MAC honor student but also a GTE/CoSIDA academic winner, while Jodie Wise (Kormanski), team leader in six categories, was named a MAC all-star. In 1996 Lori Williams was elected an All-American Scholar Athlete by the National Softball Coaches Association.

The Oller track, its surface coated with a softer, composition material, and measured out in meters, was ready for use in the spring of 1989. With the 1990s, dual meets were phased out. That decade also saw no less than twenty-six records set by men and women thinclads. Alan Hartman remained the sport's coach four seasons into the Neff presidency, winning fifteen and losing twenty-six dual meets. Darien Hamilton coached one year, Scott Devore, three years (1991–93), Philip Riccio, three years (1994–96), Kevin Burke, one year (1997), and Jon Cutright, from 1998 to the present. Cutright, on the full-time staff of the athletic department, holds a master's degree from Ohio University, his alma mater. There he was a letter-winner in both cross-country and track-and-field. He began his career at Juniata, on a part-time basis in 1993, coaching the men's and women's cross-country runners. Beginning in 1994 Juniata began competing in multi-team invitational meets during the regular season, including one of its own. Since then, the traditional MAC championships cap the competitive events.

Male track-and-field athletes set eleven of the twenty-six new records and tied one. Their names and marks are as follows: 1991—Ray Shelley, the 100 Meters (:10.78); 1992—Joseph Kibler, the 800 Meters (1:56:25) and the 1500 Meters (4:08:9), Jeffrey Hetrick, the 5K (16:15:85), and Frederick Bayer, the high jump (6'9½"); 1993—David Prudenti, the 110 high hurdles (:15.20); 1998—Michael Kenawell, the 200 Meters (:22.50), Jonathan Long, the shot put (48'55") and the discus—tying Calvin Shoenberger's 1972 heave—(147'2"), and, in the 400-Meter Relay (:45.54), Michael Kenawell, Travis Frenay, Jason Falvo, and Joel Peppetti; 1999—Scott Hobbie, the 10,000 Meters (37:25.67).

Individual record-setters for the women's track-and-field program were, by year: 1992—Kimberly Wurth, the 800 Meters (2:19.5), and the 1500 (4:48.40), the latter time making her the MAC's champion in that event and the first gold medalist since Peggy Evans in 1985, and Heather Underwood, the high hurdles (16.25); 1993—Lisa Dechano, the discus (116'10"), and Gennifer Washington, the triple jump (37'4½") and the long jump (18'2½"); 1994—Bridgette Hoff, the 400 Intermediate Hurdles (1:08.98), and Angela Hazuda, the high jump (5'5"); 1996—Nicole Norris, the 10K (43:32.40); 1997—Amy Gladfelter, the javelin (142'3"), Lisa Mueller, the 400 Meters (1:00.31), and Casey Kline, the 3K (11:24.64). Angela Gessner, a long- and triple-jump athlete, captured no records but did get MAC academic honors in 1990 and 1992, and, the latter year, made the GTE/CoSIDA District II All-America Academic Team.

Three records fell in 1998. Melissa Myers heaved the shot a new distance (43'6"). As the MAC's number-one shot putter that year, she became the third gold medalist in Juniata's track-and-field history. And her sixth-place distance at the NCAA's Division III Championships made her an All-American. In relay events, Nicole Harris, Kristin Damico, Brandi Woy, and Rose Regan set the new time for the 400-Meter (:52.18), and Harris, Regan, Diana Coulson, and Kristy Wagner for the 1600-Meter (4:10.90).

Budgetary strictures in the mid-Nineties and the need to comply with federal Title IX regulations forced the Neff administration to discontinue five men's varsity sports. Beginning the fall of 1996, the college dropped cross-country, golf, swimming, tennis, and wrestling. President Neff, a great sports enthusiast, found the decision personally painful.

For women harriers, cross-country schedules, beginning in the mid-1990s, followed the same pattern as track-and-field: multi-team invitational tournaments instead of traditional dual- or tri-team meets. Irene Chamberlain turned over the coaching job to James Payne, a Huntingdon middle-school teacher and marathon runner, in 1987. His five squads won sixteen and lost twenty-three. The 1991 women went 7-2, the best since the Chamberlain-coached team ended up 8-2-1. Terry Fike coached in 1992 and then, as earlier noted, Jon Cutright took charge in 1993. Coach Cutright took special pride in the 1995 cross-country runners. The NCAA designated the entire unit as the All-Academic Intercollegiate Cross Country Division III women's team.

Male harriers won twelve and lost forty-three for James Payne (1986–1991) before Terry Fike (2-4) and Jon Cutright (1-11) did their coaching stints. Though erased as a varsity sport in 1995, men's cross-country made a comeback in 1999. Coach Cutright had to forfeit all three meets, however, because the team fell one runner short of the MAC-mandated five-man team minimum.

In golf, the coaching duo of Drs. Arnold Tilden and Duane Stroman lasted one year into the Neff era. Their 1987 team won four and lost eight. Stroman's solo season as coach in 1988 finished up four and two. College staffers William Huston and Joseph Scialabba paired up to handle the sport for the next three years, the Blue and Gold winning fourteen and losing ten. Then Scialabba (1992–94) alone coached until golf was dropped, going 1-3. The last years on the links were mostly played at tourneys. Not since Steven Stroup's 1980 gold medal at the MAC Championships had a College Hill golfer advanced that far.

Juniata's youngest varsity sport—swimming—took to the lanes in 1988–89. The Binder Natatorium pool is Olympic-size, but most MAC colleges measure in yards. Hence Juniata keeps the time of events in distances of yards, not meters. A series of coaches looked after the aquatic sport, directing men *and* women: Scott Preston (M. A.) from 1982 to 1991, Michael McMullen (1992), Nitisha Maclay (1993–94), Gregory Scallen (1995), Thomas Getz (1996–97), and, since 1998, Director of Residential Life Kathleen Collins (M. S.), an alumna swimmer. In the eleven years from 1988–89 through the 1997–98 season, the women swam to fifty-two victories and sixty-two defeats in dual meets (6-8 for the 1998–99 season). Both sets of teams went undefeated in the 1991–92 season—the women 13-0, the men 12-0.

Most of the times set by Juniatians in swimming's initial season, especially for women, have been broken. On the women's original team, Kristin Newman (Vaughn), Mary Strapple, and Pamela Ezdebski (Prim) each put their names on the Binder Natatorium record board in their specialties. Ezdebski remains the only Juniata record-holder from the earliest years—in the 1650y Freestyle (19:32.58) and the 1000y Freestyle (11:48.51).

Members of the undefeated 1991–92 women's team set several unbeaten times during their college careers. Rica Yamaguchi, a Japanese exchange student for the 13-0 season, has claim to two marks: 200 Breaststroke (2:36.76) and the 100 Breaststroke (1:12.20). Kathryn Bucklen (Bahoric) swam to a record time in the 50y Freestyle (:25.9). The best times in the five relay events also date to the triumphant 1991–92 season. Yamaguchi, Kimmie Cass, Bucklen, and Marie Sullivan hold the times in the 200y Medley (1:58.14) and the 400y Medley (4:19.04).

The late 1990s turned up a couple more record-setters. Kirsten Kenyon set two new standards in the 1997–98 season: 200y Backstroke (2:18.70) and 100y Backstroke (1:03.14). Teammate Rebecca Koch was also a two-mark performer that season: 400y Individual Medley (5:11.27) and 200y Individual Medley (2:20.89).

The names of the 1991–92 men's team appear on the natatorium's record-posted wall in all but three events. Earlier, on the original 1988–89 squad, two performers dominated the individual races. Stephen Grater, the soccer star and John Blood Award winner, set eight marks, while Bradley Newman recorded two. Grater still has ownership of one event: 100y Butterfly (:57.26). Newman, however, would be around to swim on the 1991–92 stellar team. One of his 1988–89 times still holds—100y Backstroke (1:07.57). But in 1991–92 Newman broke his three-year-old record in the 200y Backstroke (2:03.27) and Grater's previous time for the 200y Freestyle (1:53.50). Of that undefeated team, Mark Beekey boasts the most records—four: 1650y Freestyle (17:44.00); 1000y Freestyle (10:38.50); 500y Freestyle (5:11.14) and 400y Individual Medley (4:36.61). Alexander Shubert, a 1989–93 natator and like Grater a four-year letter-winner in soccer, also put his name on the record board more than once: for the 100y Breaststroke (1:15.14), the 200y Breaststroke (2:22.36), and the 200y Individual Medley (2:08.55). Brent Parsons, for 1991–92, swam to the best time in the 100y Freestyle (:49.78). At the 1995 MACs, Timothy Lipski, another 1991–92 swimmer, broke his earlier record in the 50y Freestyle with a time of :22.44. That performance made him Juniata's first gold medalist in men's and women's swimming. The 1991–92 time set by the quartet of Lipski, Shubert, Parsons, and Newman in all four relay events was never outswam: 800y Freestyle (7:29.78), 400y Freestyle (3:20.42), 200y Freestyle (1:30.67), and 200y Medley (1:42.71).

In the net game from 1987 through 1998, the women won forty-eight and lost seventy-seven matches under four coaches. Nancy Latimore left in 1986 with a 5-4 season and was followed by Ray Pfrogner (1987–95), Ernest Post (1996), Gregory Mahosky (1997), and Ann Houck (1998-present). Pfrogner led the women to a log of 35-56 wins and losses in his nine years at the tennis tiller. Houck, a Huntingdon businesswoman, had been women's tennis coach in 1997 and the first part of 1998, before moving up to the lead spot in midseason. She carried a 13-8 coaching record into the millennial year. The 1997 netters 6-1 mark in the MAC Commonwealth League was good enough for a first-place and a spot in the conference playoffs. Pfrogner's 1994 squad featured Anne-Valerie Horvil, an exchange student from France. A MAC champion, Horvil played her way to the finals of the Rolex/ITA National Small College Championship (Divisions II and III), held at the University of Central Oklahoma. She lost for the "Super Bowl" title, however, having compiled a 9-1 log in tournament play. Julia Thaler (Morrissey) gained MAC academic honors in 1989 and 1990.

When Coach Robert Ash left in 1988, Dr. Small did tennis duty through 1991, after which Klaus Jaeger took over until the final year of 1994. Over that eight-year span, the men won thirty-four and lost sixty-two matches. The 1986 unit went 10-3, tying the number of record wins set in 1969 but losing two matches more. Three men netters of the Nineties made the MAC academic honor roll: Michael Welker (1990) and the Benner twins, William and John (1992).

Wrestling, the fifth sport to be dropped from the varsity calendar after 1994, registered a 47-53-1 mark in the nine years from 1986. William Berrier, 25-28 in the period 1986–87 to 1991–92, compiled a tally of 119-195-7 as coach since the 1968–69 season. Huntingdon middle-school mathematics teacher Michael Simpson handled the grappling sport its last three years with a log of 22-18-1. Shad Hoover, at 158 pounds, set a season record for Juniata matmen of twenty-six wins (four losses) in 1991–92. This exceeded All-American Joseph Paskill's twenty-two victories in 1979–80.

Votary of College Hill sportsdom that he was, President Neff saw an institutional—and marketing—benefit to returning to a full-time sports information director. Not since the late 1960s had Juniata athletics been given exclusive attention in the public information office. But in 1997 alumnus Melvin "Bub" Parker came to College Hill for that purpose. A 1991 communication graduate and varsity golfer, he learned the SID métier at Lafayette University and Ithaca College.

Chapter 17

JUNIATA COLLEGE AT MILLENNIUM 2000

PRESIDENT ROBERT NEFF RETIRES

On March 21, 1997, Dr. Neff told the executive committee of the board of trustees that he planned to retire following the 1997–98 academic year. He said he had recently completed a questionnaire on college presidencies; nobody had served longer than twelve years, the length of time he had been at Juniata. "It is time to retire," he concluded. Neff's announcement was followed by that of Provost Robert Hatala's, which set September 1997 as his resignation date. Both Neff's and Hatala's revelations came within weeks of Vice-President Donald Moyer's decision to accept a position in California.

The Hill was shaken at the prospect of losing its three top administrators all at once. But in his March 28 remarks to the college community, Neff stressed that "the measure of an institution's strength is its ability to move through transition smoothly."[1] He said, "As I look at the human and financial resources of the college, I know we can look forward to the next century with confidence." Neff appointed economics professor James Lakso as interim provost to ensure a smooth transition in the academic program. Foster Ulrich, once Juniata's vice-president for development, was placed in charge of advancement and marketing, also on an interim/consultative basis.

Robert Neff's twelve-year presidential tenure transformed Juniata in many ways. The college's national academic reputation soared to new heights. Its endowment quadrupled to $62,316,000 (by July 1998). Its student enrollment was sharply on the rise. Its rebuilt, aging faculty emerged stronger than ever, as did its rejuvenated board of trustees. Its physical plant—from residence halls to athletic facilities to the Swigart

Enrollment Center—underwent a major overhaul without onerously mortgaging the future. In June 1998 Juniata's financial assets approached $100.7 million. The operating budget for 1997–98 totaled $20.8 million. The departing Neff administration also left as a legacy the campus master plan: a blueprint of the new century's College Hill.

Locally, off campus, Neff led the call for a retirement community in the Huntingdon area. His hope was to keep emeriti Juniatians close to the campus as they aged to the point of preferring retirement living over maintaining their family homes. He and other business leaders persuaded the Presbyterian Homes of the Huntingdon Presbytery to make a feasibility study apropos a retired-years facility. Juniata College offered ground it owned in Oneida Township, but the study found the site unusable. Instead, the study identified another location more suitable, a forty-six-acre tract of forest land on a ridge one mile from the college, off Cold Springs Road. There, in 1991, began the development of Westminster Woods. Neff did not hope in vain. Six former College Hill-connected persons pioneered as the first residents of the community. In 1999 the directory of Westminster Woods lists the names of more than twenty individuals once associated with Juniata.

In his last months as president, Neff forged a special bond with the Class of 1998, both facing their valedictory year. At the Spring Awards Convocation in April the seniors made him an honorary member of their class. This was a fitting tribute to a president who once said he wanted to be remembered an "an advocate for students."

The professoriate had accolades for Neff also. At his last board of trustees meeting, faculty representatives Norman Siems and L. Sue Esch thanked him for his "unfailing respect for the faculty." Added Dr. Esch: "[T]he current faculty is more peaceful than those of the past, morale is high, and there is a high degree of cohesiveness among its members."[2]

Juniata College gave the outgoing president an Oller Hall musical farewell on Sunday, April 26. The Presidential Gala included a commissioned work by Paul Halley, pianist and composer for the Paul Winter Consort.

THOMAS RAY KEPPLE, JR.:
JUNIATA'S ELEVENTH PRESIDENT

A presidential search committee, chaired by Henry Gibbel and made up of trustee, faculty, alumni, administration, and student representatives, began its work the spring of 1997. John Synodinos, who had been a consultant to the search process twelve years before, again served in that capacity. The national search produced more than ninety-three applicants from twenty-five states. Three candidates were brought to campus in November to address the Juniata community. The trustees made their decision at a special meeting in Harrisburg on January 23, 1998—Robert Neff's successor would be Thomas Kepple. Student Government had already made him *its* choice. A late September *Juniatian* issue proclaimed that, in only two months' time, President Kepple "seems to have won everyone's heart."[3]

Dr. Kepple, his fiftieth birthday four months past, came to Juniata in July from the University of the South in Sewanee, Tennessee. There, with the title of Vice-President for Business and Community Relations, he had been the chief business officer and town manager. (The university's ten-thousand-acre campus included the town of Sewanee.) Prior to that he had been provost at Rhodes College in Memphis from 1986 to 1989. At Rhodes he helped raise one hundred million dollars and at Sewanee $174 million. At the time of his election as Juniata's president, Dr. Kepple headed—and still does—a nationwide effort to develop a private prepaid tuition program that would lower future tuition costs for children and grandchildren of alumni. By the time he arrived on College Hill, twenty-five colleges and universities (now up to 175 members), with over 840,000 alumni and over thirteen billion dollars in combined endowment assets, had joined the effort. He spurned the presidency of a much larger institution to accept Juniata's invitation.

A western Pennsylvania native, Kepple graduated from Westminster College in 1970 with a degree in economics and business. He received his M. B. A. (1974) and Ed.D. (1984) from Syracuse University in higher education administration. He is a Presbyterian. His wife, Patricia, a Missionary Baptist, comes prepared to assume the role of first spouse, having served as the executive assistant to the president of the University of the South. A native of Nashville, Patricia—she likes to be called "Pat"—brings southern hospitality to Huntingdon. Juniata's new-millennium president, an avid swimmer and weekend artist, is a genial, unassuming man whose warm, sincere manner invites trust and loyalty.

A focused administrator, Kepple wasted no time in building on the momentum of the Neff presidency. He pushed ahead on the seven-million-dollar renovation program already underway in the fall of 1998. He confirmed James Lakso as permanent provost and filled two other vacant key administrative posts. He beckoned an old friend, John S. Hille, to join him as vice-president for advancement and marketing. Hille, a 1970 graduate of Rhodes College, had a highly successful career at both for-profit and not-for-profit institutions. In a high-school friend, Marsha Frye Hartman, a 1970 alumna, he found his director of The Juniata Fund. David Hawsey, however, resigned as enrollment chief in the fall of 1999. Michelle Bartol, director of admissions and a 1984 Juniatian, was designated his replacement pro tempore for the rest of the academic year. After one of the college's best recruiting years ever, she officially became the dean of enrollment in June 2000—Juniata's second female in that position. Earlier that spring Tristan S. delGiudice came from Centenary College in New York, to be in charge of the physical plant.

President Kepple's inauguration took place on Saturday, April 10, 1999, in Rosenberger Auditorium of Oller Hall. The ceremony featured artistic presentations ranging from choral and piano recitals to poetry readings. Kepple's inaugural address dwelt on the theme "Uncommon Vision, Uncommon Commitment." He personified this title in the life of James Quinter, Juniata's first president, a large portrait of whom was projected on a screen behind the rostrum as Kepple began to speak. In all, a series of twenty pictures were cast on the screen to illustrate the president's main points as the speech progressed. He spoke of Juniata's strengths, the exciting opportunities the twenty-first century will bring, and what plans the college has to make the most of those opportunities. But, as he stressed, in realizing "what is our uncommon vision and commitment for the future, we must also consider our historic mission." Thomas Kepple appreciates the values of a liberal arts college with a church-related genesis.

At the beginning of his address, the president noted a recent special resolution passed by the board of trustees. It recognized the four living wives of the college's past presidents for the "unselfish and inexhaustible service they have rendered over the years to enhance the life of the college." Thus did Elizabeth Ellis, Louise Stauffer, Grace Binder, and Dorothy Neff have conferred upon them the title of "Presidential Partner Emeritus."

WILLIAM J. VON LIEBIG: JUNIATA'S GREATEST BENEFACTOR

An eighteen-million-dollar gift from William J. von Liebig of Naples, Florida, in 1999, represents the largest monetary contribution in the history of Juniata College. A native of Huntingdon, Liebig (he reassumed his family's prefix "von" as an adult) began premedical studies at Juniata in 1941. World War II, however, forced him to put his college career on hold in the second semester of his freshman year. He became an alternate lead pilot with the Eighth Air Corps in England and flew twenty-five bombing missions to Germany, earning several medals. The operations officer to whom he reported was Lt. Col. James Stewart, the movie actor, who commanded the famous 38th Bomb Group.

Following his tour of duty, von Liebig did not continue his studies at Juniata. Instead, he attended the Philadelphia College of Textiles and received a certificate. In 1953 he parlayed that certificate, his practical experience, and studies at New York University, into an M. B. A. there. After a brief stint in textile sales and manufacturing, he went to work at the Meadox Weaving Company, which he bought in 1961 and renamed Meadox Medicals, Inc. The company grew over time, gaining an international reputation for its manufacture and distribution of vascular grafts and other devices to treat cardiovascular disease. Von Liebig holds thirty-three patents in the use of textiles as grafts, replacement of human arteries, and the technological advancement of heart valves, synthetic ligaments, and catheters. Seven million people are alive today, it has been estimated, because of Meadox Medicals, Inc.[4] He received a host of achievement awards during his career from organizations such as the American Medical Association, the New Jersey Institute of Technology, and the Textile Institute in England. His massive fortune came from the sale of Meadox in the mid-1970s—$448 million.

At that time Mr. von Liebig formed the von Liebig Foundation of Naples, Florida, to support medical research, primarily for the treatment of vascular and cardiovascular disease. In 1999 it exceeded $240 million. Over the years, he and his wife Suzanne expanded their philanthropic interests to benefit education and the arts, especially in their community of Naples. In 1991 Juniata honored von Liebig with the Alumni Achievement Award, and in 1995 the trustees elected him to the board. He was scheduled to receive an honorary doctor of science degree at commencement on May 9, 1999. He died, however, on February 21, a month before his seventy-sixth birthday.

Von Liebig had virtually no contact with Juniata College after his student days until he received its Alumni Achievement Award. How was it, then, that the college became a beneficiary of his massive wealth? A New York City source told Earl Kaylor that von Liebig was at heart a Pennsylvanian all his life, that subconsciously he had never lost his love for small-town Huntingdon, his boyhood home and where a younger sister, Edith, still survives. All it took was some special people to direct his interest to College Hill.

Among them were two widows, Phyllis Henry and Beulah Replogle Lesher Baugher (thrice widowed). They served as directors of the Mifflinburg Throwing Mill in Pennsylvania along with von Liebig. Their husbands—Jewett Henry and Chalender Lesher, both deceased Juniata trustees—had been partners with von Liebig's father and uncle from the time that textile company originated in Huntingdon. Both women took their deceased spouses' place as directors. In the late Eighties they began putting forward the idea that von Liebig think seriously about including Juniata in his will (he was already in declining health).

Another couple important in the Juniata-von Liebig story were Eugene and Miriam Brumbaugh, both alumni. Miriam, daughter of former physics professor Paul Yoder, had been a classmate of von Liebig's from kindergarten through high school (1928–41) and had enrolled at Juniata the same year. Years later, in 1988, after the Brumbaughs had moved to New Orleans, von Liebig, attending a medical convention, made a surprise social call upon them. This was the first of many visits, usually a dinner date somewhere in the Crescent City. Eugene Brumbaugh, as a member of the Alumni Council in 1991 (later an alumni-elected trustee, 1995–98), was asked to serve on its Honors and Awards Committee.

Aware of von Liebig's extraordinary career and enormous wealth, Brumbaugh pushed the name of his friend for the Alumni Achievement Award. It took some convincing, but he prevailed, abetted by Harold Brumbaugh. No one else on the Alumni Council knew anything about the former Juniatian. When von Liebig came to the campus in the spring of 1991 to receive the honor, the Brumbaughs flew from New Orleans to introduce him and his wife to Donald Moyer, a newcomer to campus. Thereafter, Moyer and Robert Neff kept in close touch with the wealthy entrepreneur, revitalizing his interest in the hometown college he once had attended for a few months. By this time, the stock market had escalated von Liebig's personal wealth to nearly three-quarters of a billion dollars. In declining health for some time, the philanthropist was within weeks of personally finalizing his largesse to Juniata when he died.

The college will honor its greatest benefactor by building the twenty-two-million-dollar William J. von Liebig Center for Science. The eighty-thousand-square-foot center will house the chemistry and biology departments. A portion of the humanitarian's gift will be used to fund other programs and faculty positions including the William J. von Liebig Chair in Biomedical Sciences. Some of it will also support collaborative research projects by faculty and students. Plans call for the new science center to be located across campus from the Cloister, between South Hall and Founders. (Oneida Hall will be razed.) The completion date is projected for the year 2002.

THE MILLENNIAL CAMPUS

By fall 2000 the Kepple administration had brought the campus master plan it inherited to completion. Several campus-wide open forums months prior had dealt with landscaping and architectural projects planned for the Hill. The Martison Group did an architectural rendering of the results. The plans created a true quadrangle at the center of the campus. Eighteenth Street was closed to vehicular traffic, replaced by a broad brick pedestrian walk. A "ring road" encircles the campus from 17th to 19th streets and Scott to Moore streets. The parking lot in front of the Kennedy Sports + Recreation Center, which is connected to the ring road, was paved over, dotted by concrete islands. In the opinion of President Kepple, "Visitors to Juniata College will [now] see a campus that more accurately reflects the nature of who we are as an institution."[5] The projected von Liebig Science Center will accentuate the quadrangle effect, with walkways linking all center-campus buildings. The Kepple presidency also put the finishing touches to the soccer/field hockey fields along Cold Springs Road with the fall of 1999.

Besides a campus with an enhanced appearance, the coming millennium brought two other changes to the Hill: program headquarters conversions. In the fall of 1999 the college finished renovating the Brumbaugh-Oller House, the grand brick colonial-style home on 18th Street next to the Swigart Enrollment Center. Renamed the Oller Center, it now accommodates the International Programs and the Baker Peace Institute. Earlier in September 1998, the college infirmary had been relocated from Lesher Hall to the former Stone Church of the Brethren parsonage on Moore Street, its new name the Health and Wellness Center. The move came about to relieve housing congestion.

MILLENNIAL POTPOURRI

Faculty

The Bookend Seminar, a colloquium instituted by Provost Robert Hatala in the fall of 1996, remains popular. The original purpose of the Seminar, one each semester, was to give a forum for faculty members to report on their sabbatical research and projects. Now these sessions are scheduled more frequently and need not be sabbatical-related.

Women swept the three faculty prizes in 1999. The two Beachley honors went to philosopher Janet Lewis for teaching, and for service to biologist Debra Kirchhof-Glazier. Dr. Kirchhof-Glazier joins Karen Rosell as the only two recipients of the junior faculty and Beachley teaching prizes. Biologist Jill Keeney (Washington University Ph.D.) won the junior-faculty teaching award. The previous spring, Norman Siems had acceded to the William J. and Zella B. Book chair in physics, long held by Wilfred Norris.

In the fall of 2000 the faculty met a new registrar, Athena Fredrick. She came to Juniata from Antioch College in Yellow Springs, Ohio, where she had served as registrar from 1996 to 2000. One of her important duties was providing leadership in the transition to a new integrated student information system.

While the von Liebig millions greatly strengthened the sciences, another large benefaction helped Juniata take a big stride into the booming field of information technology (IT). Trustee John Dale (Class of 1954) and his wife Irene, née Miller (Class of 1958), donated stock worth $1,556,250 in December 1998. The IT program, implemented that fall, added a full-time position to the faculty and an administration/faculty person to oversee its operation. Its liberal arts context at Juniata uniquely blends technical training with analytical and problem-solving skills. A second gift from the Dales, this one $2.7 million in December 1999, will enable the Kepple administration to add more IT positions. This new program was named in honor of the husband-and-wife donors in 2000.

From the perspective of the *Juniatian*, the Kepple administration seemed to be determined to move the humanities into the new century "with a strong foot and a bold stride."[6] A front-page article in November 1999 exulted: "Between the Pennsylvania Collegiate Choral Festival held in the fall semester and American College Theater Festival, Juniata College is taking a firm stand on its support of the Arts, and, at the same time, broadcasting this attitude to a national audience." The choral festival held its forty-ninth annual statewide competition in October 1999, brought here by Juniata Choir Director Russell Shelley, also head of the music department.

In January 1999 Professor Andrew Belser lured to the campus the Kennedy Center/American College Theatre Festival (KC/ACTF) for Region II. The KC/ACTF gave the Hill a week's worth of the best college-level theater. In all, eight hundred thespians and other personnel from six regional states and the District of Columbia took part in five fully staged productions. There are eight regions, all competing each year for selection to the national festival at the John F. Kennedy Center in the national capital. Esther Doyle, emerita doyeme of drama at Juniata, said that "nothing of this magnitude in theater has ever happened here."

The festival gave Juniata occasion to showcase its recently refurbished and dedicated (September 1998) Rosenberger Auditorium in Oller Hall. Funding for the renovations came collectively from the Rosenberger family: W. Clemens Rosenberger and his wife, Margaret; his mother and father, the late Pauline and Lester Rosenberger; his sister, Nancy Faus, and her husband, Robert; and the Rosenberger family trust. Theater lovers also made their way to Rosenberger Auditorium for the spring-semester performance of *The Wild goose Circus* [sic]. In attendance was award-winning playwright Russell Davis, who wrote the remarkable script. He was on campus throughout rehearsals and during the performance, March 10-13, to work closely with students. He also made a cameo appearance in the play.

Dr. Margaret Gray Towne, who had taught biology at Juniata in the early 1960s, came as the J. Omar Good Visiting Professor of Evangelical Christianity, from January 1998 to May 2001. Her courses dealt with science and religion, especially the invalidity of creationism as a scientific perspective. She brought to campus her mentor, Dr. John "Jack" Horner, as a guest lecturer in her classes. Dr. Horner, curator of paleontology at the Museum of the Rockies at Montana State University, enjoyed world renown as the paleontologist of the box-office-hit movies *Jurassic Park* and *The Lost World*. Some five hundred elementary students from local school districts heard him speak in Oller Hall on the topic, "Would T-rex Really Eat Ya?" He also gave a public lecture to the college community and general public on his academic specialty—"Dinosaur Behavior."

The millennial has coincided with a year-long reassessment of the J. Omar Good program conducted by its trustees. Guided by legal counsel, the trustees have been exploring, with the Kepple administration, ways by which the Good fund can help augment the religion department. This will mean the addition of two fully endowed chairs, four prestigious scholarships, and an annual national award.

For the 1998–99 and the 1999–2000 financial years, one hundred percent of Juniata's full-time faculty members made a gift to the college. That had never happened in recent memory, and it was the first time President Kepple had witnessed such professorial commitment in all of his twenty-five years in higher education.

In December 1998 the Juniata College Museum of Art acquired fifty-one paintings by the German artist Gunther Spaltman. Spaltman's works were shown in Germany in the 1970s, their style influenced by artistic developments of the early twentieth century, such as cubism and expressionism. The Spaltman paintings complement the Worth B. Stottlemyer Collection and its range of art forms from earlier centuries. Juniata came into possession of these works through the efforts of chemistry professor William Russey, who had been a long-time friend of the late artist.

Several months earlier, in September, Juniata dedicated the Malloy-Rabinowitz Gallery at its Museum of Art. Trustee Edwin Malloy and his wife Susan, a talented artist, made possible extensive renovations to Carnegie Hall Museum of Art. (Mrs. Malloy is the daughter of the late Aaron Rabinowitz, who had been a generous friend of Beeghly Library in the 1970s.) In recognition of their benevolence, the college named one of the museum's two wings in their honor (the other wing retains the name Shoemaker). Juniata received word the day after the dedication ceremony that Mr. Malloy had passed away in New York City.

Another benefaction by the Malloys was unveiled the fall of 1999: a new sculpture titled *Juniata Quilts*. The Malloy-commissioned work was created by the Greek-born artist Peter Calaboyis, whose sculptures can be seen at places such as Atlanta's Centennial Park and the University of Chicago. *Juniata Quilts* graces the Malloy Plaza of the Tussey-Terrace residence halls.

Board of Trustees

The college lost two dedicated trustees and altruistic donors by the deaths of Edwin Malloy and William von Liebig. The millennial board represented a greater number of women than ever before: eleven of thirty-seven. In addition to the experienced quintet of Baker, Hesselbein, Michel, Simpson, and Zeller, the trustee roll in 2000 included five other women members-at-large: Carol Lake (1996), Eileen Gipprich Sill (1999), Patricia Swigart (1999), and Mary White (1999). Patricia Swigart, a non-Juniatian, replaced her husband, William, who took emeritus status after one term. Three women came on the board elected either by the alumni or the church: Sharon Cramer Faulkner, in 1998, and Aliceann Wohlbruck, in 1999, by the alumni; and Verdean Keyser, in 1996, by the Brethren.

Going into the millennial year, the board roster included, as noted in the previous chapter, a cadre of male trustees who have served a decade or longer. Other members-at-large, with fewer years on the board, and the year of their appointments, were Francis DeMar (1990), Donald Detwiler (1994), Karl Kindig (1994), Charles Pearson (1994), Timothy Statton (1998), David Andrews (1992–95; 1999), Robert McDowell (1999), and John Swigart, Jr. (1999). DeMar of Huntingdon and Pearson of State College did not graduate from Juniata. The alumni elected Richard Paulhamus (1997) and the Brethren elected Steven Holsinger (1997) and John Swigart, Jr. (1999). In May 1999 the board, in addition to William Swigart, named Charles Knox and Garry Pote emeriti trustees.

Alumni

In May 1999 Mark. H. Miller, Class of 1980, accepted from Jodie Monger (Gray) the Alumni Association's presidential gavel. He will lead his alma mater's graduates into the new millennium. For the fiscal year 1998–1999, alumni contributed $1,271,256 to The Juniata Fund, the most ever, although the percentage of donors fell below forty percent. In all, the alumni-giving record for President Kepple's first year amounted to $3,829,225. Director of Alumni Development Lynanne Schaeffer and recent Association's presidents had built up a long list of volunteers that kept alumni personally connected to the campus through their talents and time. Vice-President John Hille called Juniata's kind of volunteerism: "altruistic hedonism"—having a good time helping others. Beginning the year 2000, Juniata initiated an alumni-nominated merit-based scholarship program, which will benefit as many as twenty freshmen. That fall Lynanne Schaeffer left as director of alumni development, replaced by Michelle Koren Corby, Class of 1995.

Church-College Relations

President Thomas Kepple came to College Hill with a deep appreciation for Juniata's historic ties to the Church of the Brethren. He recognized that communications between the three church districts in Pennsylvania, represented on the board of trustees, and the college needed to be improved. The Church Relations Council, in existence since 1969, still heard complaints from some constituent congregations that Juniata was "elitist, over-priced, and disconnected from its foundations and ideals."[7]

In October 1998 the trustees passed a resolution supporting a mission statement from the Church Relations Council that read, in part: "Juniata College and the Church of the Brethren affirm their historical relationship and covenant to work together to actively support each other's unique mission." Chaplain Torin Alexander organized Brethren Heritage Week in March of 1999. A brochure publicized Juniata's Brethren roots and ideals and its evolution as a church-related college. The administration, through the Church Relations Council and David Witkovsky, chaplain since fall 1999, will make Brethren Heritage Week an annual event of worship and education. Witkovsky, a Brethren minister with pastoral experience, graduated from Elizabethtown College (1978) and received the M.Div. degree from Bethany Theological Seminary.

Student Life

The Kepple presidency greeted a student body of 1,270, the highest enrollment in over a decade. Resident Juniatians paid a general fee of $22,460 for that 1998–99 academic year. A new chapter began for Student Government: terms of office for SG officers would now begin with the spring semester and run for a calendar year, rather than for the duration of an academic year. The hope was that a change in leaders between semesters would motivate student interest in the governance process. For the first time in Juniata's history, a group of five College Hill students spoke publicly about their sexuality at an October 1998 forum sponsored by Alternate Ways of Loving. In February 1999 the United Cultures of Juniata College held its third annual celebration of Islam's Eid Holiday. (Ever since the early 1990s the two days of the Jewish Rosh Hashanah had been printed on the college's official calendar.) For the academic year 1999–2000 Roman Catholics (301) made up 35.6 percent of 846 respondents to a question on religious preferences. The number of Catholics had doubled since Juniata's centennial year. (For decades, someone from Most Holy Trinity Church in Huntingdon has ministered to campus Roman Catholics.) Methodists, as in 1976, remain the largest Protestant denomination represented. Brethren students number fifty-six, their 6.6 percentage two points higher than twenty-three years before.

The 1999 edition of *Who's Who Among Students in American Colleges and Universities* included the names of forty-six Juniatians, who were selected on the basis of academic achievement and extracurricular leadership. In the spring of 1999 Lisa Petrella, a junior in biology, became the third Juniata student to receive a Goldwater scholarship for her outstanding work in the field of molecular biology. Sharon Simpson, a previous Goldwater scholar with a program of emphasis in environment studies (1998), also won three academic honors in sports: All-USA Collegiate College Academic Third Team, National Field Hockey All-Academic Squad, and Collegiate All-American scholar. In the spring of 2000 senior Rebecca McClaine, headed for a career in medicine, was cited in *USA TODAY* as one of the nation's exemplary collegians.

Athletics

In the fall of 1998 freshman Brian Olsen revived a long-standing Juniata tradition: pep-band music at athletic events. His Screamin' Eagles started with a roster of thirty-five student instrumentalists with high-school marching band experience.

On October 17, 1999, the college welcomed back seventeen members of the Stag Bowl football team. Former coaches Walter Nadzak and Dean Rossi and long-time trainer William Germann attended the reunion. Of that 1973 unit, Germann and four players—Louis Eckerl, Michael McNeal, Stuart Jackson, and Robert Waggoner (today a National Football League field official)—have been elected to Juniata's Sports Hall of Fame.

In August 1999 head coach Thomas Gibboney resigned, and the college named Kevin Burke, former offensive coordinator, as football's nineteenth mentor. The Eagles won five and lost five in 1998 and went six and four in 1999. It was the first winning season since 1990's 7-2-1. Junior wide receiver Matthew Eisenberg had a phenomenal day against Albright College on October 2, 1999, in an away game. He made fourteen receptions for 314 yards and four touchdowns, school records for all three categories. His receiving yards also set a new MAC standard—surpassing by forty-three yards the previous high. Eisenberg went on to be tabbed the MAC offensive player of the year as well as the Commonwealth League MVP. He caught a Juniata- and Conference-record seventy-six passes for another double record 1,597 yards. He was the first College Hill offensive player to earn most valuable player honors in the MAC since David Murphy in 1984. The swift-footed receiver was also a first-team Division III All-American in *Football Gazette*. Twelve Juniata gridders made the MAC All-Commonwealth League squads, which tied the number from the 1973 Stagg Bowl team. Joseph Montrella became the first Juniata quarterback to repeat on the MAC top squad since Donald Weiss in 1967 and 1968. His 589 yards in pass-completions against Widener University in one game is a college and MAC record.

In a gesture most uncommon in the history of any college or university, the Juniata faculty unanimously passed a resolution in January 1999 recognizing Lawrence Bock, the college's legendary volleyball coach. The citation stated, in part: "Since 1996 he has been Juniata's director of athletics, administering his duties with grace, courtesy, and fairness. He has always treated members of his own teams, as well as those of competitors as students first."[8] At that time he had compiled a twenty-two-year coaching career record of 826-124. His teams had won eighteen straight MAC titles and had made fourteen appearances in the national semifinals/finals. Larry's Ladies never won a national title but finished second four times. The 1998 team finished the regular season 39-1 but lost to Central Iowa in the NCAA Division III semifinals. Meanwhile, three juniors on the 1998 squad were named to the American Volleyball Coaches Association (AVCA) Division III first team All-American list: middle hitter Kristin Hershey, outside hitter Carrie Zeller, and setter Colleen Carver.

Bock's 1999 Eagles won thirty-five and lost four in regular season play. And for the nineteenth consecutive time Juniata women won the MAC Championship. This earned the college its fifteenth overall appearance in the NCAA Division III national semifinals. Juniata hosted the nationals for the third time, having done so in 1993 and 1998. But alas! The women finished fourth again. Juniata's outside hitter Carrie Zeller was named to the all-tournament team. That season was the third time Kristin Hershey made AVCA's first team.

The 1998 men's volleyball team carried off the Molten championship crown. Its 1999 unit, 14-13 for the season, won the Division III laurels the second straight year. But at the third annual Molten national playoffs, the fellows came in fourth. For the first time, however, Coach Ryan Patton's Eagles played in the Eastern Intercollegiate Volleyball Association (EIVA) Division I semifinals. Penn State eliminated the Blue and Gold in three games. Three 1999 Juniata volleyballers made all-star teams. Junior outside hitter Roderick Kirby and senior opposite Ryan Celesnik were both named All-East (which includes Division I, II, and III players). They also earned spots on the EIVA Division III First Team, along with junior setter Michael Shaeffer. Coach Patton's three-year won-lost record stood at forty-seven and thirty-nine at the millennium.

Juniata celebrated the centennial birthday of baseball on College Hill at an April 17, 1999, Founders Day banquet. The team ended the season 22-15, with a stack of broken ash-wood bats. The NCAA had outlawed the aluminum version for 1999 as too dangerous (the velocity of the batted baseball put pitchers at peril). The ban was lifted for the 2000 season after aluminum bats were redesigned.

Coach Berrier retired at the end of the millennial season. As one of Juniata's all-time great athletes, the former athletic director and head wrestling coach will take his place alongside another legendary Hilltop athlete/coach/administrator: Philip Snider. By the time of his retirement, Berrier had chalked up four hundred-sixteen wins in thirty years of coaching baseball at his alma mater. His teams won the league championship seven times and twice the MAC title. While athletic director he increased the number of varsity sports to twenty-one, later to be cut back to sixteen in 1996. Huntingdon attorney George Zanic, Berrier's MVP second baseman and Goodale-prize winner in 1989, succeeded his mentor as baseball coach.

In women's aquatics, Coach Kathleen Collins presided over a phenomenal 1999–2000 season. In all, nine records fell, six by a couple freshman sensations and three by the relay team on which they swam. Cyndi Long took three of them: 500y Freestyle (5:33.53), 200y Butterfly (2:24.08), and 100y Butterfly (I:02.88). Alissa Schneider laid claim to the other three: 200y Freestyle (2:01.02), 100y Freestyle (:55.94), and 400y Individual Medley (4:50.26). She posted the 400-yard mark at the MACs, which made her the first gold medalist for a Juniata female swimmer. Her time in the 200-yard race at that Conference meet in February earned her a silver medal. In relay action, the unit of Schneider, Long, Jenn Dorsch, and Erin Soule recorded new times in the 200y Freestyle (1:44.61), the 400y Freestyle (3:50.01), and the 800y Freestyle (8:22.95).

The athletic seasons of 1998–99 produced a bevy of academic honors for varsity letter-winners. For 1998, volleyball's Kristin Hershey was a GTE/CoSIDA All District II scholar for the second consecutive year and received a prestigious NCAA postgraduate scholarship. Five other student-athletes won MAC academic kudos. In women's soccer there were striker Bett Bleil, midfielder Deanna Leone, and defender Erin Copeland. Men's soccer was represented by back Kevin Andrews. From women's tennis came Emily Mann.

In 1999 twenty-one athletes had a 3.20 grade-point average or better, thus earning MAC academic recognition. Women's cross-country boasted Megan McGinnis and Dody Smith. Field hockey added goalie Elizabeth Allard, back midfielder Allyson Kenyon, and midfielder/forward Candace Sanders to the list. (In addition, the trio of strikers were tabbed scholar-athletes by the National Field Hockey Coaches Association. As noted earlier, Sharon Simpson had studied her way to three prestigious academic honors while a field-hockey athlete.) The football team accounted for eight: quarterback Jamie Campbell, offensive guard Ray Ghaner, guard Colin Gillin, linebacker Andrew Grace (second straight year), defensive tackle Steven Harbaugh, wide receiver Lucas Kelleher (also a two-time honoree), defensive back Joel Peppetti, and wide receivers Timothy Lonesky and Andrew Radomsky. Men's soccer contributed four honor-roll athletes: back Kevin Andrews (second time), goalie midfielder Matthew Betting, back Gerald Knepp, and striker Scott Kucharcik. Women's soccer had midfielder Mary Cypressi make the grade. Finally, women's volleyball placed two players on the honor roll: Kristin Hershey (third time), and outside hitter Brandy Workinger. The lowest GPA represented in this group was 3.25, the highest, 3.96 (Radomsky).

Recapitulative Epilogue

In the course of one hundred twenty-five years, Juniata College has twice seen one century end and another one begin. The first time, as the Victorian Era lapped over a year or two into the 1900s, the United States found itself in the midst of profound change—from a farm-based to a factory-based economy, from a rural to an urban society, from a hemispheric to a world power. It was a time of dynamic economic, social, and cultural progress. But it was also a time of strain, dislocation, reorganization, and readjustment at all levels of American life.

Juniata College faced this first centurial transition in a tenuous state. True, it had made passable growth since its 1876 genesis, enough to qualify as a liberal arts school by the mid-1890s. At that time the trustees had even arrogated to the little countrified institution a new name, its present one, to broaden marketing appeal. But it suffered from systemic problems. It was headed by an absentee president, which resulted in tentative leadership on the campus. It was practically unknown outside the immediate Juniata Valley and a small ethnocentric religious group. There was no fortifying endowment, forcing the college to scrabble from yearly budget to yearly budget, its faculty woefully underpaid. Presenting itself as a liberal arts college, Juniata had by 1900 awarded but seven B. A. degrees, all to men.

No doubt many Juniatians entered the twentieth century with great uncertainty (though never publicly voiced) as to the future of their alma mater. Yet there is no evidence of anyone on College Hill pondering, out of long-range concern, what demands on higher education an America in mighty changeover might levy. Perhaps Juniata's unpreparedness for the times and its dubious future explain the wonderment David Emmert verbalized in 1901. The teacher-trustee wrote in his *Reminiscences*: "Even now the growth of Juniata seems like a dream, and yet it is true!"[1]

At millennium 2000, Juniata's second century's-turn experience, the nation is again caught up in a major structural shift—from a factory-based economy to a computer-based economy. The digital age, coming so rapidly—in less than two generations' time—has wrought conditions no less revolutionary or challenging than those a hundred years ago.

This sea change in contemporary American history is epitomized in the recent anxiety about Y2K, computerese for Year 2000. The fear was, because of a programming oversight years ago, that computers would misread "00" for "1900" instead of "2000." Such a glitch, experts warned, could play havoc with the way Americans did business, relied on basic services, communicated, ran the military. The federal government spent one hundred billion dollars to ensure there would be no computer meltdown on New Year's Day 2000. There was, of course, no major glitch in America, or anywhere else in the world. But the media frenzy that preceded Y2K made compellingly clear just how computerized modern life has become.

The viability of Juniata College at Y2K contrasts dramatically with the status of its ancestor circa 1900. Today Juniata stands confidently poised, strong in human and material resources. It begins the fall of 2000 with the largest enrollment ever (1294). For a decade its administrators and trustees had planned, with commendable foresight, how best to equip, in curriculum and facilities, the Juniata of the future. Early in the 1990s the Hill had affirmed a global-oriented mission and had taken the steps to attune the whole campus to a planet shrunken by the computer and microchip. In Y2K Juniata ranks among the nation's finest small colleges, a status annually attested to by appraisers of higher education.

In April 2000 President Kepple announced the "Campaign for Uncommon Outcomes." This will be a seventy-million-dollar capital drive, by far the college's most ambitious fund-raising effort ever. Beginning on Founders Day, it will end June 30, 2005. Vice-President John Hille will oversee the campaign, his trustee counterpart, Barry Halbritter, chairing the board's steering committee. Already, in December 1999, major gifts began coming in, even before the campaign had officially begun. That month alone, the college received $6,701,555—only a few thousand dollars less than it received in its best year of financial support. By fiscal year-end of 1999–2000 this figure had grown to a record $10.1 million.

Campaign plans earmark thirty-six million dollars toward five construction or renovation projects: the von Liebig Center; Brumbaugh Science Center (the business and economics department and the information technology staff will occupy the vacated chemistry wing); the Regional Performing Arts Center (a renovated Oller Hall and a theatre addition to be named for alumni donors Barry and Marlene Robinette Halbritter, Classes of 1965 and 1962, respectively); Founders Hall; and the Raystown Field Station (putting to use a five-million-dollar federal grant). A totally restored Founders Hall will cost an estimated three million dollars, the renovation of Brumbaugh Science Center ten million. Oneida Hall's demolition means temporarily relocating the financial and human resources people to a pair of remodeled college-owned residences flanking the "Pink Palace" on Moore Street. Eventually, these offices will be permanently relocated to the renewed Founders Hall.

In addition, twenty-three million dollars are slotted for the endowment, to be used for faculty chairs and development, information technology, scholarships and awards, and athletic support programs. Eleven million dollars more of the campaign's yield will be allocated to the current fund.

With the millennium, several professorial chairs have yet to be filled. Two have remained long vacant: the John Downey Benedict Professorship in English and the I. Harvey Brumbaugh Professorship in Languages. A more recent one, in peace studies, is the Elizabeth Evans Baker Professorship established in 1990. Three others will be the Elma Stine Heckler Professorship in Music, and the two in religion endowed by the J. Omar Good Fund. Mrs. Heckler was a Juniata music graduate in 1950.

On the matter of name-professorships (sixteen in all, counting five Danas), it should be noted that Juniata faces the twenty-first century blessed with three fully endowed chairs. Such a boon is almost never heard of at a college the size of Juniata. The term "fully endowed," as differentiated from "endowed" (which all name-chairs are), means that total compensation—salary and benefits—is annually defrayed by the endowment; no costs are borne by the college's current fund. Two of these professorships, both in religion and as yet unnamed, are financed by the J. Omar Good Fund. The third one, in chemistry, is covered by the H. George Foster benefaction.

The Kepple administration will make space in revamped Founders Hall for an unusual purpose, so far as most institutional shrines go. The college's pioneers in 1876, as activist Brethren, not only defied their religious heritage in starting a school, but also American mores of that era. Victorian America was a male-dominated society, a time when most colleges and universities accepted only men. It was extraordinary, therefore, that Juniata began as a coeducational school and early on gave women a prominent place in its institutional aims and governance.

Eight of the school's first thirteen students in Juniata's natal year were women. So were the first two teachers Principal Jacob Zuck hired to assist him. Between 1878 and 1888, as Chapter 5 noted, women made up a high percentage of stockholders—thirty-nine of 176. As early as 1880 a woman was elected a trustee. Thereafter, except for a few years in the 1890s, the board of trustees always had female representation, whether in times of the Great Depression or the student-depleted years of World War II.

Therefore, looking ahead to April 2001, the Kepple administration intends to commemorate Juniata's uncommon origins by recognizing the uncommon role of women in its history. A "Celebration of Juniata Women" will tell that story in one of the 125th Anniversary Year's spotlighted events. The observance will not pay tribute only to pioneering womankind in Juniata's early history. It will also salute notable female teachers and graduates down through later generations—their impact on the campus, on their families, on their communities, on their professions. Plans call for a wall hanging that depicts the many ways in which the college is woven into the "fabric" of Juniata women's entire lives. Celebration planners envision a tapestry that incorporates a piece of fabric personally meaningful to each contributing alumna (such as a swatch of a dress worn at graduation time). A booklet will describe the meaning of each cloth patch. The wall hanging is to be preserved in the cabinet room on the first floor of renovated Founders Hall.

All things considered, the term "uncommon" is not a hyperbolic way to characterize the history of Juniata College. The circumstances of its unique origins and its rise to national prominence as a private, small liberal arts college—all within a century-and-a-quarter's time—make for an atypical story. For that reason, Juniata celebrants on April 17, 2001, need not manifest a David Emmert-like sense of amazement at how far their alma mater has come. The more fitting mood would be that of Jacob Zuck at the dedicatory service for Founders Hall. Not a man known for bravado, the founding teacher declared unapologetically: "In view of our small beginning, it [would be]…less than human for us not to boast ourselves on an occasion like this."[2] That sentiment would be as excusable in April 2001 as it was in April 1879.

NOTES

Key to Abbreviations

AB — *Alumni Bulletin*
FM — *Faculty Minutes*
MAM — *Minutes of Annual Meeting*
SM — *Stockholders' Minutes*
TM — *Trustee Minutes*
TTM — *Temporary Trustee Minutes*

CHAPTER 1

1. *MAM* (1853), Art. 28.
2. *Gospel Visitor* (Mar. 1856), p.76.
3. Ibid. (Sept. 1856), p. 249.
4. There are no accurate membership data for this period of Brethren history. The figure of thirty thousand is a good guess. See *The Brethren Encyclopedia* (Philadelphia, PA, and Oak Park, IL: The Brethren Encyclopedia, Inc., 1984), IV, p. 1465.
5. *Gospel Visitor* (Sept. 1856), p. 249.
6. Ibid. (June 1857), p. 189.
7. *MAM* (1857), Art. 19.
8. *Gospel Visitor* (June 1857), p.190.
9. Ibid. (Apr. 1857), p. 110.
10. *MAM* (1858), Art. 51.
11. *A History of the Church of the Brethren in the Middle District of Pennsylvania* (Prepared and published by the District Home Mission Board, 1925), p. 497.
12. W. Arthur Cable and Homer F. Sanger, eds., *Educational Blue Book and Directory of the Church of the Brethren, 1708-1923* (Elgin, IL: Published by the General Education Board of the Church of the Brethren, 1923), p. 37.
13. *Two Centuries of the Church of the Brethren: Bicentennial Address* (Elgin, IL: Brethren Publishing House, 1908), p. 347.
14. For a biographical sketch of Henry Brumbaugh, see Earl C. Kaylor, Jr., *Henry Boyer Brumbaugh: Dunker with a Cause* (Juniata College Keepsake, 1970).
15. *Pilgrim* (Mar. 7, 1871), p. 106.
16. Gaius M. Brumbaugh, *Genealogy of the Brumbaugh Families* (New York: Frederick H. Hitchcock, 1923), p. 524.
17. Ibid., p. 522.

18. Ibid., p. 531; see also *Juniata Echo* (Jan. 1908), p. 4.
19. *Christian Family Companion* (Nov. 5, 1872), p. 696.
20. *Pilgrim* (Jan. 3, 1873), p. 6.
21. John H. Moore, *Some Brethren Pathfinders* (Elgin, IL: Brethren Publishing House, 1929), p. 252.
22. *Pilgrim* (Apr. 1, 1873), p. 103.
23. See also Ibid. (Sept. 1, 1874), p. 276.
24. David Emmert, *Reminiscences of Juniata College* (Harrisburg, PA: J. Horace McFarland Co., 1901), p. 115.
25. *Pilgrim* (July 28, 1874), p. 236.
26. Ibid. (Oct. 6, 1874), p. 316.
27. *Gospel Messenger* (May 16, 1908), p. 317.
28. Henry R. Holsinger, *History of the Tunkers and the Brethren Church* (Oakland, CA: Pacific Press Publishing Co., 1901), p. 271.
29. This account is taken from a Founders Day speech by John Brumbaugh, printed in the *Gospel Messenger* (May 16, 1908), pp. 317 f.
30. I have taken the liberty to insert the sentence, "Do it on a small scale," from another account of this conversation supplied by John Brumbaugh and recounted in Solomon Z. Sharp, *The Educational History of the Church of the Brethren* (Elgin, IL: Brethren Publishing House, 1923), p. 72.
31. D. L. Miller and Galen B. Royer, *Some Who Led* (Elgin, IL: Brethren Publishing House, 1912), p. 195.
32. Brumbaugh, *Genealogy*, p. 531.

CHAPTER 2

1. Henry R. Holsinger, *History of the Tunkers and the Brethren Church* (Oakland, CA: Pacific Press Publishing Co., 1901), p. 411.
2. This incident was told by John Brumbaugh in an article, "History of the Life of Prof. Zuck," written for the *Juniata Echo* (Apr. 1896), p. 50.
3. This journal, along with his diary for the same year, is deposited in the college Archives.
4. Wayne G. Broehl, Jr., *The Molly Maguires* (Cambridge, MA: Harvard University Press, 1964), p. 83.
5. David Emmert, *Reminiscences of Juniata College* (Harrisburg, PA: J. Horace McFarland Co., 1901), p. 5. For a profile of Emmert see Earl C. Kaylor, Jr., *The Versatile David Emmert;* printed address given on May 4, 1988, at the opening of the David Emmert Exhibit, Shoemaker Galleries, Juniata College.
6. *Gospel Messenger* (May 16, 1908), p. 317.
7. Holsinger, *History of Tunkers*, p. 412, seems to provide the most accurate account (though extremely sketchy) of this period of his life. Much of the extant biographical data on Zuck is erroneous and contradictory. I have tried to reconstruct the main outline of his life by seeking to reconcile this conflicting body of data with material I have turned up.
8. *Christian Family Companion* (Oct. 17, 1873), p. 632.
9. *Pilgrim* (Sept. 8, 1874), p. 282.
10. *Christian Family Companion and Gospel Visitor* (Sept. 28, 1874), p. 595.
11. *Gospel Messenger* (May 16, 1908), p. 317. John Brumbaugh was confused about the year and circumstances of this letter, dating it 1872 and connecting it with the Waynesboro position. They did not know each other until 1873, which was after Zuck taught there. I have taken the position that the letter was written in 1875 after Zuck was elected principal at Mt. Pleasant.
12. Undated excerpt in Zuck's scrapbook.
13. Emmert, *Reminiscences*, p. 12.
14. Ibid., pp. 16 f.

15. Quoted in Charles C. Ellis, *Juniata College: The History of Seventy Years, 1876-1946* (Elgin, IL: Brethren Publishing House, 1947), pp. 238 f.
16. *Gospel Messenger* (May 16, 1908), p. 318.
17. Ibid.
18. *Pilgrim* (May 23, 1876), p. 321.
19. *Gospel Messenger* (May 16, 1908), p. 318. See also *Juniata Echo* (Apr. 1896), pp. 56 f.
20. *Pilgrim* (Oct. 10, 1876), p. 642.
21. *Primitive Christian* (Nov. 7, 1876), p. 710.
22. The minute book for the society's earliest meetings is deposited in the college Archives.
23. *Primitive Christian* (Feb. 6, 1877), pp. 90 f.

CHAPTER 3

1. *TTM* (Jan. 27, 1877).
2. John Brumbaugh wrote of this incident in the *Juniata Echo* (Apr. 1896), pp. 51 f.
3. *TTM* (Jan. 27, 1877).
4. *Primitive Christian* (May 29, 1877), p. 330.
5. David Emmert, *Reminiscences of Juniata College* (Harrisburg, PA: J. Horace McFarland Co., 1901), p. 38.
6. Ibid., pp. 40 f.
7. Ibid., p. 20.
8. *Primitive Christian* (Nov. 20, 1877), p. 719.
9. Emmert, *Reminiscences*, p. 27.
10. *Primitive Christian* (July 31, 1877), p. 471. Italics are mine.
11. Emmert, *Reminiscences*, p. 27.
12. Ibid., p. 28.
13. *Primitive Christian* (May 29, 1877), p. 330.
14. J. Linwood Eisenberg, ed., *A History of the Church of the Brethren in the Southern District of Pennsylvania* (Quincy, PA: Quincy Orphanage Press, 1941), p. 383.
15. Emmert, *Reminiscences*, p. 43.
16. Ibid., p. 44.
17. Ibid., pp. 45 f.
18. *Gospel Messenger* (May 15, 1908), p. 318. See also Emmert, *Reminiscences*, pp. 96 f.
19. Emmert, *Reminiscences*, p. 48.
20. Ibid.
21. "Story About the Boys at Orphans' Retreat, by One of Them." College Archives.
22. Ibid.
23. Emmert, *Reminiscences*, p. 92.
24. Ibid., p. 130. See also *Primitive Christian* (Feb. 19, 1878).
25. See *Primitive Christian* (Apr. 30, 1878), p. 263, where Zuck writes of having rented a "new brick dwelling-house," which was "well adapted to the purpose and is quite convenient to the school building." Zuck's account book in the college Archives identifies the house's owner and its address.
26. Ibid. (May 28, 1878), p. 327.
27. *Primitive Christian* (Nov. 19, 1878), p. 736.
28. Ibid. (Jan. 7, 1879), p. 6.
29. Quoted from an undated excerpt in Zuck's scrapbook.
30. Emmert, *Reminiscences*, p. 77.
31. *Juniata Echo* (Apr. 1896), p. 51.
32. Emmert, *Reminiscences*, pp. 73 f.
33. Quoted in Charles C. Ellis, *Juniata College: The History of Seventy Years, 1876-1946* (Elgin, IL: Brethren Publishing House, 1947), p. 239.

34. Emmert, *Reminiscences*, p. 80.
35. Not May 10, as Emmert and Ellis say.
36. *Juniata Echo* (July 1911), p. 114.
37. Emmert, *Reminiscences*, p. 88.
38. Ibid., pp. 84 f.
39. Ibid., p. 85.

CHAPTER 4

1. *Primitive Christian* (June 24, 1879), p. 386.
2. See a letter from E. D. Kendig in Ibid. (July 15, 1879), p. 445.
3. David Emmert, *Reminiscences of Juniata College* (Harrisburg, PA: J. Horace McFarland Co., 1901), p. 38.
4. *Primitive Christian* (July 22, 1879), p. 457.
5. Mt. Morris College was scheduled to open on August 20. The Illinois Brethren had purchased the defunct plant of the Rock River Seminary, consisting of two buildings and a seven-acre campus.
6. Emmert, *Reminiscences*, p. 120.
7. *Primitive Christian* (July 22, 1897), p. 456.
8. Emmert, *Reminiscences*, pp. 122 f.
9. [Huntingdon] *The Daily News* (Nov. 19, 1934).
10. *Juniata Echo* (June 1897), pp. 83 f.
11. The author has a copy of this note, given him by an employee of Mead Products, Blair Division, Alexandria, PA.
12. Emmert, *Reminiscences*, p. 125.
13. *Golden Dawn* (Dec. 1885), p. 242.
14. She is not listed in the college catalog for 1887 and 1888, but the biographical sketch of her in Gaius M. Brumbaugh, *Genealogy of the Brumbaugh Families* (New York: Frederick Hitchcock, 1923), pp. 614 f, states that she taught the fall and spring terms of both those years.
15. Emmert, *Reminiscences*, p. 137.
16. *TM* (Mar. 9, 1880).
17. Ibid. (Sept. 11, 1880).
18. *Advance* (Mar. 1885), p. 75.
19. Ibid. (Nov. 1884), p. 59.
20. Ibid. (Feb. 1884), p. 32.
21. Circular for 1881, in Jacob Zuck's scrapbook.
22. See *Juniata Echo* (May 1907), pp. 62 f, an article in which Joseph Saylor reminisces about his years as librarian.
23. *Golden Dawn* (Dec. 1885), p. 241.
24. *Advance* (Mar. 1884), p. 31.
25. *Golden Dawn* (Mar. 1886), p. 80.
26. *Advance* (May 1884), p. 44.
27. *Golden Dawn* (Nov. 1885), p. 208.
28. See the manuscript biographical sketch of Dr. A. B. Brumbaugh, presumably written by his son, Gaius, in the college Archives.
29. Letter among the *Trustee Minutes*.
30. *Golden Dawn* (Nov. 1885), p. 208.
31. *Advance* (Aug. 1884), p. 54.
32. *TM* (Oct. 13, 1882).
33. Emmert has a very short chapter, "Some Good Work," on the orphanage in his *Reminiscences*.
34. *Golden Dawn* (Mar. 1886), p. 80. See also *Advance* (Aug. 1884), p. 52.
35. See the chapter in Emmert's book, "Beginning Life on the Hill."

36. J. Simpson Africa, *History of Huntingdon and Blair Counties, Pennsylvania* (Philadelphia: J. B. Lippincott & Co., 1883), p. 481.
37. *Golden Dawn* (June 1885), p. 62.
38. *Gospel Messenger* (Mar. 9, 1886), p. 155.
39. *Advance* (Mar. 1885), pp. 72 f. See letter from a stockholder, dated Dec. 14, 1884, and filed with the *Trustee Minutes* for that year.
40. *Golden Dawn* (May 1885), p. 11.
41. Ibid. (May 1887), p. 158.
42. The incomplete manuscript minutes of the early years of the Alumni Association and its original constitution are preserved in the college Archives.
43. This entire episode is reconstructed from several funeral speeches in Mary N. Quinter, *Life and Sermons of Elder James Quinter* (Elgin, IL: Brethren Publishing House, 1909).
44. Ibid., p. 55.
45. Ibid., p. 61.

CHAPTER 5

1. *A History of the Church of the Brethren in the Middle District of Pennsylvania* (Prepared and published by Home Mission Board, 1925), p. 408.
2. Ibid., p. 407.
3. *TM* (June 16, 1890); (July 16, 1891).
4. Ibid. (June 27, 1890).
5. Charles C. Ellis, *Juniata College: The History of Seventy Years, 1876-1946* (Elgin, IL: Brethren Publishing House, 1947), p. 43.
6. *Advance* (Aug. 1890), p. 102.
7. *Juniata Echo* (Nov. 1890), p. 5.
8. Ibid.
9. "Juniata College During the First Decade of the Twentieth Century," written in October 1967 and preserved in the college Archives.
10. Anonymous letter dated April 8, 1887, among the papers of Dr. Gaius Brumbaugh in the college Archives.
11. *Advance* (Aug. 1884), p. 56.
12. *Juniata Echo* (Aug. 1891), p. 25.
13. See David Emmert, *Reminiscences of Juniata College* (Harrisburg, PA: J. Horace McFarland Co., 1901), p. 149. Emmert was gone during this period but he does mention such drills when the gymnasium was moved to Students Hall.
14. *Juniata Echo* (Aug. 1891), p. 27.
15. *TM* (Sept. 11, 1890).
16. Ibid. (Mar. 21, 1892). Court records show he purchased the lots in his name. But I have not been able to trace out how and when the transfer to the college was made.
17. *Juniata Echo* (July 1895), p. 26.
18. *MAM* (1890), Art. 14.
19. Ibid. (1893), Report of School Visiting Elders.
20. *Juniata Echo* (June 1894), p. 3.
21. *MAM* (1897), Report of the Publishing Department.

CHAPTER 6

1. The only published book-length biography of Brumbaugh is Earl C. Kaylor, Jr.'s, *Martin Grove Brumbaugh, A Pennsylvanian's Odyssey from Sainted Schoolman to Bedeviled World War I Governor, 1862-1930* (Cranbury, NJ: Associated University Presses, 1996). See also Valentino Anthony Ciampa, "Martin Grove Brumbaugh, Educator" (unpublished Master of Arts thesis, The

Pennsylvania State College, 1937). This thesis, however, concentrates on his contributions to the public school system and does little with his governorship, while completely ignoring his two presidential stints at Juniata.
2. Ibid., p. 33.
3. Ibid., pp. 84-91.
4. Henry Brumbaugh Diary.
5. Edward Potts Cheyney, *History of the University of Pennsylvania, 1740-1940* (Philadelphia: University of Pennsylvania Press, 1940), p. 401.
6. *Juniata Echo* (June 1896), p. 94.
7. Ibid. (May 1898), p. 71.
8. Ibid. (Nov. 1897), p. 130.
9. For a comprehensive account of his work as commissioner, see Kaylor, *Martin Grove Brumbaugh*, pp. 126-168.
10. Ibid., pp. 144, 162.
11. Ibid., p. 167.
12. Ibid.
13. For a comprehensive account of his superintendency, see Ibid., pp. 208-237.
14. M. G. Brumbaugh to Trustees of Juniata College, Brumbaughana, college Archives.
15. M. G. Brumbaugh to Dr. A. B. Brumbaugh, Ibid.
16. David Emmert, *Reminiscences of Juniata College* (Harrisburg, PA: J. Horace McFarland Co., 1901), p. 158.
17. *TM* (June 26, 1899).
18. *Juniata Echo* (June 1894), p. 5.
19. Ibid. (May 1900), p. 75.
20. [Huntingdon] *Semi-Weekly News* (Sept. 11, 1902).
21. Ibid.
22. This ruling was made in 1881, but the trustees took no immediate action because the college had just been chartered in 1878. See *MAM* (1881), Art. 26.
23. *Gospel Messenger* (Apr. 10, 1894), p. 225.
24. *Juniata Echo* (July 1896), p. 111.
25. *TM* (Feb. 12, 1901).
26. *SM* (Feb. 1, 1904).
27. *TM* (Feb. 2, 1906).
28. Martin G. Brumbaugh to I. Harvey Brumbaugh, Feb. 1, 1907, Brumbaughana, college Archives.
29. There are several letters in the college Archives between college officials and George Henderson, the Philadelphia attorney who gave legal counsel dealing with this matter. On the matter of paying off the family, see George Henderson to I. Harvey Brumbaugh, July 24, 1908.
30. I. Harvey Brumbaugh to Martin G. Brumbaugh, May 17, 1907, Brumbaughana, college Archives.
31. A typewritten copy of these bylaws are in the college Archives.
32. *Gospel Messenger* (Feb. 15, 1908), p. 100.
33. *Juniata Echo* (July 1907), p. 112.
34. Ibid. (Dec. 1900), p. 164.
35. Ibid. (Jan. 1901), p. 15.
36. Ibid. (Nov. 1900), p. 148.
37. Ibid. (Feb. 1905), p. 25.
38. *TM* (Jan. 17, 1910).
39. Annual Meeting declared: "We also declare distinctly that our loyal and faithful brotherhood should neither fellowship, countenance nor tolerate those who should undertake to establish, under any pretence or color whatever, theological schools, or theological departments of schools or colleges, having in contemplation or purpose the training or graduation of any youth specially for the ministry of the Brotherhood or elsewhere...." *MAM* (1882), Art. 10.

40. W. Arthur Cable and Homer F. Sanger, eds., *Educational Blue Book and Directory of the Church of the Brethren, 1708-1923* (Elgin, IL: Published by the General Education Board of the Church of the Brethren, 1923), p. 227.
41. Ibid., pp. 317 f.
42. *AB* (Oct. 1906), p. 3.
43. *TM* (Nov. 15, 1904).
44. Ibid. (Mar. 6, 1905).
45. *Juniata Echo* (Jan. 1899), p. 2.
46. *AB* (Oct. 1909), p. 2; also *TM* (July 9, 1908).
47. *TM* (Nov. 25, 1902).
48. *Juniata Echo* (May 1905), p. 80.
49. Ibid. (Nov. 1894), pp. 10 f.
50. Ibid., pp. 12 f.
51. Henry Brumbaugh Diary.
52. Emmert, *Reminiscences*, p. 106.
53. *Juniata Echo* (Apr. 1898), p. 59.
54. Ibid. (Mar. 1901), p. 50.
55. Emmert, *Reminiscences*, p. 150.
56. *Juniata Echo* (Jan. 1897), p. 9. The student prank involved in getting the stone from Mrs. Summers is found in the March issue, pp. 44 f. M. G.'s letter of request to her is in Brumbaughana, college Archives.
57. Cassel also sold portions of his library to Mt. Morris College and the Pennsylvania Historical Association. When Mt. Morris merged with Manchester College in 1932, most of its Cassel books went to Bethany Theological Seminary. For a biographical sketch of Cassel, in manuscript, see Donald Durnbaugh, "The Great Antiquarian: Abraham Cassel, and His Collection at Juniata College." It is in the college Archives.
58. These letters are in Brumbaughana, college Archives.
59. *Juniata Echo* (Apr. 1900), p. 60.
60. See the article on "The Library of Juniata College," Ibid. (Oct. 1904), pp. 114-17.
61. *TM* (Mar. 22, 1905). President M. G. had received Carnegie's affirmative answer on March 12.
62. A copy of this cablegram is in Brumbaughana, college Archives.
63. *TM* (July 9, 1908).
64. *Juniata Echo* (May 1909), p. 81.
65. Ibid. (July 1907), p. 114.
66. His college-days diary was found among old papers in the college Archives.

CHAPTER 7

1. In 1903 the college urged parents to prosecute the Washington House proprietor for illegal liquor sales and even inquired into initiating action itself.
2. [Huntingdon] *Semi-Weekly News* (Sept. 17, 1908).
3. *Juniata Echo* (June 1896), p. 93.
4. Ibid. (Nov. 1902), p. 137.
5. The manuscript minutes of this organization from 1893-1911 are in the college Archives.
6. The Volunteer Mission Band was only unofficially connected with SVM. Then, between 1906 and 1911 for some reason, the Band was defunct. Revived the latter year, it affiliated officially with SVM in 1916.
7. At first it was simply called Mission Band but its name was changed the next November. Its manuscript minutes to Feb. 28, 1900, are in the college Archives.
8. Quoted in Winthrop S. Hudson, *Religion in America* (New York: Charles Scribner's Sons, 1965), p. 322.
9. *SM* (Feb. 19, 1900).

10. This portion of the vow is taken from the first minutes of the Girls' Christian Band, which presumably was modeled after the Boys'. These manuscript minutes are in the college Archives.
11. This petition is in the college Archives.
12. See *Juniata Echo* (Oct. 1900), p. 127. The constitution of the JAA, in manuscript, is in the college Archives, as are its minutes for 1908-10.
13. The Lyceum's early minutes are in the college Archives.
14. See the manuscript account of these debates in the college Archives as part of the Lyceum records.
15. A copy is in the college Archives.
16. This pamphlet is in the library vault. Some of Dassdorf's later correspondence with Cassel is in the college Archives.
17. *Juniata Echo* (Apr. 1905), pp. 62 f.
18. Letter dated Dec. 12, 1906, Brumbaughana, college Archives.

CHAPTER 8

1. *Juniata Echo* (Oct. 1911), p. 119.
2. *TM* (June 14, 1917).
3. Charles C. Ellis, *Juniata College: The History of Seventy Years, 1876-1946* (Elgin, IL: Brethren Publishing House, 1947), p. 192.
4. *Juniata Echo* (Jan. 1913), p. 11.
5. Ibid. (June 1921), p. 128.
6. This letter is filed with *Trustee Minutes* in the Beeghly Library vault.
7. Ibid. (Apr. 15, 1918).
8. Ibid. (Nov. 13, 1918).
9. Ibid. (Dec. 4, 1922).
10. This treatment of Holsopple was told the author by his daughter, Mrs. Naomi Adams, in a telephone conversation, June 6, 1975.
11. *TM* (Apr. 25, 1924).
12. Ibid. (Jan. 13, 1916).
13. *Juniata Echo* (May 1912), p. 71.
14. *TM* (Feb. 8, 1922).
15. *Juniata Echo* (June 1922), pp. 116 f.
16. Ibid. (Oct. 1923), p. 152.
17. See a summary statement on this subject in Herbert Hogan, "Fundamentalism in the Church of the Brethren, 1900-1931," *Brethren Life and Thought*, 5: (Winter 1960), p. 32.
18. *Gospel Messenger* (Mar. 25, 1922), p. 180.
19. Ibid. (Sept. 11, 1920), p. 542.
20. *TM* (Apr. 17, 1919).
21. Letter dated August 7, 1919, in the college Archives.
22. *AB* (Oct. 1916), p. 4.
23. *Juniata Echo* (Apr. 1919), p. 62. The college Archives has the minutes of the Council from Dec. 7, 1921 to May 3, 1922.
24. For a brief period in the fall of 1913 Earl Speicher, a Somerset County senior, was editor-in-chief of the *Echo*, but Alphaeus Dupler took over in January 1914.
25. *Juniata Echo* (Jan. 1920), p. 73.
26. Ibid. (Aug. 1922), p. 145.
27. W. Arthur Cable and Homer F. Sanger. eds., *Educational Blue Book and Directory of the Church of the Brethren, 1708-1923* (Elgin, IL: Published by the General Education Board of the Church of the Brethren, 1923), p. 622.
28. See *TM* (Apr. 26, 1920); (Apr. 17, 1922).

CHAPTER 9

1. Jennie Newcomer to *MGB* (undated letter), Brumbaughana, college Archives.
2. Frank Foster to *MGB* (May 26, 1924), Ibid.
3. C. C. Ellis to *MGB* (May 22, 1924), Ibid.
4. See the manuscript biographical sketch by Harold B. Statler, Brumbaughana, college Archives.
5. See the basic work, Wayland F. Dunaway, *A History of Pennsylvania* (New York: Prentice-Hall, Inc., 1935), p. 577. Also Robert Fortenbaugh and H. James Tarman, *Pennsylvania: The Story of a Commonwealth* (Harrisburg, PA: The Pennsylvania Book Service Publishers, 1940), pp. 314, 315.
6. J. T. Salter, *The People's Choice* (New York: The Exposition Press, 1971), pp. 27-28. See also William S. Vare, *My Forty Years in Politics* (Philadelphia: Roland Swain Co., 1933), pp. 63-64, 125-26.
7. Salter, *People's Choice*, p. 28.
8. Ibid., p. 29.
9. Statler, "M. G. Brumbaugh," p. 20.
10. *Lancaster Daily New Era* (Mar. 2, 1914).
11. *Philadelphia Inquirer* (Oct. 3, 1914).
12. *Lancaster Daily New Era* (Mar. 15, 1914).
13. Earl C. Kaylor, Jr., *Martin Grove Brumbaugh: A Pennsylvanian's Odyssey from Sainted Schoolman to Bedeviled World War I Governor, 1862-1930* (Cranbury, NJ: Associated University Presses, 1996), pp. 271-330.
14. *Juniatian* (Feb. 3, 1925).
15. *MGB* to J. S. Noffsinger (Apr. 3, 1929), Brumbaughana, college Archives.
16. See Claude Flory's "M. G. Wants Me for a Sunbeam."
17. William Faust to *MGB* (Apr. 21, 1928), Brumbaughana, college Archives.
18. *Juniatian* (Dec. 13, 1928).
19. *Juniata Echo* (Oct. 1910), p. 22.
20. *Juniatian* (Jan. 12, 1928).
21. *TM* (Oct. 24, 1925).
22. Among N. J.'s papers, preserved in the college Archives.
23. *Juniatian* (Mar. 12, 1930).
24. *AB* (Oct. 1925), p. 4.
25. Ibid., (Oct. 1927), p. 4.
26. *TM* (Dec. 2, 1924).
27. *Juniatian* (Apr. 21, 1927).
28. See Claude Flory's "M. G. Wants Me for a Sunbeam."
29. Kaylor, *Martin Grove Brumbaugh*, p. 357.

CHAPTER 10

1. Letter to the board of trustees, dated April 17, 1930, among Dr. Ellis's papers.
2. *AB* (Oct. 1931), p. 2.
3. In a paper read to the faculty, Sept. 1946.
4. *AB* (Feb. 1931), p. 6.
5. In a paper read to the faculty, Sept. 1946.
6. Quoted by Dean Clyde Stayer in an undated mimeographed script of a mock radio program honoring Dr. Ellis.
7. *Sunday School Times* (July 15, 1950), p. 601.
8. Charles C. Ellis, *Juniata College: The History of Seventy Years, 1876-1946* (Elgin, IL: Brethren Publishing House, 1947), p. 198.
9. *Juniatian* (Dec. 4, 1940).
10. Ellis, *Juniata College*, p. 196.

11. Robert Kelly, *A Survey of the Colleges of the Church of the Brethren* (Association of American Colleges, 1933), p. 14.
12. Ibid., p. 23.
13. *AB* (Oct. 1938), p. 2.
14. Ibid. (Oct. 1939), p. 3.
15. *TM* (Apr. 17, 1930).
16. *Juniatian* (Apr. 11, 1934).
17. *AB* (Oct. 1939), p. 3. President's Report.
18. *Juniatian* (Feb. 5, 1941).
19. *TM* (Oct. 20, 1938).
20. John Baker made this statement in public as well as to Earl Kaylor in private.
21. Ellis, *Juniata College*, p. 96.

CHAPTER 11

1. *The Pennsylvania Manual, 1935-36* (Harrisburg: Bureau of Publications, 1936), pp. 196 f.
2. *TM* (Oct. 15, 1942).
3. Thelma Smith Scott to Arthur and Anna Smith, March 21, 1936. A letter in the possession of Earl Kaylor.
4. *TM* (Nov. 6, 1929).
5. *AB* (Fall 1943), p. 5.
6. Ibid.

CHAPTER 12

1. *AB* (Spring 1968), p. 4.
2. Ibid.
3. Ibid., p. 2.
4. Ibid., p. 11.
5. *AB* (Spring 1963), p. 7.
6. [Huntingdon] *The Daily News* (Oct. 25, 1943).
7. *AB* (Spring 1963), p. 7.
8. Ibid. (Fall 1962), p. 8.
9. Report of the President to the Board of Trustees, June 7, 1954.
10. *FM* (Oct. 9, 1950); *TM* (Oct. 20, 1950; Apr. 16, 1951).
11. Treasurer's Report to the Board of Trustees, June 4, 1956.
12. *TM* (Sept. 8, 1967).
13. Ibid. (Mar. 2, 1968).
14. Ibid. (Apr. 21, 1958).
15. *AB* (Spring 1949), p. 3.
16. Ibid. (Summer 1953), p. 3.
17. Ibid. (Fall 1957), p. 10.
18. *Juniatian* (Sept. 17, 1966).
19. Report of the team that visited the campus, Feb. 25-28, 1962.
20. *AB* (Spring 1961), p. 9; *Juniatian* (Jan. 10, 1961).
21. Taped personal interview with Calvert Ellis.
22. *TM* (May 15, 1965).
23. *AB* (Winter 1951), p. 10.
24. Ibid. (Spring 1944), p. 10.
25. Calvert N. Ellis, *Ten Years as President*. A pamphlet in the college Archives.
26. John Baker to Calvert Ellis, Jan. 4, 1952. Presidential Papers, college Archives.
27. *AB* (Spring 1968), p. 1.

28. Built by John Cassady in 1921, the house was later sold to the Orphans' Home after the Cloister was erected. Later it was purchased by Francis McSherry, five of whose children either graduated from or attended Juniata.
29. [Huntingdon] *The Daily News* (Mar. 8, 1976). Obituary of Philip Snider.
30. Interview with Calvert N. Ellis, June 16, 1976.
31. *TM* (June 3, 1957).
32. *Juniatian* (Apr. 7, 1967).
33. Ibid. (Nov. 4, 1966).
34. *AB* (Summer 1968), p. 8.

CHAPTER 13

1. *TM* (Oct. 21, 1944).
2. *AB* (Fall 1946), p. 3.
3. Ibid. (Fall 1945), p. 5.
4. *Juniatian* (Oct. 10, 1945).
5. Calvert Ellis to John Baker, March 26, 1946. Presidential Papers, college Archives.
6. *Juniatian* (Nov. 7, 1946).
7. *TM* (Oct. 25, 1946).
8. The Yoder papers are deposited in the college Archives.
9. Janet Howell Clark to Calvert N. Ellis, June 19, 1945. Presidential Papers, college Archives.
10. *Juniatian* (Apr. 1, 1955).
11. *AB* (Fall 1950), p. 9.
12. *Juniatian* (Mar. 2, 1953).
13. Ibid. (Apr. 29, 1955; Mar. 2, 1956).
14. *AB* (Spring 1956), p. 6.
15. Ibid. (Fall 1956), p. 2.
16. *Juniatian* (Nov. 9, 1956).
17. Ibid. (Oct. 12, 1956).
18. *AB* (Summer 1957), p. 13.
19. *Juniatian* (Nov. 1, 1957).
20. *TM* (Aug. 15, 1958).
21. Ibid. (May 12, 1967), Dean of Student Affairs Report.
22. Ibid.
23. *Juniatian* (May 11, 1962).
24. The trustees bought the house from the I. Harvey Brumbaugh daughters, whose mother had lived there after selling her corner residence.
25. *AB* (Winter 1964), p. 11.
26. *Juniatian* (Mar. 19, 1965).
27. Ibid. (Apr. 23, 1965).
28. Ibid. (Feb. 18, 1966).
29. Ibid. (Mar. 8, 1967).

CHAPTER 14

1. *AB* (Feb. 1968).
2. *Juniatian* (Oct. 13, 1967).
3. *AB* (Mar. 1968).
4. Ibid.
5. Ibid.
6. *AB* (Fall 1969), p. 5.
7. Ibid. (Feb. 1972), p. 2.

8. Ibid. (Dec. 1975), p. 37.
9. For a fuller account of the J. Omar Good Fund's origin and agreement, see Earl C. Kaylor, Jr.'s essay, "J. Omar Good, The Man and His Legacy," in David W. Gill, ed., *Should God Get Tenure? Essays on Religion and Higher Education* (Grand Rapids, MI: William B. Eerdman's Publishing Company, 1997), pp. 237-245.
10. *FM* (Oct. 1968).
11. *Juniatian* (Nov. 1, 1972).
12. *The Chronicle of Higher Education* (Feb. 9, 1976), p. 3.
13. For the origins of the peace studies program at Juniata, see Marta Daniels, *Peace Is Everybody's Business: Half a Century of Peace Education with Elizabeth Evans Baker.* (Huntingdon, PA: Juniata College Press), 1999.
14. Gordon Carruth and Associates, eds., *American Facts and Dates*, 7th Edition, with a Supplement of the 70s (New York: Thomas Y. Crowell, Publishers, 1979), p. 929.
15. *AB* (Fall 1969), p. 2.
16. Carruth and Associates, *American Facts and Dates*, p. 929.
17. *Renaissance* (Dec. 15, 1970).
18. *Juniatian* (Apr. 25, 1969).
19. Ibid. (Oct. 13, 1971).

CHAPTER 15

1. John N. Stauffer. Presidential Papers, college Archives.
2. *AB* (Sept. 1975), p. 5.
3. He used this terminology in a conversation with Earl Kaylor.
4. *AB* (Sept. 1975), p. 6.
5. Jewett Henry invited Earl Kaylor to his office one day, showed him Binder's letter, and said it warranted serious consideration.
6. *AB* (Sept. 1975), p. 1.
7. Ibid. (Oct. 1975), p. 2.
8. Ibid. pp. 5-6.
9. A published transcript of the *Season* narration, illustrated with photographs and printed in magazine format, is on file in the college Archives.
10. *AB* (Feb. 1976), p. 6.
11. *TM* (May 5, 1977).
12. Ibid. (May 11, 1979). See Exhibit A.
13. *Juniatian* (Jan. 24, 1980).
14. Ibid. (Mar. 13, 1980).
15. *TM* (May 1, 1976). See attached mimeographed sheet.
16. Ibid. (July 20, 1977).
17. *AB* (July 1986), p. 20.
18. *Juniatian* (Oct. 24, 1985).
19. *AB* (Nov. 1978), p. 4.
20. Ibid. (April 1983), p. 10.
21. Ibid. (Jan. 1986), pp. 6-7.
22. Ibid. (Winter, 1991), p. 22.
23. Ibid. (July 1983), p. 3.
24. Ibid. (July 1985), p. 17.
25. Ibid.
26. *TM* (April 30, 1976); (May 1, 1976).
27. *AB* (Jan. 1986), p. 6.
28. Ibid. (June 1978), p. 12.
29. Ibid. (Nov. 1979), p. 5.

30. *Juniatian* (Feb. 2, 1984).
31. Ibid. (Feb. 15, 1979).
32. U. S. Bureau of the Census, *Statistical Abstract of the United States: 1988 (108th edition).* Washington, D. C., 1987, p. 148.
33. *Juniatian* (April 10, 1986).
34. Ibid. (May 18, 1987).
35. *TM* (Undated letter to the board of trustees at its semiannual meeting on Oct. 20, 1987).
36. *Juniatian* (April 17, 1980).
37. Ibid. (Nov. 1, 1979).
38. *TM* (Sept. 24, 1982).
39. *Juniatian* (Oct. 4, 1979).
40. U. S. Department of Education. National Center for Education Statistics. *Digest of Education Statistics, 1997,* NCES 98-015, by Thomas D. Snyder. Production Manager, Charlene M. Hoffman. Program Analyst, Claire M. Geddes, Washington, D. C.: 1997, pp. 133, 136.
41. *TM* (Oct. 9, 1982).

CHAPTER 16

1. *AB* (July 1985), p. 7.
2. *Report of the President* (1985-86), p. 2.
3. Ibid., p. 3.
4. Ibid., p. 2.
5. Ibid., p. 3.
6. *Juniata Journal* (Fall 1986). p. 1.
7. *Inauguration Program* (April 1987). p. 15.
8. Ibid., p. 18.
9. *Report of the President* (1986-87). p. 2.
10. *TM* (Oct. 15, 1988).
11. *AB* (Summer 1990), p. 5.
12. Ibid. (Spring 1994), p. 14.
13. *TM* (May 7, 1988).
14. *Memorandum to the Faculty* (June 10, 1988) from Joseph V. Stewart.
15. For the May 3, 1997, post-retirement benefits plan *see TM* for that date.
16. See Chapter 4, under *MEMORIALIZING ZUCK,* pp. 71 f.
17. The data for this section comes from a promotional pamphlet, *JUNIATA COLLEGE at a glance.*
18. *AB* (Summer 1993), p. 15.
19. Ibid. (Spring 1993), p. 6.
20. Ibid. (Fall 1998), p. 6.
21. Marta Daniels, *Peace Is Everybody's Business: Half a Century of Peace Education with Elizabeth Evans Baker* (Huntingdon, PA: Juniata College Press), 1999, pp. 130, 156.
22. Ibid. p. 133.
23. *AB* (Summer 1994). p. 13.
24. Ibid. (Summer/Fall 1995), p. 6.
25. Mr. and Mrs. Charles Gump bequested $215,000 to Juniata, all but $25,000 to go toward instructional technology. Room 201 in Good Hall is named, as Mr. Gump willed, for his brother and sister-in-law. Both brothers had attended Juniata just after World War I.
26. *Juniatian* (Feb. 26, 1987).
27. Ibid. (April 28, 1994).
28. *TM* (Oct. 20, 1990).
29. *AB* (Summer/Fall 1995). p. 2.
30. Loren Pope, *Colleges that Change Lives* (NY: Penguin Books, 1996), p. 58.
31. *Juniatian* (Feb. 2, 1996).

32. *JUNIATA COLLEGE QUICK FACTS: 1997-98.*
33. See *JUNIATA COLLEGE at a glance*, p. 7, and [State College] *Centre Daily Times* (Oct. 6, 1999), p. 3A.
34. Pope, *Colleges That Change Lives*, p. 53.
35. The data in this paragraph were taken from an article written by David Hawsey for the *Juniatian* (Feb. 28, 1997).
36. Ibid. (Sept. 10, 1992).
37. *TM* (Oct. 17, 1987).
38. *Juniatian* (Feb. 15, 1990).
39. Ibid. (April 11, 1997).
40. *Time* (Sept. 13, 1999), p. 85.
41. Ibid.
42. *Juniatian* (Jan. 28, 1997).
43. Ibid. (April 19, 1972).
44. Ibid. (Sept. 29, 1988).
45. Ibid. (Nov. 21, 1991).
46. Ibid. (Feb. 11, 1993).
47. *AB* (Summer 1994), p. 19.
48. Ibid. (Summer 1997), p. 17.
49. Ibid. (Summer/Fall 1995), p. 18.

CHAPTER 17

1. *AB* (Spring 1997), p. 2.
2. *TM* (May 2, 1998).
3. *Juniatian* (Sept. 23, 1998).
4. *Juniata College 120th Commencement Program* (Sunday, May 9, 1999).
5. *AB* (Fall 1998), p. 3.
6. *Juniatian* (Nov. 27, 1999).
7. *TM* (May 1, 1999).
8. [Huntingdon] *The Daily News* (Jan. 28, 1999), p. 5.

EPILOGUE

1. David Emmert, *Reminiscences of Juniata College* (Harrisburg, PA: J. Horace McFarland Co., 1901), p. 183.
2. Extract of a speech among the Jacob Zuck papers, college Archives.

Name Index

Abel, Elizabeth, 299
Abler, Lawrence, 199
Abu-Jamal, Mumia, 333
Adams, Kirsten (Brandt), 327
Adams, Naomi, 376
Africa, Elmer, 119
Africa, J. Murray, 99
Africa, J. Simpson, 54, 373
Agnew, Spiro, 255
Aichelle, Gary, 309
Alakoye, Ayinde, 337
Alexander, Lamar, 312
Alexander, Torin, 330, 360
Alexander, William, x, 266-267, 307
Allard, Elizabeth, 363
Amidon, David, 252
Anderson, A. S. M., 37-38
Andre, Carolyn (Beck), 300
Andrews, David, 360
Andrews, Kevin, 363-364
Apel, Edward, 157
Armstrong, Donald, 231
Arnold, Thomas, 162-163
Asendorf, William, 267
Ash, Rob, 295, 297
Ash, Robert, 345, 351
Atkins, Susy, 337
Atkinson, Louis, 54

Bach, Emma, 167
Bader, Bruce, 290
Bailey, John M., 109, 154
Baker, Anne, 322, 359
Baker, Elizabeth, 248, 250, 275, 292, 317-318

Baker, John, 117, 174, 187-188, 201-202, 211, 239-240, 248, 274-275, 277, 292, 317-318, 321, 336, 378-379
Baker, Robert, 201
Baldino, Thomas, 268
Bampton, Rose, 173
Barbash, Steven, 198, 265
Bargerstock, Charles, 203, 295
Bargiel, Diane, 338
Barker-(Hildebrandt), Susan, 294
Barlow, J. Jackson, 309, 311
Bartol, Michelle, 354
Barnes, Jeffrey, 235
Barrick, Rebecca C., 258
Bartok, Bela, 173
Barton, Bruce, 146
Basham, Lynn (Fleisher), 285
Basom, Brett, x
Baugher, Beulah Replogle Lesher, x, 356
Bauknight, Catherine, 331
Baumgaertner, Jill Palaez, 310
Baxter, Craig, 268, 310
Baxter, James, 202
Bayer, Frederick, 348
Beachley, Donovan, 195, 321
Beachley, Donovan, Jr., 275, 322
Beard, Richard, 235, 260
Bebes, Lona (Norris), 242
Bechtel, Annie, 63
Bechtell, Barbara, 232
Beckley, Mary F., 281-282

Bednarczyk, Kathleen (Walch), 300
Beeghly, Leon A., 206
Beekey, Mark, 350
Beer, Joseph, 28-29, 39-40
Beery, Adaline Hohf, 60
Beery, William, 24, 31, 36-37, 40, 49, 51, 53, 60-61, 65, 73, 75, 91, 93, 108-110, 209
Bell, Jane (Swigart), 231
Belser, Andrew, 338, 358
Benn, David, 325
Benner, John, 351
Benner, William, 351
Berger, Steven, 295
Berlanda, Mario, 235
Berrier, Grey, 235-236
Berrier, James, 236, 351
Berrier, William, x, 222, 235-236, 260, 296-297, 300-301, 343-345, 351, 363
Berthold, Robert, 236
Betting, Matthew, 364
Beyer, Joseph, 215
Biddle, Eric, 298
Biddle, John, 182
Biddle, Joseph, 155
Biddle, Josephine, 182
Biden, Joseph, 285
Bieber, Larien, 236
Bigler, Ivan, 134
Biko, Steven, 331
Binder, Frederick, 262-272, 274-278, 281, 283, 286-288, 291-296, 299, 301-

303, 305, 308-310, 322, 326, 342, 380
Binder, Grace, 264, 355
Binder, Robin, 264
Binkley, Harold, 167-169, 195, 216, 252
Blair, John C., 49-50
Blaisdell, Alice G., 231
Blaisdell, Edwin, 193, 231
Blankley, Richard, 68
Bleil, Bett, 363
Bleil, Robert, ix
Bloch, Philip, 333
Blood, John, 236, 347, 350
Blose, William, 290
Blough, Albert, 341
Blough, Amy, 347
Blough, Heather (Pavlic), 344
Blough, Percy, 201
Blough, Perry, 120
Bock, Lawrence, x, 294, 342-344, 362
Bogle, Sarah, 97
Book, William, 201
Book, William I., 195
Book, Zella B., 195
Bosserman, Linnie (Grigsby), 47
Botha, President, 286
Bourgeois, Roy, 332
Bower, Harry, 157
Bowman, Calvin, 174
Bowman, Warren, 166
Bowser, John, 193
Boyer, Ernest, 304-305
Brady, Joseph, 214
Brandau, Will, 231, 253, 290
Brashear, John, 89
Bray, James, 196
Briggs, Clayton, 192, 247
Broadwater, Barry, 235
Brosz, Christian, 333
Brougher, Mahlon, 174
Brouwer, Frederick, 229
Browdy, Louis, 226
Brown, C. Clifford, 223, 260
Brown, Charles, 221, 275, 322, 342
Brown, Jane, 290-291
Brown, Joel, 299-300
Brown, Rosann, x
Brubaker, William, 231
Brumbaugh, Andrew B. (A. B.), 9-11, 14, 23, 28, 30, 35, 38-39, 41, 45, 47, 51, 54-55, 57-60, 62, 64-65, 71, 73-74, 79, 83, 88, 95, 111, 314, 372, 374
Brumbaugh, Edwin, 158-159
Brumbaugh, Eleanor, 13
Brumbaugh, Eugene, x, 356
Brumbaugh, F. Samuel, 322, 342
Brumbaugh, Gaius, 23, 39, 46-47, 54-55, 61, 64, 71, 88, 173, 201, 369, 372-373
Brumbaugh, George, 37, 64
Brumbaugh, Harold (H. B.) vii, x, 166, 175, 203, 206-207, 209-210, 241, 275, 321-322, 327, 356
Brumbaugh, Henry, 7-8, 11-12, 14, 23-24, 26-27, 29-30, 38-39, 44, 47-48, 50, 52, 54, 58, 60, 62-69, 72, 74-77, 79, 85, 90, 94-95, 103, 119, 138, 148, 369, 374-375
Brumbaugh, Isaac Harvey, 11, 64-65, 75, 79, 83-87, 90, 97, 100, 104-105, 113-117, 119, 120-124, 129, 130-133, 137-140, 143, 147-148, 150, 165-166, 276, 374, 379
Brumbaugh, Jacob H., 30, 36, 38-39, 41, 48-49, 64-65, 73, 93, 98, 102, 107, 119, 122, 150
Brumbaugh, John, 6-10, 13-14, 20-24, 26, 28-29, 36, 40-41, 43, 47, 57, 60, 64-67, 71-73, 76, 86, 90, 100, 119, 121, 370-371
Brumbaugh, Levi, 56
Brumbaugh, Martha, 342
Brumbaugh, Martin Grove (M. G.), vii, 37, 44, 48, 52-53, 55, 57, 61-65, 75, 77-88, 90-99, 105, 112-115, 117, 119-120, 127, 136-137, 139-147, 149-152, 155, 157-161, 171-172, 174, 176, 205, 263, 292, 373-375, 377
Brumbaugh, Miriam—see Yoder
Brumbaugh, Norman J (N. J.), 64, 107-108, 150, 154-155, 187, 195
Brumbaugh, Samuel, 61
Brumbaugh, Susan, 11
Buchanan, Homer W., 38
Buchanan, Jay, 286
Buck, Hannah, 63
Buckle, Jack, 327
Bucklen, Kathryn (Bahoric), 350
Bunche, Ralph, 229
Bunn, Kenneth, 221, 234, 236
Burchinell, Thomas, 27
Burke, Kevin, 348, 362
Burkholder, Clay, 275, 321
Burt, Frederick, 102
Butler, Gertrude, 167
Buttimer, Jeffrey, 331
Button, S. D., 55
Buxbaum, Amy, 346
Buys, Peter, 127-128, 154
Bygall, Rhonda, 344

Cable, Thomas, 298
Caitlin, Anne, 207
Calaboyis, Peter, 359
Calhoun, Lucy, 307
Calian, Samuel, 243, 271
Campbell, Jamie, 363
Carfora, Juanita, 217
Carfora, Lolita, 217
Carleton, Judy (Barnett), 226
Carnegie, Andrew, 83, 97-98
Carnell, Corbin, 271, 310
Carney, Eugene, 109
Carver, Colleen, 344, 362
Casey, James, 338
Cass, Kimmie, 350
Cassady, Harry, 117
Cassady, John, 379
Cassel, Abraham, 80, 96, 111, 375-376
Cassel, Hannah, 96
Catlin, Anne, 207
Caulk, Richard, 225
Caulton, Cyrus, 251, 343
Caulton, Isabelle, 251, 343
Cawley, Jeffrey, 234
Cecil, Vernon, 135
Celesnik, Ryan, 362
Chadwick, Ryan, 309, 338
Chamberlain, Irene, 300, 349
Chaplin, John, 46
Check, Brian, 287
Cherry, Elizabeth, 192-193, 244, 306, 309-310

Cherry, Ronald, 192-193, 196, 209, 227, 242, 268, 309
Cheyney, Edward Potts, 79, 374
Christy, Michael, 307
Church, Evelyn, 192
Church, Ralph, 192, 265, 286, 310
Clark, H. Ford, 264
Clark, Martin, 248
Clarke, Cynthia—see Gilbert
Clarke, Wealthy (Burkholder), 63
Clarkson, Kris, 306, 319
Claycomb, Janet (Dodge), 327
Clem, Donald, 278
Clemens, George, 167
Clemson, Sara, 234, 244
Clouse, Robert, 271
Cohick, Sandra, 219
Coleman, Donna, 311
Coller, Christopher, 345
Collins, Constance, 267
Collins, Kathleen, x, 349, 363
Confer, Violet, x
Conner, Harold, 124, 150
Conner, Stanley, 236
Cook, Isabel, 124
Cook, Patricia, 291
Cook-Huffman, Celia, 309, 311
Cook-Huffman, Daniel, 306
Copeland, Erin, 363
Coradetti, Joseph, 260, 298
Corle, Donald, 235
Corson, Oscar, 79
Cottle, Michael, 295, 345
Coulson, Diana, 348
Coupland, Douglas, 282-283
Coursen, Amy, 285, 331
Craig, Casey, 346
Craik, Elmer, 150
Cramer, John, 275, 322
Cramer, Sharon—see Faulkner
Croft, David, 214
Cronemiller, Philip, 275, 321
Croner, Earl, 275, 321
Crosby, David, 185
Crosby, Kenneth, 192, 195, 206, 268-269
Crossey, Robert, 295-296
Crouch, Howard, 192, 268, 274, 314
Crowell, William, 235
Croyle, Jane, x

Crummy, Pressley, 167, 196-197
Cruser, George, 275, 322
Crust, Robin (Boyer), 284
Culver, Michael, 295, 347
Cumming, Janet, 241
Cutright, Jon, x, 348-349
Cuttrell, Edith—see also Hartman, 321
Cypressi, Mary, 364

Dahmus, Elizabeth, 327
Dale, Irene—see Miller
Dale, John, 217, 325, 358
Damico, Kristin, 348
Dana, Charles, 242
Daniels, Marta, 234, 254-255, 380-381
Dassdorf, Richard Arno, 111, 376
Davis, Bruce, 247
Davis, Cloyd, 137
Davis, Lincoln, 57
Davis, Russell, 358
Davis, Stanley, 206
Day, Raymond, 211, 292, 321
DeBlase, Joseph, 346
DeBlaze, Tracy (Huston), 301
Dechano, Lisa, 348
delGiudice, Tristan, 354
Delewski, Joel, 235
DeMar, Francis, 360
Deppen, John, 331
Desky, Donald, 154
Detrick, Earl, 222
Dettore, Thomas, 260
Detweiler, George, 201
Detwiler, Dale, 201, 321, 325
Detwiler, Donald, 360
Detwiler, Edgar, 69, 103, 208
Deucher, Herbert, 216, 222
Devore, Scott, 348
Diehl, Anna (Brumbaugh), 56
Diehl, Robin, 344
Diehm, Edgar, 154, 206
Diehm, G. Graybill, 247
Dills, William "Toby", 233
Docherty, George, 271
Dock, Christopher, 82
Dolnikowski, George, 192-193, 309-311, 314
Domonkos, Dorothy, 173, 181
Donaldson, James, 232, 267, 306, 309
Dore, Orville, 215, 327

Dorner, Mark, 345
Dorris, William, 35
Dorsch, Jenn, 363
Dortch, Jessiann, 272
Douthett-Desky, Mary, 154
Dove, Alice, 217, 232
Dove, Patricia, 231
Doyle, Esther, 192, 195, 212, 242, 244, 268, 358
Doyle, Robert, 228
Drews, David, 243, 309
Drexler, Barry, 222
Dubbel, Earl, 150
Dudash, Andrew, ix
Dudzik, Kenneth, 326
Duey, William, 316
Duffy, Kathleen, 300
Dugan, Miriam (Bryngelson), 127
Dungan, Al, 222
Dunkle, Jeffrey, 232-233
Dunlavy, Myron, 211-212
Dupler, Alphaeus, 93, 121-122, 147, 376
Durnbaugh, Donald, ix, 248, 310, 375
duVon, Jay, 189
Dzvonar, Mike, 214

Eckerl, Louis, 361
Edwards, Glenora (Rossell), 212
Eisenberg, Matthew, 345, 362
Eisenhart, Henry, 215
Eisenhour, Jeremiah, 256
Eisenhower, Dwight, 205, 217-218
Ellis, Calvert, 133, 135, 161, 166-168, 174, 178, 187-198, 200-204, 209-211, 213, 216, 221, 223-224, 226-228, 231-234, 237-239, 242-244, 247, 249, 253-254, 263, 265, 275, 280, 307, 321, 378-379
Ellis, Charles, viii, 88-89, 93, 106, 115-117, 121, 125-127, 138-141, 147, 161-165, 167-168, 170, 172, 174, 177, 182, 184-186, 188, 201, 213, 216-217, 249, 252, 264, 278, 321, 371, 373, 376-377
Ellis, Charles C., 275, 321
Ellis, Earle, 271

Ellis, Elizabeth, 191, 205, 242, 248, 252, 265, 280, 355
Emmert, David, viii, 11, 15, 19-20, 23, 31-33, 35-37, 42-46, 48-51, 53, 58, 65, 73, 83, 93-95, 98, 100, 111-112, 119-121, 205-206, 214, 250, 264, 366, 370-374, 382
Emmert, Denton, 201
Emrich, Jessica, 347
Engel, William, 196, 204, 234, 261, 342-343
Engle, Harold, 150, 223
Engle, Stephen, 231
Esch, Linda Sue, 268, 288, 309, 353
Esterline, Eugene, 208, 280
Evans, Dale, 225, 230
Evans, Lillian, 121, 149, 174, 213
Evans, Peggy, 294, 301, 348
Ewing, John, 31
Eyman, David, 271
Ezdebski, Pamela (Prim), 349

Faber, Anthony, 236
Fackler, Miriam, 150
Fairweather, Judy (Young), 226
Fala, Grace, 309, 321
Falkenstein, George, 61
Falvo, Jason, 348
Fattman, George, 219
Faulkner, Sharon (Cramer), 359
Faus, Nancy (Rosenberger), 227, 243, 358
Faus, Robert, 227, 244, 251, 255, 358
Fazio, Christopher, 344
Ferry, Rick, 345-346
Figg, Joseph, 338
Fike, John, 120, 208, 241
Fike, John, Jr., 227
Fike, Terry, 349
Finnegan, Betty—see Simpson
Firestone, Nicole, 344
Fischer, Jeffrey, 344
Fisher, Robert, 192, 217, 247, 270, 307, 309
Fisher, Tom, 268, 308
Fiske, Edward B., 280
Fitch, Nancy, 225
Fleck, Betty, 184

Fleck, David, 235
Flory, Claude, 146, 377
Flory, Daniel, 40
Flory, William, 201, 250
Fogelsanger, Florence (Murphy), 139, 201
Fogelsanger, John, 119-120
Fogelsanger, Luella, 121
Ford, Gavin, 297
Ford, Gerald, 246
Forney, Christopher, 340
Fort, Amelia, 346
Fort, Amy, 347
Fortson, Mary, 337
Foster, Eleanor, 310
Foster, Frank, 120, 137, 377
Foster, H. George, 310, 367
Foster, M. R., 38
Frantz, David, 59
Frazier, Patrick, 261, 296
Fredrick, Athena, 357
Frenay, Travis, 348
Friend, Paul, 208
Frye, Mardi (Dunklebarger), 261
Frye, Marsha (Hartman), x, 354
Frysinger, James, 218
Fultz, Alexa—now Cook, 261
Fusco, David, 319

Gahagen, William, 120
Galo, Roger, 296
Gardner, Robert, 236
Gargula, Edmund, 261, 294
Gasque, W. Ward, 310
Gehrett, Ada, 282
Gehrett, J. Foster, 223
Gehrett, Samuel, 282
Geiger, Mary, 88, 91, 116, 119, 128, 171, 195, 269
George, Julie (McCormick), 295
Gerko, Eric, 344
Germann, William, 223, 299, 361
Gessner, Angela, 348
Getz, Thomas, 349
Ghaner, Ray, 363
Giachetti, Brian, 345
Gibbel, Florence, 147
Gibbel, Henry B., 201
Gibbel, Henry H., 275, 303, 322, 327, 353
Gibbel, Henry R., 120, 151

Gibboney, Thomas, 345, 362
Gilbert, Cynthia (Clarke), x, 266, 307
Gilbert, Jack, 199
Gilbert, Karl, 155
Gildea, David, xi, 301, 307
Giles, J. P., 54
Gill, David, 310, 380
Gillard, Kathleen, 166, 179
Gillich, Caroline, 347
Gillies, Katherine (Dixon), 224
Gillin, Colin, 363
Gingrich, Ada, 292
Gipprich, Eileen (Sill), 359
Gladfelter, Amy, 348
Glaeser, Carl, 257-258
Glazier, Douglas, 268, 308
Gliem, Valerie, x
Glosenger, Fay, 268, 309-310, 315
Goehring, Doris, 192, 252, 338
Goldwater, Barry, 228
Gooch, James, 193, 268
Good, J. Omar, 242
Good, Jane, 343
Good, Joseph, 201, 321, 343
Good, Paul, 209
Good, Stoler, 119, 139
Goodale, Charles, 223, 341
Goodrich, Benn, 202
Gould, David, 231-232
Grabiak, Raymond, 259, 293, 296
Grace, Andrew, 364
Gracey, Carole, x
Gramm, Kent, 310
Grater, Stephen, 347, 350
Graves, Frank, 161
Gray, Glenn, 218
Green, Francis, 61
Greene, Arnold, 215, 222, 235
Greenwood, Joan (Metro), 206
Griffith, George, 135
Groff, Warren, 275, 322
Groninger, Anna (Smith), 195, 307
Grove, Donna, ix
Grove, Priscilla (Gibboney), 294
Grubb, Mary, 63
Grubb, Susan, 295, 346
Gump, Charles, 381
Guss, Evelyn, 195

Gustafson, Todd, 268
Gutshall, Edward, 156

Habakus, Shawn, 346
Haines, Amos, 90, 93, 104, 107, 121
Haines, Stephanie, 346
Halbritter, Barry, 322, 366
Hall, Roslyn, 299-300
Halley, Paul, 353
Hamilton, Darien, 348
Hamme, John B., 205
Handzelek, Jacob, 222, 297
Hannig, Kimberly, 344
Harbaugh, James, 234
Harbaugh, Steven, 364
Harden, Nancy—see Latimore
Harden, Ralph, 235, 294
Hardy, John, 280
Harrison, Charles, 79, 81
Harrity, Ralph, 216
Harroun, Herbert, 127
Harsanyi, Mary (Miller), 228
Hartland, James, 235
Hartman, Alan, 298, 300, 348
Hartman, Donald, 241, 244, 267, 288, 305
Hartman, Edith (Cutrell), 201
Hartman, Linda (Bianchi), 234
Hartman, Lloyd, 147
Hartzler, Eva, 193, 242, 268
Harvey, Charles, 259
Haskell, Jack, 261
Hatala, Robert, 305-306, 316-317, 323, 352, 357
Hatchett, Oscar, 259
Hatfield, Mark, 285
Haushalter, William, 222
Hawsey, David, x, 306, 354, 382
Hayes, Samuel, Jr., 318-319
Hazuda, Angela, 348
Heberling, Paul, 192, 231-232, 268, 270, 310, 341
Hedrick, Bayard, 172
Heidecker, Gwendolyn, 300
Heinz, Howard, 145-146
Heller, Bernice, 192
Heller, Max, 193
Helm, Daniel, 296-297, 345-346
Helms, Frances, 232-233, 306
Helsel, David L., 235
Helz, William, 317
Henderson, George, 87, 374

Henry, C. Jewett, 201, 250, 263, 275, 286, 356, 380
Henry, Phyllis, 321, 356
Henry, Tobias, 193
Herlan, Donald, 347
Herman, Ted, 317
Herritt, Alice (Stenstrom), 261, 298
Herritt, Elizabeth, 298
Herrold, Susan Kaylor, xi
Hershberger, Dorothy Lehman, 282, 323, 326
Hershberger, Rex, 323
Hershberger, William, 322
Hershey, Kristin, 344, 362-364
Hess, Nancy, 327
Hess, Samuel, 174
Hesselbein, Frances, 322, 359
Hetrick, Jeffrey, 348
Hettinger, Herman, 124, 132
Hettinger, Sarah, 192
Hickes, Paul, 249, 270, 277
Hicks, Robert, 221
Higbee, Elisha, 78
Hill, Russell, 217-218
Hille, John, x, 354, 360, 366
Himes, Scott, 307
Hirsch, Bruce, 230, 253
Hobbie, Scott, 348
Hobolinko, Joseph, 345
Hoch, Timothy, 285
Hochberg, Mark, 243, 268, 309
Hockley, Alfred, 338-339
Hockley, H. Alfred, 338
Hodges, Charles, 93
Hofelt, William, 192-193, 309
Hoff, Bridgette, 348
Hoffman, Annette, 346-347
Hoffman, Edwin, 236
Hoffman, Thomas, 298-299
Hohenshelt, Dennis, 344
Hollinger, John, 196
Holmes, Robert, 230
Holsinger, Alden, 157
Holsinger, Henry, 7-13, 15-16, 20, 39, 370
Holsinger, Steven, 360
Holsopple, Frances (Parsons), 139
Holsopple, Frank, 93, 121, 376
Hoover, Perry, 93, 121
Hoover, Shad, 351
Hope, Donald, 229

Hoppel, Beth (Barnett), 294, 344
Horner, Albert, 147
Horner, John "Jack", 358
Horvil, Anne-Valerie, 350
Houck, Ann, 350
Howden, Robert, 307
Howe, Elizabeth (Brubaker), 51, 94, 105
Howe, William, 120
Howey, Richard, 295-296
Hrach, Frank, 222
Hsiung, David, 309-310
Hunt, James, x, 219, 226, 301
Hunt, Nan, 327
Hunter, Richard, 192, 252
Huston, William, 329, 349
Hutchinson, Fred, 133
Hyatt, Dr. and Mrs. Thaddeus, 157
Hysong, Mark, 292
Hyssong, Eugene, 218

Instone, Craig, 346
Ireland, Colleen, 294

Jackson, Cecil, 214
Jackson, Stuart, 259, 361
Jaeger, Klaus, 299, 309, 347, 351
James, Arthur, 173
Janusz, Patricia (Shreiner), 327
Johnson, Amelia (Brumbaugh), 84-85, 100
Johnson, Donald, 192, 212, 230
Johnson, Lyndon, 189, 199, 224, 228
Johnson, Michele, 331
Johnson, Roger, 330
Jones, John, 307
Jones, Lynn, ix
Jones, Rodney, 227
Jubelirer, Robert, 304
Judy, Ruth, 206
Judy, Susanne (Wright), 231
Judy, Will, 175, 200, 206, 209, 281
Jula, Mark, 259
Junas, Lillian, 234
Justham, Wayne, 290

Kalinyak, Thomas, 295
Kaminsky, Edward, 267

Kauffman, Janet (Borland), 228
Kaylor, Earl, 142, 192-193, 195, 233, 236, 240, 242-244, 259, 264, 268, 309, 356, 369-370, 373-374, 377-378, 380
Kaylor, Harriet, xi
Keehner, Julia, 291, 306
Keenan, Gerald, 286
Keeney, Jill, 357
Keeny, John, 61, 78
Keim, Howard, 57
Keirns, May, 150, 167
Kellehar, Lucas, 364
Kelso, Margaret, 338
Kenawell, Michael, 348
Kennedy, Edwin, 249, 277, 280, 321
Kennedy, John, 225, 227
Kennedy, Robert, 238
Kennedy, Ruth, 277
Kensinger, Charles, 276, 306, 320
Kenyon, Allyson, 347, 363
Kenyon, Kirsten, 350
Kepple, Patricia, xi, 354
Kepple, Thomas R., vii, x, 325-326, 333, 336, 347, 353-355, 357-361, 366-367
Ketrick, Melissa, 347
Keyser, Verdean, 359
Kibler, Joseph, 348
Kichline, Ronald, 134
Kimmel, Lewis, 12-14, 29-30, 59
Kimmey, Richard, 198
Kindig, Karl, 244, 258, 360
King, Martin Luther, Jr., 229, 238, 320
King, Samuel, 160
Kinnell, Galway, 229
Kipphan, Klaus, 192, 248, 265, 268, 309
Kiracofe, Betty (Weicht), 213
Kiracofe, Edgar, 167, 184, 195, 215, 223
Kirby, Roderick, 344, 362
Kirchhof-Glazier, Debra, 268, 308-309, 357
Klepfer, Douglas, 290
Kline, Casey, 348
Kline, Joseph, 250
Knaub, Mark, 344
Knepp, Gerald, 364
Knepp, Thomas H., 293
Knepp, Tom, 155
Knepper, Lewis, 120, 147, 327
Knox, Charles, 222, 275, 322, 342, 360
Koch, Rebecca, 350
Komer, Louis, 296
Konigmacher, Annie (Brumbaugh), 112, 140, 142
Koren, Michelle (Corby), 360
Korody, Raymond, 223
Koval, Carl, 260
Krall, Julia, x
Kreider, David, 250, 261, 280, 282
Kreider, Gayle, 261, 306
Krugh, Joanne, x
Kubitz, Ida, 167
Kulp, Nancy, 271
Kulp, Todd, 288, 290
Kumada, Gisuke, 151
Kupersmith, Peter, 319
Kurl, Andrew, 344
Kurtz, Henry, 3-7
Kysor, Darwin, x, 327

Lach, Steven, 295
Lake, Carol, 359
Lakso, James, x, 243, 246, 268, 305, 314, 352, 354
Landon, Margaret, 232
Langdon, Chester, 118, 157, 174, 237
Langdon, Justina Marsteller, 155-156
Langenbacher, Mark, 280
LaPoint, Jill, 346-347
Latimore, Nancy Harden, 294-295, 298, 300, 350, 360
Latimore, William, 294, 300
Layman, Don, 222, 236
Laza, James, 111
Leaman, Bertha, 167
Lee, Louise—see Stauffer
Leedy, Scott, 253
Lehman, Dorothy—see Hershberger
Lehman, James, 229-230, 265
Leiter, Ralph, 157, 250
Lentini, Peter, 259, 295
Leonard, David, 234
Leone, Deanna, 363
Lesher, Chalendar, 201, 356
Lewis, Janet, 291, 309, 357
Lightner, Patricia, ix
Lin, Maya, 318, 338
Linetty, John, 280, 290, 307
Lingenfelter, Wesley, 299
Linton, Mary Ruth, 192-193, 212, 309
Lipski, Timothy, 350
Livengood, William, Jr., 57, 173
Loewen, James W., viii
Lonesky, Timothy, 346, 364
Long, Cyndi, 363
Long, D. Melvin, 57
Long, Hazel, 269, 309
Long, Jonathan, 348
Long, Michael, 244
Long, Ted J., 307
Long, W. Newton, 120, 250, 269, 309
Long, W. Newton, Jr., 275, 321
Loomis, Cecil, 201
Low, Clare, 232
Lucas, Renee, x
Lyon, George, 103, 110
Lyras, Evangelia "Teddy", 300
Lytle, Charles, 229

Maas, Elmer, 227, 229, 233-234
MacCrindle, Heather (Zimmerman), 292
Mack, Alexander, 9, 251
Maclay, Connie, 309
Maclay, Nitisha, 349
Mahosky, Gregory, 350
Malee, Ian, 296
Malloy, Edwin, 275, 322, 359
Malloy, Susan, 359
Malone, Perce "Pat", 134
Maloney, H. Newton, 310
Mandela, Nelson, 286, 331
Manion, Arthur, 319
Mann, Emily, 363
Mann, Keith, 309
March, Richard, 211
Marshall, Paul, 310
Martin, James, 220
Martin, Paula, 319
Martin, Thomas, 201, 248
Martin, William, 209, 266, 281
Marzio, Michael, 229-230, 234
Mason, Robert, 36-37

Masters, Henry, 192
Mathers, Nina, 347
Mathias, Frances, 221
Maxwell, Delores, 241
Maxwell, Leroy, Sr., 249
Mayher, Richard, 290
Mayley, George, 327
Mays, Morley, 193, 198, 227, 240, 278, 305
McBride, Alexander, 243-244, 265, 310
McCann, Samuel, 57
McCarthy, Eugene, 234, 255
McChesney, Margaret, x
McClaine, Rebecca, 361
McClelland, Liberty, 166
McClure, Joan (Hamm), 216
McCracken, John, 151
McCrimmon, Margaret, 150
McCullen, Kevin, 266, 306-307
McCullough, John, 260, 298-299
McDowell, Robert, 231, 360
McFadden, Robert, 248
McGinnis, Megan, 363
McGowan, Kathleen, 347
McIlroy, Mailand, 261, 343
McKenzie, Fayette, 147, 150, 166, 170
McLaughlin, Ronald, 268, 309
McMillan, Wendell, 218
McMullen, Kevin, 266
McMullen, Michael, 349
McNeal, Michael, 361
McNelly, Robert, 298
McQuaide, Delbert, 216, 219-221, 321-322
McQuown, Bernard, 222
McSherry, Francis, 205, 379
Meditch, Carl, 259, 296, 299
Mehl, Robert, 121
Merritt-(Nixon), Lynn, 337
Metzger, Irvin, 123
Metzger, Vila Gardner, 292
Meyer, George, 287
Meyers, Lauree Hersh, 310
Michel—see Richardson
Mickle, Stanford, 215-216
Mierley, Beulah, 279
Miles, Jeffrey, 295-296
Miller, Allison, 38
Miller, Blair, 215, 223, 260
Miller, Catharine (Gilkey), 344

Miller, Elizabeth, 291
Miller, Emma, 29
Miller, Herbert, 192-193, 247, 249
Miller, Howard, 59
Miller, Irene (Dale), 358
Miller, Jesse, 135
Miller, Kirsten, 231
Miller, Marjorie, 247
Miller, Mark, 360
Miller, Oliver, 12
Miller, Robert, 201, 250
Miller, Thomas, 201
Miranda, Juan, 111
Mitchell, Donald, 193, 244, 260, 268, 299, 309, 311-312
Mitchell, Robert, 184
Mock, Leroy, 235
Monger, Jodie (Gray), 327, 360
Montgomery, James, 216
Montgomery, John, 135, 201
Montgomery, William, 285
Montrella, Joseph, 362
Moore, Christopher, 234
Moore, Gary, 258
Moore, Kevin, 344
Morgan, Marjorie, 294
Morse, Paul, 231-232
Mouw, Richard, 271
Moyer, Bruce, 258
Moyer, Donald, 306, 325, 342, 352, 356
Mueller, Lisa, 348
Muir, Jill (Klinger), 301
Mullen, Charles, 222
Mumford, John, ix, x, 319, 347
Murphy, David, 295, 362
Murphy, Ross, 147
Murray, Andrew, 243, 248, 251, 270, 272, 284-285, 309, 317-318, 330
Murray, William, 215
Musselman, Miriam Schlegel, 192, 195
Musselman, Patricia, x
Musser, Robert, 297
Mutch, Andrew, 155, 292
Mutti, Laurence, 268, 309
Myers, Allan, 116, 120, 128, 137, 166
Myers, Alphia, 70
Myers, Graybill, 11

Myers, Jacob, 119
Myers, Mary Ruth—see Linton
Myers, Melissa, 344, 348
Myers, Oscar, 93, 121-122, 166
Myers, Tobias, 90-91, 93, 104, 121-122, 125, 171-172

Nadzak, Walter, 259, 295, 361
Nagengast, Emil, 311
Nathan, Hilda, 208
Neff, C. Scott, 303
Neff, Dorothy Rosewarne, 303, 355
Neff, Heather, 303
Neff, Robert, vii, x, 267, 303-310, 312-313, 315-326, 328, 331-337, 339-345, 348-349, 351-356
Newcombe, Robert, 197
Newcomer, Ewing, 107
Newcomer, Jennie—see Stouffer
Newman, Bradley, 350
Newman, Kristin (Vaughn), 349
Nicholson, Jay, 346
Nicolopoulos, Sotirios, 233-234
Nieto, José, 192, 244, 269
Nixon, Richard, 225, 244
Nolan, Thomas, 192, 244, 246, 267, 310
Noll, Mark, 271
Noll, Richard, 297
Nordin, Robert, 307
Norris, Nicole, 348
Norris, Phoebe, 47
Norris, Wilfred, 193, 195, 218, 241-242, 244, 246, 248, 257, 266-267, 309, 328, 357
North, Melissa, 347
Noyes, Chris, 330, 347
Nye, Harry, 167

O'Connell, Elizabeth, 241, 291, 306
O'Connell, Richard, 226
Oaks, Wilbur, 231
Ochiai, Ei-Ichiro, 268, 310
Oeffner, Randall, 235
Oiler, Amy, 347
Olawsky, Hugo, 31-32, 57

Oller, Anne, 298
Oller, Jack, 150, 159, 173, 183, 215, 223, 249, 275, 310
Oller, Jacob, 34, 47, 116, 173
Oller, Jefford, 135, 298
Oller, Joseph, 116-117, 119, 128, 147, 150, 159, 173
Oller, May (Wertz), 155
Oller, Rello, 173
Olsen, Brian, 361
Ondrejcak, Sally, 272
Orndorff, Christy (Osmun), 344
Orr, Nancy, 339
Orr, Scott, 339
Osborne, Larry, 254

Palmer, Cynthia, 281
Palmer, Deborah, 281
Palmer, Dorothea (Ferrier), 281
Park, Joanne, x
Parker, Catherine, 347
Parker, Melvin "Bub", x, 351
Parks, Flora Belle (Brumbaugh), 143
Parsons, Brent, 350
Parsons, Joan (Engle), x, 306
Paskill, Joseph, 297, 351
Patete, Dana, 346
Patrick, Dr. and Mrs. Robert, 279
Patterson, Wayne, 275, 321
Patton, Jenell, 330
Patton, Ryan, 344, 362-363
Paul, Wayne, 346
Paulhamus, Richard, 360
Paxton, Thomas, 226
Payne, James, 349
Pearson, Barbara, 299
Pearson, Charles, 360
Pecht, Ida, 51
Pembrooke, Evelyn, x
Pennington, Blanch, 278
Pennington, John, 278
Pennington, Sally, 290
Penny, James, 217, 232
Peppetti, Joel, 348, 364
Peregrine, Peter, 309
Perri, Gino, 295, 298
Perry, Christopher, 260
Petrella, Lisa, 361
Pfrogner, Jill Shrum, 267, 316
Pfrogner, Ray, 193, 261, 350

Phalunus, Richard, 306
Pheasant, Clayton, 250, 275-276, 280, 300, 306
Pheasant, Thomas, 322
Phillips, George, 43
Phillips, William, 258, 260, 328
Pierce, Frank, 247
Pirrello, Jamie, 286
Pollock, Charles, 261, 301, 306-307
Polte, Jarmilla, 317
Pope John Paul II, 333
Pope, Loren, 314, 326, 329, 381-382
Poska, Stephen, 296
Post, Ernest, 192, 236, 246, 269, 297, 309, 350
Pote, Garry, 275, 322, 360
Prender, Fred, 234-236, 259
Preston, Scott, 349
Price, William, 166, 208, 217
Prudenti, David, 348
Putt, Ward, 134

Quackenbos, Alan, 216
Quigg, Gerald, 203, 241-242
Quinlan, James, 280
Quinn, Kathleen, 346-347
Quinn, Richard, 224-225
Quinter, Grace (Holsopple), 121
Quinter, James, 3-8, 12, 21, 26, 28-29, 39, 42-44, 46-49, 51-55, 61-62, 64-66, 69, 72, 76, 97-98, 117, 121, 354, 373
Quinter, Mary, 96, 373

Rabenstein, Kenneth, 280
Rabinowitz, Aaron, 248, 359
Radis, Susan, 268
Radomsky, Andrew, 364
Raffensperger, Horace, 223
Read, Charles, 181
Reagan, Ronald, 285
Reber, Daniel, 88
Rebert, Jacquelyn (Wolfgang), 344
Reed, Michael, 345
Reed, Ruth, 268, 308-309
Reed, Timothy, 295
Regan, Rose, 348
Reichenbach, Bruce, 271
Reilly, JoAnn, 261, 294

Reilly, Richard, 259-260
Reilly, Robert, 243, 309
Reimer, Jennifer, 346
Reingold, I. David, 309, 311
Replogle, Harvey, 120
Ressler, Adie, 119
Rhoads, James B., 265
Rhodes, Loren, 268
Rhodes, Melvin, 197, 217, 232
Rhodes, Rhoda Metz, 208
Rhodes, Robert, 223
Riccio, Philip, 348
Rice, Charles, 166, 201, 231
Rice, Donald, 298
Richards, Robert, 237
Richardson, Harriet (Michel), 228-229, 322, 359
Richardson, Kim, 268, 309, 317
Rine, Renee, 347
Rini, Victor, 326
Risser, Stanley, 346
Ritter, William "Wild Bill", 134
Roach, Nancy (Gurdak), 300
Roberts, Katharine, 121, 130-131, 147-148, 166
Roberts, Owen, 146
Roberts, Robert, 310
Robinette, Marlene (Halbritter), 366
Robinson, Paul, 201
Robinson, Thomas, 241, 250
Robison, Janet (Bumbarger), 300
Rockwell, Donald, 167, 193, 195, 241, 255, 268, 293, 311
Rockwell, Kenneth, 192-193, 268, 303
Rodgers, Judith (Pheasant), 300
Roguish, Thomas, 298
Rohrer, Bessie, 159, 212
Roll, Brenda, x
Roller, Floyd, 241, 266
Roosevelt, Franklin, 177, 185
Roosevelt, Theodore, 81, 141, 143, 146
Root, Elihu, 81
Roppelt, Donna, 244, 254-255
Rose, Robert, 224-225
Rosell, Karen, 267, 309, 357
Rosenberger, Clarence, 208

Rosenberger, Lester, 201, 242, 358
Rosenberger, Pauline, 358
Rosenberger, W. Clemens, 243, 275, 322, 358
Rosenberry, Christopher, 345
Rosewarne, Dorothy—see Neff
Ross, Donald, 236
Ross, Jay, 120
Rosshirt, Susan, 258
Rossi, Dean, 259-260, 295, 298, 361
Rothenberger, Eugene, 222
Rowe, Barbara, 266-267, 307
Rowe, Gary, 229
Rowland, Charles, 121, 128, 180, 212
Royer, Galen, 117, 121, 370
Ruble, Duane, 235, 260
Ruby, Jodee, 307
Rummel, John, 225
Russell, John, 231
Russey, William, 193, 244, 268, 309, 359
Rutter, William, 266, 307

Sabin, Robert, 248, 271
Samseil, Lee Harvey, 233
Samuel, Earl, 235-236
Sanders, Candace, 347, 363
Sandler, Karen, 305, 308
Sanger, Homer, 91
Santos, Jeremy, x, 307
Sarni, Vincent, 275, 321
Satterlee, David, 330
Sauer, Christopher, 171
Sayer, Dorothy (Pentz), 148
Saylor, Joseph, 43, 49, 53, 55-56, 61, 65, 67, 70, 89, 93, 96, 102, 119, 121, 206, 372
Scallen, Gregory, 349
Schaaf, Don, 280
Schadler, Jill, 347
Schaeffer, Lynanne, 326, 360
Schaffner, Michael, 295
Schell, John, 213
Schell, Rosalyn, 213
Schettler, Paul, 193, 244, 268, 309
Schlesinger, Arthur, Jr., 230
Schlichter, William A., 258
Schneider, Alissa, 363

Schoenherr, Charles, 231-233, 241, 255-256
Scholl, Herman, 212
Schrock, William, 327
Schuyler, Peter, 260, 297
Schwab, Charles, 145-146
Scialabba, Dawn, x, 249
Scialabba, Joseph, x, 301, 327, 342-343, 346, 349
Scialabba, Richard, 347
Scranton, William, 189
Selby, Melina (Sterner), 344
Sell, James, 11, 75
Sell, Jesse, 75
Seltzer, Carolyn (Diercksen), 298
Severs, Kimberly, 347
Shaeffer, Michael, 363
Shaffner, Allen, 203
Sharkey, Robert, 346
Sharp, Solomon, 6-8, 12, 17, 41, 370
Shaute, Joseph, 134, 236
Shawaryn, Timothy, 344
Sheedy, Carolyn (Seckinger), 347
Shelley, Ray, 348
Shelley, Russell, x, 309, 338, 358
Sheppard, Gary, 235-236
Sherbine, Keith, 297
Sherk, Christian, 235
Sherk, Jacob, 299
Shively, Charles, 93, 121-122
Shontz, Martha, 93
Shook, James, 190-191
Shrum, Jill—see Pfrogner
Shubert, Alexander, 350
Shuck, Jack, 185
Shuler, William, 299
Sieber, Harry, 120
Siegel, Nancy, x
Siems, Norman, 268, 309, 353, 357
Sier, Marshall, 280
Sier, Zada, 280
Siersema, Ronald, 182
Sill, Eileen—see Gipprich
Sill, Jennifer, 337
Sill, Robert, 341
Silverthorn, Cora (Brumbaugh), 5, 61
Simes, Dimitri, 285
Simmons, Scott, 297

Simpson, Betty Finnegan, 275, 322, 359
Simpson, Cary, 213
Simpson, Michael, 351
Simpson, Richard, 224
Simpson, Sharon, 361, 363
Slaughter, Nancy (Lee), 177
Sloan, Permilla, x
Slough, Michael, 260
Small, Bradley, 345
Smaltz, William, 214-215, 221
Smelser, Ronald, 226-228
Smith, Anna, 378
Smith, Arthur, 378
Smith, Charles, 149
Smith, Cynthia, 252
Smith, Dody, 363
Smith, George, 214
Smith, John S., 293
Smith, Kenneth, 254-255
Smith, M. L., 38
Smith, Miriam (Wetzel), 217
Smith, Philbrook, 192, 242, 268, 309
Smith, Robert, 216
Smith, Thelma (Scott), 182, 378
Smoke, Kenneth, 167
Smolcic, Elizabeth, 317
Snavely, George, 67-68, 91
Snider, Philip, 183-184, 214-215, 222, 235-236, 260, 296, 363, 379
Snyder, Kathleen (Johnson), 254-255
Snyder, Thomas, 250, 267
Sollenberger, John, 255
Solomon, Robert, 222
Sothoron, Allen, 134
Souder, Jeremy, 332
Soule, Erin, 363
Sowell, Christine, x
Sowell, David, 309-310, 317
Spaltman, Gunther, 359
Spanier, Graham, 335
Sparr, Kelly, 346
Specter, Arlen, 332
Speer, Robert, 105
Spencer, Bruce, 226
Spencer, Edith, 167, 217, 232
Stackpole, Edward, 155
Staley, John, 222
Stambaugh, Carolyn, 339
Stambaugh, Russell, 169
Stanley, Karen, 241

Stark, Brenda, 341-342
Statler, Foster, 153
Statton, Timothy, 360
Stauffer, John, vii, 201, 239-244, 246, 248-251, 254, 256-257, 259, 262-264, 268-269, 278, 287, 310, 339-340, 380
Stauffer, Louise Lee, 242, 355
Staup, Peter, 235
Stayer, Clyde, 121, 123, 135, 166-167, 179, 231, 377
Stayer, James, 218-219
Stefanko, Kerry, 346
Stephenson, Kay (Cramer), 307
Stevenson, Adlai, 205, 217-218
Stewart, Joseph, 267, 305, 312, 381
Stofile, Ella, 331
Stoner, Belinda, 63
Stottlemyer, Quayton R., 339
Stottlemyer, Worth B., 339, 359
Stouffer, Jennie (Newcomer), 88, 119, 137, 377
Strapple, Mary, 349
Streicher, Michael, 332
Streightiff, Betty, 347
Streightiff, Thomas, 260
Stroman, Duane, 192, 244, 246, 257, 268, 273, 299, 349
Stroup, Steven, 299, 349
Stultz, John, 236
Sullivan, Marie, 350
Summers, Mrs. E. C., 96
Sunderland, Benjamin, 268
Sunderland, Klare, 249, 321-322, 325
Suplicki, Stephen, 254
Surbeck, Carlton, 306
Swartz, Milford, 182-184, 215
Swayne, David, 120
Swigart, Jane—see Bell
Swigart, John, 201, 231, 321
Swigart, John, Jr., 360
Swigart, Patricia, 325, 342, 359
Swigart, W. Emmert, 120, 205, 214
Swigart, William, 39, 41, 49-50, 60, 64-66, 69, 72, 75, 93, 95, 105, 113, 115, 119-120, 136, 173, 249, 278, 325, 327, 342, 359-360
Swigart, William J., 44, 47, 60-61, 121, 205, 214, 249
Swinderman, John, 259
Synodinos, John, 353

Tarquinio, Pat, 222
Taylor, Barnard, 204, 265-266
Taylor, Maurice, 259, 293, 322
Taylor, Deems, 161
Taylor, Newton, 216
Tendall, Carol (Carmon), 300-301
Thaler, Julia (Morrissey), 351
Thomas, Alan, 292
Thomas, Joanne, 347
Thomas, Maurice, 344
Thompson, Philip, x, 307
Thurston-Griswold, Henry, 311, 319
Tilden, Arnold, 267, 288-289, 291, 299, 305-306, 320, 349
Tilton, Edward, 97, 100, 129
Tower, Ibrook, 253, 268
Towne, Margaret Gray, 310, 358
Trent, Albert, 57
Trever, John, 310
Trexler, Peter, 193, 200, 268
Trimmer, Russell, 235, 259
Trombley, Susan, 291, 306
Trout, Harry, 157
Trout, Mary E., 88
Troy, Jack, 192, 244, 247, 310
Truman, Harry, 205, 214, 216
Turnball, David, 298
Tuten, Belle, 319
Tweardy, Claudia (Serfass), 294
Tyhurst, Alfred, 38

Ulrich, Foster, 241, 266, 275, 277, 306, 352
Ulrich, Gail, 307
Unterberger, Alayne, 331

Van Antwerp, Donna Richie, 336
Van Doren, Mark, 216
Van Kuren, Nancy, 306
Van Mater, Steven, 332
Van Ormer, Bunn, 121-122, 159
Van Ormer, Mrs. Bunn, 159
Vance, Andrew, 321
Vanderbush, Walter, 222
Vedock, Kathleen, 341
Vernocy, John, 236
Veto, Joseph, 222
Vinson, Ronald, 225
Vocke, William, 244, 273, 317
Voler, John, 298
von Liebig, Suzanne, 355
von Liebig, William, x, 325, 355-359, 366
von Moschzisker, Robert, 145
Vuille, Charles, 109

Wade, Jennifer, 347
Waggoner, Robert, 259, 361
Wagner, Harold, 215
Wagner, Kristy, 348
Wagoner, Robert (professor), 192-193, 246, 309-311
Wagoner, Robert (trustee), 275, 322-323, 325
Wald, Emma, 220
Wald, John R., 220
Wald, Lillian, 248
Wallace, JoAnn deArmas, 317
Walsh, Chad, 271
Waltenbaugh, Tay, 296
Walton, George, 184
Walton, Joseph, 80
Wampler, Benjamin, 122
Wampler, Dale, 193, 246, 268, 273, 305
Wampler, Gayle (Kreider), (Pollock), 267, 306
Ward, Frank, 180
Warfel, George, 155-156
Warmerdam, Clair, 300
Warneke, Paul, 285
Washburn, Robert, 193
Washington, Gennifer, 348
Wasner, Frank, 173
Watson, Keith, 345
Weakley, Phebe, 29, 49, 109
Weber, George, 223
Weidler, Dennis, 260
Weimer, Donna, 309
Weimer, Larissa (Crum), 344
Weinrich, Carl, 173
Weiss, Donald, 235, 259, 362
Welker, David, 346
Welker, Michael, 351
Wenger, Kenneth, 198
Wentz, Leroy, 259

Wertz, D. Maurice, 188
Wertz, Edith, 247
Wertz, Elizabeth—see Ellis
Wertz, John, 112, 281
Wertz, Ronald, 198
Westphal, Merold, 271
Westwater, James, 267
Wetzel, Vernne, 261
White, Mary, 359
Whitelegg, Richard, 173
Wickham, Conrad, 254
Wiedemer, Lisa, x
Wilde, Mary, 97
Will, Gerald, 229
Will, Homer, 167-168
Williams, Betty, 337
Williams, Donald, 259
Williams, Ruth (Replogle), 132
Williams, William, 236
Wilson, Harriet, 51
Wilson, Jerry, 51
Wilson, Martha, 51
Wilson, Martin, 271
Wilson, Woodrow, 82, 140-141, 228, 258
Wilt, Ardie, 158
Winter, Paul, 353
Wirt, George, 99-100, 102-103
Wise, Charles, 268
Wise, Jodie (Kormanski), 347

Witkovsky, David, 308, 360
Witmer, Kim, 260
Wohlbruck, Aliceann, 359
Wojcik, Michael, 285
Wolfgang, Roy, 135
Woodin, William, 146
Woodrow, Thomas, 192-193, 309-310
Woods, Helen, 291
Woodworth, Amy (Tranquillo), 281
Woodworth, Elizabeth, 281
Woodworth, Eric, 281
Woodworth, Gail (Mann), 281
Woodworth, Gwen, 281
Woodworth, Mrs. Hayden, 281
Woodworth, Philip, 281
Woodworth, Stephen, 281
Woolcock, Hope, 347
Workinger, Brandy, 364
Woy, Brandi, 348
Wright, Dale, 243, 310
Wurth, Kimberly, 348
Wyrick, Ronald, x, 307-308

Yamaguchi, Rica, 350
Yanckello, Robert, 295
Yevtushenko, Yevgeny, 337
Yocum, Bethany, ix
Yoder, Joseph, 214

Yoder, Miriam (Brumbaugh), x, 356
Yoder, Paul, 150, 356
Yohe, Christine, 232
Yohn, Charles, 319
Young, Chris, 297
Young, Danielle, 347
Young, Nanci, 299
Yount, Walter, 75

Zaleskie, Ellen (Daulerio), 301
Zanic, George, 363
Zaring, Chad, 345
Zassenhaus, Herbert, 167
Zauzig, Belinda, x
Zauzig, James, 345-346
Zbinden, Hans, 196
Zeller, Carrie, 344, 362
Zeller, Marie, 275, 322, 359
Zimmerer, Robert, 192, 268, 309
Zimmerman, Francis, 299
Zimmerman, Heather, 292
Zimmerman, Robert, 260
Zinkham, Nancy, 295, 346
Zuck, Jacob, 7, 12-49, 51, 54-55, 66-67, 69, 83, 86, 91, 98, 289, 314, 367-368, 370-372, 381-382
Zug, Glenn, 209, 250

General Index

academic reputation, 147, 196-198, 274, 283, 291-292, 314-315, 337, 352
Academy, 5, 11, 92-93, 99, 116, 123, 124, 128, 134
accreditation, 85-86, 113, 118, 122-123, 164, 171, 198, 272, 274, 315, 320
administration, 41, 146, 231-232, 241, 246, 266-267, 305-306
admissions, 197-198, 281, 327
Advance, 60-61, 70, 71, 73
alcohol problem. *see also* CASE
   Anti-Saloon League and, 132, 141-142
   binge drinking nationally and, 335
   college drinking policy and, 288-289, 335-336
   drinking and, 102, 179, 224, 242, 257-258, 287-289
Alma Mater, 103, 123, 180, 213, 220
Alternative Ways of Loving (AWOL), 321, 361
Altoona Extension Center, 170-172
alumni, 159, 178
   Association of, 61-62, 75-76, 113, 138, 156, 173-175, 178, 195, 250-251, 280-281, 327, 360, 367
   awards, 250-251, 282, 328, 355-356
   Bulletin (later called *Juniata magazine*), 111-112, 175, 186, 204, 218, 274, 282, 304
   children of, 177
   choir, 338
   church/college and, 208-209
   clubs of, 195, 209, 234, 280-281, 301
   Council of, 175, 321-324, 340, 356
   Day, 175
   directories of, 75, 175, 265
   dues for, 174-175
   endowment funds and, 75-76, 112-113, 138, 209
   financial support of, 174-175, 203, 209, 249-250, 280, 281, 302, 326-327, 360
   reunions of, 112-113, 138, 209, 281, 326
   scholarships from, 75, 138
   volunteering of, 99
   Week, 175
American Association of Universities, 171
American Association of University Women, 292
American Chemical Society (ACS), 164, 284, 333, 337
American Institute of Bangladesh Studies, 310
American Medical Association (AMA), 123
anniversary
   25th, 100
   50th, 144-146
   75th, 216
   100th, 264-266
   125th, 367
Annual Conference, 189-190, 208
art, 31, 53, 247, 292, 311, 339, 359
Association of American Colleges (AAC), 148, 189
Association of American Universities, 164, 189
Association of American Women, 214
athletic awards. see sports
Athletic Association, 106-108
athletic facilities, 219. *see also* physical education; sports
   Binder Natatorium, 349
   Brumbaugh (F. Samuel and Martha) fitness center, 342
   College Field, 206, 237, 342
   Hall of Fame Room, 342-343

hockey-soccer fields, 342
Kennedy Sports + Recreation Center, 277, 291, 304, 342-343, 357
Knox Stadium, 342
Langdon Baseball Field, 156, 237
Memorial Gymnasium, 205-206, 219, 260, 277, 342
Old/Women Gymnasium, 205, 223
Oller (Jefford F.) track, 342
Raffensperger tennis courts, 223, 342
awards, 199, 217, 218, 220-221, 224-225, 231, 250-251, 258, 282, 292-293, 322, 330, 336-337, 341, 353, 355. *see also* alumni; endowment; prizes; scholarships; sports
American Chemical Society Award, 337
American Institute of Chemists Award, 336
Arnold (Carroll C.) Communication's Award, 336
Art History Award, 336
Baker (John C.) Award, 322
Bargerstock (Charles) Award, 295, 300
Blood (John E.) Memorial Award, 236, 347, 350
Calhoun (Lucy M.) Distinguished Adminstrative Performance Award, 307
Creative Writing Awards, 336
Endowed Award, 336
Friends of the Library Award, 336
Groninger Smith (Anna) Supporting Staff Award, 307
Klinger (Jill Muir) Award, 301
Merck Index Award, 336
Mickle (Stanford) Award, 215, 295
Miller (Herbert A.) Award, 336
Native American Culture Award, 336
Rockwell Chemistry Award, 293
Schlichter (William) Award, 258
Steinberger (Samuel J. Jr.) Memorial Award, 292-293
Tutoring Award, 336
Van Antwerp (Donna Richie) Biology Award, 336

Baker-Henry Nature Preserve, 250
Baker Institute. *see* Peace and Conflict Studies
Baker (Elizabeth Evans) Peace Chapel, 318, 388
Baker (Robert) Guest House, 62, 196, 277, 279
Beeghly Foundation, 206-207
Best Buys in College Education, 274, 280
Bethany Theological Seminary, 303, 361
bible studies, 66, 88, 90-91, 198. *see also* school, theology
Blue Ridge College, 128, 144
Bookend Seminars, 357
Brethren. *see* Church of Brethren

Brethren Publishing Company, 64, 76
Brethren's Normal College, 40
Brethren's Normal School, 31-32
board of trustees. *see* trustees
Burchinell House, 27, 31, 32, 35
business community, 33-34, 38-39, 354. *see also* Program for Area Residents

Camp Kanesatake, 181
Camp Myler, 180-181
campus
  beginning location of, 9-11, 23-24, 27, 34-35, 38-39
  expansion of, 39, 42, 73, 98-99, 138, 204-207, 249-250, 357
  renovation of, 99-100, 277-279, 325-326
campus ministry. *see also* religious activiities
  CROP meal and, 284-285, 331-332
  organizations of, 330, 360-361
Campus Songs of Juniata, 110
capital campaign(s). *see also* alumni; endowment; fundraising; trustees
  Build Juniata Program, 202-203, 208-209
  Campaign for Uncommon Outcomes, 366
  Century II, 275-278, 282, 324
  Golden Jubilee, 145-146
  Greater Juniata, 116-119
  Margin of Difference, 203, 249, 275
  Transformations, 324-325
Carnegie Foundation, 97-98, 118, 122, 182
CASE (Committee on Alcohol Study and Education), 289, 326
catalog, 40, 86, 169, 276, 308, 316, 319
charter, 41
  reform of, 86-88, 119-120
Christian Family Companion, 7-8
Church Advisory Board, 74-75
Church of the Brethren, 1. *see also* Church Advisory Board; pacifism; religious activities
  abortive school ventures of, 6-7
  antieducationists of, 5-6, 10, 12
  beginning school movement of, 3-6
  Berlin and, 12-14, 33
  Brethren Campus Day and, 208
  college ties to, 163-164, 190-191
  college independence from, 29, 87, 240-241
  contributions to college by, 117-118, 120, 208, 213-214, 251
  final school movement of, 12-14
  lifestyle/thought of, 2-3, 5, 10
  as minority at college, 177
  playing down of, 28, 34-35
  portraits and, 46
  regalia bias by, 104

school struggles for, 7-12
Stone Church and, 100, 113, 128, 133, 180, 214, 308
trustees and, 173, 202
church-college relations, 360-361. *see also* Church of the Brethren
alumni affairs and, 208-209
Church Relations Council and, 251, 360
values of Christian college and, 162-164
civil rights. *see* racism
class fund agents (CFA), 327
clubs. *see also* glee club
other, 132, 139, 151, 154, 179, 181, 184, 209, 212, 234, 252-253, 283-284, 288, 291, 301, 329-330, 334, 343
co-curricular transcript (CCT), 291
coffeehouse, 231, 249, 253
College. *see also* liberal arts
Arts and Sciences, 123-125, 169
Colleges that Change Lives (Pope), 314, 326
conscientious objectors. *see* pacifists
colors, 103, 157
commencement, 226
first, 46
community service, 284-285, 318, 329-331, 333. *see also* student, demonstrations
Companion, 16
convocation, 252, 264-266
creationists, 163
cultural events, 109-110, 154-156, 179-180, 212, 219-220, 337-339. *see also* drama; music
curriculum
1879-1888 offering of, 52-54
1888-1893 offering of, 66-68
1893-1910 offering of, 88-93
1910-1924 offering of, 123-128
1924-1930 offering of, 148-150
1930-1943 offering of, 168-170
1943-1968 offering of, 198-200
1968-1975 offering of, 244-248
1975-1986 offering of, 271-274
1986-1998 offering of, 315-320

DAJUMO, 202-203, 223
dean's list, 148, 198-199
debate, 109, 132, 180
degrees, 123, 148, 168, 170, 365
depression
1876, 13, 23-24
great 1930's, 166, 172, 176-178
Detwiler Plaza, 289
Development/Trustee Council, 175, 323
donations, 214. *see also* endowment; fundraising
drama, 179, 212-213, 226, 252, 271, 323, 337-338, 358

drugs, 257
DuBois Business College, 324
Dunkerism. 2, 6-9, 10. *see also* Church of Brethren

Echo. see Juniata Echo
Elderhostel, 273-274
Ellis Center Board, 249, 253
Emeriti Association, 314
emeritus status, 270
endowment, 75-76, 112-113, 116-119, 123, 138, 177, 203, 206, 209, 242-243, 247, 249, 258, 302, 310, 317, 336, 339, 352, 361, 367
spending of, 324
Wertz Endowment for Support of Cultural Events and, 247
enrollment, 89, 176, 186, 230, 245, 283, 289-290, 293, 302, 323, 324, 328, 361, 366
exam
comprehensive (comps), 169, 218, 245-246, 254
Extension Department, 117, 149, 170-171

faculty. *see also* professorships
Beachley Distinguished Professor Award for, 195, 268, 309, 357
Beachley Distinguished Service Award for, 309, 357
children of, 194
Ellis (C.N.) Humanities Series and, 247
Folgelsanger-Murphy Lectureship and, 247
Judy Lectureship and, 200
Juniata Faulty Professional Association and, 269
junior faculty award for, 309
Lindback Distinguished Teaching Award for, 268, 309
members of 1876-1888, 31-32, 37, 40-41, 43, 48-51
members of 1888-1893, 65
members of 1893-1910, 93
members of 1910-1924, 121-122, 123
members of 1924-1930, 150-151
members of 1930-1943, 166-168
members of 1943-1968, 191-196
members of 1968-1975, 242-244
members of 1975-1986, 267-271
members of 1986-1998, 307-314
members of 1998-2000, 357-359
redefinition of Liberal Arts by, 269-270
sabbaticals for, 151, 168, 195
salaries/fringe benefits of, 168, 192-196, 269, 312-313, 367
Sears-Roebuck Award for, 309

tenure and, 196, 269-270
von Liebig (William J.) Chair in Biomedical Sciences for, 356
Family Educational Rights and Privacy Act of 1974, 251
fellowships. *see* scholarships
finances, 71-72, 113, 190, 203, 208, 302, 313, 352-353
  budget crisis of 1990's and, 323-324, 338, 349
football bowl game
  Stagg, 259, 361
  Tangerine, 221, 341
Ford Foundation for the Advancement of Education, 197, 202
Foundation for Independent Colleges, 202
founder(s). *see also* presidents
  Brumbaugh, Andrew B., 8, 9-11, 14, 23, 28-30, 33-35, 38-39, 41, 45, 47-49, 51, 54-55, 57-60, 62, 64-65, 71, 73-74, 79, 83, 88, 95, 111, 314, 372, 374
  Brumbaugh, Henry, 7-8, 11-12, 14, 23-24, 26-27, 29-30, 33, 38-39, 44, 47-48, 50, 52, 54, 58, 60, 62-69, 72, 74-77, 85, 90, 94-95, 103, 119, 138, 148, 369, 374-375
  Brumbaugh, Jacob, 30, 36, 38-39, 41, 48-49, 64-65, 73, 93, 98, 102, 107, 119, 122, 150
  Brumbaugh, John, 6-11, 13-14, 20-24, 26, 28-29, 33, 36, 40, 41, 43, 47, 57, 60, 64-67, 71-73, 76, 86, 87, 90, 100, 119, 121, 370-371
  Holsinger, Henry, 7-13, 15-16, 20, 39, 370
  Quinter, James, 1- 8, 12, 21, 26, 28-30, 39, 42-44, 46-49, 51-55, 61-62, 64-66, 69, 72, 76, 97-98, 117-118, 121, 354, 373
  Zuck, Jacob, 7, 12-49, 51, 54, 55, 66-67, 69, 83, 86, 91, 98, 289, 314, 367-368, 370-372, 381-382
Freudian fears, 129-130
Friends of the Library, 174, 213, 248, 336
fundamentalism, 125-127
fundraising, 12-14, 33-35, 38, 40, 75, 97-98, 112-113, 116-119, 172, 175, 266, 329, 355, 358. *see also* alumni; capital campaigns; endowment; trustees
  Annual Support Fund for, 249, 280, 282, 292, 302
  53 Investors Club, 209
  Five Hundred Dollar Club, 209
  Founders Club, 209, 280
  Juniata Centennial Fund, 249
  The Juniata Fund, 326, 360
  Juniata Postwar Fund, 202
  Juniata World Service Fund, 213-214
  One Hundred Dollar Club, 175
  One Thousand Dollar Club, 209

Quinter Society, 280-281
25 Year Club, 195

gays, 321
gender, 26-27. *see also* women
general facilities, 353
  Alumni Hall, 207, 304
  Baker (Robert C.) House, 62, 196, 277, 279
  Baker Refectory, 249, 285, 289, 333, 335
  Beeghly (L.A.) Library, 206-207, 271, 319
  Brumbaugh, 250, 272, 277
  Brumbaugh (Harold B.) Alumni House, 207, 282, 306-307
  Brumbaugh-Oller House, 326
  Carnegie Hall, 207, 277, 311, 326, 359
  Carnegie Library, 97-98, 100, 116, 128, 199, 206, 207
  Cyber Café, 249
  Ellis College Center, 249, 253, 265, 287, 290
  Faculty Club, 196, 205, 277
  Founders Hall, 39, 42, 99-100, 104, 138, 171, 186, 196, 214, 206, 279, 366-378
  Gehrett House, 282
  Health and Wellness Center, 357
  Home Management House, 277
  maintenance building, 205
  Mallory-Rabinowitz Gallery, 359
  Muddy Run Café, 319
  Oller Center for Peace and International Programs, 357
  Oller Hall, 171-173, 174, 179, 205, 226, 229, 231, 252, 279, 339, 354, 358, 366
  Oneida Hall, 94-96, 205, 206, 224, 250, 354, 366-377
  Practice House, 148
  Regional Performing Arts Center, 366
  Rosenberger Auditorium, 354, 358
  Science Hall, 94, 124
  Shoemaker Gallery, 207, 311
  Student Center, 217
  Students Hall, 94, 96, 100, 106, 200, 207-208, 218, 232, 250
  Swigart (William E., Jr.) Enrollment Center, 325-326, 352-353, 357
General Information Test, 182, 230
GI Bill (Veteran's Education Act), 189, 211, 217
gifted children, 315
glee club, 110, 128, 155, 180, 339
Good (Omar J.) Protestant Campus Minister, 330
Good (Omar J.) Fund, 243, 278, 310, 330, 359, 367
Gospel Messenger, 64-65, 126
Gospel Visitor, 4, 5, 6, 7
grants, 200, 246, 366

Health Fair/Wellness Day, 291
health services, 291, 323. *see also* infirmary
Hicks (Paul E.) Observatory, 270
History Day, 273
A History of the German Baptist Brethren in Europe and America, 80
honor society, 133, 139, 149, 154, 181-182, 198, 213, 245, 284, 316, 337
humanities, 198-199, 246-247, 272, 358
Humanities Cluster, 277-278
Huntingdon Board of Trade, 38-39
Huntingdon Normal Select School, 23, 25, 29,
    merger of, 30, 33
    name change of, 31-32

infirmary, 95, 171, 220, 357. *see also* health services
Institute for Civil Affairs, 318-319
instructional facilities
    Academic Classroom Building, 207
    Brumbaugh (I. Harvey) House, 199, 205, 207, 277
    Brumbaugh Science Center, 200, 204, 207, 244, 272-273, 366
    Dana Humanities Center, 277-278
    Early Childhood Education Center, 206, 272
    Good Hall, 242, 319
    Gump classroom, 319
    Manse, 277
    Pierce Laboratories, 247
    Presser Music Building, 172
    Raystown Environmental Studies Field Station, 247, 270, 319, 366
    Science Hall, 128-129, 138
    Smith (L.B.) House, 277
    Swigart Hall, 205
    von Liebig (William) Center for Science, 356-357, 366
International Programs Office (IPO), 317
internships, 318-320

J Club, 181, 184, 214, 234, 252, 301, 343
journalism, 216, 224
Juniata Activities Board. *see* Ellis Center Board
Judiciary, 219, 220, 230, 254
Juniata Business College, 67-68, 72, 91
Juniata College Artist Series (JCAS), 247
Juniata Dames, 191
Juniata Echo, 73-74, 111, 153
Juniata Quilts, 359
Juniata World Service Fund (JWSF), 213, 232, 252
Juniatian, 153-154, 211, 216, 218, 224, 232, 253, 257, 283, 286, 312-313, 331, 333-334, 338, 341

Kishacoquillas Seminary and Normal Institute, 6-8, 50
Korean War, 216-217
Kvasir, 225, 230, 253, 334

land
    donation of, 34-35, 38-39
law suits, 84-85
Leadership Conference, 181
lectureships, 200, 247
liberal arts, 88-89, 123-126, 169, 269. *see also* College, Arts & Sciences
library, 54-55
    Archives, 248
    beginning, 25
    Beeghly (L.A.) Library, 206-207, 271, 319
    Carnegie Library and, 97-98, 100, 116, 128, 199, 206, 207
    Cassel collection for, 96
    friends of, 174, 213, 248, 336
    Myers Science, 207, 271
    Quinter collection for, 97
    Swigart (William Emmert) Treasure Room, 206
literary society
    Eclectic, 39-40, 45, 68-69
    Everett, 19
    Juniata, 27, 29-30, 39
    Junior, 39-40, 68
    Oriental, 69, 109-110
    Wahneeta, 69, 109-110, 132
loans
    art, 213
    federal, 207, 221, 228, 251, 258, 328
Louisiana, 78

Mace, Centennial, 265-266
Mallory-Rabinowitz Gallery, 359
mascot
    Eagle and, 341
    Indian, 157, 183, 215, 226, 339-341
Masque, 179, 212, 226, 252. *see also* drama
Medallion, Presidential, 265
memorials, 98
Middle States Association of Colleges and Schools, 118, 122-123, 182, 189, 193, 198, 206, 246, 254, 263, 274, 315, 319, 320
Millersville State Normal School, 7, 9
mission statements, 276, 320-321
Moller organ, 173, 279
Monopoly, Mammoth, 233
motto, 103
Museum of Art, 359

music, 8, 53, 68, 91, 109-110, 127-128, 148, 154-155, 172-173, 179-180, 205, 212-213, 230, 231, 251, 253, 292, 323, 337-339, 353, 358, 367. *See also* glee club

name of college
   Brethren's Normal College as, 31-32, 40
   Brethren's Normal School as, 31-32
   Huntingdon Normal School as, 23, 25, 29, 30
   Juniata College as, 85-86
National Collegiate Alcohol Awareness Week, 326
National Endowment for the Humanities (NEH), 246, 248
National Endowment of the Arts, 272
National Newspaper Service (NNS), 224
National Normal School, 20-21
National School Public Relations Association (NSPRA), 282
National Science Foundation (NSF), 200, 311
National Student Loan Program, 258
National Student Lobby (NSL), 258
New Vienna Academy, 6-7
New Visions, 315
Nobel prize, 328
nonprofit, 86-87
Normal College, 1
Normal English Course, 40, 52
nuclear weapons, 285

observatory, 207
Orphans' Home, 58

pacifists, 136, 142, 186, 210, 265
Pathfinder, 225, 257, 283, 288
Patrick Lodge, 279
Peace and Conflict Studies (PACS), 247-248, 265, 270-272, 274-275, 310, 317-318, 330, 332, 357, 367
Pennington House, 278
Pennsylvania Association of Colleges and Universities, 189
Philadelphia Public Schools, 82
physical education. *see also* sports
   discontinuance of, 258-259
   early years for, 71, 94-96
   graduation requirement of, 106, 198
   intramurals and, 16-108, 156-157, 184, 215, 258-259, 300
   Women's Athletic Association (WAA) and, 184, 215
physical plant, 59, 280
Pilgrim, 7-10, 12-14, 21, 23, 26, 55
pin, college, 103
Planning Commission, 203, 205

politics, 136, 140-143, 218-219, 227-228, 255
president(s)
   Binder, Frederick M., 262-272, 274-278, 281, 283, 286-288, 291-296, 299, 301-303, 305, 308-310, 322, 326, 342, 380
   Brumbaugh, Henry, 7-8, 11-12, 14, 23-24, 26-27, 29-30, 33, 38-39, 44, 47-48, 50, 52, 54, 58, 60, 62-69, 72, 74-77, 85, 90, 94-95, 103, 119, 138, 148, 369, 374-375
   Brumbaugh, I. Harvey (I.H.), 64-65, 75, 79, 83-87, 90, 97, 100-101, 104-105, 113-117, 119, 120-124, 129, 130-133, 137-141, 143, 147-148, 150, 165-166, 276, 374, 379
   Brumbaugh, Martin G. (M.G.), vii, 37, 44, 48, 52-53, 55, 57, 61-65, 75, 77-99, 105, 112-115, 117, 119-120, 127, 136, 137, 139-148, 149-152, 155, 157-161, 171-172, 174, 176, 205, 263, 292, 373-375, 377
   Ellis, Calvert (C.N.), 133, 135, 161, 166-168, 174, 178, 186-198, 200-204, 209-211, 213, 216, 221, 223-224, 226-228, 231-234, 237-239, 242-244, 247, 249, 253-254, 263, 265, 275, 280, 307, 321, 378-379
   Ellis, Charles (C.C.), vii, 88-89, 93, 106, 115-117, 121, 125-127, 138-141, 147, 159-165, 166-168, 170, 172, 174, 177, 182, 184-187, 188, 201, 213, 216-217, 249, 252, 264, 278, 321, 371, 373, 376-377
   Kepple, Thomas R., Jr., vii, x, 325-326, 333, 336, 347, 352-355, 357-361, 366-367
   Neff, Robert W., vii, x, 267, 303-310, 312-313, 315-326, 328, 331-337, 339-345, 348-349, 351-356
   Quinter, James, 1- 8, 12, 21, 26, 28-30, 39, 42-44, 46-49, 51-55, 61-62, 64-66, 69, 72, 76, 97-98, 117-118, 121, 354, 373
   Stauffer, John N., vii, 201, 238-244, 246, 248-251, 254, 256-257, 259, 262-264, 268-268, 278, 287, 310, 339-340, 380
president's house, 159, 240, 264, 278
Presidential Partner Emeritus, 355
Presser Foundation, 172
Primitive Christian, 26, 27, 28, 29, 38, 46, 64
prizes, 182, 217, 220, 231, 258, 292-293, 328, 357. *see* awards
   Baker Peace Studies Prize, 292
   Barrick Language Prize, 258
   Biddle (Joseph F.) General Information Prize, 182
   Blaisdell (Alice) Geology/Math Prize, 231
   Metzger (Vila Gardner) Prizes, 292

Presidential Medallion for Meritorious
    Service, 322
Price (William) Social Science Prize, 217
Wald (John R. & Emma G.) Humanities
    Prize, 220
professorship(s). *see also* faculty
  Baker, 367
  Benedict, 194, 367
  Book, 195, 357
  Brumbaugh, Harvey (I.H.), 195, 269, 367
  Brumbaugh, Jacob H. and Rachel, 195, 268
  Brumbaugh, Martin G. (M.G.), 195, 268, 310
  Dana, 242, 268, 292, 309, 367
  endowed, 367
  Foster, 310, 367
  Geiger, 195, 269
  Good, 242, 271, 278, 309-310, 358-359, 367
  Heckler, 367
  Long (Newton & Hazel), 269, 309-310
Program for Area Residents (PAR), 318, 337
Program of Emphasis (POE), 271-272, 315-316
progressivism, 141-142
public relations, 59-60, 307
public speech, 109
publications, 60, 225
Puerto Rico, 81, 97
Pulpit Rocks, 99

Quakers, 21

race relations, 177, 218, 283, 292, 320-321, 337
racism, 227, 228-229, 240, 283, 285-286, 331, 333, 339-340
radio stations, 213, 217, 218, 221, 225, 254, 263, 287, 334
Raystown Environmental Studies Field Station, 247, 319, 333, 366
religious activities, 2-4, 25, 104-106, 117-118, 133, 144, 155, 162-164, 177, 180, 190-191, 220, 221, 226-227, 242-243, 253, 360-361. *see also* campus ministry
Renaissance, 253
residence hall(s)
  Alexander Mack House, 171
  Brumbaugh, 138, 171, 179, 181, 199, 205, 224, 250, 277
  Brumbaugh-Oller House, 326, 357
  Christopher Sauer House, 171
  Cloister, 158-159, 166, 170-171, 179, 204, 207, 287, 290, 325, 327, 332
  East Houses, 249-250
  Emmert House, 250
  Geiger House, 171, 206
  Hess Apartments, 279, 289
  Ladies, 72-73, 138

Lesher Hall infirmary, 220
Malloy Plaza, 359
Maude-Lesher, 206, 220-221, 224, 279
Mission House, 158, 279, 289
North/Sunderland, 205, 206, 218, 224, 325
Nye, 277
Pink Palace, 250, 367
private homes and, 138, 171, 206
Sherwood, 204, 206, 287
South, 206, 224, 279
Terrace Hall, 327
Tussey-Terrace, 207
retention rate, 291, 329
retirement, 313, 353
room inspections, 57
Round Top, 99, 138, 152, 223

Salem College, 7-10
scholarships, 75, 138, 177, 182, 203, 217-218, 220-221, 224-225, 228, 251, 258, 281-282, 292-293, 311, 315, 337, 341, 359, 363
  Ellis (Charles C.) Memorial Scholarship, 217
  Fulbright Fellowship, 217, 218, 224, 315
  Goldwater Scholarship, 315
  Saint Andrew's Society of Philadelphia (Mutch) Scholarship, 292, 315
  Woodrow Wilson Fellowship, 228, 258
Scholastic Aptitude Test (SAT). *see* tests
school
  business, 67-68, 72, 91-92, 124, 199, 247, 336
  education, 88-90, 93, 247, 272, 315
  music, 127-128, 338, 367
  theology, 90-91, 125-127
Science in Motion (chemistry department), 311-312
science museum, 55
sciences, 53-54, 124, 200, 270, 273, 312, 319, 356, 358
seal, 103
sectarian, non, 28
Selective Service Act, 214
Seven Points Amphitheater, 274
Shoemaker Gallery, 207, 311
small college
  purpose of, 190-191
smallpox, 35-37
smoking, 77, 179, 218, 224-225, 263, 335
sports. *see also* athletic facilities; physical education
  1899-1930 intercollegiate, 107-108, 133-135, 139, 157-158
  1930-1943 intercollegiate, 182-184
  1943-1968 intercollegiate, 214-216, 221-223, 234-237

1968-1975 intercollegiate, 259-261
1975-1986 intercollegiate, 293-301
1986-1998 intercollegiate, 343-351
1998-2000 intercollegiate, 361-364
academics and, 293, 295-296, 297, 347, 364
professional athletes from, 134, 222, 236
recognition award for, 215-216, 236, 295, 300-301, 343, 347, 348, 350, 362, 363
scholarships for, 182
Special Olympics and, 329-330
volleyball and, 182, 294-295, 301, 343-344, 362-363
women, 184, 261-262, 294-295, 298, 299-301, 343-344, 346-350, 362-364
Sports Hall of Fame, 342-343, 361
Standing Stone, 96
START, 257-258
State Science Olympiad, 312
stock
    holders of, 63, 86-88
    joint, 11, 29
Stone Church, 100, 113, 128, 133, 180, 214, 308
Stottlemyer Collection of Art, 339
strategic planning, 320-321, 323
Student Government, 152, 178-179, 181, 211-213, 217, 218-219, 225, 230, 232-233, 254-255, 257, 285, 286, 288, 290, 332, 334-335, 339-340, 353
    Council of Cooperation and, 130-131
student life, years of
    1876-1888, 30-32, 40, 55-59
    1888-1910, 69-71, 102-114
    1910-1924, 129-133
    1924-1930, 151-156
    1930-1943, 176-183
    1943-1950, 210-216
    1950-1960, 216-221
    1960-1968, 223-234
    1968-1975, 251-258
    1975-1986, 282-293
    1986-1998, 328-339
    1998-2000, 361
Student Volunteer Movement, 105
student(s), 47. *see also* enrollment; tuition
    apathy of, 328, 334-335
    commuters as, 177, 253
    demonstrations by, 223-224, 227, 229, 233-234, 238, 251, 256, 285, 331-332
    dress code for, 110, 224, 252
    financial aid for, 178, 221, 228, 292, 302, 328
    foreign, 111, 283, 316-317, 329, 350
    handbook for, 152, 225
    in loco parentis and, 102, 224, 232, 243, 252, 256
    on-campus demonstrations by, 255-256, 331

    overcrowding of, 289-290, 335
    recruitment of, 144
    social regulations of, 30-31, 102-103, 129-130, 139-140, 179-180, 224, 232, 242, 252, 256-257, 288
    stunts by, 179, 233, 287-288
    voluntary help for, 217
study aboard
    Brethren Colleges Abroad, 200, 316-317
    exchange programs and, 317
    junior year, 317, 337
sugaring, maple, 271
summer school, 92-93, 254

task force, 241
    diversity and, 320-321, 340
    mascot, 340
    smoking, 335
    technology, 319
    value-centered education by, 244-246
teacher(s)
    Brethren need for, 4
    studies for, 88-90, 124, 168, 199, 247
    two year course for, 40
    Union Teachers Institute and, 18
technology, 319-320, 334, 358, 367
tests, standardized, 291-292
    American Council of Education (ACE) and, 197
    Scholastic Aptitude Test (SAT) and, 197, 226, 291-292, 329
textbooks, 53
Toonerville Trolley, 103, 156, 177
Totem Inn, 217, 219, 230, 232, 335
tradition(s)
    All Class Night, 179, 198, 203, 218, 287-288, 338
    Candlelighting/Mantle, 133
    Casino Night, 252
    Christmas Carol reading as, 216, 252
    Christmas decorations, 217, 252, 333
    Continental Breakfast, 209
    Firelighting, 181
    Founders Day, 103, 129, 145, 195, 203, 277, 278
    freshmen "regs," 152, 180-181, 203, 213, 252, 332
    Homecoming, 139, 182, 184, 213, 226, 240, 252, 321, 330
    Lobsterfest, 332
    Madrigal Dinner, 253, 332
    May Day/Woman of the Year, 132, 177, 252
    Mountain Day, 103, 212, 220, 228, 265, 287, 332
    Move Up Day, 153, 212, 214, 252

mud volleyball, 287
Parents Day, 181, 212, 232, 252
pig roast, 333
Presidential Ball, 332
raft regatta, 253, 287
Senior Convocation, 252
Spring Awards Convocation, 353
Spring Carnival/Springfest, 232-233, 332
storming of the Arch, 226, 332
TWIRP Week, 213, 252
Tree Program, 280
trustees, 40-41, 47, 64. *see also* capital campaigns
   awards by, 322
   beginning, 29, 34, 39-40
   chairmen of, 119-120, 173, 201, 239, 275, 321-322
   change of, 119-120, 173-174, 200-204, 275-276, 321-323, 359-360
   charter reforms by, 86-88, 119-120
   donations by, 38-39, 119, 324-325
   fundraising and, 172, 242-243, 249
   faculty purging by, 121
   mascot and, 341
   mission statements and, 276, 320-321
   president and, 41, 48, 79, 83, 263, 353-354
   religion and, 139
   social awareness of, 331
   Student Government and, 254-255, 286
   student life and, 70, 288
   textbooks and, 53
tuition, 25, 30, 54, 72, 89, 178, 190, 194, 203, 214, 221, 283, 289, 328, 361

United Nations Seminar series (PACS), 270, 318
University of Pennsylvania, 78-80

vandalism, 102-103
Vietnam War, 224, 230, 233-234, 238, 245, 251, 255-256
Village, 199, 204, 207, 211
Volunteer Mission Band, 105
volunteers, 327, 329-330
Voyages, 315

Westminster Woods, 327, 353
Who's Who in American Colleges and Universities, 83, 181, 209, 337, 361
William Price Social Science Prize, 217
Williamsburg Conference Center, 278, 318
Winton Hill property, 325-326, 342
women, 328-329. *see also* gender; physical education; sports
   celebration of, 367-368
   rights of, 290-291
   student, 154
   suffrage for, 132
Women's League of Juniata College, 159, 209, 213, 258
World War I, 136, 138
World War II, 184-186, 197, 210-211

Yard, 73
yearbook(s)
   Alfarata, 111, 129, 132, 146, 153, 181, 253, 286, 334, 335
   Blossoms of Life, 111
   Fruits of Virtue, 111
   Leaves of Industry, 111
YMCA/YWCA, 106, 152, 181, 214